The Mirror and the Lamp:

ROMANTIC THEORY AND THE CRITICAL TRADITION

By M. H. ABRAMS

*It must go further still: that soul must become
its own betrayer, its own deliverer, the one
activity, the mirror turn lamp.*

WILLIAM BUTLER YEATS

OXFORD UNIVERSITY PRESS

London · Oxford · New York

OXFORD UNIVERSITY PRESS
Oxford   London   Glasgow
New York   Toronto   Melbourne   Wellington
Nairobi   Dar es Salaam   Cape Town
Kuala Lumpur   Singapore   Jakarta   Hong Kong   Tokyo
Delhi   Bombay   Calcutta   Madras   Karachi

To Ruth

Preface

THE DEVELOPMENT OF LITERARY THEORY in the lifetime of Coleridge was to a surprising extent the making of the modern critical mind. There were many important differences between, let us say, Horace's *Art of Poetry* and the criticism of Dr. Johnson, but there was also a discernible continuity in premises, aims, and methods. This continuity was broken by the theories of romantic writers, English and German; and their innovations include many of the points of view and procedures which make the characteristic differences between traditional criticism and the criticism of our own time, including some criticism which professes to be anti-romantic.

The primary concern of this book is with the English theory of poetry, and to a lesser extent of the other major arts, during the first four decades of the nineteenth century. It stresses the common orientation which justifies us in identifying a specifically 'romantic' criticism; but not, I trust, at the cost of overlooking the many important diversities among the writers who concerned themselves with the nature of poetry or art, its psychological genesis, its constitution and kinds, its major criteria, and its relation to other important human concerns. The book deals, for the most part, with the original and enduring critics of the time, rather than with the run-of-the-mill reviewers who often had a more immediate, though shorter-lived influence on the general reading public.

In order to emphasize the pivotal position of the age in the general history of criticism, I have treated English romantic theory in a broad intellectual context, and I have tried to keep constantly in view the background of eighteenth-century aesthetics from which romantic aesthetics was in part a development, and against which it was, still more, a deliberate reaction. I have described some of the relations of English critical theory to foreign thought, especially to the richly suggestive German speculations of the age, beginning with Herder and Kant, when Germany replaced England and France as the chief exporter of ideas to the Western world. I have also moved freely in time, going back to the Greek and Roman origins of aesthetic thought and ahead to various critical ideas current today. Finally, I have undertaken, although briefly, to trace the origins of prominent romantic ideas, not only in earlier aesthetic discussion, but also in philosophy, ethics, theology, and in the theories and discoveries of the natural sciences. In aesthetics, as in other provinces of inquiry, radical novelties frequently turn out to be migrant ideas which, in their native intellectual habitat, were commonplaces.

The title of the book identifies two common and antithetic metaphors of mind, one comparing the mind to a reflector of external objects, the other to a radiant projector which makes a contribution to the objects it perceives. The first of these was characteristic of much of the thinking from Plato to the eighteenth century; the second typifies the prevailing romantic conception of the poetic mind. I have attempted the experiment of taking these and various other metaphors no less seriously when they occur in criticism than when they occur in poetry; for in both provinces the recourse to metaphor, although directed to different ends, is perhaps equally functional. Critical thinking, like that in all areas of human interest, has been in considerable part thinking in parallels, and critical argument has to that extent been an argument from analogy. As this inquiry will indicate, a number of concepts most rewarding in clarifying the nature and criteria of art were not found simply in the examination of aesthetic facts, but seem to have emerged from the exploration of serviceable analogues, whose properties were, by metaphorical transfer, predicated of a work of art. From this point of view the shift from neo-classic to romantic criticism can be formulated, in a preliminary way, as a radical alteration in the typical metaphors of critical discourse.

The bringing of submerged analogies into the open puts certain old facts into a new and, it seems to me, a revealing perspective. Perhaps the attempt may deserve the measured commendation Dr. Johnson awarded to Lord Kames: He 'has taken the right method in his *Elements of Criticism*. I do not mean he has taught us anything, but he has told us old things in a new way.' There are, however, many profitable ways to approach the history of criticism. I have tried to use whatever ways seemed most pertinent, and to restrict the analysis of basic metaphors to problems in which this approach promised genuine illumination.

This book had its distant origin in a study of the writings of Johnson and Coleridge, under the stimulating direction of I. A. Richards at Cambridge University, and it was developed at Harvard University with the guidance and encouragement of my mentor and friend, the late Theodore Spencer. In the ten years and more that the work has been in progress, I have incurred many intellectual obligations which are indicated in the text and footnotes. In this place I wish to acknowledge both a Rockefeller Fellowship, which gave me an invaluable year for catching up broken threads after the war, and a grant for summer research from Cornell University. I wish also gratefully to record the material assistance of many colleagues and friends. Victor Lange and Israel S. Stamm helped me make my way through the intricacies of German criticism; and Harry Caplan, James Hutton, and Friedrich Solmsen have been valuable sources of information on classical and medieval matters. I have had access to the full resources of the Cornell and Harvard University Libraries; and H. H. King, of the Cornell Library staff, whose services were made available to me by a grant from the Cornell Graduate School, has been of great assistance in verifying quotations and in many bibliographical matters. Richard Harter Fogle and Francis E. Mineka have made a number of useful suggestions. William Rea Keast undertook to read the entire manuscript, at a time when he was heavily burdened by other enterprises; the book has benefited in a great many ways from his command of the history and methods of criticism. To my wife I owe the greatest debt, for her fortitude and her unfailing cheerfulness while doing and redoing the most laborious of the tasks needed to make ready this book.

Some of the material incorporated in the seventh chapter appeared in an article, 'Archetypal Analogies in the Language of Criticism,' *The University of Toronto Quarterly,* July 1949.

M. H. A.

Cornell University
Summer 1953

Contents

CONTENTS

THE MIRROR AND THE LAMP:

ROMANTIC THEORY AND THE CRITICAL TRADITION

I

Introduction:
ORIENTATION OF CRITICAL THEORIES

BOSWELL. 'Then, Sir, what is poetry?'
JOHNSON. 'Why, Sir, it is much easier to say what it is not. We all *know* what light is; but it is not easy to *tell* what it is.'

It is the mark of an educated man to look for precision in each class of things just so far as the nature of the subject admits.

ARISTOTLE, *Nicomachean Ethics*

TO POSE AND ANSWER aesthetic questions in terms of the relation of art to the artist, rather than to external nature, or to the audience, or to the internal requirements of the work itself, was the characteristic tendency of modern criticism up to a few decades ago, and it continues to be the propensity of a great many—perhaps the majority—of critics today. This point of view is very young measured against the twenty-five-hundred-year history of the Western theory of art, for its emergence as a comprehensive approach to art, shared by a large number of critics, dates back not much more than a century and a half. The intention of this book is to chronicle the evolution and (in the early nineteenth century) the triumph, in its diverse forms, of this radical shift to the artist in the alignment of aesthetic thinking, and to describe the principal alternate theories against which this approach had to compete. In particular, I shall be concerned with the momentous consequences of these new bearings in criticism for the identification, the analysis, the evaluation, and the writing of poetry.

The field of aesthetics presents an especially difficult problem to the historian. Recent theorists of art have been quick to profess that much, if not all, that has been said by their predecessors is wavering, chaotic, phantasmal. 'What has gone by the name of the philosophy of art' seemed to Santayana 'sheer verbiage.' D. W. Prall, who himself wrote two excellent books on the subject, commented that traditional aesthetics 'is in fact only a pseudo-science or pseudo-philosophy.'

Its subject-matter is such wavering and deceptive stuff as dreams are made of; its method is neither logical nor scientific, nor quite whole-heartedly and empirically matter of fact . . . without application in practice to test it and without an orthodox terminology to make it into an honest superstition or a thorough-going, soul satisfying cult. It is neither useful to creative artists nor a help to amateurs in appreciation.[1]

And I. A. Richards, in his *Principles of Literary Criticism,* labeled his first chapter 'The Chaos of Critical Theories,' and justified the pejorative attribute by quoting, as 'the apices of critical theory,' more than a score of isolated and violently discrepant utterances about art, from Aristotle to the present time.[2] With the optimism of his youth, Richards himself went on to attempt a solid grounding of literary evaluation in the science of psychology.

It is true that the course of aesthetic theory displays its full measure of the rhetoric and logomachy which seem an inseparable part of man's discourse about all things that really matter. But a good deal of our impatience with the diversity and seeming chaos in philosophies of art is rooted in a demand from criticism for something it cannot do, at the cost of overlooking many of its genuine powers. We still need to face up to the full consequences of the realization that criticism is not a physical, nor even a psychological, science. By setting out from and terminating in an appeal to the facts, any good aesthetic theory is, indeed, empirical in method. Its aim, however, is not to establish correlations between facts which will enable us to predict the future by reference to the past, but to establish principles enabling us to justify, order, and clarify our interpretation and appraisal of the aesthetic facts themselves. And as we shall see, these facts turn out to have the curious and scientifically reprehensible property of being conspicuously altered by the nature of the very principles which appeal to them for their support. Because many critical statements of fact are thus partially relative to the perspective of the theory within which they occur, they are not 'true,' in the strict scientific sense that they approach the ideal of being verifiable by any intelligent human being, no matter what his point of view. Any hope, therefore, for the kind of basic agreement in criticism that we have learned to expect in the exact sciences is doomed to disappointment.

A good critical theory, nevertheless, has its own kind of validity. The criterion is not the scientific verifiability of its single propositions, but the scope, precision, and coherence of the insights that it yields into the properties of single works of art and the adequacy with which it accounts for diverse kinds of art. Such a criterion will, of course, justify not one, but a number of valid theories, all in their several ways self-consistent, applicable, and relatively adequate to the range of aesthetic phenomena; but this diversity is not to be deplored. One lesson we gain from a survey of the history of criticism, in fact, is the great debt we owe to the variety of the criticism of the past. Contrary to Prall's pessimistic appraisal, these theories have not been futile, but as working conceptions of the matter, end, and ordonnance of art, have been greatly effective in shaping the activities of creative artists. Even an aesthetic philosophy so abstract and seemingly academic as that of Kant can be shown to have modified the work of poets. In modern times, new departures in literature almost invariably have been accompanied by novel critical pronouncements, whose very inadequacies sometimes help to form the characteristic qualities of the correlated literary achievements, so that if our critics had not disagreed so violently, our artistic inheritance would doubtless have been less rich and various. Also, the very fact that any well-grounded critical theory in some degree alters the aesthetic perceptions it purports to discover is a source of its value to the amateur of art, for it may open his senses to aspects of a work which other theories, with a different focus and different categories of discrimination, have on principle overlooked, underestimated, or obscured.

The diversity of aesthetic theories, however, makes the task of the historian a very difficult one. It is not only that answers to such questions as 'What is art?' or 'What is poetry?' disagree. The fact is that many theories of art cannot readily be compared at all, because they lack a common ground on which to meet and clash. They seem incommensurable because stated in diverse terms, or in identical terms with diverse signification, or because they are an integral part of larger systems of thought which differ in assumptions and procedure. As a result it is hard to find where they agree, where disagree, or even, what the points at issue are.

Our first need, then, is to find a frame of reference simple enough to be readily manageable, yet flexible enough so that, without undue violence to any one set of statements about art, it will translate as many sets as possible onto a single plane of discourse. Most writers bold enough to undertake the history of aesthetic theory have achieved this end by silently translating the basic terms of all theories into their own favorite philosophical vocabulary, but this procedure unduly distorts its subject matter, and merely multiplies the complications to be unraveled. The more promising method is to adopt an analytic scheme which avoids imposing its own philosophy, by utilizing those key distinctions which are already common to the largest possible number of the theories to be compared, and then to apply the scheme warily, in constant readiness to introduce such further distinctions as seem to be needed for the purpose in hand.

i. Some Co-ordinates of Art Criticism

Four elements in the total situation of a work of art are discriminated and made salient, by one or another synonym, in almost all theories which aim to be comprehensive. First, there is the *work,* the artistic product itself. And since this is a human product, an artifact, the second common element is the artificer, the *artist.* Third, the work is taken to have a subject which, directly or deviously, is derived from existing things—to be about, or signify, or reflect something which either is, or bears some relation to, an objective state of affairs. This third element, whether held to consist of people and actions, ideas and feelings, material things and events, or super-sensible essences, has frequently been denoted by that word-of-all-work, 'nature'; but let us use the more neutral and comprehensive term, *universe,* instead. For the final element we have the *audience:* the listeners, spectators, or readers to whom the work is addressed, or to whose attention, at any rate, it becomes available.

On this framework of artist, work, universe, and audience I wish to spread out various theories for comparison. To emphasize the artificiality of the device, and at the same time make it easier to visualize the analyses, let us arrange the four co-ordinates in a convenient pattern. A triangle will do, with the work of art, the thing to be explained, in the center.

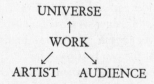

Although any reasonably adequate theory takes some account of all four elements, almost all theories, as we shall see, exhibit a discernible orientation toward one only. That is, a critic tends to derive from one of these terms his principal categories for defining, classifying, and analyzing a work of art, as well as the major criteria by which he judges its value. Application of this analytic scheme, therefore, will sort attempts to explain the nature and worth of a work of art into four broad classes. Three will explain the work of art principally by relating it to another thing: the universe, the audience, or the artist. The fourth will explain the work by considering it in isolation, as an autonomous whole, whose significance and value are determined without any reference beyond itself.

To find the major orientation of a critical theory, however, is only the beginning of an adequate analysis. For one thing, these four co-ordinates are not constants, but variables; they differ in significance according to the theory in which they occur. Take what I have called the *universe* as an example. In any one theory, the aspects of nature which an artist is said to imitate, or is exhorted to imitate, may be either particulars or types, and they may be only the beautiful or the moral aspects of the world, or else any aspect without discrimination. It may be maintained that the artist's world is that of imaginative intuition, or of common sense, or of natural science; and this world may be held to include, or not to include, gods, witches, chimeras, and Platonic Ideas. Consequently, theories which agree in assigning to the represented universe the primary control over a legitimate work of art may vary from recommending the most uncompromising realism to the most remote idealism. Each of our other terms, as we shall see, also varies, both in meaning and functioning, according to the critical theory in which it occurs, the method of reasoning which the theorist characteristically uses, and the explicit or implicit 'world-view' of which these theories are an integral part.

It would be possible, of course, to devise more complex methods of analysis which, even in a preliminary classification, would make more subtle distinctions.[3] By multiplying differentiae, however, we sharpen our capacity to discriminate at the expense both of easy manageability and the ability to make broad initial generalizations. For our historical purpose, the scheme I have proposed has this important virtue, that it will enable us to bring out the one essential attribute which most early nineteenth-century theories had in common: the persistent recourse to the poet to explain the nature and criteria of poetry. Historians have recently been instructed to speak only of 'romanticisms,' in the plural, but from our point of vantage there turns out to be one distinctively romantic criticism, although this remains a unity amid variety.

ii. Mimetic Theories

The mimetic orientation—the explanation of art as essentially an imitation of aspects of the universe—was probably the most primitive aesthetic theory, but mimesis is no simple concept by the time it makes its first recorded appearance in the dialogues of Plato. The arts of painting, poetry, music, dancing, and sculpture, Socrates says, are all imitations.[4] 'Imitation' is a relational term, signifying two items and some correspondence between them. But although in many later mimetic theories everything is comprehended in two categories, the imitable and the imitation, the philosopher in the Platonic dialogues characteristically operates with three categories. The first category is that of the eternal and unchanging Ideas; the second, reflecting this, is the world of sense, natural or artificial; and the third category, in turn reflecting the second, comprises such things as shadows, images in water and mirrors, and the fine arts.

Around this three-stage regress—complicated still further by various supplementary distinctions, as well as by his exploitation of the polysemism of his key terms—Plato weaves his dazzling dialectic.[5] But from the shifting arguments emerges a recurrent pattern, exemplified in the famous passage in the tenth book of the *Republic*. In discussing the nature of art, Socrates makes the point that there are three beds: the Idea which 'is the essence of the bed' and is made by God, the bed made by the carpenter, and the bed found in a painting. How shall we describe the painter of this third bed?

I think, he said, that we may fairly designate him as the imitator of that which the others make.

Good, I said; then you call him who is third in the descent from nature an imitator?

Certainly, he said.

And the tragic poet is an imitator, and therefore, like all other imitators, he is thrice removed from the king and from the truth?

That appears to be so.[6]

From the initial position that art imitates the world of appearance and not of Essence, it follows that works of art have a lowly status in the order of existing things. Furthermore, since the realm of Ideas is the ultimate locus not only of reality but of value, the determination that art is at second remove from the truth automatically establishes its equal remoteness from the beautiful and good. Despite the elaborate dialectic—or more accurately, by means of it—Plato's remains a philosophy of a single standard; for all things, including art, are ultimately judged by the one criterion of their relation to the same Ideas. On these grounds, the poet is inescapably the competitor of the artisan, the lawmaker, and the moralist; indeed, any one of these can be regarded as himself the truer poet, successfully achieving that imitation of the Ideas which the traditional poet attempts under conditions dooming him to failure. Thus the lawmaker is able to reply to the poets seeking admission to his city, 'Best of strangers—

we also according to our ability are tragic poets, and our tragedy is the best and noblest; for our whole state is an imitation of the best and noblest life, which we affirm to be indeed the very truth of tragedy. You are poets and we are poets . . . rivals and antagonists in the noblest of dramas. . .[7]

And the poor opinion of ordinary poetry to which we are committed on the basis of its mimetic character, is merely confirmed when Plato points out that its effects on its auditors are bad because it represents appearance rather than truth, and nourishes their feelings rather than their reason; or by demonstrating that the poet in composing (as Socrates jockeys poor obtuse Ion into admitting) cannot depend on his art and knowledge, but must wait upon the divine afflatus and the loss of his right mind.[8]

The Socratic dialogues, then, contain no aesthetics proper, for neither the structure of Plato's cosmos nor the pattern of his dialectic permits us to consider poetry as poetry—as a special kind of product having its own criteria and reason for being. In the dialogues there is only one direction possible, and one issue, that is, the perfecting of the social state and the state of man; so that the question of art can never be separated from questions of truth, justice, and virtue. 'For great is the issue at stake,' Socrates says in concluding his discussion of poetry in the *Republic,* 'greater than appears, whether a man is to be good or bad.'[9]

Aristotle in the *Poetics* also defines poetry as imitation. 'Epic poetry and Tragedy, as also Comedy, Dithyrambic poetry, and most flute-playing and lyre-playing, are all, viewed as a whole, modes of imitation'; and 'the objects the imitator represents are actions. . .'[10] But the difference between the way the term 'imitation' functions in Aristotle and in Plato distinguishes radically their consideration of art. In the *Poetics,* as in the Platonic dialogues, the term implies that a work of art is constructed according to prior models in the nature of things, but since Aristotle has shorn away the other world of criterion-Ideas, there is no longer anything invidious in that fact. Imitation is also made a term specific to the arts, distinguishing these from everything else in the universe, and thereby freeing them from rivalry with other human activities. Furthermore, in his analysis of the fine arts, Aristotle at once introduces supplementary distinctions according to the objects imitated, the medium of imitation, and the manner—dramatic, narrative, or mixed, for example—in which the imitation is accomplished. By successive exploitation of these distinctions in object, means, and manner, he is able first to distinguish poetry from other kinds of art, and then to differentiate the various poetic genres, such as epic and drama, tragedy and comedy. When he focuses on the genre of tragedy, the same analytic instrument is applied to the discrimination of the parts constituting the individual whole: plot, character, thought, and so on. Aristotle's criticism, therefore, is not only criticism of art as art, independent of statesmanship, being, and morality, but also of poetry as poetry, and of each kind of poem by the criteria appropriate to its particular nature. As a result of this procedure, Aristotle bequeathed an arsenal of instruments for technical analysis of poetic forms and their elements which have proved indispensable to critics ever since, however diverse the uses to which these instruments have been put.

A salient quality of the *Poetics* is the way it considers a work of art in various of its external relations, affording each its due function as one of the 'causes' of the work. This procedure results in a scope and flexibility that makes the treatise resist a ready classification into any one kind of orientation. Tragedy cannot be fully defined, for example, nor can the total determinants of its construction be understood, without taking into account its proper effect on the audience: the achievement of the specifically 'tragic pleasure,' which is 'that of pity and fear.' [11] It is apparent, however, that the mimetic concept—the reference of a work to the subject matter which it imitates—is primary in Aristotle's critical system, even if it is *primus inter pares*. Their character as an imitation of human actions is what defines the arts in general, and the kind of action imitated serves as one important differentia of an artistic species. The historical genesis of art is traced to the natural human instinct for imitating, and to the natural tendency to find pleasure in seeing imitations. Even the unity essential to any work of art is mimetically grounded, since 'one imitation is always of one thing,' and in poetry 'the story, as an imitation of action, must represent one action, a complete whole. . .' [12] And the 'form' of a work, the presiding principle determining the choice and order and internal adjustments of all the parts, is derived from the form of the object that is imitated. It is the fable or plot 'that is the end and purpose of tragedy,' its 'life and soul, so to speak,' and this because tragedy is essentially an imitation not of persons but of action and life. . . We maintain that Tragedy is primarily an imitation of action, and that it is mainly for the sake of the action that it imitates the personal agents.[13]

If we refer again to our analytic diagram, one other general aspect of the *Poetics* presses on our attention, particularly when we have the distinctive orientation of romantic criticism in mind. While Aristotle makes a distribution (though an unequal one) among the objects imitated, the necessary emotional effects on an audience, and the internal demands of the product itself, as determinants of this or that aspect of a poem, he does not assign a determinative function to the poet himself. The poet is the indispensable efficient cause, the agent who, by his skill, extracts the form from natural things and imposes it upon an artificial medium; but his personal faculties, feelings, or desires are not called on to explain the subject matter or form of a poem. In the *Poetics,* the poet is invoked only to explain the historical divergence of comic from serious forms, and to be advised of certain aids toward the construction of plot and the choice of diction.[14] In Plato, the poet is considered from the point of view of politics, not of art. When the poets make a personal appearance all the major ones are dismissed, with extravagant courtesy, from the ideal Republic; upon later application, a somewhat greater number are admitted to the second-best state of the *Laws,* but with a radically diminished repertory.[15]

'Imitation' continued to be a prominent item in the critical vocabulary for a long time after Aristotle—all the way through the eighteenth century, in fact. The systematic importance given to the term differed greatly from critic to critic; those objects in the universe that art imitates, or should imitate, were variously conceived as either actual or in some sense ideal; and from the first, there was a tendency to replace Aristotle's 'action' as the principal object of imitation with such elements as human character, or thought, or even inanimate things. But particularly after the recovery of the *Poetics* and the great burst of aesthetic theory in sixteenth-century Italy, whenever a critic was moved to get down to fundamentals and frame a comprehensive definition of art, the predicate usually included the word 'imitation,' or else one of those parallel terms which, whatever differences they might imply, all faced in the same direction: 'reflection,' 'representation,' 'counterfeiting,' 'feigning,' 'copy,' or 'image.'

Through most of the eighteenth century, the tenet that art is an imitation seemed almost too obvious to need iteration or proof. As Richard Hurd said in his 'Discourse on Poetical Imitation,' published in 1751, 'All *Poetry,* to speak with Aristotle and the Greek critics (if for so plain a point authorities be thought wanting) is, properly, *imitation*. It is, indeed, the noblest and most extensive of the mimetic arts; having all creation for its object, and ranging the entire circuit of universal being.' [16] Even the reputedly radical proponents of 'original genius' in the second half of the century commonly found that a work of genius was no less an imitation for being an original. '*Imitations*,' Young wrote in his *Conjectures on Original Composition,* 'are of two kinds: one of nature, one of authors. The first we call *Originals*. . .' The original genius in fact turns out to be a kind of scientific investigator: 'The wide field of nature lies open before it, where it may range unconfined, make what discoveries it can . . . as far as visible nature extends. . .' [17] Later the Reverend J. Moir, an extremist in his demand for originality in poetry, conceived genius to lie in the ability to discover 'a thousand new variations, distinctions, and resemblances' in the 'familiar phenomena of nature,' and declared that original genius always gives 'the identical impression it receives.' [18] In this identification of the poet's task as novelty of discovery and particularity of description we have moved a long way from Aristotle's conception of mimesis, except in this respect, that criticism still looks to one or another aspect of the given world for the essential source and subject matter of poetry.

Instead of heaping up quotations, it will be better to cite a few eighteenth-century discussions of imitation that are of special interest. My first example is the French critic, Charles Batteux, whose *Les Beaux Arts réduits à un même principe* (1747) found some favor in England and had immense influence in Germany, as well as in his native country. The rules of art, Batteux thought, which are now so numerous, must surely be reducible to a single principle. 'Let us,' he cries, 'imitate the true physicists, who assemble experiments and then on these found a system which reduces them to a principle.'

That Batteux proposes for his procedure 'to begin with a clear and distinct idea'—a principle 'simple enough to be grasped instantly, and extensive enough to absorb all the little detailed rules'—is sufficient clue that he will follow in method not Newton, the physicist, but rather Euclid and Descartes. In pursuance of his clear and distinct idea, he burrowed industriously through the standard French critics until, he says ingenuously, 'it occurred to me to open Aristotle, whose *Poetics* I had heard praised.' Then came the revelation; all details fell neatly into place. The source of illumination?— none other than 'the principle of imitation which the Greek philosopher established for the fine arts.' [19] This imitation, however, is not of crude everyday reality, but of 'la belle nature'; that is, 'le vrai-semblable,' formed by assembling traits taken from individual things to compose a model possessing 'all the perfections it is able to receive.' [20] From this principle Batteux goes on, lengthily and with great show of rigor, to extract one by one the rules of taste—both the general rules for poetry and painting and the detailed rules for the special genres. For

the majority of known rules refer back to imitation, and form a sort of chain, by which the mind seizes at the same instant consequences and principle, as a whole perfectly joined, in which all the parts are mutually sustained.[21]

Next to this classic instance of a priori and deductive aesthetics I shall set a German document, Lessing's *Laokoon,* published in 1766. Lessing undertook to undo the confusion in theory and practice between poetry and the graphic and plastic arts which, he believed, resulted from an uninquisitive acceptance of Simonides' maxim that 'painting is dumb poetry and poetry a speaking painting.' His own procedure, he promises, will be continually to test abstract theory against 'the individual instance.' Repeatedly he derides German critics for their reliance on deduction. 'We Germans have no lack of systematic books. We are the most expert of any nation in the world at deducing, from a few given verbal explanations, and in the most beautiful order, anything whatever that we wish.' 'How many things would prove incontestable in theory, had not genius succeeded in proving the contrary in fact!' [22] Lessing's intention, then, is to establish aesthetic principles by an inductive logic which is deliberately opposed to the procedure of Batteux. Nevertheless, like Batteux, Lessing concludes that poetry, no less than painting, is imitation. The diversity between these arts follows from their difference in medium, which imposes necessary differences in the objects each is competent to imitate. But although poetry consists of a sequence of articulate sounds in time rather than of forms and colors fixed in space, and although, instead of being limited, like painting, to a static but pregnant moment, its special power is the reproduction of progressive action, Lessing reiterates for it the standard formula: 'Nachahmung' is still for the poet the attribute 'which constitutes the essence of his art.' [23]

As the century drew on, various English critics began to scrutinize the concept of imitation very closely, and they ended by finding (Aristotle to the contrary) that differences in medium between the arts were such as to disqualify all but a limited number from being classed as mimetic, in any strict sense. The trend may be indicated by a few examples. In 1744 James Harris still maintained, in 'A Discourse on Music, Painting, and Poetry,' that imitation was common to all three arts. 'They agree, by being all

mimetic or imitative. They differ, as they imitate by different media. . .' [24]
In 1762 Kames declared that 'of all the fine arts, painting only and sculpture
are in their nature imitative'; music, like architecture, 'is productive of originals, and copies not from nature'; while language copies from nature only
in those instances in which it 'is imitative of sound or motion.' [25] And by
1789, in two closely reasoned dissertations prefixed to his translation of the
Poetics, Thomas Twining confirmed this distinction between arts whose
media are 'iconic' (in the later terminology of the Chicago semiotician,
Charles Morris), in that they resemble what they denote, and those which
are significant only by convention. Only works in which the resemblance
between copy and object is both 'immediate' and 'obvious,' Twining says,
can be described as imitative in a strict sense. Dramatic poetry, therefore,
in which we mimic speech by speech, is the only kind of poetry which is
properly imitation; music must be struck from the list of imitative arts;
and he concludes by saying that painting, sculpture, and the arts of design
in general are 'the only arts that are *obviously* and *essentially* imitative.' [26]

The concept that art is imitation, then, played an important part in neo-
classic aesthetics; but closer inspection shows that it did not, in most theories,
play the dominant part. Art, it was commonly said, is an imitation—but an
imitation which is only instrumental toward producing effects upon an
audience. In fact, the near-unanimity with which post-Renaissance critics
lauded and echoed Aristotle's *Poetics* is deceptive. The focus of interest had
shifted, and, on our diagram, this later criticism is primarily oriented, not
from work to universe, but from work to audience. The nature and consequences of this change of direction is clearly indicated by the first classic of
English criticism, written sometime in the early 1580's, Sir Philip Sidney's
The Apologie for Poetry.

iii. Pragmatic Theories

Poesy therefore [said Sidney] is an arte of imitation, for so Aristotle termeth it
in the word *Mimesis,* that is to say, a representing, counterfetting, or figuring
foorth—to speake metaphorically, a speaking picture: with this end, to teach and
delight.[27]

In spite of the appeal to Aristotle, this is not an Aristotelian formulation.
To Sidney, poetry, by definition, has a purpose—to achieve certain effects
in an audience. It imitates only as a means to the proximate end of pleasing,
and pleases, it turns out, only as a means to the ultimate end of teaching;
for 'right poets' are those who 'imitate both to delight and teach, and delight

to move men to take that goodnes in hande, which without delight they would flye as from a stranger. . .' [28] As a result, throughout this essay the needs of the audience become the fertile grounds for critical distinctions and standards. In order 'to teach and delight,' poets imitate not 'what is, hath been, or shall be,' but only 'what may be, and should be,' so that the very objects of imitation become such as to guarantee the moral purpose. The poet is distinguished from, and elevated above, the moral philosopher and the historian by his capacity to move his auditors more forcefully to virtue, since he couples 'the general notion' of the philosopher with 'the particular example' of the historian; while by disguising his doctrine in a tale, he entices even 'harde harted evill men,' unaware, into the love of goodness, 'as if they tooke a medicine of Cherries.' The genres of poetry are discussed and ranked from the point of view of the moral and social effect each is suited to achieve: the epic poem thus demonstrates itself to be the king of poetry because it 'most inflameth the mind with desire to be worthy,' and even the lowly love lyric is conceived as an instrument for persuading a mistress of the genuineness of her lover's passion.[29] A history of criticism could be written solely on the basis of successive interpretations of salient passages from Aristotle's *Poetics*. In this instance, with no sense of strain, Sidney follows his Italian guides (who in turn had read Aristotle through the spectacles of Horace, Cicero, and the Church fathers) in bending one after another of the key statements of the *Poetics* to fit his own theoretical frame.[30]

For convenience we may name criticism that, like Sidney's, is ordered toward the audience, a 'pragmatic theory,' since it looks at the work of art chiefly as a means to an end, an instrument for getting something done, and tends to judge its value according to its success in achieving that aim. There is, of course, the greatest variance in emphasis and detail, but the central tendency of the pragmatic critic is to conceive a poem as something made in order to effect requisite responses in its readers; to consider the author from the point of view of the powers and training he must have in order to achieve this end; to ground the classification and anatomy of poems in large part on the special effects each kind and component is most competent to achieve; and to derive the norms of the poetic art and canons of critical appraisal from the needs and legitimate demands of the audience to whom the poetry is addressed.

The perspective, much of the basic vocabulary, and many of the characteristic topics of pragmatic criticism originated in the classical theory of rhetoric. For rhetoric had been universally regarded as an instrument for achieving persuasion in an audience, and most theorists agreed with Cicero that in order to persuade, the orator must conciliate, inform, and move the minds of his auditors.[31] The great classical exemplar of the application of the rhetorical point of view to poetry was, of course, the *Ars Poetica* of Horace. As Richard McKeon points out, 'Horace's criticism is directed in the main to instruct the poet how to keep his audience in their seats until the end, how to induce cheers and applause, how to please a Roman audience, and by the same token, how to please all audiences and win immortality.'[32]

In what became for later critics the focal passage of the *Ars Poetica,* Horace advised that 'the poet's aim is either to profit or to please, or to blend in one the delightful and the useful.' The context shows that Horace held pleasure to be the chief purpose of poetry, for he recommends the profitable merely as a means to give pleasure to the elders, who, in contrast to the young aristocrats, 'rail at what contains no serviceable lesson.'[33] But *prodesse* and *delectare,* to teach and to please, together with another term introduced from rhetoric, *movere,* to move, served for centuries to collect under three heads the sum of aesthetic effects on the reader. The balance between these terms altered in the course of time. To the overwhelming majority of Renaissance critics, as to Sir Philip Sidney, the moral effect was the terminal aim, to which delight and emotion were auxiliary. From the time of the critical essays of Dryden through the eighteenth century, pleasure tended to become the ultimate end, although poetry without profit was often held to be trivial, and the optimistic moralist believed with James Beattie that if poetry instructs, it only pleases the more effectually.[34]

Looking upon a poem as a 'making,' a contrivance for affecting an audience, the typical pragmatic critic is engrossed with formulating the methods —the 'skill, or Crafte of making' as Ben Jonson called it—for achieving the effects desired. These methods, traditionally comprehended under the term *poesis,* or 'art' (in phrases such as 'the art of poetry'), are formulated as precepts and rules whose warrant consists either in their being derived from the qualities of works whose success and long survival have proved their adaptation to human nature, or else in their being grounded directly on the psychological laws governing the responses of men in general. The rules, therefore, are inherent in the qualities of each excellent work of art, and when excerpted and codified these rules serve equally to guide the artist in making and the critics in judging any future product. 'Dryden,' said Dr. Johnson, 'may be properly considered as the father of English criticism, as the writer who first taught us to determine upon principles the merit of composition.'[35] Dryden's method of establishing those principles was to point out that poetry, like painting, has an end, which is to please; that imitation of nature is the general means for attaining this end; and that rules serve to specify the means for accomplishing this end in detail:

Having thus shewn that imitation pleases, and why it pleases in both these arts, it follows, that some rules of imitation are necessary to obtain the end; for without rules there can be no art, any more than there can be a house without a door to conduct you into it.[36]

Emphasis on the rules and maxims of an art is native to all criticism that grounds itself in the demands of an audience, and it survives today in the magazines and manuals devoted to teaching fledgling authors 'how to write stories that sell.' But rulebooks based on the lowest common denominator of the modern buying public are only gross caricatures of the complex and subtly rationalized neo-classic ideals of literary craftsmanship. Through the early part of the eighteenth century, the poet could rely confidently on the trained taste and expert connoisseurship of a limited circle of readers, whether these were Horace's Roman contemporaries under Emperor Augustus, or Vida's at the papal court of Leo X, or Sidney's fellow-courtiers under Elizabeth, or the London audience of Dryden and Pope; while, in theory, the voices even of the best contemporary judges were subordinated to the voice of the ages. Some neo-classic critics were also certain that the rules of art, though empirically derived, were ultimately validated by conforming to that objective structure of norms whose existence guaranteed the rational order and harmony of the universe. In a strict sense, as John Dennis made explicit what was often implied, Nature 'is nothing but that Rule and Order, and Harmony, which we find in the visible Creation'; so 'Poetry, which is an imitation of Nature,' must demonstrate the same properties. The renowned masters among the ancients wrote not

to please a tumultuous transitory Assembly, or a Handful of Men, who were call'd their Countrymen; They wrote to their Fellow-Citizens of the Universe, to all Countries, and to all Ages. . . They were clearly convinc'd, that nothing could transmit their Immortal Works to Posterity, but something like that harmonious Order which maintains the Universe. . .[37]

Although they disagreed concerning specific rules, and although many English critics repudiated such formal French requisites as the unity of time and place, and the purity of comedy and tragedy, all but a few eccentrics among eighteenth-century critics believed in the validity of some set of universal rules. At about mid-century, it became popular to demonstrate and expound all the major rules for poetry, or even for art in general, in a single inclusive critical system. The pattern of the pragmatic reasoning usually employed may conveniently be studied in such a compendious treatment as James Beattie's *Essay on Poetry and Music as they affect the Mind* (1762), or more succinctly still, in Richard Hurd's 'Dissertation of the Idea of Universal Poetry' (1766). Universal poetry, no matter what the genre, Hurd says, is an art whose end is the maximum possible pleasure. 'When we speak of poetry, as an *art,* we mean *such a way or method of treating a subject, as is found most pleasing and delightful to us.'* And this idea 'if kept steadily in view, will unfold to us all the mysteries of the poetic art. There needs but to evolve the philosopher's idea, and to apply it, as occasion serves.' From this major premise Hurd evolves three properties, essential to all poetry if it is to effect the greatest possible delight: figurative language, 'fiction' (that is to say, a departure from what is actual, or empirically possible), and versification. The mode and degree in which these three universal qualities are to be combined in any one species of poetry, however, will depend on its peculiar end, because each poetic kind must exploit that special pleasure which it is generically adapted to achieve. 'For the art of every *kind* of poetry is only this general art so modified as the *nature* of each, that is, its more immediate and subordinate end, may respectively require.'

For the name of poem will belong to every composition, whose primary end is to *please,* provided it be so constructed as to afford *all* the pleasure, which its kind or *sort* will permit.[38]

On the basis of isolated passages from his *Letters on Chivalry and Romance,* Hurd is commonly treated as a 'pre-romantic' critic. But in the summation of his poetic creed in the 'Idea of Universal Poetry,' the rigidly deductive logic which Hurd employs to 'unfold' the rules of poetry from a primitive definition, permitting 'the reason of the thing' to override the evidence of the actual practice of poets, brings him as close as anyone in England to the geometric method of Charles Batteux, though without that critic's Cartesian apparatus. The difference is that Batteux evolves his rules from the definition of poetry as the imitation of *la belle nature,* and Hurd, from its definition as the art of treating a subject so as to afford the reader a maximum pleasure; and this involves his assuming that he possesses an empirical knowledge of the psychology of the reader. For if the end of poetry is to gratify the mind of the reader, Hurd says, knowledge of the laws of mind is necessary to establish its rules, which are 'but so many MEANS, which ex-

perience finds most conducive to that end.'[39] Since Batteux and Hurd, however, are both intent on rationalizing what is mainly a common body of
poetic lore, it need not surprise us that, though they set out from different
points of the compass, their paths often coincide.[40]

But to appreciate the power and illumination of which a refined and flexible pragmatic criticism is capable, we must turn from these abstract sys-
tematizers of current methods and maxims to such a practical critic as
Samuel Johnson. Johnson's literary criticism assumes approximately the
frame of critical reference I have described, but Johnson, who distrusts rigid
and abstract theorizing, applies the method with a constant appeal to specific
literary examples, deference to the opinions of other readers, but ultimately,
reliance on his own expert responses to the text. As a result Johnson's comments on poets and poems have persistently afforded a jumping-off point
for later critics whose frame of reference and particular judgments differ
radically from his own. For an instance of Johnson's procedure which is
especially interesting because it shows how the notion of the imitation of
nature is co-ordinated with the judgment of poetry in terms of its end and
effects, consider that monument of neo-classic criticism, Johnson's *Preface
to Shakespeare.*

Johnson undertakes in his *Preface* to establish Shakespeare's rank among
poets, and to do so, he is led to rate Shakespeare's native abilities against the
general level of taste and achievement in the Elizabethan age, and to measure these abilities in turn 'by their proportion to the general and collective
ability of man.'[41] Since the powers and excellence of an author, however,
can only be inferred from the nature and excellence of the works he achieves,
Johnson addresses himself to a general examination of Shakespeare's dramas.
In this systematic appraisal of the works themselves, we find that mimesis
retains for Johnson a measure of authority as criterion. Repeatedly Johnson
maintains that 'this therefore is the praise of *Shakespeare,* that his drama is
the mirrour of life,' and of inanimate nature as well: 'He was an exact surveyor of the inanimate world. . . *Shakespeare,* whether life or nature be his
subject, shews plainly, that he has seen with his own eyes. . .'[42] But, Johnson also claims, 'The end of writing is to instruct; the end of poetry is to
instruct by pleasing.'[43] It is to this function of poetry, and to the demonstrated effect of a poem upon its audience, that Johnson awards priority as
aesthetic criterion. If a poem fails to please, whatever its character otherwise,
it is, as a work of art, nothing; though Johnson insists, with a strenuous
moralism that must already have seemed old-fashioned to contemporary
readers, it must please without violating the standards of truth and virtue.

Accordingly, Johnson discriminates those elements in Shakespeare's plays which were introduced to appeal to the local and passing tastes of the rather barbarous audience of his own time ('He knew,' said Johnson, 'how he should most please'),[44] from those elements which are proportioned to the tastes of the common readers of all time. And since in works 'appealing wholly to observation and experience, no other test can be applied than length of duration and continuance of esteem,' Shakespeare's long survival as a poet 'read without any other reason than the desire for pleasure' is the best evidence for his artistic excellence. The reason for this survival Johnson explains on the subsidiary principle that 'nothing can please many, and please long, but just representations of general nature.' Shakespeare exhibits the eternal 'species' of human character, moved by 'those general passions and principles by which all minds are agitated.'[45] Thus Shakespeare's excellence in holding up the mirror to general nature turns out, in the long run, to be justified by the superior criterion of the appeal this achievement holds for the enduring tastes of the general literary public.

A number of Johnson's individual observations and judgments exhibit a play of the argument between the two principles of the nature of the world the poet must reflect, and the nature and legitimate requirements of the poet's audience. For the most part the two principles co-operate toward a single conclusion. For example, both the empirical nature of the universe and of the universal reader demonstrate the fallacy of those who censure Shakespeare for mixing his comic and tragic scenes. Shakespeare's plays, Johnson says, exhibit 'the real state of sublunary nature, which partakes of good and evil, joy and sorrow, mingled with endless variety.' In addition, 'the mingled drama may convey all the instruction of tragedy or comedy' by approaching nearer 'to the appearance of life'; while the objection that the change of scene 'wants at last the power to move' is a specious reasoning 'received as true even by those who in daily experience feel it to be false.'[46] But when the actual state of sublunary affairs conflicts with the poet's obligation to his audience, the latter is the court of final appeal. It is Shakespeare's defect, says Johnson,

that he seems to write without any moral purpose. . . He makes no just distribution of good or evil, nor is always careful to shew in the virtuous a disapprobation of the wicked. . . It is always a writer's duty to make the world better, and justice is a virtue independant on time or place.[47]

The pragmatic orientation, ordering the aim of the artist and the character of the work to the nature, the needs, and the springs of pleasure in the audience, characterized by far the greatest part of criticism from the time of Horace through the eighteenth century. Measured either by its duration or the number of its adherents, therefore, the pragmatic view, broadly conceived, has been the principal aesthetic attitude of the Western world. But inherent in this system were the elements of its dissolution. Ancient rhetoric had bequeathed to criticism not only its stress on affecting the audience but also (since its main concern was with educating the orator) its detailed attention to the powers and activities of the speaker himself—his 'nature,' or innate powers and genius, as distinguished from his culture and art, and also the process of invention, disposition, and expression involved in his discourse.[48] In the course of time, and particularly after the psychological contributions of Hobbes and Locke in the seventeenth century, increasing attention was given to the mental constitution of the poet, the quality and degree of his 'genius,' and the play of his faculties in the act of composition. Through most of the eighteenth century, the poet's invention and imagination were made thoroughly dependent for their materials—their ideas and 'images'—on the external universe and the literary models the poet had to imitate; while the persistent stress laid on his need for judgment and art— the mental surrogates, in effect, of the requirements of a cultivated audience —held the poet strictly responsible to the audience for whose pleasure he exerted his creative ability. Gradually, however, the stress was shifted more and more to the poet's natural genius, creative imagination, and emotional spontaneity, at the expense of the opposing attributes of judgment, learning, and artful restraints. As a result the audience gradually receded into the background, giving place to the poet himself, and his own mental powers and emotional needs, as the predominant cause and even the end and test of art. By this time other developments, which we shall have occasion to talk about later, were also helping to shift the focus of critical interest from audience to artist and thus to introduce a new orientation into the theory of art.

iv. Expressive Theories

'Poetry,' Wordsworth announced in his Preface to the *Lyrical Ballads* of 1800, 'is the spontaneous overflow of powerful feelings.' He thought well enough of this formulation to use it twice in the same essay, and on this, as the ground-idea, he founded his theory of the proper subjects, language, effects, and value of poetry. Almost all the major critics of the English romantic generation phrased definitions or key statements showing a parallel alignment from work to poet. Poetry is the overflow, utterance, or projection of the thought and feelings of the poet; or else (in the chief variant formulation) poetry is defined in terms of the imaginative process which modifies and synthesizes the images, thoughts, and feelings of the poet. This way of thinking, in which the artist himself becomes the major element generating both the artistic product and the criteria by which it is to be judged, I shall call the expressive theory of art.

Setting the date at which this point of view became predominant in critical theory, like marking the point at which orange becomes yellow in the color spectrum, must be a somewhat arbitrary procedure. As we shall see, an approach to the expressive orientation, though isolated in history and partial in scope, is to be found as early as Longinus' discussion of the sublime style as having its main sources in the thought and emotions of the speaker; and it recurs in a variant form in Bacon's brief analysis of poetry as pertaining to the imagination and 'accommodating the shows of things to the desires of the mind.' Even Wordsworth's theory, it will appear, is much more embedded in a traditional matrix of interests and emphases, and is, therefore, less radical than are the theories of his followers of the 1830's. The year 1800 is a good round number, however, and Wordsworth's Preface a convenient document, by which to signalize the displacement of the mimetic and pragmatic by the expressive view of art in English criticism.

In general terms, the central tendency of the expressive theory may be summarized in this way: A work of art is essentially the internal made external, resulting from a creative process operating under the impulse of feeling, and embodying the combined product of the poet's perceptions, thoughts, and feelings. The primary source and subject matter of a poem, therefore, are the attributes and actions of the poet's own mind; or if aspects of the external world, then these only as they are converted from fact to poetry by the feelings and operations of the poet's mind. ('Thus the Poetry . . .' Wordsworth wrote, 'proceeds whence it ought to do, from the soul of Man, communicating its creative energies to the images of the external world.') [49] The paramount cause of poetry is not, as in Aristotle, a formal cause, determined primarily by the human actions and qualities imitated; nor, as in neo-classic criticism, a final cause, the effect intended upon the audience; but instead an efficient cause—the impulse within the poet of feelings and desires seeking expression, or the compulsion of the 'creative' imagination which, like God the creator, has its internal source of motion. The propensity is to grade the arts by the extent to which their media are amenable to the undistorted expression of the feelings or mental powers of the artist, and to classify the species of an art, and evaluate their instances, by the qualities or states of mind of which they are a sign. Of the elements constituting a poem, the element of diction, especially figures of speech, becomes primary; and the burning question is, whether these are the natural utterance of emotion and imagination or the deliberate aping of poetic conventions. The first test any poem must pass is no longer, 'Is it true to nature?' or 'Is it appropriate to the requirements either of the best judges or the generality of mankind?' but a criterion looking in a different direction; namely, 'Is it sincere? Is it genuine? Does it match the intention, the feeling, and the actual state of mind of the poet while composing?' The work ceases then to be regarded as primarily a reflection of nature, actual or improved; the mirror held up to nature becomes transparent and yields the reader insights into the mind and heart of the poet himself. The exploitation of literature as an index to personality first manifests itself in the early nineteenth century; it is the inevitable consequence of the expressive point of view.

The sources, details, and historical results of this reorientation of criticism, in its various forms, will be a principal concern of the rest of this book. Now, while we have some of the earlier facts fresh in mind, let me indicate what happened to salient elements of traditional criticism in the essays 'What Is Poetry?' and 'The Two Kinds of Poetry,' written by John Stuart Mill in 1833. Mill relied in large part on Wordsworth's Preface to the *Lyrical Ballads,* but in the intervening thirty years the expressive theory had emerged from the network of qualifications in which Wordsworth had carefully placed it, and had worked out its own destiny unhindered. Mill's logic in answering the question, 'What Is Poetry?' is not *more geometrico,* like that of Batteux, nor stiffly formal, like Richard Hurd's; nonetheless, his theory turns out to be just as tightly dependent upon a central principle as theirs. For whatever Mill's empirical pretensions, his initial assumption about the essential nature of poetry remains continuously though silently effective in selecting, interpreting, and ordering the facts to be explained.

The primitive proposition of Mill's theory is: Poetry is 'the expression or uttering forth of feeling.'[50] Exploration of the data of aesthetics from this starting point leads, among other things, to the following drastic alterations in the great commonplaces of the critical tradition:

(1) *The poetic kinds.* Mill reinterprets and inverts the neo-classic ranking of the poetic kinds. As the purest expression of feeling, lyric poetry is 'more eminently and peculiarly poetry than any other. . .' Other forms are all alloyed by non-poetic elements, whether descriptive, didactic, or narrative, which serve merely as convenient occasions for the poetic utterances of feeling either by the poet or by one of his invented characters. To Aristotle,

tragedy had been the highest form of poetry, and the plot, representing the action being imitated, had been its 'soul'; while most neo-classic critics had agreed that, whether judged by greatness of subject matter or of effect, epic and tragedy are the king and queen of poetic forms. It serves as an index to the revolution in critical norms to notice that to Mill, plot becomes a kind of necessary evil. An epic poem 'in so far as it is epic (i.e. narrative) . . . is not poetry at all,' but only a suitable frame for the greatest diversity of genuinely poetic passages; while the interest in plot and story 'merely as a story' characterizes rude stages of society, children, and the 'shallowest and emptiest' of civilized adults.[51] Similarly with the other arts; in music, painting, sculpture, and architecture Mill distinguishes between that which is 'simple imitation or description' and that which 'expresses human feeling' and is, therefore, poetry.[52]

(2) *Spontaneity as criterion.* Mill accepts the venerable assumption that a man's emotional susceptibility is innate, but his knowledge and skill—his art—are acquired. On this basis, he distinguishes poets into two classes: poets who are born and poets who are made, or those who are poets 'by nature,' and those who are poets 'by culture.' Natural poetry is identifiable because it 'is Feeling itself, employing Thought only as the medium of its utterance'; on the other hand, the poetry of 'a cultivated but not naturally poetic mind,' is written with 'a distinct aim,' and in it the thought remains the conspicuous object, however surrounded by 'a halo of feeling.' Natural poetry, it turns out, is 'poetry in a far higher sense, than any other; since . . . that which constitutes poetry, human feeling, enters far more largely into this than into the poetry of culture.' Among the moderns, Shelley represents the poet born and Wordsworth the poet made; and with unconscious irony Mill turns Wordsworth's own criterion, 'the spontaneous overflow of feeling,' against its sponsor. Wordsworth's poetry 'has little even of the appearance of spontaneousness: the well is never so full that it overflows.'[53]

(3) *The external world.* In so far as a literary product simply imitates objects, it is not poetry at all. As a result, reference of poetry to the external universe disappears from Mill's theory, except to the extent that sensible objects may serve as a stimulus or 'occasion for the generation of poetry,' and then, 'the poetry is not in the object itself,' but 'in the state of mind' in which it is contemplated. When a poet describes a lion he 'is describing the lion professedly, but the state of excitement of the spectator really,' and the poetry must be true not to the object, but to 'the human emotion.'[54] Thus severed from the external world, the objects signified by a poem tend to be regarded as no more than a projected equivalent—an extended and articu-

lated symbol—for the poet's inner state of mind. Poetry, said Mill, in a phrasing which anticipates T. E. Hulme and lays the theoretical groundwork for the practice of symbolists from Baudelaire through T. S. Eliot, embodies 'itself in symbols, which are the nearest possible representations of the feeling in the exact shape in which it exists in the poet's mind.' [55] Tennyson, Mill wrote in a review of that poet's early poems, excels in 'scene-painting, in the higher sense of the term'; and this is

> not the mere power of producing that rather vapid species of composition usually termed descriptive poetry . . . but the power of *creating* scenery, in keeping with some state of human feeling; so fitted to it as to be the embodied symbol of it, and to summon up the state of feeling itself, with a force not to be surpassed by anything but reality.[56]

And as an indication of the degree to which the innovations of the romantics persist as the commonplaces of modern critics—even of those who purport to found their theory on anti-romantic principles—notice how striking is the parallel between the passage above and a famous comment by T. S. Eliot:

> The only way of expressing emotion in the form of art is by finding an 'objective correlative'; in other words, a set of objects, a situation, a chain of events which shall be the formula of that *particular* emotion; such that when the external facts, which must terminate in sensory experience, are given, the emotion is immediately evoked.[57]

(4) *The audience.* No less drastic is the fate of the audience. According to Mill, 'Poetry is feeling, confessing itself to itself in moments of solitude. . .' The poet's audience is reduced to a single member, consisting of the poet himself. 'All poetry,' as Mill puts it, 'is of the nature of soliloquy.' The purpose of producing effects upon other men, which for centuries had been the defining character of the art of poetry, now serves precisely the opposite function: it disqualifies a poem by proving it to be rhetoric instead. When the poet's

> act of utterance is not itself the end, but a means to an end—viz. by the feelings he himself expresses, to work upon the feelings, or upon the belief, or the will, of another,—when the expression of his emotions . . . is tinged also by that purpose, by that desire of making an impression upon another mind, then it ceases to be poetry, and becomes eloquence.[58]

There is, in fact, something singularly fatal to the audience in the romantic point of view. Or, in terms of historical causes, it might be conjectured that the disappearance of a homogeneous and discriminating reading public fostered a criticism which on principle diminished the importance of the audience as a determinant of poetry and poetic value. Wordsworth still insisted that 'Poets do not write for Poets alone, but for Men,' and that each of his poems 'has a worthy purpose'; even though it turns out that the pleasure and profit of the audience is an automatic consequence of the poet's *spontaneous* overflow of feeling, provided that the appropriate associations between thoughts and feelings have been established by the poet in advance.[59] Keats, however, affirmed roundly that 'I never wrote one single line of Poetry with the least Shadow of public thought.' [60] 'A poet is a nightingale,' according to Shelley, 'who sits in darkness and sings to cheer its own solitude with sweet sounds; his auditors are as men entranced by the melody of an unseen musician. . .' [61] For Carlyle, the poet utterly replaces the audience as the generator of aesthetic norms.

On the whole, Genius has privileges of its own; it selects an orbit for itself; and be this never so eccentric, if it is indeed a celestial orbit, we mere star-gazers must at last compose ourselves; must cease to cavil at it, and begin to observe it, and calculate its laws.[62]

The evolution is complete, from the mimetic poet, assigned the minimal role of holding a mirror up to nature, through the pragmatic poet who, whatever his natural gifts, is ultimately measured by his capacity to satisfy the public taste, to Carlyle's Poet as Hero, the chosen one who, because he is 'a Force of Nature,' writes as he must, and through the degree of homage he evokes, serves as the measure of his *reader's* piety and taste.[63]

v. Objective Theories

All types of theory described so far, in their practical applications, get down to dealing with the work of art itself, in its parts and their mutual relations, whether the premises on which these elements are discriminated and evaluated relate them primarily to the spectator, the artist, or the world without. But there is also a fourth procedure, the 'objective orientation,' which on principle regards the work of art in isolation from all these external points of reference, analyzes it as a self-sufficient entity constituted by its parts in their internal relations, and sets out to judge it solely by criteria intrinsic to its own mode of being.

This point of view has been comparatively rare in literary criticism. The one early attempt at the analysis of an art form which is both objective and comprehensive occurs in the central portion of Aristotle's *Poetics*. I have chosen to discuss Aristotle's theory of art under the heading of mimetic theories, because it sets out from, and makes frequent reference back to the concept of imitation. Such is the flexibility of Aristotle's procedure, however, that after he has isolated the species 'tragedy,' and established its relation to the universe as an imitation of a certain kind of action, and to the audience through its observed effect of purging pity and fear, his method becomes centripetal, and assimilates these external elements into attributes of the work proper. In this second consideration of tragedy as an object in itself, the actions and agents that are imitated re-enter the discussion as the plot, character, and thought which, together with diction, melody, and spectacle, make up the six elements of a tragedy; and even pity and fear are reconsidered as that pleasurable quality proper to tragedy, to be distinguished from the pleasures characteristic of comedy and other forms.[64] The tragic work itself can now be analyzed formally as a self-determining whole made up of parts, all organized around the controlling part, the tragic plot—itself a unity in which the component incidents are integrated by the internal relations of 'necessity or probability.'

As an all-inclusive approach to poetry, the objective orientation was just beginning to emerge in the late eighteenth and early nineteenth century. We shall see later on that some critics were undertaking to explore the concept of the poem as a heterocosm, a world of its own, independent of the world into which we are born, whose end is not to instruct or please but simply to exist. Certain critics, particularly in Germany, were expanding upon Kant's formula that a work of art exhibits *Zweckmässigkeit ohne Zweck* (purposiveness without purpose), together with his concept that the contemplation of beauty is disinterested and without regard to utility, while neglecting Kant's characteristic reference of an aesthetic product to the mental faculties of its creator and receptor. The aim to consider a poem, as Poe expressed it, as a 'poem *per se* . . . written solely for the poem's sake,'[65] in isolation from external causes and ulterior ends, came to constitute one element of the diverse doctrines usually huddled together by historians under the heading 'Art for Art's Sake.' And with differing emphases and adequacy, and in a great variety of theoretical contexts, the objective approach to poetry has become one of the most prominent elements in the innovative criticism of the last two or three decades. T. S. Eliot's dictum of 1928, that 'when we are considering poetry we must consider it primarily as poetry and not another thing' is widely approved, however far Eliot's own criticism sometimes departs from this ideal; and it is often joined with MacLeish's verse aphorism, 'A poem should not mean

But be.' The subtle and incisive criticism of criticism by the Chicago Neo-Aristotelians and their advocacy of an instrument adapted to dealing with poetry as such have been largely effective toward a similar end. In his 'ontological criticism,' John Crowe Ransom has been calling for recognition of 'the autonomy of the work itself as existing for its own sake'; [66] campaigns have been organized against 'the personal heresy,' 'the intentional fallacy,' and 'the affective fallacy'; the widely influential handbook, *The Theory of Literature*, written by René Wellek and Austin Warren, proposes that criticism deal with a poem *qua* poem, independently of 'extrinsic' factors; and similar views are being expressed, with increasing frequency, not only in our literary but in our scholarly journals. In America, at least, some form of the objective point of view has already gone far to displace its rivals as the reigning mode of literary criticism.

According to our scheme of analysis, then, there have been four major orientations, each one of which has seemed to various acute minds adequate for a satisfactory criticism of art in general. And by and large the historic progression, from the beginning through the early nineteenth century, has been from the mimetic theory of Plato and (in a qualified fashion) Aristotle, through the pragmatic theory, lasting from the conflation of rhetoric with poetic in the Hellenistic and Roman era almost through the eighteenth century, to the expressive theory of English (and somewhat earlier, German) romantic criticism.

Of course romantic criticism, like that of any period, was not uniform in its outlook. As late as 1831 Macaulay (whose thinking usually followed traditional patterns) still insists, as an eternal rule 'founded in reason and in the nature of things,' that 'poetry is, as was said more than two thousand years ago, imitation,' and differentiates between the arts on the basis of their diverse media and objects of imitation. Then, in an essay packed with eighteenth-century catch-lines, he ungratefully employs the mimetic principle to justify his elevation of Scott, Wordsworth, and Coleridge over the eighteenth-century poets because they imitate nature more accurately, and attacks the neo-classic rules of correctness on the ground that they 'tend to make . . . imitations less perfect than they otherwise would be. . .' [67] The mode of criticism which subjects art and the artist to the audience also continued to flourish, usually in a vulgarized form, among influential journalists such as Francis Jeffrey, who deliberately set themselves to voice the literary standards of the middle class and to preserve unsullied what Jeffrey called 'the purity of the female character.' [68]

But these are not the innovative critical writings which contributed to the predominant temper of what Shelley, in his 'Defence of Poetry,' called 'the spirit of the age'; and the radical difference between the characteristic points of view of neo-classic and romantic criticism remains unmistakable. Take such representative productions of the 1760's and '70's as Johnson's *Preface to Shakespeare,* Kames's *Elements of Criticism,* Richard Hurd's 'On the Idea of Universal Poetry,' *The Art of Poetry on a New Plan* (of dubious authorship), Beattie's *Essays on Poetry and Music,* and the first eight *Discourses* of Sir Joshua Reynolds. Place these next to the major inquiries into poetry and art of the romantic generation: Wordsworth's Prefaces and collateral essays, Coleridge's *Biographia Literaria* and Shakespearean lectures, Hazlitt's 'On Poetry in General' and other essays, even Shelley's Platonistic 'Defence of Poetry'; then add to this group such later documents as Carlyle's 'Characteristics' and early literary reviews, J. S. Mill's two essays on poetry, John Keble's *Lectures on Poetry,* and Leigh Hunt's 'What Is Poetry?'. Whatever the continuity of certain terms and topics between individual members of the two eras, and however important the methodological and doctrinal differences which divide the members within a single group, one decisive change marks off the criticism in the Age of Wordsworth from that in the Age of Johnson. The poet has moved into the center of the critical system and taken over many of the prerogatives which had once been exercised by his readers, the nature of the world in which he found himself, and the inherited precepts and examples of his poetic art.

IMITATION AND THE MIRROR

This therefore is the praise of Shakespeare, that his drama is the mirrour of life.

SAMUEL JOHNSON

It is the spectator, and not life, that art really mirrors.

OSCAR WILDE

These words are ineffectual and metaphorical. Most words are so—No help!

PERCY SHELLEY

IN THE TENTH BOOK of the *Republic* Socrates undertakes to explain the true nature of poetry, and at once introduces an analogy. The maker of an actual bed or table proceeds in accordance with the Ideas of these things. But the artist has another and easier way to make these and all other things.

What way?

An easy way enough, or rather, there are many ways in which the feat might be quickly and easily accomplished, none quicker than that of turning a mirror round and round—you would soon enough make the sun and the heavens, and the earth and yourself, and other animals and plants, and all the other things of which we were just now speaking, in the mirror.[1]

And from the properties of such mirror images, Plato goes on to evolve several unflattering consequences about the character and value of art.

This illustration is not a casual one, for in his writings Plato adverts repeatedly to the analogy of the reflector, either a mirror, or water, or else those less perfect simulacra of things that we call shadows. These he uses to clarify the inter-relations of all the items in the universe: of things, natural or artificial, to their prototypes, or Ideas; and of imitations of things, including those in the arts, to their models in the world of sense. Ordinarily, one would say that Plato introduced the reflector merely to illustrate a ready formed concept of the nature of art and of the cosmos, and the principal question to be raised is, whether the illustration is apt.

But there is another reasonable and important question: not only 'How apt is the analogy to the concept?' but 'To what extent may the concept have been generated from the analogy?'

i. Art Is Like a Mirror

The task of analyzing the nature and function of metaphor has traditionally been assigned to the rhetorician and to the critic of literature. Metaphor, however, whether alive or moribund, is an inseparable element of all discourse, including discourse whose purpose is neither persuasive nor aesthetic, but descriptive and informative. Metaphysical systems in particular are intrinsically metaphorical systems, and, in a recent book, Stephen C. Pepper has made out each of the major world views to be a kind of prodigious synecdoche, demonstrating the whole of the universe to be like one of its parts.[2] Even the traditional language of the natural sciences cannot claim to be totally literal, although its key terms often are not recognized to be metaphors until, in the course of time, the general adoption of a new analogy yields perspective into the nature of the old. And in the criticism of poetry, metaphor and analogy, though less conspicuous, are hardly less functional than in poetry itself. A particular aim of this book is to emphasize the role in the history of criticism of certain more or less submerged conceptual models—what we may call 'archetypal analogies'— in helping to select, interpret, systematize, and evaluate the facts of art.

While many expository analogues, as conventional opinion proposes, are casual and illustrative, some few seem recurrent and, not illustrative, but *constitutive:* they yield the ground plan and essential structural elements of a literary theory, or of any theory. By the same token, they select and mold those 'facts' which a theory comprehends. For facts are *facta,* things made as much as things found, and made in part by the analogies through which we look at the world as through a lens. 'I wonder,' Coleridge once remarked, 'why facts were ever called stubborn things? . . . Facts, you know, are not truths; they are not conclusions; they are not even premises, but in the nature and parts of premises.'[3]

Any area for investigation, so long as it lacks prior concepts to give it structure and an express terminology with which it can be managed, appears to the inquiring mind inchoate—either a blank, or an elusive and tantalizing confusion. Our usual recourse is, more or less deliberately, to cast about for objects which offer parallels to dimly sensed aspects of the new situation, to use the better known to elucidate the less known, to discuss the intangible in terms of the tangible. This analogical procedure seems characteristic of much intellectual enterprise. There is a deal of wisdom in the popular locution for 'What is its nature?' namely: 'What's it *like?*' We tend to describe the nature of something in similes and metaphors, and the vehicles of these recurrent figures, when analyzed, often turn out to be the attributes of an implicit analogue through which we are viewing the object we describe. And if I am right, Plato's deliberate use of analogue and parable differs from that of many other inquirers less in tactics than in candor.

The recourse to a mirror in order to illuminate the nature of one or another art continued to be a favorite with aesthetic theorists long after Plato. In Renaissance speculation the reference to a looking-glass is frequent and explicit. 'What should painting be called,' asked Alberti, 'except the holding of a mirror up to the original as in art?'[4] Leonardo repeatedly appeals to a mirror to illustrate the relation to nature both of a painting and the mind of the painter. 'The mind of the painter should be like a mirror which always takes the colour of the thing that it reflects and which is filled by as many images as there are things placed before it. . . You cannot be a good master unless you have a universal power of representing by your art all the varieties of the forms which nature produces.'[5] In literature we find Caxton's *Mirror of the World,* Barclay's *The Mirror of Minds,* and Gascoigne's *Glass of Government* and *The Steele Glass;* there are mirrors of fools and mirrors for magistrates. The analogue was especially popular for comedy, the early representative of literary realism, and a great many critics, Italian and English, cited the words that Donatus, writing in the fourth century, had attributed to Cicero, that comedy is 'a copy of life, a mirror of custom, a reflection of truth.' Thus in answer to the question, *'Quid sit comoedia?',* Ben Jonson puts in the mouth of the dramatic connoisseur, Cordatus, the alleged opinion of Cicero that it is an *'imitatio vitae, speculum consuetudinis, imago veritatis.'*[6]

As late as the middle of the eighteenth century important critics continued to illustrate the concept of imitation by the nature of a looking-glass. Dr. Johnson was fond of this parallel, and found it the highest excellence of Shakespeare that he 'holds up to his readers a faithful mirrour of manners and of life.'[7] In 1751 Bishop Warburton glossed Pope's line that 'Nature and Homer were, he found, the same' with the comment that Virgil 'had the prudence to contemplate nature in the place where she was seen to most advantage, collected in all her charms in the clear mirror of

Homer.' [8] Rousseau based his analysis of dramatic imitation on the passage in which Plato had derived the nature of imitation from the attributes of a mirror-image.[9] Bishop Hurd introduced his extended commentary on poetry in general by citing Aristotle's definition of that art as imitation, and then had recourse to Plato's mirror to demonstrate how this imitation is performed:

Again; of the endless variety of these *original forms,* which the poet's eye is incessantly traversing, those, which take his attention most, his active mimetic faculty prompts him to convert into fair and living *resemblances.* This magical operation the *divine* philosopher . . . excellently illustrates by the similitude of a *mirror; 'which,'* says he, *'as you turn about and oppose to the surrounding world, presents you instantly with a* SUN, STARS, *and* SKIES. . .' [10]

In elucidating his conception of poetry in the *Republic,* Plato himself first referred to images in a mirror, then to the work of a painter, and finally applied the distinctions drawn from both these illustrations to define the mimetic character of poetry. The progression is significant. The mirror as an analogue for poetry suffers from the conspicuous defect that its images are fleeting. Before the invention of photography the product of a painter was the best available instance of something which captures and retains a likeness. A picture, therefore, while itself a work of art, was a useful adjunct to the mirror for clarifying the less obvious mimetic quality of an art like poetry, which reflects the visible world indirectly, by the significance of its words.

Plutarch popularized the saying of Simonides that 'painting is mute poetry, and poetry a speaking picture'; and this, together with Horace's phrase, *ut pictura poesis,* taken out of context and misinterpreted as asserting a comprehensive parallelism between the two arts, became axioms in popular aesthetic wisdom. As Irving Babbitt says, quite accurately, 'It is rare to read through a critical treatise on either art or literature, written between the middle of the sixteenth and middle of the eighteenth century, without finding an approving mention of the Horatian simile . . . [or] of the equivalent saying of Simonides.' [11] In 1758 it still seemed to Dr. Johnson that 'of the parallels which have been drawn by wit and curiosity, some are literal and real, as between poetry and painting . . . which differ only as the one represents things by marks permanent and natural, the other by signs accidental and arbitrary.' [12] The probable effect on Renaissance and later artistic theory and practice of the elaborate comparisons between the details of a painting and of a poem has often been remarked. For our present purpose, it is enough to note that the appeal to painting corroborated the concept that poetry is a reflection of objects and events.

It is difficult to gauge the extent to which the characteristic preoccupations and discoveries of aesthetic theory have been fostered by the conceptual model of the reflector, whether this has been explicitly or covertly effective in determining the focus and terms of critical analysis. At one extreme we have Plato's simple and obvious derivatives from the mirror as analogue. For example, a mirror-image is only a simulacrum of an object, forced deceptively to represent three dimensions by two: hence the lowly status of art as mere appearance, far removed from the truth. Also, the sole function of a mirror is to yield a flawless and accurate image: correspondingly, when poets like Homer and Aeschylus depart from the truth of things, we have no alternative but to say that they are liars. Such criteria are sufficient for Plato's purpose, which is concerned not at all with the value of art in itself, but with demonstrating that freedom of the artist may not be suffered in a closed state formed on a timeless model, whether this be the perfect state of the *Republic* or the practically perfect state of the *Laws*. At the other extreme, we have the *Poetics*. The peculiar strength of Aristotle's analysis of tragedy consists in the degree to which he succeeds in developing a set of distinctions which, if they do not entirely escape from analogy, are specifically appropriate to a poem considered as an object of its own kind, and an end in itself.[13] Between these two poles we have the post-Aristotelian theories which, almost without exception, reverted to concepts of mimesis much closer to the attributes of a literal reflector.

The perspective afforded by more recent conceptual schemes enables us to discriminate certain tendencies common to many of those theorists between the sixteenth and eighteenth centuries who looked upon art as imitation, and more or less like a mirror. For better or worse, the analogy helped focus interest on the subject matter of a work and its models in reality, to the comparative neglect of the shaping influence of artistic conventions, the inherent requirements of the single work of art, and the individuality of the author; it encouraged the striking of a dichotomy between those elements of a work which are demonstrably representative of the real world and those further verbal and imaginative elements said to be merely 'ornamental,' introduced to give greater pleasure to the reader; and it fostered a preoccupation with the 'truth' of art, or its correspondence, in some fashion, to the matters it is held to reflect.

The long survival of the reflector as archetype demonstrates its aptness and suggestiveness as one point of departure for aesthetic theory. The endemic disease of analogical thinking, however, is hardening of the categories. For as Coleridge said, 'No simile runs on all four legs'; analogues are by their nature only partial parallels, and the very sharpness of focus afforded by a happily chosen archetype makes marginal and elusive those qualities of an object which fall outside its primitive categories. While a work of art, for instance, is very like a mirror, it is also, in important respects, quite different, and not many critics have been able to keep the derived aesthetic categories flexible, and sufficiently responsive to data outside their immediate scope. The history of modern criticism, as we shall see, may in some part be told as the search for alternative parallels—a heterocosm or 'second nature,' the overflow from a fountain, the music of a windharp, a growing plant—which would avoid some of the troublesome implications of the mirror, and better comprehend those aspects and relations of an aesthetic object which this archetype leaves marginal or omits.

ii. The Objects of Imitation: the Empirical Ideal

The theorist who held that art reflected nature was committed to looking 'out there,' rather than into the artist, for the subject matter of a work. He was at once confronted by the conspicuous fact that the image is rarely a facsimile of any single object or event in the external world, and sometimes presents to the spectator a kind of being for which there is no precedent whatever in the world of sense. This deviation of art from reality has always been a cardinal problem for aesthetic philosophy, and the main basis for the charge by writers indifferent or hostile to art that it is trivial, or positively mischievous. Classic and neo-classic defenders of art alike solved the problem by claiming that poetry imitates not the actual, but selected matters, qualities, tendencies, or forms, which are within or behind the actual—veridical elements in the constitution of the universe which are of higher worth than gross and unselected reality itself. In reflecting these, the mirror held up to nature reflects what, in opposition to 'real nature,' English critics often called 'nature improved,' or 'heightened,' or 'refined,' or in the French phrase, *la belle nature*. This, said Batteux, is not 'le vrai qui est; mais le vrai qui peut être, le beau vrai, qui est représenté comme s'il existoit réellement, & avec toutes les perfections qu'il peut recevoir.' [14] True to their pragmatic point of view, most eighteenth-century theorists added that the justification for this procedure lay in the need to delight (and sometimes, to enlighten) the reader. 'Nothing can please persons of taste,' Hume said, 'but nature drawn with all her graces and ornaments, *la belle nature*. . .'[15] James Beattie summed up the prevailing opinion when he wrote:

For I presume, it was long ago evident;—that the end of Poetry is to please . . . and, consequently, that poetry must be, not according to real nature, but according to nature improved to that degree, which is consistent with probability, and suitable to the poet's purpose. And hence it is that we call Poetry AN IMITATION OF NATURE.

Dr. Johnson also held that on moral grounds, the mirror must be selective: it is necessary 'to distinguish those parts of nature which are most proper for imitation,' for it would 'be as safe to turn the eye immediately upon mankind, as upon a mirrour which shows all that presents itself without discrimination.'[16]

In recent criticism (as, to some extent, in the early Renaissance theory of painting) the concept that art is imitation, together with its analogy to a mirror, usually signalizes a demand for artistic realism, but in neo-classic criticism these concepts were standard components in the theory that art is 'ideal,' in the general sense that it properly represents an improvement upon things as we find them. The specific nature of the ideal—of those elements in the universe held to be the proper objects for artistic imitation —was described in varied fashions; but these descriptions fall readily into two main classes. The first is an empirical theory of the artistic ideal, of which the *Poetics* of Aristotle was the prototype; it maintains that the models and forms for artistic imitation are selected or abstracted from the objects of sense-perception. The other is a transcendental theory, deriving from Plato, or more accurately, from later philosophers whose aesthetic theory is made in part with building-blocks hewn out of the Platonic dialogues. This theory specifies the proper objects of art to be Ideas or Forms which are perhaps approachable by way of the world of sense, but are ultimately trans-empirical, maintaining an independent existence in their own ideal space, and available only to the eye of the mind.

The poet, Aristotle had said, does not describe 'the thing that has happened, but a kind of thing that might happen. . . Hence poetry is something more philosophic and of graver import than history, since its statements are of the nature rather of universals, whereas those of history are singulars.' The precise significance of this famous doctrine has had to be interpreted with only limited aid from other passages in the *Poetics*.

By reference to other writings of Aristotle, Professor McKeon reconstructs his intention in this way:

In imitation the artist separates some form from the matter with which it is joined in nature—not, however, the 'substantial' form, but some form perceptible by sensation—and joins it anew to the matter of his art, the medium which he uses. . . Art imitates nature; the form joined to matter in the physical world is the same form that is expressed in the matter of the art.[17]

Many eighteenth-century critics cited the passage from Aristotle, but few interpreted it according to the philosophy of formal and material causes. Instead, they gave diverse explanations of the artistic departure from the actual, and a single critic often proposed several explanations, which he presented either as alternative formulations, or as applying to diverse kinds of poetic subject matter or poetic genres. This explanation was at the same time a norm: good art was said to differ in these ways from the world as it is; and all art, to be good, *must* differ in these ways. Here are the principal empirical descriptions of that 'nature' which is to be imitated by art:

(1) Pleasant and beautiful objects or aspects of existing things. As René Rapin phrased this simple doctrine, in his commentary on Aristotle: for a poet 'it is not enough to exhibit *Nature,* which in certain places is *rude* and *unpleasant;* he must choose in *her* what is *beautiful,* from what is *not*. . .'[18] And Richard Hurd, after citing Aristotle on imitation, goes on to explain that 'the office of genius is but to select the fairest forms of things, and to present them in due *place* and *circumstance*. . .'[19]

(2) Objects which are synthesized from parts found separately in nature. Proponents of this somewhat more complex doctrine of the composite ideal refer, with a unanimity which makes indifference to boredom the *sine qua non* of research, to the old story of the painter Zeuxis who (in Pliny's version), when he desired to represent Juno, 'had the young maidens of the place stripped for examination, and selected five of them, in order to adapt in his picture the most commendable points in the form of each.'[20] While 'history represents what has really happened in nature,' says the writer of an essay sometimes attributed to Oliver Goldsmith,

the sculptor or statuary composed the various proportions in nature from a great number of different subjects, every individual of which he found imperfect or defective in some one particular, though beautiful in all the rest; and from these observations, corroborated by taste and judgment, he formed an ideal pattern, according to which his idea was modelled, and produced in execution. Everybody knows the story of Zeuxis, the famous painter of Heraclea. . .[21]

(3) The central tendency, or statistical average, of the form of each biological species. This formula was applied especially to the representation of visual objects in the plastic arts, a matter of configuration in space rather than of the intangible principles of human psychology and action, and therefore, in theory, capable of precise determination. 'From a reiterated experience, and a close comparison of the objects in Nature,' said Joshua Reynolds, the most thorough expositor of this concept, '. . . an artist becomes possessed of the idea of that central form, if I may so express it, from which every deviation is deformity.' [22] Eleven years earlier (1759), in the *Idler* No. 82, Reynolds had described the central form in statistical terms. The initial hypothesis is that 'every species of the animal as well as the vegetable creation may be said to have a fixed or determinate form, towards which Nature is continually inclining.' Within each species 'perfect beauty is oftener produced by Nature than . . . any one kind of deformity.' Reynolds illustrates his premise by the analogy of the pendulum, vibrating in different planes through the same central point; translated into the parlance of latter-day statistics, the ideal form may be said to be the 'mode'—which is at one time the central and most frequent value—in a normal distribution of the variates of a biological trait.

(4) The generic human type, rather than the individual. It would seem that when the learned neo-classicist surveyed mankind from China to Peru, he saw a world of identical men, somewhat transparently diversified by an increment of local and individual differences. 'There is such an uniformity in the state of man,' as Johnson stated the pervasive commonplace of his age, 'considered apart from adventitious and separable decorations and disguises, that there is scarce any possibility of good or ill, but is common to human kind.' [23] By reflecting those aspects in which all men have been, are, and always will be the same, an artist has the best available guarantee that his writings will interest the audience both of his own day and of all time. For 'nothing can please many, and please long, but just representations of general nature. Particular manners can be known to few, and therefore few only can judge how nearly they are copied.' [24] Therefore it is Shakespeare's great excellence that his characters 'act and speak by the influence of those general passions and principles by which all minds are agitated. . . In the writings of other poets a character is too often an individual; in those of *Shakespeare* it is commonly a species.' [25]

(5) The prominent, uniform, and familiar aspects of the outer and inner world. In descriptions of the objects of sense, according to Imlac's famous dictum, the poet 'does not number the streaks of the tulip'; that is to say,

he is to represent only those broad visual qualities of mass, form, color, light, and shade by which any person casually identifies the class—man, tree, tulip—of which the individual is a member. As Imlac goes on to say:

He is to exhibit in his portraits of nature such prominent and striking features, as recall the original to every mind; and must neglect the minuter discriminations, which one may have remarked, and another have neglected, for those characteristicks which are alike obvious to vigilance and carelessness.[26]

The rationale of this doctrine, as it is to be found in Johnson and Reynolds, is that a reader will not be pleased unless he is reminded of what he himself has seen already.[27] Furthermore, when broadly defined, the concept of imitation was held to include not only the people and things of the visible world, but also sentiments and thoughts. Poets, as Joseph Warton wrote in 1756, imitate 'objects material or animate, extraneous or internal. . .' And on the assumption that, whether objects or ideas, these 'lie equally open to the observation of all, and are perfectly similar,' he concludes that all descriptions 'that are faithful and just, MUST BE UNIFORM AND ALIKE. . .'[28] On a similar premise of the basic uniformity of human nature, and on the inference drawn from this premise that the currency of an idea is the best evidence of its validity and its enduring interest, is founded the opinion, most familiar in Pope's rendering, that

> True Wit is Nature to advantage dressed,
> What oft was thought, but ne'er so well expressed.

It has seemed to some later commentators that the neo-classic stress on the typical, the uniform, the salient, and the familiar as ideals of poetic imitation makes originality, or even diversity, impossible: that in the last analysis the doctrine implies that all serious poems must have one sole hero, Everyman, presented in a generalized milieu, uttering platitudes, describing what all men have seen already, and exhibiting the permanent principles of human action in situations that might happen to anyone. What we often overlook, however, is that the particular and the circumstantial were not employed as simple and exclusive contraries of the general and uniform; as Reynolds put it, 'he that does not at all express particulars, expresses nothing';[29] and in many passages, these critics proposed achieving the general by the just selection of those particulars which are most widely possessed. In addition, as R. S. Crane impresses on us, the neo-classic theorist was apt to pose the standard of aesthetic excellence, like that of moral excellence, in terms of a mean between extremes, or else in terms of a conjunction of opposite qualities.[30] Taken in its full context, the recommendation of the typical, general, and familiar as basic requirements of art usually turns out to be accompanied by a statement of the need for the leavening qualities of individuality, particularity, and novelty as well.

Johnson's total view is often misinterpreted because he usually argues to the single point or document at issue, by an appeal to only so much of the general principle as the case requires. Although he praises Shakespeare's characters, for example, because they are species, he later goes on to say that 'characters thus ample and general were not easily discriminated and preserved, yet perhaps no poet ever kept his personages more distinct from each other.'[31] Imlac's admonition to the poet to describe the general properties and familiar appearances of nature must be taken in conjunction with Johnson's acclaim of Shakespeare as 'an exact surveyor of the inanimate world' whose 'descriptions have always some peculiarities,' together with his admiration for James Thomson because he 'at once comprehends the vast, and attends to the minute' and combines a 'wide expansion of general views' with an 'enumeration of circumstantial varieties.'[32] And although Johnson cites the saying of La Bruyère 'that we are come into the world too late to produce any thing new' in either description or sentiment, he nevertheless refutes Pope's account of true wit as simply 'what oft was thought,' and substitutes a 'more adequate definition' expressed as a union of extremes. Wit, he says, is that 'which is at once natural and new,' and 'though not obvious, is, upon its first production, acknowledged to be just. . .'[33] (Johnson's doctrine might be paraphrased in this way: the best thoughts in poetry are so proportionable to essential human nature that, upon first annunciation, they come home to all men as though innovation were reminiscence.) Originality, therefore, is excellent, provided it does not exclude its contrary; accordingly, Johnson reserves his highest praise for such passages as four stanzas in Gray's *Elegy* which, he says, 'are to me original: I have never seen the notions in any other place; yet he that reads them here persuades himself that he has always felt them.'[34]

Read completely rather than in selected passages, then, Johnson may be said to locate the highest and rarest excellence in the representation of the individualized type, the circumstantially general, and the novel-familiar. Nevertheless Johnson, and still more Reynolds, Hurd, and other advocates of what A. O. Lovejoy calls 'uniformitarian' aesthetics, give the more prominent place to the second term in each of these pairs of contraries; the norms that loom largest, as we read through his applied criticism, are the typical, the general, and the familiar. Some of Johnson's contemporaries reversed this balance, with respect at least to descriptions of the visible scene, and gave greater emphasis to the role of particularity in achieving poetic excellence. Thus Joseph Warton said that 'the use, the force, and the excellence of language, certainly consists in raising, *clear, complete,* and *circumstantial* images'; and warned that 'I think I can perceive many symptoms, even among writers of eminence, of departing from these *true,* and *lively,* and *minute,* representations of Nature, and of *dwelling in generalities.*' [35] And among extremists (few in number, it should be noted, and very limited in influence), the bi-polar statement of aesthetic norms gave way entirely to a new formulation in terms of a single value. Edward Young's plea for originality, novelty, individuality, and 'singulars' is not qualified by reference to the need for contrary qualities. The Reverend J. Moir, who, in 1785, gathered his fugitive pieces into a collection called *Gleanings,* is almost unknown as a critic, but if anything preaches an even more radical, if less eloquent, doctrine than does Young. 'Uniformity of temper and manners,' he wrote in an essay on the 'Genius of Poetry,' 'in every situation, fools have dignified with the name of philosophy, but men of sense know to be dullness.' So much for the doctrine of uniform human nature as the foundation for standards of aesthetic excellence; the doctrine that men take pleasure in the familiar appearance fares no better. 'The mind of man is equally fond and full of variety. We dislike most, if not all things, in proportion as we know them.' [36] In a short essay, 'Originality,' Moir joins these views to the tradition of the original genius. He it is who possesses such acuity of perception that 'every new inspection of the most common and familiar phenomena of nature discovers a thousand new variations, distinctions, and resemblances.' As opposed to the compositions of 'ordinary minds,' who 'never particularize or examine the objects of their respective senses,' Moir says, 'original genius never rests in generals, never runs in a circle, but gives, in vivid, glowing, and permanent characters, the identical impression it receives.' [37]

In the Age of Johnson, then, we find standards for art running the gamut from a primary emphasis on typicality, generality, and 'large appearances,' to the unqualified recommendation of particularity, uniqueness, and a microscopic depiction of detail. For our purpose, however, it is important to note that these discussions and disagreements took place mainly within a single aesthetic orientation. Whether art is to represent a composite of scattered beauties, generic humanity, average forms, and familiar appearances, or whether unique characteristics, undiscovered particularities, and ultraviolet discriminations—all these forms and qualities are conceived to be inherent in the constitution of the external world, and the work of art continues to be regarded as a kind of reflector, though a selective one. The artist himself is often envisioned as the agent holding the mirror up to nature, and even the originality of a genius is explained in large part by his possessing the zeal and acuity to invent (in the root sense of 'discover') aspects of the universe and of human nature hitherto overlooked, and the imaginative ingenuity to combine and express familiar elements in new and surprising ways. Nature's world, as Sidney had said, 'is brazen, the poets only deliver a golden'; but the dynamics of the transformation, so far as they are discussed, consist not of emotional and imaginative stresses peculiar to the poet, but of the legitimate human demands, common to poet and audience, for illumination and delight.

iii. The Transcendental Ideal

Plotinus, for one, showed how a philosopher might retain the frame of Plato's cosmos and yet avoid Plato's derogation of the arts simply by allowing the artist to by-pass the sensible world in order to imitate the Ideas at first hand. By this sleight, the work of art is conceived to reflect the ideal more accurately than does imperfect nature itself.

Still the arts are not to be slighted on the ground that they create by imitation of natural objects; for . . . we must recognize that they give no bare reproduction of the thing seen but go back to the Ideas from which Nature itself derives, and, furthermore, that much of their work is all their own; they are holders of beauty and add where nature is lacking. Thus Pheidias wrought the Zeus upon no model among things of sense but by apprehending what form Zeus must take if he chose to become manifest to sight.[38]

This Neoplatonic justification for the deviation of art from reality had profound effects when it was strongly revived in the aesthetic theory of sixteenth-century Italy.[39] Here was an argument to elevate art from the realm of flux and shadows to an eminence over all human pursuits, in close connection to the Ideas and to God himself. The artist, from being a craftsman, became (in a momentous new aesthetic metaphor) a creator, for it was sometimes said that of all men the poet is likest God because he creates according to those patterns on which God himself has modeled the universe. In this way, the theory of Ideas, which Plato had used to depress the traditional artist to a level of social utility below that of an honest shoemaker, became—and has to this day remained—the resource by which a critic reaches the stratosphere of panegyric for the arts.

Another effect of this version of the artistic ideal was, potentially, no less important. From the first, post-Platonic theorists tended to assign a double residence to the Ideas; in addition to the region of their transcendental subsistence, they were given a secondary location within the human mind itself. The arts, Plotinus had declared, 'go back to the Ideas from which Nature itself derives,' but in a statue 'this form is not in the material; it is in the designer before ever it enters the stone. . .' [40] And more than two centuries earlier, in a passage which was to become the most important source of the concept, Cicero had called upon Plato himself as witness that art imitates Ideas, and that Ideas inhabit the mind. No beauty in art, he says, can equal the beauty of which it is a copy, and this model is not available to the external senses, but only to thought and imagination.

Nor did [Phidias], when he formed Jupiter or Minerva, have before his eyes a model which he followed strictly, but in his own mind did he have an extraordinary idea of beauty, this he contemplated, on this he fixed his attention, and to rendering this he directed his art and his hand. . . These forms of things Plato calls *ideas* . . . and these, he maintains, do not arise occasionally in our minds, but are permanently present in reason and intelligence; other things are born, die, flow, disappear, and never remain long in the same condition. [41]

Both in the Renaissance and later, Platonist aesthetics followed this tradition and customarily located the Ideas both within and without the mind. Now it is a matter of consequence, for both aesthetic theory and practice, whether the Ideas are to be sought for in their own ideal space or by turning the eye of the mind inward. In the latter instance, the work is conceived to imitate something inside the artist himself; and when its criterion is thus made both intuitive and introspective, art readily slips its moorings in the public world of sense experience and begins to rely instead on a vision which is personal and subjective. As Erwin Panofsky points out, it is significant that Neoplatonism in the theory of art reached its zenith contemporaneously with the height of Mannerism in the practice of art. The transition from the empirical to the intuitive ideal may be plausibly correlated with the transition from the solid naturalism of Leonardo to the twisted landscapes and attenuated figures of El Greco, who, according to the anecdote, refused to leave a darkened room because 'the daylight disturbed his inner light.' [42]

To be sure, Renaissance Platonism guaranteed the impersonality of the artist's vision by making metaphysical provision for linking the Idea in the individual mind to the universal and unchanging Ideas of the world-pattern. The connection might be established by positing the existence of memory-traces of the divine archetype, said to have been stamped into the intellect before birth; it was sometimes supported by an elaborate optical analogy, according to which rays of archetypal beauty, streaming from the countenance of God, are reflected in three mirrors, one in the angels, a second in the souls of men, a third in the material world.[43] But without the need for verifying the inner norm empirically, this guarantee was far from secure, and the temporal mind of man is a treacherous storehouse for an eternal and immutable Idea. It becomes vulnerable to contamination by the personal and idiosyncratic, and the supra-rational ecstasy of Neoplatonic introspection may imperceptibly be replaced by more mundane emotions. We may trace something of this process after the Renaissance, in the strange metamorphoses that the Idea underwent in some varieties of German metaphysics and aesthetics after the eighteenth century,[44] when it was translocated from its changeless domicile beyond the moon into the tumultuous milieu of human passions, or even, into the strange depths of the unconscious abysm of the mind. In 1774 Goethe's Werther evidences something like this change. 'I feel,' he writes, 'that I never was a greater artist than now.'

My friend! when darkness closes in upon my eyes, and the earth around me and the heaven dwell in my soul like the form of a beloved mistress; then do I often think longingly: Oh couldst thou only express, couldst thou breathe forth upon this paper, all that lives so full and warm in thyself, that it might become the mirror of thy soul, as thy soul is the mirror of the infinite God![45]

The divine Idea beamed from God into the soul's mirror, thence to be projected on the written page, has become one with the erotic fantasies and fevered emotions of the artist-hero of the *Sturm und Drang.*

The transcendental version of the ideal in art was known to English critics of the eighteenth century in the rendering of Cicero, and quite frequently, through the commentaries of Platonizing Italian critics as well.[46] Occasionally we hear direct echoes of the doctrine, as when John Dennis by violence construes Horace's line, 'Respicere exemplar vitae morumque jubebo,' as a counsel 'not to draw after particular Men . . . but to consult that innate Original, and that universal Idea, which the Creator has fix'd in the minds of every reasonable Creature'; a gloss which is later repeated

by Richard Hurd.[47] The metaphysical implications of this manner of thinking, however, were alien to the this-worldly and empirical-minded theorists
of English neo-classicism. Almost without exception these writers psycholo-
gized the Platonic Idea, and empiricized the method of achieving it. Sir
Joshua Reynolds provides us with an interesting example. Speaking at the
top of his eloquence in the peroration to an address celebrating the removal
of the Royal Academy to Somerset Place, he says: 'The beauty of which
we are in quest is general and intellectual; it is an idea that subsists only
in the mind; the sight never beheld it, nor has the hand expressed it. . .'[48]
Ever since Coleridge, this and similar passages have been cited as evidences
of Reynolds' 'Platonism.' But Reynolds himself makes clear that the transcendental idiom is for him only an encomiastic manner of speaking, not
to be taken literally. In his Third Discourse he quotes Proclus, together
with the standard passage from Cicero, on the Idea of beauty in the mind,
and then carefully guides his students to an interpretation which will reconcile these statements with an empirical philosophy. 'Enthusiastic admiration,' he says, 'seldom promotes knowledge.'

We ought to allow for, and we ought to commend, that strength of vivid expression, which is necessary to convey, in its full force, the highest sense of the most
complete effect of art; taking care, at the same time, not to lose in terms of
vague admiration that solidity and truth of principle upon which alone we can
reason, and may be enabled to practise.

His own position is that 'this great ideal perfection and beauty are not to
be sought in the heavens, but upon the earth.' The only procedure for finding it is 'a long habit of observing what any set of objects of the same kind
have in common,' which will result in 'an abstract idea of their forms more
perfect than any one original. . .'[49]

Emphasis on the intellectual location of artistic ideas accustomed critics
to the concept of the work of art as a mirror turned around to reflect aspects
of the artist's mind; occasionally, it even passed over into statements characterizing art as a form of expression, or communication. Reynolds, for example, could say, 'Imitation is the means, and not the end of art: it is employed by the Sculptor as the language by which his ideas are presented to
the mind of the spectator.'[50] But whether these ideas are held to be replicas
of transcendental archetypes or, as in Reynolds, are defined as the abstraction
of like elements from a class of sensible particulars, they maintain their
theoretical grounding in the nature of the external universe. Taken in its

context, this statement of Reynolds is at far remove from the doctrines most characteristic of the next generation of critics, that the content of art has an internal origin, and that its shaping influences are not the Ideas or principles informing the cosmic structure, but the forces inherent in the emotions, the desires, and the evolving imaginative process of the artist himself.

ROMANTIC ANALOGUES OF ART
AND MIND

'Didn't I tell you so?' said Flask; 'yes, you'll soon see this right whale's head hoisted opposite that parmacetti's.'

In good time, Flask's saying proved true. As before, the Pequod steeply leaned over towards the sperm whale's head, now, by the counterpoise of both heads, she regained her even keel; though sorely strained, you may well believe. So, when on one side you hoist in Locke's head, you go over that way; but now, on the other side, hoist in Kant's and you come back again; but in very poor plight.   MELVILLE, *Moby-Dick*

POETRY IS THE SPONTANEOUS overflow of powerful feelings.' Wordsworth's metaphor, 'overflow,' suggests the underlying physical analogy of a container—a fountain or natural spring, perhaps—from which water brims over. This container is unmistakably the poet; the materials of a poem come from within, and they consist expressly neither of objects nor actions, but of the fluid feelings of the poet himself. A coherent theory of poetry which takes its departure from this type of analogy, instead of from imitation, will clearly favor very different emphases and criteria. The orientation is now toward the artist, the focus of attention is upon the relation of the elements of the work to his state of mind, and the suggestion, underlined by the word 'spontaneous,' is that the dynamics of the overflow are inherent in the poet and, perhaps, not within his deliberate control. Wordsworth himself anchored his theory to the external world by maintaining that 'I have at all times endeavoured to look steadily at my subject,' and declared that the emotion was recollected in tranquillity and that the spontaneity of its overflow was merely the reward of a prior process of deliberate thought. He reasoned also that since this thought has found and rendered instinctive the connection of the poet's feelings to matters really important to men, the final overflow cannot but accomplish a 'worthy purpose' with respect to the poet's audience. The extreme consequences latent in the central analogue to which Wordsworth gave impetus in England—the elimination, for all practical purposes, of the conditions of the given world, the requirements of the audience, and the control by conscious purpose and art as important determinants of a poem—did not appear in that country until three decades later, in such critics as Keble, Carlyle, and John Stuart Mill.

i. Metaphors of Expression

Repeatedly romantic predications about poetry, or about art in general, turn on a metaphor which, like 'overflow,' signifies the internal made external. The most frequent of these terms was 'expression,' used in contexts indicating a revival of the root meaning *ex-pressus,* from *ex-premere,* 'to press out.' As A. W. Schlegel wrote in 1801, referring to the vocal signs of feeling, 'The word expression (Ausdruck) is very strikingly chosen for this: the inner is pressed out as though by a force alien to us.'[1] 'Poetry,' said John Stuart Mill, is 'the expression or uttering forth of feeling';[2] and 'utter' in its turn derives from the Old English word for 'out,' and is cognate with the German 'aüssern.' 'Behold now the whole character of poetry,' wrote an anonymous contemporary in *Blackwood's Magazine;* 'it is *essentially* the *expression of emotion.*'[3] In his version of the doctrine, the Reverend John Keble focusses upon the pressure in 'expression,' and develops a definition of poetry as personal catharsis which he opposes to Aristotle's mimesis, as this had been traditionally interpreted.

Poetry is the indirect expression in words, most appropriately in metrical words, of some overpowering emotion, or ruling taste, or feeling, the direct indulgence whereof is somehow repressed. . .

Aristotle, as is well known, considered the essence of poetry to be *Imitation.* . . *Expression* we say, rather than *imitation;* for the latter word clearly conveys a cold and inadequate notion, of the writer's meaning. . .[4]

These definitions of the 1830's agree that poetry expresses emotions, but earlier in the century there had been variety of opinion as to just what mental elements are externalized in a poem. The common definition of the fine arts, Coleridge wrote in 'Poesy or Art' (1818), is that they all, 'like poetry, are to express intellectual purposes, thoughts, conceptions, sentiments, that have their origin in the human mind. . .'[5] 'Poetry is the music of language,' Hazlitt had written the year before, 'expressing the music of the mind.'[6] Shelley declared that 'poetry, in a general sense, may be defined to be "the expression of the imagination"';[7] and that same year (1821) Byron complained to Tom Moore, 'I can never get people to understand that poetry is the expression of *excited passion* . . .'[8] Finally, Leigh Hunt reconciled these differences by the simple device of a definition which, as David Masson has remarked, is 'constructed on the principle of omitting nothing that any one would like to see included.'[9] Poetry (to quote Hunt's definition only in part) is 'the utterance of a passion for truth, beauty and power, embodying and illustrating its conceptions by imagination and fancy, and modulating its language on the principle of variety in uniformity.'[10]

Wordsworth's contemporaries were fertile inventors of other terms parallel to 'overflow' and 'expression,' and frequently the same author presents us with a variety of these alternatives. To Mill, for example (and each of these terms could be duplicated in various other critics), poetry is not only an 'expression,' and an 'uttering forth,' but 'the exhibition of a state or states of human sensibility,' and also, 'the thoughts and words in which emotion spontaneously embodies itself.'[11] Sir Walter Scott includes this last metaphor in a description which is rare among the major critics of the time because, by characterizing art as communication, it brings the audience to a parity with the stress of the artist's own feelings as a cause of artistic production. The painter, orator, and poet each has the motive

of exciting in the reader, hearer, or spectator, a tone of feeling similar to that which existed in his own bosom, ere it was bodied forth by his pencil, tongue, or pen. It is the artist's object, in short . . . to communicate, as well as colours and words can do, the same sublime sensations which had dictated his own composition.[12]

Byron characteristically prefers metaphors of greater daring, dash, and grandiosity.

> Thus to their extreme verge the passions brought
> Dash into poetry, which is but passion . . .[13]

At a more titanic level still, Byron introduces a volcano as analogy; poetry 'is the lava of the imagination whose eruption prevents an earthquake.'[14] And it is also Byron who offers the interesting parallel between poetic creation and childbirth, resulting in a poetic offspring at once separable from and blended with the spirit and feelings of the father-poet (or is it the mother-poet?).

'Tis to create, and in creating live
A being more intense, that we endow
With form our fancy, gaining as we give
The life we image, even as I do now.
What am I? Nothing: but not so art thou,
Soul of my thought! with whom I traverse earth,
Invisible but gazing, as I glow
Mix'd with thy spirit, blended with thy birth,
And feeling still with thee in my crush'd feelings' dearth.[15]

Allusions to poetry as a representation or image, as well as the implied analogy of art with a mirror, survive in the criticism of the early nineteenth century, but usually with a difference. The modern poet, wrote W. J. Fox in 1833, 'delineates the whole external world from its reflected imagery in the mirror of human thought and feeling.'[16] Often the reflector is reversed, and images a state of mind rather than of external nature. So Hazlitt wrote that 'it is the perfect coincidence of the image and the words with the feelings we have . . . that gives an instant "satisfaction to the thought."'[17] This reoriented version of poetic representation was equally current in the criticism of the German romantic writers. 'Poetry,' Novalis said, 'is representation of the spirit, of the inner world in its totality.'[18] And Tieck: 'Not these plants, not these mountains, do I wish to copy, but my spirit, my mood, which governs me just at this moment. . .'[19]

The use of painting to illuminate the essential character of poetry—*ut pictura poesis*—so widespread in the eighteenth century, almost disappears in the major criticism of the romantic period; the comparisons between poetry and painting that survive are casual, or, as in the instance of the mirror, show the canvas reversed in order to image the inner substance of the poet.[20] In place of painting, music becomes the art frequently pointed to as having a profound affinity with poetry. For if a picture seems the nearest thing to a mirror-image of the external world, music, of all the arts, is the most remote: except in the trivial echoism of programmatic passages, it does not duplicate aspects of sensible nature, nor can it be said, in any obvious sense, to refer to any state of affairs outside itself. As a result music was the first of the arts to be generally regarded as non-mimetic in nature; and in the theory of German writers of the 1790's, music came to be the art most immediately expressive of spirit and emotion, constituting the very pulse and quiddity of passion made public. Music, wrote Wackenroder, 'shows us all the movements of our spirit, disembodied.'[21] Hence the utility of music to define and illustrate the nature of poetry, particularly of the lyric, but also of poetry in general when this came to be conceived as a mode of expression. Friedrich Schlegel was of the opinion that when Simonides, in a famous phrase, characterized poetry as a speaking picture, it was only because contemporary poetry was always accompanied by music that it appeared superfluous to him to remind us 'that poetry was also a spiritual music.' [22]

Correspondingly, in England, Hazlitt said of poetry: 'It is the music of language, answering to the music of the mind. . . There is a near connection between music and deep-rooted passion. Mad people sing.' [23] John Keble plainly indicates the extent to which music has replaced painting as poetry's nearest relation, and the accompanying reversal of orientation from universe to artist. Music and poetry 'it is universally allowed . . . are twin sisters,' for music, of all arts, most closely approaches poetry 'on that side of its effect which is concerned in piercing into, and drawing out to the light, the secrets of the soul. . .' [24]

The passages quoted so far suggest that to poetize is a unilateral activity, involving only materials inherent in the poet. No less characteristic of romantic theory is a set of alternative analogies implying that poetry is an interaction, the joint effect of inner and outer, mind and object, passion and the perceptions of sense. Thus Shelley illustrates his initial definition of poetry as 'the expression of the imagination' by reference to that favorite romantic toy, the Aeolian lyre. Athanasius Kircher laid claim to having invented this instrument in 1650. In the course of the next hundred years it became a popular piece of household furniture, and its pensive moods, its insubstantial and fairy sounds, and, above all, the fact that its music could literally be attributed to nature rather than art, made it a favorite subject for poets after the mid-eighteenth century. [25] It is noteworthy, however, that not until the nineteenth century did the wind-harp become an analogy for the poetic mind as well as a subject for poetic description.

Man [Shelley says] is an instrument over which a series of external and internal impressions are driven, like the alternations of an ever-changing wind over an Aeolian lyre, which move it by their motion to ever-changing melody. But there is a principle within the human being, and perhaps within all sentient beings, which acts otherwise than in the lyre, and produces not melody alone, but harmony, by an internal adjustment of the sounds or motions thus excited to the impressions which excite them. [26]

The Aeolian lyre is the poet, and the poem is the chord of music which results from the reciprocation of external and internal elements, of both the changing wind and the constitution and tension of the strings. As Shelley at once goes on to explain, when a savage 'expresses the emotions produced in him by surrounding objects . . . language and gesture, together with plastic or pictorial imitation, become the image of the combined effect of those objects, and of his apprehension of them.' [27]

Other critics used other analogies of similar properties. Hazlitt opens his most important aesthetic essay, 'On Poetry in General' (1818), with a definition which closely parallels Shelley's Aeolian lyre, including its implications of automatism and of a pre-established harmony between objective stimulus and poetic response.

> The best general notion which I can give of poetry is, that it is the natural impression of any object or event, by its vividness exciting an involuntary movement of imagination and passion, and producing, by sympathy, a certain modulation of the voice, or sounds, expressing it.[28]

Amid the wealth of sometimes confused imagery with which Hazlitt expands and plays upon one or another part of this theme, we find the mimetic mirror familiar in older aesthetic theory. But since a mirror, whether turned to face the poet or the world without, can only reflect what is presented from a single direction, Hazlitt complicates the analogy by combining the mirror with a lamp, in order to demonstrate that a poet reflects a world already bathed in an emotional light he has himself projected.

> Neither a mere description of natural objects, nor a mere delineation of natural feelings, however distinct or forcible, constitutes the ultimate end and aim of poetry. . . The light of poetry is not only a direct but also a reflected light, that while it shews us the object, throws a sparkling radiance on all around it. . .[29]

Coleridge's lecture 'On Poesy or Art' (1818) is grounded on Schelling's metaphysics of a psycho-natural parallelism, according to which the essences within nature have a kind of duplicate subsistence as ideas in the mind. This world-view provides a new set of metaphors in which to convey the romantic theme that art is a joint product of the objective and the projected. Art is 'the mediatress between, and reconciler of, nature and man. It is, therefore, the power of humanizing nature, of infusing the thoughts and passions of man into everything which is the object of his contemplation. . .' 'Poetry also is purely human; for all its materials are from the mind, and all its products are for the mind.' Yet 'it avails itself of the forms of nature to recall, to express, and to modify the thoughts and feelings of the mind.' And, in what may stand as a summary for this leitmotif of romantic thought about art:

Now so to place these images [of nature] totalized, and fitted to the limits of the human mind, as to elicit from, and to superinduce upon, the forms themselves the moral reflections to which they approximate, to make the external internal, the internal external, to make nature thought, and thought nature,—this is the mystery of genius in the Fine Arts.[30]

In these central predications about the nature of poetry, taken out of their theoretical contexts, the principal difference from earlier criticism is a difference in metaphor. But whether poets or speakers in prose, we cannot discuss the activities of mind without metaphor. In the generation of Wordsworth and Coleridge, the transformation of the key images by which critics pictured the process and product of art is a convenient index to a comprehensive revolution in the theory of poetry, and of all the arts.

ii. Emotion and the Objects of Poetry

The habitual reference to the emotions and processes of the poet's mind for the source of poetry altered drastically the established solutions to that basic problem of aesthetics, the discrepancy between the subject matter in poetry and the objects found in experience. According to the central tradition hitherto, poetry departs from fact principally because it reflects a nature which has been reassembled to make a composite beauty, or filtered to reveal a central form or the common denominator of a type, or in some fashion culled and ornamented for the greater delight of the reader. To the romantic critic, on the other hand, though poetry may be ideal, what marks it off from fact is, primarily, that it incorporates objects of sense which have already been acted on and transformed by the feelings of the poet.

Wordsworth said that 'I have at all times endeavoured to look steadily at my subject.' This statement is often taken to be no more than a recommendation for objective accuracy and particularity. Wordsworth's 'subject,' however, is not merely the particularized object of sense, any more than it is the neo-classic ideal.

The ability to observe with accuracy things as they are in themselves, and with fidelity to describe them, unmodified by any passion or feeling existing in the mind of the describer . . . though indispensable to a Poet, is one which he employs only in submission to necessity, and never for a continuance of time: as its exercise supposes all the higher qualities of the mind to be passive, and in a state of subjection to external objects.[31]

This thesis Wordsworth insisted on again and again; for example, in 1816: 'Throughout, objects . . . derive their influence not from what they are actually in themselves, but from such as are bestowed upon them by the minds of those who are conversant with or affected by those objects.' [32] In the same vein, Thomas De Quincey wrote, refuting Erasmus Darwin's opinion that nothing is poetic that does not present a visual image: 'The fact is that no mere description, however visual or picturesque, is in any instance poetic *per se,* or except in and through the passion which presides.' [33] 'Descriptive poetry,' according to J. S. Mill, as opposed to the descriptions of a naturalist, 'consists, no doubt, in description, but in description of things as they appear, not as they *are.*' [34]

In eighteenth-century theory, the minor topic of the way feelings may enter into and alter objects of sense had been discussed under the heading of 'style,' as one of various justifying causes of certain figures of speech. In the nineteenth century, this problem moves into a position at the very center of poetic theory. Often the matter is left in terms of analogy. Feelings project a light—especially a colored light—on objects of sense, so that things, as Mill said, are 'arranged in the colours and seen through the medium of the imagination set in action by the feelings.' [35] Or the metaphor is biological rather than optical; while 'it recalls the sights and sounds that had accompanied the occasions of the original passions,' said Coleridge, 'poetry impregnates them with an interest not their own by means of the passions. . .' [36] At other times the descriptions are more explicit, and give examples of the way objects of sense are fused and remolded in the crucible of emotion and the passionate imagination. Hazlitt's 'On Poetry in General' reads as though it were itself a spontaneous overflow of feeling without logical sequence, but it incorporates in very short scope a surprising number of current aesthetic ideas. The poetic imagination, he says, represents objects 'as they are moulded by other thoughts and feelings, into an infinite variety of shapes and combinations of power.' Agitation, fear, love, all distort or magnify the object, and 'things are equal to the imagination, which have the power of affecting the mind with an equal degree of terror, admiration, delight, or love.' As an example:

When Iachimo says of Imogen,

> '—The flame o' th' taper
> Bows toward her, and would under-peep her lids
> To see the enclosed lights'—

this passionate interpretation of the motion of the flame to accord with the speaker's own feelings, is true poetry.[87]

Of all his contemporaries, Coleridge was the most concerned with the problem of how the poetic mind acts to modify or transform the materials of sense without violating truth to nature. Toward its solution, as we shall see farther on, he formulated the keystone of his critical system, his theory of imagination. In this characteristic passage he considers the role of emotion in the process of such transformation:

Images, however beautiful, though faithfully copied from nature, and as accurately represented in words, do not of themselves characterize the poet. They become proofs of original genius only as far as they are modified by a predominant passion; or by associated thoughts or images awakened by that passion . . . or lastly, when a human and intellectual life is transferred to them from the poet's own spirit,

'Which shoots its being through earth, sea, and air.' [38]

Coleridge's last example of the modifying action of passion, that of animating the inanimate—the transference of the life of the observer to the things he observes—was eminently the preoccupation of romantic poets and theorists. 'Poetry puts a spirit of life and motion into the universe,' as Hazlitt put it.[39] 'What is a Poet?' Wordsworth asks, and answers that he is a man 'who rejoices more than other men in the spirit of life that is in him; delighting to contemplate similar volitions and passions as manifested in the goings-on of the Universe, and habitually impelled to create them where he does not find them.' [40] To the recording and discussion of such occasions, when the impressed characters of danger and desire

did make
The surface of the universal earth
With triumph, and delight, and hope, and fear,
Work like a sea,

Wordsworth devoted a number of his best poems and the climactic passages of the *Prelude*. The habitual reading of passion, life, and physiognomy into the landscape is one of the few salient attributes common to most of the major romantic poets. Correspondingly, in literary criticism the valid animation of natural objects, traditionally treated as one form of the rhetorical device of prosopopoeia, or personification, now came to be a major index to the sovereign faculty of imagination, and almost in itself a sufficient criterion of the highest poetry.

In the main, therefore, romantic critics substituted the presentation of a world that is instinct with the poet's feelings for the depiction of the universal and typical as the property which distinguishes poetry from descriptive discourse. But even though the question of the ideal in poetry thus lost the special position it had held in earlier theory, romantic critics by no means ceased, in relevant contexts, and in terms adapted to their new principles, to argue the topic they had inherited from their predecessors. On this their opinions ranged from Shelley's Platonistic formulation that poetry 'lays bare the naked and sleeping beauty' of the world 'which is the spirit of its forms,'[41] through Blake's violent marginalia on Reynolds' *Discourses* that 'to Generalize is to be an Idiot. To Particularize is the Alone Distinction of Merit,'[42] to Hazlitt's interpretation of the ideal (resembling the German theory of the 'characteristic') as the quintessence of a single object. The ideal, says Hazlitt, who was especially concerned with the objective correlate of artistic subject matter, is not 'an abstraction of general nature' nor 'a *mean* or average proportion,' for this would be to reduce all productions of art 'to one vague and undefined abstraction, answering to the word *man.*' The true ideal is achieved 'by singling out some one thing or leading quality of an object, and making it the pervading and regulating principle of all the rest'; for 'a thing is not more perfect by becoming something else, but by *being more itself.*'[43] With the exceptions of Blake and Hazlitt, however, there is little tendency in the major English critics to follow the extremists of the later eighteenth century and substitute an unqualified particularity, originality, and uniqueness for the older virtues of generality and universality. Wordsworth, for example, agrees with what he has been told is Aristotle's opinion, that the object of poetry 'is truth, not individual and local, but general and operative.'[44] Coleridge also confirms 'the principle of Aristotle, that poetry as poetry is essentially *ideal,*' and that its persons must possess 'generic attributes.' He repeats as well the common eighteenth-century formula that poetry represents a just mean between the extremes of the general and familiar and the individual and novel, but restates it according to his own characteristic logic of the fusion and reconciliation of opposites. What is required is 'an involution of the universal in the individual'; the imagination acts by reconciling the opposites of 'the general, with the concrete . . . the individual, with the representative; the sense of novelty and freshness, with old and familiar objects'; and, he says, 'that just proportion, that union and interpenetration of the universal and the particular . . . must ever pervade all works of decided genius and true science.'[45]

iii. Changing Metaphors of Mind

The change from imitation to expression, and from the mirror to the fountain, the lamp, and related analogues, was not an isolated phenomenon. It was an integral part of a corresponding change in popular epistemology—that is, in the concept of the role played by the mind in perception which was current among romantic poets and critics. And the movement from eighteenth- to early nineteenth-century schemes of the mind and its place in nature is indicated by a mutation of metaphors almost exactly parallel to that in contemporary discussions of the nature of art.

The various physical analogues which make up the ground plans or conceptual schemes for those 'modes of inmost being,' as Coleridge called them, which 'can not be conveyed save in symbols of time and space,'[46] are sometimes explicitly formulated. At other times they merely intimate their existence by the structure of the metaphors with which men refer to the mental processes. To elucidate the nature of sense-perception, memory, and thought, Plato, for example, appealed to the reflection of images in a mirror, as well as to paintings, the writing of characters in the pages of a book, and the stamping of impressions into a wax plate.[47] Aristotle also said that the receptions of sense 'must be conceived of as taking place in the way in which a piece of wax takes on the impress of a signet-ring without the iron or gold.'[48] Thus John Locke—who more than any philosopher established the stereotype for the popular view of the mind in the eighteenth century—was able to levy upon a long tradition of ready-made parallels in giving definition to his view of the mind in perception as a passive receiver for images presented ready-formed from without. The mind in Locke's *Essay* is said to resemble a mirror which fixes the objects it reflects.[49] Or (suggesting the *ut pictura poesis* of the aesthetics of that period) it is a *tabula rasa* on which sensations write or paint themselves.[50] Or (employing the analogy of the *camera obscura,* in which the light, entering through a small aperture, throws an image of the external scene on the wall) external and internal senses are said to be 'the windows by which light is let into this *dark room.*'

For, methinks, the understanding is not much unlike a closet wholly shut from light, with only some little openings left, to let in external visible resemblances, or ideas of things without: would the pictures coming into such a dark room but stay there, and lie so orderly as to be found upon occasion, it would very much resemble the understanding of a man, in reference to all objects of sight, and the ideas of them.[51]

Alternatively, the mind is a 'waxed tablet' into which sensations, like seals, impress themselves.[52]

The analogies for the mind in the writings of both Wordsworth and Coleridge show a radical transformation. Varied as these are, they usually agree in picturing the mind in perception as active rather than inertly receptive, and as contributing to the world in the very process of perceiving the world. Wordsworth's *Prelude,* as completed in 1805, provides us with an anthology of mental schema whose properties are in accord with the initial plan of that poem, which, as Coleridge said more than three decades later, was, 'I believe, partly suggested by me. . . He was to treat man as man— a subject of eye, ear, touch, and taste, in contact with external nature, and informing the senses from the mind, and not compounding a mind out of the senses.'[53] The thirteenth book of that poem ends, in fact, with the manifestation of 'a new world,' ruled by laws

> Which do both give it being and maintain
> A balance, an ennobling interchange
> Of action from without and from within;
> The excellence, pure function, and best power
> Both of the object seen, and eye that sees.

The Copernican revolution in epistemology—if we do not restrict this to Kant's specific doctrine that the mind imposes the forms of time, space, and the categories on the 'sensuous manifold,' but apply it to the general concept that the perceiving mind discovers what it has itself partly made—was effected in England by poets and critics before it manifested itself in academic philosophy. Thus generally defined, the revolution was a revolution by reaction. In their early poetic expositions of the mind fashioning its own experience, for example, Coleridge and Wordsworth do not employ Kant's abstract formulae. They revert, instead, to metaphors of mind which had largely fallen into disuse in the eighteenth century, but had earlier been current in seventeenth-century philosophers outside of, or specifically opposed to, the sensational tradition of Hobbes and Locke. Behind these philosophers was Plotinus' basic figure of creation as emanation, in which the One and the Good are habitually analogized to such objects as an overflowing fountain, or a radiating sun, or (in a combination of the two images) to an overflowing fountain of light. 'Were one writing a book on the philosophic significance and use of similes,' B. A. G. Fuller has said, 'I am not sure but that one would have to count this first, both in point of its aptness, and of its central place and controlling function in thought.' [54] If Plato was the main source of the philosophical archetype of the reflector, Plotinus was the chief begetter of the archetype of the projector; and both the romantic theory of knowledge and the romantic theory of poetry can be accounted the remote descendants of this root-image of Plotinian philosophy.

In discussing the human perception of the divine overflow, Plotinus explicitly rejected the concept of sensations as 'imprints' or 'seal-impressions' made on a passive mind, and substituted the view of the mind as an act and a power which 'gives a radiance out of its own store' to the objects of sense.[55] Similar metaphors of mind were particularly prevalent in the philosophy of the 'Cambridge Platonists' (more Plotinists, actually, than Platonists), whom Wordsworth had read, and Coleridge had studied intensively. In these writers, the familiar figure of the spirit of man as a candle of the Lord easily lent itself to envisioning the act of perception as that little candle throwing its beams into the external world. I shall cite excerpts from one chapter of Nathanael Culverwel's *An Elegant and Learned Discourse of the Light of Nature,* because it serves as a convenient inventory of analogies for the mind as receptor or projector—as mirror or lamp. The *Discourse* was written before general knowledge of the full implications of Hobbes's major works had sharpened the point at issue, and Culverwel sets out to represent 'unto you, as *indifferently* as I can, the *state* of this great *Controversie.*' In this dispute he takes Plato and Aristotle to have been the chief protagonists.

'Now the *Spirit of man* is the *Candle of the Lord,*' he says, for the Creator, himself 'the fountain of Light,' furnished and beautified this *'lower part* of the *World* with *Intellectual Lamps,* that should shine forth to the *praise* and *honour* of his Name. . .'

This makes the *Platonists* look upon the *Spirit of Man* as the *Candle* of the *Lord* for illuminating and irradiating of *objects,* and darting *more light* upon them, than it receives *from* them. . . And, truely, he might as well phansie such *implanted Ideas,* such *seeds* of *Light* in his *external* Eye, as such *seminal Principles* in the Eye of the *mind* . . . (Aristotle) did not *antedate* his own *Knowledge* . . . but plainly profess'd, that his *Understanding* came *naked* into the World. He shews you . . . an *abrasa tabula.* . . This makes him set open the *windows* of *sense,* to welcome and entertain the *first dawnings,* the *early glimmerings* of *morning light.* . . As he could perceive no *connate Colours,* no *Pictures,* or *Portraictures* in his *external* Eye: so neither could he find any *signatures* in his *Mind,* till some *outward Objects* had made some *impression* upon . . . his *soft* and *pliable Understanding,* impartially prepared for every *Seal.*

Culverwel's own hesitant conclusion (for he has some inclination to the opinion that this is 'a *Question* which cannot be *determined* in this Life') is that we may look upon the understanding as a glass '*nakedly* receiving, and *faithfully* returning all such *colours,* as fall upon it. Yet the *Platonists* in this were commendable, that look'd upon the *Spirit* of a *Man* as the *Candle* of the *Lord;* though they were deceiv'd in the time when 'twas *lighted.'* [56] For an unqualified commitment to an absolute idealism, expressed in the image of the spirit of man as an outflowing fountain, we may turn to this passage from an essay by the Platonizing Puritan, Peter Sterry:

Thus is the Soule, or Spirit of every man all the World to Him. The world with all Varietie of things in it, his owne body with all it's parts, & changes are himselfe, his owne Soule, or Spirit springing up from it's own ffountaine within itselfe into all those fformes, & Images of things, which it seeth, heareth, smelleth, tasts, feeles, imagineth, or understandeth. . . The Soule often looking upon this, like Narcissus upon his owne fface in the ffountaine, forgets it to be itselfe, forgets that itselfe is the fface, the shadow, & the ffountaine, so it falls into a fond Love of itselfe in it's owne shadowie ffigure of itselfe.[57]

As in the English Platonists, so in the romantic writers, the favorite analogy for the activity of the perceiving mind is that of a lamp projecting light. Wordsworth, describing in the *Prelude* his boyish communings with nature, affirms in a sequence of metaphors, 'I still retain'd My first creative sensibility.' 'A plastic power Abode with me, a forming hand,' and then:

> An auxiliar light
> Came from my mind which on the setting sun
> Bestow'd new splendor. . .[58]

Coleridge, on first hearing the *Prelude* read aloud, adopted Wordsworth's favorite image of radiance to describe its theme—although he combined the figure of the lamp of the mind with the figure of external nature as mirror: 'Theme hard as high!'

> . . . of moments awful,
> Now in thy inner life, and now abroad,
> When power streamed from thee, and thy soul received
> The light reflected, as a light bestowed. . .[59]

Nor is the formulation confined to these two friends; the effusive Christopher North, for example, employs the lamp to support the proposition that 'we create' nine-tenths at least of what appears to exist externally. . .' They who ponder on the pages of 'the living Book of Nature . . . behold in full

the beauty and the sublimity, which their own immortal spirits create, reflected back on them who are its authors.'[60]

The familiar Neoplatonic figure of the soul as a fountain, or an outflowing stream, is also frequent in romantic poetry, although this too is usually
reformed to imply a bilateral transaction, a give-and-take, between mind and
external object. Wordsworth, who spoke of poetry as an 'overflow of feeling,'
also spoke of whatever he 'saw, or heard, or felt' on his visit to the Alps as

> but a stream
> That flowed into a kindred stream; a gale
> Confederate with the current of the soul. . .'[61]

This image of confluent streams, like that of the lamp, Coleridge reiterated
in the poem he wrote in response to the *Prelude*.[62] We must also take special
note of the image of the wind-harp, which both Wordsworth and Shelley
used as a construct for the mind in perception as well as for the poetic mind
in composition.[63] (It is a curious twist of intellectual history that Athanasius
Kircher, who claimed the invention of the Aeolian lyre, also perfected the
camera obscura which had been employed as a mind-scheme by John
Locke,[64] so that the same man was in part responsible for the artifacts used
to give structure to antipodal views of the human mind.) As early as 1795
Coleridge had suggested the harp as an analogue for the thinking mind:

> And what if all of animated nature
> Be but organic harps diversely fram'd,
> That tremble into thought, as o'er them sweeps
> Plastic and vast, one intellectual breeze,
> At once the Soul of each and God of all?

—a proposal no sooner made than recanted, for the sake both of his fiancée
and 'The Incomprehensible,' as mere bubbles 'on vain Philosophy's aye-bab-
bling spring.'[65] Even at that stage in his thinking, Coleridge was apparently
troubled by the necessitarian implications which emerged clearly in Shelley's
later use of the same image. 'There is a Power by which we are surrounded,'
Shelley says, 'like the atmosphere in which some motionless lyre is sus-
pended, which visits with its breath our silent chords at will.' Even the 'most
imperial and stupendous qualities,' though active 'relatively to inferior portions of its mechanism,' are nevertheless 'the passive slaves of some higher
and more omnipotent Power. This Power is God'; and those who have 'been
harmonized by their own will . . . give forth divinest melody, when the
breath of universal being sweeps over their frame.'[66]

A number of romantic writers then, whether in verse or prose, habitually pictured the mind in perception, as well as the mind in composition, by sometimes identical analogies of projection into, or of reciprocity with, elements from without. Usually, in these metaphors of the perceiving mind, the boundary between what is given and what bestowed is a sliding one, to be established as best one can from the individual context. Sometimes, as in Coleridge's formulation of the 'coalescence of subject and object' in the act of knowing, there is not, nor can there be, any attempt to differentiate the mental addition from that which is given, for as in the philosophy of Schelling from which Coleridge borrowed these terms, we are confined to a knowledge of the product, as against the raw materials, of the perceptual amalgam. In other instances—as in Wordsworth's expression of his state of mind at Cambridge,

> I had a world about me; 'twas my own,
> I made it; for it only liv'd to me,
> And to the God who look'd into my mind—[67]

the suggestion is of a kind of Fichtean absoluteness, in which all objects resolve into a product of the Ego. But in most passages the implication is that the content of perception is the joint product of external data and of mind; and we are sometimes enabled, very roughly, to make out various positions of the line between inner and outer as, in different poetic contexts, it advances and retreats:

(1) In Wordsworth's early passage from 'Tintern Abbey,'

> All the mighty world
> Of eye, and ear,—both what they half create,
> And what perceive,

the elements created in the act of perception may well be nothing more than Locke's secondary sense-qualities. Wordsworth himself draws attention in a note to the source of this passage in Young's *Night Thoughts*. Our senses, Young had said,

> Give taste to fruits; and harmony to groves;
> Their radiant beams to gold, and gold's bright fire . . .
> Our senses, as our reason, are divine
> And half create the wondrous world they see.
> But for the magic organ's powerful charm
> Earth were a rude, uncolour'd chaos still.
> Objects are th' occasion; ours th' exploit . . .
> Man makes the matchless image, man admires. . .[68]

The reference to the secondary qualities as constituting the mind's addition to perception is here unmistakable, and brings to the fore an interesting aspect of the Lockean tradition. For though Locke had said that in acquiring the simple ideas of sense the mind, like a mirror, is passively receptive, he had gone on to make a further distinction. Some simple ideas are 'resemblances' of primary qualities which 'are in the things themselves'; but the simple ideas of secondary qualities, such as colors, sounds, smells, tastes, have no counterpart in any external body. In Locke's dualism, then, we have the view that our perception of the sensible world consists partly of elements reflecting things as they are, and partly of elements which are merely 'ideas in the mind' without 'likeness of something existing without.' [69] Locke, therefore, implicitly gave the mind a partnership in sense-perception; what Young did was to convert this into an active partnership of 'giving,' 'making,' and 'creation.' In this simple metaphoric substitution, we find Locke's sensationalism in the process of converting itself into what is often considered its epistemological opposite.

(2) A number of passages imply that objects, possessed of their full complement of primary and secondary sense-qualities, are given from without, and that the observer contributes to perception feeling-tones and aesthetic qualities—or at any rate, any especially rich, intense, or profound sense of beauty or significance in the visible scene. 'The auxiliar light' which came from Wordsworth's mind 'on the setting sun Bestow'd new splendor,' and heightened the song of birds and the murmur of fountains.[70] In the familiar text on the 'spots of time,' when Wordsworth revisited a scene 'in the blessed time of early love,' there fell upon it

> The spirit of pleasure and youth's golden gleam;
> And think ye not with radiance more divine
> From these remembrances, and from the power
> They left behind?
>   . . . this I feel,
> That from thyself it is that thou must give
> Else never canst receive.[71]

The image of the mind as projective of aesthetic or other emotional quality had been anticipated by certain English writers of the eighteenth century, and was another part of the indigenous tendency toward the concept of creative perception which developed within the confines of the English empirical tradition. Thus Hume compared vice and virtue 'to sounds, colours, heat and cold, which according to modern philosophy, are not qualities in objects, but perceptions in the mind. . .' [72] So also with beauty, which is not (in the example of a geometrical figure) 'a quality of the circle. . . It is only the effect, which that figure produces upon the mind.' And then Hume slips over into the alternative figures of a projective lamp, of production, and even of creation:

Thus the distinct boundaries and offices of *reason* and of *taste* are easily ascertained. . . The one discovers objects, as they really stand in nature, without addition or diminution: The other has a productive faculty, and gilding or staining all natural objects with the colours, borrowed from internal sentiment, raises, in a manner, a new creation.[73]

Formulations of the mind as projective of aesthetic qualities are particularly common among those eighteenth-century theorists who infused their Locke with a tincture of Neoplatonism. Thus Akenside cried, echoing Plotinus' favorite metaphor,

> Mind, mind, alone, (bear witness, earth and heaven!)
> The living fountains in itself contains
> Of beauteous and sublime—

though, in a later edition of the *Pleasures of the Imagination,* he prudently substituted 'He, God most high' for 'Mind, mind, alone' as the well-spring of the aesthetic fountains.[74]

(3) Most frequently, however, the mind is imaged by romantic poets as projecting life, physiognomy, and passion into the universe. The mere postulation of an animate universe was no novelty; Isaac Newton's ubiquitous God, constituting duration and space and sustaining by his presence the laws of motion and gravitation, and the World-Soul of the ancient Stoics and Platonists, are often to be found dwelling amicably together in the nature-poetry of the eighteenth century. What is distinctive in the poetry of Wordsworth and Coleridge is not the attribution of a life and soul to nature, but the repeated formulation of this outer life as a contribution of, or else as in constant reciprocation with, the life and soul of man the observer. This same topic was also central in the literary theory of these writers, where it turns up repeatedly in their discussions of the subject matter of poetry, their analyses of the imaginative process, and their debates on poetic diction and the legitimacy of personification and allied figures of speech.

The reason for this common concern of the early nineteenth-century philosophy of nature and of art is not hard to find. It was an essential part of the attempt to revitalize the material and mechanical universe which had emerged from the philosophy of Descartes and Hobbes, and which had been recently dramatized by the theories of Hartley and the French mechanists of the latter eighteenth century. It was at the same time an attempt to overcome the sense of man's alienation from the world by healing the cleavage between subject and object, between the vital, purposeful, value-full world of private experience and the dead postulated world of extension, quantity, and motion. To establish that man shares his own life with nature was to reanimate the dead universe of the materialists, and at the same time most effectively to tie man back into his milieu.

The persistent objective of Coleridge's formal philosophy was to substitute 'life and intelligence . . . for the philosophy of mechanism, which, in everything that is most worthy of the human intellect, strikes *Death*.' And the life transfused into the mechanical motion of the universe is one with the life in man: in nature, he wrote in 1802, 'everything has a life of its own, and . . . we are all *One Life*.' [75] A similar idea constitutes the leitmotif of Wordsworth's *Prelude*. In a crucial passage, for example, Wordsworth describes how the infant in his mother's arms, seeing a world 'irradiated' by a sense of her love, comes to feel at home in the universe.

> No outcast he, bewildered and depressed:
> Along his infant veins are interfused
> The gravitation and the filial bond
> Of nature that connect him with the world.

But more is achieved than the mere linkage of feeling; the child becomes integral with the external world by the strongest of all bonds, through participating in its very creation and so sharing with it attributes of his own being. Through the faculties of sense, the mind creates—

> Creator and receiver both,
> Working but in alliance with the works
> Which it beholds.[76]

The culmination of this process of domiciliation came in his seventeenth year when, by a process he opposes to 'analytic industry,' he found not only his senses and feelings but his life allied to an all-pervasive life in nature, and with bliss ineffable,

> . . . felt the sentiment of Being spread
> O'er all that moves and all that seemeth still.

This experience of the one life within us and abroad cancels the division
between animate and inanimate, between subject and object—ultimately,
even between object and object, in that climactic ALL IS ONE of the mystical
trance-state,

> then, when the fleshly ear,
> O'ercome by humblest prelude of that strain,
> Forgot her functions, and slept undisturbed.[77]

Wordsworth here refers to his relation with nature in terms of 'filial
bonds'; we must add the remarkable passage from the conclusion to the first
book of *The Recluse* in which he replaces the familial by conjugal metaphors. That great undertaking, the intended crown of his poetic career, he
announces in unmistakable terms, is to be a 'spousal verse'—a prodigious
prothalamion celebrating the marriage of mind and nature, the consum-
mation of the marriage, and the consequent creation (or procreation?) of
a living perceptual world. 'Paradise, groves Elysian, Fortunate Fields—'

> the discerning intellect of Man,
> When wedded to this goodly universe
> In love and holy passion, shall find these
> A simple produce of the common day.
> —I, long before the blissful hour arrives,
> Would chant, in lonely peace, the spousal verse
> Of this great consummation:—, and, by words
> Which speak of nothing more than what we are,
> Would I arouse the sensual from their sleep
> Of Death, and win the vacant and the vain
> To noble raptures; while my voice proclaims
> How exquisitely the individual Mind
> (And the progressive powers perhaps no less
> Of the whole species) to the external World
> Is fitted:—and how exquisitely, too—
> Theme this but little heard of among men—
> The external World is fitted to the Mind;
> And the creation (by no lower name
> Can it be called) which they with blended might
> Accomplish:—this is our high argument.[78]

Two of the greatest and most representative poems of the early nineteenth century, Wordsworth's 'Intimations of Immortality' and Coleridge's
'Dejection,' turn on the distinction between data and addenda in sense experience. In both poems, the theme concerns an apparent change in the
objects of sense, and is developed in terms of mental schemes which analo-

gize the mind to something which is at once projective and capable of receiving back the fused product of what it gives and what is given to it. Wordsworth's 'Ode' employs, with dazzling success, the familiar optical metaphors of light and of radiant objects—lamps and stars. His problem is one of a loss of 'celestial light' and 'glory' from meadow, grove, and stream. The solution inheres in the figure (not uncommon, as we know, in Neoplatonic theologians) of the soul as 'our life's star,' 'trailing clouds of glory' at its rising, but gradually, in the westward course of life, fading 'into the light of common day,' though leaving behind recollections which 'Are yet the fountain-light of all our day.' [79] But if maturity has its loss of 'splendor in the grass, of glory in the flower,' it has its compensating gains, and the mind, though altered, retains its power of radiant give-and-take with the external world:

> The clouds that gather round the setting sun
> Do take a sober coloring from an eye
> That hath kept watch o'er man's mortality.

Coleridge's 'Dejection,' on the other hand, memorializes not merely an alteration but the utter loss of the reciprocating power of the mind, leaving it a death-in-life as a passive receptor of the inanimate visible scene. In the short third and fourth stanzas, in which Coleridge five times iterates the dependence of nature's life on the inner life of man, he strikes the full diapason of metaphors for the active and contributive mind, some familiar, others seemingly of his own invention. The mind is a fountain, a source of light, the generator of a cloud that conveys life-giving rain, a musical voice like that of a wind-harp whose echo mingles with the sounds of outer origin; there is even the suggestion of a Wordsworthian marriage with nature. And the fifth stanza, proposing 'joy' as the indispensable inner condition for the 'effluence' and return of life, most subtly recapitulates all these figures, optical, acoustical, meteorological, and marital:

> Joy, Lady! is the spirit and the power,
> Which, wedding Nature to us, gives in dower
>   A new Earth and new Heaven,
> Undreamt of by the sensual and the proud—
> Joy is the sweet voice, Joy the luminous cloud—
>   We in ourselves rejoice!
> And thence flows all that charms or ear or sight,
>   All melodies the echoes of that voice,
> All colours a suffusion from that light.

But it is not until the resolution in the closing stanza, when Coleridge prays that the Lady to whom the poem is addressed may retain the power he has lost, that we come upon the crowning metaphor of an eddy. The figure implies a ceaseless and circular interchange of life between soul and nature in which it is impossible to distinguish what is given from what received:

> To her may all things live, from pole to pole,
> Their life the eddying of her living soul!

This version of the perceptual mind as projecting life and passion into the world it apprehends is the one which most approximates the concurrent formulations of the mind active in the highest poetic composition—as Coleridge implies when he says, in 'Dejection,' that the failure of his power to project 'the passion and the life' marks the failure also of his 'genial spirits' and his 'shaping spirit of imagination.' We may say, then, by way of summary, that in the theory of Coleridge (partly though not consistently paralleled by that of Wordsworth) the primary and already creative act of perception yields the 'inanimate cold world' of the ever-anxious crowd. This coincides roughly with the inert world of both empirical philosophy and of common sense, which is perceived only in so far as it serves our practical interests and aims. This world includes Peter Bell's yellow primrose, but nothing more; daffodils set moving by the breeze, but neither gleeful nor dancing; the moon radiant in a bare sky —with the proviso that it is not the moon but the poet who 'doth with delight look round him when the heavens are bare.' The subsequent and higher act of re-creation, among its other functions, by projecting its own passion and life, transforms the cold inanimate world into a warm world united with the life of man, and by that same act, converts matter-of-fact into matter-of-poetry—and according to Coleridge's conception, into the highest poetry, because it is the product of the 'secondary imagination.'

We must not leave the subject of the romantic analogues of mind without citing one that was Coleridge's favorite, and destined to alter more drastically the conceptions of mind, art, and the universe than all the apparatus of lamps, fountains, and wind-harps we have come upon thus far. This was the archetype (potentially present in the Platonist's figure of the 'seeds of light' in the mind) representing the mind not as a physical object or artifact, but as a living plant, growing out into its perception. To mental mechanism, Coleridge often and explicitly opposes the concept of life and growth. In a central passage of *The Statesman's Manual,* Coleridge discovers 'correspondences and symbols' of the highest faculty of man in the growth of a plant and its power to assimilate outer elements to which its respiration has already made contribution. Looking at a plant in a flowery meadow, he says, 'I feel an awe, as if there were before my eyes the same power as that of the reason—the same power in a lower dignity, and therefore a symbol established in the truth of things.'

Lo!—with the rising sun it commences its outward life and enters into open communion with all the elements, at once assimilating them to itself and to each other. At the same moment it strikes its roots and unfolds its leaves, absorbs and respires, steams forth its cooling vapour and finer fragrance, and breathes a repairing spirit, at once the food and tone of the atmosphere, into the atmosphere that feeds it. Lo!—at the touch of light how it returns an air akin to light, and yet with the same pulse effectuates its own secret growth, still contracting to fix what expanding it had refined.[80]

In any period, the theory of mind and the theory of art tend to be integrally related and to turn upon similar analogues, explicit or submerged. To put the matter schematically: for the representative eighteenth-century critic, the perceiving mind was a reflector of the external world; the inventive process consisted in a reassembly of 'ideas' which were literally images, or replicas of sensations; and the resulting art work was itself comparable to a mirror presenting a selected and ordered image of life. By substituting a projective and creative mind and, consonantly, an expressive and creative theory of art, various romantic critics reversed the basic orientation of all aesthetic philosophy. Consider now the further innovative possibilities in Coleridge's archetypal plant. Through this perspective, Coleridge saw the mind as growing into its percepts, conceived of the activity of the poetic imagination as differing from this vital, self-determining, assimilative process in degree rather than kind, and thus was able to envision the product of artistic genius as exhibiting the mode of development and the internal relations of an organic whole. But that is a subject for a later chapter.

THE DEVELOPMENT OF THE EXPRESSIVE THEORY OF POETRY AND ART

A profound silence ensuing, he began by explaining his design. 'Gentlemen,' says he, 'the present piece is not one of your common epic poems . . . there are none of your Turnuses or Didos in it; it is an heroical description of nature. I only beg you'll endeavour to make your souls unison with mine, and hear with the same enthusiasm with which I have written. . . For you must know, gentlemen, that I am myself the hero.'

OLIVER GOLDSMITH, *Letters from a Citizen of the World*

To GENERALIZE ABOUT A LARGE and complex intellectual movement is almost inevitably to lay down convenient simplifications which must be qualified in the sequel. I have emphasized the novelty of early nineteenth-century criticism, in its contrast to the main tendencies of the theory of art during the preceding two thousand years. Even though the characteristic patterns of romantic theory were new, many of its constituent parts are to be found, variously developed, in earlier writers. By shifting the focus and selecting the examples, we can readily show that romantic aesthetics was no less an instance of continuity than of revolution in intellectual history. In the course of the eighteenth century, some elements of the traditional poetics were attenuated or dropped, while others were expanded and variously augmented; ideas which had been central became marginal, and marginal ideas became central; new terms and distinctions were introduced; until, by gradual stages, a reversal was brought about in the prevailing orientation of aesthetic thinking. A summary account of this process, in both England and Germany, will help make clear what is hereditary and what distinctive in the terminology and methods of the many romantic theories which turn on the concept that poetry is the expression of feeling, or of the human spirit, or of an impassioned state of mind and imagination. For convenience of exposition, I shall proceed topically, positing separately and in sequence developments that were in fact concomitant and interdependent.

i. Si vis me flere. . .

Within its pragmatic design, ancient rhetorical theory incorporated a number of elements which can be traced, in a straight line of descent, to central components of romantic theory: the attention, for example, to 'nature,' or innate capacity in the orator and poet, in addition to his art and acquired skills; the tendency to conceive of the invention, disposition, and expression of material as mental powers and processes, and not only as the overt manipulation of words; and the common assumption that irrational or inexplicable occurrences, such as inspiration, divine madness, or lucky graces, are indispensable conditions of the greatest utterance. What is particularly noteworthy, for our present concern, is the stress that rhetoricians had always put on the role of the emotions in the art of persuasion. Aristotle said that to stir the emotions of the hearers is one of the three modes of achieving persuasion. Cicero defined the three aims of the orator to be 'conciliating, informing, and moving the audience,' and added that the speaker must himself achieve a state of excitement if he is to evoke emotions in his auditors, for 'no mind is so susceptible of the power of eloquence, as to catch its blaze, unless the speaker, when he approaches it, is himself in flames.'[1] For the aim of persuasion, Horace substituted pleasure or profit and transferred the concept of the exhibition and evocation of feeling from rhetoric into poetic:

> Non satis est pulchra esse poemata; dulcia sunto
> Et quocumque volent animum auditoris agunto.
> . . . si vis me flere, dolendum est
> Primum ipsi tibi. . .[2]

'If you would have me weep, you must first show grief yourself'—around this maxim, often amalgamated (especially when tragedy was in question) with Aristotle's account of the evocation and purgation of pity and terror, revolved much neo-classic discussion of the emotional element in poetic art. The assertion that eighteenth-century critics read by reason alone is gross calumny. Readers of no age have demanded more, or more violent, emotion from poetry, and not only the sentimentalists, but the most judicial readers as well. Johnson's praise of Shakespeare—

> His powerful strokes presiding Truth impressed
> And unresisted passion stormed the breast—

is not empty declamation, as the intensity of Johnson's response to *Hamlet,* and to the closing scenes of *Lear* and *Othello,* demonstrates. And at least in the lyric forms, the successful evocation of feeling from the reader was held to entail a prior state of feeling in the poet. In Cowley's poem on the death of Hervey, says Johnson,

> There is much praise, but little passion. . . When he wishes to make us weep, he forgets to weep himself. . .[3]

In the typical neo-classic interpretation, however, the spontaneous surge of feeling in the poet was not held to be the indispensable originating condition of poetry. The poet, it was indicated, cultivates an appropriate state of feeling in himself, as one of various artful means to which he resorts for affecting his readers. As Boileau expressed the doctrine, it is necessary that passion 'chercher le coeur, l'échauffe et le remue.'

> Le secret est d'abord de plaire et de toucher;
> Inventez des ressorts qui puissent m'attacher.

And to this end, the poet was advised to assume the feelings he wishes to evoke; 'Pour me tirer des pleurs, il faut que vous pleuriez.'[4] The principle entered also into the romantic concept that feeling is the essence of poetry; but the way in which Carlyle employed the Horatian tag reveals the reversal in emphasis and the replacement of artfulness by spontaneity. The excellence of Burns, Carlyle says, is 'his *Sincerity.*'

> The passion that is traced before us has glowed in a living heart. . . He speaks forth what is in him, not from any outward call of vanity or interest, but because his heart is too full to be silent. . . This is the grand secret for finding readers and retaining them: let him who would move and convince others, be first moved and convinced himself. Horace's rule, *Si vis me flere,* is applicable in a wider sense than the literal one.[5]

ii. Longinus and the Longinians

Something approaching the nineteenth-century displacement of the audience by the author as the focal term of reference is to be found in one classical rhetorician, Longinus—the exemplar and source of many characteristic elements of romantic theory. His treatise, of course, was not concerned specifically with poetry, nor with any poem in its entirety, but only with the one quality of 'the sublime,' that cardinal excellence from which 'the greatest poets and writers have derived their eminence.' His pursuit of this quality cuts across the conventional divisions of discourse as well as the boundary between verse and prose; sublimity is to be found in Homer, Demosthenes, Plato, the Book of Genesis, and a love-lyric of Sappho. Of the five sources of the sublime, the first two—'the power of forming great conceptions' and 'vehement and inspired passion'—are largely a matter of innate genius, as opposed to the other three—figurative language, noble diction, and elevated composition—which are more the result of art. Of these five, the native and instinctive elements play the greater part; and, if it must come to a choice, the grand, if flawed, products of natural genius must be preferred to that impeccable mediocrity which can be achieved by art alone. Above all, the emotions are a prime consideration among the sources of sublimity, for 'I would affirm with confidence that there is no tone so lofty as that of genuine passion, in its right place, when it bursts out in a wild gust of mad enthusiasm and as it were fills the speaker's words with frenzy.'[6]

A conspicuous tendency of Longinus, therefore, is to move from the quality of a work to its genesis in the powers and state of mind, the thought and emotions, of its author. Furthermore, even though figurative language is on the whole a matter of art, Longinus attributes a particularly bold and frequent use of metaphors to the promptings of passion in the speaker, since 'it is the nature of the passions, in their vehement rush . . . to demand hazardous turns as altogether indispensable.' The fifth source of sublimity, the composition or arrangement of words, is also 'a wonderful instrument of lofty utterance and of passion'; and 'by means of the blending and variation of its own tones it seeks to introduce into the minds of those who are present the emotion which affects the speaker. . .'[7] In the final analysis, therefore, the supreme quality of a work turns out to be the reflected quality of its author:—'Sublimity is the echo of a great soul.'[8]

In various other ways Longinus prefigured what were to become familiar themes and methods in romantic criticism. His reliance on ecstasy instead of analysis as the criterion of excellence anticipated the substitution of taste and sensibility for the analytic and judicial procedure of earlier criticism. As we shall see, the opinion of some nineteenth-century critics that only the intense and necessarily brief fragment is quintessential poetry had its origin in Longinus' emphasis on the transport that results from the lightening revelation, the shattering image, or the stunning burst of passion. We find in him, moreover, the germ of a new manner of applied criticism, as eighteenth-century commentators recognized when they spoke of Longinus as 'himself that great Sublime he draws'; he is the spiritual ancestor of critical impressionism.[9] It is necessary only to substitute the generic term 'poetry,' for Longinus' qualitative term, 'sublimity,' quite to assimilate much of *Peri Hupsous* to the romantic pattern—although, strangely, the triumph of his perspective only occurred when Longinus himself had lost his earlier prestige and was rarely cited by practicing critics. The consonance of his treatise with the familiar romantic tradition is the reason why many latter-day students of criticism who find Aristotle schematic, Horace worldly, and the rhetoricians trivial, respond to Longinus as animating and 'modern.'

The full effect of Longinus' critical example was slow to make itself apparent. All record of the document disappeared until Robortello published it in 1554; and even after Boileau's translation of 1674, through its numerous editions, had added Longinus to the general heritage of classical criticism, the new terms and dicta for a long time continued to be accommodated within the structure of mimetic and pragmatic theory without affecting its over-all design. But those few early critics who, because of their special literary interests, emulated Longinus in turning to the mental and emotional capacities of the author as a major source of poetic effects demonstrated forthwith the subversive possibilities in Longinian ideas.

John Dennis, the 'Sir Tremendous Longinus' of the farce, *Three Hours after Marriage,* was the first Englishman whose critical theory showed the impact of *Peri Hupsous* in fundamentals rather than details. As presented in essays written at the turn of the century, the skeleton of Dennis' system is traditional enough. In *The Advancement and Reformation of Poetry* (1701), he defines poetry as 'an Imitation of Nature, by a pathetick and numerous Speech.'[10] This imitation has as its purpose the moving of effects in the reader; and in *The Grounds of Criticism in Poetry,* written three years later, Dennis gives a representative statement of the neo-classic frame of critical reference:

We have said above, that as Poetry is an Art, it must have a certain End, and that there must be Means that are proper for attaining that End, which Means are otherwise call'd the Rules. . . Poetry then is an Art, by which a Poet excites Passion (and for that very Cause entertains Sense) in order to satisfy and improve, to delight and reform the Mind . . . the subordinate [End] is Pleasure, and the final one is Instruction.

In his stubborn defense of traditional rules founded on the presumed needs of the audience, Dennis is more conservative than many Augustans, and his derivation of particular rules is rigidly syllogistic; thus: 'For if the End of Comedy is to please, and that End is to be attained by the *Ridiculum,* why then the *Ridiculum* ought to be spread throughout it.' [11]

It is in expanding that element of his definition which identifies the medium (what he calls 'the Instrument') of imitation as 'a pathetick and numerous Speech,' that Dennis expands upon the concepts derived from Longinus, and this puts something of a strain on his pragmatic framework. Passion is justified, properly enough, as a means toward moving the reader, for the ulterior end of pleasure and the ultimate end of instruction. But in Dennis' further treatment, the emotional element becomes an inordinate part of a poem. Passion, he says, 'distinguishes its very Nature and Character. For, therefore,' he adds, probably echoing Milton's comment in his *Letter on Education,* 'Poetry is Poetry, because it is more Passionate and Sensual than Prose.' [12] For Dennis, as for many nineteenth-century critics, its emotive, and not its mimetic character, is what at bottom distinguishes poetry from prose:

Passion then, is the Characteristical Mark of Poetry, and, consequently, must be every where: For where-ever a Discourse is not Pathetick, there it is Prosaick. . . For without Passion there can be no Poetry, no more than there can be Painting. And tho' the Poet and the Painter describe Action, they must describe it with Passion . . . and the more Passion there is, the better the Poetry and the Painting. . . [13]

What Dennis has done is to elaborate upon *Peri Hupsous* by making the emotions, which to Longinus had been only one of several sources of the single quality of sublimity, into the indispensable—almost the sufficient— source and mark of all poetry. Longinus, Dennis insists, was mistaken in saying 'that Loftiness is often without any Passion at all'; sublimity 'is never without Enthusiastick Passion,' and this one source in fact 'takes in all the Sources of Sublimity which Longinus has establish'd.' [14]

As formulated by Dennis, various other Longinian doctrines are brought into approximation with prominent elements of romantic theory. Genius and passion are a matter of 'Nature,' not art; figurative language is regarded as 'the natural Language of the Passions'; and meter 'may be said to be both the Father and Child of Passion.' In consequence, the qualities of a great poem reveal something of the author, for the greater 'the Enthusiastick Passions . . . the more they show the Largeness of Soul, and Greatness of Capacity of the Writer.' [15] Wordsworth, who in his early period may have known Longinus, as he did Aristotle, only by hearsay, approvingly cites Dennis' theory of the passions in a letter of 1814.[16] There is no evidence, however, that Wordsworth had read Dennis before the Preface of 1800, nor is there occasion to assume that he had, for there were to be much closer anticipations of Wordsworth's doctrines before the close of the eighteenth century.

Dennis, an enthusiast for religious subject matter in poetry, pointed out that Longinus had drawn many instances of sublimity from references to pagan religion, as well as one instance from the Book of Genesis itself: 'God said, Let there be light, and there was light.' In the mid-eighteenth century, another critic whose specific concern was with religious poetry turned to Longinus as his model, and with even more interesting results. Bishop Lowth, who succeeded Joseph Spence in the Chair of Poetry at Oxford, published in 1753 *Lectures on the Sacred Poetry of the Hebrews,* which he had delivered in Latin between 1741 and 1750. Such an elaborate and comprehensive critical examination of the Hebrew Bible, considered as a collection of poetic documents, was bound to have a radical impact on the accepted system of criticism. The poetry of the Bible deviated conspicuously from many of the criteria inherited from Greek and Roman practice and precepts, but at the same time its divine origin and subject matter enforced the highest estimation of its excellence as literature, as well as revelation.[17] Furthermore, the Bible has no instance of the epic genre, and as Lowth points out, only the Song of Solomon and Job can be regarded as even rudimentary approaches to the dramatic form. In discussing the Prophets, the Psalms, and the other Biblical writings, therefore, Lowth has very little to say on such standard topics as plot, or characters, or the traditional art of poetry. His dominant concern is with language and style—especially with the 'sublimity' in which the Hebrew poetry has no peer—and with the source of these elements in the conceptions and passions of the sacred writers.

In his discussion of the special quality of Hebrew style, Lowth posits a distinction between prose as the language of reason and poetry as the language of emotion which looks back to Dennis' use of passion to differentiate poetic from prosaic language, and ahead to Wordsworth's statement that 'Poetry is passion,' the opposite of 'Matter of Fact, or Science.' As we shall see in the sixth chapter, this distinction ultimately became a division of all discourse into the two categories of 'referential' and 'emotive' language.

The language of reason is cool, temperate, rather humble than elevated, well arranged and perspicuous. . . The language of the passions is totally different: the conceptions burst out into a turbid stream, expressive in a manner of the internal conflict. . . In a word, reason speaks literally, the passions poetically. The mind, with whatever passion it be agitated, remains fixed upon the object that excited it; and while it is earnest to display it, is not satisfied with a plain and exact description, but adopts one agreeable to its own sensations, splendid or gloomy, jocund or unpleasant. For the passions are naturally inclined to amplifications; they wonderfully magnify and exaggerate whatever dwells upon the mind, and labour to express it in animated, bold, and magnificent terms.

Figurative language, thus, is the spontaneous and instinctive product of feeling, which modifies the objects of perception; and Lowth derides those theories, which the rhetoricians 'have so pompously detailed, attributing that to art, which above all things is due to nature alone. . .'[18]

Lowth had already announced his adherence to the view that poetry has 'utility as its ultimate object, and pleasure as the means by which that end may be effectually accomplished.'[19] Also, those critics are right who say poetry is imitation: 'Poetry is said to consist in imitation: whatever the human mind is able to conceive, it is the province of poetry to imitate.' But both these propositions, according to Lowth, are reconcilable with his view that poetry 'derives its very existence from the more vehement emotions of the mind.' For of all forms of literary imitation, that one is in the highest degree effective which, like 'by far the greater part of the sacred poetry,' reflects not external matters, but the affections of the poet himself:

Since the human intellect is naturally delighted with every species of imitation, that species in particular, which exhibits its own image, which displays and depicts those impulses, inflexions, perturbations, and secret emotions, which it perceives and knows in itself, can scarcely fail to astonish and to delight above every other.[20]

While Lowth exemplifies a fairly common tendency in the criticism of his day to emphasize the poetic representation of passion, rather than of people or actions, he is notable for conceiving the poem as a mirror which, instead of reflecting nature, reflects the very penetralia of the poet's secret mind. Is not the so-called enthusiasm of early poets, he asks, a 'style and expression . . . exhibiting the true and express image of a mind violently agitated? when, as it were, the secret avenues, the interior recesses of the soul are thrown open; when the inmost conceptions are displayed?' Such self-revelation is a conspicuous attribute of Hebrew poetry, 'in part at least, if not in the whole.'

Frequently, instead of disguising the secret feelings of the author, it lays them quite open to public view; and the veil being, as it were, suddenly removed, all the affections and emotions of the soul, its sudden impulses, its hasty sallies and irregularities, are conspicuously displayed.[21]

This emphasis on violent agitation, secret feelings, and self-revelation, and the use of the theological concept of 'veiled' discourse, inevitably suggest the concepts of poetry which John Keble was to explore so thoroughly almost a century later. It does not surprise us, therefore, to find that Keble (who incidentally was the only important romantic critic to refer frequently to Longinus) paid specific tribute to 'that exquisite course of lectures upon "The Sacred Poetry of the Hebrews"' of his predecessor in the Oxford Professorship. The line from Lowth to Keble is direct, and so is the line from Lowth to another theologian who was to alter profoundly the standard doctrines of the nature of poetry—Johann Gottfried Herder, who acknowledged his reliance on Lowth's *Lectures* in his book *Vom Geist der ebraischen Poesie,* published in 1782.

iii. *Primitive Language and Primitive Poetry*

It was standard procedure in Wordsworth's day, when characterizing poetry, to refer to its conjectured origin in the passionate, and therefore, naturally rhythmical and figurative, outcries of primitive men. This belief displaced Aristotle's assumption that poetry developed from man's instinct to imitate, as well as the pragmatic opinion that poetry was invented by sages to make their civil and moral teachings more palatable and more memorable. The theory that poetry was engendered in emotion, and specifically, in religious emotion, had been proposed by John Dennis as early as 1704. 'Religion at first produc'd [poetry], as a Cause produces its Effect. . . For the Wonders of Religion naturally threw them upon great Passions, and great Passions naturally threw them upon Harmony and figurative Language. . .'[22] A similar theory was still further developed by Bishop Lowth. The notion, as Steele put it in his fifty-first *Guardian* paper, that 'the first poets were found at the altar'—usually merged with the ancient doctrine of divine inspiration and with Longinian concepts of the importance of passion—had considerable vogue throughout the latter part of the eighteenth century.[23]

Much of the opinion about the emotional origin of poetry, however, had an independent source in speculations concerning the origin of language in general. For the most part, the linguistic theory inherited from the ancients emphasized the relation of words to things—whether this relation was conceived to be from nature or by convention—and it usually attributed the origin of language to divine fiat, or to the deliberate invention of a culture-hero, or to a rational social covenant.[24] The great exception is the doctrine of the Epicureans, as we know it from the extraordinary fifth book of *De rerum natura*. Lucretius posits primordial man to have been endowed only with instincts, passions, and the mere potentiality of reason; hence, 'to suppose that someone . . . distributed names amongst things, and from this that men learnt their first words, is folly.' The origin of language was natural, spontaneous, and emotional; the race first distinguished things 'by varying sounds to suit varying feelings.'

Therefore if different feelings compel animals, dumb though they are, to utter different sounds, how much more natural it is that mortal men should then have been able to mark different things by one sound or another.[25]

Lucretius attributed the origin of poetry and the other arts, as distinct from language, to later and non-expressive modes of activity. But in addition to this opinion there persisted a tradition, subscribed to by such widely studied writers as Strabo and Plutarch, which reversed Lucretius' chronology and held verse to have antedated prose as a form of artful discourse.[26] The Lucretian theory that language began as a spontaneous expression of feeling was bound sometime to merge with the concurrent belief that the first elaborated form of language was poetic, into the doctrine that poetry preceded prose *because* poetry is the natural expression of feeling.

Such a merger can be discerned in the vast and tenebrous speculations of Giambattista Vico. He had studied Lucretius carefully when, in the late seventeenth century, the Epicurean philosophy had been the fashion among the *avant garde* of Neapolitan intellectual circles.[27] In his *Scienza Nuova* (1725) Vico cited the standard classical authorities on the priority of poetry to prose, as well as the reports by travelers concerning the prevalence of song among the American Indians; he also made frequent reference to the doctrines of Longinus. These elements, among others from diverse sources, Vico audaciously developed into what he called 'the master key' of his massive new science of humankind: the hypothesis that men in the first age after the flood thought, spoke, and acted imaginatively and instinctually, and therefore poetically; and that these early poetic expressions and activities contained the seeds of all the later arts, sciences, and social institutions. The post-diluvian giants, according to Vico, were dominated by sense and imagination, not by reason, and their first mode of thought was passionate, animistic, particularistic, and mythical, rather than rational and abstract; therefore they 'were by nature sublime poets.' For poetic sentences 'are formed with senses of passions and affections, in contrast with philosophic sentences, which are formed by reflection and reasoning.'[28] Articulate language developed in part from the vocal mimicry of natural sounds, and, in part, from interjections 'articulated under the impetus of violent passions' —'the first dull-witted men were moved to utterance only by very violent passions. . .' Since men naturally 'vent great passions by breaking into song,' the primordial emotional language must have been at the same time poetry and song, and, of necessity, densely figurative.[29] Thus, he grandly claims, are overthrown 'all the theories of the origin of poetry from Plato and Aristotle down to Patrizzi, Scaliger, and Castelvetro,' as well as the two common errors of grammarians, that, since tropes were the ingenious inventions of writers, 'prose speech is proper speech, and poetic speech improper; and that prose speech came first, and afterwards speech in verse.'[30] In Vico, as in the English Longinians, the development of an emotional theory of poetry is accompanied by a tendency to divide all language into the two basic categories of rational and emotional, prose and poetry.

There is a notable correspondence between Vico's ideas and the theory of the emotional genesis of language, poetry, and song proposed by Thomas Blackwell in his *Enquiry into the Life and Writings of Homer* (1735). There is no evidence, however, that Blackwell knew the *Scienza Nuova,* the first edition of which had been published only ten years before, and in all probability the similarity between these theorists resulted from a reliance on the same classical texts, combined and expanded under the influence of that interest in origins which was part of the intellectual climate of the time.[31] Language began, Blackwell supposes, in 'certain rude accidental Sounds' which the 'naked Company of scrambling Mortals emitted by Chance,' and which were uttered in a higher note than we do now, 'occasioned, perhaps, by their falling on them under some *Passion,* Fear, Wonder, or Pain. . .' When, on the return of the prompting passions, they 'put several of these *vocal* Marks together, they wou'd then seem *to sing*. . . And hence came the ancient Opinion, which appears so strange to us, "That Poetry was before Prose." ' The ancient language, before the formation of society, must have been full of the boldest metaphor, since this is the natural character of 'Words taken wholly from rough Nature, and invented under some Passion, as Terror, Rage, or Want (which readily extort Sounds from Men). . .' With the advance of human society and the achievement of a tolerable security come the new emotions of admiration and wonder, and the words of mankind then 'express these Feelings.' Of this stage, the present-day Turks, Arabs, and American Indians are surviving representatives; they speak seldom, usually with emotion, and when they 'give a loose to a fiery Imagination, they are poetical, and full of Metaphor.' [32]

Theorizing about linguistic and poetic origins became a popular occupation among Scottish writers of the mid-eighteenth century—Blair, Duff, Ferguson, Monboddo, and others—who had in common an absorbing interest in the reconstruction of the genesis and prehistoric development of human arts and institutions. (Men 'who love to talk of what they do not know,' is the way Dr. Johnson drily characterized such conjectural historians.[33]) Thomas Blackwell had probably been the teacher of some of these men at Marischall College, Aberdeen, and his work on Homer was certainly known to the intellectual circles in both Aberdeen and Edinburgh. A number of these Scottish theorists maintained that poetry had been instinctive and emotional in origin, and coeval, or almost coeval, with the birth of language itself.[34] The most elaborate contemporary discussion of the emotional genesis of art, however, was by an Englishman, John Brown. In *A Dissertation on the Rise . . . of Poetry and Music* (1763), Brown traced the development of art in 'savage Life, where untaught Nature rules,' and where such passions as love, joy, hate, and sorrow, 'thrown out by the three Powers of *Action, Voice,* and articulate *Sounds,*' in the course of time refine themselves into a combined art work which is at once song, dance, and poetry.[35]

What later on the German philologist, Max Müller, was jocosely to call the 'pooh-pooh' theory of language and poetic origins achieved international currency in the course of the eighteenth century. As early as 1746, Condillac introduced these ideas into France, in his *Essai sur l'origine des conaissances humaines.*[36] In his posthumous *Essai sur l'origine des langues,* Rousseau, whose general emphasis upon the primacy of instinct and feeling influenced the emotive theory of art, insisted that since man began not by reasoning, but by feeling, the first words were cries extorted by passion, and the first languages were song-like, passionate, figurative, and therefore the language of poets, not of geometers.[37] In Germany, Hamann combined a mystical view of the divine inspiration of language in the garden of Eden with the assumption that this pristine speech was musical and poetic.[38] His young contemporary, Herder, said in 1772 that language had been both expressive and mimetic in origin, and therefore doubly poetic:

What so many of the ancients have advanced, and so many of the moderns have repeated, viz. that poetry is older than prose, may be thus explained. For what was the first language but a collection of the first elements of poetry? An imitation of resounding, active, ever moving nature, taken from the interjections of all beings, and animated by interjections of human feeling.[39]

And the concept that speech and poetry were co-original in the press of feeling, and that even in their developed forms they are analogous as expressions of spirit, became a commonplace in the linguistic speculations of the German romantic generation.[40]

It was, then, a widely held doctrine, in the second half of the century, that although in its developed state poetry had become mainly an art of managing elaborate means for achieving deliberate ends, in its natural and primitive state it had been an entirely instinctive outburst of feeling. An important aspect of this way of thinking was that the range of poetry denoted by the terms 'primitive' or 'natural' was, for many critics and historians, extraordinarily large, diverse, and vaguely defined. The assumptions were, as Blair put it, that 'mankind never bear such resembling features as they do in the beginnings of society,' and also that 'it is not from the age of the world, but from the state of society, that we are to judge of resembling times.'[41] On this basis the earliest—or supposedly earliest—documents of the most disparate cultures, and in widely separated eras, were frequently said to exhibit the uniform attributes of the primitive mind: Homer's epics, the sacred Hebrew writings (which Lowth held to be 'the only specimens of the primeval and genuine poetry'),[42] Runic odes, and (after this had burst into the public ken) the elegiac eloquence of Ossian. The poets of culturally 'primitive' peoples of the contemporary world—the American Indian, the South Sea Islander, and Gray's savage youth repeating his 'loose numbers wildly sweet' in 'Chili's boundless forests'—were sometimes put into the same category. These minstrels in turn were held to be poetically akin to the folk balladers of Scotland and England, as well as to the 'natural' and 'artless' poetical threshers, shoemakers, and washer-women of modern vintage, who had been happily protected by social barriers from the refinements of civilization and advanced literary art. Finally, all these songsters were asserted by some critics to possess qualities in common with those 'natural geniuses' in a more highly developed cultural milieu who, whether through ignorance of models or strength of innate poetic faculty, composed from nature rather than from art—Shakespeare, for example, warbling 'his native woodnotes wild,' and Spenser, whose 'wildly-warbled song' the youthful Thomas Warton compared favorably even to Pope's 'happiest art.' [43]

To all this mélange of examples, running the full gamut of time, place, cultural provenience, literary type, and aesthetic worth, were often attributed certain common poetic qualities. It is the nature of these qualities, and their role in later criticism, that makes what would otherwise be a curious aberration of sociological speculation into an important phase in the development of critical theory. The defining character of all these poets was that they composed from nature, hence spontaneously, artlessly, and without forethought either of their design or their audience. Like the aborigines in whose outcries, extorted by passion, poetry had originated, these men were said to poetize under the stress of personal feeling; and their compositions were often characterized by various metaphors of the internal-made-external which were to become the key terms of much romantic commentary on poetry in general. Early poetry, said William Duff in his *Essay on Original Genius* (1767), 'being the effusion of a glowing fancy and an impassioned heart, will be perfectly natural and ORIGINAL'; and the poetic genius of 'the uncultivated ages of the world' acknowledges no law 'excepting its own spontaneous impulse, which it obeys without control. . .' [44] Ossian's only art, according to Blair, lies 'in giving vent to the simple and natural emotions of the heart,' and 'the heart, when uttering its native language, never fails, by powerful sympathy, to affect the heart.' His poetry

deserves to be styled, *The poetry of the heart*. It is . . . a heart that is full, and pours itself forth. Ossian did not write, like modern poets, to please readers and critics. He sung from the love of poetry and song.[45]

Or, in the alternate metaphor of Adam Ferguson, the primitive poet 'delivers the emotions of the heart, in words suggested by the heart; for he knows no other.' [46] Most important of all is the fact that many of these theorists about primitive poetry were also 'primitivists': they maintained that the characteristic qualities of primitive poetry are the enduring criteria of the greatest poetry in any age. The enthusiasm, vehemence, and the fire of the products of uncultivated ages, Blair said, 'are the soul of poetry,' and the primary qualities of Ossian 'are the great characteristics of true poetry.' [47]

Recognizably, we have, in such passages as I have quoted, the scattered materials that were to become part and parcel of romantic theory, and that were to reappear not only in Wordsworth's doctrine that all good poetry is the spontaneous overflow of feeling but also in the basic theory of critics who had no inclination toward cultural primitivism, or even (like John Stuart Mill) were specifically anti-primitivistic in their thinking.

English theorists of the eighteenth century, with a few exceptions we shall notice later, did not expand their accounts of primitive poetry into a systematic theory of poetry in general.[48] Like Dennis and Lowth earlier in the century, even the ardent primitivist, if he set himself to a formal and systematic discussion of poetry and its kinds, usually reverted to the traditional pattern of analysis; and he kept this aspect of his theory relatively insulated from his admiring description of the poetry of natural genius as a spontaneous mode of emotional and imaginative expression. In his *Essay on Original Genius,* William Duff reiterated the ancient parallel between poetry and painting as arts which have for their end the representation of characters, passions, and events; held that 'both accomplish this end by IMITATION'; [49] and devoted a major portion of his essay to a long and conventional analysis of the epic genre. In Blair's *Lectures on Rhetoric and Belles Lettres,* there is a distinct cleavage between those sections that are primitivistic and expressive and those that are conventionally rhetorical and pragmatic in their emphases. The collapse of the neo-classic structure of criticism occurred only when the concept of the urgency and overflow of feeling, from being only a part, and a subordinate part, of poetic theory, became the central principle of the whole. We may suppose that this event was delayed until, for the first time since Aristotle, epic and tragedy lost their dominant status among the poetic kinds and gave place to the lyric as the prototype and most representative single form of poetry in general.

iv. The Lyric as Poetic Norm

The lyric form—used here to include elegy, song, sonnet, and ode—had long been particularly connected by critics to the state of mind of its author. Unlike the narrative and dramatic forms, most lyrics do not include such elements as characters and plot, which can be readily explained (according to the common mirror-interpretation of mimesis) as imitations of external people and events. The majority of lyrics consist of thoughts and feelings uttered in the first person, and the one readily available character to whom these sentiments may be referred is the poet himself.[50] There soon developed a decided tendency to decry, particularly in amatory and elegiac poems, the expression of feelings that lacked conviction or were obviously engineered by the poet for the lyric occasion. Sir Philip Sidney complained that many of the songs and sonnets of his day carried no persuasion of actual passion in the author. Boileau disparaged elegists 'Qui s'affligent par art'—

> Il faut que le coeur seul parle dans l'élégie.

Dr. Johnson taxed the elegies and love poems of Cowley with a similar defect, and approximated the idiom of contemporary primitivists in charging that 'Lycidas' 'is not to be considered as the effusion of real passion.'[51]

The expressive character sometimes attributed to lyric poems offered no real challenge to the mimetic and pragmatic definitions of poetry in general, so long as lyrics remained the unconsidered trifles among the poetic kinds. Their lack of magnitude and of profitable effect, and the very fact that, in lieu of representative elements, their subject matter was considered to be principally the author's own feelings, consigned them to a lowly status in the scale of the genres. In many critics, the attitude to these poems ran the narrow gamut between contempt and condescension. According to Rapin, 'A Sonnet, Ode, Elegy, Epigram, and those little kind of Verses . . . are ordinarily no more than the meer productions of Imagination, a superficial wit, with a little conversation of the World, is capable of these things.'[52] Temple held that among the moderns, wits who cannot succeed in heroic poetry content themselves 'with the Scraps, with Songs and Sonnets, with Odes and Elegies. . .'[53]

The soaring fortunes of the lyric may be dated from 1651, the year that Cowley's Pindaric 'imitations' burst over the literary horizon and inaugurated the immense vogue of the 'greater Ode' in England. To account for the purported fire, impetuosity, and irregularity of these poems, critics were wont to invoke Longinus' concept of the sublime and its sources in enthusiasm and vehement passion; and to attribute this lofty quality to any poetic kind was inevitably to elevate its stature. The Pindaric and pseudo-Pindaric were soon split off from pettier lyrics and lesser odes, and assigned a place next to the greatest of the traditional forms. By 1704 John Dennis grouped together 'Epick, Tragick, and the greater Lyrick poetry' as the highest literary genres, to be distinguished from the lesser Poetry of comedy, satire, 'the little Ode,' elegy, and pastoral; and Dennis' example was soon followed even by more traditional theorists.[54] The prestige of the greater lyric, as well as of the other lyric forms, was strongly abetted by the opinion that the poetry of the Bible was mainly lyrical, and the claim that the Psalms of David, as well as passages from the narrative books, were the Hebrew equivalent of the odes of Pindar.[55] Of course, those who believed that poetry had originated in the overflow of feeling also believed that the earliest poems were lyric—either proto-ode or proto-elegy, as the theorist assumed the religious or erotic passions to have been the more powerful and compulsive to expression. And the growing critical interest in the lyric had its counterpart in the increasing cultivation of its various kinds by the poets in the generation of the Wartons, Gray, and Collins—

> Trick'd in antique ruff and bonnet,
> Ode, and elegy, and sonnet.

All these forces showed themselves indirectly, in passing comments, and in critical judgments which merely implied the alteration of critical premises, before they resulted in a deliberate reconstruction of the bases of poetic theory. There was a conspicuous tendency, for example, to identify as 'pure poetry,' or 'the most poetical poetry,' or 'la vraie poésie,' those particular poems or passages which were thought to be peculiarly the product of passion and rapture. Because the great ode is the boldest and most rapturous by nature, Joseph Trapp said, it 'is, of all kinds of Poetry, the most poetical. . .' 'The ode, as it is the eldest kind of poetry, so it is more spiritous, and more remote from prose, than any other,' wrote Edward Young in his Preface to *Ocean, An Ode* (1728), and enthusiasm is its 'soul.'[56] A similar idea of what constitutes quintessential poetry was at the heart of Joseph Warton's famous critical estimate of the writings of Pope. His finding that the 'species of poetry wherein Pope Excelled . . . is not the most excellent one of the art' was one against which even the most rigorous neo-classic critic could not have demurred, but the grounds on which Warton identified the highest species of poetry plainly indicate the newer directions of critical thinking. As against the 'Man of Wit' and the 'Man of Sense,' the 'true Poet' and writer of 'PURE POETRY' is stamped solely by 'a creative and glowing IMAGINATION, "acer spiritus ac vis". . .' Warton's instances of poems that are 'essentially poetical' include not only epic and drama, but an ode of Akenside, as well as Milton's 'L'Allegro' and 'Il Penseroso.' Pope did not write 'the most *poetic* species *of poetry*' because he did not 'indulge' his imagination and stifled his 'poetical enthusiasm.' Hence Pope does not transport the reader, and although he is foremost among the second order of poets, 'he has written nothing in a strain so truly sublime, as the *Bard* of *Gray*.'[57]

A few writers of the latter part of the century mark themselves off from their contemporaries because they deliberately set out to revise the bases of the neo-classic theory of poetry. Sir William Jones is remembered chiefly as a liberal jurist and an Orientalist who pioneered in the study of Sanskrit. But in 1772 he published a volume of translations and 'imitations' of Arabic, Indian, and Persian poems to which he added an important 'Essay on the Arts Called Imitative.' There we find a conjunction of all the tendencies we have been tracing: the ideas drawn from Longinus, the old doctrine of poetic inspiration, recent theories of the emotional and imaginative origin of poetry, and a major emphasis on the lyric form and on the supposedly primitive and spontaneous poetry of Oriental nations. It was Jones's distinction, I think, to be the first writer in England to weave these threads into an explicit and orderly reformulation of the nature and criteria of poetry and of the poetic genres.

Jones opens his essay by rejecting unequivocally 'the assertion of Aristotle, that all poetry consists in imitation'—one of those maxims, he thinks, 'repeated a thousand times, for no other reason, than because they once dropped from the pen of a superior genius.' Of the arts of poetry and music, 'we cannot give a precise definition . . . till we have made a few previous remarks on their origin'; and he goes on to offer evidence 'that poetry was originally no more than a strong and animated expression of the human passions.'[58] Like various critics half a century later, Jones conjectures that each poetic species had its source in an appropriate emotion: religious and dramatic poetry originated in joy at the wonders of the creation, elegies in grief, moral and epic poetry in the detestation of vice, and satires in hate. There follows this definition:

Consistently with the foregoing principles, we may define original and native poetry to be the language of the violent passions, expressed in exact measure, with strong accents and significant words.[59]

Plainly Jones employs the lyric not only as the original poetic form, but as the prototype for poetry as a whole, and thereby expands what had occasionally been proposed as the differentia of one poetic species into the defining attribute of the genus. As he says, 'in defining what true poetry ought to be . . . we have described what it really was among the Hebrews, the

Greeks and Romans, the Arabs and Persians.' Undeniably the lyrics, the hymns, the elegies of the Greeks, like the 'sacred odes, or psalms' of David, the Song of Solomon, and the prophecies of the inspired writers, 'are truly and strictly poetical; but what did David or Solomon imitate in their divine poems? A man, who is really joyful or afflicted, cannot be said to imitate joy or affliction.'

Jones extends the expressive concept to music and painting. Even if we admit, he says, the very dubious proposition that the descriptive elements in these forms are imitation, it remains the fact 'that mere description is the meanest part of both arts.' He goes on to set up a simple scale by which to measure the relative worth of the constituents of any work of art:

If the arguments, used in this essay, have any weight, it will appear, that the finest parts of poetry, musick, and painting, are expressive of the passions . . . that the inferior parts of them are descriptive of natural objects, and affect us chiefly by substitution.[60]

Jones's theory shows that inversion of aesthetic values which reached its climax in the theory of John Stuart Mill, some sixty years later. The 'imitative' elements, hitherto held to be a defining attribute of poetry or art, become inferior, if not downright unpoetic; in their place those elements in a poem that express feeling become at once its identifying characteristic and cardinal poetic value.

v. Expressive Theory in Germany: Ut Musica Poesis

These developments were not confined to England. In Germany, a conjunction of similar influences produced a comparable result; and in the late eighteenth century, it was the German, more than the English formulations of the new poetics, which achieved currency throughout western Europe.

J. G. Sulzer's *Allgemeine Theorie der schönen Künste,* a four-volume encyclopedia of aesthetics first issued in 1771-4, is exactly contemporary with Sir William Jones's 'Essay on the Arts Called Imitative,' and is remarkably parallel in its tenor; and even more than Jones, Sulzer anticipates many details of romantic expressive theories. The preliminary frame of Sulzer's theory is pragmatic. 'One can regard each work of the fine arts as an instrument, by which one produces a certain effect on the minds of men.'[61] In many of his articles, however, Sulzer's disposition is to take his theoretical departure from the soul of the artist in the process of composition—'the ground of poetry,' as he says in 'Dichtkunst,' 'is to be sought in the genius of the poet.' The result, again and again, is to put the author at the center of the theory, and to make the moral and pleasurable effect on the audience a fortunate by-product of the author's spontaneous expression of feeling.

Like Jones, Sulzer renounces the doctrine, reigning 'from Aristotle up to this day,' that the arts 'originated in imitation, and their essence consists in the imitation of nature.' This may be true for the graphic arts, 'but eloquence, poetry, music, and dance clearly originated in the fullness of lively feelings, and the desire to utter them, in order to please ourselves and others.' [62] When the poet is in a state of enthusiasm, his 'thoughts and feelings irresistibly stream out in speech,' and he 'turns all his attention to that which goes on in his soul; forgets the outer circumstances which surround him. . .' [63] In this self-absorption, the poet becomes oblivious not only to the external world, but to his actual or possible audience; so that poetry, in ceasing to be mimetic, almost ceases to be pragmatic. Only eloquence, Sulzer says, as John Stuart Mill was to say later, 'constantly has the listener, upon whom it wants to produce an effect, before its eyes.'

The poet is . . . put into a passion, or at least into a certain mood, by his object; he can not resist the violent desire to utter his feelings; he is transported. . . He speaks, even if no one listens to him, because his feelings do not let him be silent.[64]

The state of feeling from which a poem flows naturally exhibits itself in a rhythmical speech which is regularized as verse, and in a figurative and picturesque language which are the 'natural effect of the poetic mood.' As for the genres of poetry, Sulzer declares that Aristotle's attempt to discriminate these by reference to the means, object, and manner of imitation was subtle but useless. He suggests as an alternative that we distinguish the main species of poetry on the basis of 'the various grades of the poetic mood, and the subspecies according to the accidents of the subject matter or form.' [65] We also discover in Sulzer the almost infallible accompaniment of this perspective in criticism, the emergence of the lyric as the type and epitome of the purest poetry. The lyric, Sulzer holds, was the primordial form of poetry; and today, all artists agree

that odes constitute the highest poetic kind, that they display the characteristics of a poem to a higher degree, and are more purely a poem, than any other genre. . . The fashion in which the odist in each instance utters his thoughts and his feelings has more of the poetic in it, than . . . [that] of the epic poet, or any other poet.

And like Poe later on, Sulzer maintains that the intensity of this quintessential poetic form sets a limit to its magnitude, 'for this state of mind, by its very nature, can not long endure.'[66]

Sulzer's contemporaries of the Storm and Stress, with their emphasis on original genius, independence from rules, and the feeling heart, were even more insistent on the autonomy of the artist in the aesthetic scheme. Young Goethe, in fact, was outraged that Sulzer should continue to claim at all that the aim of poetry is 'the moral betterment of the people.'

For the one thing that matters is the artist, so that he feels none of the blissfulness of life except in his art, so that, absorbed in his instrument, he lives therein with all his feelings and powers. As for the gaping public, and whether when it has finished gaping it can justify why it has gaped, what difference does that make?[67]

Herder, who affirmed that poetry originated in the natural overflow of primitive feelings, made this the condition of all genuine poetry. 'So is it for the poet. He must express feelings. . . You must express the whole tone of your feeling in your phrases, in the ordonnance and connection of your words. . .'[68] The post-Kantian critics supplemented the hereditary terms of rhetoric and poetic with a large and complicated vocabulary drawn from recent philosophy, and (by taking their stand in the 'subject' or 'spirit' instead of in the 'object' or 'material') assimilated the theory of art to the 'Copernican revolution' in general metaphysics. 'Each one who is in a position to put his state of feeling into an object,' Schiller wrote to Goethe in 1801, 'so that this object compels me to pass over into that state of feeling . . . I call a poet, a maker.'[69] In his Berlin lectures on literature and art (1801-2), A. W. Schlegel, like Sulzer, rejected Aristotle's and Batteux's definitions of art as imitation; the composition of poetry, he says instead, 'is no other than an eternal mode of symbolizing: we either seek an outer covering for something spiritual, or we draw something external over the invisibly inner.'[70] Some romantic extremists, inspired by the philosophy of Fichte, made the work of art out to be, in a fashion even more absolute than the world of perception, an expression of unadulterated spirit. In all genuine art, wrote Novalis in his *Fragmente,* 'an idea, a spirit is realized, produced from within outward,' and a work of art 'is the visible product of an ego.' 'Poesy is the representation of the spirit, of the inner world in its totality. Even its medium, words, indicates this, for they are the outer revelation of that inner realm.'[71]

In 1813 Mme de Staël informed the French, and all Europe, of the new way of thinking in the chapter, 'De la poésie,' of her book, *De l'Allemagne*. Hers is a cloudy and sentimentalized version of the doctrines she had learned from August Schlegel and other early romantic theorists, but it indicates the extent to which the new critical viewpoints were collateral, although at this time still largely independent, in Germany and England. 'The gift of revealing by speech what one feels in the depths of the heart is very rare,' she says, but the poet manages 'to disengage the sentiment imprisoned in the depth of the soul; poetic genius is an interior disposition. . .' It has been said 'that prose was artificial and poetry natural: in fact, uncivilized nations always commence with poetry, and as soon as a strong passion agitates the soul, the most vulgar men . . . call to their aid external nature to express the inexpressible which takes place within them.' She herself grows lyrical on the subject of lyric poetry, which 'is expressed in the name of the author himself.' To conceive 'the true grandeur of lyric poetry, one must wander in thought into the ethereal regions . . . and regard the whole universe as a symbol of the emotions of the soul.' And of any true poet it may be said that he 'conceives his whole poem at once in his soul; were it not for the difficulties of language he would, like the sybil and the prophets, improvise the sacred hymns of genius.' [72]

The movement of ideas in German criticism in the late eighteenth century cannot be understood without some reference to the discussions of music, for in the general transition to an expressive theory of aesthetics, music, in Germany, bore the relation to the genera of art that the lyric bore to the species of poetry.

In the opening section of the *Poetics*, Aristotle described most flute-playing and lyre-playing as modes of imitation, and in the *Politics*, he characterized rhythm and melody as the one medium which can present direct likenesses of anger, courage, temperance, and other qualities of character.[73] Neo-classic writers, as we know, usually interpreted imitation narrowly, as representation in a medium which has some properties in common with the subject it represents. When these theorists turned their attention to music they, like Aristotle, conceived it to be an imitation primarily of passion—but specifically, as a sonal imitation of the noises that passion makes. As the Abbé Du Bos wrote in 1719:

Wherefore as the painter imitates the strokes and colors of nature, in like manner the musician imitates the tones, accents, sighs, and inflexions of the voice; and in short all those sounds, by which nature herself expresses her sentiments and passions.[74]

In the spate of English writings on music after the mid-century,[75] the mimetic aspect of that art was progressively minimized. There was wide agreement that instrumental music, dissociated from words, can reproduce only sound and motion, and is therefore imitative only in the trivial passages in which it simulates the cries of birds and the gurgle of running water, or in the very limited sense that the rise and fall of a musical phrase is in accord with height and depth in the natural world. As James Beattie wrote in 1776, the critics have erred in thinking that music imitates the human voice in passion. 'What resemblance is there between Handel's *Te Deum,* and the tone of voice natural to a person expressing, by articulate sound, his veneration of the Divine Character and Providence?' So, with due apology to Aristotle, and intending no disrespect to music, he 'would strike it off the list of imitative arts.' [76] Music, by its nature the weak spot in the theory of imitation, as this theory was usually interpreted in the eighteenth century, was thus the first of the arts to be severed from the mimetic principle by a critical consensus.

These critics agreed in finding the essence of music in what they called 'expression.' It is important to observe, however, that for the most part this term was not used to denote the origin of musical content in the affections of the composer, but its power of raising affections in the listener. Charles Avison, who seems to have popularized the use of this word in his *Essay on Musical Expression* (1753), defined expression as 'the power of *exciting* all the most agreeable passions of the soul.' [77] Or as Adam Smith succinctly explained what had become a technical term:

The effect of instrumental Music upon the mind has been called its expression. . . Whatever effect it produces is the immediate effect of that melody and harmony, and not of something else which is signified and suggested by them: they in fact signify and suggest nothing.[78]

By the main line of English theorists, therefore, music was defined in terms of its effects, as a tonal medium for evoking or specifying feeling in the listener.

There was a concurrent mode of speculation, however, which put a different interpretation upon the 'expressiveness' of music. It will be recalled that speculators concerning the origins of language and art, from Vico and Blackwell on, had maintained that music and poetry were a twin birth from the emotional travail of primitive men. Some theorists held that even in its developed form, music remains essentially the formalized expression of passion, and that, in consequence, music is the sister art of poetry, and not painting, as had been hitherto implied in the popular maxim, *ut pictura poesis*. In his *Dissertation on Poetry and Music* (1763), for example, John Brown presented the theory that music had, in its rudest origin, been the natural incantation of passion, that this had then been regularized into melody and, through the development of purely musical conventions and the accretion of meaningful 'associations,' had come, even in the absence of vocal accompaniment, to be an intelligible vehicle—a kind of language—for communicating emotions.[79]

In England, however, the lyrical poem seems to have been the root consideration out of which developed the concept that all art is emotional expression. In Germany, on the other hand, music came to be regarded as the art that is most purely expressive. The earliest music, Herder wrote in 1769, expressed passion; and this expression, when ordered and modulated, 'became a wonder-music of all the affections, a new magical language of the feelings.' Music is extremely obscure in its significance, and therefore all the more appropriate to feeling; while expression in speech, because the meanings of its words are 'arbitrary and therefore not so intimately bound up with the nature of the feelings . . . will clarify, but . . . only to divert and weaken' the emotion. And Herder turns to music, as earlier critics had turned to painting, in order to specify the character of poetry. Unlike painting and sculpture, poetry 'is the music of the soul. A sequence of thoughts, pictures, words, tones is the essence of its expression; in this does it resemble music. . . Ode and idyll, fable and the speech of passion, are a melody of thoughts. . .'[80]

The *Frühromantiker* pressed these ideas of Herder to an extreme. They sometimes talked of music as though it were the very essence and form of the spirit made patent—a play of pure feeling in time, unaltered by its physical medium. 'So is it,' Wackenroder said, 'with the mysterious stream in the depths of the human spirit—speech reckons and names and describes its changes in a foreign material; music streams it out before us as it is in itself. . . In the mirror of tones the human heart learns to know itself. . .'[81] Thus also Novalis: 'The musician takes the essence of his art out of himself —and not the slightest suspicion of imitation can befall him.'[82] And A. W. Schlegel: 'The musician has a language of feeling independent of all external objects; in verbal language, on the contrary, the expression of feeling always depends on its connection with the idea. . .' Even lyric poetry must avail itself of reference to an object, hence serves 'only indirectly for the expression of feeling.'[83] German critics, therefore, tend to use music as the apex and norm of the pure and nonrepresentative expression of spirit and feeling, against which to measure the relative expressiveness of all other forms of art. 'Music, plastic art, and poetry are synonyms,' wrote Novalis in his cryptic *Fragments*. 'Painting, plastic art are therefore nothing but figurations [*Figuristik*] of music.' 'Painting, plastic art—objective music. Music—subjective music or painting.'[84]

The melomania of so many German critics is one clue to the differences, not only between German and English criticism, but between German and English literary practice. English critics held that the lack of determinate representation and meaning in purely instrumental music is a deficiency, and that to achieve its full effect, music must wed itself to poetry. 'A fine instrumental symphony,' James Beattie said, '. . . is like an oration delivered with propriety, but in an unknown tongue. . .' But when words are sung to the same air, 'all uncertainty vanishes, the fancy is filled with determinate ideas, and determinate emotions take possession of the heart.'[85] In Germany, writers such as Tieck, Wackenroder, and E. T. A. Hoffmann (following the lead of Herder) praised symphonic music as the art of arts, just because it is indefinite, innocent of reference to the external world, and richly, because imprecisely suggestive. The attempt to make literature aspire to the condition of music motivated the description by German writers of sounding forms, musical fragrance, and the harmony of colors, and furthered that general synesthetic abandon which Irving Babbitt was to interpret as a symptom of the dissolution of all the boundaries and distinctions on which a rational civilization depends.[86] In another aspect, literature was made to emulate music by substituting a symphonic form—a melody of ideas and images, a thematic organization, a harmony of moods—for the structural principles of plot, argument, or exposition. These phenomena had some parallel in England, in the inter-sensory images of Keats and Shelley, the dream-fugues of De Quincey, and the quasi-musical structure of Coleridge's later odes; but there the procedure was casual, and without a specific rationale in aesthetic theory. In both countries alike, nevertheless, inquiry into the non-representative character of music joined with many collateral influences to strain and then shatter the frame of neo-classic theory, and to reorient all critical discussion toward the new magnetic north of the expressive and creative artist.

vi. Wordsworth, Blair, and The Enquirer

Two English documents which were published late in the eighteenth century, both of which may well have been known to Wordsworth, weave various of the threads we have discriminated into a pattern very like the one in Wordsworth's Preface of 1800. A summary of these two writings will help us to distinguish both the origins and the originality of Wordsworth's poetic doctrines.

Hugh Blair's *Lectures on Rhetoric and Belles Lettres* was published in 1783, but had been read at the University of Edinburgh for the twenty-four years preceding. It belonged to a class of writings, fairly common after the mid-century, which served simultaneously as manuals of oratory, composition, poetics, and general aesthetics. The earlier chapters survey such topics as taste, genius, the sublime and beautiful, and the elements of style; and they depart from the commonplace more in arrangement than in content. Then, before entering upon an extended and conventional discussion of the poetic kinds and their respective rules, Blair inserts a lecture on the 'Nature of Poetry' which is off the main road of traditional criticism.

Blair begins with the question, 'What is Poetry? and wherein does it differ from Prose?'. He rejects both the answer that the essence of poetry is fiction and that its defining character is imitation. 'The most just and comprehensive definition which, I think, can be given to poetry, is, "that it is the language of passion, or of enlivened imagination, formed, most commonly, into regular numbers."' Only in a codicil does Blair add—what had hitherto been the usual mode of defining poetry—a statement of the effect intended on the reader: 'the primary aim of a poet is to please, and to move; and, therefore, it is to the imagination, and the passions, that he speaks.' [87]

For evidence of 'the truth and justness of the definition,' Blair appeals to the conjectural origin of poetry, and to the kind of poetry described by travelers as still current among such primitive people as the North American Indians—lyric forms, 'rude effusions, which the enthusiasm of fancy or passion suggested to untaught men.' The language of primigenial poets was characterized by 'the employment of bold figures of speech'; for words would appear in the order 'most accommodated to the cadence of the passion,' and objects would be described not 'such as they really are, but such as passion makes us see them.' The same passionate impulse prompts 'a certain melody, or modulation of sound, suited to the emotions'; in this way arose both poetic meter and the art of music. And in considering the effect on poetry of advances in civilization, Blair goes on to suggest something close to Wordsworth's distinction between the genuine language of feeling and the mechanical simulation of this language by artful poets who substitute ornament for emotion. 'In its ancient original condition,' poetry spoke

the language of passion, and no other; for to passion, it owed its birth. . . In after-ages, when poetry became a regular art, studied for reputation and for gain, authors . . . endeavoured to imitate passion, rather than to express it; they tried to force their imagination into raptures, or to supply the defect of native warmth, by those artificial ornaments which might give Composition a splendid appearance.[88]

The first of the many editions of Blair's *Lectures* was published while Wordsworth was still at Hawkeshead Grammar-School, and the book was very widely used as a school text. We have no direct evidence that Wordsworth had read the *Lectures*,[89] however; and one critical essay, which appeared only four years before Wordsworth's Preface, approximates his formulations more strikingly still.

This essay, 'Is Verse Essential to Poetry?' appeared in the *Monthly Magazine* for July 1796, as one of a series signed 'The Enquirer.' The writer is now known to have been the Reverend William Enfield, essayist, anthologist, and author of a book on taste.[90] The Enquirer cites Blair's *Lectures* (together with the Platonic doctrine of inspiration) as the source of his theory of poetry. He incorporates Blair's opinions that poetry had its genesis 'in the rude state of nature' when 'men felt strong passions and expressed them strongly' in a language which 'would be bold and figurative' and would sometimes 'flow in a kind of wild and unfettered melody,' and that in any age, the 'excited state of mind, which poetry supposes, naturally prompts a figurative style.' He parallels Wordsworth in his comments about poetic diction. 'Whatever is the natural and proper expression of any conception or feeling in metre or rhyme, is its natural and proper expression in prose'; modern poetry violates the standard of prose diction only 'because the taste of the moderns has been refined to a degree of fastidiousness, which leads them to prefer the meretricious ornaments of art to the genuine simplicity of nature.' On two important issues, in particular, The Enquirer takes a more decisive stand than had Blair. First, he considers and unconditionally rejects the modes of defining poetry which, either as alternatives or as complements, had been the keystones of critical theory. 'Aristotle makes the essence of poetry to consist in imitation,' he declares, and cites Vossius, Batteux, and Trapp as modern adherents to this doctrine. Other critics, such as Racine, Hurd, and Johnson, 'have chosen to derive their definition of poetry from its *end;* though they have been by no means agreed, whether that end be principally to instruct or to please.'

Those writers appear to have approached nearest to a true definition of poetry, who have understood it to be the immediate offspring of a vigorous imagination and quick sensibility, and have called it the language of fancy and passion. . . Poets are still considered as men inspired by the power of imagination, and pouring forth the strong language of fancy and feeling.

Second, he rejects Blair's distinction between poetry and prose, and substitutes an antithesis between rational and emotive language which was destined to play a prominent role both in the theory of poetry and in the general theory of language:

The terms *poetry* and *prose* are incorrectly opposed to each other. Verse is, properly, the contrary of *prose;* and because poetry speaks the language of fancy, passion, and sentiment, and philosophy speaks the language of reason, these two terms should be considered as contraries, and writing should be divided, not into poetry and prose, but into *poetry* and *philosophy.*[91]

It is apparent that a good deal of the content of Wordsworth's Preface of 1800 derives from the ideas we have been tracing—although Wordsworth expanded these rudimentary speculations into a critical commentary far more subtle, comprehensive, and philosophical than any of its antecedents in the eighteenth century. It is equally apparent, however, that Wordsworth's theory of poetry was also based on his own practice as a poet, and on his insights into his own processes in the act of composing. And not only Wordsworth's theory, but romantic poetics in general unmistakably took its special character, in considerable part, from the special character of the poems for which it served as a rationale. This survey of the roots of the expressive theory of poetry, accordingly, would not be complete, if we did not raise the question of the way in which this theory was related to contemporary poetic practice.

vii. Expressive Theory and Expressive Practice

When Wordsworth characterized 'all good poetry' as the spontaneous overflow of feeling, it clearly was not epic or tragedy, but the lyrical poem or passage that he had in mind as exemplary. And in most theorists of Wordsworth's generation, the lyric has become the essentially poetic form, and usually, the type whose attributes are predicated of poetry in general. The lyric, Coleridge said, echoing earlier critics, English and German, 'in its very essence is poetical'; and John Stuart Mill declared that 'lyric poetry, as it was the earliest kind, is also . . . more eminently and peculiarly poetry than any other. . .' [92] By a gradual and natural progression, the stone rejected by early theorists has become the headstone of the corner of the temple of art.

The resort to the lyric as the paradigm for poetic theory—which first manifested itself at the time of the lyric revival in the generation of Gray, Collins, and the Wartons—was of course accompanied, in the romantic period, by a cultivation of this form to a degree, and in a·variety of excellence, which was without precedent in literary history. It was not only that romantic poets exploited the song, the elegy, and the ode. They also tended to lyricize those poems which Aristotle had characterized as 'possessing a certain magnitude,' by substituting for character, plot, or exposition, other elements which had earlier constituted the materials only of the pettier forms. As A. C. Bradley said of 'The Long Poem in Wordsworth's Age,' 'the center of interest is inward. It is an interest in emotion, thought, will, rather than in scenes, events, actions. . .' [93]

Concurrently we discover a tendency to convert the lyric 'I' from what Coleridge called the 'I-representative' to the poet in his proper person, and to express experiences and states of mind which can be verified from the testimony of the poet's private letters and journals. Even in the contemporary practice of narrative or dramatic forms, the reader is often invited to identify the hero with his author. Deliberate self-projection in the guise of fiction got under way in the novel, with Rousseau's *Nouvelle Héloïse* blazing the trail for such later examples of the *roman personnel* as Goethe's *Werther*, Friedrich Schlegel's *Lucinde*, Tieck's *William Lovell*, and Chateaubriand's *René*. In England, however, the author usually chose to project himself in the medium of verse. It was readily discovered by contemporary readers that Byron's heroes represented an aspect of his own daemonic personality. But the summit of what Keats unkindly called the 'egotistical sublime' was achieved by Wordsworth. He conceived his incompleted masterwork, *The Recluse*, on an analogy with the traditional epic form, and particularly with Milton's *Paradise Lost*. But before beginning this work, it seemed to Wordsworth 'a reasonable thing that he should take a review of his own mind,' and record his findings in the fourteen autobiographical books of *The Prelude*. And once chosen, the epic subject of *The Recluse* turns out to be a very modern one; namely, 'the sensations and opinions,' as Wordsworth tells us, 'of a poet living in retirement,' incorporated in a poem of which 'the first and third parts . . . will consist chiefly of meditations in the Author's own person.' [94] Finally, in a passage which somewhat humorlessly betokens the shift in critical perspective, Wordsworth declares that all his poems, long or short, and on whatever subject, are to be viewed as components of a Gothic cathedral, in which the poet himself constitutes the principle of unity. *The Prelude,* he says, has to *The Recluse* the same relation 'as the ante-chapel has to the body of a gothic church'; while the minor poems already published

will be found by the attentive Reader to have such connection with the main Work as may give them claim to be likened to the little cells, oratories, and sepulchral recesses, ordinarily included in these edifices.[95]

In the romantic period, then, much of the major poetry, like almost all the major criticism, circles out from the poet as center. Late in this period, some critics came to believe that in all ages, the long poetic forms had been not only expressive but self-expressive. Writing in the 1830's, it seemed to John Keble that the lyric poem, being short, is subject to fickle moods and simulated passions and, being written in the first person, is relatively incapable of providing what he calls the 'expedient of shifted responsibility,' under guise of which a poet may unreservedly expose his intimate feelings. Keble therefore expresses strong doubts whether lyric writers may be ranked among what he calls 'primary poets.' Primacy belongs to the long, fictional genres of drama and epic, in which, because the poet speaks 'his own thoughts through another's lips, modesty is observed, while the agitated, full heart is relieved.' [96] In Keble's particular version, expressive theory, which had begun by raising the lyric to the status of poetic norm, has outgrown its prototype, and ends by reducing it to its original position in the lower reaches of the poetic hierarchy—although for entirely new and characteristic reasons.

Varieties of Romantic Theory:
WORDSWORTH AND COLERIDGE

A copy of the universe is not what is required of art; one of the damned thing
is ample.   REBECCA WEST

I have no great opinion of a definition, the celebrated remedy for the cure of
this disorder. . . We are limited in our inquiry by the laws to which we have
submitted at our setting out.   EDMUND BURKE

AN ORIENTATION IN AESTHETIC theory is not an idea, or even a premise,
but a habitual direction of reference; and to find that the romantic
critics usually looked to the poet when they talked about the nature of
poetry does not justify the assumption that they had any specific body of
doctrine in common. Because of their hospitality to ideas from many sources,
romantic critics in fact exhibit greater diversity in philosophical presuppo-
sitions, descriptive vocabulary, dialectical motifs, and critical judgments than
the writers of any earlier period. The subject of this and the following
chapter will be the rich variety of critical methods and resources exhibited
by the major literary theorists of the early nineteenth century.

As a preliminary to this analysis, however, we may notice that there are
a limited number of assertions about poetry which turn up so persistently,
although in very different theoretical frames, that they may perhaps be
called *the* romantic complex of ideas about poetry. The romantic 'movement' in England is largely a convenient fiction of the historian, but one
document, Wordsworth's Preface to the *Lyrical Ballads* of 1800, written to
justify on universal grounds an 'experiment' in poetic language, does have
something of the aspect of a romantic manifesto. In part the Preface (together with the passages and appendix Wordsworth added in 1802) owes
its special position to the fact that it presented a set of propositions about

the nature and criteria of poetry which were widely adopted by Wordsworth's contemporaries, including those who were least in sympathy with what they supposed to be Wordsworth's own poetic aims. All these propositions rely upon the basic assertion, which usually serves as the definition of poetry, that:

(1) Poetry is the expression or overflow of feeling, or emerges from a process of imagination in which feelings play the crucial part.

Statements to this effect, we know, are to be found in almost all the important critics of the period, and in more or less easy conjunction with philosophical theories as disparate as Wordsworth's sensationism and Shelley's Platonism, the organic idealism of Coleridge and the positivism of John Stuart Mill.

(2) As the vehicle of an emotional state of mind, poetry is opposed not to prose, but to unemotional assertions of fact, or 'science.'

'Much confusion,' Wordsworth complained, 'has been introduced into criticism by this contradistinction of Poetry and Prose, instead of the more philosophical one of Poetry and Matter of Fact, or Science.'[1] It had been common since antiquity to oppose poetry to history, and to base this distinction on the ground that poetry imitates some form of the universal or ideal instead of the actual event. The usual procedure of romantic critics was to substitute science for history as the opposite of poetry, and to ground the distinction on the difference between expression and description, or between emotive language and cognitive language. As one author wrote in *Blackwood's Magazine* in 1835, 'Prose is the language of *intelligence,* poetry of *emotion.*'[2]

(3) Poetry originated in primitive utterances of passion which, through organic causes, were naturally rhythmic and figurative.

In Wordsworth's version, 'The earliest poets of all nations generally wrote from passion excited by real events; they wrote naturally, and as men: feeling powerfully as they did, their language was daring, and figurative.'[3] Coleridge believed that poetry, as the instinctive utterance of feeling, must have seemed to early men a more natural and less remarkable language than prose; 'it was the language of passion and emotion; it is what they themselves spoke and heard in moments of exultation, indignation, etc.'[4] Though romantic critics disagreed violently on the merits of primitive poetry, most of them accepted the hypothesis that it had its inception in passionate utterance—rather than, as Aristotle had assumed, in an instinct for imitation.[5]

(4) Poetry is competent to express emotions chiefly by its resources of figures of speech and rhythm, by means of which words naturally embody and convey the feelings of the poet.

In opposition to the earlier doctrine that figurative language and meter are primarily ornaments used to heighten the aesthetic pleasure, the typical romantic opinion was that expressed by Wordsworth: There is no need in poetry to deviate from ordinary language 'for elevation of style, or any of its supposed ornaments: for, if the Poet's subject be judiciously chosen, it will naturally, and upon fit occasion, lead him to passions the language of which, if selected truly and judiciously, must necessarily be dignified and variegated, and alive with metaphors and figures.' [6] From this it follows that:

(5) It is essential to poetry that its language be the spontaneous and genuine, not the contrived and simulated, expression of the emotional state of the poet.

On this thesis, Wordsworth (and in a carefully qualified way, Coleridge) based his attack on the 'mechanical adoption' of figures of speech to which he attributed the debased diction of eighteenth-century poetry. On it depends also the general romantic use of spontaneity, sincerity, and integral unity of thought and feeling as the essential criteria of poetry, in place of their neo-classic counterparts: judgment, truth, and the appropriateness with which diction is matched to the speaker, the subject matter, and the literary kind.[7]

(6) The born poet is distinguished from other men particularly by his inheritance of an intense sensibility and a susceptibility to passion.

A poet, as Wordsworth said, differs from other men because he is 'endowed with more lively sensibility, more enthusiasm and tenderness . . . a man pleased with his own passions and volitions, and who rejoices more than other men in the spirit of life that is in him. . .' [8] Writing later in defense of Robert Burns, he added that this constitution of genius, since it inclines him to pleasure, 'is not incompatible with vice, and . . . vice leads to misery—the more acute from the sensibilities which are the elements of genius. . .' [9] Coleridge also said that sensibility 'both deep and quick' and depth of emotion are essential components of genius, although he insisted that no less essential are the opposing powers of impersonality and 'energy of thought.' [10] Shelley emphasized the 'delicate sensibility' and vulnerability to temptation of the born poet, and John Stuart Mill drew an elaborate portrait of the 'poet by nature' as one who inherits 'fine senses' and 'a nervous organization . . . so constituted, as to be more easily than common organizations, thrown, either by physical or moral causes, into *states* of enjoyment or suffering. . .'[11] Later Mill went on to say that, with so fine an emotional texture, the poet cannot but suffer in the present competitive society—

not from mortified vanity, but from the poetic temperament itself, under arrangements of society, made by and for harder natures; and in a world, which, for any but the unsensitive, is not a place of contentment ever, nor of peace till after many a hard-fought battle.[12]

We are on the way, by this time, to the stereotype of the *poète maudit,* endowed with an ambiguous gift of sensibility which makes him at the same time more blessed and more cursed than the other members of a society from which he is, by the destiny of inheritance, an outcast.

(7) The most important function of poetry is, by its pleasurable resources, to foster and subtilize the sensibility, emotions, and sympathies of the reader.

Romantic poetry remains poetry with a purpose, but in place of 'solas and doctryne,' its aim becomes primarily to cultivate the affective elements of human nature. As Wordsworth put what became a commonplace of his age: 'The end of Poetry is to produce excitement in co-existence with an overbalance of pleasure,' and its effect is 'to rectify men's feelings,' to widen their sympathies, and to produce or enlarge the capability 'of being excited without the application of gross and violent stimulants.'[13]

These or similar propositions have, since the early nineteenth century, persisted as integral parts of an expressive aesthetics. Eugene Véron, who in his *Esthétique* of 1878 wrote one of the fullest accounts of art as the expression of feeling, includes and expands upon all seven of Wordsworth's theses. And a number of these points, variously reinterpreted and reorganized, continue to be made by theorists with an expressive bias, who are as doctrinally diverse in other ways as Benedetto Croce and I. A. Richards.

i. Wordsworth and the Eighteenth Century

Wordsworth, then, the first great romantic poet, may also be accounted the critic whose highly influential writings, by making the feelings of the poet the center of critical reference, mark a turning-point in English literary theory. It is nevertheless remarkable that Wordsworth was more thoroughly immersed in certain currents of eighteenth-century thinking than any of his important contemporaries. There is, for example, almost none of the terminology of post-Kantian aesthetic philosophy in Wordsworth. Only in his poetry, not in his criticism, does Wordsworth make the transition from the eighteenth-century view of man and nature to the concept that the mind is creative in perception, and an integral part of an organically inter-related universe. To recall the material of the preceding chapter, furthermore, is to recognize the extent to which Wordsworth incorporates in his poetic theory eighteenth-century speculations on the emotional origin of language, prevalent ideas about the nature and value of primitive poetry, together with the results of a century of developments in Longinian doctrines, and substitutes this amalgam for neo-classic theories which had been based more substantially on Aristotle, Horace, Cicero, and Quintilian. Dr. Johnson would have been pained by most of Wordsworth's critical conclusions, but he would have found little occasion for surprise either in the technical vocabulary or in the reasoning by which these conclusions were established.

Wordsworth remained within a well-defined tradition in the general pattern of his criticism, no less than in its details. Throughout the Preface, Wordsworth has recourse to a basic standard for establishing validity, whether in the aims of the poet or the criteria of the critic—the common nature of men, always and everywhere. This is the system to which A. O. Lovejoy has given the name, 'Uniformitarianism,' and which he has shown was a leading principle in normative provinces of thought—moral, theological, and political, as well as aesthetic—in the seventeenth century and through most of the eighteenth century.[14]

This way of thinking depends on the assumption that human nature, in its passions and sensibilities no less than its reason, is everywhere fundamentally the same; and it educes the consequence that the shared opinions and feelings of mankind constitute the most reliable norm of aesthetic, as of other values. To cite Hugh Blair, in matters of taste, the standard must be 'the common sentiments and feelings of men.' 'For the universal feeling of mankind is the natural feeling; and because it is the natural, it is, for that reason, the right feeling.' [15] In this doctrine a great many eighteenth-century critics were well agreed; and they also shared the opinion that, since the earliest poets were endowed by nature with all the necessary faculties and powers for writing great poetry, the earliest productions—the *Iliad*, for example—are in certain respects without a peer. Dr. Johnson has Imlac say, 'It is commonly observed that the early writers are in possession of nature, and their followers of art: that the first excel in strength and invention, and the latter in elegance and refinement.' [16]

The theorists we now single out as aesthetic primitivists departed from this quite orthodox neo-classic opinion mainly in emphasis and detail. For one thing, they not only noted, but deplored the replacement of nature by art in the course of literary history; and for another, they specified the superiority of the primitive poet to consist particularly in the simple and uniform purity of his feelings and imagination, and in the uninhibited spontaneity and candor with which he gave those feelings expression. 'In the infancy of societies,' as Blair said, '[men's] passions have nothing to restrain them, their imagination has nothing to check it. They display themselves to one another without disguise, and converse and act in the uncovered simplicity of nature.' Hence, because it was then free from the restraints and refinements of civility, 'poetry, which is the child of imagination, is frequently most glowing and animated in the first ages of society.' [17]

According to one common eighteenth-century variant of this point of view, the elemental and uniform—and, therefore, the normal—aspects of human nature and products are to be found not only in 'chronological,' but in 'cultural' primitives, including people dwelling in civilized nations but insulated by caste or rural habitat from the artifice and complications of culture. In its aesthetic application, this presumption was one reason for the vogue in the eighteenth century of poets who were either peasants or proletarians—Stephen Duck, the Thresher Poet; Mary Collier, the Poetical Washerwoman; Henry Jones, the Poetical Shoemaker—from whose ranks the one aspirant to make good was the Poetical Plowboy, Robert Burns.[18]

Wordsworth was not a chronological primitivist, for unlike Blair, he did not believe that in certain major respects, man's best poetic age lies behind him. In a letter written in 1809 for Coleridge's periodical, *The Friend,* he even suggests a cautious commitment to the belief that, by and large, there is a 'progress of human nature towards perfection' in both moral dignity and intellectual power.[19] But the critical theory he held during those early years of the nineteenth century, when he formulated his most important literary pronouncements, may in all fairness be classified as a form—though a highly refined and developed form—of cultural primitivism. Wordsworth's cardinal standard of poetic value is 'nature,' and nature, in his usage, is given a triple and primitivistic connotation: Nature is the common denominator of human nature; it is most reliably exhibited among men living 'according to nature' (that is to say, in a culturally simple, and especially a rural environment); and it consists primarily in an elemental simplicity of thought and feeling and a spontaneous and 'unartificial' mode of expressing feeling in words. In 1802 he wrote a letter to the youthful Christopher North which exhibits his characteristic normative procedure, and provides

us with an illuminating gloss on the Preface to the *Lyrical Ballads* which
he had written two years before. 'Whom must poetry please?' Wordsworth
asked.

I answer, human nature as it has been [and ever] will be. But, where are we to
find the best measure of this? I answer, [from with]in; by stripping our own
hearts naked, and by looking out of ourselves to[wards men] who lead the
simplest lives, and most according to nature; men who have never known false
refinements, wayward and artificial desires, false criticisms, effeminate habits of
thinking and feeling, or who having known these things have outgrown them.

To find 'fair representatives of the vast mass of human existence,' we must
leave the class of 'gentlemen, persons of fortune, professional men, ladies';
we must 'descend lower, among cottages and fields, and among children.' [20]

Wordsworth is not an ideal expositor, and he complains frequently in
his letters that writing prose came hard to him and induced muscular
cramps, a nervous sweat, and despondency of spirit. The argument of the
Preface to the *Lyrical Ballads* is not pellucid, but it clears up considerably,
I think, once we recognize how persistent is its reference, in each area of
discussion, to the norm of what Wordsworth called 'human nature as it
has been [and ever] will be,' of which the simple Cumberland dalesman
is assumed to be the nearest existing approximation. Thus:

(1) The subject matter of poetry. Wordsworth tells us that his purpose
was, above all, to trace 'the primary laws of our nature: chiefly, as far as
regards the manner in which we associate ideas in a state of excitement.'
To illustrate these generically human laws,

humble and rustic life was generally chosen, because in that condition, the essential passions of the heart find a better soil in which they can attain their maturity,
are less under restraint, and speak a plainer and more emphatic language; because
in that condition of life our elementary feelings coexist in a state of greater simplicity . . . because the manners of rural life germinate from those elementary
feelings . . . and are more durable; and, lastly, because in that condition the
passions of men are incorporated with the beautiful and permanent forms of
nature. . . Such a language, arising out of repeated experience and regular feelings, is a more permanent, and a far more philosophical language, than that which
is frequently substituted for it by Poets. . .[21]

Dr. Johnson was Wordsworth's chief example of a bad critic, but it is
instructive to notice how close is the parallel, in concept and critical idiom,
between Wordsworth's justification of his ballad characters and Johnson's

praise of Shakespeare's comic characters. Shakespeare's characters, Johnson had said,

act upon principles arising from genuine passion, very little modified by particular forms . . . they are natural, and therefore durable. . . The uniform simplicity of primitive qualities neither admits increase, nor suffers decay. . .

If there be, what I believe there is, in every nation, a style which never becomes obsolete . . . this style is probably to be sought in the common intercourse of life, among those who speak only to be understood, without ambition of elegance.[22]

Wordsworth, then, was quite in agreement with Johnson that the poet properly concerns himself with the general and uniform elements, passions, and language of human nature; he merely differed in regard to the place these qualities are best exemplified in real life. This difference, however, led in practice to a drastic break with traditional poetic decorum. To Wordsworth, a mad mother, an idiot boy, or a child who cannot know of death were as appropriate subjects for serious poetry as Achilles or Lear. The poetic representation of these people was not intended to be a shift from the universal and normal to the deviant and abnormal, as some critics have charged from his day to this. On the contrary, by a simple extension of the most widely held premise of neo-classic thought—an extension for which there was ample precedent even in Johnson's lifetime—Wordsworth turned in his poetry to those feelings and thoughts whose very presence in peasants, children, and idiots is what proves them to be the property, not of the cultivated classes alone, but of all mankind. In such characters, as Wordsworth declared, 'the elements are simple, belonging rather to nature than to manners, such as exist now and will probably always exist. . .'[23] On these grounds Wordsworth rationalized the great and important extension of literary sympathies and subject matter which he exemplified in his poetic practice.

In Wordsworth's theory, the 'essential passions' and 'unelaborated expressions' of humble people serve not only as the subject matter of poetry, but also as the model for the 'spontaneous overflow' of the poet's own feelings in his act of composition. In the last analysis, Wordsworth refers the questions of subject matter, of diction, of characterization, and of all the elements of a poem to what in his system is the logically primitive category:

(2) The nature of the poet. 'Taking up the subject, then, upon general grounds, let me ask, what is meant by the word Poet? What is a Poet?' Wordsworth's answer is that he is 'a man speaking to men,' different from

other men not in kind, but merely in degree of sensibility, passion, and power of expression. Hence, 'where the Poet speaks through the mouths of his characters,' the subject 'will naturally, and upon fit occasion, lead him to passions,' of which the language will be that really spoken by men. On those other occasions, 'where the Poet speaks to us in his own person and character,' he also feels, and therefore speaks, as the representative of uniform human nature.

But these passions and thoughts and feelings are the general passions and thoughts and feelings of men. . . The Poet thinks and feels in the spirit of human passions. How, then, can his language differ in any material degree from that of all other men who feel vividly and see clearly? [24]

The fact that he grounded poetry in his own feelings made Wordsworth, as he realized, especially vulnerable to the contemporary charge that these feelings might be peculiar to himself, and capriciously linked to trivial subjects. 'I am sensible,' he admitted, 'that my associations must have sometimes been particular instead of general.' His defense is that though, being human, he is fallible, a poet's best guide to universal human feeling is his own feeling. An author cannot, without danger, defer to 'the simple authority of a few individuals, or even of certain classes of men . . . his own feelings are his stay and support.' [25]

Wordsworth next considers a possible inference from his expressive theory of poetry which was, in fact, one day to become a justification for coterie poetry and private symbolism. Might not a poet be allowed to abandon a universal language and 'to use a peculiar language when expressing his feelings for his own gratification or that of men like himself?' To this, Wordsworth objects that 'Poets do not write for Poets alone, but for men' [26]— which brings us to a third area of his argument:

(3) The audience. Wordsworth was as certain as any neo-classic critic had been that poetry must produce 'immediate pleasure,' that it must appeal to the constant and uniform susceptibilities of men, and that, therefore, as Dr. Johnson had put it, 'by the common sense of readers, uncorrupted with literary prejudices, after all the refinements of subtilty and the dogmatism of learning, must be finally decided all claim to poetical honours.' [27] But here Wordsworth was confronted with a difficulty, for one of the main concerns of his Preface was to justify his own poetic principles and practice against the indifference or adverse judgments of the great majority of readers in his own day. Exactly parallel had been the chronic dilemma of many neo-classic theorists, who had found the equalitarian implications of

a reliance upon the voice of men in general to come into conflict with their own cultivated aesthetic preferences. Dr. Johnson boldly put his reliance on the common reader; but other critics not only derogated the consensus of their own time and place in favor of the consensus of the ages, but disqualified all but a very few men as competent to speak for man in general. The train of logic by which this surprising conclusion could be achieved is evident in Lord Kames's *Elements of Criticism.* What is uniform among men, according to Kames, is 'not only invariable, but also *perfect,* or *right. . .*' But to determine the standard of taste 'common to the species,' we cannot 'rely on a local or transitory taste; but on what is the most general and the most lasting among polite nations.' In consequence, not only are 'savages' to be disfranchised, but also 'those who depend for food on bodily labour,' as well as any other men who 'by a corrupted taste are unqualified for voting. The common sense of mankind must then be confined to the few that fall not under these exceptions.' [28]

Wordsworth also employs a rationale of exclusion, although of course he reverses Kames's bias by looking toward, rather than away from 'those who depend for food on bodily labour' as the best practical index to the general sense of mankind. As he wrote in his letter to Christopher North, poetry must please 'human nature as it has been and ever will be,' but this is very poorly represented by much of human nature as it now exists, because a great proportion of the reading public has been perverted by 'false refinements' and 'artificial desires.' A great poet, therefore, instead of conforming himself to, ought rather

to rectify men's feelings, to give them new compositions of feeling, to render their feelings more sane, pure, and permanent, in short, more consonant to nature. . .[29]

On such grounds as these, Wordsworth writes in the Conclusion to his Preface of 1800, he believes that fulfilment of his aims would produce 'genuine poetry; in its nature well adapted to interest mankind permanently.' Fifteen years later, the 'unremitting hostility' with which his poems continued to be opposed by some critics motivated him to expand upon this thesis in the Essay Supplementary to the Preface. This time he proceeds by drawing a distinction between the passing and fallible voice of 'the Public' and that eternal and universal norm which emerges, through time, as the voice of 'the People.'

Is it the result of the whole, that, in the opinion of the Writer, the judgment of the People is not to be respected? The thought is most injurious. . . The People have already been justified, and their eulogium pronounced by implication, when it was said, above—that, of *good* poetry, the *individual,* as well as the species, *survives.* And how does it survive but through the People? . . . The voice that issues from this Spirit is that Vox Populi which the Deity inspires. Foolish must he be who can mistake for this a local acclamation, or a transitory outcry—transitory though it be for years, local though from a Nation.[30]

(4) The diction of poetry. In any theory that poetry is an expression of feeling, the question of diction tends to become primary. For the feelings of the poet are most readily conceived to overflow, not into plot or into characters, but into words, and it becomes the major task of the critic to formulate the standards by which the language of poetry is to be regulated and judged.

That Wordsworth's deliverances on this subject—to which he devoted the greater part of his Preface—were peculiarly dark and equivocal is attested by the endless disputes about his meaning from his day to our own. Much of the difficulty arises from his repeated formulation of the poetic norm as a selection of 'the real language of men,' or 'the language really spoken by men,' and from the associated statement that there can be no *'essential* difference between the language of prose and metrical composition.'[31] The total context makes it plain that (despite some wavering because of the ambiguity of the word 'real') Wordsworth's chief concern is not with the single words or the grammatical order of prose discourse, but with figurative departures from literal discourse, and that Wordsworth's main intention is to show that such deviations are justifiable in verse only when they have the same psychological causes that they have in the 'artless' speech of every day. Those who have thought to confound Wordsworth's argument by demonstrating that in his own poetry he uses a larger vocabulary and a different syntactic ordonnance than a peasant does, have largely missed the point. In Wordsworth's theory the relation between the language of 'Tintern Abbey' and the speech of a Lake Country shepherd is not primarily one of lexical or of grammatical, but of genetic equivalence. Both forms of discourse, he would claim, are instances of language really spoken by men under the stress of genuine feeling.

Once more Wordsworth's argument is clarified if we look at it in the perspective of eighteenth-century criticism. In his use, the term 'real' as the norm of poetic language is for the most part interchangeable with the term 'natural'—'the real language of *nature'* is one of his phrases—and 'nature,' as elsewhere in Wordsworth, connotes several attributes. First, the language of nature is not the language of poets as a class, but the language of mankind. It is not colored, as Wordsworth says, by a diction 'peculiar to him as an individual Poet or belonging simply to Poets in general.'[32] Second, it is exemplified in the language uttered by 'the earliest poets,' who 'wrote naturally, and as men'; and in prose, its best present instance is 'the simple and unelaborated expressions' of essential passions by men living close to nature.[33] Third, considered genetically, natural language is the instinctive and spontaneous overflow of feeling into words, and is therefore opposed to the deliberate adaptation of means to end, and of the adherence to specifically poetic conventions, which characterize 'art.' The one qualification Wordsworth sets to this principle is the necessity 'of giving pleasure,' which involves a selection to remove what would be 'painful or disgusting in the passion'; but, he is quick to say, this does not require the poet 'to trick out or elevate nature'—those words 'which are the emanations of reality and truth.'[34]

In short, in setting the standard of poetic diction, Wordsworth adopts and elaborates the old antithesis between nature and art and, like the aesthetic primitivists of the preceding age, declares himself for nature. This is implied throughout the Preface, and made explicit in his tripartite essay *Upon Epitaphs,* one part of which was published in *The Friend* in 1810, and the other two first printed from manuscript in Grosart's *The Prose Works of William Wordsworth* (1876). Even though the total essay is Wordsworth's longest piece of sustained criticism and devotes itself, like the Preface, to combating the notion that 'what was natural in prose would be out of place in verse,'[35] it has not received adequate attention from students of Wordsworth's literary theory.

'I vindicate,' he begins the third part of the essay, 'the rights and dignity of Nature.'

I have said that this excellence is difficult to attain; and why? Is it because nature is weak? No! Where the soul has been thoroughly stricken . . . there is never a want of *positive* strength; but because the adversary of Nature (call that adversary Art or by what name you will) is *comparatively* strong. . . [Of the verse epitaphs in *Elegant Extracts*] there is scarcely one which is not thoroughly tainted by the artifices which have over-run our writings in metre since the days of Dryden and Pope.[36]

It is clear that Wordsworth is opposing Pope's theory, as well as his practice, of poetic language. 'True Wit,' Pope had said, 'is Nature to advantage dressed,' and 'true expression' consists in giving thoughts their just and appropriate 'dress' and ornament. 'It gilds all objects, but it alters none.' False wit, on the other hand, results when poets are 'unskill'd to trace The naked nature . . . And hide with ornaments their want of art.' [37] But to Wordsworth, all such wit is false wit, and all art—in the meaning of the deliberate adjustment of phrase to sentiment and of rhetorical ornament to phrase —serves only to pervert what he calls 'genuine' poetry. Rejecting 'art' in the neo-classic sense of the term, Wordsworth also rejects the related concept of language as the dress of thought, and of figures as the ornaments of language.[38]

When we turn back to the Preface and Appendix to the *Lyrical Ballads,* we find that Wordsworth justifies figures of speech generally, and the different kinds of figures severally, only when, instead of being 'supposed ornaments,' they are 'naturally' suggested by passion.[39] 'Poetic diction,' he explains, originated at that period in the history of poetry when, through 'a mechanical adoption' of figures of speech, men 'frequently applied them to feelings and thoughts with which they had no natural connexion whatsoever.' The result was a poetic language (and here Wordsworth unmistakably reveals that he uses 'real' as a synonym of 'natural') 'differing materially from the real language of men in *any situation,*' although in time, 'the taste of men becoming gradually perverted, this language was received as a natural language.' [40] The same antithesis between the language of nature and of art, together with the rejection of art, prompts the epithets Wordsworth applies to the characteristic diction of the eighteenth-century poets. This diction is 'artificial,' and the result of 'false refinement or arbitrary innovation'; detached from the laws of human nature, and therefore 'arbitrary and capricious'; 'spoken by rote' rather than 'instinctively ejaculated'; and in consequence, it replaces the natural and universal language of men by 'a family language,' passed on from father to son 'as the common inheritance of Poets.' [41]

By showing that Wordsworth's theory had its roots in earlier primitivistic doctrine, I should by no means be taken to condemn, or even to derogate, Wordsworth's achievement. The attempt to correct earlier tendencies to formalize and freeze the 'art' of poetry by emphasizing the opposing element of 'nature' was historically justifiable, and validated at least in the pragmatic sense that the theory was the working hypothesis, and so helped shape the procedure, of one of the great and original poets of the language. Wordsworth's criticism rests on the solid basis of his recognition of the greatness, and the potentialities as literary models, of the ballads, songs, and stories of oral tradition. It rests also on his perception of the possibilities as literary subject matter of the ways and speech of men living close to the soil, comparatively insulated from the rapid changes of life and manners in the urban world. And if neither the literature nor manners of the folk are 'artless' in the way Wordsworth asserted, and if his attempt to generalize from their attributes to all of poetry is open to serious objection, still Wordsworth, by doctrine and example, brought into the literary province the store of materials which has since been richly exploited by writers from Thomas Hardy to William Faulkner.

In addition, Wordsworth succeeded in elaborating and qualifying the doctrines of earlier enthusiasts for the primitive so as to convert them into a reputable and rewarding, if not in itself a wholly adequate, contribution to our critical tradition. Certainly Wordsworth did not conceive of the great poet as a thoughtless and instinctive child of nature. Just as he required the poet to keep his eye on the subject, and reminded him that he writes not for himself, but for men, so he affirmed that good poems are produced only by a man who has 'thought long and deeply. For our continued influxes of feeling are modified and directed by our thoughts, which are indeed the representatives of all our past feelings. . .' In this way, he refined the key assumption of aesthetic primitivism into the conception of a spontaneity which is the reward of intelligent application and hard-won skills—a spontaneity, as F. R. Leavis has said, 'supervening upon complex development,' and a naturalness 'consummating a discipline, moral and other.' [42] Wordsworth's own practice, as this is described in Dorothy Wordsworth's *Journals,* also gives ample evidence that once they have been composed, poems may be subjected to long and arduous revision. It is the strength of Wordsworth's expressive theory, therefore, that he brings into its purview elements of the older conception that poetry is a deliberate art; it is its peculiarity that these elements are carefully relegated to a temporal position before or after the actual coming-into-being of the poem. For in the immediate act of composition, the best warrant of 'naturalness,' Wordsworth insists, is that the overflow of feeling be spontaneous, and free both from the deliberate adaptation of conventional language to feeling and from the deliberate bending of linguistic means to the achievement of poetic effects.

It is worth emphasizing, finally, that although Wordsworth repudiates the opinion that nature in poetry must be 'to advantage dressed,' he consents to the opinion that it may be 'what oft was thought.' In one instance, Wordsworth overtops Dr. Johnson in his demand for uniformity, instead of originality, in the materials of poetry. Johnson, like Wordsworth, was interested in mortuary verse, and had anticipated him in writing essays on epitaphs. Johnson had selected a composition of Pope's for special praise because in it 'there is scarce one line taken from common places.' For this Wordsworth reprimands him:

It is not only no fault but a primary requisite in an epitaph that it shall contain thoughts and feelings which are in their substance common-place, and even trite. It is grounded upon the universal intellectual property of man,—sensations which all men have felt and feel in some degree daily and hourly;—truths whose very interest and importance have caused them to be unattended to, as things which should take care of themselves.

The next sentence, however, marks the point at which the two theorists part company: 'But it is required,' says Wordsworth, 'that these truths should be *instinctively* ejaculated or should rise irresistibly from circumstances. . .'[43]

That the great romantic poet should exceed the great neo-classic critic in his quest for uniformity will not seem anomalous if we remember that Johnson, on his part, had balanced his demand for common truths by requiring what 'is at once natural and *new*,' and if we remember also that none of the English romantic poets was of Novalis' opinion that 'the more personal, local, temporal, and peculiar [*eigentümlicher*] a poem is, the nearer it is to the center of poetry.'[44] In England the high-water mark of the worship of uniqueness and originality had come and passed with Young's *Conjectures*. In his demand that the content of poetry be what is central to all mankind, Wordsworth was at one with Boileau, Pope, and Johnson; the substitution of poetry as the overflow of feeling, however, for poetry as a pleasure-giving imitation enforced a change in the application of this criterion. Since a poet is 'a man speaking to men,' to express his spontaneous feelings is the best way to insure a universal content and to appeal to what is universal in mankind. This way of thinking, severed from Wordsworth's insistence that the poet's eye be kept on his subject, was to reach its theatrical extreme in the formulation of Victor Hugo:

Hélas! quand je vous parle de moi, je vous parle de vous. Comment ne le sentezvous pas? Ah! insensé, qui crois que je ne suis pas toi.[45]

ii. Coleridge on Poems, Poetry, and Poets

That Coleridge's applied criticism is independent of—or even a happy escape from—his general philosophic principles is an error common to Coleridgeans and to many anti-Coleridgeans as well. At its extreme, this opinion results in the conclusion that Coleridge's critical method 'would today be called impressionistic,' and 'is something like Anatole France's "adventures of the soul among masterpieces." ' [46] Even T. M. Raysor, in his indispensable edition of Coleridge's Shakespeare criticism, is misleading when he says that in Coleridge's analysis of Wordsworth's theories in the *Biographia Literaria,* the general ideas 'are inductive generalizations based upon . . . personal experience,' and 'not in any sense a deduction of art from a metaphysical system, like that branch of philosophy which we call aesthetics.' [47] Coleridge himself repeatedly attacked as false the absolute opposition of deduction to induction. In criticism as in science, to his way of thinking, empirical investigation without a prior 'idea' is helpless, and discoveries can only be made by the prepared spirit. As Coleridge expressed it, with his genius for analogy, observation is to meditation only 'as eyes, for which [meditation] has pre-determined their field of vision, and to which, as to *its* organ, it communicates a microscopic power.' [48] And in applied criticism, he says, 'I should call that investigation fair and philosophical, in which the critic announces and endeavours to establish the principles, which he holds for the foundation of poetry in general. . .' [49] The truth of the matter is, that beyond any critic of comparable scope, Coleridge can hardly consider a literary fact without explicit reference to first principles. He never completed his projected philosophical system which would include the bases of poetry and criticism among the *omne scibile,* but he proceeded far enough in the undertaking to demonstrate that his metaphysical premises, far from being alien to his critical practice, reappear as the chief critical principles which make possible his characteristic insights into the constitution and qualities of specific poems.

As in his philosophy, so in his criticism, Coleridge roots his theory in the constitution and activity of the creative mind.

I labored at a solid foundation, on which permanently to ground my opinions, in the component faculties of the human mind itself, and their comparative dignity and importance. According to the faculty or source, from which the pleasure given by any poem or passage was derived, I estimated the merit of such poem or passage.[50]

The mind, the relative status and play of the productive faculties, is for Coleridge at once the source and the test of art. So systematically does his discussion of poetry involve its causes in the mental processes of the poet, that we may profitably postpone considering a number of his leading ideas until we come to deal with the romantic psychology of poetic invention.

At this point, we have a convenient opportunity to contrast Coleridge's theory with Wordsworth's, by observing how Coleridge—in the central, longest, and most closely reasoned portion of his *Biographia Literaria*—applies his major critical principles to the examination of Wordsworth's theory of poetry and poetic diction.

Coleridge's disagreement with Wordsworth was not a long-delayed afterthought, nor (as has sometimes been charged) a result of the estrangement between the poets; and it was a disagreement in fundamentals, not in details. Only two years after the Preface of 1800, Coleridge had written to Southey that 'although Wordsworth's Preface is half a child of my own brain,' I 'rather suspect that somewhere or other there is a radical difference in our theoretical opinions concerning poetry; this I shall endeavour to go to the bottom of. . .' [51] Coleridge's critique of Wordsworth in the *Biographia,* it is apparent, was the fruit of some fourteen years of meditation on the topic.

Coleridge makes clear in the *Biographia,* that he objects not to the validity of Wordsworth's 'experiment' in a new poetic style, but to those passages which seem 'to contend for the extension of this style to poetry of all kinds,' and that he objects to such passages 'as erroneous in principle.' [52] Wordsworth's basic opposition of 'nature,' in various senses, to 'art' must have been conspicuous enough to any of his contemporaries familiar with the patterns of late eighteenth-century criticism. Coleridge's elaborate dialectic is designed in large measure to show that this opposition cannot be sustained, and that great poems are 'natural' only in a sense which involves those very qualities of purpose, the proportioning of parts to whole and of means to end, and the election of specifically poetic conventions, which are the defining characteristics of an art.

Coleridge begins his critique by explaining his ideas 'first, of a POEM; and secondly, of POETRY itself, in *kind,* and in *essence.*' For Wordsworth, the justification of poetic meter had proved a particularly troublesome problem, because, although the natural language of feeling may be broadly rhythmical, the use in poetry of highly regular stress and stanza patterns would seem a matter not of nature, but of artifice and convention. He had consequently been forced to depart from the main lines of his argument, and to explain meter (in a formula resembling the theories of artful poetic ornament he was attacking) as a 'charm' which is 'superadded' to natural language. This charm is justifiable because it yields a supplementary pleasure and tempers the pain of 'the deeper passions,' yet does not interfere with the passions, nor open the way to any 'other artificial distinctions of style.'

Yet meter, he holds, 'is but adventitious to composition.' [53] In opposition to Wordsworth, Coleridge expressly defines a poem in such a way as to make meter an essential attribute. He thus separates poems not only from works of science or history, but from works of fiction which are written in prose:

The final definition then, so deduced, may be thus worded. A poem is that species of composition, which is opposed to works of science, by proposing for its *immediate* object pleasure, not truth; and from all other species (having *this* object in common with it) it is discriminated by proposing to itself such delight from the *whole,* as is compatible with a distinct gratification from each component *part.*[54]

By defining a poem as a means to an 'object,' 'purpose,' or 'end' (terms which he employs as synonyms), Coleridge, quite in the tradition of neo-classic criticism, establishes the making of poems to be a deliberate art, rather than the spontaneous overflow of feeling. In an earlier lecture, he had put the matter in such a way as to bring in the expression of feeling, but under subordination to deliberate purpose: 'It is the *art* of communicating whatever we wish to communicate, so as both to express and produce excitement, but for the purpose of immediate pleasure; and each part is fitted to afford as much pleasure, as is compatible with the largest sum in the whole.' [55] The component parts of a poem, including the feelings it expresses, are so many means to achieving the definite aim of pleasure; and meter, in this context of discussion, is regarded as 'a studied selection and artificial arrangement' for the purpose of affording the optimal pleasure in each part of a poem. Meter is not, however, as Wordsworth and many earlier theorists had maintained, merely a supernumerary charm, for in a harmonious or organized whole the change in any part involves an alteration of the rest; hence, 'if metre be superadded, all other parts must be made consonant with it.' 'I adduce . . . the principle,' Coleridge says later on in the argument, 'that *all* parts of an organized whole must be assimilated to the more *important* and *essential* parts.' [56]

So much for poems as finished metrical products, or (as Coleridge terms it) as 'species of composition.' Now Coleridge performs a significant and highly characteristic maneuver. 'But if this should be admitted as a satisfactory character of a *poem,* we have still to seek for a definition of *poetry.*' For in writers so diverse as Plato, Taylor, Burnet, and Isaiah, we find 'poetry of the highest kind,' even though it lacks meter and has truth rather than pleasure for its immediate object; while a poem itself 'neither can be, or ought to be, all poetry.' To define what he elsewhere called 'poetry in

its highest and most peculiar sense'—those supreme achievements of the
creative mind which can be sustained only for limited passages, whether
in prose or verse—Coleridge turns from the finished product to its etiology
in the poet, and from a definition in terms of rational ends to a definition
in terms of the combination and play of the mental faculties in composition. In this 'strictest use of the word'—

What is poetry? is so nearly the same question with, what is a poet? that the
answer to the one is involved in the solution of the other. For it is a distinction
resulting from the poetic genius itself. . .

The poet, described in *ideal* perfection, brings the whole soul of man into activity. . . He diffuses a tone and spirit of unity, that blends, and (as it were)
fuses, each into each, by that synthetic and magical power, to which we have
exclusively appropriated the name of imagination. This power . . . reveals itself
in the balance or reconciliation of opposite or discordant qualities. . .[57]

Here we find the typical movement of Coleridge's criticism; he begins
with the product, but after a point, moves into the process. So long as his
concern is with the development of terms for the classification and critical
analysis of 'species of composition,' he re-adapts to his purpose the time-
tested distinctions of medium, subject matter, diction, and ends, which had
constituted the main tools of criticism since the ancient rhetoricians. But
when Coleridge addresses himself to the problem of establishing the criteria
for evaluating poetry 'in its highest . . . sense,' his criticism becomes genetic and, by making the poet's mind and powers the focus of aesthetic
reference, shows its consonance with the central tendency of his age.

In this passage, Coleridge introduced into English criticism an important
concept, and one which has reappeared to play a leading role in the critical
writings of our own generation.[58] This is the appeal to inclusiveness as the
criterion of poetic excellence—to the co-existence in a poem of 'opposite or
discordant qualities,' provided that these have been blended or 'reconciled'
into unity by the synthetic power which Coleridge attributes to the imagination. The concept, it is important to notice, is not adventitious in Coleridge's criticism, nor even specifically aesthetic in its origins. It is merely
the application in the province of aesthetics of the generative principle which
underlies Coleridge's metaphysical system in its totality.

'Grant me a nature having two contrary forces,' Coleridge had written
in an earlier chapter of the *Biographia,* 'the one of which tends to expand
infinitely, while the other strives to apprehend or *find* itself in this infinity,
and I will cause the world of intelligences with the whole system of their

representations to rise up before you.'[59] In a series of theses, he went on to summarize the main tenets of this 'Dynamic Philosophy,' in order, he explicitly says, to apply them 'to the deduction of the Imagination, and with it the principles of production and of genial criticism in the fine arts.' We must begin, he tells us, with 'a truth self-grounded, unconditional and known by its own light.' That principle is to be found in 'the SUM or I AM'—that 'spirit, self, and self-consciousness' which may be described 'as a perpetual self-duplication of one and the same power into object and subject, which presuppose each other, and can exist only as antitheses.' And in the generative power of this perpetually self-renewing opposition, in the mind of an individual, between subject and object, between infinite and finite—'in the existence, in the reconciling, and the recurrence of this contradiction consists the process and mystery of production and life.'[60]

The dynamic conflict of opposites, and their reconciliation into a higher third, is not limited to the process of individual consciousness. The same concept serves Coleridge as the root-principle of his cosmogony, his epistemology, and his theory of poetic creation alike. This is the point that Coleridge tries to make in his cryptic and oft-ridiculed comment: 'The primary IMAGINATION I hold to be the living Power and prime Agent of all human Perception, and as a repetition in the finite mind of the eternal act of creation in the infinite I AM. The secondary Imagination I consider as an echo of the former. . .'[61] All genuine creation—everything that is not a mimicking of given models, or a mere reassembly of given elements into a whole which is novel in its pattern but not in its parts—derives from the generative tension of opponent forces, which are synthesized, without exclusion, in a new whole. The imagination, in creating poetry, therefore echoes the creative principle underlying the universe. Conversely, the whole universe, both in its continuous generation 'in the infinite I AM' and in the repetition of that act in the process of perception by individual human minds, may be said to consist, just as a great poem does, in the productive resolution of contraries and disparates.

In Coleridge's criticism, accordingly, the imaginative synthesis of discordant or antithetic aesthetic qualities replaces Wordsworth's 'nature' as the criterion of highest poetic value; and this on grounds inherent in Coleridge's world-view. Neo-classic critics, as we know, had often posed the aesthetic norm in terms of a mean, or a proper combination, of extremes. Many of these extremes reappear in Coleridge's list of the kinds of contraries reconciled in poetry, but converted into the new triadic rhythm of thesis-antithesis-synthesis. The imaginative reconciliation is 'of sameness, with difference; of the general, with the concrete; the idea, with the image; the individual, with the representative; the sense of novelty and freshness, with old and familiar objects; a more than usual state of emotion, with more than usual order. . .' [62] Among other things (and this brings us back to the crux of Coleridge's debate with Wordsworth), the greatest poetry reconciles the opposites of nature and art, and 'while it blends and harmonizes the natural and the artificial, still subordinates art to nature.'

In the remainder of his argument against Wordsworth's theory Coleridge tries repeatedly to demonstrate that this poetic resolution of nature and art, in place of a reliance on nature unalloyed, is not an empty triumph of dialectic, but can be confirmed by the facts of poetic composition. Notice first that he heartily concurs with Wordsworth in grounding valid figures of speech in natural passion—though this may be the passion not of the poet proper, but of his invented characters—and in condemning the pure 'artifice' of much recent poetry. As far as Wordsworth 'has evinced the truth of passion, and the *dramatic* propriety of those figures and metaphors in the original poets, which, stripped of their justifying reasons' are 'converted into mere artifices of connection or ornament,' and as far as he has distinguished the latter from 'the natural language of empassioned feeling,' he 'deserves all praise, both for the attempt and for the execution.' [63] What he takes exception to, Coleridge informs us, is Wordsworth's attendant argument that 'the proper diction for poetry in general consists altogether in a language taken, with due exceptions from . . . the natural conversation of men under the influence of natural feelings,' and that such conversation is best exemplified in 'low and rustic life.' Against this form of cultural primitivism, Coleridge argues cogently and in detail, first, by appealing to the violation of this standard in the subject matter and language of many of Wordsworth's own poems, and second, by demonstrating that the special conditions of rural life conduce rather to grossness and narrowness than to excellence in feeling and language.[64]

There remains Wordsworth's more general contention that the standards of poetry are those of the natural language of feeling in ordinary speech, and that in consequence, as Coleridge quotes Wordsworth, 'there neither is or can be any essential difference between the language of prose and metrical composition.' Coleridge replies that there are 'modes of expression' which are 'fit and natural' in prose, but 'disproportionate and heterogeneous in metrical poetry'; and, on the other side, there is an ordonnance of words and a use of figures of speech appropriate to a serious poem which would be 'vicious and alien' in a correct prose.[65]

In other words, the canon of naturalness which applies to ordinary feel-ingful discourse has no necessary jurisdiction over 'poetry,' especially when this occurs in the medium of a 'poem,' which is a form of art having its proper ends and selected means (including diction) to achieve those ends. Coleridge's first effort now is to bridge the gap between his earlier defini-tions of 'poetry' and 'poem,' in order to show how the synthesizing activity of imagination is able to find expression in such a contrived medium, and by a process that is at once spontaneous *and* deliberate, natural *and* artful. This he does by supplementing his earlier analysis of a completed poem in terms of its ends with an analysis of what he calls 'metrical poetry'—poetry in the medium of a poem—in terms of its psychological origins. From this altered standpoint, meter turns out to be one of the products of that con-flict and resolution of contraries which is the genetic principle—the 'imagi-nation'—of poetry as a whole.

And first from the *origin* of metre. This I would trace to the balance in the mind effected by that spontaneous effort which strives to hold in check the workings of passion. It might be easily explained likewise in what manner this salutary antagonism is assisted by the very state, which it counteracts; and how this bal-ance of antagonists became organized into metre . . . by a supervening act of the will and judgement, consciously and for the foreseen purpose of pleasure.[66]

It is in this respect, as Coleridge had said somewhat earlier, that 'the sense of musical delight, with the power of producing it, is a gift of im-agination.' And from this approach, those poems which are genuine poetry are seen to unite, and so reconcile, both natural language and artifice, both spontaneity and voluntary design. 'As the *elements* of metre owe their exist-ence to a state of increased excitement, so the metre itself should be ac-companied by the natural language of excitement.' Yet 'as these elements are formed into metre *artificially,* by a *voluntary* act, with . . . design,' these conditions too 'must be reconciled and co-present. There must be not only a partnership, but a union; an interpenetration of passion and of will, of *spontaneous* impulse and of *voluntary* purpose.' By parity of reasoning, those figures of speech which in their primitive origin were entirely the natural expression of passion must be employed according to different and more complex standards in the artful discourse of a poem, which is directed to-ward the end of yielding aesthetic pleasure.

Again, this union can be manifested only in a frequency of forms and figures of speech (originally the offspring of passion, but now the adopted children of power) greater than would be desired or endured, where the emotion is not voluntarily encouraged and kept up for the sake of . . . pleasure. . . It not only dictates, but of itself tends to produce, a more frequent employment of picturesque language than would be natural in any other case.[67]

We find here, among other things, Coleridge's attempt to subtilize the crudity and supplement the inadequacy of the doctrine that poetry, at the moment of composition, is the spontaneous overflow of feeling, *tout simplement*. The valid language of poetry, for example, must be traced back not to one, but to two sources of feeling, of which the second is peculiar to poetic composition. As Coleridge explains it: Poetry, 'Mr. Wordsworth truly affirms, does always imply PASSION,' and every passion has 'its characteristic modes of expression.' But in addition, 'the very *act* of poetic composition *itself* is, and is allowed to imply and to produce, an unusual state of excitement, which of course justifies and demands a correspondent difference of language.'[68]

Coleridge focuses his discussion, however, on refuting the general antithesis between nature and art which is the substratum of all Wordsworth's theory. He proves himself to be thoroughly aware that Wordsworth's reasoning is only a new application of an old strain in Western thought, for he quotes against his friend the classic refutation of the primitivistic point of view. The passage is that in which Shakespeare has Polixenes refute Montaigne's preference for nature, as opposed to art, by pointing out that art (the intervention of man's planning and skill) 'itself is nature.' 'We may,' Coleridge concludes,

in some measure apply to this union [of spontaneous impulse and voluntary purpose in poetry] the answer of POLIXENES, in the Winter's Tale, to PERDITA's neglect of the streaked gilly-flowers, because she had heard it said,

> There is an art which in their piedness, shares
> With great creating nature.
> 　　　*Polixenes:* Say there be;
> Yet nature is made better by no mean,
> But nature makes that mean; so, ev'n that art,
> Which, you say, adds to nature, is an art,
> That nature makes.[69]

In sum, Coleridge holds that the greatest poetry is, indeed, the product of spontaneous feeling, but feeling which, by a productive tension with the impulse for order, sets in motion the assimilative imagination and (balanced by its antagonists, purpose and judgment, and supplemented by the emotion inherent in the act of composition itself) organizes itself into a conventional medium in which the parts and the whole are adapted both to each other and to the purpose of effecting pleasure. The paradox that what is natural in poetry includes art, and results from an interpenetration of spontaneity and voluntarism, is not merely an abstract product of Coleridge's philosophical frame of reference. The fact is attested by the creative poets of all ages who, in various idioms, assert that they write according to prior plan and as the result of skills acquired by laborious practice, but that on occasion the central idea takes control and evolves itself in a way contrary to their original intention, and even to their express desire; yet retrospect shows that they have written better than they knew.

Let us attend to Coleridge's attempt to grapple with one other aspect of the same problem. Wordsworth had assumed that there is no practical alternative between relying on the spontaneous promptings of nature (best exemplified in the speech of common folk) and the arbitrary and capricious fiat of the poet, 'upon which no calculation whatever can be made.' Coleridge's reply is that there exist valid 'principles of writing,' from which we can derive *'rules* how to pass judgement on what has been written by others.'

But if it be asked, by what principles the poet is to regulate his own style, if he do not adhere closely to the sort and order of words which he hears in the market, wake, high-road, or ploughfield? I reply; by principles, the ignorance or neglect of which would convict him of being no *poet,* but a silly or presumptuous usurper of the name! By the principles of grammar, logic, psychology!

Coleridge is not appealing from artless nature to the codified rules of doctrinaire forms of neo-classicism. The principles of grammar, logic, and psychology apply; but in the practice of the poet, such knowledge must be 'rendered instinctive by habit'; then it reappears as 'the representative and reward of our past conscious reasonings, insights, and conclusions, and acquires the name of TASTE.' It is not by the observation of other people, but 'by the power of imagination proceeding upon the *all in each* of human nature,' and therefore 'intuitively,' that a poet will know what language suits different states of emotion, as well as 'what intermixture of conscious volition is natural to that state; and in what instances such figures and colors of speech degenerate into mere creatures of arbitrary purpose.' Finally, Coleridge demonstrates how poetry can be natural yet regular, lawful without being legislated, and rationally explicable after the fact although intuitive at the moment of composition, by replacing the concept of rules imposed from outside by the concept of the inherent laws of the imaginative process:

Could a rule be given from *without,* poetry would cease to be poetry, and sink into a mechanical art. . . The *rules* of IMAGINATION are themselves the very powers of growth and production.[70]

In this passage, Coleridge equates the orderliness of the imaginative process with the process of 'growth.' And, as we shall see when we come back to Coleridge's theory from a different point of view, the 'nature' that Coleridge, unlike Wordsworth, ultimately appeals to in art is basically a biological nature. Correspondingly, Coleridge's concept of poetic creativity which we have been detailing—that self-organizing process, assimilating disparate materials by an inherent lawfulness into an integral whole—borrows many of its characteristic features from the conceptual model of organic growth.

It was above all in his exploitation of this new aesthetics of organism that Coleridge, more thoroughly than Wordsworth, was the innovative English critic of his time. At the same time, it was, paradoxically, because he retained a large part of the neo-classic critical tenets and terms which Wordsworth minimized or rejected that Coleridge's criticism is much more flexible and practicable—more adequate to the illumination of a great diversity of specific poems—than Wordsworth's. The logical maneuver by which Coleridge managed this feat, through sharply differentiating 'poetry' from a 'poem,' is awkward, and has certainly led to a wide misunderstanding of his intention. But by it, he was enabled to maintain his double view, capable alternately of dwelling on a poem as a poem, and on a poem as a process of mind. By this device, he was also able to make use of the pregnant concept of a poem as a quasi-natural organism, without sacrificing the indispensable distinctions and analytic powers of the concept that the writing of poems is basically a rational and acquired art of adapting parts to parts, and of bending means to foreseen ends. By this device, finally, he remained free to maintain that the judging of poems (as his eighteenth-century schoolmaster, Bowyer, had so strenuously impressed on him) must proceed on the assumption that poetry has 'a logic of its own, as severe as that of science; and more difficult, because . . . dependent on more, and more fugitive causes.'[71]

Varieties of Romantic Theory:
SHELLEY, HAZLITT, KEBLE, AND OTHERS

Will you believe me? I am almost ashamed to confess the truth, but I must say that there is hardly a person present who would not have talked better about their poetry than the poets did themselves.
                                                                    PLATO, *Apology*

The question should fairly be stated, how far a man can be an adequate . . . critic of poetry who is not a poet, at least *in posse?* . . . But there is yet another distinction. Supposing he is not only a poet, but is a bad poet? What then?
                                                        COLERIDGE, *Anima Poetae*

THOMAS LOVE PEACOCK's 'Four Ages of Poetry,' published in 1820, may be read as a shrewd and caustic parody of Wordsworth's poetic tenets, especially of those he held in common with the primitivistic theorists of the preceding century. Peacock agrees that primitive language is naturally poetical—'the savage indeed lisps in numbers, and all rude and uncivilized people express themselves in the manner which we call poetical'—but himself draws the conclusion that poetry is a useless anachronism in this era of reason, science, metaphysics, and political economy.[1] In the present age of brass the poet, while actually reviving the barbarism and superstition of the age of iron, 'professes to return to nature and revive the age of gold.' By a sequence of enthymemes, Peacock parodies the logic by which this return to nature is usually justified: 'Poetical impressions can be received only among natural scenes: for all that is artificial is anti-poetical. Society is artificial, therefore we will live out of society. The mountains are natural, therefore we will live in the mountains.' Wordsworth's contention that 'I have at all times endeavoured to look steadily at my subject' has its mocking echo in Peacock's comment that the Lake Poets 'contrived, though they had retreated from the world for the express purpose of seeing nature as she was, to see her only as she was not.' Wordsworth himself, Peacock says, 'cannot describe a scene under his own eyes without putting into it [some] phantastical parturition of the moods of his own mind.' The doctrine of the overflow of powerful feeling has its derisory counterpart too. 'The highest inspirations of poetry are resolvable into three ingredients: the rant of unregulated passion, the whine of exaggerated feeling, and the cant of factitious sentiment. . .'[2] It is idle to inquire about the exact boundaries between the serious and the playful in this witty essay. Peacock cannot be pinned down. He had the eye of the born parodist, before which everything pretentious writhes into caricature. If he was a poet who mocked at poets from a Utilitarian frame of satirical reference, he was a Utilitarian who turned into ridicule the belief in utility and the march of intellect, as well as a critic who derided the contemners of poetry, after having himself derided the poetry they contemned.

i. Shelley and Romantic Platonism

Peacock was also a loyal friend who did not scruple to pillory his friends in his inimitable novels. And it was the Scythrop of *Nightmare Abbey* who sprang to the defense of poetry against Peacock's essay; although, as Shelley good-humoredly wrote to Peacock, his was a championship by 'the knight of the shield of shadow and the lance of gossamere.'[3] But Shelley left his sense of humor behind when he launched into his 'Defence of Poetry' in 1821, and though he opposes the arguments of the 'Four Ages' more systematically and in detail than a cursory reading would indicate, he never quite escapes the disadvantage of one who responds to raillery with a solemn appeal to the eternal verities.

Shelley happened to be reading Plato's *Ion* when he received Peacock's article, and had only recently translated the *Symposium,* as well as portions of some others of the more mythic dialogues. There is more of Plato in the 'Defence' than in any earlier piece of English criticism, even though it is a Plato who has obviously been seen through a vista of Neoplatonic and Renaissance commentators and interpreters. But Shelley was also familiar with the poetic theory of Wordsworth and other contemporaries,[4] had been a close student of the English sensational psychologists, and continued to support the benevolistic ethics that Godwin had adopted from his English predecessors.[5] In the 'Defence' these various traditions remain imperfectly assimilated, so that one can discriminate two planes of thought in Shelley's aesthetics—one Platonistic and mimetic, the other psychological and expressive—applied alternately, as it were, to each of the major topics under discussion. The combination effected a loosely articulated critical theory, no doubt, but resulted also in a set of magnificent passages on the power and the glory of art unmatched by the other apologists for poetry who have succumbed to the allure of the Platonic world-picture, with its radiant Essences behind the fleeting shadows of this world of becoming.

On the level of Platonism, we find Shelley proposing a mimetic theory of the origin of art, in rebuttal to Peacock's unflattering speculation that it is a commodity invented by the bard who is 'always ready to celebrate the strength of [the king's] arm, being first duly inspired by that of his liquor.' 'In the youth of the world,' says Shelley, 'men dance and sing and imitate natural objects, observing in these actions, as in all others, a certain rhythm or order.' This order originates in man's 'faculty of approximation to the beautiful,' and may itself 'be called the beautiful and the good.' [6] The objects imitated by the great poet are the eternal Forms discerned through the veil of fact and particularity. Poetry 'strips the veil of familiarity from the world, and lays bare the naked and sleeping beauty, which is the spirit of its forms.' And the analogue Shelley employs to clarify the relation of imitation to ideal is the standard one of the mirror, conceived, as by many Renaissance Platonists, to reflect the Ideas more accurately than do the particulars of the natural world.

A poem is the very image of life expressed in its eternal truth. . . A story of particular facts is as a mirror which obscures and distorts that which should be beautiful: poetry is a mirror which makes beautiful that which is distorted.[7]

Shelley's essay demonstrates, in its most uncompromising form, the tendency of a Platonic aesthetic to cancel differences, by reducing everything to a single class, and by subjecting this class to a single standard of judgment. Since the realm of Essences is the residence of all modes of value, 'to be a poet is to apprehend the true and the beautiful, in a word, the good'; in consequence, any aesthetic judgment inescapably involves a moral and ontological judgment as well. These several values, in turn, are ultimately the attributes of a single Form of Forms; and Shelley goes beyond Plato and approximates Plotinus, for whom all considerations had been drawn irresistibly into the vortex of the One. 'A poet,' as Shelley puts it, 'participates in the eternal, the infinite, and the one.' [8] Even in the most narrow sense of 'poetry,' defined as representation in the medium of figurative and harmonious language, Shelley employs the word so as to include the writings of Plato, Bacon, and all the 'authors of revolutions in opinion,' as well as Shakespeare, Dante, and Milton.[9] When, on the other hand, poetry is defined in what Shelley calls 'the most universal sense of the word,' it includes all imitations of the realm of Essence, whether in the medium of 'language, colour, form,' or 'religious and civil habits of action.' In this usage, poetry collapses into a single category with all the important human activities and products.

But poets, or those who imagine and express this indestructible order, are not only the authors of language and of music, or the dance, and architecture, and statuary, and painting; they are the institutors of laws, and the founders of civil society, and the inventors of the arts of life, and the teachers, who draw into a certain propinquity with the beautiful and the true, that partial apprehension of the agencies of the invisible world which is called religion.[10]

Plato ironically had set up poets to be competitors of philosopher-statesmen in the art of imitation, 'rivals and antagonists in the noblest of dramas,' but always at an insuperable disadvantage, because the traditional poet operates at two removes from the Forms of things. In Shelley's theory, writers of drama and epic also penetrate to the eternal Forms, hence are no longer inferior rivals of lawmakers and statesmen, but their co-workers and compeers—even their superiors, because the plasticity of poetic language makes it an incomparable medium for reproducing without distortion the 'indestructible order.'[11]

Shelley goes on to give a résumé of the history of poetry and its moral influences, by way of corrective to Peacock's serio-comic account of its progress through the four ages. But the theory of Ideas makes a very blunt instrument for dealing with history. If Platonic literary criticism is a criticism without real distinctions, Platonic literary history is a history essentially without change; for according to this outlook, the poetry of every age, so far as it is truly poetry and not its simulacrum, reapproximates the same unaltering pattern. In Shelley's essay, therefore, all the greatest single poems lose their particular locations in time and place, lose even their identity, and are viewed as though they were fundamentally simultaneous and inter-convertible. Since a poet participates in the eternal and the one,

as far as relates to his conceptions, time and place and number are not. The grammatical forms which express the moods of time, and the difference of persons, and the distinction of place, are convertible with respect to the highest poetry without injuring it as poetry; and the choruses of Aeschylus, and the book of *Job,* and Dante's *Paradise,* would afford, more than any other writings, examples of this fact, if the limits of this essay did not forbid citation. The creations of sculpture, painting, and music, are illustrations still more decisive.[12]

In this general annulment of distinction between the characters in a single poem, between individual poems, between poems and the products of other arts, and between the arts and all other pursuits of men, it is entirely to be expected that the traditional genres of poetry should also fall together. Comedy, for example, no less than tragedy, must be 'universal, ideal, and sublime.' As for tragedy and epic, it is only by a regrettable necessity that they reproduce the vice, the evil, the struggle, and the suffering which are the all-but-gratuitous attributes of the fleeting many, instead of the unalloyed perfection of the One.

But a poet considers the vices of his contemporaries as a temporary dress in which his creations may be arrayed, and which cover without concealing the eternal proportions of their beauty. . . It is doubtful whether the alloy of costume, habit, &c., be not necessary to temper this planetary music for mortal ears.[13]

We could not spare Shelley's essay from our literature, and as, specifically, a *defense* of poetry, it has no rhetorical equal. Its greatness, however, is not of a kind to make it in any important degree useful for the practical criticism of poems. For all its planetary music, has any critical essay of comparable scope and reputation ever contained less of specifically *literary* criticism?

We can also make our way through the 'Defence of Poetry' on another level of discussion; one on which Shelley comes closer to the characteristic ideas and idiom of the critics of his own time. Like the Neoplatonists, Shelley implies that the Ideas have a double subsistence, both behind the veil of the material world and in the minds of men;[14] and this view, we remember, had, in earlier criticism, sometimes resulted in statements that poetry is an expression, as well as an imitation, of Ideas. But in Shelley's version of these opinions, the poet sometimes turns out to express not only Platonic Ideas, but also human passions, and other mental materials, which he describes in the alien psychology of English empiricism.

In the second paragraph of his essay, Shelley defines poetry, 'in a general sense,' as 'the expression of the imagination,' and he pictures the process on the analogy of a wind-harp, with the poetry the combined product of an external impression and an internal adjustment and contribution. In this mode, we get an account of the primitive origin of poetry which is no longer merely mimetic, but resembles that of Blair and Wordsworth by making poetry the product of an emotional response to sensible objects.

The savage . . . expresses the emotions produced in him by surrounding objects in a similar manner; and language and gesture . . . become the image of the combined effect of those objects, and of his apprehension of them. Man in society, with all his passions and his pleasures, next becomes the object of the passions and pleasures of man; an additional class of emotions produces an augmented treasure of expressions; and language, gesture, and the imitative arts, become at once the representation and the medium. . .

That art whose medium is language is of greater excellence than those whose media are color, form, and motion, in part because language, the product of imagination, 'is a more direct representation of the actions and passions of our internal being.' In this context, Shelley, like many of his contemporaries, reverses the aesthetic mirror in order to make it reflect the lamp of the mind: the language of poetry 'is as a mirror which reflects,' but the materials of the other arts 'as a cloud which enfeebles, the light of which both are mediums of communication.' [15]

A combination of Platonism and psychological empiricism, and of the mimetic and expressive point of view, runs all through the 'Defence.' For example, Shelley says that poetry strips the veil from the forms of the world, but a few sentences later, suggests an alternative possibility: 'And whether it spreads its own figured curtain, or withdraws life's dark veil from the scene of things, it equally creates for us a being within our being.' [16] The greatest poems (including Dante's *Paradiso*), all mirroring the universal Forms, are interconvertible; yet each also mirrors its particular author, so that the writings of Dante and Milton 'are merely the mask and the mantle in which these great poets walk through eternity enveloped and disguised.' [17] The 'imagination,' of which poetry is the product and expression, is the mental organ for intuiting 'those forms which are common to universal nature and existence itself.' It is also said to be the 'principle of synthesis,' and in its genesis and activity, this faculty turns out to resemble closely the 'sympathetic imagination' developed by the empirical and associationistic moralists of eighteenth-century England to explain how an individual can conceive an identity with other individuals. Shelley describes the poet as envisioning his Ideas in isolation from an audience, like a nightingale who 'sings to cheer its own solitude'; nevertheless, the effect of his poetry is centrally moral, because it enlarges and strengthens 'the great instrument of moral good'—that sympathetic imagination by which man puts himself 'in the place of another and of many others.' In the process of creation, the poet is held to ascend to the 'eternal regions' for his materials; but his inspiration is also explained in psychological terms as the result of 'evanescent visitations of thought and feeling,' and as an emergence from the subliminal depths of the creative mind itself. Finally, Shelley describes beautifully the process by which subject matter is transformed into poetry, in a metaphor for expression we have not met with heretofore:

[Poetry] arrests the vanishing apparitions which haunt the interlunations of life, and veiling them, or in language or in form, sends them forth among mankind, bearing sweet news of kindred joy to those with whom their sisters abide—abide, because there is no portal of expression from the caverns of the spirit which they inhabit into the universe of things.[18]

Distant and devious products of Platonic Ideas and the Platonic cosmos also make their appearance in other aesthetic commentaries of the period. 'No Man of Sense,' wrote William Blake, 'can think that an Imitation of the Objects of Nature is the Art of Painting.' Like poetry and music, painting must be elevated from 'facsimile representations of merely mortal and perishing substances . . . into its own proper sphere of invention and vision-ary conception.' This 'Vision or Imagination is a Representation of what Eternally Exists, Really & Unchangeably,' and constitutes 'in that Eternal World the Permanent Realities of Every Thing which we see reflected in this Vegetable Glass of Nature.'[19] In his 'On Poesy or Art,' modeled on an essay of Schelling's, Coleridge employed the Neoplatonic concept of the *natura naturans,* a dynamic principle which operates not only behind the particulars of the external world, but also in the mind of man. The artist must copy, not the *natura naturata,* but the essence 'which is within the thing.' The co-presence of the Ideas of art both in mind and nature, how-ever, opened the way to Coleridge for a display of dialectical virtuosity. Since to copy the *'Naturgeist,* or spirit of nature,' is equivalent to externaliz-ing one's own 'living and life-producing ideas,' Coleridge in the space of a few pages can describe poetry as an 'imitatress of nature,' as an art 'to express' elements 'which have their origin in the human mind,' and as 'a reconcile-ment of the external with the internal.'[20] By the fitful light of Carlyle's rhetoric, we can sometimes discern a remotely kindred cosmology; and here, as in Shelley, the Platonic scheme serves to cancel any essential distinction between poets and all the other great agents on the stage of the world. The hero-poet, together with the man-gods, prophets, priests, and kings, lives 'in the True, Divine and Eternal, which exists always, unseen to most, under the Temporary, Trivial.' Carlyle follows approvingly Fichte's exposition of the true literary man as a priest teaching all men 'that all "Appearance," whatsoever we see in the world, is but as a vesture for the "Divine Idea of the World," for "that which lies at the bottom of Appearance."'[21]

We may, in conclusion, notice an article, 'Real and Ideal Beauty,' which appeared anonymously in *Blackwood's Magazine* for 1853. The author founds his theory on Plato's 'system of beauty of which little is now known, and still less is understood.' He discards the earlier theories that the ideal is 'an average of humanity,' or the eclectic choice of 'the best points out of a multitude of fine forms,' and he vigorously renounces the sensationism of Locke and the associationist aesthetics of his own time.[22] Ideal beauty springs 'not from any mere inspection of external particulars, but from . . . a discernment of the true ideas of form with which the human mind is itself endowed'—ideas which appear as 'image after image in the mirror of the phantasy or imagination.'[23] When he comes to describe the process of artistic composition, however, the author conceives of it on the analogue of the creation of the universe; and now his model is not the Demiurge of Plato's *Timaeus,* who copied the world from an unchanging pattern, but rather the Absolute of Plotinus, who generated the world by a process of endless self-emanation. The One, Plotinus had said, 'being perfect . . . overflows, and thus its superabundance produces an Other.' Similarly, now, with the poet:

Creation, with Genius, is an expansion, a flowing-forth, of the soul—when it takes heed of nothing but its own promptings, and bounds along without thinking how it goes. . . [The mind] is melting all her ideas into one golden stream, which she pours forth with a joy that takes note of nothing but itself.[24]

Hence, this intended Platonic theory of poetic creation, by adopting the root-metaphor of Plotinus' philosophy, ends in a close metaphoric parallelism with Wordsworth's naturalistic doctrine of the spontaneous overflow of powerful feeling.

ii. Longinus, Hazlitt, Keats, and the Criterion of Intensity

To the extent that he placed preponderant emphasis on the great conceptions and vehement passion of the author, rather than on the other and more 'artful' sources of sublimity, Longinus adumbrated in classical times the conceptual pattern which underlies the typical romantic theory of poetry in general. Within this frame, an aspect of Longinian theory is worth singling out, because at the hands of certain critics of the early nineteenth century it was converted into one of the most familiar modern criteria of aesthetic value.

In Longinus' treatment, sublimity is said to be the product of an inspired moment of passion, rather than of cool and sustained calculation. It follows that: (1) This highest quality of style invests only a short passage of verse and prose, as against 'skill in invention, and due order and arrangement' which emerge 'as the hard-won result not of one thing nor of two, but of the whole texture of the composition.' Accordingly, Longinus' instances of sublimity range only from a single phrase or sentence—'Let there be light, and there was light'—to short passages from Sappho, Homer, and Demosthenes. (2) This fragment bursts suddenly upon the auditor, with an effect of intensity, shock, and illumination: 'flashing forth at the right moment,' sublimity 'scatters everything before it like a thunderbolt.' The sublimity of Demosthenes, for example, is characterized by 'speed, power, and intensity,' and 'may be compared to a thunderbolt or flash of lightning.' (3) We auditors recognize the sublime not by an act of analytic or comparative judgment, but by our transport (*ekstasis*), and by 'the spell it throws over us.' [25]

The tendency to isolate a supremely poetic quality—'pure poetry,' the 'poetry of a poem'—and to locate this quality in the electrifying and transporting image or passage, rather than in the larger aspects of plot or design, is visible in all eighteenth-century critics who felt strongly the impact of Longinus. To choose a relatively late example: in assessing the position of Pope as a poet, Joseph Warton discriminates 'Pure Poetry,' the result of 'a creative and glowing IMAGINATION,' from the lesser products of wit and sense. It is, among other things, because Pope, having stifled his imagination and 'poetical enthusiasm,' 'does not frequently ravish and transport his reader' that he is placed in a rank below Homer and Milton, of whom it can be said 'that no man of a true poetical spirit, *is master of himself while he reads them.*' [26]

To such contemporary attempts to derogate Pope, Johnson countered with the question, 'If Pope be not a poet, where is poetry to be found?' [27] By 1825, however, the editor of the Oxford edition of Johnson's *Works,* though otherwise sympathetic to his author, felt constrained to use an expanded form of Warton's criteria in order to define the limits of Johnson's own critical sensibility:

With respect to Johnson's powers as a critic, we confess that he had but little natural taste for poetry, as such; for that poetry of emotion which produces in its cultivators . . . an intensity of excitement, to which language can scarcely afford an utterance, to which art can give no body, and which spreads a dream and a glory around us. All this Johnson felt not, and, therefore, understood not; for he wanted that deep feeling which is the only sure and unerring test of poetic excellence. He sought the didactic in poetry, and wished for reasoning in numbers.[28]

'Intensity,' which has since come to rival, and sometimes supersede, older terms like 'nature,' 'truth,' and 'universality' as a first order criterion for poetic value, would appear to be a romantic development from the tradition of *Peri Hypsous*. In this passage we find that norm clearly emerging, together with other tenets, easily evolved from Longinian elements, all of which have since become equally familiar: that by a stroke beyond the reach of art 'poetry, as such' expresses a mode of feeling which is all but ineffable; that its primary appeal is not to the judgment, but the sensibility; and that its effect is suggestive and hypnotic, leaving the reader in a state of mind resembling a dream.

Reference of poetry to supreme moments of unsustainable feeling and imaginative impetus made it common for romantic theorists to focus upon the short and incandescent passage as the manifestation of poetry at its highest. 'When composition begins,' Shelley declared, 'inspiration is already on the decline,' and poets must fill the gaps between the incandescent moments by an 'intertexture of conventional expressions.' [29] Aristotle had said that plot is the soul of tragedy, but Coleridge held that 'Passion must be [the] Soul of Poetry'; or alternatively, that the imagination is 'the SOUL that is everywhere' in a work of poetic genius. Coleridge emphasizes the organic integration effected by the imagination, and specifically denies that the proportion of 'striking passages' is 'a fair criterion of poetic excellence.' His definition of poetry as the product of 'the whole soul of man' in action, however, leads to the claim that 'a poem of any length neither can be, or ought to be, all poetry,' but merely 'in keeping' with the transcendant passages; [30] and his specific examples of imaginative poetry range only from a couplet in *Venus and Adonis* through the storm scene in *King Lear*. In a fashion going far beyond Coleridge, the poetic quotations and anthologies of De Quincey, Lamb, and Hunt give evidence of an almost total fragmentation of poetic works into supernal lines, excerpts, and scenes.

William Hazlitt's favorite criterion, 'gusto,' involves a flash of intensity in both the artist's conception and effect. Thus, 'Milton had as much of what is meant by *gusto* as any poet. He forms the most intense conception of things, and then embodies them by a single stroke of his pen. Force of style is perhaps his first excellence.' [31] Hazlitt's theory and practice, more than that of any of his fellow critics, also demonstrates another derivation from the Longinian emphasis on critical responsiveness and 'enthrallment,' rather than judgment. Hazlitt typically applies his criticism, not to the analysis of design, ordonnance, and the inter-relations of parts, but to the representation in words of the aesthetic qualities and feeling-tones of a work of art. 'In art, in taste, in life, in speech, you decide from feeling, and not from reason; that is, from the impression of a number of things on the mind, which impression is true and well-founded, though you may not be able to analyze or account for it in the several particulars.' In his essay 'On Criticism,' Hazlitt renounces both the 'modern or metaphysical school of criticism,' which 'supposes the question, *Why?* to be repeated at the end of every decision,' and 'the dry and meagre mode of dissecting the skeletons of works' of the older school.

A genuine criticism should, as I take it, reflect the colours, the light and shade, the soul and body of a work:—here we have nothing but its superficial plan and elevation. . . We know every thing about the work, and nothing of it. The critic takes good care not to baulk the reader's fancy by anticipating the effect which the author has aimed at producing.[32]

The critic, then, in place of analysis and an inquiry into causes, undertakes to formulate a verbal equivalent for the aesthetic effects of the work under consideration. Longinus had long ago indicated how this might be done, in passages such as that which defines the quality of the *Odyssey* by means of the extended similes of the setting sun and the ebbing tide. Gibbon, for one, had described the novelty in Longinus' way 'of criticizing a beautiful passage'—'He tells me his own feelings upon reading it; and tells them with such energy, that he communicates them.'[33] Hazlitt gives frequent and striking examples of his more elaborate and subtle attempts to capture in words what he calls 'the true and general impressions of things,' by the use of comparisons to other sense-experiences, and even to other sense-modalities. As an example, here is a small part of his critique of two paintings by Titian. Either picture

is like a divine piece of music, or rises 'like an exhalation of rich distilled perfumes.' In the figures, in the landscape, in the water, in the sky, there are tones, colours . . . woven together into a woof like that of Iris. . . There is not a distinct line in the picture—but a gusto, a rich taste of colour is left upon the eye as if it were the palate, and the diapason of picturesque harmony is full to overflowing.[34]

We are well on the way to critical impressionism: to Pater's declaration that the first step in criticism 'is to know one's impression as it really is,' and to such examples of the method as the critical prose-poem by which he conveys his impression of the Mona Lisa.

Keats, who found Hazlitt's 'depth of taste' one of the three things to rejoice at in his age, and who unmistakably followed Hazlitt as his guide in literary speculation, emphasized more than any of his contemporaries the image-and-intensity aspect of the Longinian heritage. 'I look upon fine Phrases like a Lover,' he said, referring to Shakespeare's dramas and Milton's *Paradise Lost*. Charles Cowden Clarke has fixed forever the picture of Keats reading: how his 'features and exclamations were ecstatic' at 'the more passionate passages' of Spenser's *Epithalamion,* and how, as he went 'ramping' through the *Faerie Queene,* 'he especially singled out epithets' for their 'felicity and power.' [35] Keats maintained specifically that 'the excellence of every art is its *intensity*'; and although Longinus was probably not known to him at first hand, the three poetic axioms he announced to the publisher of his *Endymion* read like a gloss upon some doctrines of *Peri Hypsous:* '1st. I think Poetry should surprise by a fine excess and not by Singularity—it should strike the Reader as a wording of his own highest thoughts, and appear almost a Remembrance.' (Longinus had said that at contact with the true sublime our soul 'is filled with joy and vaunting, as though it had itself produced what it has heard.') '2nd. Its touches of Beauty should never be half way thereby making the reader breathless rather than content . . . and this leads me to another axiom. That if Poetry comes not as naturally as the Leaves to a tree it had better not come at all.' [36]

In answer to Hunt's question, 'Why endeavour after a long Poem?', Keats justified the sustained poetic effort, but in such a way as to exhibit still his proclivity for fragments that come on one with a fine suddenness. 'Do not the Lovers of Poetry like to have a little Region to wander in where they may pick and choose, and in which the images are so numerous that many are forgotten and found new in a second Reading?' [37] In 1838, however, John Stuart Mill asserted flatly that all genuine poems must be 'short poems; it being impossible that a feeling so intense . . . should sustain itself at its highest elevation for long together . . . a long poem will always be felt . . . to be something unnatural and hollow. . .' [38] In the extremity to which this view was pressed by Edgar Allan Poe a decade later, a long poem becomes 'simply a flat contradiction in terms,' and the 'absolute effect of even the best epic under the sun, is a nullity. . .' Poe's line of reasoning, based on intensity as the defining quality of poetry, is by now familiar to us. 'It is needless to demonstrate that a poem is such, only inasmuch as it intensely excites, by elevating, the soul; and all intense excitements are, through a psychal necessity, brief.' Brevity, in fact, must, within limits, 'be in direct ratio to the intensity of the intended effect'; and this effect is further defined as involving 'suggestiveness,' and as 'thrilling us to the soul.' According to Poe, 'Beauty is the sole legitimate province of the poem'; his use of 'beauty,' even more plainly than that of Keats, is in the lineage of Longinus' 'sublime,' in its literal meaning of 'elevation.'

When, indeed, men speak of Beauty, they mean, precisely, not a quality, as is supposed, but an effect—they refer, in short, just to that intense and pure elevation of *soul—not* of intellect, or heart—upon which I have commented. . .[39]

However widely they differ in other ways, Longinian critics, from John Dennis on, who appeal to elevation of soul and to quintessential passages as the chief test for poetry, seem to unite in an antipathy to the writings of Pope. Matthew Arnold, for example: In his Preface to the Poems of 1853, Arnold had appealed to Aristotle's discussion of poetry as an imitation of an action, in order to attack both modern subjectivism and the tendency to judge poetry by its parts, rather than by the whole—by its 'separate thoughts and images,' its 'brilliant things,' and the turns of expression 'which thrill the reader with a sudden delight.'[40] But in his later criticism, he himself emphasized 'the grand style'—Longinus' sublimity, as interpreted with the help of Joshua Reynolds' *Discourses*—which 'is the last matter in the world for verbal definition to deal with adequately'; 'one must feel it in order to know what it is.'[41] Arnold's basic essay, 'The Study of Poetry' (1880), employs a measuring stick for poetry which is calibrated primarily in characterological terms—'high seriousness,' 'largeness, freedom, shrewdness, benignity,' and so on—but he supplemented this scale of value by a recourse to touchstones for detecting 'high poetic quality' in general. For such a purpose, 'short passages, even single lines, will serve our turn quite sufficiently'; and the reason for Arnold's preference of concrete passages over abstract analyses is that the attributes of 'a high quality of poetry' are 'far better recognized by being felt in the verse of the master, than by being perused in the prose of the critic.' Joseph Warton had remained content to call Pope a poet, even though only a 'Poet of Reason'; but by applying the touchstone of

Absent thee from felicity awhile . . .

Arnold concludes that Pope and Dryden are not properly poets at all, but 'classics of our prose.'[42] In the writings of immoderate critics, the intense poetic fragment becomes explosive. 'If I feel physically as if the top of my head were taken off,' said Emily Dickinson, 'I know that it is poetry.'[43]

A. E. Housman, in corroborating Arnold's low estimate of eighteenth-century verse, demonstrated that he also belonged among the left-wingers in the Longinian tradition. We recognize the ancient hallmarks of the approach. The highest poetry is 'lofty or magnificent or intense,' it transports with rapture, and shakes the soul. 'Poems very seldom consist of poetry and nothing else,' for 'that thrilling utterance' is usually combined with other ingredients which give a non-poetic kind of pleasure. Housman concludes that he cannot define poetry except by its effect—or as he puts it, 'by the symptoms which it provokes in us'—and these symptoms turn out to be a physical, or even a physiological, syndrome: a bristling of the skin, a precipitation of water to the eyes, and a sensation like a spear through the pit of the stomach.[44]

iii. Poetry as Catharsis: John Keble and Others

Latent in the term 'expression' is the notion of something that is forced out by a pressure from within. The alternative metaphor, 'overflow,' by suggesting the fluid nature of feeling, also involves a question in regard to the hydrodynamics of the poetic process. It was to be expected that some romantic critics should find the impulse to composition in the pressure of pent-up feeling, or in the urgency of unfulfilled desires. And naturally enough, Aristotle's description of the cathartic effect of tragedy upon the pity and fear of its auditors was generalized to include all emotions in all forms of poetry, and silently shifted to denote the healing expenditure of feeling in the poet himself.

That emotions exert a kind of psychic pressure, and that their suppression is morbid and their verbal expression a therapeutic measure, had long been a maxim in folk-psychology. 'Give sorrow words,' Malcolm counseled Macduff,

> the grief that does not speak
> Whispers the o'er fraught heart and bids it break.

The Elizabethan critic, George Puttenham, applied this concept to explain one kind of lyric, the 'forme of poetical lamentations,' as an homeopathic remedy by which the poet plays physician to his auditors, 'making the very greef it selfe (in part) cure of the disease.'[45] In the latter part of the eighteenth century, poets began to testify that, in their experience, diverse kinds of literary composition served them as a personal therapy. Burns wrote in 1787 that 'my Passions . . . raged like so many devils, till they got vent in rhyme; and then conning over my verses, like a spell, soothed all into quiet.'[46] To reassure George and Georgiana Keats against taking fright at his wooing of easeful death in the sonnet, 'Why did I laugh tonight?' Keats wrote them that after composing the poem, 'I went to bed, and enjoyed an uninterrupted Sleep. Sane I went to bed and sane I arose.'[47] Byron declared that 'it comes over me in a kind of rage every now and then . . . and then, if I don't write to empty my mind, I go mad.' He did not hesitate to extend his private experience to poets in general. Poetry

is the lava of the imagination whose eruption prevents an earthquake. They say poets never or rarely go mad . . . but are generally so near it that I cannot help thinking rhyme is so far useful in anticipating and preventing the disorder.[48]

Related to this view is the concept that the compulsion to poetry lies in the disproportion between man's desires, or man's ideals, and the world of reality. Aristotle, defining poetry as imitation, had attributed its origin merely to the human instinct for mimicry, and for taking delight in the imitations of others.[49] Longinus, on the other hand, set current the suggestion that writers who achieve sublimity are activated by the fact that 'not even the entire universe suffices for the thought and contemplation within the reach of the human mind. . .'[50] The most important document in this development was Francis Bacon's *Advancement of Learning*. The use of 'fained historie,' or narrative and dramatic fiction, 'hath been to give some shadowe of satisfaction to the minde of Man in those points wherein the Nature of things doth denie it.' That the poet has the power to reform nature, delivering a golden for a brazen world, had been a commonplace of Renaissance criticism. What Bacon added to this concept was a theory of the dynamics of the idealizing process, in the compelling desires of man for 'a more ample Greatness, a more exact Goodnesse, and a more absolute varietie then can bee found in the Nature of things.' These desires remould the shadows of things when reality proves recalcitrant:

And therefore [Poesie] was ever thought to have some participation of divinesse, because it doth raise and erect the Minde, by submitting the shewes of things to the desires of the Mind, whereas reason doth buckle and bowe the Minde unto the Nature of things.[51]

Some eighteenth-century critics tended to merge the statements of Longinus and Bacon into a single doctrine. As Richard Hurd said, 'fiction,' which is essential to poetry, is to be ascribed to 'something in the mind of man, sublime and elevated, which prompts it to overlook all obvious and familiar appearances, and to feign to itself other and more extraordinary. . . . ' [52] In this period, however, all theories of this kind were strictly qualified. The desires that may validly shape the matter of poetry are those common to all men, and are restricted to the noble modes of aggrandizing, beautifying, moralizing, and multiplying the variety of given nature. In one fashion, indeed, men of this age conceived the imagination to picture the fictional satisfactions for all kinds of desires, whether general or personal, noble or ignominious—in the activity they sometimes called castle-building, and we call wishful thinking. Dr. Johnson, for one, was acutely aware of the immense disproportion between what a man wants and what he is likely to get, and of the strength of the impulse to make up the difference in phantasy; this observation is the theme of many of his best writings in verse and prose. 'The Dangerous Prevalence of Imagination,' he says, exhibits itself in revery, when a man 'must find pleasure in his own thoughts, and must conceive himself what he is not; for who is pleased with what he is?'

He then expatiates in boundless futurity, and culls from all imaginable conditions that which for the present moment he should most desire, amuses his desires with impossible enjoyments, and confers upon his pride unattainable dominion.[53]

Johnson, of course, had no intention of applying his analysis of the imagination in wish-fulfillment to the valid play of this faculty in poetry. In that province, its function is to exemplify truth in an imaginative instance, for 'poetry is the art of uniting pleasure with truth, by calling imagination to the help of reason.' [54] To find a conflation of the sources of art and the daydream we must look ahead to certain critics of the romantic generation.

William Hazlitt defined poetry in general as 'the natural impression of any object or event . . . exciting an involuntary movement of imagination and passion, and producing, by sympathy, a certain modulation of the voice, or sounds, expressing it.' It is 'the language of the imagination and the passions,' or alternatively, it is 'natural imagery or feeling, combined with passion and fancy.' [55] Tragedy, no less expressive than the lyric, is 'the most impassioned species' of poetry. And in the narrative form, Dante 'interests by exciting our sympathy with the emotion by which he is himself possessed'; his great power 'is in combining internal feelings with external objects.' [56]

One of Hazlitt's contributions to the expressive theory of poetry stems from his persistent interest in the impulses, the inner forces which compel human action, including the creation of poetry. A salient aspect of the romantic era in general was the sharpened 'Inner Sense,' as Coleridge called it, for the goings-on of the mind, and a new power, by those poets and critics who are 'accustomed to watch the flux and reflux of their inmost nature, to venture at times into the twilight realms of consciousness.' [57] Coleridge himself had no equal as a microscopic analyst of the interplay of sensation, thought, and feeling in the immediate cross-section, or 'fact of mind.' Hazlitt differed from Coleridge in that his psychological occupation was less with the nuances of a mental event than with its springs and motives, and particularly, with the secret motives, hidden from the world, and sometimes from the agent himself.

Hazlitt's chief complaint against the current psychology of rationalism and of hedonistic calculus was its failure to take into account the complex urgencies underlying behavior. Bentham, he said, 'has not allowed for the wind.' 'We are the creatures of imagination, passion, and self-will more than of reason or even of self-interest.' [58] In his own theory, Hazlitt, who had set out in his youth to be a philosopher, amalgamated Hobbes's principle that the power-drive is the prime human motive with La Rochefoucauld's readiness to look for the Ego hidden behind the curtain. His paper 'On Depth and Superficiality,' published in *The Plain Speaker,* may be recommended as a demonstration. In it Hazlitt lays bare 'the intricate folds and delicate involutions of our self-love'; points to the hunger for 'power,' or 'downright love of pain and mischief for the interest it excites,' as 'the root of all the evil, and the original sin of human nature'; and adumbrates the mental mechanisms of suppression and hidden conflict in describing the 'obscure and intricate way' in which 'unconscious impressions necessarily give a colour to, and re-act upon our conscious ones.' [59] In his essay 'On Dreams,' we find a neat epitome of the Freudian concepts of the repression of unwelcome desires, and the partial release of unconscious thought in sleep.

We may sometimes discover our tacit, and almost unconscious sentiments, with respect to persons and things in the same way. We are not hypocrites in our sleep. The curb is taken off from our passions, and our imagination wanders at will. When awake, we check these rising thoughts, and fancy we have them not. In dreams, when we are off our guard, they return securely and unbidden. . . Infants cannot disguise their thoughts from others; and in sleep we reveal the secret to ourselves.[60]

In numerous passages, Hazlitt surrenders the poetic imagination, like the imagination of the dreamer, to the motive power of unrealized desires.

In the essay 'On Poetry in General,' into which he crammed all the odds and ends of his poetic speculation, he makes the point that

> if poetry is a dream, the business of life is much the same. If it is a fiction, made up of what we wish things to be, and fancy that they are, because we wish them so, there is no other nor better reality.

Hazlitt then characteristically misquotes from memory Bacon's explanation of poetry as 'conforming the shows of things to the desires of the soul,' and interprets this doctrine in a way that eliminates the earlier restriction of poetry to the desires for more grandeur, variety, and morality than the real world affords. 'We shape things according to our wishes and fancies, without poetry; but poetry is the most emphatical language that can be found for those creations of the mind "which ecstasy is very cunning in." ' [61] Elsewhere he writes that 'poets live in an ideal world, where they make everything out according to their wishes and fancies.' He even suggests that one impulse to art is the need to compensate for a physical defect. Thus Byron's 'miss-shapen feet' contributed to his genius; they 'made him write verses in revenge.'

> There is no knowing the effect of such sort of things, of defects we wish to balance. Do you suppose we owe nothing to Pope's deformity? He said to himself, 'If my person be crooked, my verses shall be strait.' [62]

To this theory, that at least some literature is a form of *Wunschbild,* Hazlitt adds the doctrine that it provides an emotional catharsis for its author. Rousseau had already confessed that *La Nouvelle Héloïse* originated in the compulsive daydreams in which he compensated for his frustrations as a lover,[63] and Goethe was soon to describe in *Dichtung und Wahrheit* how his youthful despairs and disappointments had transformed themselves into *Die Leiden des jungen Werthers,* which he wrote in four weeks 'almost unconsciously, like a somnambulist.' 'I felt, as if after a general confession, once more happy and free, and justified in beginning a new life.' [64] Hazlitt himself, in his complex and tangled personality, was strongly subject to the impulse for public confession. In his *Liber Amoris,* he poured out the humiliating details of his unrequited passion for the coquettish daughter of his lodging-house keeper, not, as in *Werther* or *The New Héloïse,* transformed into fiction, but under the sole and readily penetrated disguise of anonymity.[65] Why, Hazlitt asks in his essay 'On Poetry in General,' are we 'as prone to make a torment of our fears, as to luxuriate in our hopes of good?' The answer is, 'Because we cannot help it. The

sense of power is as strong a principle in the mind as the love of pleasure.'
Under the heading of 'the sense of power,' Hazlitt elaborates the concept,
which has since become a familiar element in expressive theories, of the
capacity of art to master, by objectifying, the chaotic press of emotion. 'This
is equally the origin of wit and fancy, of comedy and tragedy, of the sublime and pathetic.' In all these forms, the motive is the relief that attends
upon our identifying and making conscious, and, therefore, manageable, the
importunity of unarticulated feelings and desires.

The imagination, by thus embodying and turning them to shape, gives an obvious relief to the indistinct and importunate cravings of the will.—We do not
wish the thing to be so; but we wish it to appear such as it is. For knowledge
is conscious power; and the mind is no longer, in this case, the dupe, though it
may be the victim of vice or folly.[66]

Hazlitt's exposition of 'the sense of power' may have contributed to De
Quincey's well-known distinction between 'the literature of power' and 'the
literature of knowledge' which he substituted for Wordsworth's distinction
between 'poetry' and 'matter of fact, or science.' In the third of his *Letters
to a Young Man* (1823), in which he first expanded upon his thesis, De
Quincey gave credit to Wordsworth himself for this, 'as for most of the
sound criticism of poetry.'[67] But De Quincey's description of the communication of power as the occasion on which one is 'made to feel vividly,
and with a vital consciousness, emotions which . . . had previously lain un-
awakened, and hardly within the dawn of consciousness' suggests, rather,
Hazlitt's 'On Poetry in General,' published only five years before. Under
the influence of the traditional theory of rhetoric, in which De Quincey
prided himself on being adept, he based the initial antithesis between the
literature of knowledge and that of power on the relation of utterance to
hearer: 'The function of the first is—to *teach;* the function of the second
is—to *move;* the first is a rudder; the second, an oar or a sail.'[68] In his
essay on 'Style,' however, De Quincey substituted for this distinction the
German antithesis between subjective and objective writing, and described
the discrimination and objectification of feeling as a process in the writer
himself. In his characteristic eddyings and dallyings with the subject, De
Quincey (whose reputation as a critical theorist is over-inflated) succeeds
in muddying the already turbid distinction. Subjective writing turns out to
include the extraordinary combination of theology, geometry, metaphysics,
and 'meditative poetry'; while the natural sciences are classed with Homeric

poetry as forms of objective writing. But De Quincey's analysis of the nature of literary subjectivity is worth quoting:

In very many subjective exercises . . . the problem before the writer is to project his own inner mind; to bring out consciously what yet lurks by involution in many unanalysed feelings; in short, to pass through a prism and radiate into distinct elements what previously had been even to himself but dim and confused ideas inter-mixed with each other. . . Detention or conscious arrest is given to the evanescent, external projection to what is internal, outline to what is fluxionary, and body to what is vague. . .[69]

De Quincey allows for the existence of an objective kind of poetry; and Hazlitt, although he gives an important role to personal desires in shaping the poetic design, insists that the terminal product must be particularized and concrete, and holds that the intensity of the poet's emotional response is a condition for his grasping and realizing the essential qualities and sensuous particulars of the world without. He also joins this theory to a denunciation of contemporary poets (including Wordsworth and Byron) who depart from tradition in writing about themselves rather than about other men and things, and so express personal moods and feelings without finding for them, as we might now say, an objective correlative:

The great fault of a modern school of poetry is, that it is an experiment to reduce poetry to a mere effusion of natural sensibility; or what is worse, to divest it both of imaginary splendour and human passion, to surround the meanest objects with the morbid feelings and devouring egotism of the writers' own minds. Milton and Shakespeare did not so understand poetry.[70]

One writer of the romantic period, however, made no distinction between objective and subjective poetry, or between expression and self-expression. Everything, in fact, that earlier critics had conjectured about the emotional dynamics and therapeutic function of poetic composition was but a prelude to the amplification given this theme in the criticism of the Reverend John Keble.

Keble revised and published in 1844, under the title *De poeticae vi medica*, the lectures he had delivered from the Chair of Poetry at Oxford between the years 1832-41. The lectures were delivered in Latin, according to the tradition that persisted until the incumbency of Matthew Arnold, and their somewhat bravura quality is emphasized by the lecturer's device of setting off a lyric of Robert Burns from its Latin context by translating it into Theocritan Greek. Keble dedicated his book, in terms most laudatory, to William Wordsworth. In addition to his many echoes of Wordsworth's criticism in detail, his basic theory is in considerable part a single-minded exploitation of Wordsworth's principle of poetry as the spontaneous overflow of feeling; although this principle is joined by Keble to ideas from quite different sources, and interpreted in a way Wordsworth had never intended. The book has received remarkably scant attention, even after its translation into English by E. K. Francis in 1912. Yet, if we take into account the authoritative position from which they were voiced, Keble's *Lectures* must surely be regarded as, under their pious and diffident surface, the most sensationally radical criticism of their time. They broach views of the source, the function, and the effect of literature, and of the methods by which literature is appropriately read and criticized, which, when they occur in the writings of critics schooled by Freud, are still reckoned to be the most subversive to the established values and principles of literary criticism.

Keble's most compendious statement of his position is the definition of poetry he proposed in a review of Lockhart's *Life of Scott,* written while he was in the process of delivering his Oxford lectures.

Poetry is the indirect expression in words, most appropriately in metrical words, of some overpowering emotion, or ruling taste, or feeling, the direct indulgence whereof is somehow repressed.[71]

In his *Lectures on Poetry,* he supports this position by pointing to the origin of poetry in the passionate outcries of savages, and validates this speculation, in the cavalier fashion of eighteenth-century primitivists, by quoting instances of 'primitive' song indiscriminately from the Hebrew, Old Norse, Lappish, Polynesian, and North American Indian, all having their origin in 'the desire to relieve thoughts that could not be controlled.'[72] All the arts, including music, sculpture, and architecture, are linked by expressing feeling in diverse media; thus, 'the poetry of painting simply consists in the apt expression of the artist's own feeling. . .'[73]

From the same point of departure, that poetry 'gives healing relief to secret mental emotion,' Keble goes on, in a way that 'has occurred to no one, as far as I know,' to reorder drastically the poetic kinds. First, he distinguishes between the class of primary poets 'who, spontaneously moved by impulse, resort to composition for relief and solace of a burdened or over-wrought mind,' and the worthy but lowly class of secondary poets who 'imitate the ideas, the expression, and the measures of the former.' Within the province of primary poetry, 'it will follow that there will be as many and as many kinds of poems as there are emotions of the human mind.'[74]

By this stroke of logic, Keble hurls down the structure of the genres which, with relatively minor modifications and exceptions, had endured as a corner-stone of criticism from Aristotle through the neo-classic period. For the mimetic and pragmatic differentiations based on the subjects imitated, the means and manner of imitation, and the kind of effects to be achieved in the audience, he substitutes a simple classification based on the mental dispositions and emotions which a poem expresses. This classification, he tells us, is adapted from Quintilian's rhetorical distinction between *pathos* and *ethos*. *Ethos,* as Keble interprets it, is a matter of long-term character traits; *pathos* is a passing impulse of feeling, short, intense, and overpowering.[75] Under the expression of *pathos,* Keble groups the traditional forms of lyric, elegy, and some modes of satire; under the rubric of *ethos* he includes the epic, dramatic, and narrative forms (produced by poets who by nature are 'fond of action'), as well as georgics and eclogues (produced by those dominated by a love for 'restful things, the country, or quiet pursuits'). And as the emotional lyric forms had most exercised eighteenth-century critics who attempted to demonstrate that all poetry is imitation, so now tragedy and epic, the extended presentations of men in action, prove least amenable, Keble admits, to his attempt to ground poetry in 'the surging unrest of a passionate spirit.' His solution depends mainly on showing that these expanded forms are projected equivalents of *ethos,* or the deep-rooted and persistent sentiments and needs that compose the poet's permanent character.

We see, therefore, that there is nothing irrational in the contention that even an Epic may serve the purpose of the most fervid poet and soothe deep-rooted and vital yearning.

. . . [Such poems] reflect the character of a lifetime, and tastes which have become familiar to the mind by long association.[76]

The thesis that poetry is the imagined fulfillment of ungratified personal desire—which had appeared as an erratic but recurrent suggestion in what De Quincey described as the 'abrupt, insulated, capricious and . . . non-sequacious' course of Hazlitt's criticism [77]—is at the heart of Keble's poetic theory. The play of poetic imagination, he says, 'paints all things in the hues which the mind itself desires.' Nothing, in fact, is felt to be 'touched with poetic feeling' which 'does not by some refined consolation appease a yearning desire which for the present is denied satisfaction.' [78] And for Keble, very much as for Byron, poetry, in the last analysis, is a release of the affects in words, affording relief from threatening inner pressures. In place of Byron's volcano, however, Keble introduces the less spectacular mechanical analogy (modeled, he says, on the ancient notion that poetic inspiration is a form of insanity) of 'a safety-valve, preserving men from actual madness.' [79]

Keble's chief importance, historically considered, is in his thesis that there is a conflict of motives in poetic creation, and in his view that poetry is, therefore, not a direct, but a disguised form of self-expression. This concept, as Keble says, 'is the very pivot on which our whole theory turns.' [80] The impulse to express one's emotions is 'repressed,' in Keble's term, 'by an instinctive delicacy which recoils from exposing them openly, as feeling that they never can meet with full sympathy.' [81] There ensues a conflict in poets between the need for relief on the one side, and the 'noble and natural' requirements of reticence and shame on the other; a conflict which threatens 'their mental balance.' Poetry is a divinely bestowed medicine because, by means of 'those indirect methods best known to poets,' it is able to satisfy opposed motives by giving 'healing relief to secret mental emotion, yet without detriment to modest reserve.' It is, therefore, 'the art which under certain veils and disguises . . . reveals the fervent emotions of the mind.' [82]

It may seem odd that this radical, proto-Freudian theory, which conceives literature as disguised wish-fulfillment, serving the artist as a way back from incipient neurosis, should come out of the doubly conservative environment of High-Anglicanism and the Oxford Chair of Poetry. But the very fact that Keble was more a theologian than a critic goes far to explain the nature of his poetics. Ideas, which in theology have become matter of course and inert, may become alive and drastically innovative when transferred— as Keble patently transferred them—into the alien soil of aesthetics. Keble himself gives us the clue to the source of his formulas, in his frequent allusions to poetry as something near allied to religion, almost a sacrament. He compares the motive for veiled self-expression in poetry to the instinct that made the Fathers of the Church take every care 'lest opponents and mockers should attain knowledge of sacramental mysteries and the keywords of the faith'; [83] and his basic concept of veiled self-revelation had its roots in a well-established theological opinion in regard to the nature of God. Various religious observances also suggest Keble's view of the poetic function. There is, for example, the parallel with the healing relief of prayer, and also with the disburdening of guilt in the privacy of the confessional—as a leader in the Oxford Movement, Keble frequently regretted that in the Anglican Church, auricular confession was voluntary rather than the rule.[84] The parallelism between the poetic theories of Keble and Freud may be taken as one more evidence of the extent to which psychoanalysis is a secularized version of religious doctrine and ritual.[85]

Keble's consonance with Freud extends to his analysis of the psychology of the reader. Those who fasten upon certain poems with enthusiasm, he says, 'believe themselves to have lighted, at last, upon a unique mental solace.' And 'the peculiar delight which some men feel in some poetry will be found, if analyzed, mainly to depend'—not 'on the subject, or the skill of creating it'—but 'on the sympathy they feel for the character of the author, indirectly made known to them through his verses.'[86] Here is further evidence of how completely traditional poetics gets reversed by such an uncompromising commitment to the view that poetry is self-expression. To enjoy literature is to reachieve the catharsis of its creator; the question of taste reduces mainly to the congruence of one's emotional needs with those of a particular writer; when the reader looks at the work, what he finds is a veiled reflection of its author. It will not be a surprise when we find, later on, that according to Keble, the chief task of practical criticism is to reconstruct in detail, from the traces left in a poem, the sentiments and temperament of the poet who wrote it.

iv. The Semantics of Expressive Language: Alexander Smith

There are some marked similarities between the ideas expounded by Keble in his third and fourth lectures, and the theses developed by John Stuart Mill in the exactly contemporary essays on poetry which he published in the *Monthly Repository* for 1833. Like Keble, Mill apparently derived many elements of his theory from Wordsworth; he wrote to John Sterling in 1831 that no one can converse with Wordsworth 'without feeling that he has advanced that great subject [the theory of poetry] beyond any other man. . .'[87] Mill's definition of poetry as 'the expression or uttering forth of feeling' resembles that of Keble. Both writers also separate poetry from oratory on the grounds that a poet pours out his feelings without reference to an audience; trace the presence of 'poetry,' or emotive expression, in each of the non-literary arts in turn; redefine the poetic genres on the basis of the kind of feelings they express; and propose a fundamental distinction, on related grounds, between what Keble calls primary and secondary poets, and Mill calls poets by nature and poets by culture. Mill diverges from Keble by omitting any but minor references to the cathartic function of poetry, and by emphasizing instead—as we should expect from a disciple, though a truant disciple, of Bentham—the distinction in logical function and criteria between the expressive language of poetry and the descriptive language of science.[88]

The semantics of poetry, however, was explored with greater explicitness, detail, and cogency by a contemporary writer who has been totally lost to sight in the history of criticism and linguistic theory. In *Blackwood's Magazine* for December 1835, appeared an article entitled 'The Philosophy of Poetry,' signed with the initial 'S,' which, the present editors of the magazine inform me, was contributed by an A. Smith of Banff, Scotland. Through the courtesy of the Town Clerk of Banff, I have a note from a local newspaper of some thirty years ago describing an Alexander Smith who in all probability was the author of the article—a man educated at King's College, Aberdeen, who, because of ill health, resigned a position as school-teacher to become Postmaster of Banff from 1827 until his death in 1851. Alexander Smith also published a treatise on *The Philosophy of Morals* in 1835, and an article demolishing the pretensions of 'Phrenological Ethics' in the *Edinburgh Review* for January 1842,[89] but 'The Philosophy of Poetry' is his only literary essay I have been able to identify. It deserves to be republished in its entirety, on its own account, and also because it anticipates the analysis of poetry by recent semantic theorists even more closely than Keble's criticism anticipates the literary doctrines of Freud.

Smith approaches the basic question, 'Wherein does *poetry* differ from *prose?*' with Scottish equanimity. Those who regard poetry 'with enthusiasm,' he complains, 'have seemed to shrink from too narrow an examination . . . as if they felt that they might thereby dissipate a charming illusion'—a charge which perhaps exposes the change in the attitude to poetry since the days when Dr. Johnson had fixed it with his nearsighted but incisive gaze. Smith himself, he tells us, has enough sense of the charms of poetry to incline him to speculation, but within such bounds as to enable him to pursue his speculation 'with the most philosophical composure.'[90]

Since 'verse is not essential to poetry,' the problem is one of discriminating '*poetry*, as opposed to prose.'

The essential distinction between poetry and prose is this:—prose is the language of *intelligence*, poetry of *emotion*. In prose, we communicate our *knowledge* of the objects of sense or thought—in poetry, we express how those objects *affect* us.

Later Smith presents a definition of poetry resembling that of Mill:

Behold now the whole character of poetry. It is *essentially* the *expression of emotion;* but the expression of emotion *takes place* by measured language (it may be verse, or it may not)—harmonious tones—and figurative phraseology.[91]

He is careful to distinguish poetry from eloquence by a difference in ends. 'While the sole object of poetry is to transmit the *feelings* of the speaker or writer, that of eloquence is to convey the *persuasion* of some *truth.* . .' He also sets out to show that his definition has scope enough to include all the poetic genres; his recasting of the traditional classification, however, is less radical than that of Keble, because the base for his distinction is not the kinds of emotions expressed, but the kinds of subject matter evoking the emotions. 'In an epic or narrative poem, some event, or connected chain of events, is narrated with the various feelings which arise from the view of such event or events,' and the aim of expressing and evoking feeling in the most effective way is sufficient to account for the selection, arrangement, and unity of the parts. Similarly with the other kinds: poetry will be descriptive, or didactic, or satirical, in accordance as it 'conveys an expression of the feelings' excited by natural objects, or by 'the contemplation of general truths,' or by 'the view of human vice, folly, and weakness.'[92]

Such doctrines differ from opinion current in the mid-1830's in detail rather than in essence. Smith's new departure consists in identifying and examining poetry as, basically, a linguistic activity—as an expressive, in opposition to a cognitive, use of language. 'Acts or states of intelligence are those in which the mind perceives, believes, comprehends, infers, remembers. Acts or states of emotion are those in which it hopes, fears, rejoices, sorrows, loves, hates, admires, or dislikes.' Prose is the language of the first of these states, poetry of the second.[93]

The recognition that language is capable of expressing emotion is as old as classical rhetoric, which had maintained that words will evoke emotions from the hearer, and so be persuasive, to the degree that they indicate a similar affective state in the speaker. Hobbes and other English empiricists had pointed to the importance of the fact that words, 'besides the signification of what we imagine of their nature, have a signification also of the nature, disposition, and interest of the speaker. . .'[94] Eighteenth-century Longinians, such as Lowth, tended to distinguish between 'the language of reason' and 'the language of the passions.' Edmund Burke, in the section on language of his essay on *The Sublime and Beautiful,* brought both the concepts of rhetoric and the philosophy of Locke to bear on the problem of how words in poetry are able to evoke emotions in the reader:

> We do not sufficiently distinguish, in our observations upon language, between a clear expression and a strong expression. . . The former regards the understanding: the latter belongs to the passions. The one describes a thing as it is; the latter describes it as it is felt.[95]

In this tradition, Alexander Smith's important innovations consist in deliberately reversing the rhetorical point of view to make the evocation of feeling in the auditor incidental to the expression of feeling in the poet; in extending the discrimination between descriptive and expressive language to strike a basic dichotomy through all linguistic usage; in identifying poetry in general with the language of expression; and above all, in exploring the linguistic and logical problems raised by this division far more thoroughly than had any earlier theorist. Smith's discussion of poetry, therefore, is quite comparable to that in the writings of I. A. Richards; for Richards also grounded both his semantic and poetic theory on the opposition between the 'symbolic' (or 'scientific') use of words for 'the support, the organization and the communication of references,' and the 'emotive' use of words 'to express or excite feelings and attitudes,' and went on to identify poetry as 'the supreme form of emotive language.'[96] The same antithesis, under a variety of names, has been widely adopted in the last thirty years as a solvent for the perennial problems of philosophy, morals, propaganda, law, and all other forms of human discourse. Rudolph Carnap, for example, in his popular exposition of logical positivism in *Philosophy and Logical Syntax,* set out to demonstrate that not only poetry, but metaphysics and normative ethics as well, are forms of 'expressive,' as opposed to 'representative' language; and Carnap's account of the difference between these modes of language, though more cursory and omissive, in its essentials parallels that of Alexander Smith.[97]

Now, what are the distinctions with which Smith supplements his initial definition of poetry? First, he refines the crude assertion that any emotional exclamation constitutes poetry (Hazlitt, for one, had spoken of 'oaths and nicknames' as 'only a more vulgar sort of poetry').[98] Smith differentiates three uses of the term. In the basic sense, 'every expression of emotion is poetry'; in another sense, 'we only call the expression of emotion *poetry,* when it expands itself to a certain extent, and assumes a peculiar defined form'; in a third use, 'poetry' is only apparently a descriptive, but actually a laudatory term—what Charles L. Stevenson has recently called a 'persuasive definition.' 'We say,' Smith writes, 'that a composition, in its essential nature poetical, is not *poetry*—as meaning, that it is not good poetry. . .'[99] He then introduces a further discrimination, simple enough, but a fertile source of confusion even in some recent discussions of the topic, between the description of emotion and the expression of emotion:

By the *language of emotion,* however, I mean the language in which that emotion vents itself—not the description of the emotion, or the affirmation that it is felt. . . Between such and the expression of emotion, there is much the same difference as that which exists between the information a person might give us of his feeling bodily pain, and the exclamations or groans which his suffering might extort from him.

This point requires amplification. Poetic expression is not 'mere *exclamation*. Feeling can only be expressed so as to excite the sympathy of others . . . with reference to a cause or object moving that feeling.' In this way, Smith safeguards his theory from the charge (which a few unwary passages in I. A. Richards' earlier writings have invited, despite many other passages of a contrary import) that 'emotive language' is opposed to 'reference,' or at least, that the emotive is relatively independent of the referential function.[100] In Smith's analysis, poetry is not non-referential, but more than *merely* referential. It is, in fact, tightly dependent for communicating feeling upon allusion to the kind of objects which are the occasion for such feeling; and its essential difference from prose does not consist in the presence or absence of reference, but in the purpose for which it is uttered. Poetry, in other words, can be distinguished from prose because it employs reference for an expressive, instead of an assertional purpose:

The essential character, however, of a poetical narrative or description, and that which distinguishes it from a merely prosaic one, is this—that its direct object is not to convey information, but to intimate a subject of feeling, and transmit that feeling from one mind to another. In prose, the main purpose of the writer or speaker is to inform, or exhibit truth. The information may excite emotion, but this is only an accidental effect.[101]

The difficulty in discriminating between the two uses of language is the fact that there is often no verbal or grammatical clue to this difference in ends —'words of precisely the same grammatical and verbal import, nay, the *same words,* may be either prose or poetry . . . according as they are uttered, merely to inform or to express and communicate emotion.' This generalization Smith illustrates with a variety of passages, such as this one:

'My son Absalom' is an expression of precisely similar import to 'my brother Dick,' or 'my uncle Toby'. . . It would be difficult to say that 'oh! Absalom, my son, my son,' is not poetry; yet the grammatical and verbal import of the words is exactly the same in both cases. The interjection 'oh,' and the repetition of the words 'my son,' add nothing whatever to the meaning; but they have the effect of making words which are otherwise but the intimation of a fact, the expression of an *emotion* of exceeding depth and interest. . .[102]

The feelings expressed, Smith says, 'may be called the soul of poetry. Let us next consider the peculiarities of its bodily form, and outward appearance.' On this topic, he agrees with what by this time was the commonplace opinion that poetic meter and rhyme 'are *but more artificial dispositions of the natural expressions of feeling.'* [103] He maintains further that 'the language of emotion is generally *figurative* or *imaginative* language,' because 'the mind, anxious to convey not the truth or fact with regard to the object of its contemplation, but its own feelings as excited by the object, pours forth the stream of its associations as they rise from their source.' This too is in accord with the established opinion of the time, but the interest of Smith's treatment inheres in the detail of his discussion. For example, the connection between feeling and expressive figure, Smith holds, is not a one-way causal sequence, but an interaction. 'It is often not very easy to say whether the feeling is the parent of the image by which it expresses itself, or whether, on the contrary, the image is the parent of the feeling. The truth seems to be, that they produce and reproduce one another.' And Smith's generalizations are strengthened by his discerning analyses of particular poetic instances. Take, for example, a part of the *explication de texte* he applied to the opening line of Gray's 'Elegy,' 'The curfew tolls the knell of parting day.'

The vital character of this line, as constituting it poetry, is, that it is not the mere *fact* or *truth*—(namely, that the tolling of the bell is a sign of the ending of the day)—that the words of the poet aim at communicating, but his emotion in regard to the fact. . . The sound of the bell, intimating the close of day, he invests, for the moment, with the import of the death knell summoning a soul from life; and the epithet 'parting,' bespeaks the similitude of his present frame of mind to that excited by the interruption of a cherished intercourse with an animated being—with a companion, a friend, a lover.[104]

The inadequacies of Smith's essentially grammatical theory, as an approach to the problems of poetry in general, are clear enough. It represents an extreme instance of the tendency in expressive theories (already evident in Wordsworth's criticism) to put the emphasis on the diction, at the expense of other poetic components. The classification of poetry at one end of a simple bipolar distribution of all forms of discourse makes but a crude instrument for specifically literary analysis. Smith characteristically focuses upon the single line, isolated from the poem as a whole, and on its material and formal differences—rhythmic, syntactic, figurative, and logical—from an equivalent assertion of simple fact. He ignores non-linguistic elements such as character or plot, and hardly makes a start at explaining why poetry 'expands itself,' as he puts it, and 'assumes a peculiar defined form.' As a result, he provides no means for analyzing and clarifying the constitution and structure of a poem in its totality. But such limitations are representative of all the over-simple theories of poetry as an expression of feeling current in his decade. Within these limits, Smith demonstrates a clear discernment of some fundamental logical issues raised by such a theory, and an uncommon sense of the need for referring constantly from theory to poetic examples, as well as a notable acuteness in their semantic analysis.

The rigorous analytics of Alexander Smith serves as a counterweight for the easy effusiveness and loosely articulated impressionism of some writers in this period—a mode of procedure which has sometimes been unjustly attributed to romantic criticism in the large. On the premise that poetry expresses feeling, we find certain critics using the word 'poetry' in a diffusive sense, not only for the language which exhibits feeling, but also for feelings which are not expressed in words, and even for objects and events which are merely typical occasions for feeling. William Hazlitt, for one, was subject to whirling off in this way, at those times when he gave his journalistic pen free rein. 'Poetry is the language of the imagination and the passions.' But poetry is not to be found only in books; 'wherever there is a sense of beauty, or power, or harmony, as in the motion of a wave of the sea, in the growth of a flower . . . *there* is poetry in its birth.' The emotions themselves are poetry. 'Fear is poetry, hope is poetry, love is poetry, hatred is poetry,' and, therefore, to be a poet, we need do no more than experience an emotion. The child is a poet 'when he first plays at hide-and-seek,' 'the countryman, when he stops to look at the rainbow,' and 'the miser, when he hugs his gold.' [105]

I shall quote one other critic to show how readily extempore effervescence bubbled over into the new dialect of poetry as feeling. In his review of Tennyson's *Poems* of 1832, John Wilson (Christopher North) characteristically refused to define poetry 'because the Cockneys have done so,' and immediately went on to define it. 'Everything is poetry which is not mere sensation. We are poets at all times when our minds are makers.' The 'inferior animals,' since they 'modify matter much in their imaginations,' are also poets.

The stock-dove, therefore, under stress of erotic feeling becomes a poet, and even a droning beetle is a mute, inglorious Wordsworth.

Thus all men, women, and children, birds, beasts, and fishes, are poets, except versifiers. Oysters are poets. Nobody will deny that, who ever in the neighbourhood of Prestonpans beheld them passionately gaping, on their native bed, for the flow of tide. . . Nor less so are snails. . . The beetle, against the traveller borne in heedless hum, if we knew all his feelings in that soliloquy, might safely be pronounced a Wordsworth.[106]

Although this is hardly intended to be more than glib foolery, it is not without its significance for the historian. The passage demonstrates the kind of critical jargon which had become the equivalent, in the 1830's, for the cant of imitation, nature, rules, beauties, and faults of the Dick Minims of Johnson's generation.

VII

The Psychology of Literary Invention:
MECHANICAL AND ORGANIC THEORIES

> In the word *Reason* may be seen one of that numerous set of names of *fictitious entities,* in the fabrication of which the labours of the Rhetorician and the Poet have been conjoined. In *Reason* they have joined in giving us a sort of *goddess:* a goddess, in whom another goddess, *Passion,* finds a constant antagonist. . . It is not by any such mythology, that any clear and correct instruction can be conveyed.
>
> Jeremy Bentham
>
> What thou art we know not;
> What is most like thee?
>
> <div align="right">Shelley, <i>To a Skylark</i></div>

WHAT WE NOW CALL the psychology of art had its origin when theorists in general began to think of the mind of the artist as interposed between the world of sense and the work of art, and to attribute the conspicuous differences between art and reality, not to the reflection of an external ideal, but to forces and operations within the mind itself. This development was, in large part, the contribution of the critics (and especially the English critics) of the seventeenth and eighteenth centuries, who expanded the passing allusions to the mental faculties in ancient and Renaissance theorists into an extensive psychology of both the production and appreciation of art. In this aspect, English criticism, of course, participated in the tendency of English empirical philosophy, which characteristically tried to establish the nature and limits of knowledge by an analysis of the elements and processes of the mind. Early in the seventeenth century, Francis Bacon included poetry in his great register of human knowledge as a part of learning which is to be explained by reference to the action of imagination. In the middle of the century, Thomas Hobbes, answering Davenant's Preface to *Gondibert,* introduced, on the basis of his earlier philosophical speculation, a brief and popularized account of the place of

sense-experience, memory, fancy, and judgment in the production of poetry.[1] The speed with which suggestions such as these were caught up
and expanded was extraordinary. One hundred years later few philosophers
omitted the discussion of literature and the other arts in their general investigations of the mind, while almost all systematic critics (in conformity
with Hume's suggestion, in the introduction to his *Treatise,* that the science of human nature is propaedeutic to the science of criticism, as well
as of logic, morals, and politics) incorporated into their aesthetic theory a
general treatment of the laws and operations of the mind. By 1774, Alexander Gerard had published his *Essay on Genius,* which remained for a
century the most comprehensive and detailed study devoted specifically to
the psychology of the inventive process.

It should be remarked that there was less absolute novelty in this contribution to criticism than appears at first. Much of the procedure was, very
simply, to translate the existing commonplaces of traditional rhetoric and
poetic into the novel philosophical vocabulary of mental elements, faculties,
and events. A glance at Alexander Gerard's footnotes, for example, will
show that he relies on all the standard critics from Aristotle to Bishop
Hurd, and that although he professes to found his theory entirely on experiment and induction, he usually establishes or bolsters his generalizations
by citing the authority of experts, among whom Cicero and Quintilian bulk
even larger than Locke and Hume. Furthermore, the psychological idiom
is very often used normatively rather than descriptively, and serves the critic
largely as a device for setting up standards of literary performance and
evaluation. In such normative discussions, mental terms, such as fancy and
judgment, are mainly surrogates for more or less precisely defined sets of
opposing qualities in the objective work of art. As one instance, when Rymer
wrote concerning 'Oriental' poets: '*Fancy* with them is predominant, is wild,
vast, and unbridled, o're which their *judgment* has little command or authority: hence their conceptions are monstrous, and have nothing of exactness, nothing of resemblance or proportion' [2]—he named the faculties not
in order to describe the workings of the mind, but in order, summarily, to
derogate what in art is wild and unconfined, and to laud the contrary qualities of exactness and decorum. Some seventy-five years later, Joseph Warton,
writing about the 'imagination' exhibited in Shakespeare's *Tempest,* correlates this psychological term with approximately the same aesthetic qualities
of wildness and irregularity: his preferences, however, have changed. Shakespeare, he says, 'has there given the reins to his boundless imagination, and
has carried the romantic, the wonderful, and the wild, to the most pleasing

extravagance.'[3] The antithesis and changing balance between imagination, or fancy, and judgment was one of the chief frames of discussion within which eighteenth-century critics of art fought out their version of the enduring battle between convention and revolt.

Our sole concern in this chapter, however, will be with descriptive psychology—what some theorists liked to call 'the science of the mind'—and specifically, with the attempt to describe what goes on in the mind in the process of composing a poem. If we penetrate through differences of terminology and detail, we are struck immediately with the extent to which eighteenth-century writers agreed in their basic conception of the psychology of invention. Against this uniform tradition of previous psychology in England, Coleridge was the center of revolt. Scholars have recently emphasized that Coleridge himself was indebted to English precedent for some of his leading ideas, but it is misleading to stress the continuity of Coleridge's mature psychology of art with that which was current in eighteenth-century England. In all essential aspects, Coleridge's theory of mind, like that of contemporary German philosophers, was, as he insisted, revolutionary; it was, in fact, part of a change in the habitual way of thinking, in all areas of intellectual enterprise, which is as sharp and dramatic as any the history of ideas can show.

I have spoken before of the role of analogy in shaping the structure of a critical theory. Nowhere is this role more conspicuous than in discussions of the psychology of art. The only direct evidence in regard to the nature of the mental processes are those shadowy and fugitive items available to introspection, and these are 'modes of inmost being,' as Coleridge said, to which we 'know that the attributes of time and space are inapplicable and alien, but which yet can not be conveyed save in symbols of time and space.'[4] Expressed in the terms of our day: mental events must be talked about metaphorically, in an object-language which was developed to deal literally with the physical world. As a result, our conception of these events is peculiarly amenable to the formative influence of the physical metaphors in which we discuss them, and of the underlying physical analogies from which these metaphors are derived. The basic nature of the shift from psychological criticism in the tradition of Hobbes and Hume to that of Coleridge can, I think, be clarified if we treat it as the result of an analogical substitution—the replacement, that is to say, of a mechanical process by a living plant as the implicit paradigm governing the description of the process and the product of literary invention. I shall begin by sketching the main outlines of the theory that was dominant prior to Coleridge, against which his own writings after the year 1800 were a continuous protest.

i. The Mechanical Theory of Literary Invention

It was of great moment to literary criticism that modern psychology was largely developed in the seventeenth century, during the smashing triumphs of the natural philosophers in the field of mechanics. For it is clear that the course of English empirical philosophy was guided by the attempt, more or less deliberate, to import into the psychical realm the explanatory scheme of physical science, and so to extend the victories of mechanics from matter to mind.[5] In the next century David Hume subtitled his *Treatise* 'An attempt to introduce the experimental method of reasoning into moral subjects,' and set himself to emulate Newton by eschewing hypotheses and ascending 'from careful and exact experiments' to the simplest and most universal causes, in order to found a science of human nature 'which will not be inferior in certainty, and will be much superior in utility to any other of human comprehension.'[6] David Hartley explained that he had taken the doctrine of vibrations from Newton, and the doctrine of association from Locke and his followers, and professed to model his own research on 'the method of analysis and synthesis recommended and followed by Sir Isaac Newton.'[7] Philosophers whose concern was with the operations of the literary mind also laid claim to the methods and certainty of natural science. Lord Kames believed that he had established his 'elements of criticism' by examining 'the sensitive branch of human nature' and ascending 'gradually to principles, from facts and experiments';[8] and Alexander Gerard declared that his aim was to extend 'the science of human nature' into the *terra incognita* of genius, and (despite the admitted difficulties of conducting experiments on the mind) 'to collect such a number of facts concerning any of the mental powers, as will be sufficient for deducing conclusions concerning them, by a just and regular induction.'[9] To some optimists of the later part of the century, it seemed that their rules for composing and judging a poem had a sanction in a science of mind which was no less secure and determinative than the science of nature. James Beattie wrote in 1776:

It would be no less absurd, for a poet to violate the *essential* rules of his art, and justify himself by an appeal from the tribunal of Aristotle, than for a mechanic to construct an engine on principles inconsistent with the laws of motion, and excuse himself by disclaiming the authority of Sir Isaac Newton.[10]

Here, in summary, are the aspects of the eighteenth-century theory of literary invention, common to most writers in the empirical tradition, which reflect the nature of their mechanical archetype:

(1) *The elementary particles of mind.* The empirical psychology is unreservedly elementaristic in its method: it takes as its starting point, its basic datum, the element or part. All the manifold contents and goings-on of the mind are assumed to be analyzable into a very limited number of simple components, and the procedure of the theorist is to explain complex psychological states or products as various combinations of these atoms of mind. The sole elements, or 'ideas,' entering into the products of invention are assumed to be wholes or parts, literally, of *images*—exact, although fainter replicas of the original perceptions of sense.

The assumption that ideas are images is implied by Hobbes's characterization of the contents of mental discourse as 'decaying sense.' In Hume's locked internal world, the only differentia between sense impressions and ideas is the greater 'force and vivacity' of the former. 'The one,' he says, 'seems to be in a manner the reflexion of the other. . .' [11] Hume's implicit metaphor of an idea as a mirror-image of sensation, so pervasive in eighteenth-century discussions of the mind, becomes explicit in Gerard's description of the ideas in memory: 'Like a mirrour, it reflects faithful images of the objects formerly perceived by us. . . It is in its nature a mere copier. . .' [12]

To the philosophical school of Locke, the ultimate, unanalyzable particles of mental content were, of course, the replicas of the simple qualities of sense—blue, hot, hard, sweet, odor-of-rose—plus the replicas of the feelings of pleasure and pain. But when they talked of the making of poetry, both philosophers and literary theorists tended to take as the unit of the process that bundle of simple qualities constituting either the whole, or a splintered fragment, of a particular object of sense. Furthermore, in most discussions of poetic invention, these mental units were assumed to be primarily, if not exclusively, visual images, replicas of the objects of sight. Coleridge remarked acutely that the 'mechanical philosophy' insists on a world of mutually impenetrable objects because it suffers from a 'despotism of the eye'; [13] and in literary theories this despotism was strengthened by the long rhetorical tradition that a speaker is most emotionally effective when he visualizes and evokes the scene he describes. As Addison said flatly, in *Spectator* 416, 'We cannot indeed have a single Image in the Fancy that did not make its first Entrance through the Sight. . .' Later, Lord Kames held that because the ideas of all the other senses are 'too obscure for that operation,' the imagination, in 'fabricating images of things that have no existence,' is limited to dividing and recombining the 'ideas of sight.' [14]

(2) *The motions and combinations of the parts.* Images move in sequence across the mind's eye. If these recur in the same spatial and temporal order as in the original sense-experience, we have 'memory.' But if the integral images of the objects of sense recur in a different order, or else if segmented parts of such images are combined into a whole never present to sense, we have 'fancy,' or 'imagination'—terms almost always used synonymously to apply to all non-mnemonic processions of ideas, including those that go into the making of a poem.

To typify the action of imagination, theorists often adduced the ancient example of mythological grotesques which obviously lack a precedent in sense.[15] In 1677 Dryden quoted Lucretius (who had early attempted to extend material atomism to the activities of the soul) in order to establish the possibility of imaging hippocentaurs, chimeras, and other 'things quite out of nature' by 'the conjunction of two natures, which have a real separate being.' [16] Similar instances of mental collocations had been cited by Hobbes, and were picked up by Hume,[17] and they became a standard component in critical discussions of poetic invention. Gerard, for example, points out that even when the poet's imagination 'creates' new wholes 'such as are properly its own,' the 'parts and members of its ideas have been conveyed separately by the senses. . .'

When Homer formed the idea of *Chimera,* he only joined into one animal, parts which belonged to different animals; the head of a lion, the body of a goat, and the tail of a serpent.[18]

The concept that the inventive process, in its boldest flights, consists in the severance of sensible wholes into parts and the aggregation of parts into new wholes, united even antagonistic schools of eighteenth-century philosophy. The Scottish philosopher, Dugald Stewart, followed the initiative of Thomas Reid in objecting to the tendency, from Locke through Hume, to disintegrate all of mental content into mere sequences of sensations and ideas, and in stressing instead the concept of mental faculties and 'powers.' He also anticipated (and perhaps influenced) Coleridge in distinguishing between the imagination and the fancy—the fancy, according to Stewart, constituting a lower faculty that proffers sensible materials upon which the imagination operates by its complex powers of 'apprehension,' 'abstraction,' and 'taste.' Yet Stewart's analysis of the poetic imagination follows the eighteenth-century pattern: its creative power consists only in the fact that it is able 'to make a selection of qualities and of circumstances, from a variety of different objects, and by combining and disposing these to form a new creation of its own.' [19]

We must not project into Stewart's word, 'creation,' or into 'original' and 'plastic,' which also became attached to the 'imagination' in the second half of the century, a significance opposed to psychological atomism. All of these terms, as we shall see, carried important consequences for criticism, and 'plastic' is especially interesting because it was adopted from cosmogonists who, in express opposition to a purely atomistic and mechanical philosophy, had employed the word to signify a vital principle, inherent in nature, which organizes chaos into cosmos by a self-evolving formative energy.[20] As a term in the psychology of literature, therefore, 'plastic' from the first carried the latent implications of Coleridge's creative 'esemplastic' imagination. But in eighteenth-century usage, when the details get filled in, we recognize the standard imaginative process, consisting of the division and recombination of discretes to form a whole which may be novel in its order, but never in its parts. The word 'create,' as John Ogilvie warned, must not be interpreted 'as relating to discoveries purely *original,* of which the senses receive no patterns.' The ideas of sense and of reflection—

these are indeed by what we term a plastic imagination associated, compounded, and diversified at pleasure. . . But in the whole of this process, the originality obviously results from the manner in which objects are selected and put together, so as to form upon the whole an unusual combination.[21]

(3) *The laws of associative attraction.* As the principle governing the sequence and conjunction of ideas, and rendering the imagination 'in some measure, uniform with itself in all times and places,' Hume—building upon suggestions in Aristotle and in his English predecessors—posited the concept of the association of ideas. 'The qualities, from which this association arises, and by which the mind is after this manner convey'd from one idea to another, are three, *viz.* Resemblance, Contiguity in time or place, and Cause and Effect.' [22] Ten years later, in 1749, David Hartley published a version of associative theory, developed independently of Hume, in which he set out to demonstrate rigorously that all the complex contents and processes of mind are derived from the elements of simple sensation, combined by the single link of contiguity in original experience. And very quickly the general concept of association, although with diverse predications of the number and kinds of associative connections, became incorporated into standard theories of the literary imagination.[23]

There is a conspicuous parallelism between this basic pattern of mental activity and the elementary concepts of matter, motion, and force composing Newton's science of mechanics—although shorn, naturally, of the quantitative aspects of Newton's formulation. (1) The unit ideas of mind correspond to Newton's particles of matter. Ideas, Hume pointed out, 'may be compar'd to the extension and solidity of matter,' for, unlike impressions, they 'are endow'd with a kind of impenetrability, by which they exclude each other, and are capable of forming a compound by their conjunction, not by their mixture.' [24] (2) The motion of ideas in sequence or 'trains' is the mental equivalent of the motion of matter in physical space. (3) The 'uniting principle' or 'gentle force' (as Hume characterized association) adds the concept of a force effecting that motion; while the uniform operations of this force in 'the laws of association' are analogous to Newton's uniform laws of motion and gravitation.

So, at least, it seemed to some of the more systematic theorists concerning the science of the mind. Hume himself drew the parallel between the principles of association (even though he regarded these as a statistical tendency rather than an 'inseparable connection') and the law of gravitation.

These are therefore the principles of union or cohesion among our simple ideas. . . Here is a kind of ATTRACTION, which in the mental world will be found to have as extraordinary effects as in the natural, and to shew itself in as many and as various forms.[25]

In Hartley's system of psycho-physiological parallelism, the association of ideas frankly becomes the introspective correlate to the operation of the mechanical laws of motion in the nervous system.[26] And for a thoroughgoing materialistic monist such as Holbach, of course, mind disappears entirely, and its processes are reduced to the 'action and re-action of the minute and insensible molecules or particles of matter' in that particular area of the universal machine which constitutes a human brain.[27]

(4) *The problem of judgment and artistic design.* It is the need for giving a satisfactory account of the order and design in the completed work of art which perplexes, if it does not confound, the attempt at a pure mechanism of mind. The problem was aggravated for the eighteenth-century psychologist of invention because, as I have said, his procedure was mainly to translate the existing theory of poetry into mental terms, and this theory incorporated two elements entirely alien to elementarism and the mechanical categories of mind. One of these elements was the central Aristotelian concept of 'form,' and of an artistic 'unity' in which the transposition, re-

moval, or addition of any part will dislocate the whole. The other was the rhetorical and Horatian concept of art as, basically, a purposeful procedure, in which the end is foreseen from the beginning, part is fitted to part, and the whole is adapted to the anticipated effect upon the reader. But as Alexander Gerard, for one, pointed out, according to the principles of associationism any one idea 'bears some relation to an infinite number of other ideas,' so that the ideas collected merely according to this relation will 'form a confused chaos,' and 'can no more be combined into one regular work, than a number of wheels taken from different watches, can be united into one machine.'[28] Otherwise stated: if the process of imagination is conceived as images moved by purely mechanical, or efficient causes of attraction—each present image pulling in the next automatically, according to the accident of its inherent similarity or of its contiguity in past experience—how are we to explain that the result is a cosmos instead of a chaos? And how are we to account for the difference between the incoherent associations of delirium and the orderly, productive associations of a Shakespeare?

The equivalent problem of explaining design in the physical universe had been the stumbling block of a mechanical philosophy ever since the atoms of Democritus. 'How,' Cicero had asked, can the Epicureans 'assert the world to have been made from minute particles . . . coming together by chance or accident? But if a concourse of atoms can make a world, why not a porch, a temple, a house, a city, which are works of less labor and difficulty?'[29] In the seventeenth century, the strong revival of atomism in the physical sciences made for a counter-emphasis—hardly less pronounced among the atomists than among their opponents—on the need for a supplementary principle to account for the manifest order of the physical universe. Despite his reluctance to frame hypotheses, Newton himself, following the example of Boyle and other scientific predecessors, solved the problem of the genesis of law, order, and beauty in the world-machine by drawing, as it were, a *deus ex machina*. 'This most beautiful system of the sun, planets, and comets,' he said, 'could only proceed from the counsel and dominion of an intelligent and powerful Being'[30]—that is, from the execution of a design by a purposeful God. And of course, this theological argument from design in physical nature became one of the most familiar of philosophical concepts in both eighteenth-century prose and poetry.[31]

In this respect, as in others, mechanical psychology repeated the pattern of mechanical cosmology. In his felicitous verses on the poems of Sir Robert Howard (1660), Dryden—who had studied Hobbes, and whose own imagination was enthralled by the Lucretian account of chaos falling into order by the chance concourse of atoms—considered, only to reject, the claim of mental atomism to have dispensed with the mental equivalent of Providence in explaining the creation of a poem:

> No atoms, casually together hurl'd,
> Could e'er produce so beautiful a world.
> Nor dare I such a doctrine here admit,
> As would destroy the providence of wit.[32]

David Hume subjected the theological argument from design to a wonderfully acute critique in his *Dialogues concerning Natural Religion.* Yet in his *Enquiry,* after expounding the role of the association of ideas, he found it necessary to postulate the existence of a controlling design in the mind of the productive artist.

In all compositions of genius, therefore 'tis requisite that the writer have some plan or object . . . some aim or intention in his first setting out, if not in the composition of the whole work. A production without a design would resemble more the raving of a madman, than the sober efforts of genius and learning.

 [Events or actions in narratives] must be related to each other in the imagination, and form a kind of *Unity,* which may bring them under one plan or view, and which may be the object or end of the writer in his first undertaking.[33]

Alexander Gerard attempted to integrate his concept of a 'main design' with the mechanical operation of imagination, by postulating that the presence of the supervisory design doubles the strength of certain associative links, and so enables relevant ideas to over-rule their irrelevant rivals.[34] Most theorists of mind, however, followed the model of physico-theological speculation in a very simple and direct way: they merely brought the intelligent Artisan of the world-machine indoors and converted him into a mental agent or faculty (called interchangeably 'judgment,' 'reason,' or 'understanding') which supervises and reviews the mechanical process of association.

 Even Gerard felt constrained to supplement, in this way, his concept of the 'main design' as an automatic control over imaginative association.

Every work of genius is a whole, made up of the regular combination of different parts, so organized as to become altogether subservient to a common end. . . But however perfectly the associating principles perform this part of their office, a person will scarce reckon himself certain of the propriety of that disposition, till it has been authorized by judgment. Fancy forms the plan in a sort of mechanical or instinctive manner: judgment, on reviewing it, perceives its rectitude or its errors, as it were scientifically; its decisions are founded on reflection, and produce a conviction of their justness.[35]

The passage is perfectly representative; and except for a few stubborn mechanists like Hartley and Holbach, the eighteenth-century psychologist developed his scheme of the mind by combining two analogies. One was the analogy of a mechanism, in which the images of sense follow one another according to the laws of mental gravitation. The other was the analogy of an intelligent artisan, or architect, who makes his selection from the materials so proffered, and then puts them together according to his pre-existent blueprint or plan.

This concept of a teleological designer, superimposed on a mechanical scheme of mind, was achieved at considerable cost to the hoped-for 'science of the mind.' In Newton's world-system a final cause had been adduced only to explain the genesis of the universe, with God's omnipresence thereafter—except for his rare intervention in the way of a miracle, or to correct the irregularities of certain celestial bodies—serving mainly to guarantee the continuity of the mechanical laws of cause and effect.[36] In the system of mind, however, final causes were permitted to interfere with the uniform operation of the laws of association in each several instance of purposive thinking. Furthermore, the very concept of a prior design (conceived to be a kind of master-image in the mind) posed a tacit challenge to the primary empirical assumption that there is no mental content which has not entered through the senses. Obviously, this design could not be an innate Idea. Neither could it be derived from direct perception, either of the works of nature or the works of earlier poets, for this is to set up a regress in which at some point original invention has to be introduced; and original invention, after all, is the very phenomenon we have set out to explain.[37]

The endeavors of associationists to cope with these difficulties in the concept of aesthetic design is a most interesting aspect of their writings. Gerard, for example, following his normal routine of converting the topics of rhetoric into mental terms, comes, in due course, to the subject of 'disposition,' which (citing Cicero and Quintilian) he describes as the ordered arrangement of invented materials into 'the economy of the whole.' Here he discovers that the distinction between prior design and later fulfillment, and the underlying parallel between the internal process of genius and the deliberate and successive operations of an artisan, do not square with the facts of observation.

The operations of genius in forming its designs, are of a more perfect kind than the operations of art or industry in executing them. . . An architect contrives a whole palace in an instant; but when he comes to build it, he must first provide materials, and then rear the different parts of the edifice only in succession. But to collect the materials and to order and apply them, are not to genius distinct and successive works.

In the first stage of invention, 'the notion of the whole is generally but imperfect and confused,' and only emerges as the process goes on. Hence 'this faculty bears a greater resemblance to *nature* in its operations, than to the less perfect energies of *art*.' And to illustrate the special properties of the workings of 'nature,' Gerard hits upon an analogue pregnant with implications for literary psychology—the analogue of vegetable growth.

When a vegetable draws in moisture from the earth, nature, by the same action by which it draws it in, and at the same time, converts it to the nourishment of the plant: it at once circulates through its vessels, and is assimilated to its several parts. In like manner, genius arranges its ideas by the same operation, and almost at the same time, that it collects them.[38]

That is, when substituted for mechanism and artisanship as the paradigm for the inventive process, a plant yields the concept of an inherent potential design, unfolding spontaneously from within, and assimilating to its own nature the materials needed for its nourishment and growth. As we shall see, German theorists, under the spur of similar problems, were already beginning to explore the possibilities of the plant as the archetype of imagination, but this suggestion fell on stony ground in the England of 1774. Gerard himself, pursuing the analysis of literary design, at once reverts to the standard combination of mechanical association and supervisory architect. 'Thus imagination,' he says, 'is no unskilful architect,' for 'it in a great measure, by its own force, by means of its associating power, after repeated attempts and transpositions, designs a regular and well-proportioned edifice.'[39]

ii. Coleridge's Mechanical Fancy and Organic Imagination

Not until four decades after Gerard's *Essay on Genius* do we find in England a full development of the organism as aesthetic model. In order to sharpen the contrast between the categories of mechanical and organic psychology, I shall postpone, until the next chapter, discussion of the general history of organic theory, and go directly to its deliberate and elaborate application in Coleridge's description of the process and products of literary invention.

At the heart of Coleridge's theory is his laconic differentiation between fancy and imagination, in the thirteenth chapter of the *Biographia Literaria* (1817). As opposed to imagination, fancy

has no other counters to play with, but fixities and definites. The Fancy is indeed no other than a mode of Memory emancipated from the order of time and space; while it is blended with, and modified by that empirical faculty of the will, which we express by the word CHOICE. But equally with the ordinary memory the Fancy must receive all its materials ready made from the law of association.

In his lengthy prolegomenon to this passage, in which he reviews and criticizes the history of mental mechanism through its culmination in Hartley, Coleridge expressly tells us that he intends his faculties of memory and fancy to incorporate everything that is valid in the associative theory of the eighteenth century, 'and, in conclusion, to appropriate the remaining offices of the mind to the reason, and the imagination.' [40] And in fact, Coleridge's description of fancy skillfully singles out the basic categories of the associative theory of invention: the elementary particles, or 'fixities and definites,' derived from sense, distinguished from the units of memory only because they move in a new temporal and spatial sequence determined by the law of association, and subject to choice by a selective faculty—the 'judgment' of eighteenth-century critics.[41] Formerly, this had been the total account of poetic invention. But after everything which can be, has been so explained, Coleridge finds a residue which he attributes to the 'secondary imagination.' This faculty

dissolves, diffuses, dissipates, in order to recreate; or where this process is rendered impossible, yet still at all events it struggles to idealize and to unify. It is essentially *vital,* even as all objects (*as* objects) are essentially fixed and dead.

The historical importance of Coleridge's imagination has not been overrated. It was the first important channel for the flow of organicism into the hitherto clear, if perhaps not very deep, stream of English aesthetics. (Organicism may be defined as the philosophy whose major categories are derived metaphorically from the attributes of living and growing things.) Consider first the antithetic metaphors by which Coleridge, in various passages, discriminates his two productive faculties. The memory is 'mechanical' and the fancy 'passive'; fancy is a 'mirrorment . . . repeating simply, or by transposition,' and 'the aggregative and associative power,' acting only 'by a sort of juxtaposition.' [42] The imagination, on the contrary, 'recreates' its elements by a process to which Coleridge sometimes applies terms borrowed from those physical and chemical unions most remote, in their intimacy, from the conjunction of impenetrable discretes in what he called the 'brick and mortar' thinking of the mechanical philosophy. Thus, imagination is a 'synthetic,' a 'permeative,' and a 'blending, fusing power.' [43] At other times, Coleridge describes the imagination as an 'assimilative power,' and the 'coadunating faculty'; these adjectives are imported from contemporary biology, where 'assimilate' connoted the process by which an organism converts food into its own substance, and 'coadunate' signified 'to grow together into one.' [44] Often, Coleridge's discussions of imagination are explicitly in terms of a living, growing thing. The imagination is, for example, 'essentially *vital*,' it 'generates and produces a form of its own,' and its rules are 'the very powers of growth and production.' [45] And in such passages, Coleridge's metaphors for imagination coincide with his metaphors for the mind in all its highest workings. The action of the faculty of reason Coleridge compares in detail to the development, assimilation, and respiration of a plant—thus equating knowing with growing and (to borrow a coinage from I. A. Richards) 'knowledge' with 'growledge.' [46]

Indeed, it is astonishing how much of Coleridge's critical writing is couched in terms that are metaphorical for art and literal for a plant; if Plato's dialectic is a wilderness of mirrors, Coleridge's is a very jungle of vegetation. Only let the vehicles of his metaphors come alive, and you see all the objects of criticism writhe surrealistically into plants or parts of plants, growing in tropical profusion. Authors, characters, poetic genres, poetic passages, words, meter, logic become seeds, trees, flowers, blossoms, fruit, bark, and sap. The fact is, Coleridge's insistence on the distinction between the living imagination and the mechanical fancy was but a part of his all-out war against the 'Mechanico-corpuscular Philosophy' on every front. Against this philosophy he proposed the same objection which is found in the writings of a distinguished modern heir of organic theory, A. N. Whitehead. The scheme was developed, said Coleridge, under the need 'to submit the various phenomena of moving bodies to geometrical construction' by abstracting all its qualities except figure and motion. And 'as a *fiction of science*,' he added, 'it would be difficult to overvalue this invention,' but Descartes propounded it 'as *truth of fact*: and instead of a World *created* and filled with productive forces by the Almighty *Fiat*, left a lifeless Machine whirled about by the dust of its own Grinding. . .'[47] What we need in philosophy, he wrote to Wordsworth in 1815, is

the substitution of life and intelligence (considered in its different powers from the plant up to that state in which the difference in degree becomes a new kind (man, self-consciousness), but yet not by essential opposition) for the philosophy of mechanism, which, in everything that is most worthy of the human intellect, strikes *Death,* and cheats itself by mistaking clear images for distinct conceptions. . .[48]

Coleridge, with considerable justification, has been called the master of the fragment, and has been charged with a penchant for appropriating passages from German philosophers. Yet in criticism, what he took from other writers he developed into a speculative instrument which, for its power of insight and, above all, of application in the detailed analysis of literary works, had no peer among the German organic theorists. And in an important sense, the elements of his fully developed criticism, whether original or derivative, are consistent—with a consistency that is not primarily logical, or even psychological, but analogical; it consists in fidelity to the archetype, or founding image, to which he has committed himself. This is the contradistinction between atomistic and organic, mechanical and vital—ultimately, between the root analogies of machine and growing plant. As Coleridge explored the conceptual possibilities of the latter, it transformed radically many deeply rooted opinions in regard to the production, classification, anatomy, and evaluation of works of art. The nature of these changes can be brought to light if we ask what the properties are of a plant, as differentiated from those of a mechanical system.

Our listing of these properties is greatly simplified, because Coleridge has already described them for us, in the many, though generally neglected, documents in which he discusses the nature of living things. These begin with a long letter written at the age of twenty-four,[49] two years before his trip to Germany and his study of physiology and natural science under Blumenbach; and they culminate with his *Theory of Life,* which incorporates various concepts from the German *Natur-Philosophen* and from the discoveries and speculations of English 'dynamic' physiologists such as Hunter, Saumarez, and Abernethy.[50] To place passages from Coleridge's biology and his criticism side by side is to reveal at once how many basic concepts have migrated from the one province into the other.

What, then, are the characteristic properties of a plant, or of any living organism?

(1) The plant originates in a seed. To Coleridge, this indicates that the elementaristic principle is to be stood on its head; that the whole is primary and the parts secondary and derived.

In the world we see every where evidences of a Unity, which the component parts are so far from explaining, that they necessarily pre-suppose it as the cause and condition of their existing *as* those parts; or even of their existing at all. . . That the root, stem, leaves, petals, &c. [of this crocus] cohere to one plant, is owing to an antecedent Power or Principle in the Seed, which existed before a single particle of the matters that constitute the *size* and visibility of the crocus, had been attracted from the surrounding soil, air, and moisture.[51]

'The difference between an inorganic and organic body,' he said elsewhere, 'lies in this: In the first . . . the whole is nothing more than a collection of the individual parts or phenomena,' while in the second, 'the whole is everything, and the parts are nothing.' [52] And Coleridge extends the same principle to non-biological phenomena: 'Depend on it, whatever is grand, whatever is truly organic and living, the whole is prior to the parts.' [53]

(2) The plant *grows*. 'Productivity or Growth,' Coleridge said, is 'the first power' of all living things, and it exhibits itself as 'evolution and extension in the Plant.' [54] No less is this a power of the greatest poets. In Shakespeare, for example, we find '*Growth* as in a plant.' 'All is growth, evolution, *genesis*—each line, each word almost, begets the following. . .' [55] Partial and passing comparisons of a completed discourse or poem to an animal body are to be found as early as Plato and Aristotle,[56] but a highly developed organismic theory, such as Coleridge's, differs from such precedents in the extent to which all aspects of the analogy are exploited, and above all in the extraordinary stress laid on this attribute of growth. Coleridge's interest is persistently genetic—in the process as well as in the product; in becoming no less than in being. That is why Coleridge rarely discusses a finished poem without looking toward the mental process which evolved it; this is what makes all his criticism so characteristically psychological.

(3) Growing, the plant assimilates to its own substance the alien and diverse elements of earth, air, light, and water. 'Lo!' cries Coleridge eloquently, on this congenial subject:

Lo!—with the rising sun it commences its outward life and enters into open communion with all the elements, at once assimilating them to itself and to each other. . . Lo!—at the touch of light how it returns an air akin to light, and yet with the same pulse effectuates its own secret growth, still contracting to fix what expanding it had refined.[57]

Extended from plant to mind, this property effects another revolution in associationist theory. In the elementarist scheme, all products of invention had consisted of recombinations of the unit images of sense. In Coleridge's organic theory, images of sense become merely materials on which the mind feeds—materials which quite lose their identity in being assimilated to a new whole. 'From the first, or initiative Idea, as from a seed, successive Ideas germinate.'

Events and images, the lively and spirit-stirring machinery of the external world, are like light, and air, and moisture, to the seed of the Mind, which would else rot and perish. In all processes of mental evolution the objects of the senses must stimulate the Mind; and the Mind must in turn assimilate and digest the food which it thus receives from without.[58]

At the same time the 'ideas,' which in the earlier theory had been fainter replicas of sensation, are metamorphosed into seeds that grow in the soil of sensation. By his 'abuse of the word "idea,"' Locke seems to say 'that the sun, the rain, the manure, and so on had made the wheat, had made the barley. . . If for this you substitute the assertion that a grain of wheat might remain for ever and be perfectly useless and to all purposes non-apparent, had it not been that the congenial sunshine and proper soil called it forth—everything in Locke would be perfectly rational.' [59] To Coleridge, the ideas of reason, and those in the imagination of the artist, are 'living and life-producing ideas, which . . . are essentially one with the germinal causes in nature. . .' [60]

(4) The plant evolves spontaneously from an internal source of energy—'effectuates,' as Coleridge put it, 'its own secret growth'—and organizes itself into its proper form.[61] An artefact needs to be made, but a plant makes itself. According to one of Coleridge's favorite modes of stating this difference, in life 'the unity . . . is produced *ab intra*,' but in mechanism, '*ab extra*.' 'Indeed, evolution as contra-distinguished from apposition, or superinduction *ab aliunde,* is implied in the conception of life. . .' [62] In the realm of mind, this is precisely the difference between a 'free and rival originality' and that 'lifeless mechanism' which by servile imitation imposes an alien form on inorganic materials. As he says, echoing A. W. Schlegel:

The form is mechanic when on any given material we impress a pre-determined form . . . as when to a mass of wet clay we give whatever shape we wish it to retain when hardened. The organic form, on the other hand, is innate; it shapes as it develops itself from within, and the fullness of its development is one and the same with the perfection of its outward form.[63]

In this property of growing organisms, Coleridge finds the solution to the problem which, we remember, had worried the mechanists, both of matter and of mind; that is, how to explain the genesis of order and design by the operation of purely mechanical laws. To say, Coleridge declares, that 'the material particles possess this combining power by inherent reciprocal attractions, repulsions, and elective affinities; and are themselves the joint artists of their own combinations' is 'merely to shift the mystery.' Since, by Coleridge's analysis, an organism is inherently teleological—since its form is endogenous and automotive—his own solution of the mystery has no need for the mental equivalent of an architect either to draw up the preliminary design or to superintend its construction. For

herein consists the essential difference, the contra-distinction, of an organ from a machine; that not only the characteristic shape is evolved from the invisible central power, but the material mass itself is acquired by assimilation. The germinal power of the plant transmutes the fixed air and the elementary base of water into grass or leaves. . .[64]

Parenthetically, it may be pointed out that Coleridge resolved one problem only to run up against another. For if the growth of a plant seems inherently purposeful, it is a purpose without an alternative, fated in the seed, and evolving into its final form without the supervention of consciousness. 'The inward principle of Growth and individual Form in every seed and plant is a *subject*,' said Coleridge. 'But the man would be a dreamer, who otherwise than poetically should speak of roses and lilies as *self-conscious* subjects.'[65] To substitute the concept of growth for the operation of mechanism in the psychology of invention, seems merely to exchange one kind of determinism for another; while to replace the mental artisan-planner by the concept of organic self-generation makes it difficult, analogically, to justify the participation of consciousness in the creative process. We shall see that, in some German critics, recourse to vegetable life as a model for the coming-into-being of a work of art had, in fact, engendered the fateful concept that artistic creation is primarily an unwilled and unconscious process of mind.[66] Coleridge, however, though admitting an unconscious component in invention, was determined to demonstrate that a poet like Shakespeare 'never wrote anything without design.'[67] 'What the plant is by an act not its own and unconsciously,' Coleridge exhorts us, 'that must thou *make* thyself to become.' [68] In Coleridge's aesthetics, no less than in his ethics and theology, the justification of free-will is a crux—in part, it would appear, because this runs counter to an inherent tendency of his elected analogue.

(5) The achieved structure of a plant is an organic unity. In contradistinction to the combination of discrete elements in a machine, the parts of a plant, from the simplest unit, in its tight integration, interchange, and interdependence with its neighbors, through the larger and more complex structures, are related to each other, and to the plant as a whole, in a complex and peculiarly intimate way. For example, since the existing parts of a plant themselves propagate new parts, the parts may be said to be their own causes, in a process of which the terminus seems to be the existence of the whole. Also, while the whole owes its being to the co-existence of the parts, the existence of that whole is a necessary condition to the survival of the parts; if, for example, a leaf is removed from the parent-plant, the leaf dies.

Attempts to define such peculiarities of living systems, or the nature of 'organic unity,' are at the heart of all organismic philosophies. Sometimes Coleridge describes organic relation on the model of Kant's famous formula in the *Teleological Judgment;* in Coleridge's wording, the parts of a living whole are 'so far interdependent that each is reciprocally means and end,' while the 'dependence of the parts on the whole' is combined with the 'dependence of the whole on its parts.' [69] Or, following Schelling, he formulates it in terms of the polar logic of thesis-antithesis-synthesis. 'It would be difficult to recall any true Thesis and Antithesis of which a living organ is not the Synthesis or rather the Indifference.'

The mechanic system . . . knows only of distance and nearness . . . in short, the relations of unproductive particles to each other; so that in every instance the result is the exact sum of the component qualities, as in arithmetical addition. . . In Life . . . the two component counter-powers actually interpenetrate each other, and generate a higher third including both the former, 'ita tamen ut sit alia et major.' [70]

Alternatively, Coleridge declares that in an organism the whole spreads undivided through all the parts. 'The physical life is in each limb and organ of the body, all in every part; but is manifested as life, by being one in all and thus making all one. . .' [71]

These formulae, like the others, are duly transferred from natural organisms to the organic products of invention.

The spirit of poetry, like all other living powers . . . must embody in order to reveal itself; but a living body is of necessity an organized one,—and what is organization, but the connection of parts to a whole, so that each part is at once end and means! [72]

That function of synthesizing opposites into a higher third, in which the component parts are *alter et idem,* Coleridge attributes, in the aesthetic province, to the imagination—'that synthetic and magical power,' as he describes it in the *Biographia Literaria,* which 'reveals itself in the balance or reconciliation of opposite or discordant qualities.' And the affinity of this synthesis with the organic function of assimilating nutriment declares itself, when Coleridge goes on at once to cite Sir John Davies' description of the soul, which 'may with slight alteration be applied, and even more appropriately, to the poetic IMAGINATION':

> Doubtless this could not be, but that she turns
>   Bodies to spirit by sublimation strange,
> As fire converts to fire the thing it burns,
>   As we our food into our nature change. [73]

To Coleridge, therefore, imaginative unity is not a mechanical juxtaposition of 'unproductive particles,' nor a neo-classic decorum of parts in which (as Dryden translated Boileau), 'Each object must be fixed in the due place'—

> Till, by a curious art disposed, we find
> One perfect whole of all the pieces joined. [74]

Imaginative unity is an *organic* unity: a self-evolved system, constituted by a living interdependence of parts, whose identity cannot survive their removal from the whole.

It is a curious attribute of an organismic philosophy that on the basis of its particular logic, in which truth is achieved only through the synthesis of antitheses, it is unable to deny its metaphysical opposite, but can defeat it only by assimilating it into 'a higher third,' as Coleridge said, 'including both the former.' Accordingly, despite Coleridge's intoxication with the alchemical change wrought in the universe by his discovery of the organic analogy, he did not hesitate to save, and to incorporate into his own theory, the mechanical philosophy he so violently opposed. Mechanism is false, not because it does not tell the truth, but because it does not tell the whole truth. 'Great good,' he wrote in his notebook, 'of such revolution as alters, not by exclusion, but by an enlargement that includes the former, though it places it in a new point of view.'[75] Coleridge's fully developed critical theory, therefore, is deliberately syncretic, and utilizes not one, but two controlling analogues, one of a machine, the other of a plant; and these divide the processes and products of art into two distinct kinds, and by the same token, into two orders of excellence.

Again and again, Coleridge uses his bifocal lens to discriminate and appraise two modes of poetry. One of these can be adequately accounted for in mechanical terms. It has its source in the particulars of sense and the images of memory, and its production involves only the lower faculties of fancy, 'understanding,' and empirical 'choice.' It is therefore the work of 'talent,' and stands in a rank below the highest; its examples are such writings as those of Beaumont and Fletcher, Ben Jonson, and Pope. The other and greater class of poetry is organic. It has its source in living 'ideas,' and its production involves the higher faculties of imagination, 'reason,' and the 'will.' Hence it is the work of 'genius,' and its major instances are to be found in the writings of Dante, Shakespeare, Milton, and Wordsworth. For while talent lies 'in the understanding'—understanding being 'the faculty of thinking and forming judgments on the notices furnished by sense'—genius consists in 'the action of reason and imagination.' As part of what it learns from sense-experience, talent has 'the faculty of appropriating and applying the knowledge of others,' but not 'the creative, and self-sufficing power of absolute *Genius*.' The 'essential difference' is that between 'the shaping skill of mechanical talent, and the creative, productive life-power of inspired genius,' resulting in a product modified '*ab intra* in each component part.'[76]

'The plays of B[eaumont] and F[letcher],' for example, 'are mere aggregations without unity; in the Shakespearean drama there is a vitality which grows and evolves itself from within,' so that 'Shakespeare is the height, breadth, and depth of genius: Beaumont and Fletcher the excellent mechanism, in juxtaposition and succession, of talent.'[77] Similarly, Ben Jonson's work 'is the produce of an amassing power in the author, and not of a growth from within.'[78] And to conclude, here is a passage epitomizing the analogical method of Coleridge's applied criticism. The lesser Elizabethans, he tells us, merely took objects available to sense and assembled them into new combinations of discrete parts.

What had a grammatical and logical consistency for the ear, what could be put together and represented to the eye, these poets took from the ear and eye, unchecked by any intuition of an inward possibility, just as a man might fit together a quarter of an orange, a quarter of an apple, and the like of a lemon and of a pomegranate, and make it look like one round diverse colored fruit.

To this collocative activity Coleridge opposes the organic process: 'But nature, who works from within by evolution and assimilation according to a law, cannot do it.' Immediately, these concepts of growth, assimilation, and biological law are translated from nature to the poetic mind.

Nor could Shakespeare, for he too worked in the spirit of nature, by evolving the germ within by the imaginative power according to an idea—for as the power of seeing is to light, so is an idea in the mind to a law in nature.[79]

iii. The Associative Imagination in the Romantic Period

In spite of his valiant efforts, Coleridge failed to give any substantial check to the elementarist philosophy of mind in England. The attempt to account for all the contents and actions of the mind by a minimal number of sensory elements and a minimal number of associative laws continued to dominate the psychology of the age. Indeed, the system only achieved its most detailed and uncompromising statement in 1829, with the *Analysis of the Phenomena of the Human Mind* of James Mill—'the reviver and second founder,' as his son said, of Hartley's associationist psychology.[80]

The elder Mill had little interest in poetry, and in formulating the laws of association he felt no need to make special provision for the poetic process. The associative connections of the poet differ no whit from those of merchant, lawyer, or mathematician; poetic ideas 'succeed one another, according to the same laws. . . They differ from them by this only, that the ideas of which they are composed, are ideas of different things.'[81] When, in 1859, John Stuart Mill edited his father's book, although he inserted corrections of many other passages, he let this observation pass without challenge. Some twenty-six years earlier, however, in that period when he had zealously applied himself to solving the secret of poetry, he had written, in seeming contradiction to his father's doctrine:

What constitutes the poet is not the imagery nor the thoughts, nor even the feelings, but the law according to which they are called up. He is a poet, not because he has ideas of any particular kind, but because the succession of his ideas is subordinate to the course of his emotions.[82]

It turns out, however, that the younger Mill remained an associationist, more open-minded, though hardly less thorough-going, than his father. He merely adapted the earlier theory to his own view that poetry is 'the expression or uttering forth of feeling'[83] by delivering to the feelings the total control over the associative process. That association may involve not only sensory images, but also the feelings (themselves often regarded as aggregates of elementary pleasures and pains), was a doctrine coeval with the modern form of the theory itself. It had also been noted by theorists in the associationist tradition that a feeling or mood may help steer the course of association; Gerard, for one, demonstrated that 'a present passion' often suggests 'trains of ideas which derive their connexion, not from their relation to one another, but chiefly from the congruity to the . . . passion.'[84] Mill's innovation was merely to take what had hitherto been a part and make it the total explanation of the specifically poetic process of invention.

'Whom, then, shall we call poets?' Mill asks, and answers: 'Those who are so constituted, that emotions are the links of association by which their ideas, both sensuous and spiritual, are connected together.' He specifically substitutes a determining feeling for the determining design or plan posited by earlier associationists, in order to account for the formation of an aesthetic whole:

At the centre of each group of thoughts or images will be found a feeling; and the thoughts or images are only there because the feeling was there. All the combinations which the mind puts together, all the pictures which it paints, the wholes which Imagination constructs out of the materials supplied by Fancy, will be indebted to some dominant *feeling,* not as in other natures to a dominant *thought,* for their unity and consistency of character—for what distinguishes them from incoherencies.[85]

In this passage, Coleridge's organic imagination, although casually distinguished from the fancy, is reduced once more to a mechanical faculty combining particles of ideas, and the unity achieved by this process is not an organic unity, but a unity of emotional coherence. In the best poems of Shelley—the prime example, according to Mill, of the natural poet—'unity of feeling' is 'the harmonizing principle which a central idea is to minds of another class . . . supplying the coherency and consistency which would else have been wanting.'[86]

Even when we turn to those contemporaries who were poets or critics by profession, we find little support or understanding of what Coleridge aimed to achieve by his theory of the imagination. We do find in characteristic romantic discussions of imagination a superlative evaluation of the function and status of this faculty; a frequent lapse of what had recently been an almost universal recourse to associative laws to explain its workings; a pre-occupation with the office of the emotions in poetic invention; and a stress on the power of poetic imagination to modify the objects of sense. Not infrequently, we also hear echoes of Coleridge's antithesis between fancy and imagination, but the distinction is usually desultory and tends to collapse entirely, because unsupported by the firm understructure of Coleridge's philosophical principles.

Six years before the appearance of the *Biographia Literaria,* Charles Lamb used a concept of imagination to justify his preference of Hogarth's extraordinary engraving, 'Gin Lane,' over Poussin's celebrated 'Plague of Athens':

There is more of imagination in it—that power which draws all things to one— which makes things animate and inanimate, beings with their attributes, subjects and their accessories, take one colour, and serve to one effect. . . The very houses . . . seem drunk—seem absolutely reeling from the effect of that diabolical spirit of phrenzy which goes forth over the whole composition.[87]

This passage was justly admired by Wordsworth; and it is safe to assume that Coleridge would have agreed that this power of coadunating every part, with no detail left irrelevant, and even the houses made obeisant to the passion, is a gift of imagination—the faculty, as he said, 'that forms the many into one.'[88] But Lamb, though a gifted and sensitive literary commentator, was disinclined to speculation or theoretical construction, and has little more to say on the matter.

Hazlitt, on the other hand, considered himself to be a philosopher as well as critic, and a number of his comments on the poetic imagination also approximate those of Coleridge. 'The imagination is that faculty which represents objects, not as they are in themselves, but as they are moulded by other thoughts and feelings into an infinite variety of shapes and combinations of power.' Among the illustrations of this faculty Hazlitt includes Coleridge's favorite, the madness of Lear:

Again, when [Lear] exclaims in the mad scene, 'The little dogs and all, Tray, Blanche, and Sweetheart, see, they bark at me!' it is passion lending occasion to imagination to make every creature in league against him. . .[89]

In addition Hazlitt, like Coleridge, objected to the atomism and analytic rationalism of eighteenth-century psychology. But his own psychology, as we noticed in the preceding chapter, was a dynamic one, focusing on the nisus, the intricate urgencies underlying human behavior, and viewing the literary imagination both as the organ of sympathetic self-protection and as a compensatory instrument which 'gives an obvious relief to the indistinct and importunate cravings of the will.' [90] For Coleridge's organic idealism, Hazlitt had no sympathy whatever. He wrote a derisory review of Coleridge's *Statesman's Manual,* ending with a citation of the central passage in which Coleridge analyzed a growing plant in order to read it 'in a figurative sense' for correspondences 'of the spiritual world.' This excerpt Hazlitt labeled 'Mr. Coleridge's Description of a Green Field,' and on it he commented: 'This will do. It is well observed by Hobbes, that "it is by means of words only that a man becometh excellently wise or excellently foolish." ' [91]

We turn now to Wordsworth, whose poetry had first opened Coleridge's eyes to the need of positing the existence of a faculty of imagination, who had been in close communication with Coleridge at the very time when that theorist was maturing his anti-mechanistic philosophy, and who entirely agreed with his friend that the inveterate elementarism of eighteenth-century thought,

> Viewing all objects unremittingly
> In disconnection dead and spiritless;
> And still dividing, and dividing still,

wages 'an impious warfare with the very life Of our own souls.' It might confidently be expected that Wordsworth's extensive differentiation between fancy and imagination—developed to sanction the segregation, in the edition of 1815, of his 'Poems of the Fancy' from his 'Poems of the Imagination'— would show essential conformity to that of Coleridge.

On one point, Wordsworth, indeed, is unreservedly at one with Coleridge: in the opinion, as he gravely affirms, that he has himself demonstrated that he possesses imagination, in poems 'which have the same ennobling tendency as the productions of men, in this kind, worthy to be holden in undying remembrance.' [92] Some of his descriptions of the faculty, too, are consonant with those of Coleridge. In an imaginative simile—or as he puts it, when the faculty is 'employed upon images in a conjunction by which they modify each other'—'the two objects unite and coalesce in just comparison.' In other instances, Wordsworth's imagination, like Coleridge's, 'shapes and *creates*' by 'consolidating numbers into unity. . .' Two of Wordsworth's examples of poetic imagination (Lear on the heath, and Milton's description of the coming of the Messiah to battle) were afterward cited by Coleridge as well. [93] And upon first reading, it did seem to Coleridge, as he tells us in the fourth chapter of the *Biographia,* that Wordsworth's theory only differed from his own 'chiefly perhaps, as our objects were different.' Eight chapters farther along, however, Coleridge expressed a change of opinion: 'After a more accurate perusal of Mr. Wordsworth's remarks on the imagination . . . I find that my conclusions are not so consentient with his as, I confess, I had taken for granted.' [94]

The reasons for Coleridge's disappointment with Wordsworth's discussion are not far to seek. The imagination, Wordsworth says, is creative; yet, he asks, 'is it not the less true that Fancy, as she is an active, is also, under her own laws and in her own spirit, a creative faculty?' [95] Worse still, Wordsworth indicates not only that fancy is creative, but that imagination is *associative:* both powers alike serve 'to modify, to create, and to associate.' At one point Wordsworth describes imagination as a mode of dissection and recombination in almost exactly the terms of Dugald Stewart, referred to earlier in this chapter. 'These processes of imagination,' he says, 'are carried on either by conferring additional properties upon an object, or abstracting from it some of those which it actually possesses,' thus enabling it to act on the mind 'like a new existence.' [96] Finally, Wordsworth takes specific issue with Coleridge's differentiation, written for Southey's *Omniana* (1812), between the imagination as the 'shaping and modifying power' and the fancy as 'the aggregative and associative power.' 'My objection,' Wordsworth declares, is 'only that the definition is too general.'

To aggregate and to associate, to evoke and to combine, belong as well to the Imagination as to the Fancy; but either the materials evoked and combined are different; or they are brought together under a different law, and for a different purpose.[97]

To this Coleridge feels compelled to reply in the *Biographia* that 'if, by the power of evoking and combining, Mr. Wordsworth means the same as, and no more than, I meant by the aggregative and associative, I continue to deny, that it belongs at all to the imagination. . .' [98]

This dispute may seem much ado about a purely verbal difference. But from Coleridge's point of view, Wordsworth's vocabulary showed a regressive tendency to conflate the organic imagination with mechanical fancy, by describing it once again in terms of the subtraction, addition, and association of the elements of sensory images; and in doing this, Wordsworth had incautiously given the key to their position away to the enemy. According to A. N. Whitehead, 'Wordsworth in his whole being expresses a conscious reaction against the mentality of the eighteenth century,' and the nature-poetry of the romantic revival (of which *The Excursion* is Whitehead's prime example) 'was a protest on behalf of the organic view of nature.' [99] The truth is, however, that in his critical writings, Wordsworth retained to a notable degree the terminology and modes of thinking of eighteenth-century associationism. But to Coleridge, the metaphoric failure to maintain the difference in kind between mechanism and organism, in the crucial instance of the faculties of fancy and imagination, threatened collapse to the dialectic structure of his total philosophy.

The further degeneration of Coleridge's distinction is plainly evident in Leigh Hunt's anthology, which he entitled *Imagination and Fancy*. In Hunt's introductory essay the difference between these faculties resolves into a difference between levity and gravity in the poet's attitude.

[Poetry] embodies and illustrates its impressions by imagination, or images of the objects of which it treats . . . in order that it may enjoy and impart the feeling of their truth in its utmost conviction and affluence.

It illustrates them by fancy, which is a lighter play of imagination, or the feeling of analogy coming short of seriousness, in order that it may laugh with what it loves, and show how it can decorate with fairy ornament.[100]

A similar procedure has been followed by most commentators on Coleridge's theory of imagination, whether they deplore or admire Coleridge as a critic. As did the writers in Coleridge's life-time, so many succeeding writers have either made the difference out to be a trivial one between serious and playful poetry, or else, on various grounds, have melted the two processes, that Coleridge so painstakingly separated, back into one.[101] It is a final irony that I. A. Richards, who takes the crucial import of the distinction between fancy and imagination more seriously than any critic since Coleridge himself, and who attacks vigorously earlier efforts to conflate the distinction, goes on to do very much the same thing. Writing as a Benthamite or materialist 'trying to interpret . . . the utterance of an extreme Idealist,' he translates the difference between the products of the faculties into that of the number of 'links' or 'cross-connections' between their 'units of meaning.' These relations, quite comparable to the links of 'similarity' between 'ideas' in standard associationist analysis, serve once again to convert Coleridge's distinction in kind into a quantitative difference along a single scale. But Richards differs from other commentators in his awareness of what he is about. He undertakes deliberately to substitute for Coleridge's description one that he finds more congenial and, for his purposes, fruitful, however conscious that his 'refreshed atomism—a counting of inter-relations' might 'sometimes have been repugnant, as suggesting mechanical treatment, to Coleridge himself.'[102]

The history of such philosophical disagreement makes it exceedingly dubious that this difference can ever be resolved by rational argument. Any logical and semantic analysis of the key terms in the dispute—'part,' 'unity,' 'relations,' 'links,' 'similarities,' 'coadunation,' 'growth,'—finally gets down to an appeal to the observed facts, and about these facts there is blank disagreement. When those of us whom Coleridge (with scant justice to the historical figure) called 'Aristotelians' confront his example of an imaginative passage—

> Look! how a bright star shooteth from the sky
> So glides he in the night from Venus' eye—

we see a patent combination of parts; and we go on to explain its difference from Coleridge's illustration of fancy,

> Full gently now she takes him by the hand,
> A lily prison'd in a gaol of snow,
> Or ivory in an alabaster band;
> So white a friend engirts so white a foe,

as a matter of the multiplicity and intimacy of the relations between these parts. When Coleridge, speaking for the 'Platonists' who for him constituted the remainder of the planet's population, looked at the first pair of lines, he saw a simple integral of perception, in which constituent parts are isolated, properly enough, for purposes of critical analysis, but at the price of altering their character and momentarily destroying the whole.

In our day those who wish to save the division between things-as-they-are and things as they appear to some other person, tend to account for Coleridge's stubbornness in this matter by referring to the non-rational elements of his personality; F. L. Lucas, for example, speculates that Coleridge's longing for unity 'may be mere homesickness for the womb.'[103] Coleridge himself preferred to explain such differences in perception on rational grounds. 'Facts, you know, are not truths; they are not conclusions; they are not even premises, but in the nature and parts of premises.'[104] The crucial difference lies in the choice of the initial premises (often, if I have not been mistaken, the analogical premises) of our reasoning, and the validity of the choice is measured by the adequacy of its coherently reasoned consequences in making the universe intelligible and manageable. If this criterion incorporates our need to make the universe emotionally as well as intellectually manageable, is not that the most important requirement of all?

VIII

The Psychology of Literary Invention:
UNCONSCIOUS GENIUS AND ORGANIC GROWTH

For if a house or other such final object is to be realized, it is necessary that such and such material shall exist, and it is necessary that first this and then that shall be produced, and first this and then that set in motion, and so on in continuous succession, until the end and final result is reached, for the sake of which each prior thing is produced and exists. As with these productions of art, so also is it with the productions of nature. . .

ARISTOTLE, *De partibus animalium*

The deeper anyone descends into himself, into the construction and source of his noblest thoughts, the more will he cover his eyes and feet and say: 'What I am, that have I become. Like a tree have I grown: the germ was there; but air, earth, and all the elements, which I did not myself provide, had to make their contribution to form the germ, the fruit, the tree.'

J. G. HERDER, *Vom Erkennen und Empfinden der menschlichen Seele*

It is all a Tree: circulation of sap and influences, mutual communication of every minutest leaf with the lowest talon of a root, with every other greatest and minutest portion of the whole.

THOMAS CARLYLE, *The Hero as Poet*

To PUT THE WHOLE before the part, the living and growing before the fixed and lifeless, and to use the former to explain the latter, is an intellectual procedure with a long and complex history. Elements from the speculations of both Plato and Aristotle entered into the gradual development of an organistic philosophy. Plato's Timaeus proposed the doctrine that a soul had been diffused through the body of the world by the Demiurge, 'wherefore, using the language of probability, we may say that the world became a living creature. . .'[1] The concept of an *anima mundi* recurs, with many variations, in the Stoic philosophers, in Plotinus, in Giordano Bruno and other thinkers of the Italian Renaissance, as well as in the Platonizing English divines of the seventeenth century. Newton's hypothesis of a ubiquitous God, willing the movement of all physical bodies 'within his boundless uniform sensorium,'[2] together with Shaftesbury's more purely Platonistic conception of 'that single ONE' who is 'original soul, diffusive, vital in all, inspiriting the whole,'[3] became a commonplace of physico-theology in eighteenth-century prose and verse; and so helped to keep alive the view that the universe is in some fashion a living thing, instead of a machine run by an absentee mechanic. Ultimately, the World-Soul was incorporated into the Nature-Philosophy of the German romantics. In the earlier and cruder versions of the concept, sometimes found in Renaissance theory, the world had been said to be, in literal fact, an immense animal in its constitution and functions, and even in its method of procreation. When in German theory this concept was subtilized, and the universe held to be not literally an animal, but animal-like, and only to the extent that it is most appositely described by categories derived from living and growing organisms, the old cosmological myth achieved the status of a coherent and all-inclusive metaphysic.

To this development, Aristotle, in his turn, had contributed the concepts that natural things are distinguished from artificial things in that they have an internal source of motion, instead of an external efficient agent, and that biological coming-to-be is a progressive determination of form unfolding from within. These Aristotelian ideas eventually contributed to organic theory the central conceptions of genesis and development, but only after they had been taken out of a philosophical context that was in many ways alien to organic thinking. For one thing, as Werner Jaeger points out, Aristotle's interest was not in the process but in the end-result of growth. 'What interests him is the fact, not that something *is coming to be,* but that *something* is coming to be; that something fixed and normative is making its way into existence—the form.'[4] Furthermore, to extend the categories specific to biology to all other areas of intellection, after the fashion of a fully developed organicism, violates Aristotle's ruling methodological principle that each science has its particular subject matter and mode of procedure.

In the seventeenth and eighteenth centuries, Aristotle's 'teleological' explanation of nature, with its emphasis on inherent formal and final causes, persisted in the science of biology after it had been banished from inquiries into the physical world. Its survival there set the stage for the discovery, by German thinkers of the later eighteenth century, that the nature and events of the physical universe in all its parts, and of human beings in all their processes and productions, manifestly exhibit the properties that, by a strange obtuseness, had hitherto been predicated solely of living and growing things. The excitement and energy with which this discovery was prosecuted was a natural reaction to the boundless pretensions of the mechanical point of view, which radical theorists had pushed beyond the theological and other limits set up by both Newton and Descartes. As Goethe described the response to Holbach's *System of Nature* among the members of his circle at Strasbourg in 1770:

We did not understand how such a book could be dangerous. It appeared to us so dark, so Cimmerian, so deathlike, that we found it difficult to endure its presence, and shuddered at it as at a specter. . .

How hollow and empty did we feel in this melancholy, atheistical half-night, in which earth vanished with all its images, heaven with all its stars. There was to be an eternal matter in eternal motion, and by this motion, right and left and in all directions, without anything further, were to be produced the infinite phenomena of existence.[5]

Similarly repelled, a more systematic philosopher, Friedrich Schelling, constructed an opposing world-view, based on the concept of the organism. Once abroad, the two opponent schemes demonstrate a curious history of mutual infiltration. Since both mechanism and organicism (implicitly asserting that all the universe is like some one element in that universe) claim to include everything in their scope, neither can stop until it has swallowed up the archetype of the other. In consequence, as the extreme mechanist claimed organisms to be higher-order machines, so the extreme organicist, in his philosophical counter-attack, maintained that physical things and processes are simply more rudimentary forms of organism.

My topic, however, is not the fascinating history of the general philosophy of organism, but only the increasing tendency to view a work of art, in its becoming and being, as endowed with organic properties. It will be convenient to order this exposition around three inter-related topics, which turn up repeatedly as the pivotal elements in the development of an organismic theory of art: the topics of 'natural genius,' of inspired composition, and of the literary 'grace,' or spontaneous stroke of invention totally beyond the reach of deliberate intention, method, or rule. Such concepts were equally uncongenial to the central neo-classic view of art as a deliberate craft of ordering means to ends, and to the mechanical scheme of associative invention with which this theory was so often combined. As a result, they were sometimes ignored or denied by traditional theorists; but more frequently, they were accepted as indubitable but somewhat anomalous facts of composition and left on the periphery of critical theory in the form of critical 'mysteries.' These mysteries of earlier theory became the very facts most easily comprehended by a criticism which analogized the artistic process to the spontaneous growth of a plant. The momentous historical shift from the view that the making of a work of art is a supremely purposeful activity to the view that its coming-into-being is, basically, a spontaneous process independent of intention, precept, or even consciousness, was the natural concomitant of an organic aesthetics. But, it will appear, no sooner were such 'irrational' aspects of artistic invention satisfactorily accommodated in the new theory, than a different order of facts, hitherto readily taken into account, became, in their turn, recalcitrant to explanation.

i. Natural Genius, Inspiration, and Grace

We may begin with Addison's distinction, which he did not invent, but sharpened and popularized, between the genius who is born—the 'natural genius'—and the genius who is made. Natural geniuses, a class comprising Homer, Pindar, the Old Testament poets, and Shakespeare, are 'the prodigies of mankind, who by the mere strength of natural parts, and without any assistance of art or learning, have produced works that were the delight of their own times, and the wonder of posterity.' The second class of geniuses, differing in kind rather than in excellence, 'are those that have formed themselves by rules, and submitted the greatness of their natural talents to the corrections and restraints of art'; among them are numbered Plato, Virgil, and Milton. With natural genius, Addison associates other concepts which recur as leitmotifs in the critical tradition we are pursuing. Such authors are characterized by 'a natural fire and impetuosity' and 'noble sallies of imagination,' and achieve works that are 'nobly wild and extravagant,' 'sublime,' as well as 'singular in their kind, and inimitable.' They are also subject to inspiration; Pindar, for example, exhibits 'that divine impulse which raises the mind above itself, and makes the sounds more than human.' Finally, Addison illustrates the difference between the natural and the artful genius by the difference between the plants in a natural state, and those in a formal garden:

[Natural genius] is like a rich soil in a happy climate, that produces a whole wilderness of noble plants rising in a thousand beautiful landskips, without any certain order or regularity. In the other it is the same rich soil under the same happy climate, that has been laid out in walks and parterres, and cut into shape and beauty by the skill of the gardener.[6]

Behind Addison's thesis, of course, was the ancient question whether a poet is born or made; as Horace said,

> Natura fieret laudabile carmen an arte
> Quaesitum est.

And very early, inspiration—whether regarded as a celestial or mundane form of madness—was said to be either the constant accompaniment or the actual equivalent of the *ingenium* with which a poet is endowed by nature. 'Hence it is,' according to Aristotle, 'that poetry demands a man with a special gift for it, or else one with a touch of madness in him. . .'[7] This conjunction of nature and inspiration became commonplace in the Renaissance. The argument for 'October' in Spenser's *Shepheards Calender* is typical: Poetry is 'no arte, but a divine gift and heavenly instinct not to be gotten by laboure and learning, but adorned with both; and poured into the witte by a certain *enthousiasmos* and celestiall inspiration.'[8] In Addison's version, 'genius' has come to signify the integral poet as well as the inborn poetic power, while innate endowment is held to be not only a necessary but (in a certain few cases) a sufficient condition for the achievement of the greatest poetry.

Pope's Prefaces to his edition of Shakespeare and to his translation of Homer's *Iliad* have many points in common with Addison's *Spectator* 160, and proved almost as influential on later theory. Shakespeare is supremely the poet of nature and inspiration, and also (because independent of prior models) a complete original.

If ever any author deserved the name of an *Original*, it was Shakespear. Homer himself drew not his art so immediately from the fountains of Nature; it . . . came to him not without some tincture of the learning, or some cast of the models, of those before him. The poetry of Shakespear was inspiration indeed: he is not so much an Imitator, as an Instrument of Nature; and 'tis not so just to say he speaks from her, as that she speaks through him.

To these ideas, Pope joins the idea of 'felicity,' which in his time, as we shall see in a moment, was almost a technical term of criticism: in his 'sentiments' Shakespeare often exhibits 'a talent very peculiar, something between penetration and felicity.' Pope concludes by comparing the distinction between Shakespearean and 'more finished and regular' dramas to that between 'an ancient majestic piece of Gothic architecture' and 'a neat modern building.'[9] But in his earlier Preface to the *Iliad*, he had echoed and expanded Addison's parallel between natural genius and a natural landscape. The 'invention' which characterizes all great geniuses is equatable with nature, and 'as in most regular gardens, Art can only reduce the beauties of Nature to more regularity'; the *Iliad* is compared to 'a wild paradise,' and also to a single item within a garden—a growing tree.

A work of this kind seems like a mighty tree which rises from the most vigorous seed, is improved with industry, flourishes, and produces the finest fruit. . .[10]

The various ideas associated with natural genius posed a number of problems to eighteenth-century critics which require our consideration:

(1) *Poetic inspiration.* Inspiration (or, in its Greek form, 'enthusiasm') is the oldest, most widespread, and most persistent account of poetic invention. If we compare the various forms in which the doctrine has been presented over the centuries, we find a recurrent area of agreement amid differences. Where poets and apologists for poetry largely agree is in their description of the facts of an extraordinary experience to which at least some poets are susceptible while composing; where they differ is in the theory they adduce to explain these facts.

The experience of poetic inspiration is said to differ from normal ideation in possessing some or all of these four characteristics: (a) The composition is sudden, effortless, and unanticipated. The poem or passage springs to completion all at once, without the prior intention of the poet, and without that process of considering, rejecting, and selecting alternatives which ordinarily intervenes between the intention and the achievement. (b) The composition is involuntary and automatic; it comes and goes at its own pleasure, independently of the will of the poet. (c) In the course of composition, the poet feels intense excitement, usually described as a state of elation and rapture, but occasionally said to be racking and painful in its initial stages, though followed by a sense of blissful relief and quiescence. (d) The completed work is as unfamiliar and surprising to the poet as though it had been written by someone else.

The earliest and most tenacious theory adduced to explain these phenomena attributed the poem to the dictation of a supernatural visitant. All good poets, Socrates told Ion the rhapsode, in a dialogue whose pervading irony escaped many later readers, 'compose their beautiful poems not by art, but because they are inspired and possessed.' 'God himself is the speaker, and . . . through them he is conversing with us.'[11] The Hebrew singers claimed that they kindled to communicate the word of God: 'I kept silent, yea even from good words. . . And while I was thus musing, the fire kindled and at last I spoke with my tongue.' Later tradition assimilated the pagan doctrine of inspiration to the 'mysteries' of Christian faith; and in the Renaissance, when the attribution of secular poems to Apollo and the muses had largely become a transparent fiction of the sonneteer, the tradition of Holy Writ remained more vital.[12] Robert Herrick's 'Not Every Day Fit for Verse' is worth quoting because it so neatly summarizes the facts claimed for inspired composition.

> 'Tis not ev'ry day, that I
> Fitted am to prophesie:
> No, but when the Spirit fils
> The fantastick Pannicles:
> Full of fier; then I write
> As the Godhead doth indite.
>
> Thus enrag'd, my lines are hurl'd
> Like the Sybell's, through the world,
> Look how next the holy fier
> Either slakes, or doth retire;
> So the Fancie cooles, till when
> That brave Spirit comes agen.

The theory of a supernatural afflatus, it will be noted, fulfills all the requirements of a good hypothesis; it is simple, intelligible, and comprehends all the facts. That the poem is dictated to the poet by a visitor from without accounts for its spontaneity, involuntarism, and unfamiliarity; that the visitor is divine accounts for the accompanying ecstasy. But animistic hypotheses, assigning mental phenomena to the will of a supernatural being, passed out of favor in the latter seventeenth century. Any recourse to 'enthusiasm' in that age was dangerous, because it suggested the claim of disorderly religious zealots to have private access to God. In addition, the sensationalist theory of mind, with its reliance on the mechanical motions and combinations of conscious, mirror-like images, afforded no place either for the mysterious facts or the supernatural theory of inspiration. Thomas Hobbes hailed Davenant's attack on the poet's claim to be inspired, and wondered why a man, 'enabled to speak wisely from the principles of nature and his own meditation, loves rather to be thought to speak by inspiration, like a Bagpipe.'[13] Most importantly, the notion that some poetry is spontaneous was out of harmony with the Horatian tradition that poetry, although requiring native talent, is in practice a laborious and formal craft. In 1576 Castelvetro insisted that the notion of divine frenzy had originated in an ignorance of the art of poetry, and had been fostered by the vainglory of poets; to write a poem of real value, the poet must work deliberately, must 'sapere il perchè.'[14]

By the eighteenth century, the Horatian point of view had been reinforced by the rationalism of French neo-classicists and had largely lost the Platonic coloring with which it had been endowed by Renaissance critics. Johnson was skeptical toward Gray's notion that he could not write but 'at happy moments,' and toward Richardson's report of the dependence of Milton's poetic faculty upon 'an *impetus* or *oestrum*.' [15] According to Reynolds, only they who never look beyond the finished product to the 'long labour and application of an infinite number and infinite variety of acts' which went into its making, will conclude that an art can be achieved 'by those only who have some gift of the nature of inspiration bestowed upon them.' [16]

Many eighteenth-century poets, however, continued to lay claim to inspiration in polished couplets, and asked divine assistance in invocations which were hardly less pure formulas than the 'Hail, Muse! et cetera' with which Byron opens a canto of *Don Juan*. And in the main, even the more rigid theorists admitted the existence of inspiration, but in their brisk and business-like way, insisted that it be subject to the control of judgment, decorum, and the rules. 'Though his Discourse,' Rapin had said, 'ought in some manner to resemble that of one inspired; yet his Mind must always be serene, that he may discern when to *let his Muse run mad,* and when to govern his Transports.' [17] Some critics, accepting the facts of inspired composition, specifically substituted a natural for a supernatural hypothesis to account for their appearance. Alexander Gerard's discussion is especially interesting because it undertakes to give a detailed psychological explanation of enthusiasm—'a very common, if not an inseparable attendant of genius'—without violating the assumptions of the associationist theory of mind.

When an ingenious track of thinking presents itself, though but casually, to true genius, occupied it may be with something else, imagination darts alongst it with great rapidity; and by this rapidity its ardour is more inflamed. The velocity of its motion sets it on fire, like a chariot wheel which is kindled by the quickness of its revolution. . . Its motions become still more impetuous, till the mind is enraptured with the subject, and exalted into an extasy. In this manner the fire of genius, like a divine impulse, raises the mind above itself, and by the natural influence of imagination actuates it as if it were supernaturally inspired. . . By elevating and enlivening the fancy, [enthusiastick ardour] gives vigour and activity to its associating power, enables it to proceed with alacrity in searching out the necessary ideas. . .[18]

Here are the traditional facts of inspiration, but explained now in exclusively mechanical terms of space, time, and motion: the more than usual speed of the motion of associated ideas accounts for the suddenness and seeming spontaneity of the composition, while the mechanical phenomenon of friction serves, very handily indeed, to explain its fire and ecstasy.

To establish a contrast, we may glance ahead fifty years to Shelley's discussion of the same literary phenomena. Peacock's *Four Ages of Poetry* came to Shelley's hand while he was in the process of reading Plato's *Ion,* and he had earlier recommended to Peacock himself the discussion of poetic madness in the *Phaedrus,* by way of antidote to 'the false and narrow systems of criticism which every poetical empiric vents' in this age.[19] In his 'Defence of Poetry,' Shelley insists that valid poetic composition is uncontrollable, automatic, and ineffably joyous. 'A man cannot say, "I will compose poetry."' It is 'an error to assert that the finest passages of poetry are produced by labour and study'; when they come, the evanescent visitations are 'elevating and delightful beyond all expression.' Shelley echoes the ancient theory concerning 'the visitations of the divinity in man,' and like earlier Neoplatonists, suggests also that poetic inspiration is to be identified with the blissful contemplation of the sempiternal Forms. But then, after his wont, he shadows forth a third hypothesis, this time naturalistic, according to which inspiration is an empirical phenomenon of the mind itself:

For the mind in creation is as a fading coal, which some invisible influence, like an inconstant wind, awakens to transitory brightness; this power arises from within, like the colour of a flower which fades and changes as it is developed, and the conscious portions of our natures are unprophetic either of its approach or its departure.

And he goes on to introduce a parallel between the inventive process and embryonic growth.

A great statue or picture grows under the power of the artist as a child in the mother's womb; and the very mind which directs the hands in formation is incapable of accounting to itself for the origin, the gradations, or the media of the process.[20]

Though he starts with the Platonic facts, Shelley ends with a theory which is not in Plato. An inspired poem or painting is sudden, effortless, and complete, not because it is a gift from without, but because it grows of itself, within a region of the mind which is inaccessible either to awareness or control. The 'birth and recurrence' of poetry, he says again, 'have no necessary connexion with the consciousness or will.' And as he re-formulates the matter in a letter written that same year:

The poet and the man are two different natures; though they exist together they may be unconscious of each other, and incapable of deciding upon each other's powers and efforts by any reflex act.[21]

The concept of a compartmentation between the creative and the conscious mind, the description of inspired invention in terms of gestation and growth—these are not unusual in Shelley's generation, but are remote from the earlier interpretations of inspiration either as a ghostly dictation or as a matter of psychic heat and celerity. To trace the emergence of such ideas during the preceding century, we must look to certain speculations conducted in a radical spirit, outside the main course both of Horatian criticism and of associationist psychology.

(2) *Poetic grace.* Neo-classic criticism made allowance for another attribute of invention, 'grace,' which is not only, like inspiration, beyond the scope of art, but even of critical understanding. The concept, under various terms, had been anticipated in antiquity, and in the Italian Renaissance 'la grazia' was widely used to connote a quality, difficult to describe, which is a free gift of nature or heaven, hence to be achieved negligently, if at all, and never by effort or rule.[22] One alternate name for such a quality was 'felicity,' which Bacon, for one, ascribed to music, and by extension, to painting. 'Not but I think a painter may make a better face than ever was; but he must do it by a kind of felicity, (as a musician that maketh an excellent air in music,) and not by rule.'[23] In 1660, paying tribute 'To My Honor'd Friend Sir Robert Howard, on His Excellent Poems,' Dryden developed an elaborate poetic logic around this concept. The 'native sweetness' of Howard's verse excels its 'art,' and is comparable to the 'wild notes,' uninformed by art, of cageless birds. In them is 'no sign of toil'; therefore, either 'your art hides art,'

> Or 't is some happiness that still pursues
> Each act and motion of your graceful Muse.
> Or is it fortune's work . . . ?

To the quality of grace there was soon attached the phrase, 'the I-don't-know-what,' which had been current in Spain and Italy, and afterward in France, before being adopted in England. Such a quality, Bouhours pointed out (in a dialogue entitled 'Le je ne sais quoi') is to be found both in natural objects and in works of art, and is indefinable as well as unpredictable. 'Sa nature est d'être incompréhensible et inexplicable'; it is a 'mystery,' a charm in sensible objects 'which touches the heart,' to be known only by the effects it produces. 'Grace,' 'felicity,' 'mystery'—the modification,

by this time, of aesthetic by religious ideas is unmistakable. Father Bouhours even ventures explicitly to equate aesthetic grace with God's free gift
of mercy, for what is grace in the latter sense 'but a supernatural *je ne sais
quoi* that one can neither explain nor comprehend?' [24] A few years later the
notion was given further sanction by a founding father of neo-classic doctrine, René Rapin. In Rymer's translation of Rapin's *Reflections on Aristotle's Treatise of Poesie* we find a stress on the enigmatic character of literary grace, together with a list of alternative names for this quality which
passed at once into standard usage:

> Yet is there in *Poetry* as in other *Arts*, certain *things* that *cannot be expressed*,
> which are (as it were) *Mysteries*. There are no Precepts to teach the *hidden
> Graces*, the insensible *Charms*, and all that *secret power* of Poetry, which passes
> to the *Heart*, as there is no *method* to teach to *please*, 'tis a pure effect of *Nature*.[25]

Also in 1674 Boileau published his influential translation of Longinus, and
soon afterward, the doctrine of the *je ne sais quoi* was merged with Longinus' 'transport,' and his elevation of irregular grandeur over flawless mediocrity; and all these qualities together were attributed particularly to
the writings of a 'genius.' [26]

    The *locus classicus* in which Pope discusses the *je ne sais quoi* in his
Essay on Criticism is a compendious version of what had gone before. 'True
ease in writing,' Pope says, 'comes from art, not chance'; yet there is a province left for composition outside the jurisdiction of art and rules.

> Some beauties yet no precepts can declare,
> For there's a happiness as well as care.
> Music resembles Poetry, in each
> Are nameless graces which no methods teach,
> And which a master-hand alone can reach.

These beauties are a matter of 'lucky licence,' and Pegasus may

> From vulgar bounds with brave disorder part,
> And snatch a grace beyond the reach of art,
> Which without passing through the judgment, gains
> The heart, and all its end at once attains. . .
> Great wits sometimes may gloriously offend,
> And rise to faults true Critics dare not mend.[27]

And later even such a rationalist as Johnson left room for the occurrence
in poetry of 'nameless and inexplicable elegancies which appeal wholly to
the fancy, from which we feel delight, but know not how they produce it,
and which may well be termed the enchantresses of the soul.' [28]

Within the artful province of neo-classicism, then, a preserve was set up to afford asylum to certain spontaneous and mysterious products of pure 'nature.' The *je ne sais quoi* in a work of art, recognized only by the intuitions of sensibility, cannot be explained in terms of its causes, nor precisely defined, nor even named except by a phrase which is an expression of our ignorance. There is often the implication that these happy chances have a way of occurring only to poets capable of calculating well; but when they luckily occur, he knows not how, they license him not only to transcend existing rules, but even to 'offend,' or break these rules, in order to achieve a sublimer poetry than rules can comprehend. Poetic inspiration, as we have seen, was no longer seriously attributed to Divinity; but in his commentary on Pope's description of the 'grace beyond the reach of art,' Bishop Warburton, like Father Bouhours, emphasized the affinity between these poetic mysteries and the supra-rational and contra-rational mysteries of the Christian faith. Pope, he says, points to beauties that rules can neither enable us 'to execute or taste.'

Being entirely the gift of heaven, art and reason have no further share in them than just to regulate their operations. These sublimities of poetry (like the mysteries of religion, some of which are above reason, and some contrary to it) may be divided into two sorts, such as are above rules, and such as are contrary to them.[29]

In this instance, as in so many others with which this book deals, theological concepts were brought into criticism with radical effect. Warburton's comment implies that, in criticism as in religion, faith takes over where reason must have its stop, and that with respect to certain poetic excellences we have no alternative to sheer acceptance, believing where we cannot prove.

(3) *Natural genius.* As the most inclusive concept, natural genius involved these questions and raised others as well. A poet of this order, in Addison's phrase, composes 'by the meer Strength of natural Parts,' without precedent either in concrete examples or in codified precepts and rules. Yet, all theorists agreed, it is from the products of such a genius that critics abstract the rules which they apply to the practice of later poets. As Pope described the way in which 'learned Greece' established her rules (*Essay on Criticism*, I, 98-9):

> Just precepts thus from great examples giv'n,
> She drew from them what they deriv'd from Heav'n.

By what process of mind, however, did a natural genius accord with rules without being aware of them? The 'invention' of geniuses who, like Homer and Shakespeare, were supposed to have written in the total absence or ignorance of earlier models also posed in an acute form the related problem which, as we saw in the preceding chapter, confronted critics in formulating the psychology of 'original' genius in all times, and of all degrees. That problem is, how are we to explain the mental origin of the 'design' of a work of literature for which there exists no prototype either in nature or in art?

James Harris sets the issue, in considering the case of authors who may be said 'to have excelled, not by Art, but by Nature; yet by a Nature, which gave birth to the perfection of Art.'

If these great writers were so excellent before Rules were established, or at least were known to them, what had they to direct their Genius, when Rules (to them at least) did not exist?

For critics who, like Harris, had a sufficient tincture of Platonism to entertain the possibility of ideas engraved in the mind at birth, the solution was simple. 'There never was a time, when rules did not exist.' 'We cannot admit, that Geniuses tho' prior to Systems, were prior also to Rules, because Rules from the beginning existed in their own Minds, and were a part of that immutable Truth, which is eternal and every where.' [30] Other critics, whose emphasis was on the artful element in poetry, minimized in other ways the difference in procedure for achieving excellence, whether by originality or by imitation, and whether before or after the availability of rules. Thus Joshua Reynolds, who considered the question at some length in his Sixth Discourse, pointed out that the genius is one who, while transcending 'any known and promulgated rules,' yet works according to subtler and tacit rules 'by a kind of scientific sense.'

It cannot be by chance, that excellencies are produced with any constancy or any certainty, for this is not the nature of chance; but the rules by which . . . such as are called men of Genius, work, are either such as they discover by their own peculiar observations, or of such a nice texture as not easily to admit being expressed in words. [31]

Critics of a different inclination, however, differentiated sharply between the poet of art and the poet of nature, and sought out concepts that would liberate the latter entirely from reliance on models or on the rational adaptation of means to ends. Shakespeare, Pope had said, is 'an Instrument of Nature, and 'tis not so just to say he speaks from her, as that she speaks through him': the phrasing implies that the poet may be a vehicle of productive forces outside his responsibility or control, and suggests the problem of how to explain the operation of that 'nature' in the production of poetic masterpieces. We find some tendency in Pope's own lifetime to identify the element of nature in the natural genius with those instinctive activities of animals, which, because they evolve entirely from inherited dispositions, are examples of unlearned behavior *par excellence*. Long before, Milton had equated the composition of Shakespeare (who was and remained the chief poet around whom these concepts developed) with the instinctive singing of a bird, when he described L'Allegro attending the stage to hear

> sweetest Shakespear fancies childe
> Warble his native wood-notes wilde—

a passage that later prompted Joseph Warton's rhetorical question, in *The Enthusiast,*

> What are the lays of artful Addison,
> Coldly correct, to Shakespear's warblings wild?

And in 1690 Sir William Temple employed the analogy of the totally instinctive 'art' of bees to illustrate the natural, free, unlearned quality—the 'Grace'—in poetic composition.

The Truth is, there is something in the *Genius* of Poetry too Libertine to be confined to so many Rules; and whoever goes about to subject it to such Constraints loses both its Spirit and Grace, which are ever Native, and never learnt, even of the best Masters. . . [Poets] must work up their Cells with Admirable Art, extract their honey with infinite Labour, and sever it from the Wax with such Distinction and Choyce as belongs to none but themselves to perform or to judge.[32]

By 1732 Fontenelle, while admitting the need in poetry for 'natural talent' and 'enthusiasm,' so long as they remain under control of a presiding reason, found it necessary to decry the tendency to reduce all poetic capacity to the automatism of blind instinct.

What! is that which is most valuable in us to be that which depends least on us . . . and has the greatest conformity with the instinct of animals? For this enthusiasm and this furore, properly understood, reduce to veritable instincts. Bees make a work, true enough, but remarkable only in that they make it without meditation and without knowledge.[33]

But to account for the workings of nature in the mind of genius, other theorists turned from analogy with the instincts of birds and insects to analogy with the growth of a vegetable—an even lower form of life, but as it turned out, infinitely more pregnant of concepts for the theory of artistic creativity.

ii. Natural Genius and Natural Growth in Eighteenth-Century England

As A. O. Lovejoy has pointed out, the term 'nature,' in the usage in which it was opposed to 'art,' possessed two main areas of application. In reference to the mind of man, 'nature' designated those inborn attributes 'which are most spontaneous, unpremeditated, untouched by reflection or design, and free from the bondage of social convention.' In reference to the external world, it designated those parts of the universe which come into being independently of human effort and contrivance.[34] The element of nature in natural genius, of course, was comprehended under the first of these applications; but it was easy, in these discussions, to make the transition from human nature to external nature and to compare the natural products of mind to the products of the vegetable world. Addison and Pope, we remember, used the contrast between 'a wilderness of noble plants' and a garden shaped 'by the skill of the gardener' to illustrate the difference between the natural and the artful kinds of genius.[35] Genius, the Abbé du Bos also said, 'is therefore a plant which shoots up, as it were, of itself; but the quality and quantity of its fruit depends in a great measure on the culture it receives.'[36]

A most important document in the development of the vegetable concept of genius is Young's *Conjectures on Original Composition,* published in 1759. The attributes of 'natural genius' which are described in this essay are for the most part expanded from elements already present in Addison's essay; the principal novelty is Young's contempt for, and almost total abandonment of, the traditional rhetorical framework of art, with its emphasis on study, example, precept, and the skillful manipulation of means to end. Hence Addison's class of artful geniuses, the peers of the geniuses of nature, survives only in Young's contemptuous reference to the 'infantine genius . . . which like other infants, must be nursed, and educated, or it will come to naught.' An adult genius like Shakespeare, on the contrary, 'comes out of Nature's hand . . . at full growth, and mature,' apparently endowed at birth not only with the requisite mental powers but with sufficient knowledge as well. 'Learning is borrowed knowledge; genius is knowledge innate, and quite our own.' Young attributes to genius the standard characteristic of inspiration—'genius has ever been supposed to partake of something divine. *Nemo unquam vir magnus fuit, sine aliquo afflatu divino'* —as well as the power to effect 'natural unstudied graces,' which 'lie without the pale of learning's authorities, and laws. . . There is something in poetry beyond prose reason; there are mysteries in it not to be explained, but admired.' [37]

A striking aspect of Young's essay is his persistent, if unsystematic, way of alluding to the invisible architectonics of original invention in metaphors of vegetable growth. The mind of genius 'is a fertile and pleasant field' of which '*Originals* are the fairest flowers.' 'Nothing *Original* can rise, nothing immortal, can ripen, in any other sun' but that 'of our own genius.' 'An evocation of vegetable fruits depends on rain, air, and sun; an evocation of the fruits of genius no less depends on externals.' Most notable is this terse antithesis:

An *Original* may be said to be of a *vegetable* nature; it rises spontaneously from the vital root of genius; it *grows,* it is not *made. Imitations* are often a sort of *manufacture* wrought up by those *mechanics, art* and *labour,* out of pre-existent materials not their own.[38]

The passage might almost serve as a précis of Coleridge's basic distinction, half a century later, between mechanical making and organic growth, between the reordering of given materials by artificers like Beaumont and Fletcher, and the vital emergence of an original form in the plays of Shakespeare. An important difference, of course, is that for Coleridge (in specific opposition to the psychology of associationism as well as aspects of the neoclassic theory of art), the 'pre-existent materials' of the mechanical fancy comprehend the fixities and definites of all sense perception, and not merely the elements imitated from earlier works of art.

Neither member of Young's antithesis is unprecedented. The word 'mechanical' had been frequently used, with derogatory connotation, to distinguish those elements in a work which merely conform to structural rules, such as the unities, from the genuinely artistic performance, which comprehends subtler beauties and the inspired and lucky strokes of free imagination. Addison, for one, thus discriminated between 'the mechanical rules' and 'the very spirit and soul of fine writing'—'something more essential to the art, something that elevates and astonishes the fancy, and gives a greatness to the mind of the reader.' [39] Young's innovation is first, in setting up the growth of a plant as the contrary of mechanical manufacture, and second, in using the plant unequivocally as the analogue for the process, and not only the product, of genial creativity. In thus transferring the emphasis to the development of a work of art, Young imports from vegetable life certain attributes destined to become important concepts in organic aesthetics. As opposed to objects which are 'made' by 'art and labour,' the original work is *vital*, it *grows, spontaneously*, from a *root*, and (by implication) unfolds its original form from within outward.

In addition, Young—no less enamored of mystery in art than Sir Thomas Browne in religion—expands the realm of the mysterious poetic graces until he heralds the division of the creative mind into a conscious and commonplace surface and an inscrutable and fathomless depth. 'Another often sees that in us,' he tells us, 'which we see not in ourselves; and may there not be that in us which is unseen by both?' Young may even be taken to suggest that poetic inspiration can be explained as a sudden emergence out of this obscure profound of human nature:

Few authors of distinction but have experienced something of this nature, at the first beamings of their yet unsuspected genius on their hitherto dark Composition: The writer starts at it, as at a lucid meteor in the night; is much surprized; can scarce believe it true. . . This sensation, which I speak of in a writer, might favour, and so promote, the fable of poetic inspiration.[40]

Although he thus transfers the origin of inspired poetry to the poet's own mind, Young retains the ancient attitudes appropriate to an inspiring divinity. 'Therefore dive deep into thy bosom,' he exhorts the poet, 'contract full intimacy with the stranger within thee . . . let thy genius rise (if a genius thou hast) as the sun from chaos; and if I should then say, like an *Indian, Worship it,* (though too bold) yet should I say little more than my second rule enjoins, (*viz.*) *Reverence thyself.*' For as he had said earlier, with regard to the intellectual world, '*genius*, is that god within.'[41] So, in this extraordinary composition of a seventy-six-year-old cleric we find adumbrated, however scatteredly, the essential attributes of the romantic genius as we shall find him characterized by Fichte, Jean Paul, and Carlyle. He is a double-man compounded of knowable and unknowable elements, Godlike and venerable, as inscrutable to himself as to others, creative by processes which are vital and spontaneous like the self-effecting growth of a tree, whose greatest work springs unanticipated out of the darkness into the light of his consciousness.

In the development toward an organic aesthetics the third Earl of Shaftesbury was also important, but more by the nature of his great influence on

German writers than by his proper doctrine. The true poet, he said, is 'a second Maker.' 'Like that sovereign artist or universal plastic nature, he forms a whole, coherent and proportioned in itself, with due subjection and subordinacy of constituent parts.' Despite his use of 'plastic,' however, Shaftesbury envisions formative nature, on the model of Plato's Demiurge, as creating a fixed and finished universe according to a timeless and changeless pattern. The poet who imitates the creator by modeling his work, in turn, on 'the inward form and structure of his fellow-creature,' is thus, as Shaftesbury says, an 'architect in the kind.' [42] Shaftesbury's aesthetic emphasis, furthermore, is consistently on the Horatian virtues of decorum, learning, deliberate craftsmanship, 'the rules of writing' and 'the truth of art.' He accordingly finds Shakespeare rude, incoherent, and deficient 'in almost all the graces and ornaments,' ridicules authors who rely on genius alone, and holds that only those feeble readers who respond to the beauties of poetry without knowledge of their cause will term them 'the *je ne scay quoy,* the unintelligible or the I know not what,' and suppose them 'to be a kind of charm or enchantment of which the artist himself can give no account.' [43] It was only by endowing his 'inward Form' with a kind of entelechy, and interpreting his 'universal plastic nature' as a mode of development from the inside out, that German writers later converted Shaftesbury's completed and static cosmos, whether of nature or art, into an endlessly growing, never finished, process of organic development.

There is very little more of the organic motif in English literary criticism of the eighteenth century. The only other important passage I know is Gerard's description of the mental procedure of genius in forming its original design. This, he said, 'bears a greater resemblance to nature in its operations, than to . . . *art';* and (it may be recalled from the preceding chapter) Gerard went on to interpret the operation of nature in terms of a vegetable organizing itself by the same action through which it draws in and assimilates its food.[44] To find any further development of this pattern of aesthetic ideas we must turn first to Germany, and then to the writings of those English theorists who had themselves been appreciably Germanized.

iii. German Theories of Vegetable Genius

An index to the difference in the critical climate of the two countries is the fact that in England, Young's *Conjectures* attracted only minor attention, while in Germany the essay was translated twice within two years of its publication in 1759, and became a primary document in the canon of the Storm and Stress. Its special popularity in Germany is attributable in part to the verve and absoluteness with which Young preached literary independence and originality, in a country where youthful writers were chafing at the long subjection of the native literary tradition to foreign models and rules. But in addition, German thought was much more receptive than English to Young's suggestions that a great work of literature grows out of the impenetrable depths of the mind of genius.

The dominant English psychology of empiricism had no place either for the concept of growth or of the subliminal in the activities of mind.[45] The psychology of Leibniz, on the other hand, so influential in Germany in the latter eighteenth century, was favorable to both these concepts. Leibniz emphasized the essential community of all monads, from the human soul, down through the vegetable kinds, to the monads of apparently inorganic substances. The real, as opposed to phenomenal nature, is living and organic throughout this hierarchy, and each monad, of every degree, is 'a perpetual living mirror of the universe,' possessing within itself the simultaneous perception of everything, everywhere, whether past, present, or future.[46] Man is distinguished from the lower orders in the scale of being because in his soul some few of these perceptions arrive at a sufficient degree of clarity to achieve 'apperception,' or awareness. Still, even in the soul of man, the mass of *petites perceptions* which remain below awareness incalculably exceeds the tiny area which becomes available to consciousness. As Leibniz describes this domain of unconscious ideation:

There is at every moment an infinity of *perceptions* within us, but without apperception and without reflexion; that is to say, changes in the soul itself of which we are not conscious [s'apercevoir], because the impressions are either too small and too numerous or too closely combined. . .[47]

Furthermore, according to the principle of 'pre-established harmony,' the process of perception within each 'windowless' monad keeps in phase with the course of external events through an inner source of motion. To literary theorists, Leibniz's province of confused and unconscious perceptions, eternally evolving themselves, in the mind of man, into a state of greater distinctness and articulation, both helped to suggest, and offered an obvious locus to which they might assign, the secret, plant-like maturation of a work of art in the mind of genius.

We detect such a merger of traditional aesthetic concepts with Leibnizian metaphysics, in the very act of developing into an organic scheme of literary psychology, in Johann Georg Sulzer's *Allgemeine Theorie der schönen Künste,* a four-volume dictionary of aesthetic terms first issued in 1771-4. Sulzer begins his article 'Erfindung' (Invention) by expounding Leibniz's theory that no ideas are absolutely new, but that all are latently present in the mind, until, in correlation with external circumstance, one of them becomes clear enough to emerge into consciousness. Pursuing the implications of such a theory for aesthetic invention, Sulzer arrives at the psychological 'mystery' that certain conceptions clarify and develop independently of the intention or attention of the artist.

It is a remarkable thing, belonging among other mysteries of psychology, that at times certain thoughts will not develop or let themselves be clearly grasped when we devote our full attention to them, yet long afterwards will present themselves in the greatest clarity of their own accord, when we are not in search of them, so that it seems as though in the interim they had grown unnoticed, like a plant, and now suddenly stood before us in their full development and bloom. Many a conception ripens gradually within us, and then, freeing itself as though of its own accord from the mass of obscure ideas, emerges suddenly into the light. Every artist must rely on such happy expressions of his genius, and if he cannot always find what he diligently seeks, must await with patience the ripening of his thoughts.[48]

In the 'glückliche Äusserungen des Genies,' Sulzer is clearly concerned with the standard literary mystery of the *je ne sais quoi* and the 'happiness as well as care.' More explicitly than Young (whose essay he also knew), he characterizes the process as one of self-effecting growth and flowering, and assigns it to a mental region impervious to awareness. In an article, 'Begeisterung,' Sulzer employs a similar hypothesis to account for the related mystery of poetic inspiration. No one, he says, 'has sufficiently fathomed the depths of the human soul' to explain the extraordinary ease, copiousness, and lack of personal responsibility which all artists of genius assure us they sometimes feel in the act of invention.

It is a thing known from experience, but difficult to explain, that the thoughts and ideas which ensue from the persistent contemplation of an object—whether these be clear or obscure—gather together in the soul and there germinate unnoticed, like seeds in a fruitful soil, and finally at the proper moment come suddenly to light. . . At that instant we see the relevant object—which up to then has hovered before us darkly and confusedly like a formless phantom—standing before us in a form clear and complete. This is the genuine instant of inspiration.[49]

Facts of composition which, as Sulzer points out, had formerly been attributed to the intervention of an external power, can now be assigned to the secret mental burgeoning of seed-ideas which, after generating their completed form, burst above the limen of awareness.

This pattern of thinking which Sulzer occasionally applied to special problems of artistic invention was at that very time being extended by J. G. Herder to comprehend the universe in all its aspects and functions. In spite of its over-all formlessness and its chaotic detail, Herder's essay 'On the Knowing and Feeling of the Human Soul,' published in 1778, must be accounted a turning point in the history of ideas. To the elementaristic and mechanical explanation of nature and man, body and mind, Herder vehemently opposed views woven out of Leibniz's monadology, Shaftesbury's pantheism, and biological science, especially Albrecht Haller's theory that the essential aspect of living organisms is its *Reizbarkeit*—its power to respond to external stimuli by a self-contraction or expansion. Herder's essay thus heralds the age of biologism: the area of the most exciting and seminal discoveries having shifted from physical science to the science of life, biology has begun to replace Cartesian and Newtonian mechanics as the great source of concepts which, migrating into other provinces, were modifying the general character of ideation.

The central phenomenon to which Herder points, in order to expose the inadequacy of the mechanical view of nature, is the life process of a plant:

Behold yon plant, that lovely structure of organic fibers! How it turns and rotates its leaves to drink the dew which refreshes it! It sinks and twists its root until it stands upright; each shrub, each little tree bends itself toward fresh air, so far as it is able; the blossom opens itself for the advent of its bridegroom, the sun. . . With what marvelous diligence a plant refines alien liquors into parts of its own finer self, grows, loves . . . then ages, gradually loses its capacity to respond to stimuli and to renew its power, dies. . .

The herb draws in water and earth and refines it into its own elements; the animal makes the lower herbs into the nobler animal sap; man transforms herbs and animals into organic elements of his life, converts them to the operation of higher, finer stimuli.[50]

The qualities of this plant—its growth, its responsiveness to its environment and assimilation of elements from that environment into its own integrated substance, its self-sustained life and ultimate death—Herder generalizes, after his unsystematic fashion, into the categories of his world-view. Nature is an organism, and man, inextricably a part of that living whole, is in himself an organic and indissoluble unity of thought, feeling, and will, exhibiting in his own life the same powers and functions as the nature without. In application to aesthetics, Herder, unlike Young and Sulzer, uses the plant as the prototype for the development of an art form in the soil of its own time and place, instead of for the genesis of a single work in the mind of an artist. The drama of the Greeks and the drama of Shakespeare, for example, each grew out of the peculiar conditions of its own age and cultural milieu. The product of this growth was a richly various and living whole; and as a play of Shakespeare now evolves before the reader, it can in its turn be conceived as a process in which the later parts grow out of the earlier ones. King Lear, for example, 'even in the first scene of the play carries within him all the seeds of his fate toward the harvest of the darkest future.' Characters, actions, attendant circumstances, motives, in such a play —'all are in motion, continuously developing into a single whole,' in which no component can be altered or displaced, and which, like the universe, is filled with 'one interpenetrating, all-animating soul.' [51]

Alternatively, an individual genius may himself be envisioned as an unconsciously growing plant. This poet is not so much unconscious of the ideas germinating in his creative imagination, as he is un*self*-conscious, in the sense that he remains unaware of his own powers and potentialities.

Nature has noble shoots enough, but we detect them not, and trample them under foot, because for the most part we value genius for its formlessness, and for the too-early ripeness or exaggeration of its growth. . .

Every noble human species sleeps, like any good seed, in silent germination: is there, and remains unaware of itself. . . How does the poor shoot know, and how should it know, what impulses, powers, vapors of life streamed into him at the instant of his coming into being? [52]

This special deduction from the prototype of the growing plant, making the true genius out to be one who is born to blush unrecognized, by himself or others, until the full and unanticipated flowering of his powers, looks back to Edward Young, and ahead to Schiller, Fichte, and other theorists of the later German school.[53]

Alexander Pope had said that the works of Shakespeare, the poet of nature, are to more regular works as a Gothic edifice is to a modern building. In his essay *On German Architecture* (1772), the young Goethe, under the influence of the ideas of Herder, described Gothic architecture, in contrast to buildings constructed according to rules, as the organic product of growth in the mind of genius. A genius is one 'out of whose soul the parts emerge, grown together into an eternal whole,'—such a whole as we find represented in the Cathedral at Strasbourg. 'For there is in man a formative nature' which creates from its materials 'a characteristic whole.' Such art, 'whether born of crude savagery or of a cultivated sensibility, will always be a complete whole, and a living one.' [54]

Goethe is distinctive among aesthetic organologists in that he was himself a research biologist as well as a theorist of art. He deliberately pursued these as mutually illuminating kinds of activity, each new hypothesis or discovery he made in biology duly reappearing in the form of new organizing principles or insights in the field of his criticism. 'As I have looked upon nature,' he wrote to Frau von Stein from Italy, 'so do I now look upon art, and I am now achieving what I have striven after for so long, a more perfect conception of the highest things which men have made. . .' [55] In the journal of his epoch-making trip to Italy, Goethe records the emergence of his theory of plant metamorphosis—'in botany I have hit upon an *en kai pan* that has set me in astonishment'—and goes on to say that he has also found a principle for explaining a work of art which is 'really also an egg of Columbus,' and a kind of master-key to critical theory. The analogy between a natural organism and a work of art, earlier implicit in his discussion of medieval architecture, is now more explicitly applied to the products of classical antiquity, although with a new emphasis on the lawfulness of the natural process in both its manifestations:

These high works of art, like the highest works of nature, were produced by men according to true and natural laws. Everything arbitrary, fanciful falls together: here is necessity, here is God.[56]

This view of artistic invention as a process of nature within the realm of mind becomes a cardinal theme in the aesthetic theory of Goethe's mature years. 'A perfect work of art,' he wrote in 1797, 'is a work of the human spirit, and in this sense also a work of nature.' A year later he pointed out that 'nature is separated from art by a monstrous chasm, which even the genius cannot overpass without outside aid.' Yet the separation can be bridged, if the artist is capable

of penetrating into the depths of the object as well as into the depths of his own spirit, and of producing in his works not merely something which is easily and superficially effective, but in rivalry with nature, something spiritually-organic [Geistig-Organisches], and of giving his work such a content and form that it will seem at once natural and above nature.

And just as in his biological speculations Goethe's emphasis is on development, and on the metamorphosis of part into part and kind into kind, sc in his criticism his persistent concern is with the genesis and coming-into-being of a work of art. 'Ultimately, in the practise of art, we can only vie with nature when we have at least to some extent learned from her the process that she pursues in the formation of her works.' [57]

Immanuel Kant's basically static and taxonomic approach to the questions of art, and of the faculties involved in its making, seems to be at an extreme from the organic theories *des werdenden Gedichts,* yet elements of his *Critique of Judgment* contributed importantly to the development of such theories by other hands. Under this single title Kant investigated the problems both of the productive genius and of the nature of living things, and in the latter province particularly, he gave philosophical definition and elaboration to concepts which heretofore had been relatively undeveloped and vague. To Goethe, who hailed the treatise with delight after its appearance in 1790, it seemed that Kant's joining of the problems of poetry and biology confirmed his own view that these are essentially parallel phenomena. Kant intended to indicate, he wrote in 1792, 'that a work of art must be treated like a work of nature, a work of nature like a work of art, and the value of each must be developed out of itself and regarded in itself.' [58]

Kant developed his entire view of the productive genius around the problem which, we saw earlier in this chapter, had puzzled earlier critics: how the genius is able to form a work of art without rules or conscious method, yet achieve a product from which critics later draw the rules of art. This paradox the philosopher, who had read widely in English as well as German criticism, found congenial to his favorite tactic of posing dilemmas from which to extricate himself. The fine arts, he said, 'must necessarily be regarded as arts of *genius*,' and genius is to be defined as 'the innate mental aptitude (*ingenium*) *through which* nature gives the rule to art.'

It cannot indicate scientifically how it brings about its product, but rather gives the rule as *nature.* Hence, where an author owes a product to his genius, he does not himself know how the *ideas* for it have entered into his head, nor has he it in his power to invent the like at pleasure, or methodically, and communicate the same to others in such precepts as would put them in a position to produce similar products.[59]

The problem, as Kant elaborates it, is that genius, through the operation of 'nature,' produces exemplary works which seem to be necessarily in accord with ends, yet without being aware either of those ends or of the means by which to effect them, and without having it in his power either to will or to describe the productive process. Kant later demonstrates that a kind of mirror-image of this paradoxical working of 'nature' in the mind of genius is to be found in that other, or phenomenal, 'nature' of living organisms. The phenomenal world in all its elements is mechanical, completely determined, a chain of causes and effects perceived in accordance with the invariant forms imposed on sense by the human understanding. But to make intelligible to ourselves the organic existences in this phenomenal world, we are constrained to view them, not as a system of efficient causes, but as 'natural purposes'; that is, as though organisms were things which develop toward ends which are inherent in the organism itself, and therefore not by means of a combination of parts to achieve a previsioned plan or design. As the representative instance of such natural purpose, Kant analyzes the organic constitution of a tree, which he opposes to the purely mechanical functioning of a watch. Each tree has its genesis in another of the same species; as it grows, it proceeds to generate itself by compounding and incorporating its own substance; and in it, each part seems to exist for the sake of the other parts and of the whole, at the same time that the whole depends for survival on the existence of its parts.[60]

As the fruit of a century's endeavors, then, Kant formulates the view of a natural organism as immanently but unconsciously teleological, a 'self-organising being' which, possessing both its own *moving* power' and its own *formative* power,' develops from the inside out, and in which the relations between the parts and the whole can be restated in terms of an inter-relationship of means and end. 'An organised product of nature is one in which every part is reciprocally purpose (end) and means.' Kant warns us repeatedly that this concept of an organism as a natural purpose is merely a philosophy of as-if; that it is, in his terms, not a 'constitutive,' but merely 'a regulative concept for the reflective Judgment, to guide our investigation about objects of this kind by a distant analogy with our own causality according to purposes.' [61] But to Goethe and to other aesthetic organologists it proved irresistible to make such a purely internal teleology a constitutive element in living nature, and then to go beyond Kant and indentify completely the unconsciously purposeful process and product of 'nature' in the mind of genius with the unconsciously purposeful growth, and the complex inter-adaptations of means to ends, in a natural organism. Thus Friedrich Schlegel described Goethe's *Wilhelm Meister,* in 1798:

The inherent drive of this thoroughly organized and organizing work to form itself into one whole expresses itself in the larger as in the smaller combinations. No pause is fortuitous and insignificant, and . . . everything is at the same time means and end.[62]

Of the various post-Kantian theorists I shall single out two, Friedrich Schelling and Jean Paul Richter, who made important additions to the psychology of the creative process. Schelling's *System of Transcendental Idealism* (1800) sets out from the antithesis between 'subject' and 'object,' or between what the author alternatively calls 'intelligence' and 'nature,' 'the conscious' and 'the unconscious,' the 'freedom' exhibited in the human choice of ends and the 'necessity' exhibited by the involuntary processes of nature. This dynamic opposition sets Schelling's dialectic in motion, and from it he 'deduces,' seriatim, all the constitution of the natural world and all the powers of mind. But, Schelling says, 'the system of knowledge can be regarded as completed only when it returns to its principle.' In other words, he needs a concept which will close the dialectical circle and resolve the initial opposition by combining both intelligence and nature, conscious and unconscious, reflective freedom and blind necessity. Such a concept Schelling discovers in the activity of genius in producing a work of art; hence he is able to make the triumphant claim that the creative process of imagination is 'the general organon of philosophy, and the keystone of its arch.' [63]

In this characteristic document of romantic philosophy in Germany, the extraordinary importance attributed to aesthetic invention may be regarded as the climax of a general tendency of the time to exalt art over all human pursuits. But the concept of genius lent itself to Schelling's metaphysical requirements only because he could take for granted the long-standing critical tradition we have been tracing: that the inventive genius combines in himself the elements both of art and of nature, both the process of adapting means to freely chosen ends according to knowable rules and a reliance on a blind spontaneity outside his knowledge or control. The productive activity, as Schelling phrases the idea, includes 'what is generally called art . . . that which is practised with consciousness, deliberation, and reflection, and can be taught and learned,' and also that which cannot 'be achieved by application or in any other way, but must be inherited as a free gift of nature.' [64] And by appealing not only to this theory, but to the facts underlying it—the testimony of artists concerning 'inspired' composition and the occurrence of an unanticipated 'grace' in a work of art—Schelling converts what would otherwise be a dance of bloodless abstractions into an at least potentially usable theory of the creative mind.

The depositions of all artists, Schelling says, anciently explained as inspiration by a divinity, show 'that they are driven involuntarily to the production of their work,' and that the completion of the work results 'in a feeling of an infinite harmony,' which the artist 'ascribes, not to himself, but to a voluntary grace of his nature.'

The artist is driven to production involuntarily, and even against an inner resistance (hence the sayings of the ancients: 'pati Deum,' etc.; hence above all the idea of inspiration by means of another's breath). . . . No matter how purposeful he is, the artist, with respect to that which is genuinely objective in his production, seems to be under the influence of a power that sunders him from all other men and forces him to express or represent things that he himself does not entirely fathom, and whose significance is infinite.[65]

Schelling himself introduces a half-metaphysical, half-psychological explanation of these facts. What sets the poet's process going is the insistent demand for closure by the ultimate contradiction between the conscious and the unconscious, working 'at the roots of his whole being.' The natural and unconscious (*bewusstlos*) element in the act of creation is the internal representative of the unconscious development of things in external nature which, while seeming products of 'the blindest mechanism,' are 'adaptive to ends without being explicable in terms of ends.' The blissful feeling of release at the conclusion of the process signalizes the resolution of this 'last and uttermost contradiction,' by virtue of which the 'infinite division of opposed activities' from which philosophy has set out is 'completely annulled.' And that marvelous productive faculty, by which alone we are both 'able to think and to reconcile contradictions,' Schelling finally and dramatically identifies as *die Einbildungskraft*—the imagination.[66]

Although not the first to introduce 'the unconscious' into the artistic process, Schelling is, more than anyone, responsible for making that Protean term an ineluctable part of the psychology of art. His theory, for example, provoked two great contemporaries to declare themselves on this issue. In his essay on 'Naïve and Sentimental Poetry' (1795), Schiller had already associated the 'naïve,' or natural, genius with the processes of external nature, and described the resulting poetry (in the familiar terms) as a mystery to the poet himself, 'a happy chance,' in which all is done 'through nature' rather than reflection, and through an 'internal necessity' from which 'nothing is so remote as the arbitrary will.' [67] When in 1801 Schiller wrote to Goethe, to take issue with an aspect of Schelling's theory, he used Schelling's own terminology:

I fear that in their ideas, these Idealist-gentlemen take too little notice of experience; in experience, the poet begins entirely with the unconscious . . . and poetry, it seems to me, consists precisely in being able to express and communicate that unconscious—i.e., to carry it over into an object. . . The unconscious united with awareness constitutes the poetic artist.

Goethe responded that he himself would go even farther: 'I believe that everything which the genius does as genius, eventuates unconsciously. The man of genius can also operate rationally, after careful consideration, from conviction, but all that only happens secondarily.' [68]

In Jean Paul's Orphic ejaculations on the nature of genius, as set forth in his *Vorschule der Aesthetik* (1804), we can dimly make out some familiar traits. Genius is a harmony of all the powers of man, and includes two aspects, one of conscious reflection (*Besonnenheit*) and the other of the unconscious (*das Unbewusste*), 'the mightiest element in the poet.' This latter is an innate power which, in a man like Shakespeare, works 'with the blindness and sureness of an instinct,' impenetrable to the awareness of the artist himself, and related in its process to the divine wisdom 'in the slumbering plant and in the instinct of animals.' However necessary it may be, reflection, taken by itself, is merely mechanical and imitative. Only 'seemingly innate and involuntary poetry' provides the inner material which 'makes that genial originality which the imitator seeks merely in the form and manner.' [69]

There is in Richter's concept of the unconscious, however, another and sinister component which sets it off from Schelling's postulate, and also gives it an important place in the development of the present psychology of art. Richter, building on earlier suggestions of the chaos, the darkness, and the mysterious depths in the creative mind, develops the night-side of the unconscious, so that in his writings we find ourselves halfway from Leibniz to that later inheritor of the depth-psychology of German romanticism, Carl Jung. Leibniz's doctrine of the obscure and chaotic realm of *petites perceptions* had been merely a rational hypothesis to establish the possibility of universal innate ideas which, in their independence both of awareness and of phenomenal time and place, can simultaneously correspond to what is past, or passing, or to come. Jung's 'collective unconscious' is likewise common to all human souls and independent of time and locality, but it has also become a primordial abyss whence emerge the monsters of our dreams and night-fears, and also the visions of our myth makers, poets, and seers. Its experience, Jung says, 'arises from timeless depths; it is foreign and cold, many sided, demonic and grotesque. A grimly ridiculous sample of the eternal chaos.' Its visions, for all we can say, may be 'of the beginning of things before the age of man, or of the unborn generations of the future.' [70] Richter, foreshadowing this development, speaks of the unconscious as an abyss 'of which we can hope to fix the existence, not the depth,' and as an instinct which eternally 'has a presentiment of and demands its objects without regard to time, because these dwell beyond the reaches of time.' It is, furthermore, the common origin of dreams, the sense of terror and guilt, demonology, and myth:

It does not matter what we call this supra-mundane angel of the inner life, this death's-angel of the worldly in men, or how we reckon up its indications; enough if in its disguises we fail not to recognize it. At one time it shows itself to men deeply enveloped in guilt . . . as a being before whose presence (and not its actions) we are terrified; this feeling we call the fear of ghosts. . . Again the spirit shows itself as The Infinite, and man prays.

It first gave us religion—the fear of death—Greek Fate—superstition—and prophecy . . . belief in a devil . . . romanticism, that embodied spirit-world, as well as Greek mythology, that spiritualized world of the body.

This source of dreams is a source also of poetry. The genius, in fact, 'is in more than one sense a sleep-walker; in his clear dream he is capable of more than in waking, and in darkness does he mount every height of reality.' [71]

The writings of August Wilhelm Schlegel provide a compendious summary of German concepts of organic invention, and also enable us to close this section on a calmer note. Unlike most of his contemporaries, the older Schlegel had a tidy mind. In the lectures he read in Berlin between 1801 and 1804, he collected and ordered the ideas contributed by thinkers from Leibniz through Kant to Friedrich Schlegel and Schelling, trimmed away some of the accrued extravagance and a good deal of the rhetoric, and most importantly, brought them down to the consideration of specific questions in the history and analysis of works of art. The true philosopher sees everything 'as an eternal becoming, an unintermitted process of creation.' No living organism can be understood from the standpoint of materialism alone, because its nature is such 'that the whole must be conceived before the parts,' and it can only be made intelligible as 'a product which produces itself,' exhibiting in the process 'an endless reciprocation, in which each effect becomes a cause of its cause.' [72] And a work of art exhibits the organic properties of a work of nature. For art, 'creating autonomously like nature, both organized and organizing, must form living works, which are first set in motion, not by an outside mechanism like a pendulum, but by an indwelling power like the solar system, and which, when they are completed, turn back upon themselves [*in sich selbst zurückkehren*].' In this productive process, Schlegel agrees with Schelling, instinctive nature and conscious judgment operate together, and 'it destroys the whole organism of art' to regard these as separate or sequential activities. True genius

is precisely the most intimate union of unconscious and self-conscious activity in the human spirit, of instinct and purpose, of freedom and necessity.[73]

Schlegel's Berlin lectures remained in manuscript until long after his death, but his Viennese lectures *On Dramatic Art and Literature,* delivered in 1808 and published in 1809-11, achieved almost immediate translation into several languages, and served as the chief vehicle for acquainting Western Europe, at first hand, with the new German aesthetics. There is less of obviously biological thinking in these lectures than in the earlier series; but in them Schlegel applies the earlier antithesis between mechanism and organism to the distinction—which Coleridge found so illuminating—between mechanical form, achieved by imposing rules from without, and organic form, achieved only by a process analogous to natural growth.

Form is mechanical when it is imparted to any material through an external force, merely as an accidental addition, without reference to its character. . . Organic form, on the contrary, is innate; it unfolds itself from within, and reaches its determination simultaneously with the fullest development of the seed. . . In the fine arts, just as in the province of nature—the supreme artist—all genuine forms are organic. . .

Coleridge found equally congenial the insistence in these lectures on the self-conscious and calculating element in Shakespeare's inventive process, upon which Schlegel elaborated in preparation for his analysis of the art of Shakespeare's individual plays. The activity of such a genius, Schlegel says, 'is, it is true, natural to him, and in a certain sense unconscious'; but, he insists, Shakespeare's compositions also exhibit learning, reflection, and the deliberate management of means to effects upon the audience. 'To me [Shakespeare] is a profound artist, not a blind and wildly coursing genius. What has been babbled on this subject I hold, in general, to be a mere fable, a blind and extravagant illusion.' [74]

iv. Unconscious Invention in English Criticism

In his *Lectures on Metaphysics and Logic,* delivered 1836-56, Sir William Hamilton, after crediting German philosophers with having developed the concept of the unconscious, claimed that he was the first English writer seri-

ously to propose that 'the mind exerts energies, and is the subject of modifications, of neither of which it is conscious.'[75] Hamilton was mistaken, for the
notion of an unconscious element in the inventive process had already become almost a commonplace of English literary criticism. It is true that no
English critic made any essential advance upon the Germans: but then, these
writers had explored the subject so thoroughly that even von Hartmann's
monumental study of *The Philosophy of the Unconscious* (1868), in the section devoted to the unconscious growth-like processes of artistic genius, presented no ideas which had not been formulated in Germany half a century
before.

With the end of the eighteenth century in England, even the more sober
poets began to testify to an experience of unwilled and unpremeditated verse.
Walter Scott wrote:

Nobody knows, that has not tried the feverish trade of poetry, how much it depends upon mood or whim . . . in sober reality, writing good verse seems to
depend upon something separate from the volition of the author. I sometimes
think my fingers set up for themselves, independent of my head.[76]

Keats's axiom that poetry must come 'as naturally as the leaves to a tree'
was grounded in his own mode of composition which, as he described it
to Woodhouse, waited upon the 'happier moment' when, in the full play of
all his faculties, he could write as one 'almost inspired.' Often, after Keats
had written down some thought or expression, Woodhouse says, it 'struck
him with astonishment and seemed rather the production of another person
than his own. . . It seemed to come by chance or magic—to be as it were
something given to him.'[77] Keats's heavily corrected and inter-written manuscripts, like those of Shelley and other contemporaries, demonstrate that
poetic vision by no means obviated revision; but, most romantic poets insisted,
at its inception a poem is an involuntary and unanticipated *donnée*. Wordsworth's postscript to 'The Waggoner,' written in 1805, may be regarded as
a versified supplement to his discussion of the spontaneous overflow of feeling in the Preface of 1800. 'Timid scruples' long checked the writing of this
poem, but 'Nature might not be gainsaid'; and disclaiming personal responsibility, Wordsworth postulates a 'shy spirit' as the only begetter of the verse.

> Nor is it I who play the part,
> But a shy spirit in my heart,
> That comes and goes—will sometimes leap
> From hiding places ten years deep.

And in the sonnet, 'A poet!—He hath put his heart to school,' Wordsworth exhorted the poet to let 'Thy art be nature,' and illustrated the process by the free growth of a meadow-flower and a forest-tree.

Other writers of the period offered elaborate theories in prose to account for the element of 'nature' in the act of composition. Shelley, as we have seen, supplemented the concept of inspiration as a vision of the eternal Forms with that of inspiration as the growth of a work of art, like 'a child in the mother's womb,' outside the limits of consciousness. In the essay 'Is Genius Conscious of Its Powers?' written five years after Shelley's 'Defence of Poetry,' Hazlitt used a similar figure to account for the traditional facts of inspired composition and the 'happiness as well as care.'

The definition of genius is that it acts unconsciously; and those who have produced immortal works have done so without knowing how or why. . . . Correggio, Michael Angelo, Rembrandt, did what they did without premeditation or effort— their works came from their minds as a natural birth—if you had asked them why they adopted this or that style, they would have answered, *because they could not help it* . . . Shakespeare himself was an example of his own rule, and appears to have owed almost everything to chance. . . The true inspiration of the Muse . . . leaves us little to boast of, for the effect hardly seems to be our own.[78]

In the instance of Correggio, he adds, under an 'involuntary, silent impulse,' the 'work grew under his hand as if of itself.' Elsewhere, Hazlitt explicitly analogized the process to a growing plant. The 'instinct of the imagination,' the sign of genius, 'works unconsciously, like nature, and receives its impressions from a kind of inspiration.' More explicitly:

Milton has given us a description of the growth of a plant—

> —So from the root
> Springs lighter the green stalk. . .

And we think this image might be transferred to the slow and perfect growth of works of imagination.[79]

The extreme claimant for poetic automatism was, of course, William Blake. Of his *Milton* he said, in 1803:

I have written this Poem from immediate Dictation, twelve or sometimes twenty or thirty lines at a time, without Premeditation and even against my Will; the Time it has taken in writing was thus render'd Non Existent, and an immense Poem Exists which seems to be the Labour of a Long life, all produc'd without Labour or Study.[80]

Like his German contemporaries, Blake waged war against Bacon, Newton, and Locke, and for an alternative to the elementarism and mechanism of the 'Philosophy of Five Senses,' turned to the cabalistic tradition, and to Paracelsus, Boehme, Swedenborg, and other occult writers. As a result he sketched out a world-view which came remarkably close to that of German romantic philosophy: a view based on the generative power of opposites— 'Without Contraries is no progression'—and terminating in the concept of an organically inter-related universe, where any part involves the whole and we can 'see a World in a grain of sand.' To explain the compulsiveness, ease, and completeness of poetic composition, however, Blake did not draw upon these concepts, but reverted to the oldest Vatic theory, in a form which attests that he was himself subject to a visionary experience approaching hallucination. 'Inspiration and Vision was then, and now is, and I hope will always Remain, my Element, my Eternal Dwelling Place. . .' 'I write,' he said, 'when commanded by the spirits, and the moment I have written I see the words fly about the room in all directions.' [81]

One British critic, Thomas Carlyle, exceeded even his German forbears in the claims he made for the absolute sovereignty of the unconscious in all valid activity, whether in the literary, political, or moral domain. As early as 1827, Carlyle, reviewing the 'new criticism' (this is Carlyle's term) of Kant, Herder, Schiller, Goethe, Richter, and the Schlegels, remarked penetratingly that a common element in these various systems was the stress on poetry as a living, growing whole, and that the primary question with these critics concerned the mysterious mechanism by which 'Shakespeare organised his dramas.' [82] Four years later, Carlyle announced the essentials of his own philosophy in the essay, 'Characteristics,' which he fabricated out of strands taken from a variety of German writers. In this essay we find Schiller's concept of the naïve genius as a harmonious and unreflective creator, assimilated to Fichte's view that the genius is a seer of the Divine Idea who remains totally unaware of his own powers and growth-like processes. Always, the sign of right performance is unconsciousness, so that 'on the whole, "genius is ever a secret to itself."' [83] Carlyle also uses 'unconscious,' after Richter's fashion, to stand for an impenetrable area in the mind which is every man's inheritance of the primordial realm of chaos. Underlying the surface film of consciousness is the 'bottomless boundless Deep'; the roots of life 'stretch down fearfully to the regions of Death and Night'; and only 'in these dark, mysterious, depths . . . if aught is to be created, and not manufactured, must the work go on.' [84]

Carlyle preserves enough fossilized remains of older concepts to enable the resourceful student, from this one essay, to reconstruct the total history of the theory that the greatest works of art are products of unconscious growth. This is the process, Carlyle tells us, which had once been imputed to divine inspiration, and he himself continues to interpret it as a quasi-religious 'mystery.' 'Unconsciousness is the sign of creation. . . So deep, in this existence of ours, is the significance of Mystery.' [85] Conjoined to this concept is the equally ancient antithesis between art and nature, for which Carlyle provides us also with a list of parallel or synonymous opposites: conscious *vs.* unconscious, voluntary and purposive *vs.* involuntary and spontaneous, manufacture *vs.* creation, death *vs.* life, mechanical *vs.* dynamic. [86] And persistently, in Carlyle's choice of his figures of speech, we discern the extent to which the paradigm of the secret and silent growth of a plant has steered his conception of the completely unpremeditated and unconscious development of a work of art. As Carlyle says of Shakespeare—who remains, as he had been since Milton, the cardinal instance of the poet of nature—

[Shakespeare's] is what I call an unconscious intellect. . . Novalis beautifully remarks of him, that those Dramas of his are Products of Nature too . . . Shakespeare's Art is not Artifice; the noblest worth of it is not there by plan or precontrivance. . . Such a man's works, whatsoever he with utmost conscious exertion and forethought shall accomplish, grow up withal *un*consciously, from the unknown deeps in him;—as the oak-tree grows from the Earth's bosom, as the mountains and waters shape themselves; with a symmetry grounded on Nature's own laws. . . How much in Shakespeare lies hid . . . like *roots,* like sap and forces working underground! [87]

Like Coleridge before him, Carlyle uses the epithet 'mechanical' to indict not only the neo-classic theory of art but also Locke's picture of the mind as 'a Shape, a Visibility . . . as if it had been some composite, divisible and reunitable substance,' [88] as well as the world-view of Newtonian science and French materialism. The profound difference between these two thinkers is that Carlyle, setting up 'nature' as norm, interprets it so as to condemn all 'art,' and to set as the ideal in all human concerns the reliance on the unconscious and the instinctual.

For in all vital things, men distinguish an Artificial and a Natural . . . the artificial is the conscious, mechanical; the natural is the unconscious, dynamical. Thus, as we have an artificial Poetry, and prize only the natural; so likewise we have an artificial Morality, an artificial Wisdom, an artificial Society. [89]

v. Coleridge and the Aesthetics of Organism

Before he read German philosophy Coleridge had familiarized himself with such important antecedents of German organology as Plotinus, Giordano Bruno, and Leibniz, as well as Boehme and other writers in the occult tradition. There are few key ideas in Coleridge's cosmology and theory of knowledge which had not been anticipated in some fashion by Schelling, and there can be no doubt that Coleridge based on the formulations of A. W. Schlegel both his central antithesis between mechanical and organic art and a good deal of his practical commentary on Shakespeare and other dramatists. In the light of the community of background, however, we can understand Coleridge's feeling that in the German thinkers he found what he had already thought and was just on the point of saying himself. Certainly in his criticism he appropriated nothing that he did not assimilate to his own principles, he restated little that he did not improve, and he succeeded better than any of his predecessors in converting the organic concept of the imagination into an inclusive and practicable method for specifically literary analysis and evaluation.

Organic thinking in aesthetics, as this came to Coleridge from Germany, was by no means confined to the process of artistic invention. It penetrated all aspects of criticism, sometimes providing a new formulation and focus for existing opinions, and sometimes generating novel categories for chronicling, interpreting, and evaluating works of art. Before we leave the subject, it will be worthwhile to sketch, in rough outline, some of the more prominent aspects of the organic point of view, outside the domain of literary psychology.

(1) *Organic history.* By transplanting the seed-idea from the mind of the poet to the collective mind of a nation or era, theorists were enabled to apply organic categories to the phylogeny, as well as the ontogeny of art: an artistic genre or a national literature, seen as a *Gesamtorganismus,* was conceived to grow in time as a single work grows in the imagination of the individual artist.

The life-cycle of an organism—birth, maturity, decay, death—had, of course, been one of the most ancient paradigms on which to model the conception of history. In a full-fledged organology, which exploits the detailed possibilities of living and growing things, any human product or institution is envisioned as germinating, without anyone's deliberate plan or intent, and as fulfilling its destiny through an inner urgency, feeding on the materials of its time and place in order to proliferate into its ultimate and living form. All of Greek art, Friedrich Schlegel thus wrote in 1795-6, constitutes a single growth whose 'seed is grounded in human nature itself,' and which possesses a 'collective force' as its dynamic and guiding principle. And in its historical course, each 'advance unfolds out of the preceding one as if of its own accord, and contains the complete germ of the following stage.' [90]

It hardly needs to be said how strongly a mode of thinking patterned on a growing plant fostered the genetic habit of mind. From this point of view, to understand anything is to know how it has come about. Much that has hitherto been conceived as Being is now seen as itself a Becoming—the universe itself is a process, and God's creation is a continuant. Change, instead of a meaningless Heracleitean flux, is conceived to be the orderly emergence of inner forms, and is held to constitute the very essence of things; and the ancient distrust of mutability is annulled. 'Truth,' said Carlyle, quoting Schiller, *immer wird, nie ist;* never *is,* always *is a-being';* and in change 'there is nothing terrible, nothing supernatural: on the contrary, it lies in the very essence of our lot and life in this world.' [91]

One important result of the organic theory of history was to provide a new rationale for the theory of cultural pluralism. From the seventeenth century on, 'the doctrine of circumstances,' applied to the monuments of literature, had resulted in widespread empirical inquiry into the local and temporal conditions, physical or cultural, which had influenced Homer's epics, the Hebrew Bible, the tragedies of Sophocles, or the dramas of Shakespeare. In the eighteenth century, the view was increasingly emphasized that the products of genius, since they are differently conditioned, may differ, and differ validly, without necessarily approaching or receding from a single norm of excellence. 'To judge therefore of Shakespear by Aristotle's rules,' Pope said in 1725, 'is like trying a man by the laws of one country, who acted under those of another.' [92] Half a century later the founding father of historical organology, J. G. Herder, replacing these jurisprudential with biological figures of speech, shows how readily the relation of different plant-species to diverse conditions of climate and soil translates itself into a thoroughgoing theory of aesthetic relativism. In considering the applicability to Shakespeare of Aristotle's rules, founded on the local drama of the Greeks, Herder writes:

The first and last question is: 'What is the nature of the soil? What is it adapted to? What has been sown therein? What is it able to bear?'—And heavens! how far are we here from Greece! History, tradition, customs, religion, spirit of the time, of the people, of feeling, of language—how far away from Greece! . . . The nature, virtue, and perfection [of Shakespeare's creation] rests on this fact, that it differs from the former; that out of the soil of his time, precisely this other plant grew up.[93]

The opposition of vegetable categories to a single-form, single-measure theory of literary genres is epitomized in the following passage from Coleridge's manuscripts. Poets of the Italian and English Renaissance are

like fair and stately plants, each with a living principle of its own, taking up into itself and diversely organising the nutriment derived from the peculiar soil in which [each?] grew. . . In all their hues and qualities they bear witness of their birth-place and the accidents and conditions of their inward growth and outward expansion.[94]

(2) *Organic evaluation.* The essential categories of organicism fostered characteristic and important criteria of aesthetic value. These are opposed to the main inclination of taste, in French and early English classicism, for the simple, the clear, the concordant, and the complete. Organic criteria bear a resemblance to the aesthetic qualities which were collected, in the course of the eighteenth century, under the rubric of 'the sublime,' but are formulated in distinctive terms, and with a novel rationale. For example, organic growth is an open-ended process, nurturing a sense of the promise of the incomplete, and the glory of the imperfect. Also, as a plant assimilates the most diverse materials of earth and air, so the synthetic power of imagination 'reveals itself,' in Coleridge's famous phrase, 'in the balance or reconciliation of *opposite* or *discordant* qualities.' And only in a 'mechanical' unity are the parts sharply defined and fixed; in organic unity, what we find is a complex inter-relation of living, indeterminate, and endlessly changing components.

Consider also, in this application, Coleridge's organismic version of the Great Chain of Being, which he adapted to his biological theory from the speculations of Schelling and Henrik Steffens. In *The Theory of Life,* Coleridge defines life as 'the power which discloses itself from within as a principle of *unity* in the *many,*' or 'of unity in *multëity*'; this power 'unites a given all into a whole that is presupposed by all its parts.' (The same principle, in his aesthetic writings, serves for Coleridge to define 'the Beautiful'— 'that in which the *many,* still seen as many, becomes one,' or in other words, 'Multëity in Unity.')[95] From this definition of life Coleridge derives the criteria of the rank of any individual or species in nature. 'The unity will be more intense in proportion as it constitutes each particular thing a whole of itself; and yet more, again, in proportion to the number and interdependence of the parts which it unites as a whole.' The index to the status of an organism on the ladder of nature, therefore, is a product of two factors, which he calls 'extension' and 'intensity'—in other words, inclusiveness and organization, the number and diversity of the component parts and the tightness of their integration into the whole. Lowest in the scale are the metals, which as 'elements, or simple bodies,' constitute 'the form of unity with the least degree of tendency to individuation.' At the apex is man, the 'one great end of Nature,' her 'ultimate production of the highest and most comprehensive individuality.' [96]

It is obvious that this scale of nature may readily be generalized into a comprehensive standard of value, ethical and aesthetic. In the province of conduct, this standard manifests itself as the Faustian ideal of insatiability, and the unceasing quest at once to include, and to assimilate to one's own integrity, the fullest measure of the most diverse experience. For a work of art, the gauge of greatness becomes, jointly, the richness—the quantity and diversity—of the component materials, and the degree to which these are bound together in the interdependence characteristic of an organic whole. Though all beauty is multeity in unity, the degree of beauty varies directly with the multeity: a work of art, as Coleridge puts it, will be 'rich in proportion to the variety of parts which it holds in unity.' [97]

On these grounds, Coleridge, like the German critics with whom he has a close affinity, elevated the variegated multeity in unity of modern or 'romantic' art over what he regarded as the simpler unity of more uniform materials in the products of the Greeks and Romans. The key to the difference between the Athenian and Shakespearean drama is 'that the very essence of the former consists in the sternest separation of the diverse in kind; the latter delights [in variety].' [98] Accordingly, Coleridge apotheosized Shakespeare for the very qualities which some even of his fervent neo-classic admirers had attributed to the barbarity of his age and audience. From the standpoint of organic theory, the measure of Shakespeare's greatness is precisely the diversity and seeming dissonance of the materials of his plays: the reconciliation into unity of tragedy and farce, laughter and tears, the trivial and sublime, kings and clowns, the high style and low, pathos and puns; and the delineation in high tragedy of man as at once the glory, jest, and riddle of the world. Shakespeare, Coleridge maintains, adheres 'to the great law of nature that opposites tend to attract and temper each other,' and he produces a whole 'by the balance, counteraction, inter-modifications, and final harmony of differents.' And as against the perfectly finished classic models, we find to admire in him the infinite promise of the never completed:

Upon the same scale we may compare Sophocles with Shakespeare: in the one there is a completeness, a satisfying, an excellence, on which the mind can rest; in the other we see a blended multitude of materials, great and little, magnificent and mean, mingled, if we may so say, with a dissatisfying, or falling short of perfection, yet so promising of our progression that we would not exchange it for that repose of the mind which dwells on the forms of symmetry in acquiescent admiration of grace.[99]

Organic analogies, together with organic categories of value, have been making a notable reappearance in modern criticism. Recently, for example, Cleanth Brooks announced:

One of the critical discoveries of our time—perhaps it is not a discovery but merely a recovery—is that the parts of a poem have an organic relation to each other. . . The parts of a poem are related as are the parts of a growing plant.

On this discovery, he bases the present renaissance of practical criticism, and to it he attributes 'the best hope that we have for reviving the study of poetry and of the humanities generally.' [100] Brooks's own first-order criteria for poetry—wit, irony, paradox, and the requirement, in any great poem, that an attitude be qualified by its opposite—as Brooks himself points out,[101] may be regarded as involved in Coleridge's standard of the reconciliation of heterogeneous elements. These criteria, however, have been cut loose from their roots in Coleridge's metaphysical principles and from their context in a highly developed organic theory of art, and also narrowed, somewhat after the fashion of the concept of 'romantic irony' put forward by Coleridge's German contemporaries, Friedrich Schlegel and Ludwig Tieck.

(3) *Organic law*. Coleridge followed Schelling in maintaining that the artist's mind, repeating the workings of external nature, where we find a 'co-instantaneity of the plan and the execution,' contains in itself a similar unconscious purposefulness. 'Hence there is in genius itself an unconscious activity; nay, that is the genius in the man of genius.' [102] Coleridge, therefore, like the German theorists, holds that literary invention involves the natural, unplanned, and unconscious process by which things grow. But Coleridge is also cautious to avoid the anarchical tendency evident in some earlier rebels against external rules by exploiting simultaneously another possibility in the growing plant—the aspect of biological laws.

In England, we remember, the nearest approach to equating literary invention with natural growth had occurred in a writer, Edward Young, who had for all practical purposes eliminated the aspect of art and orderly procedure in the concept of the original genius. With Young, in this latter aspect, can be associated the extreme aesthetic primitivists of the mid-eighteenth century and later who fell into the trap of assuming that there is but a single and universal *poesis* or 'art' of poetry, and that this art is identical with the forms implicit in classical writings. For these critics (as for their opposite numbers, the very few English critics who were doctrinaire adherents of rules), the sole alternative to this one kind of art was artlessness, and the sole alternative to neo-classic rules was irregularity, lawlessness, and chance. Because Shakespeare, for example, gave pleasure independently of classic models and neo-classic rules, the single option was to assign his success to his artlessness as a nursling of nature, warbling his native wood-notes wild. 'Poetry knows no rules,' wrote Robert Heron. 'Is not Genius . . . [Nature's] superior, her king, her god?' Lasting fame is won only by a soul 'free as the mountain winds.' [103]

The logic inherent in the organic view of composition could demonstrate that this choice between rules and lawlessness was a false dilemma. A plant grows independently of imposed controls, yet in strict obedience to natural laws. By parallel reasoning, in the imagination of genius the alternative to external rules is not lawlessness, but the inherent lawfulness of organic development. Such an inference, often suggested in German organology, played a vital part in the evolution of Goethe's critical thinking. For Goethe himself had passed through the stage of aesthetic and moral antinomianism of the *Genieperiode,* which was the German equivalent of the movement of cultural primitivism in British thinking; and Goethe's transition to his later 'classicism' was marked above all by his growing emphasis on the reign of law in art and life—although for him, this was a law for man constructed on the analogy of the law for things.[104] As Goethe said during his crucial Italian journey, the high works of classic art were produced, 'like the highest works of nature, according to true and natural laws.' And he declared later, artists 'finally form the rules out of themselves according to laws of art which lie just as truly in the nature of the formative genius as the great and universal nature eternally maintains its organic laws.' [105]

When we turn to Coleridge, we find that he persistently put in opposition to neo-classic rules the concept of the silent reign of law in external living nature. In the growth of trees 'there is a law which all the parts obey,' in conformity with the 'essential principle.' So Shakespeare worked in the spirit of nature, which 'works from within by evolution and assimilation according to a law'; and 'the *rules* of Imagination,' we remember, are to Coleridge 'the very powers of growth and production.' [106] But recourse from rules to the laws of organic growth confronted Coleridge with another, and very serious, problem. The nature of this difficulty is clearly pointed out in Walter Pater's shrewd, though short-sighted essay on Coleridge as critic and poet. Coleridge, Pater observed, came close to identifying art with a natural organism; and, after citing several relevant passages from Coleridge's criticism, Pater entered this objection:

What makes his view a one-sided one is, that in it the artist has become almost a mechanical agent: instead of the most luminous and self-possessed phase of consciousness, the associative act in art or poetry is made to look like some blindly organic process of assimilation.[107]

The laws of the inanimate world, that is, are fixed and given laws, and operate without consciousness or the possibility of choice; so that in discarding external rules, Coleridge seems in danger of falling into a total artistic automatism.

Of this danger, Coleridge himself was well aware. The unconscious activity may indeed be 'the genius in the man of genius,' but, he also insisted—

What then shall we say? even this; that Shakespeare, no mere child of nature; no automaton of genius; no passive vehicle of inspiration possessed by the spirit, not possessing it; first studied patiently, meditated deeply, understood minutely, till knowledge, become habitual and intuitive . . . at length gave birth to that stupendous power. . .

Coleridge's constant and most emphatic iteration, in fact, is that poetry brings 'the whole soul of man into activity'; that the imagination is 'first put in action by the *will* and understanding, and retained under their irremissive, though gentle and unnoticed, controul'; and that 'great as was the genius of Shakespeare, his judgment was at least equal.'[108] When Clarence D. Thorpe defended the thesis that no critic ever 'had more to say for the value of intellect and reason than Coleridge,'[109] he pointed to a side of Coleridge's theory that Pater, like Irving Babbitt and others after him, totally overlooked.

Coleridge's central problem, therefore, was to use analogy with organic growth to account for the spontaneous, the inspired, and the self-evolving in the psychology of invention, yet not to commit himself so far to the elected figure as to minimize the supervention of the antithetic qualities of foresight and choice. Coleridge's attempt to reconcile these antitheses took varied forms. The judgment of Shakespeare, he says in one instance, 'was the birth and living offspring of his genius even as the symmetry of a body results from the sanity and vigour of the life as the organizing power.' In his best and most sustained passage on the subject, Coleridge contrasts Shakespeare's 'living power' and 'free and rival originality' with the 'lifeless mechanism' of servile imitators of ancient forms, in such a way as to make lawful organic development incorporate both art and rules:

Imagine not I am about to oppose genius to rules. . . The spirit of poetry, like all other living powers, must of necessity circumscribe itself by rules, were it only to unite power with beauty. It must embody in order to reveal itself; but a living body is of necessity an organized one. . .

No work of true genius dare want its appropriate form; neither indeed is there any danger of this. As it must not, so neither can it, be lawless! For it is even this that constitutes it genius—the power of acting creatively under laws of its own origination. . . Nature, the prime genial artist, inexhaustible in diverse powers, is equally inexhaustible in forms. . . And even such is the appropriate excellence of her chosen poet, of our own Shakespeare, himself a nature humanized, a genial understanding directing self-consciously a power and an implicit wisdom deeper than consciousness.[110]

'Directing self-consciously a power and an implicit wisdom deeper than consciousness.' In this way did Coleridge, like A. W. Schlegel, apply the theory based on organism to the solution of the problems in which, as we saw, that theory had its provenience: How a genius, composing independently of set examples and rules, can produce works which are at once regular, exemplary, and the source of rules; how, though writing with seeming freedom, inspiration, and a happy spontaneity, he nevertheless follows a process which turns out to be strictly directed toward an end—in short, how the element of 'nature' in the natural genius can be reconciled to his undoubted achievement of a most complex and elaborate 'art.' The solution is that genius, however free from prior precept, is never free from law; knowledge, diligence, and the reflective judgment, as a preliminary and accompaniment to creation, are necessary but not sufficient conditions to the highest aesthetic achievement; eventually, the work of imagination must start spontaneously into independent life and by its own energy evolve its final form in the same way that a tree grows. Acting thus under 'laws of its own origination,' achieving works each of which is unique, the genius gives the laws by which his own products are to be judged; yet these laws are universal laws which he himself must necessarily obey, because his composition proceeds in accordance with the order of the living universe. Typically, in this mode of romantic criticism, belief in the complete autonomy and the unique originality of the individual work went hand in hand with a confidence in universal principles of value. There is, of course, no logical inconsistency in this position. A work of art may in theory demand to be enjoyed by everyone, yet differ radically from every other work of art in existence.

LITERATURE
AS A REVELATION OF PERSONALITY

Shakespeare is above all writers, at least above all modern writers, the poet of nature; the poet that holds up to his readers a faithful mirrour of manners and of life.

SAMUEL JOHNSON

[Shakespeare's] works are so many windows, through which we see a glimpse of the world that was in him.

THOMAS CARLYLE

To know a work of literature is to know the soul of the man who created it, and who created it in order that his soul should be known.

J. MIDDLETON MURRY

THE GRAND QUESTION 'usual with the best of our own critics at present,' Carlyle wrote in 1827, 'is a question mainly of a psychological sort, to be answered by discovering and delineating the peculiar nature of the poet from his poetry.' [1] There could be no more striking antithesis to the practice of critics (with the partial exception of Longinus) from the dawn of speculation about art through the greater part of the eighteenth century. So long as the poet was regarded primarily as an agent who holds a mirror up to nature, or as the maker of a work of art according to universal standards of excellence, there was limited theoretical room for the intrusion of personal traits into his product. Accordingly, practical criticism busied itself chiefly with the poem itself, its relation to the world it reflected, and its relation to the rules of writing and to the susceptibilities of the audience on which these rules were grounded. The writing of the lives of poets and artists was carried on as one branch of general biography, intended to memorialize men of note in all areas of endeavor. But once the theory emerged that poetry is primarily the expression of feeling and a state of mind—and even, in its extreme form, that poetry is the fictional gratification of desire—a natural corollary was to approach a poem as a revelation of what Carlyle called the 'individual specialties' of the author himself. Schleiermacher wrote in 1800, in the idiom of contemporary idealism:

If the introspection of the spirit into itself is the divine source of all plastic art and poetry, and if the spirit finds within its own being all that it can represent in its immortal works: shall not the spirit, in all its products and compositions, which can represent nothing else, also look back upon itself? [2]

For good or ill, the widespread use of literature as an index—as the most reliable index—to personality was a product of the characteristic aesthetic orientation of the early nineteenth century.

Before undertaking an account of this strange innovation, which swept everything before it in applied criticism for more than a century, it will prove useful to make a few broad distinctions. We shall be concerned with three kinds of ostensibly critical activity, and although each relies on the same assumption that art and personality are correlated variables, the difference between them is important. One looks to an author for the explanation of his work; another reads an author out of his work; and the third reads a work in order to find its author in it. The first type is primarily an investigation of literary causes; *tel arbre, tel fruit,* as Sainte-Beuve, its famed exponent, put it—the attempt is to isolate and explain the special quality of a work by reference to the special quality of the character, life, lineage, and milieu of its author. The second type is biographical in aim: it sets out to reconstruct the author as he lived, and uses the literary product merely as a convenient record from which to infer something about his life and character. The third, however, claims to be specifically aesthetic and appreciative in purpose: it regards aesthetic qualities as a projection of personal qualities, and in its extreme form, it looks upon the poem as a transparency opening directly into the soul of its author. 'Where it is worth the trouble,' Herder said as early as 1778, 'this *living reading,* this divination into the soul of the author, is the *sole* mode of reading, and the most profound means of self-development.' [3] Or in F. L. Lucas' more recent and more moderate rendition of this ideal:

I have found by spontaneous experience more and more that even the aesthetic pleasure of a poem depends for me on the fineness of the personality glimpsed between its lines; on the spirit of which the body of a book is inevitably the echo and the mould. [4]

In the critical discourse of such readers, therefore, the primary qualities of a good poem are, literally, attributes of the mind and temper of its composer: sincerity, integrity, high seriousness, shrewdness, benignity—and so on, through the whole of the characterological resources of the language.

In addition, we may profitably distinguish the level at which a critic pursues the connection between art and temperament, whether his aim is explanatory, biographical, or appreciative. First, a literary product may be taken to reflect the powers, faculties, and skill of its producer—

> Immortal flowers of poesy,
> Wherein, as in a mirror, we perceive
> The highest reaches of a human wit,

as Christopher Marlowe expressed this near-tautology long ago. On the next level, there is held to be a particularity in the style, or general cast of language, which serve as an index to the particularity of its author's cast of mind. But on the third level, the style, structure, and subject matter of literature are said to incorporate the most persistent, dynamic elements of an individual mind; the basic dispositions, interests, desires, preferences, and aversions which give continuity and coherence to a personality. In the sweeping statement of a critic of our own time, Edmund Wilson:

The real elements, of course, of any work of fiction, are the elements of the author's personality: his imagination embodies in the images of characters, situations, and scenes the fundamental conflicts of his nature or the cycle of phases through which it habitually passes. His personages are personifications of the author's various impulses and emotions: and the relations between them in his stories are really the relations between these.[5]

The correlation of the style and certain limited attributes of a work both with the powers and general cast of the author's mind occasionally appeared in classical rhetoric and poetic; it was a prominent element in the theory of Longinus; and it became a fairly frequent subject for comment in the criticism of the seventeenth and eighteenth centuries. The distinctive characteristic in the applied criticism of many romantic critics, English and German, is the extent to which this general approach to literature superseded others, and above all, the development and exploitation of interpretation at the third of these levels. Certain of these critics even went on to distinguish between the personal attributes which an author projects directly into his work and those which he disguises and distorts in order to hide certain facts from his readers, or from himself. As a result we find the division of a work of literature into a surface reference to characters, things, and events, and a more important covert symbolism which is expressive of elements in the nature of its author. Furnished with the proper key, the romantic extremist was confident he could decipher the hieroglyph, penetrate to the reality behind the appearance, and so come to know an author more intimately than his own friends and family; more intimately, even, than the author, lacking this key, could possibly have known himself.

i. Style and the Man

The theory of art has always harbored doctrines which imply some limited correspondence between the nature of the artist and the nature of his product. One familiar instance, the proposition that artistic excellence can only be the consequence of moral excellence, was introduced by Plato, but was better known to Renaissance critics in the simpler version of the geographer, Strabo: 'It is impossible for one to become a good poet unless he has previously become a good man.' [6] The doctrine was readily correlated with the view that art is a vehicle of moral instruction; as Ben Jonson said, they who will consider that a poet is 'a Master in manners,' who can 'inflame *growne-men* to all great vertues,' will 'easily conclude to themselves the impossibility of any mans being the good *Poët*, without first being a good *Man*.' [7] The verso of this tenet—that bad poetry is an index to bad morals—was, of course, urged particularly against poets inclined to the indecorous in subject màtter; while these habitually offered in their defense the contrary maxim, *Lasciva est nobis pagina, vita proba*.[8] On the whole such protests were vain. That a writer reveals his moral character in his art continued to be generally maintained through the eighteenth century and (with sharply divergent interpretations of the nature of morality and the mode of its artistic expression) by Goethe, Coleridge, Shelley, Carlyle, Ruskin, Arnold, and others in the nineteenth century.

Another doctrine, early and widely held, implied that certain aspects of a work reflect more of the particularity of a man than merely his moral excellence. George Puttenham, in *The Arte of English Poesie* (1589), following ample precedent in Italian criticism, held that style is the ornament and dress of poesy, and as such, must be adjusted to the 'matter and subject' of a literary work. Nonetheless there remains a natural and pervasive individuality of language independent of the internal requirements of a work, and this, Puttenham holds, is the literary equivalent of physiognomy, and expresses character:

And because this continuall course and manner of writing or speech sheweth the matter and disposition of the writers minde more than one or few words or sentences can shew, therefore, there be that have called stile the image of man, *mentis character*. . . For if the man be grave, his speech and stile is grave; if light-headed, his stile and language also light; . . . if it be humble, or base and meeke, so is also the language and stile.[9]

The treatment of style as literary physiognomy, as well as the dress of thought, flourished through the eighteenth century. It will be noted that this concept contains two implicit assertions: (1) There is an individuality about a man's writing which distinguishes his work from that of other authors; we recognize a 'Virgilian quality' or a 'Miltonic quality.' (2) This literary trait is correlated with the character of the man himself; the Virgilian quality of style is the equivalent of some aspect of Virgil as he lived. The relation of both these assertions to certain widely held eighteenth-century critical ideas requires some comment.

The position of many eighteenth-century critics was that valid art is constructed according to universal standards, to appeal to sensibilities which men possess in common. But many critics left a place in their view of art for an epiphenomenal 'style,' or 'manner,' which is peculiar to each artist. Boswell tells us that he asked Dr. Johnson 'if there was as clear a difference of styles in language as in painting . . . ?' Johnson replied:

Why, Sir, I think every man whatever has a peculiar style, which may be discovered by nice examination and comparison with others: but a man must write a great deal to make his style obviously discernible. As logicians say, this appropriation of style is infinite *in potestate*, limited *in actu*.[10]

In the most systematic of all expositions of uniformitarian theory, the 'Discourse on Poetical Imitation,' Richard Hurd demonstrated that because of 'the necessary uniformity of *nature* in all her appearance, and of *common sense* in its operations upon them,' poets must all copy the same 'permanent objects,' and according to that universal '*form* which governs each species' of poetry. Yet even Hurd saved a theoretical place for originality and individuality, not in 'the *matter*, but MANNER of imitation'; that is, either in the '*general* turn or manner of writing, which we call a *style*,' or in 'the peculiarities of *phrase and diction*.'[11] If not in what is said, then at the very least in *how* it is said—in the adverbial, if not in the substantive mode—the personal idiom of an author is permitted validly to exhibit itself. This distinction is drawn sharply in Bishop Warburton's acid comment on Young's unqualified advocacy, in his *Conjectures*, of originality and uniqueness in all aspects of a work: 'Dr. Young is the finest writer of nonsense of any of this age.

And had he known that original composition consisted in the manner and not the matter, he had wrote with common sense.'[12]

Furthermore, 'style is the image of character,' as Edward Gibbon phrased what was often an associated point of view.[13] Hurd himself had gone on to say that literary manner corresponds to mental disposition:

A style in writing, if not formed in express imitation of some certain *model,* is the pure result of the disposition of the mind, and takes its character from the predominant quality of the writer. Thus, a *short and compact,* and a *diffused and flowing* expression are the proper consequences of certain corresponding characters of the human genius. . . A polite and elegant humour delights in grace and ease and perspicuity. A severe and melancholic spirit inspires a forcible but involved expression.[14]

An anonymous writer for the *British Magazine* in 1760, therefore, was thoroughly mistaken when he supposed that 'it has not hitherto occurred to any of the critics, that an author's peculiar character is stampt upon his works, and may be discovered under the disguise of different forms in all his compositions.'[15] The opinion was already commonplace that although poetry is imitation, style is the man. This assertion was not self-contradictory, for, it was affirmed, it is the matter which mirrors the world, and the manner which mirrors the man.

As early as the seventeenth century, there were occasional attempts to put this critical postulate to biographical use. Thomas Sprat's *Account of the Life and Writings of Mr. Abraham Cowley,* written in 1668, is representative. There is scarcely an author 'that has handled so many different Matters in such various sorts of Style.'

Yet this is true of them all, that in all the several shapes of his Style there is still very much of the likeness and impression of the same mind: the same unaffected modesty, and natural freedom, and easie vigour, and chearful passions, and innocent mirth, which appear'd in all his Manners.[16]

In addition, the established practice of drawing detailed critical parallels between writers of diverse times and places encouraged some comparison between their temperaments as well. In his Preface to *King Arthur,* Sir Richard Blackmore said that Homer's 'Fire burns with extraordinary Heat and Vehemence . . . Virgil's is a clearer and a chaster flame'; and he found this disparity between the characteristic inspiration of these authors to be reflected in the difference between their protagonists. 'Methinks there is the same Difference between these two great Poets, as there is between their Heros.

Homer's Hero, Achilles, is Vehement, Raging and Impetuous. . . Aeneas, the Hero of the Latine Poet, is a calm, Sedate Warriour.' [17] Dryden vigorously attacked Blackmore in his 'Preface to the Fables' (1700), but did not scruple, in the same essay, to employ and expand upon Blackmore's parallel, and to apply it more specifically to characterological purposes. 'In the works of the two authors we may read their manners and natural inclinations, which are wholly different.'

Our two great poets being so different in their tempers, one choleric and sanguine, the other phlegmatic and melancholic; that which makes them excel in their several ways is, that each of them has followed his natural inclination, as well in forming the design, as in the execution of it. The very heroes shew their authors: Achilles is hot, impatient, revengeful . . . Aeneas patient, considerate, careful of his people, and merciful to his enemies.[18]

Clearly, Dryden here tracks the signs of the 'manners and natural inclinations' of a writer beyond the limits of style, in any narrow sense, and into the design, the characterization, and the action of a literary work. The passage reflects Dryden's personal interest in individual differences. It goes, I believe, just about as far in this direction as any critic was to go for almost a hundred years, despite the vigorous growth of the biographical art, the increasing tendency to appraise an author's literary work in the context of his biography, and the rapid proliferation and refinement of the terminology for psychological analysis. Johnson's procedure in writing the most famous of all literary *Lives* is a case in point.

The tradition within which Johnson worked, of prefatory biography combined with a critical notice, would seem to offer a constant solicitation to the critic to supplement characterological data from evidences in the poems, and to use biographical facts to illuminate the poetry. His treatment of an important author usually falls into three parts: an initial record of biographical facts, including the occasion and the public reception of his more notable poems; an appraisal of the poet's intellectual character; and finally a critical examination of the poems themselves. And in the light of romantic practice, or even of some examples in Johnson's own lifetime, it is notable how rarely, and with what limitation of purpose and material, he crosses over from external to internal sources of biographical evidence, or from an analysis of a poem, and of the resources and genius of the author evidenced by the poem, to a consideration of the details and idiosyncrasies of the poet's temperament.

Joseph Wood Krutch seems to assert the contrary in his distinguished life of Johnson. The chief novelty in Johnson's method is that he is sometimes led 'to seek in poetry the personality of the poet,' and this, Krutch holds, establishes a connection between the criticism of Johnson and that of the romantic period. He cites one example.

'Pope and Swift,' he remarks in passing, 'had an unnatural delight in ideas physically impure.' No statement could be simpler but, simple as it is, it is sufficient to suggest how readily Johnson passed from an analysis of writing to an analysis of the writer.[19]

But neither the critical assumption nor this specific observation was novel in Johnson's time,[20] nor is the type of comment a frequent or distinctive attribute of Johnson's critical procedure. It is quite true that Johnson loved best, as he said, the biographical part of literature, but this was characteristic of his humanism; his business, as Rasselas put it, 'is with man,' and with a reading of what Johnson called 'the great book of mankind.' Krutch is also right in noting as a characteristic property of Johnson's criticism, the reference of a work to the intellect that produced it. Johnson's basic interest, however, is not a 'romantic' interest in the revelation of personality, but, as W. R. Keast has shown, a humanistic interest in the measure the work affords of the knowledge, acquired skill, and native genius of its maker, abstracted from the literary examples and opportunities then available, and gauged against 'the general and collective ability of man.' [21] Reference to such obvious peculiarities as those of Swift are usually made in the attempt to discover the failings which have hindered a writer from realizing the full scope of his powers. 'There is always,' as Johnson said in a central passage of his Preface to Shakespeare, 'a silent reference of human works to human abilities,' and 'the enquiry how far man may extend his designs, or how high he may rate his native force, is of far greater dignity than in what rank we shall place any particular performance.' [22]

How far Johnson's procedure is from the use of a poem as an index to temperamental particularities may be judged from his comment on such an attempt by a contemporary biographer. Patrick Murdock, in his 'Account of the Life and Writings of James Thomson,' had written:

It is commonly said, that the life of a good writer is best read in his works; which can scarce fail to receive a peculiar tincture from his temper, manners, and habits; the distinguishing character of his mind, his ruling passion, at least, will there appear undisguised. . .

As for [Thomson's] more distinguishing qualities of *mind* and *heart,* they are better represented in his writings, than they can be by the pen of any biographer.

There, his love of mankind, of his country and friends; his devotion to the
Supreme Being . . . shine out on every page.[23]

Johnson's comment is brief, pungent, and decisive:

The biographer of Thomson has remarked, that an author's life is best read in
his works: his observation was not well-timed. Savage, who lived much with
Thomson, once told me, how he heard a lady remarking that she could gather
from his works three parts of his character, that he was a 'great lover, a great
swimmer, and rigorously abstinent'; but, said Savage, he knows not any love but
that of the sex; he was perhaps never in cold water in his life; and he indulges
himself in all luxury that comes within his reach.[24]

The extent to which the biographical use of literature was originally rooted
in the neo-classic interest in mankind, and developed out of the rhetorical
concept that style is an image of mind, is revealed by the most thorough
and systematic exposition of the theory I have found in eighteenth-century
Britain. This is an essay read to the Royal Irish Academy in 1793-4 by the
Reverend Robert Burrowes, with the resoundingly informative title: *On
Style in Writing, considered with respect to Thoughts and Sentiments as
well as Words, and indicating the Writer's peculiar and Characteristic Disposition, Habits and Powers of Mind.* Burrowes contends that the traditional consideration of style from the point of view of its appropriateness to
the subject matter and to the literary kind overlooks its important use as the
distinctive mark of 'an author's peculiar habits of thinking.' He justifies his
own enterprise by the central tenet of neo-classic humanism:

If the proper object of mankind be man, an enquiry into the varieties of the
human mind, a discovery of them in their natural effects, in the style of thought,
traced out through the medium of literary productions and style of language,
could not fail of being highly useful.[25]

Burrowes sets up various salutary caveats against an unprincipled search for
the 'habits and dispositions' reflected in a style. Conclusions drawn from
purely literary evidences must be validated by 'an accurate biographical account,' drawn from external sources; application of the method, therefore,
to ancient writers, about whom few facts are available, can at best result
only in 'probable conjecture.' Furthermore, such literary forms as the pastoral
are too conventional, and the dramatic too impersonal, for the author to discover himself in them.[26] He then goes on to list the kinds of clues which,
given the appropriate circumstances, will assist the detective reader in track-
ing the dispositions of the writer, and these herald strikingly a number of the

interpretative stratagems employed by biographical critics of a later day. Here are some examples:

When a man quits the direct path, it is always to go by some way which he likes better. . . The digressions of an author are, in like manner, indications of what is agreeable to his dispositions, for he cannot expatiate on what he dislikes.

Metaphors and similes he will seek in those sources which his prior occupations have made familiar and his habits have endeared to his taste.

[From] the various lights in which the same subjects appear to different writers, and from their different modes of treating them the characteristic differences of their own understandings obviously appear. .

The choice of [his subject] is an act directed by the habits and dispositions of the author, and therefore indicative of these.

Man has been said to be a bundle of habits: habit then will account for the frequent recurrence of a kindred train of thinking in the mind of the same person. . .

The frequent recurrence of any one topic gives information of the same sort.[27]

When Burrowes finally comes to give 'some specimens of this theory applied . . . in the writings of known authors,' the results are conventional and unexciting enough. His most penetrating remark is that Goldsmith has drawn all his principal personages on a single pattern; all are awkwardly ignorant of the world and are amiably virtuous. 'His Good-natured Man, Young Marlow, and Vicar of Wakefield agree in this particular with each other, because in this particular they all agree with the author himself.'[28] Burrowes' theory, shrewd and empirical-minded as it is, represents a kind of hypertrophy of one strand of neo-classic literary theory. It was written very late in the eighteenth century, and in the meantime, the total fabric of traditional criticism had been strangely altered by immersion in the deep sea of German metaphysical and aesthetic speculation.

ii. Subjective and Objective, and Romantic Polysemism

To permit an uninhibited and all-embracing reading of literature for the nuances of personality—what Walter Pater was to call 'imaginative criticism,' that act of 'creation' which 'penetrates, through the given literary or artistic product, into the mental and inner constitution of the producer'[29] —we must suppose that the general framework of ideas within which criticism operated had to undergo two important changes. First, each author must be regarded as unique, different in essentials from all other authors. Second, not only the style but the characters, ordonnance, and total subject matter of a work of literature must be regarded as molded by, and, therefore, as expressing, the shaping forces in the personality of its author. Both these conditions were fulfilled as early as the 1770's, in the writings of J. G. Herder. 'The deepest ground of our being,' he wrote in his epoch-making essay, *Vom Erkennen und Empfinden der menschlichen Seele* (1778), 'is individual, in feelings as well as thoughts . . . All the species of animals are perhaps not so distinct from one another as a man is from men.' Edward Young and a few other dissidents from the reigning uniformitarianism had already claimed that all men are born originals, and therefore would best fulfil the aesthetic intention of nature by writing original poems.[30] Herder adds the explicit concept that genuine works of literature express the dynamics of the individual temperament; to this the corollary is that 'creative' reading uses the text as a 'Divination in die Seele des Urhebers.'

One ought to be able to regard each book as the impression [*Abdruck*] of a living human soul. . . The more discreet and judicious reader . . . endeavors rather to read the spirit of the author than the book; the farther he penetrates into this, the brighter and more coherent does everything become. The life of an author is the best commentary on his writings, provided that he is genuine, and in harmony with himself. . .

Each poem, especially a great and complete poem, a work of the soul and of life, is a dangerous betrayer of its author, and often when he believes that he is betraying himself least. Not only do you discern, as the populace will have it, the poetic talents of the man; you also discern which of his faculties and propensities were the ruling ones; the manner in which he got his images; how he regulated and disposed these and the chaos of his impressions; the most intimate places of his heart and often the fated course of his life as well. . . Such reading is emulation, a stimulus to discovery: we mount with [the author] to creative heights, or else discover the error and the deviation at its inception.[31]

The total poem, hitherto an image of manners and life, has become 'a dangerous betrayer of its author.' But what was the source of the interesting and important romantic variant of this concept, that poetry is not a direct, but an indirect and disguised expression of the author's temperament—and therefore, that the author is at the same time in, and not in his poem? It can be shown, I think, that this critical paradox, in its early appearance, was theological in its origin, and Kantian in the philosophical vocabulary by which it was justified. To the comparatively uncomplicated terminology, stemming mainly from ancient rhetoric and poetic, with which critics had earlier attacked the problems of art, German critics, especially in the 1790's, assimilated a Pandora's box of new terms and concepts. These were in considerable part imported from Kant's epistemology and aesthetics, but with admixture from Christian theologians, as well as various rather disreputable specialists in mysticism and the occult. The result was indubitably to extend the range and subtlety of aesthetic analysis, although at the expense of crosshatching the relatively simple distinctions with which critics up to that time had been content.

One of the results was to complicate the discussion of the extent to which art is impersonal or self-expressive by introducing a set of cross-distinctions revolving about the terms 'subjective' and 'objective.' That fecund but disorderly thinker, Friedrich Schlegel, who introduced the distinction between classic and romantic which has turned out to be equally indispensable and unmanageable to literary critics and historians, helped also to popularize other contraries which are scarcely less attractive, or less equivocal. During his phase of youthful Grecomania, he tried to isolate the supposedly opposite qualities of ancient and modern art so as to bring into focus the superiority of the former. 'Das Wesentlich-Antike' he characterized by a number of overlapping or correlated attributes; from our present point of view, the most important of these was an unconditional *Objektivität*. In Schlegel's use, this term did not, as it usually does today, connote realism—writing done with the eye on the object—but specifically excluded realism, as well as self-expression. That is to say, the objective art of the ancients, without reference either to reality or to private interests, reveals nothing more of the individual writer than his capacity to achieve the one uniform excellence according to the universal laws of beauty.[32]

In 'das eigentümlich Moderne,' the identifying attribute which Schlegel most frequently opposes to *Objektivität* is not *Subjektivität*,[33] but *das Interessante*. This term he uses in an old sense, close to its Latin etymon; it signifies a lack of *dis*interestedness, and the intervention in a work of the attitudes and proclivities of the author himself.[34] The work of such a poet (and here Schlegel finally brings into his theory terms of the traditional rhetoric) is also said to show 'manner,' or 'an individual turn of the mind, and an individual state of sensibility,' as opposed to 'style,' which signifies an impersonal mode of expression according to the uniform laws of beauty.[35] And modern art, in its lack of 'universality,' combines subjectivity and realism, self-revelation and 'the characteristic,' or representation of external particulars.

In this lack of universality, in this domination of the mannered, the characteristic, and the individual, there declares itself the radical tendency of the poetry and of the total aesthetic structure of modern times toward interestedness.[36]

In the course of the years 1797-8, Schlegel re-christened 'interessante Poesie' as 'romantische Poesie,' and precipitately transferred his admiration and allegiance from the classical to the newer mode of poetizing.[37] A. O. Lovejoy has demonstrated the decisive role played in this famous conversion by Schiller's essay, *Über naive und sentimentalische Dichtung,* published in 1795.[38] According to Schiller, naïve poetry, characteristic of the ancients, is an immediate, detailed, and particularized representation of the sensuous surface of life.[39] Modern, or 'sentimental,' man, on the other hand, no longer in unity either with nature or himself, tends in poetry to substitute his ideal for the given reality, and also 'can suffer no impression without immediately attending to its own part in the performance, and by reflection, projecting outside and opposite itself that which it has in itself.'[40] In naïve poetry, therefore, the poet is realistic, impersonal, and elusive; but in sentimental poetry, the poet is constantly present in his work and solicits our attention to himself:

Wholly unconfiding, [the naïve poet, ancient or modern] flees the heart that seeks him, the longing that wishes to embrace him. . . The object possesses him utterly. . . Like the Deity behind this universe, he stands behind his work; he is himself the work, and the work is himself; a man must be no longer worthy of the work, or be incapable of mastering it, or be tired of it, even to ask after its author.

So appear to us, for example, Homer among the ancients and Shakespeare among the moderns. . . When at a very early age I first learned to know the latter poet, his coldness, his insensibility repelled me. . . Misled as I was through acquaintance with modern poets to seek at once the poet in the work, to meet *his* heart, to reflect *with him* upon his theme—in short, to see the object in the subject—I could not bear that in this instance the poet could nowhere be seized, and would nowhere abide my question [*und mir nirgends Rede stehen wollte*].[41]

In Schiller's essay, Shakespeare, because 'the object possesses him utterly,' is a naïve poet born out of his time; therefore he, like God, is not visible in his work. But precisely because he agreed that Shakespeare was supreme in representing the particulars of external nature, Schlegel had put him in the camp of the moderns, rather than the ancients: he is 'the pinnacle of modern poetry.' And therefore, to Schlegel, Shakespeare inevitably exhibits that other symptom of the modern syndrome: 'In [Hamlet] the spirit of its author is at its most visible.' 'It has often been remarked, that the original impress of his individual manner is unmistakable and inimitable.' [42]

On the question of Shakespeare, then, the two critics were at first in flat opposition: to Schlegel, he was inveterately subjective, but to Schiller, impregnably objective. A student of the *Romantiker*, A. E. Lussky, has recently argued, very convincingly, that it soon occurred to Schlegel that he and Schiller might both be right. It is possible, Schlegel thought, that the literary qualities of 'objectivity' and 'interestedness' are not incompatible, so that a modern writer may at the same time be in, and aloof from, his own dramas. This is a seeming contradiction, but one which had sanction in an ancient and persistent concept about the relation of God to the universe. And the recourse to theology for resolving the paradox of Shakespeare had been suggested by Schiller himself, in the passage comparing that poet to 'the Deity behind this universe' who 'stands behind his work' yet 'is himself the work.' [43]

Lussky deals with this insight as the origin of Schlegel's celebrated concept of 'romantic irony,' which holds that a romantic author, while remaining impersonal, nonetheless manifests his power and love with respect to his artistic creation. I should like, however, to emphasize a different aspect of Schlegel's achievement, and to look at it from a different point of view. What Schlegel did, in effect, was to give new application to the Renaissance metaphor of the poet as creator, with its implicit analogy between God's creation of the world and the artist's making of a poem. Once adopted, this analogy opened the way for the introduction into criticism of a rich stock of linked ideas, accumulated over centuries of theological speculation, about the nature of God's activity in making this world. In the next chapter we shall have occasion to examine some important aesthetic inferences concerning the valid likenesses and differences between God's world and the other world created by the poet. At the moment, let me remark only this curious consequence, that in Schlegel's writings the parallel between creator and poet serves as the intellectual model for conceiving a poem as a disguised projection of its author.

Ultimately, this concept goes back to a very old idea as to God's relation to his created universe. The primitive text setting forth this idea is in Paul's Epistle to the Romans, 1.20: 'For the invisible things of Him from the creation of the world are clearly seen, being understood by the things that are made, even His eternal power and Godhead. . .' The Church Fathers in the early Middle Ages, inveterate allegorizers, expanded greatly on this passage.[44] And in their interpretation, the Pauline text was glossed to mean that the world of sense is indeed what it appears to be, a structure of physical objects; but that it is at the same time a mirror and mystical typology of the attributes—the power, the love, and the glory—of the Creator himself. For God has declared himself in two manifestations, in the Holy Scriptures, and also in the Great Book of Nature. And as the Scriptures are manifold in meaning, embodying both literal and typological significance, so with the Book of Nature, though this possesses a duplicity peculiar to itself. It declares to us not only God's creation in and for itself; through the veil of its tangible surface, it also declares to us, 'visibly invisible,' its Author. As Milton later expressed the commonplace, in his *Paradise Lost:*

> To us invisible or dimly seen
> In these thy lowest works, yet these declare
> Thy goodness beyond thought, and Power Divine.

Some medieval writers, such as Aquinas and Dante (in his 'Letter to Can Grande della Scala'), had maintained that secular works of literature may, like the Scriptures, be made 'polysemous,' or significant both of literal and various kinds of allegorical truths. Schlegel now proposes what, in distinction from the medieval theory, we may call romantic polysemism. According to Schlegel, a 'romantic' work may be multiple in meaning, but in the particular sense of having, like God's creation, bi-directional reference—both outward and inward, 'objective' and 'subjective.' As Lussky has said, proceeding from the proportion, 'as God is to His creation, so the great modern artist is to his literary creation,'

Schlegel could conclude—and it is evident that he did so—that just as God, despite His transcendence, is immanent in the world, showing 'the invisible things of him . . . by the things that are made,' so also the typical modern writer, Shakespeare in this instance, despite his transcendence of his works by virtue of his objectivity, is plainly immanent in them and reveals his invisible presence by the things that he has made.[45]

As we shall see later in this chapter, this pregnant idea was to be independently derived and much more thoroughly exploited by the English critic, John Keble, but it was clearly expressed a number of times by Schlegel; for example, in this passage written in 1801, dealing with the tales of Boccaccio:

I maintain that the novella is very well adapted to represent a subjective mood and point of view—even of the deepest and most peculiar sort—indirectly and symbolically [*sinnbildlich*], as it were. . . But by what magic do [some tales of Cervantes] agitate our inmost soul, and seize it with divine beauty, except by virtue of the fact that everywhere the feeling of the author—even the innermost depths of his most intimate individuality—gleams through, visibly invisible; or else because, as in the *Curioso Impertinente,* he has expressed views which, because of their very peculiarity and depth, had either to be expressed in this way or not at all. . . Precisely that which is indirect and veiled in this mode of communication may lend it a higher charm than anything which is immediately lyrical. In a similar way the novella itself is, perhaps, particularly adapted to this indirect and secret subjectivity, because in other respects it tends very much to the objective.[46]

Here, in a phrasing which—with its allusions to symbolism, divine beauty, and veiled meanings, and its oxymoron of the 'visibly invisible'—is taken directly from medieval and Renaissance typology, there emerges clearly the familiar modern view that certain works of literature are dual symbol-systems, pointing in two directions, ostensibly representing the outer world, but indirectly expressing the author. In its early form, what we now think of as the Freudian theory of literature was mainly the result of applying medieval hermeneutics to secular works of fiction and poetry.

iii. Subjective and Objective in English Theory

It is already apparent that, from their earliest uses in criticism, the terms 'subjective' and 'objective' were both multiple and variable in their meanings. This ambiguity greatly complicates the story of the romantic attempts to use literature as an index to temperament; and it will, I think, prove helpful to preface that story with an outline of some of the major variations in the application of the terms.

Subjective-objective in their various connotations, together with the diverse pairs of contraries with which these words were often associated, served both as historical and as critical terms, and therefore were used alternately to define (1) the salient character of a period of art; (2) the over-all character of a work of art, no matter what its period; (3) specific aesthetic qualities which may be found, separately or united, in any work of art. A fourth use of these terms complicated their roles still further: (4) subjective and objective sometimes served as the terminal values on a scale which was employed to grade the several genres of poetry. In this application, which was adumbrated by both Friedrich and August Schlegel, the lyric was held to be the thoroughly subjective form, the epic was usually put at the opposite extreme of pure objectivity, and the drama regarded as a composite form somewhere in between.

This complex of related antitheses—subjective and objective, naïve and sentimental, classical and romantic, style and manner, and the rest—migrated over into the vocabulary of English and American criticism mainly during and after the second decade of the nineteenth century. Some Englishmen —notably Coleridge, H. C. Robinson, Lockhart, De Quincey, and Carlyle —discovered these terms by reading Schiller, or the brothers Schlegel, or Goethe, in the original. Many more, like Hazlitt, depended primarily on Madame de Staël's rendering of German theory in her *L'Allemagne,* or on English versions of such documents as A. W. Schlegel's *Lectures on Dramatic Art and Literature* (translated in 1815).[47] And in England these terms preserved the varied applications, the ambiguities, and the sliding usages they had had in Germany. 'German dulness, and English affectation,' John Ruskin complained in 1856, 'have of late much multiplied among us the use of two of the most objectionable words that were ever coined by the troublesomeness of metaphysicians—namely, "Objective" and "Subjective." No words can be more exquisitely, and in all points, useless.'[48]

Let Coleridge's use of 'subjective' and 'objective' represent for us some of this variety. In expounding Milton's three adjectives, 'simple, sensuous, and passionate,' which Coleridge regards as an adequate summary definition of poetry, he makes the point that 'the second condition, sensuousness, insures that framework of objectivity, that definiteness and articulation of imagery,' without which poetry evaporates into day-dreaming, while 'the third condition, passion, provides that neither thought nor imagery shall be simply objective, but that the *passio vera* of humanity shall warm and animate both.'[49] In this sense, no poetry is purely objective, for passion is essential, and passion makes it more than 'simply objective'—and presumably, therefore, subjective. Elsewhere, however, Coleridge contracts 'objective' so as to make it specifically applicable to the poetry of the ancients; 'subjective' then becomes a historical term characterizing medieval and modern poetry. 'It is this inwardness or subjectivity, which principally and most fundamentally distinguishes all the classic from all the modern poetry.'[50] In a third use, 'subjectivity' is further narrowed, and at the same time subdivided, so as to connote attributes which may apparently be possessed by any individual poet or composition:

There is no subjectivity whatever in the Homeric poetry. There is a subjectivity of the poet, as of Milton, who is himself before himself in everything he writes;

and there is a subjectivity of the *persona,* or dramatic character, as in all Shakespeare's great creations, *Hamlet, Lear,* etc.[51]

Finally, subjective and objective become defining attributes of poetic species, independently, it would seem, of either epoch or authorship. The elegy

may treat of any subject, but it must treat of no subject *for itself;* but always and exclusively with reference to the poet himself. . . The elegy is the exact opposite of the Homeric epic, in which all is purely external and objective, and the poet is a mere voice.

The true lyric ode is subjective too. . .[52]

In conclusion, here is a passage from that great popularizer of German ideas, Henry Crabb Robinson, who in brief compass includes a number of critical terms drawn from Schiller and the Schlegels—'objective,' 'subjective,' 'naïve,' 'sentimental,' 'style,' 'real,' 'ideal'—and attempts to reconcile their various significations. The source is an article on Goethe in the *Monthly Repository* (1833), a periodical which in its brief span included some of the more interesting aesthetic speculation of its time.

The epic is marked by this character of style,—that the poet presents his *object* immediately and directly, with a total disregard of his own personality. He is, as it were, an indifferent and unimpassioned narrator and chronicler. . . The opposite class of poetry is the *lyric,* in which the poet gives mainly objects as they are reflected in the mirror of his own individuality. And this certainly is the essential character of odes, elegies, songs, &c. These same classes, designated generally, as the *objective* and *subjective,* were called by Schiller the naïve and the sentimental, and they have also been named the real and the ideal. In general, modern poets belong to the subjective class. . . The dramatic poet must unite the powers of both in an equal degree. In the plan of his drama, in the relation of the characters to each other, all in subordination to the purpose of the work, he must have the epic impartiality; but in the execution, he is lyric.[53]

The dialectical variability of these terms, however confusing to the student of criticism, was not, in the best critics, the result of intellectual confusion, but a way of converting a rigid into a flexible analytic instrument. For example, employment of the distinction between objectivity (in the most common sense, implying impersonality) and subjectivity of various kinds enabled Coleridge and other exponents to adjust the characterological interpretation of literature to the particular author and work, and to waive this interpretation entirely when dealing with writers to whom it was considered inapplicable. Some extremists, however, admitted no limit to this mode of interpretation. Regarding all poetry—at any rate, all genuine poetry—as a projection of individual thought, feeling, and desire, they carried their pursuit of personality into poets of all periods, writing in any form. Poetry which is not 'tinctured with the character and leanings of the poet as by some mysterious aroma,' Keble maintained, is 'absolutely not poetry at all.' [54] And Newman, who in this respect was a faithful follower of Keble, translated the same concept into terms of subjective and objective; all literature, in his rendering, is subjective by definition. Literature 'is essentially a personal work . . . [it] is the expression of that one person's ideas and feelings,—ideas and feelings personal to himself. . . In other words, literature expresses, not objective truth, as it is called, but subjective; not things, but thoughts.' [55]

So much by way of theoretical groundwork. I shall devote the rest of this chapter to the attempts, in the earlier nineteenth century, to convert expressive theory into critical practice, and to reconstruct the life story and character of a writer from his imaginative writings. For economy's sake, I shall omit the discussions of such contemporaries as Byron, whom everyone knew to wear his heart on his sleeve, and focus upon the attempts to deal with three older poets, each an Olympian, and each posing the biographical critic with a distinctive problem in interpretation: Shakespeare, Milton, and Homer.

iv. The Paradox of Shakespeare

The disagreement between Schlegel and Schiller whether Shakespeare was subjective or objective continued to divide English critics, although the majority concurred with Schiller that in Shakespeare 'the poet could nowhere be seized,' rather than with Schlegel, that in his work 'the spirit of its author is the most visible.' One of the chief themes of Coleridge's criticism is his insistence that Shakespeare is with Homer, and is opposed to Milton, Chaucer, and most other poets, in keeping his personal self aloof from his writings. In one passage Coleridge, like Schiller, applies to Shakespeare the analogy of the relation of God to his creation, though he figures God as the depersonalized immanent Deity of Spinoza:

Shakespeare is the Spinozistic deity—an omnipresent creativeness . . . Shakespeare's poetry is characterless; that is, it does not reflect the individual Shakespeare. . .

Nevertheless he is not, like Homer, 'objective,' but 'subjective,' though his subjectivity is of that peculiar sort, the 'subjectivity of the *persona,* or dramatic character.' [56] For his characters are drawn not by the induction of types from external individuals, but 'by the simple force of meditation: he had only to imitate certain parts of his own character . . . and they were at once true to nature, and fragments of the divine mind that drew them. . .'[57] Shakespeare, therefore, can be said to 'imitate certain parts of his own character,' and yet be 'universal, and in fact [have] no manner.'[58]

Coleridge explains this paradox of Shakespeare's union of subjectivity and God-like impersonality in several alternate ways. In metaphysical terms (we have discussed these in an earlier chapter), Shakespeare, in his introspective meditation, imitates not the *natura naturata,* 'his own nature, as an individual person,' but the *natura naturans,* that universal potentiality 'of which his own personal existence was but one [modification].'[59] Restated psychologically in terms of *Einfühlung,* he 'darts himself forth, and passes into all the forms of human character and passion. . . Shakespeare becomes all things, yet forever remaining himself.'[60] Coleridge also employs for Shakespeare's peculiar power the term 'sympathy,' first developed by eighteenth-century associationists primarily as an ethical concept, and then extended, even in that century, to explain how a poet is able to annul space and the isolation of his individual nervous system and become, for the nonce, the personality he contemplates:

The sympathy of the poet with the subjects of his poetry is particularly remarkable in Shakespeare and Chaucer; but what the first effects by a strong act of imagination and mental metamorphosis, the last does without any effort, merely by the inborn kindly joyousness of his nature. How well we seem to know Chaucer! How absolutely nothing do we know of Shakespeare![61]

Like Coleridge, William Hazlitt believed that in Milton 'you trace the bias and opinions of the man in the creations of the poet,' but that Shakespeare, almost alone among poets, had 'the faculty of transforming himself at will into whatever he chose. . . He was the Proteus of human intellect.'[62] Hazlitt's explanation of Shakespeare's unique faculty, however, is put solely in terms developed from English psychology. The 'capacious soul' of Shakespeare is the greatest example of 'an intuitive and mighty sympathy.'

He was the least of an egoist that it was possible to be. He was nothing in himself; but he was all that others were, or that they could become. . . He had only to think of any thing in order to become that thing, with all the circumstances belonging to it. . . The poet may be said, for the time, to identify himself with the character he wishes to represent, and to pass from one to another, like the same soul successively animating different bodies.[63]

And John Keats, the most thoroughly empathic of his contemporaries, who admired Hazlitt and attended his lectures on Shakespeare, expressed a similar conception of Shakespeare's impersonality. 'The genius of Shakespeare was an *innate universality*—wherefore he laid the achievement of human intellect prostrate beneath his indolent and kingly gaze.' [64] Keats extended this quality to define the poetical character in general. 'It is not itself—it has no self—it is every thing and nothing.' A poet 'has no Identity—he is continually infor[ming] and filling some other Body.' [65]

Critics who hungered for an intimate acquaintance with Shakespeare the man found a seemingly ready and easy access to him in his sonnets. For however successfully Shakespeare may have kept his private affairs out of his dramas and narrative poetry, do not the sonnets speak out in the first person, and with the most convincing passion, about explicit people and events? Merely assume that you can identify the lyrical voice with the author's own, and you have cleared the way to startling revelations about Shakespeare's life and deepest feelings.

In the eighteenth century, Shakespeare's sonnets, like his other non-dramatic writings, had been omitted from most editions of his collected works, and were ignored or contemned by his critics. Steevens' comment is notorious, that 'the strongest acts of Parliament that could be framed, would fail to compel readers into their service.' The growth of interest in the sonnets is synchronous with the development of the biographical bias in criticism. Apparently, August Wilhelm Schlegel hit upon the crucial discovery when he wrote, in an article for Schiller's *Horen* (1796), that the sonnets 'are valuable primarily because they seem inspired by a love and friendship that were not imaginary.' [66] In his *Lectures on Dramatic Art and Literature,* delivered in 1808, he expanded upon this theme:

It betrays more than ordinary deficiency of critical acumen in Shakespeare's commentators, that none of them, so far as we know, have ever thought of availing themselves of his sonnets for tracing the circumstances of his life. These sonnets paint most unequivocally the actual situation and sentiments of the poet; they make us acquainted with the passions of the man; they even contain remarkable confessions of his youthful errors. [67]

After John Black's translation of the *Lectures* in 1815, Schlegel was often claimed as patron by English literary detectives into Shakespeare's private history, and in 1827 Wordsworth gave the group their slogan—'With this key, Shakespeare unlocked his heart.' [68] By 1838, Charles Armitage Brown, who had been a close friend of Keats, devoted an entire book to *Shake-*

speare's Autobiographical Poems which established the basic pattern for many later commentaries. Shakespeare's true lovers, as Brown discloses the motive for such researches, 'would know all about him; they would see him face to face, hear him speak, be in his companionship, live with him altogether.' The personal history Brown extracts from the sonnets is the now familiar one involving a beloved friend, a rival poet, and a dark mistress. Some of Shakespeare's conduct, Brown admits, was of questionable morality; but from the sequence as a whole, the critic issues with an image which was not only standard for that age of Bardolatry, but reappears in such modern restorations of Shakespeare's portrait as that of Caroline Spurgeon.

When I open the pages of Shakespeare, my reason sees nothing but the product of a superior mind, aided and strengthened by the keenest observation and the deepest study. Yes, one thing more . . . a spirit of goodness within him. . . A kindliness of nature, an inexhaustible charity, an ardent love of all created things.[69]

It remains to say something of those who, instead of regarding the sonnets as the one chink in Shakespeare's chain-mail of impersonality, operated on the assumption that he is self-revealed in all his writings. In England, the early decades of the nineteenth century produced a variety of books and articles devoted to reconstructing Shakespeare's moral, political, and religious beliefs from his plays. Hartley Coleridge's essay, 'Shakespeare a Tory and a Gentleman' (1828), whose title speaks for itself, is representative. Jones Very's two essays on Shakespeare (1838) are more interesting to us than most. They were written by a young American who believed that he himself composed to the dictation of the Holy Ghost. They contain a number of critical concepts which were still relatively novel even in England, and they propose an early version of the theory that Shakespeare is to be identified with Hamlet—a Hamlet interpreted not as suffering from romantic abulia, but as fearful of death through very excess of a passion for life and action. Very concurs in the opinion that the secret of Shakespeare's creative ability is his powerful projective sympathy. 'With the ever-surprised mind of a child, he was always transformed into the object he saw,' and so strongly 'as to seem for the time to have no other individuality.' But it is a mistake to assume, in consequence, that the real Shakespeare is none of his characters; he is *all* of his characters. 'This view of Shakespeare will lead us to look upon his characters as the natural expression of his own, as its necessary growths or offshoots.'[70] And the very difficulty we find in interpreting Hamlet derives from the fact that Shakespeare had employed this character beyond all others 'for the expression of his own feelings'; its obscurity arises 'from too close a connexion with his own mind.' [71]

But Carlyle was king among those who read an author not for what he made, but for what he was. It is true that he adopted the German distinction between manner and mannerlessness, and the prevailing opposition between writers such as Byron, 'who painted nothing else than himself,' on the one side, and Homer, Shakespeare, and Goethe, on the other. One characteristic of Goethe, for instance, is his 'universality; his entire freedom from Mannerism.'

As hard is it to discover in his writings . . . what sort of spiritual construction he has, what are his temper, his affections, his individual specialities. For all lives freely within him: . . . he seems not this man, or that man, but a man. We reckon this to be the characteristic of a Master in Art of any sort; and true especially of all great Poets. How true is it of Shakspeare and Homer! Who knows, or can figure what the Man Shakspeare was, by the first, by the twentieth, perusal of his works? [72]

But for Carlyle absence of manner was not, as to most critics, equivalent to absence of self-revelation, but merely a greater challenge to the reader. For 'to transform into *shape,* into *life,* the opinion, the feeling that may dwell in him . . . in its widest sense, we reckon to be essentially the grand problem of the Poet.' Even in Goethe's, 'as in every man's writings, the character of the writer must lie recorded,' and Goethe's 'opinions, character, personality . . . with whatever difficulty, are and must be decipherable in his writings.' [73] Carlyle typically names his essays for a writer—'Jean Paul Friedrich Richter,' 'Goethe,' 'Burns'—and concerns himself very little with their art, and very much with their lives, and their personal and moral quality.

Carlyle deals in this way with Shakespeare, 'The Hero as Poet.' He applies to Shakespeare's relation to his subject matter the old analogue of the mimetic mirror, but by an interpretative tour de force, converts the very perfection with which Shakespeare reflects the world into a revelation of the reflector. 'And is not Shakespeare's *morality,* his valour, candour, tolerance, truthfulness . . . visible there too? Great as the world! No *twisted,* poor convex-concave mirror, reflecting all objects with its own convexities and concavities; a perfectly *level* mirror;—that is to say withal, if we will understand it, a man justly related to all things and men, a good man.' His joyful tranquillity is notable, yet 'those *Sonnets* of his will even testify expressly in what deep waters he had waded, and swum struggling for his life.' But in contrast, 'observe his mirthfulness, his genuine overflowing love of laughter!' So intent is Carlyle's single-minded search in literature for a communion of souls that the effects on Shakespeare's dramas of the very causes which had hitherto served as the defining qualities of an 'art'—the requirements of his medium, the nature of his conventions, and the demands of his audience—constitute for Carlyle so many opaque waste-stretches between those 'bursts of radiance' which illuminate the man himself.

But I will say, of Shakspeare's works generally, that we have no full impress of him there; even as full as we have of many men. His works are so many windows, through which we see a glimpse of the world that was in him. . . Such bursts, however, make us feel that the surrounding matter is not radiant; that it is, in part, temporary, conventional. Alas, Shakspeare had to write for the Globe Playhouse: his great soul had to crush itself, as it could, into that and no other mould. It was with him, then, as it is with us all. No man works save under conditions. . . *Disjecta membra* are all that we find of any Poet, or of any man.[74]

From such beginnings there developed the largest mass of conjectural biography under which any author has ever staggered on his way to immortality. The rough impressionism of Carlyle's portrait of Shakespeare gave way to more and more elaborate detail. As the patient accumulation of external evidence, supported by techniques for analyzing changes of versification in the dramas themselves, yielded greater assurance about the chronology of Shakespeare's writings, there emerged the developmental biography, in which Shakespeare's plays are regarded as single episodes in the immense drama of Shakespeare's inner life—that 'tragedy of tragedies' as Frank Harris called it, 'in which "Lear" is only one scene.' In 1874 Edward Dowden formulated the biographical stereotype of 'In the Workshop,' 'In the World,' 'Out of the Depths,' 'On the Heights'—Shakespeare's life being rounded with *The Tempest*.[75] According to similar or alternate schemes, Shakespeare has been unriddled from his plays by a number of able critics, from David Masson to Dover Wilson. But the romantic war over the question whether we are at all justified in reading Shakespeare out of his plays is far from settled. Such formidable antagonists as G. L. Kittredge and E. E. Stoll still maintain, like Schiller and Coleridge before them, that Shakespeare's writings reveal only the artist, and that Shakespeare the man must remain a mystery.

v. Milton, Satan, and Eve

Romantic critics were unanimous that, without complication of objectivity and mannerlessness to veil his image, John Milton, as Coleridge put it, 'himself is in every line of *Paradise Lost*.'[76] The reasons for this opinion are plain enough. Then as now, Milton as a person was incomparably better known than any earlier poet. His triple function as politician, scholar, and poet had made him the subject of a number of commentators and biographers, and the self-descriptions in his prose writings are so many and lengthy as, gathered together, to make up an autobiography of formidable dimensions. By mingling expressly personal utterances with the epic narrative in *Paradise Lost,* he solicits critics to seek him in other passages not written in the first person. His style is relatively homogeneous, whether it is he or an invented character who speaks; and his characters lend themselves to biographical interpretation because they are relatively few, and are developed in large, bold strokes without that complexity and infinite variety which has exercised, when it has not daunted, the pursuers of the essential Shakespeare.

The parallel between Milton's circumstances after the Restoration and those of the vanquished hero of *Samson Agonistes,* eyeless in Gaza, was too patent to pass unnoticed, even in the eighteenth century.[77] But most romantic critics chose rather to seek Milton in *Paradise Lost,* where extraction of the personal element required a more intricate strategy than the simple equation of author with protagonist, and also promised more startling results. We remember that Shakespeare was often paralleled with God the Creator, and was even endowed with the suitable attributes of omniscience, omnipotence, and beneficence. A common prototype for Milton, however, was precisely God's Great Opposite; but if the resulting portrait of the poet was not God-like, neither was it of one who is 'less than Archangel ruined, and the excess of glory obscured.'

For more than a century after his great epic was published, no one doubted that Milton's whole-souled purpose had been, as he had represented it, 'to justify the ways of God to men,' or that his sympathies were anything but unreservedly on the side of Omnipotence in His suppression of the Satanic rebellion. There was indeed some observation that by choosing a fable in which Satan is a central, active, and temporarily victorious figure, Milton had slipped into the inadvertency of making him, in a sense purely technical, the epic hero. Dryden introduced this impeachment in 1697; John

Dennis, some seven years later, agreed that 'the Devil is properly his Hero, because he gets the better.' And despite the counter-claim of Addison that the hero is the Messiah, and of Blackmore that the hero is Adam, Chesterfield in 1749 continued to maintain 'with Mr. Dryden, that the Devil is in truth the Hero of Milton's poem; his plan, which he lays, pursues, and at last executes, being the subject of the poem.' [78] A political enemy of the Great Rebellion such as Dr. Johnson might charge that Milton's republicanism was founded on his temperamental 'desire of independence,' and that he 'felt not so much the love of liberty as repugnance to authority,' [79] but for a long time, it apparently occurred to no one to correlate this reading of Milton's character with his unintended elevation of Satan to the position of formal protagonist in *Paradise Lost*.

Later on the leading role of Satan was given a different emphasis. In 1787 Robert Burns, smarting under the oppressor's wrong and the insolence of office, light-heartedly gave birth to the attitude of romantic Satanism, soon to reappear, with some change, as Byronism:

I set as little by kings, lords, clergy, critics, etc. as all these respectable Gentry do by my Bardship. . . I am resolved to study the sentiments of a very respectable Personage, Milton's Satan—'Hail horrors! hail, infernal world'!

And a few months later: 'Give me a spirit like my favorite hero, Milton's Satan.' [80] Satan has come to be the hero not for technical reasons but because the reader rather inclines to take his side in the war between heaven and hell.

This process reached its culmination in William Blake. Blake was acquainted with the tradition of the multiple significance of the Bible, and also with the development of various forms of literary cryptology in the theory and practice of the cabalists, Swedenborg, and other votaries of the occult. He himself read habitually not for the surface content but seeking always to uncover veiled allegories of man's spiritual estate. It is not surprising that by the union of this principle with his proto-Freudian psychology, Blake formulated what is, I believe, the earliest instance of that radical mode of romantic polysemism in which the latent personal significance of a narrative poem is found not merely to underlie, but to contradict and cancel the surface intention. In Blake's reading, the defeat of Satan is construed as the lamentable and pestilence-breeding victory of repressive reason over man's passion and desire, that 'Energy' which 'is Eternal Delight.'

Those who restrain desire, do so because theirs is weak enough to be restrained; and the restrainer or reason usurps its place & governs the unwilling. . .

The history of this is written in Paradise Lost, & the Governor or Reason is call'd Messiah.

Most significant is Blake's remarkable postscript. In this, the inversion of the poem's ostensible purpose is attributed to an aspect of Milton's character unknown to the author himself, but revealed by the unconscious fervor and freedom with which he depicted the affairs of Satan.

Note: The reason Milton wrote in fetters when he wrote of Angels & God, and at liberty when of Devils & Hell, is because he was a true Poet and of the Devil's party without knowing it.[81]

This was written about 1793. A quarter of a century later, Shelley gave this view its classic statement in his 'Defence of Poetry'; and whatever we may now think of Shelley's interpretation—or ignorance—of Milton's intellectual convictions, the passage has no peer for the cogency with which it expresses the intractable artistic problem involved in Milton's matching of infinitely unequal protagonists. Shelley took it as a matter of course that in the epics of both Dante and Milton, the narrative surface is but the tangible vesture of the poet's own spirit.

The distorted notions of invisible things which Dante and his rival Milton have idealized, are merely the mask and the mantle in which these great poets walk through eternity enveloped and disguised.

As to how far these poets 'were conscious of the distinction which must have subsisted in their minds between their own creeds and that of the people,' Shelley, unlike Blake, does not commit himself. But of this he is certain, that Paradise Lost, properly deciphered, refutes the theology it purports to advance.

. . . Milton's poem contains within itself a philosophical refutation of that system, of which, by a strange and natural antithesis, it has been a chief popular support. . . Milton's Devil as a moral being is as far superior to his God, as one who perseveres in some purpose which he has conceived to be excellent in spite of adversity and torture, is to one who in the cold security of undoubted triumph inflicts the most horrible revenge upon his enemy, not from any mistaken notion of inducing him to repent of a perseverance in enmity, but with the alleged design of exasperating him to deserve new torments.[82]

Surprisingly, we must class John Keble with this group of critics, for he joined Johnson's opinion that Milton is a rebel by temperament with the belief that Satan is the hero of Paradise Lost, in order to suggest that the first fact was the unconscious cause of the second. Unlike his heretical predecessors in this way of thinking, needless to say, the High Churchman noted the phenomenon only to deplore it.

It is a well-known complaint among many of the readers of Paradise Lost, that they can hardly keep themselves from sympathizing, in some sort, with Satan, as the hero of the poem. The most probable account of which surely is, that the author himself partook largely of the haughty and vindictive republican spirit, which he has assigned to the character, and consequently, though perhaps unconsciously, drew the portrait with a peculiar zest.[83]

When Coleridge reconstructed the character of Milton, his unspoken assumptions were similar, but his findings discrepant. He agreed, it is true, that Milton had written himself into all the characters of the poem, including Satan. In 1833 he wrote:

In the *Paradise Lost*—indeed in every one of his poems—it is Milton himself whom you see; his Satan, his Adam, his Raphael, almost his Eve—are all John Milton; and it is a sense of this intense egotism that gives me the greatest pleasure in reading Milton's works.[84]

But Coleridge had made manifest, in a lecture delivered fifteen years before, that he did not believe Milton's secret sympathies had betrayed the professed purpose of the poem. 'As to Milton's object:—It was to justify the ways of God to man!' The character of Satan, as Milton intended, 'is pride and sensual indulgence, finding in self the sole motive of action.' The intimate revelation of Milton's personal sympathies and wants, Coleridge suggests, is to be found in his heartfelt descriptions of the connubial felicities in the Garden of Eden:

In the description of Paradise itself you have Milton's sunny side as a man. . .
The love of Adam and Eve in Paradise is of the highest merit—not phantomatic, and yet removed from everything degrading. . .
No one can rise from the perusal of this immortal poem without a deep sense of the grandeur and the purity of Milton's soul, or without feeling how susceptible of domestic enjoyments he really was, notwithstanding the discomforts which actually resulted from an apparently unhappy choice in marriage.[85]

Only read this last sentence with Coleridge's own principle, that a subjective author writes himself into his work, in the foreground of the mind, and the thought is irresistible: *de te fabula*. For what author was more subjective than Coleridge; and to whom could the statement that he was 'susceptible of domestic enjoyments' despite an 'unhappy choice in marriage' be more aptly applied? Which leads us to the further discovery that each of these portraits of Milton bears a notable likeness to the portraitist. Coleridge, miserably unhappy with Sara Fricker and in love with Sara Hutchinson, saw Milton in a similar predicament, longing for a wife comely and tractable as Eve. Blake re-created Milton in his own antinomian image. And if it seemed to Shelley that Milton projected his hatred of tyranny in the character of Satan, Shelley's own life was a classic case history of rebellion, according to the psychoanalytic scheme: rebellion primarily against the father, and derivatively against those projected father-imagos, kings and the Deity. It would appear, then, that a biographical interpretation of a work may, on its own principles, be interpreted by the biography of the interpreter; and this opens up the vista of an infinite regress.

On the other hand, the fact that these descriptions of Milton differ does not in itself demonstrate that any one of them is necessarily wrong. A diversity—even a seeming antithesis—of imputed characteristics is resolvable in the concept of the many-sidedness of human nature; and it is at least possible that Milton was both Satan and Adam, too. And that is exactly what a few romantic critics suggested.

As we might expect, Hazlitt was confident that 'it is rarely that a man even of lofty genius will be able to do more than carry on his own feelings and character, or some prominent and ruling passion, into fictitious and uncommon situations.' To this rule Shakespeare is an exception, but not Milton. 'Milton has by allusion embodied a great part of his political and personal history in the chief characters and incidents of Paradise Lost. . . You trace the bias and opinions of the man in the creations of the poet.' [86] Some years earlier, in an analysis of *Paradise Lost,* he had found the character of Satan and the domestic scenes in Eden to be of equivalent importance. 'In a word, the interest of the poem arises from the daring ambition and fierce passions of Satan, and from the account of the paradisaical happiness, and the loss of it by our first parents.' Satan is the indubitable hero —in fact, 'the most heroic subject that ever was chosen for a poem.' But Hazlitt offered a theory, more subtle than most, that Satan expresses a dual attitude in his creator, of religious acquiescence and impatience of authority:

Some persons may think that he has carried his liberality too far, and injured the cause he professed to espouse by making [Satan] the chief person in his poem. Considering the nature of his subject, he would be equally in danger of running into this fault, from his faith in religion, and his love of rebellion; and perhaps each of these motives had its full share in determining the choice of his subject.

At the same time, Hazlitt rhapsodized even more than Coleridge over the happiness of Adam and Eve. (We recall that Hazlitt was both a political radical and an unhappily married man.)

It is true, there is little action in this part of Milton's poem; but there is much repose, and more enjoyment. . .

What need was there of action, where the heart was full of bliss and innocence without it! They had nothing to do but feel their own happiness, and 'know to know no more.' [87]

To cite one other instance: John Sterling, disciple of Coleridge and Carlyle, was in this respect a trinitarian. He formulated a concept of Milton as a union of Satan, Adam, and Jehovah as well.

That Milton's grandest, as well as his most trivial writings are undisguised fragments and glimpses of Milton's individual self, all will admit. . . His moral reason, exalted into the region of pure intelligence, and invested with crystalline glory, constitutes, not suggests, the highest beings of his Heaven. His austere, concentrated, often baffled human affections are the originals of his earthly personages. And his passionate and gloomy self-will, like his shadow thrown by a flash of lightning upon the snow-wall of an Alpine ridge, supplies the shapes and the demoniac stature of his nether spirits.[88]

The position, then, that Milton reveals his predilections in Pandemonium as well as Paradise is not untenable, for there is no characterological reason why a flaming rebel, proud as Lucifer, could not have been the vicarious lover of a submissive Eve. The question is, were these empirically possible traits the actual attributes of Milton, as he lived?

Recent opponents of the Satanic interpretations of Milton stress the fact that it was not until public belief in the firm theological understructure of *Paradise Lost* had weakened that the role of Satan in the cosmic epic began to seem an equivocal one. Furthermore, there is almost invariably a circularity in this interpretative procedure: a selection from external testimony about the writer is used as a guide to his poetic self-revelation, and this data is invoked to validate the portrait after it has already entered into its composition.

But whatever the logical and empirical difficulties involved, pursuit of Milton in *Paradise Lost* was continued with unflagging energy by post-romantic critics, and later was given added impetus by the popularization of Freudian concepts. E. M. W. Tillyard's equation of Satan with Milton, or at least with one aspect of Milton, has made its way into textbook histories of literature; while others of our critics, like some of their romantic prototypes, attribute to Milton the dual role of Satan and Adam. This latter is essentially the view emerging from the lengthy inquiry of Denis Saurat in *Milton, Man and Thinker,* and it is neatly summarized by Middleton Murry:

There is, of course, a wealth of unconscious poetic richness in Milton: of which the most astonishing manifestation is the passionate unconscious sympathy with the rebellious energy of Satan, and the most attractive the lovely pictures of the sensuous innocence of our first parents in Paradise.[89]

Furthermore, just as the early division over the question whether Shakespeare was subjective or objective survives in our day, so modern commentators on Milton—even those who oppose romantic interpretations of the man—are no less unanimous than the romantics that Milton reveals himself in his poems. Douglas Bush, for example, has written a trenchant critique of the unprincipled use of biography in Miltonic criticism, turning 'biographical conjecture into biographical fact,' then making 'this conjecture the basis of much of [the] analysis of the later poems, *Paradise Lost* in particular.' Yet he urges a mode of reading which is itself a lineal descendant of romantic polysemism, translating objective reference into spiritual revelation.

It is . . . essential to our full appreciation of the major poems that we should realize . . . what these late works represent in their author's spiritual evolution: that the militant and confident revolutionist has lost his faith in mass movements . . . that he has learned upon his pulses that 'In His will is our peace.' But all the essential knowledge we get from the works themselves, with help from Milton's other writings, not from biography.[90]

To most modern critics, as to Shelley, Milton's great poem (whatever more it may be) is 'the mask and mantle' in which the poet walks through eternity; they differ only about the nature of the man behind the mask.

vi. The Key to Homer's Heart

There remain to be chronicled the adventures of the boldest, most pertinacious, and most methodical of the romantic explorers of personality. Everyone admitted Milton was subjective; some maintained that even Shakespeare was subjective; but the Reverend John Keble pursued personality into what by universal consent was impregnably objective, the poetry of Greek and Roman antiquity, and above all, the epic poetry of Homer. Keble was not in the least deterred by the fact that the *Iliad* had been the very rock on which German critics built their theories of the objective and the naïve, or by the knowledge that a number of contemporary investigators affirmed that Homer was not a person at all, but a composite myth—'a mere concrete name,' as Coleridge said, 'for the rhapsodies of the Iliad.' [91]

It will be recalled that Keble's central tenet is that true poetry satisfies conflicting motives—the pressure of personal passions and desires to seek imaginative satisfaction, and the force of modesty, which shrinks from revelation of the private self—by its capacity 'to give utterance sparingly, and only under veils and disguises, to the deepest feelings.' [92] All such poetry, therefore, has a double significance, whether this be the professed duality of 'allegorical symbolism' or the implicit duality (combining external reference and self-expression) of the ostensibly non-allegorical poem:

Whether, therefore, throughout the whole course of a poem one story is really told in fact and substance, another outwardly in words—which is the characteristic of Allegory: or whether we make the true tenor of a poem to depend not so much upon the things described as upon the spirit and temper of the poet, in either case it is clear that the force and beauty of true poetry is two-fold. For not only are the direct themes of the poem themselves expressed with lucidity and beauty, but the whole work is tinctured with the character and leanings of the poet as by some mysterious aroma. [93]

It is clear that Keble (apparently independently of Friedrich Schlegel) achieved the notion that a work of literature unites subjective and objective reference by carrying theological concepts over into literary criticism. He was, of course, deeply read in the writings of the Church Fathers, and while his Oxford lectures on poetry were still in progress, he wrote *Tract* 89 to support these writers in the view that, just as the Scriptures have manifold senses, so the sensible objects of the natural world are also *verba visibilia*—

> Characters of the great Apocalypse,
> The types and symbols of Eternity,
> Of first, and last, and midst, and without end,

as Wordsworth expressed his secularized version of the ancient typology. [94] The two forms of multiple significance are closely related, for 'consider,' Keble tells us, 'what this really comes to. The Author of Scripture is the Author of Nature.' To support this thesis, Keble quotes the basic text from Paul's Epistle to the Romans, 'The invisible things of Him from the creation of the world are clearly seen, being understood by the things that are made.' He quotes also this revealing comment from St. Irenaeus (a theologian of the second century whose complete works Keble translated into English) to illustrate 'the analogy between God's visible dealings with us, and His invisible dispensations':

The Word was made the dispenser of the Father's grace for the profit of men, on account of which he made so many arrangements . . . on the one hand maintaining the invisibility of the Father, lest at any time man should become a contemner of God . . . on the other hand, manifesting God to the sight of men by many arrangements, lest man, falling altogether away from God, should cease to be.[95]

In the same tract, Keble clinches the case for us by explicitly drawing the parallel between Creator and poet, cosmos and poem:

If we suppose Poetry in general to mean the expression of an overflowing mind, relieving itself, more or less indirectly and reservedly, of the thoughts and passions which most oppress it . . . may it not be affirmed that [God] condescends in like manner to have a Poetry of His own, a set of holy and divine associations and meanings, wherewith it is His will to invest all material things? [96]

To Keble, it is evident, God in creating the world was not only a poet; he was a Wordsworthian poet, whose creation was the spontaneous, though disguised overflow of powerful feeling.

If the process of composition is thus conceived to be a kind of encoding, the task of criticism becomes one of decoding; and Keble shamelessly undertakes to lift the veils with which the ancient poets—Greek and Roman, epic, tragic, and lyric—had modestly screened their intimate selves. Of all these poets, Homer is chosen for the most searching analysis. 'There is no writer known to us,' Keble declares confidently, 'who more simply and openly exhibits, in almost every part of his poem, his real character and feeling.' [97]

Carlyle is his only match in England for scorn of what Keble called mere outward 'ornament and prettiness' (that is, poetry-as-such), and for the dogged reading of poetry for personality. Keble's biographical procedure, however, is as orderly and detailed as Carlyle's is impressionistic and panoramic. In the course of reconstructing the temperament of Homer, for example, Keble takes pains to catalogue what he calls 'tests of an author's bias and disposition'—in other words, principles for reasoning from literary effects to psychological causes, in purpose not unlike the famous Canons of Induction that his contemporary, John Mill, proposed for the discovery of causal relations in general. Robert Burrowes, we remember, had earlier specified some guides to investigators of the ways that style reflects the man, but it is highly improbable that Keble had read *The Transactions of the Royal Irish Academy*. Since Keble's principles continue to be the assumptions of biographical critics in our own day, and since they have never been given a more explicit or exhaustive inventory, it will be worth while to summarize Keble's exposition, and also to supplement it by giving each principle the convenience of a name.

(1) The Canon of the Significant Theme. The first clue to an author's disposition is to be found by a 'careful analysis of the plan of the work, both as a whole and in detail. . .' From 'the subject of the Iliad,' and 'the course of the poem itself,' for example, Keble infers that Homer 'had the same outlook on life as the old heroes,' but that, living in a later age, he 'betook himself to composition in order to appease in some measure his restless, burning passion for bygone days and departed heroes.'[98] Keble's underlying assumption here, as in all his investigations, is that each personality has a single key, 'one prevailing character or element, the centre of attraction,' which constitutes its 'ruling taste or passion.'[99] The ancestors of this concept, obviously, were the ancient theory of humors and its historical successor, the idea of 'a ruling passion.' It was to live on, among later connoisseurs of literary temperament, as Sainte Beuve's 'faculté première,' Arnold's 'essential character,' and Pater's 'personal formula.'

(2) The Canon of Identification with the Hero. Keble also holds that 'nothing appears of greater value and importance when endeavouring to estimate the poet's genius and qualities as a whole, than a thorough acquaintance with the character to whom he designedly accords the leading part.' Of the author of the *Iliad* 'you might safely say he would have wished, had he not been Homer, to be Achilles.'[100] Sometimes the sentiments of the hero duplicate those of his creator, as the result of a process Keble calls 'the transference of the poet's own passion and disposition to actual characters.' Indeed, Keble goes so far as to reverse the standard evaluation of the lyric as the most subjective and the epic as the most objective poetic form. 'Our judgement of the real disposition and attitude of lyric writers is generally less easy to form' because the poet's 'most intimate feelings' shrink from expression in the glaring publicity of a lyric utterance in the first person. Dramatic and epic poets, on the other hand, can avail themselves of the 'expedient of shifted responsibility.'

Opinions are expressed, judgements passed, praise and blame are meted out, not however as the utterances of Homer or Aeschylus, but as those of an Achilles or a Prometheus. . . When a man speaks his own thoughts through another's lips modesty is observed, while the agitated, full heart is relieved.[101]

(3) The Canon of Fervor. Passing on 'to other tests whereby the leanings and preferences of great poets are wont to declare themselves,' Keble cites as

one significant index to a poet 'the subjects upon which he enthusiastically delights to discourse.' Passages that stand out from their context by their *energeia,* fervor, and by the freedom and richness of their versification, according to this application of Longinus' doctrines, are particularly apt to be rooted in personal feeling. 'When the poet approaches subjects which stand highest in his regard and are dear to his soul, the poem, precisely then, flows in freer vein. . . Verses [with] glowing words or large and deep meaning testify that then, at all events, the author is adopting no conventional form, but writing from the inmost sincerity of his heart.' [102]

(4) The Canon of Imagery. 'Homer's mind and disposition,' Keble says, 'can be inferred not only from his story, but from his imagery and the comparisons which he draws from every quarter, and from the choice which he makes of poetic ornament and beauty, to illustrate both the language and the subjects of which he treats.' [103] This principle of 'l'image est l'homme même' is, of course, one which Caroline Spurgeon made so immensely popular not long ago in her quest for the 'personality, temperament, and quality of mind' of Shakespeare. The underlying assumption is that the vehicles of the metaphors and similes uttered by dramatic characters are relatively independent of external dramatic requirements and relatively uncensored by modesty, hence peculiarly conditioned by the personal bias of the author himself.[104] The way Keble applies this device is sufficiently illustrated by the following passage:

There remains what is, perhaps the most fruitful field of all: the many kinds of birds and beasts, tame and wild; whose sports, food, fierce contests, and whole manner and habit of living afford a rich source of splendid imagery. . . Whatever examples Homer takes of this sort, they all seem to be proper to *hunters* or *shepherds*. And so they are exactly what might be looked for in such a man, as we, moved by many independent reasons, infer that he must have been.[105]

(5) The Canon of Style. What had earlier been regarded as the sole element of a work which mirrors the poet rather than the world, Keble relegates to the position of last and least of the indices to personality. 'But I press on to the subject reserved for the last—the style of language, namely, affected by the author of the *Iliad*. For no less on this account than from his mode of thought and choice of comparisons, I apprehend that he stands out, first as a warrior, next as a countryman, finally as of humble birth and poor in station.' [106]

How extraordinarily up-to-date Keble's technique was becomes apparent if we compare it with Donald A. Stauffer's recent exposition of his devices for construing Shakespeare's moral ideas from his dramas; or, in the field of psychology, with Henry A. Murray's report on the most meticulous and elaborately controlled attempt yet made to establish an experimental basis for what he calls 'the subtle matter of deducing the personality of an author from his writings.' Many of Murray's 'variables of psychological significance' correspond to Keble's canons; for example, 'the motives and actions of the major characters,' 'repetitions of mood, sentiment, action, theme, plot,' and 'emotions or actions of unusual intensity.' [107] In fact, Keble was hardly less scientific in his method than the modern psychologist. He was thoroughly aware, he said, that the reconstruction of literary personality is 'sure to be tinged more or less with the peculiar views of the person carrying it on.' He therefore hailed the appearance of Lockhart's *Life of Walter Scott* as a kind of *experimentum crucis* for validating by independent external evidence the character of the writer previously inferred from his works:

How much to our purpose, either in the way of confirmation or correction, must be the appearance of such a life as this. . . The biography may serve as an actual experiment, to verify or disprove the conclusions, which the theory as applied to the poems would give.[108]

Adapted as they now are to the pungent sauces of post-Freudian criticism, our palates find bland enough Keble's discovery that Homer, like Miniver Cheevy, was born too late and dominated by a nostalgia for 'what was not'; that his occupations were manual and rural; that he was courageous, yet kindly, and a lover of nature, birds, and animals; that he revered the gods; and that although a poor man himself, he was in politics a conservative and a supporter of the aristocracy.[109] And for all his scientism Keble, like his contemporaries, ends up with a poet made patently after his own image, or at least after his own ideals. The Homer who emerges from Keble's pages is a Tory, a backward-looking romantic, and a sentimental, all-but-Christian gentleman. He turns out, in fact, to bear an almost comical likeness to Keble's earlier portrait of Sir Walter Scott. It is only just, however, to apply to Keble the historical estimate, and to acknowledge him as the founding father of what is now one of the most prominent and intensively cultivated systems of critical premises and procedures.

In later discussions of literature as disguised or (to use a term found in Keble) 'unconscious' autobiography, the original oxymoron of the visibly-invisible God not infrequently manifests its continued presence, although with variable emphasis, according to the individual critic, on the relative visibility or invisibility of the poet in his poem. The figure was a great favorite with Flaubert, who clearly connected it to the root-analogue between the poet and God the Creator:

The author in his work ought to be like God in the universe, present everywhere, and visible nowhere. Since art is a second nature, the creator of this nature ought to act in analogous ways, so that one may feel in all its atoms, and in every aspect, a hidden, infinite impassibleness.[110]

In a well-known lecture, George Lyman Kittredge revived the image of Shakespeare as an immanent deity, but like Schiller, in such a rendering as to enjoin further speculation. Shakespeare is subjective, yet inscrutable. 'For his creatures are like those of God.' 'Unquestionably the man is there, the real Shakespeare is somehow latent in his plays: but how is one to extract him?' He 'pervades and vivifies the whole but eludes analysis and defies extraction. . .'[111] But D. S. Savage, in a recent book called *The Personal Principle,* employs the same parallel to prove precisely the opposite point. The following analogy, Savage declares, 'seems to me a permissible one.'

God remains invisible and we perceive His creation, which is His creation and not His expression or embodiment. And in the same way when we read a poem we enter the poet's projected and stylized world of experiences and perceptions; his creation, and not his expression or embodiment. But we are surely entitled to see the imprint of the poet's personality . . . within his work, stamping it with his unique image, no less than we see the image of God imprinted upon the divine creation.[112]

I said earlier that the mind moves from the better known to the less known, assimilating new materials through metaphor and analogy. We may conclude with an interesting example of how an idea which was once taken as a base-term may in the course of time become a mystery and itself require analogical clarification. In his book on *God and the Astronomers,* Dean W. R. Inge, considering the question of God and the cosmos, said: 'I sometimes think that the analogy of a poet and his work—say Shakespeare and his plays—is the most helpful in forming an idea of the relation of God to the world. . . It is the expression of His mind. . . Whatever we can learn about nature teaches us something about God.'[113] By an irony of intellectual history, it is God's relation to His work which must now be explained, and Dean Inge appeals to the concept of the creative poet in order to illuminate the very analogue from which it had once been engendered.

X

The Criterion of Truth to Nature:
ROMANCE, MYTH, AND METAPHOR

The natural appetite or taste of the human mind is for TRUTH; whether that truth results . . . from the agreement of the representation of any object with the thing represented; or from the correspondence of the several parts of any arrangement with each other. . .

A picture that is unlike, is false. Disproportionate ordonnance of parts is not right; because it cannot be true, until it ceases to be a contradiction to assert, that the parts have no relation to the whole.

JOSHUA REYNOLDS, *The Seventh Discourse*

IF POETRY IS CONCEIVED to be an imitation or representation of nature, we may expect as the cardinal requirement that poetry be 'true,' that it accord in some sense to the nature it reflects. In neo-classic criticism the word 'truth,' or an equivalent, is indeed the aesthetic standard of standards; truth (as Boileau said in a passage which became proverbial) is beauty.

> Rien n'est beau que le vrai: le vrai seul est aimable;
> Il doit régner partout, et même dans la fable:
> De toute fiction l'adroite fausseté
> Ne tend qu'à faire aux yeux briller la vérité.[1]

Even taste, it could be maintained, no less than reason, is an organ for perceiving truth. John Dennis wrote:

That which we call Taste in Writing, is nothing but a fine Discernment of Truth. But as Truth must be always one, and always the same to all who have Eyes to discern it; he who pleases one of a true Taste at first, is sure of pleasing all the World at last.[2]

Truth may indeed be 'always one, and always the same,' but the aesthetic senses in which the term was used are legion. Sometimes the criterion involved the double demand that a work exhibit an inner decorum or mutual correspondence of its parts, as well as a correspondence to its model in external nature. In its turn, the demand that a work correspond to nature was no less variable in its significance than the word 'nature' itself. In spite of this variety, however, we can discern a strong tendency to consider that even the ideal nature reflected in a poem must be consonant with the content and laws of the experienced world. A poem might be said to imitate primarily 'la belle nature,' or quasi-Platonic Ideas, or vaguely Aristotelian universals, or generic types. But for the critics in the philosophical tradition of empiricism (and that is, for the great majority of eighteenth-century English critics), all these ideals were held to be derived, in some fashion, from the world of sense-experience, and still responsible, if indirectly, to the known constitution and order of nature.[3] As George Campbell expressed the point in his *Philosophy of Rhetoric* (1776):

Nay, even in those performances where truth, in regard to the individual facts related, is neither sought nor expected, as in some sorts of poetry and in romance, truth still is an object to the mind, the general truths regarding character, manners, and incidents. When these are preserved, the piece may justly be denominated true, considered as a picture of life, though false, considered as a narrative of particular events. And even these untrue events must be counterfeits of truth, and bear its image. . .[4]

The pressure of the principle of imitation, as this was usually interpreted by post-Restoration critics, was therefore toward conformity to the world known by the enlightened man. As a result, many critics were faced with the problem of reconciling such traditional poetic elements as classic myth, romantic magic and fairy-lore, even figurative deviations from literal fidelity of statement, with the cardinal criterion of truth to nature. The eighteenth-century attempts to explain and justify these materials are interesting in themselves, and in some instances engendered a new and non-mimetic conception of poetry that was destined to have surprising consequences in the critical theory of our present century. In addition, to consider the differences between the management of this problem by certain eighteenth-century critics and by such later theorists as Wordsworth and Coleridge is to achieve a fresh insight into some fundamental distinctions between representative neo-classic and romantic approaches to poetry.

i. Truth and the Poetic Marvelous

Many an enlightened reader after the middle of the seventeenth century was confident that man's knowledge of the constitution and order of nature had been drastically corrected within the very recent past. If the new philosophy called all in doubt, it soon emerged with new and unshakable certainties. For some thousands of years, Abraham Cowley sang in his ode 'To the Royal Society,' 'Philosophy . . . has still been kept in Nonage,' until 'Bacon at last, a mighty Man, arose' and 'like Moses, led us forth' to a glimpse of

> These spacious countries but discover'd yet;
> Countries where yet in stead of Nature, we
> Her Images and Idols worship'd see. . .

We must not mistake what, for contemporary poets, was the most significant character of this nature newly revealed. It was not, as one is apt to think after the brilliant exposition by Alfred North Whitehead, the abstract system of physical hypothesis—the mechanical order of particles in motion, endowed only with primary sense-qualities, which had been postulated by Descartes and Newton. Neither critic nor poet succumbed to the fallacy of misplaced concreteness, and held that nature is 'a dull affair, soundless, scentless, colourless; merely the hurrying of material, endlessly, meaninglessly'; nor did he believe that 'the poets are entirely mistaken. They should address their lyrics to themselves, and should turn them into odes of self-gratulation on the excellency of the human mind.' [5] When a poet entertained 'that great modern discovery,' as Addison called it, 'that lights and colours . . . are only ideas in the mind, and not qualities that have any existence in matter,' he was usually inspired, like Addison, to praise not his own excellence, but the foresight and bounty of Providence which motivated Him 'to add supernumerary ornaments to the universe, and make it more agreeable to the imagination.' [6]

The new nature which had a quick and direct impact on criticism and the practice of poets was not the universe of high-level scientific abstraction, but something on the concrete level of common sense. From this point of view, empiricism altered the face of nature primarily by annihilating the figments of classical and post-Christian superstition and delusion. In his *Leviathan,* Hobbes went out of his way to point out that only from an ignorance 'of how to distinguish Dreams, and other strong Fancies, from Vision and Sense,' did there rise the pagan worship of 'Satyres, Fawnes, Nymphs and the like,' as well as the present opinion 'that rude people have

of Fayries, Ghosts, and Goblins; and of the power of witches.'[7] Or as Thomas
Sprat described the new world of science in the *History of the Royal Society*,
to which Cowley's Ode had been a prefix: 'Poets of old devis'd a thousand
false Chimaeras. . .'

> But, from the time in which the *Real Philosophy* has appear'd, there is scarce
> any whisper remaining of such *horrors*. . . The course of things goes quietly
> along, in its own true channel of *Natural Causes* and *Effects*. For this we are
> beholden to *Experiments;* which though they have not yet compleated the Dis-
> covery of the true world, yet they have already vanquish'd those wild inhabitants
> of the false world, that us'd to astonish the minds of Men.[8]

Thus was it brought sharply to public attention that the 'true World' of the
present was entirely disparate from the 'false worlds' which had been imitated by the poets of the great past. Joseph Glanvill and others attempted
to save the credit of witchcraft, as an element essential to religious faith in
a non-material realm, but most informed men of the time left no place in the
world either for the gods of Homer, or for what Sir William Temple con-
temptuously called 'the visionary Tribe of *Faries, Elves,* and *Goblins,* of
Sprites and of *Bul-beggars'*[9] of the more recent Christian romancers.

It was this 'true World' that poets were frequently enjoined to reflect in
their poetry. To be sure, Christian hostility to pagan myth had long before
invaded the province of poetry; in addition, the new philosophers were not
the first to disbelieve in magic and witchcraft, and had been anticipated by
various Puritan writers in their antagonism to the materials of the romances.[10]
But a distinctive element in criticism after the mid-seventeenth century was
the systematic campaign to eliminate the discrepancy between poetry and
reality, conducted mainly by men who were themselves poets, and also
either in, or on the fringe of, the movement of empirical philosophy. A crucial
event in this development was the publication of Davenant's unfinished epic,
Gondibert (1651), which came furnished with a preface by Davenant, an
answer by Hobbes, and prefatory poems by Waller and Cowley. These
jointly, as Mark Van Doren says, 'prescribed the materials for the new
poetry' and compose 'almost a text-book of the new aesthetics.'[11] Davenant,
declaring that the business of poets is to 'represent the Worlds true image,'
censured the practice of Tasso in his epic

> because his errors, which are deriv'd from the Ancients, when examin'd, grow in
> a great degree excusable in them, and by being his, admit no pardon. Such are
> his Councell assembled in Heaven, his Witches Expeditions through the Air, and
> enchanted Woods inhabited with Ghosts.[12]

Both Waller and Cowley commended Davenant for renouncing in his own epic the fairy land of gods, monsters, and fairies. Hobbes's *Answer to Davenant,* corroborating both his opinions and his practice, has the cadence and finality of a critical manifesto. The structure of a poem, he says, ought to be 'such as an imitation of humane life requireth.' 'Poets are Painters. . .'

There are some that are not pleased with fiction, unless it be bold, not onely to exceed the *work,* but also the *possibility* of nature: they would have impenetrable Armors, Inchanted Castles, invulnerable bodies, Iron Men, flying Horses. . . [But] as truth is the bound of Historical, so the Resemblance of truth is the utmost limit of Poeticall Liberty. . . Beyond the actual works of nature a Poet may now go; but beyond the conceived possibility of nature, never.[13]

It was Aristotle, of course, who had made the discussion of possibility and probability a standard element in poetic theory. But to Aristotle, poetic probability had been an effect less of conformity to the external order of things than of the relations of the parts within the work itself; probability, thus conceived, can assimilate even the empirically impossible, so that 'a likely impossibility is always preferable to an unconvincing possibility.' To Hobbes, truth and likelihood in poetry have become simply a matter of correspondence to the known order of nature. Poetry must imitate the external world as it is; must represent—not single events in past time, or poetry would be history, and the right of poetry to fiction is not here in question, but—the *kinds* of objects that we know to exist, and the *kinds* of events that we know to be possible, on the basis of an empirical knowledge of nature and nature's laws.

A number of critics in the following century echoed or paralleled Hobbes's interpretation of the principle of imitation. The specifically Christian supernatural, which had the double advantage of being both marvelous and true, was of course often excepted for poetry; although some critics also discountenanced such materials on the ground that they are insusceptible of properly poetic treatment. Some critics justified pagan marvels as essential to the epic poem for the effects of 'astonishment' and 'admiration' which were its indispensable characteristics, but condemned their use in the other poetic forms. Thus Addison lauded the machinery of Homer and Virgil, but derided the occurrence of mythical beings in the minor genres of modern poets, in which 'nothing can be more ridiculous than to have recourse to our Jupiters and Junos.'[14] Other writers refused to allow any exception whatever from the criterion of truth to the actual world. 'For Poetry being an Imitation of Nature,' wrote Sir Richard Blackmore, author of that unreadable epic, *Prince Arthur,* 'that can never be a regular Performance, which represents Things that never did or can exist.' His own interpretation makes probability a matter of statistical frequency and quotidian realism, where 'nothing is admitted that does not frequently fall under Observation, and is the common Result of Physical and Moral Causes.' [15]

Some of the most potent voices of the time were raised against the deviation of poetry from its model in empirical nature. 'To draw chimeras,' said Hume, 'is not, properly speaking, to copy or imitate. The justness of the representation is lost, and the mind is displeased to find a picture, which bears no resemblance to any original.' [16] Lord Kames developed an elaborate psychological construction in order to demonstrate that even in an epic poem, 'no improbable incident ought to be admitted: that is, no incident contrary to the order and course of nature'; and he employed this argument to decry not only the romantic 'imaginary beings' of Tasso, but even Homer's deities, which 'do no honour to his poems.' [17] It was Dr. Johnson, of course, who waged the most strenuous war against false gods in poetry. 'Of the ancient poets,' he says, 'every reader feels the mythology tedious and oppressive.' In modern poetry, he allows 'a transient allusion, or slight illustration,' and admits that although in *Paradise Lost* such allusions are not 'always used with notice of their vanity . . . they contribute variety to the narration, and produce an alternate exercise of the memory and the fancy'; [18] but he does not spare either Milton's *Lycidas,* or Pope's *St. Cecilia's Day,* or the odes of Gray for the degree to which they violate truth by the 'puerilities of obsolete mythology.' [19]

ii. The Logic of Deviation from Empirical Truth

But the critics who, in the name of truth, proposed to banish from poetry all gods, spirits, and impossibilities were contending against one of the weightiest of poetic traditions. On the example of the *Iliad* and *Aeneid,* confirmed by Aristotle's dictum that the marvelous is required in the epic, many critics held, with Pope, that Homer's gods 'continue to this day the Gods of Poetry'; some even claimed mythological machinery to be the essence, the very 'soul,' of an epic poem. [20] Even more effective, in the long run, was the growing passion for what Joseph Warton fervently called 'the romantic, the wonderful, the wild'—that is, the materials of witchcraft and enchantment which were coming to be extravagantly admired in such Renaissance poets as Tasso, Spenser, and Shakespeare. For the adherents of *le merveilleux,* whether pagan or romantic, the problem was: how to justify for poetry, which is an imitation of nature, the representation of materials and happenings which do not exist in nature? Typically, the procedure was to retain the criterion of truth or empirical probability, but so to adjust it as to permit the poet, in the memorable phrase of Father Bouhours, to lie ingeniously. The fabulous world, as the Jesuit said, is patently false, but 'il est permis, il est même glorieux à un Poete de mentir d'une manière si ingenieuse.' [21]

The reasoning which validated deviation from the order of nature depended upon the almost universal neo-classic principle that poetry is, indeed, an imitation of nature, but only as a means to the ultimate purpose of moving and pleasing the reader. 'For I presume, it was long ago evident,' wrote James Beattie, 'that the end of Poetry is to please';

—that if, according to real nature, it would give no greater pleasure than history, which is a transcript of real nature;—that greater pleasure is, however, to be expected from it, because we grant it superior indulgence, in regard to fiction, and the choice of words. . .[22]

In conformity with this basic pattern, poetic prodigies, antique or modern, could be defended in various areas of discussion. For example, with reference to the elements composing a poem, the duality of means (imitation) and end (pleasure) was often reflected in the distinction between substance and ornament; truth constitutes the basic subject matter, but myth and other literal impossibilities are necessary to embellish truth and rescue it from languor. Boileau said, concerning the fabulous elements in the epic poem:

> Ainsi, dans cet amas de nobles fictions,
> Le poëte s'égaye en mille inventions,
> Orne, élève, embellit, aggrandit toutes choses. . .
> Sans tous ces ornemens le vers tombe en langueur. . .[23]

Alternatively, when the question concerned the general norms of literary excellence, the discussion was often conducted in terms of a mediation between extremes. 'Indeed,' as Hugh Blair summed up this concept, 'I know nothing more difficult in epic poetry, than to adjust properly the mixture of the marvellous with the probable; so as to gratify and amuse us with the one, without sacrificing the other.' [24]

But progressively criticism, following the logic of the definition of poetry as an instrument for achieving effects, transferred the locus of discussion from external nature to human nature—that of the poet's audience—and interpreted truth or probability as conformity to the expectations or responsiveness of the reader. The French terms indicate this shift. The basic requirement is not *le vrai,* but *le vraisemblable,* not verity but verisimilarity; and 'le vraisemblable,' according to Rapin, 'est tout ce qui est conforme à l'opinion du public.' [25] In the course of eighteenth-century theory, therefore, the discussion of the poetic marvelous involved an ever more elaborate analysis of the psychology of poetic illusion, or the 'waking dream,' as Kames called it. In this region of inquiry, the difference between opponents and proponents of the marvelous in poetry became mainly a difference in opinion about the kind and degree of empirical impossibility that the normal reader will find credible. At one extreme are the critics who agreed with Hume that 'the mind is displeased to find a picture, which bears no resemblance to any original.' At the other, we find Thomas Twining, who agreed wholeheartedly with what he thought to be the opinion of Aristotle, that the end of poetry is pleasure, and that therefore we must justify in poetry 'not only impossibilities, but even absurdities, where that end appears to be better answered with them, than it would have been without them.' 'If it is our interest to be cheated, it is her duty to cheat us.' [26]

Even extremists like Twining, however, agreed that the normal reader requires special qualities in poetic fictions, before he can be enticed, by the promise of pleasure, into forsaking a dowerless truth. Chief among these qualities are:

(1) Conformity of the fiction to popular belief. The rationalists among modern critics, according to Twining, have not always seen 'the power of popular *opinion* and *belief* upon poetical credibility. . .' [27] A few decades after the appearance of *Gondibert* and its prefatory pieces, Dryden had explicitly refuted the doctrines of Davenant, Cowley, and Hobbes, by pleading as a sufficient basis for poetic fictions the existence of widespread belief concerning matters 'depending not on sense':

And if any man object the improbabilities of a spirit appearing, or of a palace raised by magic; I boldly answer him, that an heroic poet is not tied to a bare representation of what is true, or exceeding probable. . . 'Tis enough that, in all ages and religions, the greatest part of mankind have believed the power of magic, and that there are spirits and spectres which have appeared. This, I say, is foundation enough for poetry. . .[28]

There is the suggestion in Dryden of the uniformitarian argument that universality and permanence of opinion is one valid evidence of possibility in matters of fact. Such wide consent, Dryden says, is enough to prove concerning specters and magic 'that for aught we know, they may be in nature.' [29] Later writers, however, who entirely agreed with the philosophers that ghosts and enchantments are merely a widespread illusion, appealed to the force of this popular belief as an auxiliary to the pleasure-principle in breaking down the resistance to fictions in the skeptical reader. Witches, charms, and fairies, Addison held, were largely a product of the pious frauds practiced by moralists 'before the world was enlightened by learning and philosophy.' Yet these things still have probability enough for poetry, because 'at least we have all heard so many pleasing relations in favour of them, that we do not care for seeing through the falsehood, and willingly give ourselves up to so agreeable an imposture.' [30]

(2) Self-consistency. Verisimilitude was often held to depend in large part on the skill of an artist in making a supernatural character (in Beattie's phrase) 'consistent with itself, and connected with probable circumstances.' [31] Richard Payne Knight was of the opinion that *poetical probability* does not arise so much from the resemblance of the fictions to real events, as from the consistence of the language with the sentiments, of the sentiments and actions with the characters, and of the different parts of the fable with each other.' [32] Thomas Twining proposed in the case of imaginary persons and false events, poetic 'probability, nature, or truth' depends upon an unconscious inferential process, in which the reader is induced tacitly to accept certain postulates contrary to fact, from which all the rest follows by natural consequence.[33]

In spite of these attempts by the amateurs of the supernatural to justify its use by a system of grant and limited license, the poetry of myth and magic was not the forte of eighteenth-century writers. Although he maintained that 'they, who deceive, are honester than they who do not deceive,' even such an admirer of poetic prodigies as Richard Hurd 'would advise no modern poet to revive these faery tales' in his own age of unbelief.[34] The fictions of romance were for the most part driven out of serious poetry to lead a disheartened half-life in the Gothic novel. The best achievements in this form, the tales of Anne Radcliffe, provide a counterpart in practice to the attempts to reconcile fiction and truth, with their inevitable denouements to render assurance that the seeming wonders were in perfect accord with the laws of science after all. And in the classic age, the classic gods were, with a few fine exceptions in Collins and Gray, subdued to a subsistence hardly less bloodless than that of 'Inoculation, Heavenly Maid,' and the other personifications mainly engendered by a capital letter.[35] Except, that is, in the licensed genre of burlesque; the liveliest machinery in the period is to be found in Pope's mock-epic *Rape of the Lock*.[36]

iii. The Poem as Heterocosm

We also find in eighteenth-century criticism the beginnings of a more radical solution to the problem of poetic fictions, one which would sever supernatural poetry entirely from the principle of imitation, and from any responsibility to the empirical world. The key event in this development was the replacement of the metaphor of the poem as imitation, a 'mirror of nature,' by that of the poem as heterocosm, 'a second nature,' created by the poet in an act analogous to God's creation of the world. In the preceding chapter, we discovered that this parallel between God and the poet, and between God's relation to his world and the poet to his poem, fostered the earliest appearance of the doctrine, so widespread today, that a poem is a disguised self-revelation, in which its creator, 'visibly invisible,' at the same time expresses and conceals himself. It turns out that the same parallel helped generate a conception of a work of art which seems equally modern, is hardly less widely current, and (having largely lost the marks of its origin) is often presented in explicit opposition to the cognate thesis that a poem is the expression of personality. This is the concept, at the heart of much of the 'new criticism,' that poetic statement and poetic truth are utterly diverse from scientific statement and scientific truth, in that a poem is an object-in-itself, a self-contained universe of discourse, of which we cannot demand that it be true to nature, but only, that it be true to itself.

The word 'create,' applied to literary invention, has become a colorless, almost a dead metaphor; and as Logan Pearsall Smith has commented, the latest hat is even more likely than the latest poem to be heralded as 'a new creation.' Yet this stock term is the residue of a metaphor which only four centuries ago was new, vital, and—because it equated the poet with God in his unique and most characteristic function—on the verge, perhaps, of blasphemy. That there is some connection between artist and divinity is, of course, as old as the belief that poetry is sponsored and inspired by the gods; and in classic times, the divine origin of the world was sometimes illustrated by reference to the activity of a sculptor or other human artisan. But the explicit reference of the poet's invention to God's activity in creating the universe appears to have been a product of Florentine writers in the later fifteenth century. Cristoforo Landino, a member of Ficino's Platonic 'Academy,' in his *Commentary on Dante* (1481) cited Plato's *Ion* and *Phaedrus*, as well as the evidence in the Latin term, *vates*, that a poet is a seer, and went on to join these pagan ideas to Jewish and Christian speculations about God's act of genesis:

And the Greeks say 'poet' from the verb 'piin' [sic], which is half-way between 'creating,' which is peculiar to God when out of nothing he brings forth anything into being, and 'making,' which applies to men when they compose with matter and form in any art. It is for this reason that, although the feigning of the poet is not entirely out of nothing, it nevertheless departs from making and comes very near to creating. And God is the supreme poet, and the world is His poem.[37]

Similar statements became fairly common in the literary theorists of the cinquecento. Shelley later repeatedly cited what he described as 'the bold and true words of Tasso: *Non merita nome di creatore, se non Iddio ed il Poeta';* the sense, although not the phrasing, is indeed to be found in Tasso,[38] as well as in a number of his predecessors and contemporaries. The most influential statement was that by Scaliger in 1561, who pointed out, in his crabbed Latin, that poetry excels all other arts in that, while these 'represent things themselves just as they are, in some sort like a speaking picture, the poet represents another nature and varied fortunes, and in so doing makes himself, as it were, another God.' Because the poetic art 'fashions images more beautiful than reality of those things which are, as well as images of things which are not,' it does not seem 'as in the case of the other arts, to narrate things like an actor, but like another God, to produce the things themselves [res ipsas . . . velut alter deus condere].'[39]

  The concept was introduced into English criticism by Sir Philip Sidney. The Roman name for poet, he says, was *vates,* a prophet, and the Greek name was *poeta,* from *poiein,* 'to make.' The incomparable name of maker is appropriate, for while all other arts have the works of nature for their principal object,

onely the poet, disdayning to be tied to any such subjection, lifted up with the vigor of his owne invention, dooth growe in effect into another nature, in making things either better than nature bringeth forth, or, quite a newe, formes such as never were in Nature, as the *Heroes, Demigods, Cyclops, Chimeras, Furies,* and such like. . .

And he adds, let us 'give right honor to the heavenly Maker of that maker, who . . . set [man] beyond and over all the workes of that second nature; which in nothing he sheweth so much as in Poetrie, when with the force of a divine breath he bringeth things forth far surpassing her dooings. . .'[40] To this idea, Sidney's contemporary, George Puttenham, joined the portentous word 'create'; in ecclesiastical Latin, *creare* was the common word to connote the orthodox concept that God made the world 'out of nothing.' If poets, said Puttenham, 'be able to devise and make all these things of them selves, without any subject of veritie,' then 'they be (by maner of speech) as creating gods.' [41]

The passage from Sidney holds in suspension many of the ideas of which we are in pursuit, but these occupy a marginal, and not a determinative position in Sidney's essay. His stated task is the defense of poetry, and having confounded Gosson and other Puritan detractors by his etymological evidence that, of all men, the poet in dignity is nearest God, Sidney goes on at once to a less honorific but 'more ordinary opening of him, that the truth may be the more palpable.' The resulting definition, on which the substance of his theory turns, drops the theological for the traditional critical metaphors, and introduces the standard reference of a poem to this world, and to the audience for whom it is written. Poesy is 'an arte of imitation,' a 'mimesis, that is to say, a representing, counterfeiting, or figuring foorth . . . with this end, to teach and delight.' Later on, the rudimentary concept that the artist is a God-like creator of a second nature was kept alive by Neoplatonists, Italian and English, and the term 'creation' was more or less casually applied to poetry by writers like Donne, Dennis, and Pope.[42] The potentialities of this comparison, however, were developed chiefly by those critics who were intent on explaining and justifying the supernatural elements in a poem which could not have been copied from life. Gradually it became evident that it was possible to rescue these beings from Limbo by contending that the poetic supernatural does not imitate God's created nature, but constitutes a second, super-nature created by the poet himself.

The germ of this notion was already present in Sidney's comment that the poet grows 'into another nature' particularly in bringing forth 'forms such as never were in nature, as the heroes, demigods, cyclops, chimeras. . .' Cowley picked up and expanded upon this passage,[43] and Dryden later praised Shakespeare's invention because in Caliban he seems 'to have *created* a person which was not in Nature.' [44] But to Addison must go the credit for compounding these suggestions and making them strongly effective in the critical tradition, in his eclectic, but endlessly suggestive, papers on 'The Pleasures of Imagination.' In 'the fairy way of writing,' Addison says in the *Spectator* 419, 'the poet quite loses sight of nature' and presents persons—fairies, witches, magicians, demons—which have 'no existence, but what he bestows on them.' Far from being contemptible, such writing is more difficult than any other because the poet 'has no pattern to follow in it, and must work altogether out of his own invention.' And the world of spirits and chimeras which Sprat had proscribed as 'a false world,' in opposition to the true world of science, Addison lauds as a second world, valid in itself, and only analogous to the one we owe to God. In such poetry 'we are led, as it were, into a new creation, and see the persons and manners of another species!' Poetry is thus not limited to imitation of the world of sense; 'it has not only the whole circle of nature for its province, but makes new worlds of its own,' and 'shews us persons who are not to be found in being. . .'[45]

From these passages developed various important ideas which are usually held to be radically innovative by historians of eighteenth-century criticism. Following the suggestion in Addison, succeeding commentators, rapidly carrying out the psychologizing of the traditional *ars poetica* which is distinctive of their century, specifically took the creative act indoors and delegated it to the faculty of imagination. A prime source of the concept of 'the creative imagination'—which elevates the imagination above the reason and all other faculties by its hidden claim that this is the mental process re-enacting God—was the endeavor to account for fantastic poetic characters which are most utterly 'original,' because they had to be invented without the assistance of prior forms in sense. A characteristic excellence of Shakespeare, Joseph Warton wrote as early as 1753, is his 'lively creative imagination.'

Of all the plays of Shakespeare, the Tempest is the most striking instance of his creative power. He has there given the reigns to his boundless imagination, and has carried the romantic, the wonderful, and the wild, to the most pleasing extravagance.

In this play the poet has 'wonderfully succeeded' in forming a character 'totally original,' for 'the monster Caliban is the creature of his own imagination, in the formation of which he could derive no assistance from observation or experience.'[46]

Warton's comment suggests another development. The poet's creativity resides peculiarly in his non-realistic inventions; it is in these, therefore, that he comes nearest to God; and the appropriate attitude to Divinity, of course, is one of adoration. Shakespeare, it was further agreed, is superlative among poets in this manner of creation. As Addison said, 'Shakespeare has incomparably excelled all others' in the fairy way of writing, and 'it shows a greater genius in Shakespeare to have drawn his Caliban, than his Hotspur, or Julius Caesar: the one was to be supplied out of his own imagination, whereas the other might have been formed upon tradition, history, and observation.'[47]

Dr. Johnson maintained that this 'is the praise of Shakespeare, that his drama is the mirrour of life,' but to readers of another inclination, the highest praise of Shakespeare was that some of his dramas exhibit beings that could not possibly have been mirrored from this life. A powerful influence in the genesis of Shakespeare idolatry, in the most nearly literal sense of 'idolatry,' was the awe experienced before the man who emulated God in 'creating' Caliban, Oberon, the witches in *Macbeth,* and—not Hamlet, who after all was such a man as can be found in nature, but the ghost of Hamlet's father.[48]

Our concern, however, is with another derivative from the basic analogy between God and the poet. If the making of a poem—or rather, in the present context, the making of certain poetic elements—is a second creation, then to poetize after this fashion is to recapitulate the original cosmogony. Hence it becomes important for critical theory which of the competing theories of the creation of the world are transferred from philosophy into the psychology of poetic invention: whether the Hebraic account of a creation *ex nihilo* by fiat and (in Sidney's words) 'the force of a divine breath'; or the theory in Plato's *Timaeus* of a Demiurge who copied from an eternal pattern; or Plotinus' doctrine of emanation from a perpetually overflowing One; or the Stoic and Neoplatonic tradition of an endlessly generative Soul in Nature itself.

Echoes of all these schemes are to be found, in one or another eighteenth-century critic, as accessories to the root-analogue of the poet as creator. The most extensive and influential application of cosmogony to poetry, however, occurs in the writings of the Swiss friends and co-workers, Johann Bodmer and Johann Breitinger. Breitinger's *Critische Dichtkunst,* published in 1740, devotes itself in considerable part to the problem of reconciling the 'marvelous,' which he regards as an element essential to poetry, with the no less essential criterion of 'probability.' The whole of Bodmer's companion piece, published that same year under the compendious title, *Critical Treatment of the Marvelous in Poetry and its Relation with the Probable in a Defence of John Milton's Poem of Paradise Lost,* is dedicated to the same task. Both critics rely heavily on Addison's *Spectator* papers; in fact Bodmer's work is mainly an expansion of Addison's treatment of 'the fairy way of writing,' and of his detailed analysis of *Paradise Lost.* In these writers, the chief novelty is the emphasis on the productive powers of the poet and especially, the elaboration of the imaginative coming-into-being of the poetic marvelous, on the paradigm of Leibniz's description of the way God created the world in which we live.

Briefly, according to Leibniz, God had present to him at the creation an infinite number of 'possibles,' or model essences. He could not bring all these possibles over into existence, because existence may only be achieved by a set of 'compossibles'—that is, by a system of essences which may exist together, because they are neither self-contradictory nor otherwise incompatible. From the alternative sets of such compossibles, or model worlds, God, in accordance with his excellence, selected the best of all possible worlds for realization.[49]

The Swiss critics translated this structure of ideas into a theory of the poetic process; obviously, the metaphysical distinction between the infinite number of 'possible' species and the finite number of existents in this world was wonderfully convenient for explaining how it is that the poet, in Addison's words, creates 'another species.' The marvelous, Breitinger said, closely following Addison, arises when the poet 'through the power of his imagination [*Phantasie*] creates entirely new beings,' whether by personifying abstractions, or animating inanimate things and humanizing animals, or, like Milton and the ancient poets, by materializing the invisible world of gods and spirits. And since poetry is 'an imitation of the creation and of nature not only in the real, but also in the possible,' its composition, emulating this power of God, is itself 'a kind of creation.'[50] As Bodmer phrased the same concept, the feat of giving visible and bodily form to invisible spirits Milton performed 'by means of a kind of creation which is specific to poetry.' This operation of the poet is

exactly the same as that by which things which are merely possible are brought over out of this condition into the condition of real existence. . . This mode of creation is the chief work of poetry, which is distinguished from history and science by this very fact, that it always prefers to take the material of its imitation from the possible rather than from the existing world.[51]

Bodmer bids us, accordingly, to approach the work of Milton with the humility and reverence appropriate to one standing 'highest among men on the Ladder of Being,' just a little below the angels, and exhibiting in his productions an unfathomable power comparable to that of God himself.[52]

The task of the poet, then, is not merely to imitate real nature, but (as Bodmer has it) 'to imitate the powers of nature in transferring the possible into the condition of reality.'[53] This parallel between the poetic process and Leibniz's cosmogony is readily extended to a parallel between the poetic product and Leibniz's cosmology. The poem-in-being is a world of its own, and as such, needs only exhibit those internal relations which determine the compossibility of any set of model entities, whether realized by God in his creation, or by the poet in his. In the most inclusive sense, says Breitinger, 'everything can be called probable which is possible through the infinite power of the Creator of nature, hence everything that does not stand in contradiction with those first and universal principles upon which rests all knowledge of truth.' And the probability of a poem 'consists in this, that the details accord with the intention, that they are grounded in one another, and that they show no contradiction among themselves.' [54]

In such passages, poetic probability has been freed from all reference to outer reality and made entirely a matter of inner coherence and non-contradiction. And by the severance of the poetic universe from the empirical universe, we achieve the logical distinction between two kinds, or 'universes,' of truth—between what Breitinger called 'rational truth' and 'imaginative truth,' and Bodmer, 'rational truth' and 'poetic truth.' 'The poet,' as Bodmer said, 'troubles himself not at all with rational truth [*das Wahre des Verstandes*],' but only with poetic truth. This

is not without a certain reason and order—it has for the imagination and the senses its sufficient reason, it has no internal contradiction, and one part of it is grounded in the others. . . For our part, we shall seek for metaphysics among the teachers of metaphysics, but demand from the poet only poetry; in this we shall be satisfied with the probability and the reason which lies in its coherence with itself. . .[55]

In brief, we find emerging in these critics of 1740 (although amid more traditional and sometimes conflicting ideas) these important aesthetic consequences of the root-analogue between poet and creator: the poem of the marvelous is a second creation, and therefore not a replica nor even a reasonable facsimile of this world, but its own world, *sui generis,* subject only to its own laws, whose existence (it is suggested) is an end in itself.

Goethe's dialogue, 'On Truth and Probability of the Work of Art,' written half a century later, exhibits some of the potentialities of this approach to the problems of art. One kind of truth is irrelevant to the opera, since it is not its office 'to represent in probable fashion what it imitates'; yet we cannot deny it 'an inner truth' of self-consistency, 'which springs out of the consequence of its being a work of art.'

If the opera is a good one, it constitutes a little world in itself, in which everything proceeds according to positive laws, which will be judged according to its own laws, and felt according to its own characteristic qualities.

It follows that 'artistic truth and natural truth are entirely distinct.' Yet a perfect work of art gives the illusion of being a work of nature, because, as a work of the human spirit, it is 'above nature, but not out of nature'; and 'the genuine amateur of art sees not only the truth of what is imitated but also . . . what is supernatural [*das Überirdische*] in the little art-world.' Or as Goethe phrased the concept a year later:

The artist, grateful to the nature which produced him, gives back to her a second nature, but one which has been felt, thought out, and humanly perfected.[56]

In England, Richard Hurd, without either the detail or elaborate metaphysical substructure of the German theorists, faced similar problems and reached comparable conclusions. In his *Letters on Chivalry and Romance* (1762), Hurd explicitly set himself to defend the romantic marvelous of poets like Tasso against the attacks in the writings of Davenant and Hobbes. These documents, he says, 'open'd the way' to a 'new sort of criticism'; and with historical acumen, Hurd attributes the decline of pagan gods and 'Gothic Faeries' to the growing rationalism of the seventeenth century, which finally drove out 'the portentous spectres of the imagination,' until 'fancy, that had wantoned it so long in the world of fiction, was now constrained, against her will, to ally herself with strict truth, if she would gain admittance into reasonable company.' [57] But, he insists, the maxim of 'following Nature,' in the sense equating nature with the world of experience, although valid for such realistic species as the drama, is not relevant to the epic, a 'more sublime and creative poetry,' which addresses itself 'solely or principally to the Imagination.' Hurd quotes from the Spectator paper on the fairy way of writing, and expands Addison's concept of this poetry as a 'new creation' in such a way as to distinguish the world of poetry from the world of experience, and poetic truth (or self-consistency) from philosophical truth (or correspondence to empirical nature).

So little account [he says ironically] does this wicked poetry make of philosophical or historical truth: All she allows us to look for, is *poetical truth;* a very slender thing indeed, and which the poet's eye, when rolling in it's finest frenzy, can but just lay hold of. To speak in the philosophic language of Mr. Hobbes, It is something much *beyond the actual bounds, and only within the conceived possibility, of nature.*

. . . A poet, they say, must follow *Nature;* and by Nature we are to suppose can only be meant the known and experienced course of affairs in this world. Whereas the poet has a world of his own, where experience has less to do, than consistent imagination.

He has, besides, a supernatural world to range in. He has Gods, and Faeries, and Witches at his command. . .[58]

Richard Hurd, like Bodmer and Breitinger, paralleled the poet to the Creator in order to account for and certify the supernatural creatures in a poem. In a variant application of the same analogy, the concept of creation was applied to account for characters who, although invented by the poet, are convincingly lifelike, and endowed with the self-consistency of the people in God's own creation. In this realistic development, the English Platonist, Shaftesbury, occupies somewhat the pivotal position that Addison does for the theorists of the poetic marvelous. Shaftesbury's *Advice to an Author,* first published in 1710, ridicules Shakespeare and other poets who employ supernatural materials, whether in the form of romantic marvels or the prodigies of the Christian Scriptures.[59] What Shaftesbury recommends is the invention of characters such as we find in this life. To explain this achievement, Shaftesbury revives the Renaissance analogue, but with two important innovations: the creation is not of the cosmos, but, specifically, of man; and it is conceived on the model of Greek, instead of Hebraic myth:

But for the man who truly and in a just sense deserves the name of poet, and who as a real master, or architect in the kind, can describe both men and manners, and give to an action its just body and proportions, he will be found, if I mistake not, a very different creature. Such a poet is indeed a second *Maker;* a just Prometheus under Jove. Like that sovereign artist or universal plastic nature, he forms a whole, coherent and proportioned in itself, with due subjection and subordinacy of the constituent parts. . . The moral artist . . . can thus imitate the Creator. . .[60]

This passage seems to have had surprisingly little effect in English criticism, but it had a great vogue in Germany, as Oskar Walzel has shown in his articles on 'Das Prometheussymbol von Shaftesbury zu Goethe.'[61] In 1767, Lessing described the poetic other-world of realistic characters in terms comparable to Breitinger's description of the other-world of the marvelous. He would, he said, have had no objection to Marmontel's departing from the historical models in his Soliman and Roxelane—

if only I had found that, though they are not of this real world, they still might belong to another world; to a world whose events are connected in a different order, but just as closely connected, as in this one . . . in short, to the world of a genius which—let me be permitted, without naming him, to indicate the Creator through his noblest creature—which, I say, in order to imitate in miniature the Highest Genius, transposes, exchanges, diminishes, increases the elements of the present world, in order to make of it a separate whole. . .

Consistency:—there must be nothing self-contradictory in the characters. . .[62]

Explicit recourse to Shaftesbury's Prometheus myth sometimes had consequences alien to the earlier, and usually reverently qualified, parallels of
the poet to Jehovah. The rebels of the *Genieperiode* exploited the element
of Promethean defiance against vested authority, in order to attack the
code of poetic rules. In the teeth of 'all Frenchmen and infected Germans,'
the youthful Goethe flung this challenge: 'Nature! Nature! Nothing so
completely nature as Shakespeare's characters. . . He emulated Prometheus,
formed his people on his model feature for feature, but in colossal dimensions . . . and then animated them all with the breath of his spirit. . .' [63]
Later Goethe developed Prometheus into a symbol for the poet's painful
but necessary isolation, in his creativity, from both men and the gods. [64]
Even earlier than Goethe, Herder had adopted the Prometheus simile, and
he modified the Leibnizian heterocosmology of earlier commentators into
the view that a Shakespeare play—in the complex inter-relations of its characters and actions, and in its quick changes of time, place, and scene—is,
like the primal creation itself, a great and living whole. [65] Whether in the
discussion of the creative marvelous or of creative realism, Shakespeare remained the cardinal example of the poet as divinity.

A number of these diverse developments from the analogy between the
poet and the Creator were brought together in the Berlin Lectures of that
eclectic systematizer, August Schlegel. In them he attacked the doctrine that
art must imitate nature, which is used to ban from art, in the name of
probability, 'everything bold, great, wonderful, and extraordinary.' Of poetry we may validly demand only the appearance of truth; this appearance
may be assumed by things 'which can never be true,' and 'depends merely
on the fact that a poet, by the magic of his presentation, knows how to
transport us into a strange world, in which he can rule according to his
own laws.' [66] It will have been noted that Shaftesbury combined the idea
that the poet is a moulder of men, like Prometheus, with the totally un-
related idea (based on the analogue of the generative world-soul) that the
poet forms a whole like 'universal plastic nature.' In Schlegel's lectures, this
curious conjunction is maintained and expanded. Nature as a whole, he
says, is organized, and art must imitate the productive power of nature.

That means it must—creating autonomously like nature, itself organized and
organizing—form living works which are not set in motion through an alien
mechanism, like a pendulum-clock, but through an indwelling power. . . In this
manner did Prometheus imitate nature, when he formed man out of the clay of
the earth, and animated him with a spark stolen from the sun. . . [67]

In this romantic rendering, the concept of the heterocosm comprehends not only selected poetic elements, whether natural or supernatural, but a great poem in its entirety. And through the displacement, as creative principle, of both Jehovah, Demiurge, and Prometheus by an indwelling Soul of Nature, the role of a deliberate supervisory artisan, whether *deus* or *alter deus,* dwindles: the real and poetic worlds alike become self-originating, autonomous, and self-propelling, and both tend to *grow* out into their organic forms.

For English writers of the earlier nineteenth century, 'create' had for the most part become a routine critical term, but in some uses it continued to manifest its metaphorical vitality. Shelley, for example, who employed the word, in its various grammatical forms, a score of times in his 'Defence of Poetry,' reverted to an interpretation of the method of creation close to that of the Renaissance Neoplatonists. Poetry, 'created by that imperial faculty' of imagination, is 'the creation of actions according to the unchangeable forms of human nature, as existing in the mind of the Creator, which is itself the image of all other minds.' By thus repeating the primal act of creation, poetry produces a new world:

It makes us the inhabitants of a world to which the familiar world is a chaos. . . It creates anew the universe, after it has been annihilated in our minds by the recurrence of impressions blunted by reiteration.[68]

Carlyle revived the Renaissance attempt to disclose the secret of poetry by way of etymology. The poet is *Vates,* a prophet or seer into 'the Divine Idea of the World'; but since to see thus profoundly is also to create, the Latin *Vates* and Greek *Poeta* fall together—'Creative, we said: poetic creation, what is this but *seeing* the thing sufficiently?' [69]

Only in the philosophy and criticism of Coleridge, however, is creation a central and thoroughly functional metaphor. We can take advantage of the perspective afforded by the history of this term to look again at the key passage in the *Biographia Literaria* which has puzzled and irritated so many commentators:

The primary IMAGINATION I hold to be the living Power and prime Agent of all human Perception and as a repetition in the finite mind of the eternal act of creation in the infinite I AM. The secondary Imagination I consider as an echo of the former . . . differing only in *degree,* and in the *mode* of its operation. It dissolves, diffuses, dissipates, in order to recreate. . .

Coleridge has added a third term—the mind in perception—to the existing analogy between the poet and the creative God. The result is a triple parallel. At its base is the ceaseless self-proliferation of God into the sensible universe. This creative process is reflected in the primary imagination by which all individual minds develop out into their perception of this universe, and it is echoed again in the secondary, or re-creative imagination which is possessed only by the poet of genius. As early as 1801, Coleridge had written that the perceiving mind is not passive, but 'made in God's Image, and that, too, in the sublimest sense, the *Image of the Creator*. . .' Three years later he added that the poetic imagination is also 'a dim analogue of creation—not all that we can *believe,* but all that we can *conceive* of creation.' [70] (As Professor Muirhead has said, Coleridge's world of imagination is the world of sense twice-born.) In Coleridge's cosmogony, therefore, the fixed Forms of the Renaissance Platonists and the static 'possibles' of Bodmer and Breitinger, subsisting timelessly in their ideal space, start into motion and become internal and endlessly self-evolving seed-Ideas of the world; and the workings of this universal plastic nature are reiterated, within the mind of man, in the procedure of the 'esemplastic' imagination when creating a poem.

In English, unlike German romantic criticism, the heterocosmic analogue —the parallel between writing poetry and creating the universe—was used to illuminate the process more than the product of literary invention. It remained for English critics later in the century to explore the full possibilities of the parallel as a ground for the concept that the poem-in-being is its own and utterly self-sufficient world. A. C. Bradley's Oxford lecture, 'Poetry for Poetry's Sake,' published in 1901, is a revealing document in this tradition. On the one side, the lecture epitomizes what had been most tenable in the aesthetic doctrine of Art for Art's Sake (which, in its common form, had really been a moral doctrine of Life for Art's Sake). On the other side, it formulates what has since become the central position of present-day critics who (without noticing the incongruity) cite as a truth MacLeish's poetic statement that a poem does not state truth but simply exists:

> A poem should be equal to:
> Not true. . .
>
> A poem should not mean
> But be.

Poetry, Bradley pointed out fifty years ago, is not an imitation, but 'an end in itself,' and its '*poetic* value is this intrinsic worth alone.'

For its nature is to be not a part, nor yet a copy, of the real world . . . but to be a world by itself, independent, complete, autonomous; and to possess it fully you must enter that world, conform to its laws, and ignore for a time the beliefs, aims, and particular conditions which belong to you in the other world of reality. . .

[Life and poetry] are parallel developments which nowhere meet, or, if I may use loosely a word which will be serviceable later, they are analogues. . . They have different *kinds* of existence.

Behind this concept of a poem as its own world, does there not still loom, dim but recognizable, the generative analogue of the *Deus Creator*? Pure poetry, Bradley says, 'springs from the creative impulse of a vague imaginative mass pressing for development and definition. . . And this is the reason why such poems strike us as creations, not manufactures. . .'[71] The Renaissance metaphor of the heterocosmos, fully developed, now appears as one of the competing systems which lay claim to unlimited scope in the province of aesthetics—as one form of that system which, in the introductory chapter, I called the objective theory of art.

Two of the most thoughtful of our practicing critics may serve as final instances that the heterocosmic metaphor remains a vital one. In his recent book, *Rage for Order,* Austin Warren presents this statement of his critical outlook: The poet's 'final creation' is 'a kind of world or cosmos; a concretely languaged, synoptically felt world; an ikon or image of the "real world."' And the critic, in his desire to discover 'the systematic vision of the world which is the poet's construction,' must make the assumption 'that the cosmos of a serious poet is, intuitively and dramatically, coherent.'[72] Elder Olson, a member of the second generation of neo-Aristotelian critics at the University of Chicago, announces that the aim of his theory of the lyric is to deal with a work of art '*qua* work of art'—a mode of criticism to which 'only one treatise—the *Poetics* of Aristotle—is relevant. . .' When he comes to deal with the problem of poetic truth, he illustrates Aristotle's concept of probability by an analogue of much more recent provenience than the writings of the Greek master. 'Poetic statements' are not propositions, and 'since they are not statements about things which exist outside the poem, it would be meaningless to evaluate them as true or false. . .'

In a sense, every poem is a microcosmos, a discrete and independent universe with its laws provided by the poet; his decision is absolute; he can make things good or bad, great or small, powerful or weak, just as he wills; he may make men taller than mountains or smaller than atoms, he may suspend whole cities in the air, he may destroy creation or re-form it; within his universe the impossible becomes the possible, the necessary the contingent—if he but says they do.[73]

Here the description of the poet's creativity is modeled, not on Leibniz's God, whose actions, after all, are limited by the logic of contradiction and the laws of compossibility, but on a more ancient prototype—the peremptory and absolute fiat of Jehovah in the Book of Genesis.

iv. Poetic Truth and Metaphor

The problem of mythical beings was not the only one which the criterion of truth to nature presented for literary theorists. It was, for example, an old observation that the traditional statements of poets—who were prone to call a man a lion and a woman a goddess, and to avail themselves of every device for exaggeration and distortion—did not correspond to the facts of experience. In the later seventeenth century, the general need to scrutinize and justify such figurative language was made acute by vigorous attacks from several quarters. Writers on pulpit and civil eloquence sometimes blamed the effectiveness of religious zealots, and even the recent civil war, on the inherent deceptions of metaphor, and demanded drastic remedy. 'Had we but an Act of Parliament to abridge Preachers the use of fulsom and luscious Metaphors,' Samuel Parker wrote in 1670, 'it might perhaps be an effectual Cure of all our present Distempers.' [74] In addition, the New Philosophy in England, from Bacon on, quite properly incorporated a program of semantic reform which would eliminate verbal, as well as pagan, 'idols' from nature, and develop a language austerely adapted to the description and manipulation of pure fact. Speaking for the Royal Society, Thomas Sprat (who, we remember, also celebrated the triumph of experiment over the 'false Worlds' of ancient superstition) employed the old rhetorical concepts of *res* and *verba* to recommend that natural philosophers match their combinations of words precisely to the combination of things in nature. 'Specious *Tropes* and *Figures*,' however justifiable in the past, ought now to be banished 'out of all *civil Societies,* as a thing fatal to Peace and good Manners.' Since they also bring 'mists and uncertainties on our knowledge,' the Royal Society has constantly resolved 'to return back to the primitive purity and shortness, when men deliver'd so many *things* almost in an equal number of *words*,' and has exacted 'a close, naked, natural way of speaking . . . as near the Mathematical plainness as they can. . .' [75]

The tendency of recent scholarship has been to assume that these were linguistic recommendations of universal scope, and greatly to exaggerate the immediacy and extent of their influence on the language of poetry. The fact is that many of the reformers made explicit exception for poetry, in addition to certain forms of prose, as modes of discourse whose difference in purpose required a different technique of language. It was recognized that although poetry might well spare the representation of beings which lack a prototype in sense, it could hardly survive without the privilege of metaphoric deviation from literal truth. Hobbes, who denied to poets the use of fabulous beings 'beyond the conceived possibility of nature,' and who banished metaphor from all discourse whose end is the 'rigorous search of truth,' held, nonetheless, that when the end is rather 'to please and delight our selves and others, by playing with our words, for pleasure or ornament, innocently,' a good wit may with utmost propriety supply

similitudes, that will please, not onely by illustration of discourse, and adorning it with new and apt metaphors; but also, by the rarity of their invention.[76]

The influence upon poetry of the demand for a literal and mathematically plain discourse in science and sermons was patent, but usually indirect; one way in which it acted was to stimulate both poets and critics to re-examine and to redefine the permissible limits of metaphor in the language of a poem.

Justification of the apparent falsity of figurative language was frequently bound up with the defense of the poetic marvelous. In his 'Heroic Poetry and Poetic Licence' (1677), consideration of the warrant for metaphor and hyperbole leads Dryden to the question, 'If poetry be imitation,' then how are hippocentaurs, angels, and immaterial substances, which are 'things quite out of nature,' to be imaged, and how can they be authorized? His principal answer is to claim 'Poetic Licence,' or 'the liberty which poets have assumed to themselves, in all ages, of speaking things in verse, which are beyond the severity of prose.' With respect to 'the thought or imagination of a poet,' this license consists in the use of fictions, and with respect to the expression of that thought, in tropes and figures.[77] Figurative deviations from literal truth, then, like supernatural deviations from the course of nature, are to be justified by a special grant, but subjected to special restraints. 'You are pleased with the image,' Dryden said, 'without being cozened by the fiction.' As Hume later put the case for metaphor, with his usual point and clarity:

Many of the beauties of poetry and even of eloquence are founded on falsehood and fiction, on hyperboles, metaphors, and an abuse or perversion of terms from their natural meaning. To check the sallies of the imagination, and to reduce every expression to geometrical truth and exactness, would be most contrary to the laws of criticism; because it would produce a work, which, by universal experience, has been found the most insipid and disagreeable. But though poetry can never submit to exact truth, it must be confined by rules of art.[78]

In their discussion of this problem, eighteenth-century English critics were apt to recall *La Manière de bien penser* (1687) of Father Bouhours, whose balanced doctrines made him particularly useful for the simultaneous defense of linguistic freedom and the attack on the excesses, or 'false wit,' of the poets of the preceding century.[79] Bouhours' basic criterion for validating 'thoughts' in poetry is truth. 'You may judge as you please,' says Eudoxus, speaking for the author, 'but I cannot admire that which is not true.' This criterion is held to involve a simple correspondence between words and thoughts, thoughts and things, and is derived specifically from the ancient analogy of the mimetic mirror. To the question, 'What is the exact Notion of a true thought?' Eudoxus replies:

Thoughts . . . are the Images of things, as words are the Images of Thoughts: and generally speaking, to think is to Form in ones self the Picture of any Object spiritual or sensible. Now Images and Pictures are true no further than they resemble: so a Thought is true when it represents things faithfully: and it is false, when it makes them appear otherwise than they are in themselves.

Philanthus, the interlocutor, opposes the observation that wit 'generally turns most upon Fictions, upon Ambiguities, upon Hyperboles, which are but so many Lyes.' In his answer, Father Bouhours adapts to this topic the medieval notion that in poetry pagan deities and fiction in general are (in the common metaphor) but veils over the hidden truth. The fabulous world of Apollo and the muses, he says, are allowable lies, because they only conceal and adorn the truth. In a parallel fashion, 'what is figurative is not false, and Metaphors have their Truth as well as Fictions.' They 'deceive no man,' and we may say 'that Metaphors are like transparent Veils, thro' which we see what they cover.'[80] As George Granville phrased the concept, in his curious *rifacimento* of Bouhours' first dialogue called 'An Essay upon Unnatural Flights in Poetry' (1701):

> As Veils transparent cover, but not hide,
> Such metaphors appear, when right apply'd;
> When, thro' the phrase, we plainly see the sense,
> Truth, when the meaning's obvious, will dispense.[81]

The various modes of discussing figurative language—each attempting to retain, while mitigating, the requirement of truth to fact—parallel the various defenses of the poetic supernatural, even in detail. The chief difference was a lesser attention to the means of making these poetic devices acceptable to the reader (on the assumption that there is not the resistance to figurative distortion that there is to impossible beings and events), and a greater stress on trope and metaphor as ornaments and variations upon the literal sense, entailed by the pragmatic requirement that a poem move and please the reader. As James Beattie summarized this logic:

> If it appear, that, by means of Figures, Language may be made more *pleasing* . . . it will follow, that to Poetic Language, whose end is to *please* by imitating *nature,* Figures must be not only ornamental, but necessary.[82]

The pleasurable purpose of poetry not only justifies a figurative departure from a literal imitation of nature: it compels it.

In some important eighteenth-century discussions, the correspondence between the treatment of supernatural subject matter and of tropical language extended even to the employment of the analogy between poet and Creator. Certain kinds of deviations from literal language came to be treated, not as ornaments, or veiled reflections of truth, but as instances of the poetic creation of another world, peopled with its own manner of non-empirical beings. In the text and gloss of his Pindaric ode, 'The Muse,' Cowley had already included the animation and personification of 'Beasts, Trees, Waters, and other irrational and insensible things,' together with centaurs and fairies, as elements in the poet's God-like creation of 'a new World.' In his papers on 'The Pleasures of the Imagination,' Addison spoke of the personification of 'passion, appetite, virtue, or vice'—including Virgil's Fame, Milton's Sin and Death, and 'a whole creation of the like shadowy persons in Spenser' —as examples of the way poetry 'makes new worlds of its own, shews us persons who are not to be found in being. . .' In fact, one can say of the invention of all 'similitudes, metaphors, and allegories':

> It has something in it like creation. It bestows a kind of existence, and draws up to the reader's view several objects which are not to be found in being. It makes additions to nature, and gives greater variety to God's works.[83]

And Bodmer and Breitinger faithfully followed Addison by including the personification both of abstractions and of inanimate nature among the products of that creative act by which a poet, emulating Divinity, brings possibility over into the realm of being.

Only a few years after the appearance of the *Spectator* papers, John Hughes published an essay 'On Allegorical Poetry' as part of the introduction to his edition of *The Fairy Queen* (1715). Following the etymological method of Renaissance critics, Hughes wrote that in allegory,

the Power of raising Images or Resemblances of things, giving them Life and Action, and presenting them as it were before the Eyes, was thought to have something in it like Creation: And it was probably for this fabling Part, that the first Authors of such Works were call'd *Poets* or *Makers*. . .

Because it is merely the type and shadow of a hidden truth, allegory 'has a liberty indulg'd to it beyond any other sort of Writing whatsoever. . . Allegory is indeed the *Fairy Land* of Poetry, peopled by Imagination. . .' Its fable 'consists for the most part of fictitious Persons or Beings, Creatures of the Poet's Brain, and Actions surprising, and without the Bounds of Probability or Nature.' [84]

The conception of prosopopoeia as a second creation not only accompanied the rise of Spenser to high estate but also served to rationalize that cardinal instance of the new poetry in the age of Collins, Gray, and the Wartons— the allegoric and 'sublime' ode. As Joseph Warton wrote in 1753:

It is the peculiar privilege of poetry . . . to give Life and motion to immaterial beings; and form, and colour, and action, even to abstract ideas; to embody the Virtues, and Vices, and the Passions. . . Prosopopoeia, therefore, or personification, conducted with dignity and propriety, may be justly esteemed one of the greatest efforts of the creative power of a warm and lively imagination.[85]

Thus by the mid-century, what had once been a purely rhetorical figure had become an act of creation, the result of a mental process having its analogue in God's peopling of this world, of which, naturally, the effect on the reader is a sublime astonishment and enlargement of soul. As a result, poetic personification, together with the fairy way of writing, was elevated to the highest achievement of poetic imagination. 'By the vigorous effort of a creative Imagination,' said William Duff of visionary and allegorical poetry, the poet 'calls shadowy substances and unreal objects into existence.' For the imagination of the truly original genius, 'finding no objects in the visible creation sufficiently marvellous and new, or which can give full scope to the exercise of its power, naturally bursts into the ideal world,' where its success 'will be proportionable to the plastic power of which it is possessed.' [86]

v. *Wordsworth and Coleridge on Personification and Myth*

According to the most fundamental neo-classic frame of reference, language is the 'dress' of thought, and figures are the 'ornaments' of language, for the sake of the pleasurable emotion which distinguishes a poetic from a merely didactic discourse. These elements must be joined to form a consistent whole according to the basic neo-classic unifying principle of the decorum or proportionableness of parts—a complex requirement, involving adjustment to the poetic kind, and the matter signified, as well as the character and emotional state of the speaker depicted. This third requirement led theorists to attend particularly to the role of the speaker's passion in justifying figurative language. These, said Dryden, joining the doctrines of Horace and Longinus,

are principally to be used in passion, when we speak more warmly, and with more precipitation than at other times: for then, *si vis me flere, dolendum est primum ipsi tibi;* the poet must put on the passion he endeavours to represent. . . This boldness of expression is not to be blamed, if it be managed by the coolness and discretion which is necessary to a poet.[87]

As eighteenth-century criticism became more Longinian and psychological, the causes of figures in the passion of the speaker were explored in increasing detail, and the emphasis shifted from the emotions of the characters who were imitated, or from the emotions a poet assumed in order to portray such characters more effectively, to the 'natural' and uncontrived emotions of the poet himself. In Wordsworth's critical writings, a part becomes the whole. The genetic reference to the poet's own affective state, together with that to the creative operations of the poet's mind, are now the sole warrant for all valid poetic figures of speech.

Since he insisted that genuine poetry is the natural language in which thoughts and their associated feelings spontaneously embody themselves, Wordsworth found it necessary to heal the cleavage between thought and expression, language and figure, by substituting an integrative for the separative analogues most frequent in earlier rhetoric. Thoughts and feelings, he says, must have a 'vital union,' and not be 'artificially connected.' In the 'artifices which have over-run our writings in metre since the days of Dryden and Pope,' those feelings which are the pure emanations of Nature, those thoughts which have the infinitude of truth, and those expressions which are not what the garb is to the body but what the body is to the soul . . . all these are abandoned for their opposites. . . If words be not (recurring to a metaphor before used) an incarnation of the thought, but only a clothing for it, then surely will they prove an ill gift. . .[88]

In thus opposing the body-and-soul of traditional philosophy and religion to the body-and-garment, garment-and-ornament of traditional rhetoric Wordsworth had been anticipated by a few German critics,[89] and was followed by various English critics. De Quincey credited to Wordsworth the distinction he himself elaborated at some length between style as a 'separable ornament' or 'dress,' and style as 'the incarnation of thoughts.' [90] And ever since the romantic period, metaphoric formulations implying the living integrity of thought and expression, matter and manner, content and form have been commonplaces of literary criticism.

In his discussion of the style of valid poetry, Wordsworth took special exception to the personifications of abstract ideas, 'a mechanical device of style,' except (this, as always, is his ruling sanction) as they are 'occasionally prompted by passion.' [91] 'How ridiculous,' Coleridge said, 'would it seem in a state of comparative insensibility to employ a figure used only by a person under the highest emotion, such as the personification of an abstract being.' Reading with the expectation of finding passion behind such figures, Coleridge found in 'sundry odes and apostrophes to abstract terms' of the eighteenth century only 'the madness prepense of pseudo-poesy, or the startling *hysteric* of weakness over-exerting itself. . .' [92]

But what disturbed these two readers even more in the poetry of the preceding century was the facile use of that other kind of personification—invidiously identified, since Ruskin's time, as 'the pathetic fallacy'—which animates, not abstractions, but concrete particulars, by attributing life, emotion, and physiognomy to objects of the physical world. The passages from Dryden, Gray, and Cowper which Wordsworth quotes as instances of vicious poetic diction invariably include what seem to him 'glossy and unfeeling' lines that ascribe humanity to nature: the morning 'smiles' and fields are 'cheerful,' the mountains 'seem to nod their drowsy head,' and the valleys and rocks

Ne'er sighed at the sound of a knell,
Or smiled when a sabbath appeared.[93]

Wordsworth's indignation stems from the fact that he himself viewed with a religious reverence those experiences in which he gave a moral life and feeling 'to every natural form, rock, fruit, or flower'; these were the high results of his 'creative sensibility,' and the sovereign resource of his own poetry in its crowning passages. The unforgivable sin of the eighteenth-century poet, therefore, was to use such personification as a rhetorical convention. To Wordsworth's point of view, this dared to alter a natural object in cold blood, without justification in the power of natural and spontaneous passion to enter into, and so remake, the facts it perceives. And by a curious turn of circumstance, Wordsworth, condemning this resource of the eighteenth-century odists, proposes the very warrant for its legitimate use which they had developed for him. Joseph Warton, we remember, had said that 'to give life and motion to material things' by prosopopoeia is a product 'of the creative power of a warm and lively imagination.' So Wordsworth: Not idly do poets 'Call upon the hills and streams to mourn, And senseless rocks'—only provided they speak

> In these their invocations, with a voice
> Obedient to the strong *creative* power
> Of human passion.[94]

More thoroughly and systematically than Wordsworth, Coleridge moved the discussion of this, and other figures of speech, to the province of the powers and creative processes of the mind. It has not, I think, been adequately noted that almost all the examples of the secondary, or 're-creative' imagination which Coleridge explicitly cites in his criticism would fall under the traditional headings of simile, metaphor, and (in the supreme instances) personification. The products of imagination Coleridge adduces most frequently are instances of the poet's power to animate and humanize nature by fusing his own life and passion with those objects of sense which, as objects, 'are essentially fixed and dead.' Imagination acts 'by impressing the stamp of humanity, of human feeling, over inanimate objects. . .' Objects are not 'faithfully copied from nature,' but 'a human and intellectual life is transferred to them from the poet's own spirit,

> "Which shoots its being through earth, sea, and air." '

In this power of giving dignity, passion, and life to the objects he presents, Shakespeare 'in his earliest, as in his latest, works surpasses all other poets. . .

> Full many a glorious morning have I seen
> *Flatter* the mountain tops with soverign eye.'

And at its highest, this mode of imagination shows itself in *Lear,* 'where the deep anguish of a father spreads the feeling of ingratitude and cruelty over the very elements of heaven.'[95] Coleridge, no less than Wordsworth, scorned the actual use of personification in the poetry of the Wartons and their contemporaries. Nevertheless, their earlier concept of this figure as the product of the creative imagination—appropriately modified to accord with his own theory of imaginative re-creation as reconciling the opposites of mind and matter, subject and object, the living and the dead—occupies a crucial position in his own philosophy of poetry.

In the writings of Wordsworth and Coleridge, the question of myth and the supernatural, like that of figurative departures from literal speech, is usually examined genetically, with reference to the emotions and powers of the poet. These critics were no longer especially exercised about the truth of mythology in relation to the 'known order and course of nature,' or about devices for making it acceptable to the skeptical reader; for, to the romantic point of view, the main problem concerning the pagan gods has come to be their adequacy, as symbols and means of expression, to the poet himself. This is the theme of Coleridge's expanded translation of a passage in Schiller's *Die Piccolomini:*

> The intelligible forms of ancient poets,
> The fair humanities of old religion . . .
> . . . all these have vanished.
> They live no longer in the faith of reason!
> But still the heart doth need a language, still
> Doth the old instinct bring back the old names. . .[96]

In *The Excursion,* Wordsworth described the genesis of myth in the feelings and imagination of the primitive mind, in the course of his attack against the skeptical empiricism of the preceding century, with its 'repetitions wearisome of sense, Where soul is dead, and feeling hath no place.' In ancient times

> The imaginative faculty was lord
> Of observations natural,

so that when the lonely herdsman of pagan Greece chanced to hear

> A distant strain, far sweeter than the sounds
> Which his poor skill could make, his fancy fetched,
> Even from the blazing chariot of the sun,
> A beardless Youth, who touched a golden lute,
> And filled the illumined groves with ravishment.[97]

At about the same time, Wordsworth revived the serious use of pagan myth in his 'Laodamia' and other poems. Although, he told Miss Fenwick, by reason of disgust with 'the hacknied and lifeless use' of mythology in the late seventeenth and eighteenth centuries,

I abstained in my earlier writings from all introduction of pagan fable—surely, even in its humble form, it may ally itself with real sentiment—as I can truly affirm it did in the present case.[98]

And in a graceful but derivative essay, 'On the Poetical Use of the Heathen Mythology' (1822), Hartley Coleridge (citing the relevant passages from both *The Piccolomini* and *The Excursion*), noted the contemporary revitalization of myth in Keats, Shelley, and Wordsworth; attributed its genesis to 'an instinct' which induced nations 'to weave a fabric of fables, accommodated to the wants and yearnings of their own minds'; and predicted its continued use in poetry because of 'the pregnancy of its symbols, and the plastic facility with which it accommodates itself to the fancy and feelings of mankind.' [99]

As we would expect, S. T. Coleridge ultimately relegates the problem of non-realistic poetry, as he does that of poetic personification, to consideration of the imaginative process. In the *Biographia,* he promised an essay 'on the uses of the supernatural in poetry, and the principles that regulate its introduction,' which would concern itself with 'the powers and privileges of the imagination.' [100] This promise he did not keep. We know from his other writings, however, that to his way of thinking, the Greek pantheon exhibited an inherent limitation which allied it more to allegorical personification than to the animating and creative imagination of a Shakespeare. In 1802 he wrote a remarkable letter to the poet, Sotheby, which signalizes a profound change in his critical thinking, and provides a key to his later philosophy both of poetry and of mind. A few years earlier, Coleridge had revered and emulated the sonnets of William Bowles. Now he takes exception to Bowles's persistent device (in the familiar convention of the meditative-descriptive poem of the preceding century) of setting up a natural scene merely as the occasion for a parallel with human life, sentiments, and morality.

Nature has her proper interest, and he will know what it is who believes and feels that everything has a life of its own, and that we are all *One Life.* A poet's heart and intellect should be *combined,* intimately combined and unified with the great appearances of nature, and not merely held in solution and loose mixture with them, in the shape of formal similes.

Consideration of the limits of such a formal equation, rather than imaginative fusion, between ethos and object leads Coleridge to consider what he regards as the similar limits of Greek mythology, in terms of the faculty of mind involved in its genesis:

All natural objects were *dead,* mere hollow statues, but there was a Godkin or Goddessling *included* in each. . . At best it is but fancy, or the aggregating faculty of the mind, not imagination or the *modifying* and coadunating faculty. This the Hebrew poets appear to me to have possessed beyond all others, and next to them the English. In the Hebrew poets each thing has a life of its own, and yet they are all our life.[101]

Like Dr. Johnson and other empirical-minded critics, then, Coleridge disparages ancient fable, but for new and distinctive reasons. Hellenic myth, as he says, converts ideas into 'finites,' and is 'in itself fundamentally allegorical'; and allegory he defines elsewhere as 'but a translation of abstract notions into a picture-language,' and as 'empty echoes which the fancy arbitrarily associates with apparitions of matter.' [102] When used, in Coleridge's term, 'as a *poetic* language,' [103] the mythic gods demonstrate something like the deficiencies of the personified abstractions of the eighteenth-century poets. Because Venus and Apollo, Proteus and Old Triton, were from their very origin finished, fixed, and finite emblems, they can at best be only the objects—the 'fixities and definites'—manipulated by the lower faculty, the fancy, as opposed to the 'symbols'—'living educts of the imagination,' Coleridge defines them—of the Hebrew Bible.[104] And in Coleridge's description of the all-animating, 'coadunating' imagination of the Hebrew psalmists and prophets, we recognize the same creative faculty which enabled Shakespeare to fuse mind and percept, life and nature, by shooting his being 'through earth, sea, and air.'

In spite of his own greater respect for Hellenic fable, Wordsworth consented to this statement of its deficiencies. The grand storehouse of poetical imagination, he said in 1815, are 'the prophetic and lyrical parts of the Holy Scriptures,' and the works of Milton and Spenser; in Greece and Rome,

the anthropomorphitism of the Pagan religion subjected the minds of the greatest poets too much to the bondage of definite form; from which the Hebrews were preserved by their abhorrence of idolatry.[105]

Concomitantly with the romantic theory of personification, symbol, and the supernatural we find romantic poets employing these elements with an inventive freedom, vitality, and puissance unprecedented in literature. William

Blake, who like some of his German contemporaries thought a mythology essential to poetry, felt that 'I must Create a System or be enslav'd by another Man's,' [106] and constructed a pantheon by fusing his own visions with fragments of existing systems. Shelley, like Blake, exploited the possibilities of symbolism; and his astonishing 'Ode to the West Wind,' while still recognizably in the tradition of prosopopoeia and allegory represented by Collins' 'Ode to Evening,' weaves around the central image of the destroying and preserving wind, the full cycle of the myths of death and regeneration, vegetational, human, and divine. Coleridge, followed by Keats, discovered the power of the poem modeled on popular lore and legend, which in the eighteenth century—despite the occasional claim for the God-like creativity of a supernatural imagination—had been only dimly adumbrated in the factitious terrors of the Gothic tale. And many romantic writers shared the capacity of imagination (as Coleridge employed the term) to suspend the distinction between living and lifeless, and to perceive the universe as animated, both as a whole and in its parts.

Wordsworth's special achievement is nearer to being unique, for in some of his most effective passages he not only vivifies the natural scene, but seems to revert to the very patterns of thought and feeling memorialized in communal myths and folk-lore. Coleridge explicitly maintained that Wordsworth, in the power of imagination, 'stands nearest of all modern writers to Shakespeare and Milton; and yet in a kind perfectly unborrowed and his own.' [107] This characteristic and unborrowed power is found, not in Wordsworth's formal mythological poems, but in the many passages (of which several are cited by Coleridge) in which his imagination, rejecting all hereditary symbols, and without violence to the truth of perception, operates as myth in process rather than on myth in being. At such times, under the ministry of guilt and fear, natural objects are metamorphosed into 'huge and mighty forms, that do not live like living men,' and solitary living men are reduced to the condition of natural phenomena, until, as Coleridge says of the visionary effect—

> The simplest, and the most familiar things
> Gain a strange power of spreading awe around them.[108]

Symbolism, animism, and mythopeia, in richly diverse forms, explicit or submerged, were so pervasive in this age as to constitute the most pertinent single attribute for defining 'romantic' poetry.[109] The major commentators, as we have seen, no longer defended these materials as ornaments of the literal sense which serve the need for moving and pleasing the reader without violating the requirement for truth. Instead, they made them out to be, like all the essential materials of poetry, the natural expression of imagination when re-creating the world of sense under the stimulus of passion. But the earlier conflict between 'the true world' of science and the allegedly 'false world' of poetry did not cease on that account. It merely shifted its grounds and broadened its scope; and we find romantic poets faced with the charge that, by the all-comprehensive criterion of science, the passions are deceptive and the products of imagination illusory, hence that poetry is false not only in its parts, but in its entirety.

XI

SCIENCE AND POETRY
IN ROMANTIC CRITICISM

AUDREY. I do not know what poetical is. Is it honest in deed and word? Is it a true thing?

TOUCHSTONE. No, truly; for the truest poetry is the most feigning.

SHAKESPEARE, *As You Like It,* III, iii.

We shall be safe while we are aware that virtue and beauty are as intimately related as beauty and truth, and as eternally distinct.

HARRY LEVIN, 'Literature as an Institution.'

THE TRADITIONAL SCHEME underlying many eighteenth-century discussions of the relation of poetry to other discourse may be summarized in this way: poetry is truth which has been ornamented by fiction and figures in order to delight and move the reader; the representation of truth, and nothing but the truth, is non-poetry; the use of deceptive or inappropriate ornaments is bad poetry. For Wordsworth and the Wordsworthians, on the other hand, the equivalent paradigm was this: poetry is the overflow or expression of feeling in an integral and naturally figurative language; the representation of fact unmodified by feeling is non-poetry; the simulated or conventional expression of feeling is bad poetry. The first-order criterion now becomes the relation of a poem to the feeling and state of mind of the poet; and the demand that poetry be 'true' (in the sense of correspondence to 'the known order and course of affairs') gives way to the demand that poetry be 'spontaneous,' 'genuine,' and 'sincere.' If poetry is not 'obviously the spontaneous outburst of the poet's inmost feeling,' declared John Keble, it is 'not poetry at all.'[1]

An index to this change is the kind of non-poetic discourse most frequently set up as the antithesis, or logical opposite, of poetry. Ever since Aristotle, it had been common to illuminate the nature of poetry, conceived as an imitation of an action, by opposing it to history. History, it was frequently said, represents single actions in past time, whereas poetry represents the typical and recurrent forms of actions, or else it represents events not as they are, but as they might be, or ought to be. But to Wordsworth, the appropriate business of poetry is 'to treat of things not as they *are* . . . but as they *seem* to exist to the *senses,* and to the *passions,*' and as worked upon 'in the spirit of genuine imagination.'[2] The most characteristic subject matter of poetry no longer consists of actions that never happened, but of things modified by the passions and imagination of the perceiver; and in place of history, the most eligible contrary to poetry, so conceived, is the unemotional and objective description characteristic of physical science. Wordsworth therefore replaced the inadequate 'contradistinction of Poetry and Prose' by 'the more philosophical one of Poetry and Matter of Fact, or Science,'[3] and similar formulations became a standard port of departure in romantic discussions of poetry. It is the 'union of passion with thought and pleasure,' Coleridge said, in his characteristic combination of the new with the old, 'which constitutes the essence of all poetry, as contradistinguished from science, and distinguished from history civil or natural.'[4] Or as John Stuart Mill phrased it, the 'logical opposite' of poetry is 'not prose, but matter of fact or science.'[5]

Such statements are intended only as logical devices for isolating and defining the nature of poetic discourse. The prevalence of philosophic positivism, however, which claimed the method of the natural sciences to be the sole access to truth, tended to convert this logical into a combative opposition. To some writers, it seemed that poetry and science are not only antithetic, but incompatible, and that if science is true, poetry must be false, or at any rate, trivial. The eighteenth-century critic had been concerned mainly with justifying the occasional deviations from empirical possibility in the preternatural and figurative components of a poem. For various nineteenth-century critics, the problem became more crucial and comprehensive. If poetry as a whole is not 'true,' in the way that science is true, how are we to demonstrate that it is a legitimate use of language, and that it serves any useful purpose in men's lives? And in an age increasingly science-minded, what assurance is there that poetry will even endure? These continue to be the pivotal questions of much aesthetic speculation in the present day. What R. S. Crane recently called 'the morbid obsession of [the "new critics"] with the problem of justifying and preserving poetry in an age of science'[6] is a legacy from the prepossessions and preoccupations of some of the new critics of the earlier nineteenth century.

i. Positivism vs. Poetry

We may begin with Jeremy Bentham for a bald and uncompromising statement of the basic points at issue. Bentham represents a culmination of a tendency of the new philosophy in England, empirical in pretension and practical in orientation, to derogate poetry in comparison with science. Distortion of reality is congenital to poetry; and this distortion, it was said, is justified in so far as it conduces to pleasure and profit, and (it is to be hoped) after a fashion not unduly mischievous. Bacon admitted that 'it appeareth that poesie serveth and conferreth to magnanimitie, moralitie, and to delectation,' but observed that 'imagination hardly produces sciences; poesy (which in the beginning was referred to imagination) being to be accounted rather as a pleasure or play of wit than a science.'[7] We remember that Thomas Hobbes, who with some charity might himself be accounted a poet, found it advisable to bring poetry closer to fact by maintaining that 'the Resemblance of truth is the utmost limit of Poeticall Liberty.' Although Locke followed Hobbes in excepting poetry from his condemnation of the deceptiveness of 'figurative speeches and allusions,' he did so grudgingly. 'I confess, in discourses where we seek rather pleasure and delight than information and improvement, such ornaments . . . can scarce pass for faults.' In his *Thoughts Concerning Education,* Locke (echoing the opinion of the Elizabethan Puritans that poets are wantons, as well as useless) does not disguise his contempt for the unprofitableness of a poetic career, either to the poet himself or (by implication) to others. Parnassus is 'a pleasant Air, but a barren Soil,' and 'Poetry and Gaming, which usually go together, are alike in this too, that they seldom bring any Advantage but to those who have nothing else to live on.'[8] Asked for his judgment of poetry, Newton answered: 'I'll tell you that of Barrow:—he said, that poetry was a kind of ingenious nonsense.'[9]

Bentham carried to their extreme two aspects of earlier empiricism: (1) the determination of all value by the 'felicific calculus' of measuring pleasures against pains, and (2) the reform of language, primarily through the elimination or control of 'fictitious entities,' so that its primary function of stating objective truth might be most completely achieved. Accordingly, Bentham asked two questions concerning poetic discourse: 'Is it of any use?' and 'Is it true?'

To the first question Bentham replied that poetry is indubitably useful, because it affords pleasure to some human beings. As he put it, in perhaps the strangest of all definitions of poetry, a poem is a work

purely and commonly avowedly fictitious, put together, and commonly sent abroad for the purpose of affording what is called amusement; amusement—viz. an assemblage of pleasures of a particular sort, commonly termed pleasures of the imagination.

In so far as it gives pleasure, Bentham submits, poetry is as valuable as push-pin—or, if less valuable, only because it gives pleasure to a lesser number, for 'everybody can play at push-pin: poetry and music are relished only by a few.' [10]

On the basis of the requirement of truth, however, Bentham discovered in poetry a fatal flaw which, by opening the way to greater ultimate pains, more than cancels the immediate pleasure. John Stuart Mill tells us that Bentham entertained no favor toward poetry because he believed words 'were perverted from their proper office when they were employed in uttering anything but precise logical truth'; one of Bentham's aphorisms was, 'All poetry is misrepresentation.' [11] On his own testimony, the game of push-pin is always innocent, but poetic pleasure is grounded on falsehoods in narration, description, allusion, and moral judgment—all with the end of inciting the emotion against the reason.

Indeed, between poetry and truth there is a natural opposition: false morals, fictitious nature. The poet always stands in need of something false. When he pretends to lay his foundations in truth, the ornaments of his structure are fictions; his business consists in stimulating our passions, and exciting our prejudices. Truth, exactitude of every kind, is fatal to poetry.[12]

So, after many centuries, we find Jeremy Bentham following Plato's lead by banishing the lying poets from his society, which, like that of Plato, was to be planned and administered by philosophers. He even recalls Plato's indictment of Homer for degrading the gods. 'Homer is the greatest of poets. . . Can any great advantage be derived from the imitation of his gods and heroes?' [13]

These aspects of Bentham's thought were exploited by a highly vocal and polemically expert band of followers, especially in that section of the Utilitarian organ, the *Westminster Review* (established in 1824) which Bentham grudgingly surrendered to what he called 'literary insignificancies.' To the first issue of the journal, Peregrine Bingham contributed an article which 'did a good deal,' according to John Mill, 'to attach the notion of hating poetry to the writers in the Review.' [14] Bingham expressed the opinion that by exercising the imagination, poetry vitiates the reason, whereas 'truth can be attained no otherwise than by a minute and comprehensive examination of all the details of a subject.' To this he coupled the charge that the medieval revival in literature is a symptom and stimulus of political reaction, enticing us back along the path of progress to a time when 'the mind of man was still cradled in infantine weakness.'[15] As the greatest happiness of the greatest number became increasingly identified with technological progress, material accretion, and social reform, even the modest hedonistic utility that Bentham had not denied to poetry was sometimes stripped from it. 'Ledgers do not keep well in rhyme,' wrote one reviewer, 'nor are three-deckers built by songs, as towns were of yore'; and in what way is the pursuit of poetry 'to conduce towards cotton-spinning; or abolishing the poor-laws?'[16] Added to this was an attack on literary culture as an instance of what a later exponent of the tradition was to name 'conspicuous waste.' The acquisition of literature, it was said, serves pre-eminently as an emblem of wealth and of exemption from any useful employment. The reviewer of Irving's *Tale of a Traveller,* for example, maintained that to identify their circle and ward off encroachers, the upper class 'have studiously avoided cultivating a taste for any thing that savours of exertion or utility; and as far as they take any pains, bestow it in a contrary direction.' They send their children to learn to make Latin verses and acquire archaic styles for no better reason than to 'distinguish them from those who have been unable to spend some thousands of pounds in its acquirement.'[17]

In this context, Peacock's sketch of the status of poetry in *The Four Ages of Poetry* may be viewed as an application of standard Utilitarian theory by a writer who was the friend of James Mill, and the ablest of the literary contributors to the *Westminster Review*—though the reader is never comfortably certain whether the voice is that of Peacock or of Peacock's Mr. MacQuedy, habitué of Crotchet Castle and representative of the Steam Intellect Society. Poetry employs an ornamental and figurative language to arouse emotions, at the expense of truth, for 'pure reason and dispassionate truth would be perfectly ridiculous in verse.' 'As the sciences of morals and of mind advance towards perfection,' and 'as reason gains the ascendancy in them over imagination and feeling,' poetry necessarily falls behind. 'We may here see how very slight a ray of historical truth is sufficient to dissipate all the illusions of poetry'; and unfortunately for the poet, we know 'that there are no Dryads in Hyde-Park nor Naiads in the Regents-canal.' Peacock goes Bentham one better, and dismisses poetry as totally without utility in the present day. 'It cannot claim the slightest share in any one of the comforts and utilities of life of which we have witnessed so many and so rapid advances'; and the poet 'in the present state of society is . . . a waster of his own time, and a robber of that of others.' [18]

As John Mill points out in his *Autobiography,* by no means all Utilitarians were enemies of poetry, and G. L. Nesbitt, in his *Benthamite Reviewing,* reminds us also that men passionately dedicated to reform, who perceived that the great bulk of genteel literature was solidly dedicated to the status quo, 'were excusably concerned with living by bread when, as they often pointed out, bread was so dear that many people could not buy any.' [19] But the various writers who did follow the lead of Bentham picked out and sharpened the two fundamental questions for contemporary apologists for poetry. First, how to justify its departures from truth to fact? And second, how to demonstrate its utility for mankind?

ii. Newton's Rainbow and the Poet's

Keats was one among the lovers of poetry to whom it seemed that matter of fact or science is not only the opposite but the enemy of poetry, in a war in which the victory, even the survival, of poetry is far from certain. Keats's utterances on poetry are written with the unphilosophical informality and the volatility of mood proper to the personal letter; it is difficult to interpret many of them, and perilous to take any one as his ultimate judgment. But it is clear that in one recurrent frame of mind, Keats could not accept Wordsworth's opinion that the valid aim of poetry is to treat things 'as they *appear.*' To the younger poet, either poetry treats things as they are, or it is a delusion.

'Kean! Kean!' exclaimed Keats, reviewing a Shakespearean performance in December of 1817. 'Have a carefulness of thy health . . . in these cold and enfeebling times! . . . for romance lives but in books. The goblin is driven from the hearth, and the rainbow is robbed of its mystery.' [20] Only a week later, at Benjamin Haydon's 'immortal dinner,' Charles Lamb, as chance would have it, introduced the same subject. In 'a strain of humour beyond description,' Lamb abused the painter for putting Newton's head into his 'Jerusalem.' 'And then he and Keats agreed that [Newton] had destroyed all the poetry of the rainbow by reducing it to the prismatic colors.' [21] If the toast of 'confusion to mathematics' which they drank on that occasion was a Bacchic whimsy, the idea nevertheless haunted Keats, and after some eighteen months, he presented it again, entirely seriously, in *Lamia.* The central figure of the serpent-woman in that poem is a complex and equivocal symbol, but the familiar passage on Newton's rainbow demonstrates that in part it signifies the poet's vision, in opposition to the scrutiny of 'cold philosophy,' which, Keats says, will 'empty the haunted air' and 'unweave the rainbow.' The opinion that Newton's analysis of the rainbow in his *Opticks* is of special concern to the poet had a long history, but the opinion that this analysis was a threat to poetry was much later in origin. A summary of the poetic fortunes of Newton's rainbow will clarify both Keats's ideas and the romantic shift in the concept of poetry.

Various seventeenth-century theorists agreed that the new philosophy had eliminated from the poet's world the materials of myth and superstition; but, it was held, if science took something away from literature, it gave something more valuable in return. It is high time, as Thomas Sprat said, to dismiss the wit of ancient fable and religion, especially since 'they were only *Fictions* at first: whereas *Truth* is never so well express'd or amplify'd, as by those Ornaments which are *Tru* and *Real* in themselves.' He adds:

It is now therefore seasonable for *Natural Knowledge* to come forth, and to give us the *understanding* of new *Virtues* and *Qualities* of things. . . This charitable assistance *Experiments* will soon bestow.[22]

Various writers of the following century consented to both these observations. As late as 1777, for example, John Aikin wrote *An Essay on the Application of Natural History to Poetry* in which, on the principle that 'nothing can be really beautiful which has not truth for its basis,' he decried modern use of 'the trite and hackneyed fables of ancient poets,' and recommended instead 'the accurate and scientific study of nature.'[23] Accordingly, the physical discoveries of Newton, far from being viewed as inimical to poetry, were embraced as a rich source of poetic material which combined the rare advantages of novelty and the best scientific sanction. In *Newton Demands the Muse,* Marjorie Nicolson shows the extent to which eighteenth-century poets joyously pillaged Newton's *Opticks*. The enlightened few, wrote James Thomson in *The Seasons,* are above 'superstitious horrors,' and poetry, fortunately, is now tutored by philosophy, 'Effusive source of evidence and truth.'[24] These days only the ignorant swain views the rainbow as a 'bright Enchantment,' for thanks to Newton, the sage-instructed eye sees it as a 'showery Prism,' unfolding the 'various Twine of Light.'[25] And in his poem 'To the Memory of Sir Isaac Newton,' Thomson declares that the rainbow is but the more poetic, now that its mystery has surrendered to intellect, on the apparent principle that Newton alone has looked on beauty bare:

> Did ever poet image ought so fair,
> Dreaming in whispering groves by the hoarse brook?
>
> .   .   .   .
>
> How just, how beauteous the refractive law.[26]

In the same poem, Thomson himself exemplifies the process of transforming Newton's refractive law into poetry. Newton had written:

This Image or Spectrum PT was coloured, being red at its least refracted end T, and violet at its most refracted end P, and yellow green and blue in the intermediate Spaces.[27]

Poetized, this becomes: Newton 'Untwisted all the shining robe of day,' and

> To the charm'd eye educed the gorgeous train
> Of parent-colours. First the flaming Red
> Sprung vivid forth; the tawny Orange next . . .
> . . . and then, of sadder hue,
> Emerged the deepen'd Indigo, as when
> The heavy-skirted evening droops with frost;
> While the last gleamings of refracted light
> Died in the fainting Violet away.

Truth is made poetry through the current device of 'ornamenting' statements by means of simile, personification, and incipient allegory. In this way, Thomson puts back into the prismatic phenomena the sensuousness and drama—even, in the implied figure of the scientist as a magician, the mystery and enchantment—which Newton had methodically excluded from his experimental observations.

But some amateurs of romance, acknowledging the efficacy of the new philosophy in dispelling what are admitted illusions, were not so certain the gains outweighed the losses. For 'a great deal of good sense,' Bishop Hurd wrote in 1762, we have exchanged 'a world of fine fabling; the illusion of which is so grateful to the *charmed Spirit*. . .' [28] Thomas Warton maintained that the improvement of society in general is at the expense of poetry. For 'ignorance and superstition . . . are the parents of imagination'; and by 'the force of reason and inquiry,' poetry gained 'much good sense, good taste, and good criticism,' but at the cost of parting 'with incredibilities that are more acceptable than truth, and with fictions that are more valuable than reality.' [29]

Before the end of the eighteenth century, we begin also to hear suggestions that not only scientific skepticism, but the scientific description of natural phenomena, is the enemy rather than the benefactor of poetry. Mrs.

Montagu in 1769 agreed with Hurd that the new philosophy, by dispelling fables, destroyed the golden age of poetry; she also indicated her doubt about Thomson's assertion that by 'untwisting' light and the rainbow, Newton had opened new materials for poetry. 'Echo, from an amorous nymph, fades into voice, and nothing more; the very threads of Iris's scarf are untwisted. . .'[30] Twenty years later, a writer who signed himself 'GHM,' defining poetry as 'the language of passion and feeling,' attributed its decline both to the loss of a 'strong propensity to the marvellous' and to the incompatibility between the habitual perceptions of scientist and poet. In a statement anticipating passages in both Wordsworth and Keats, he said that, as opposed to poetical description,

philosophical description exhibits objects as they really are; their reasons and causes, not as they appear to be. . . Thus a botanist disregards the beauty of a flower, and is only intent upon its internal construction.

For this reason poetry was at its height when writers described the 'beauty of the works of nature, before Newton discovered the true system of the world.' 'As soon as men begin to philosophise, they become less fit for works of imagination.'[31]

In the next century, the Utilitarian opponents of poetry, as we saw, accepted the proposition that the progress of reason and imagination, of science and poetry, must be inversely related, and merely modulated the threnody into a song of thanksgiving. One man who was both historian and poet put this theory of cultural history in its most unqualified form, and explicitly on the grounds that the scientific and poetic descriptions of the sensible world are not reconcilable. 'We think,' wrote Macaulay in 1825, 'that, as civilisation advances, poetry almost necessarily declines.' The progress of knowledge is from 'particular images to general terms,' and from concrete perception to generalization, but 'analysis is not the business of the poet. His office is to portray, not to dissect.' After his apodeictic fashion, Macaulay leaves us no alternative. No person in these enlightened times can write or even enjoy poetry 'without a certain unsoundness of mind.' The truth of poetry is 'the truth of madness. The reasonings are just; but the premises are false.'

We cannot unite the incompatible advantages of reality and deception, the clear discernment of truth and the exquisite enjoyment of fiction.[32]

In this historical context, we can discriminate the separate strands in Keats's indictment of science in *Lamia*.

> Do not all charms fly
> At the mere touch of cold philosophy?
> There was an awful rainbow once in heaven:
> We know her woof, her texture; she is given
> In the dull catalogue of common things.
> Philosophy will clip an Angel's wings,
> Conquer all mysteries by rule and line,
> Empty the haunted air, and gnomed mine—
> Unweave a rainbow, as it erewhile made
> The tender-person'd Lamia melt into a shade.

First, cold philosophy dispels the charms of myth and fairy-lore—it empties 'the haunted air, and gnomed mine'—but like Hurd and Warton, Keats cannot agree with James Thomson that such materials are easily spared. Also, philosophy breaks down the rainbow into its physical components and causes; 'we know her woof, her texture,' and this knowledge 'unweaves' the rainbow, and substitutes a dull, abstract thing for the beauty and mystery of concrete perception. In maintaining, with Lamb, that Newton 'had destroyed all the poetry of the rainbow by *reducing* it to the prismatic colors,' Keats accedes to the fallacy (in which he has been joined by numerous professional philosophers) that, when a perceptual phenomenon is explained by correlating it with something more elementary than itself, the explanation discredits and replaces the perception—that only the explanation is real, and the perception illusory. And to Keats, if not to Thomson, the ability to versify and dramatize the new scientific 'truths' was no adequate payment for the 'life of sensations,' and the 'indolent' surrender to the sensuous concrete which is integral to his characteristic poetry.

As a consequence, the presumed conflict between the poet's vision and the scrutiny of the scientist raises the question not merely, as in Hurd and Warton, of poetic decline, but, as in Macaulay, of poetic survival. For Keats, in his moments of depression, accepts the exclusive disjunction of some contemporary positivists: either science or poetry; if Newton describes reality, then the poet's rainbow is an illusion; if science in general is true, then poetry in general is false. The basic theme in *Lamia,* as in so many of Keats's major poems, is that of illusion against reality. And after all, as Keats himself sets up the story, Apollonius, the cold philosopher, was right. Lamia was indeed, as he said, a serpent; and all her furniture, according to the passage from Burton's *Anatomy of Melancholy* which Keats quoted as his source, 'no substance but mere illusions.' So far as Lamia and her phantom palace symbolize the poet's view of the world, they reflect Keats's opposition

of the 'authenticity of the imagination' to 'consequitive reasonings,' and his
recurrent fear that the subject matter of his poetry is the vestige of a magical
view of the world, vulnerable to the cold stare of reason.

Keats exemplifies a romantic tendency to shift the debate about the discrepancy between science and poetry from the question of poetic myth and
fable to the difference between the visible universe of concrete imaginative
observation and that of scientific analysis and explanation. Whether they
agreed or disagreed with Keats's conclusions, many writers followed his procedure by pointing to an object traditionally consecrated to poets—if not
the rainbow, then the glow-worm, the lily, the star, or the cloud—in order
to contrast its traditional poetic depiction to its description in the science of
optics, biology, astronomy, or meteorology.

In the same year that *Lamia* appeared (1820), Thomas Campbell's 'To
the Rainbow' gave further evidence that the happy marriage of poetry and
Newton's *Opticks* was ending in recriminations and divorce. 'I ask not
proud Philosophy,' Campbell cried, 'To teach me what thou art.'

> Can all that optics teach, unfold
>   Thy form to please me so,
> As when I dreamt of gems and gold
>   Hid in thy radiant bow?
>
> When Science from Creation's face
>   Enchantment's veil withdraws,
> What lovely visions yield their place
>   To cold material laws!

Nine years later Poe's sonnet 'To Science' echoed phrases from *Lamia,* and
posed even more bitterly the conflict between the 'dull realities' of Science
with its 'peering eyes,' and the consecration and the poet's dream.

> Hast thou not torn the Naiad from her flood,
> The Elfin from the green grass, and from me
> The summer dream beneath the tamarind tree? [33]

Almost all the important romantic theorists commented on the disparity
between imaginative and scientific perception, and deplored the disproportionate development of the latter in recent times. It is important to recognize, however, that by far the greater number refused to admit that there
is any inherent and inescapable conflict between science and poetry, or that
scientific progress necessarily entails poetic decline. The most common procedure was to regard these, when properly employed, as parallel and com-

plementary ways of seeing, and to hold that while analysis yields truth, this is not the whole truth, and cannot, in vigorous and flexible minds, unweave the poet's rainbow.

Wordsworth, for example, had been present at Haydon's famous dinner, but with customary prudence had refused, pending further inquiry, to drink Keats's toast. 'And don't you remember,' Haydon wrote to Wordsworth, many years after the event, 'Keats proposing "Confusion to the memory of Newton," and upon your insisting on an explanation before you drank it, his saying: "Because he destroyed the poetry of the rainbow by reducing it to a prism." ' [34] The caution is understandable in a poet who had a Renaissance responsiveness to the grandeur of man's intellectual exploration of the universe, and who was also aware of the contributions of the 'nature-study' fostered by science to the power of exact description which he held to be a necessary, if not sufficient condition for poetry. Later Wordsworth was to expand a brief allusion to Newton's statue at Cambridge into three lines surpassing all the windy panegyrics of the preceding century—

> Newton with his prism and silent face,
> The marble index of a mind for ever
> Voyaging through strange seas of Thought, alone.[35]

We must not mistake Wordsworth's contempt, in his *Lyrical Ballads,* for the 'meddling intellect' which murders to dissect, and for the 'philosopher' who would peep and botanize on his mother's grave, for a general attack against science. Other passages make it clear that these lines are to be read only as his judgments against the fallacy of misplaced abstraction, and against the scientist whose laboratory habits are so indurate that he continues to analyze where only imagination and feeling are relevant.[36] In the Preface to these *Ballads,* Wordsworth said that poetry, being grounded in man's emotional nature, incorporates, and has nothing to fear from the narrower 'knowledge' of science: 'Poetry is the first and last of all knowledge—it is as immortal as the heart of man.' In this passage of sustained eloquence, he not only echoes the opinion of Sprat and the eighteenth-century enthusiasts that poetry will assimilate 'the remotest discoveries of the Chemist, the Botanist, or Mineralogists,' but passes beyond them to herald the poetry of *machinisme* and the industrial revolution. 'If the labours of Men of science should ever create any material revolution . . . in our condition,' the poet 'will be at his side, carrying sensation into the midst of the objects of the science itself.' [37] I must add Wordsworth's comment to Isabella Fenwick, which can be read as a belated rebuttal to Keats's toast at the Haydon dinner:

Some are of the opinion that the habit of analysing, decomposing, and anatomizing is inevitably unfavourable to the perception of beauty. . . We are apt to ascribe to them that insensibility of which they are in truth the effect and not the cause. . . The beauty in form of a plant or an animal is not made less but more apparent as a whole by more accurate insight into its constituent properties and powers.[38]

Wordsworth's published comments established the common pattern of his day for resolving the supposed conflict between poetry and science. Shelley, who was as saturated in scientific fact as any eighteenth-century versifier of physics or botany, held no commerce with the opinion that what he called 'Science and her sister Poesy,' need be at odds. Scientific developments, he admits, have momentarily outgrown the assimilative capacity of our imagination and creative faculty; but he follows Wordsworth, although on other philosophical grounds, in envisioning poetry as the larger class 'which comprehends all science, and that to which all science must be referred.'[39] And in America, William Cullen Bryant, writing in 1825, refused to deplore the supersession of 'mysteries,' myth, and superstition by the 'new wonders and glories' of science, nor see any reason that, 'because the chemist prosecutes his science successfully, therefore the poet should lose his inspiration.'[40]

To Coleridge the threat of science to poetry lay, more profoundly, in the mistaken and unbounded metaphysical pretensions of atomism and mechanism—in Coleridge's view, a useful working hypothesis for physical research which had been illicitly converted first into fact, and then into a total world-view. In his alternative statement in terms of the faculties and their functions: that which produced the diverse errors and *malaises* of the mechanistic eighteenth century, in politics, morals, and art, was 'the growing alienation and self-sufficiency of the understanding,' which, as the faculty of 'the science of *phenomena*,' is properly employed only 'as a tool or organ.'[41] But Coleridge, who was himself an amateur biologist, of course proposes not the disjunctive, 'Either poetry or science,' but the conjunctive, 'Both poetry and science.' Though a poem is opposed in aim to 'works of science,' the highest poetry is the largest, most inclusive utterance—'the whole soul of man [in] activity'—including both the emotional and the rational elements, and involving the faculty productive of science as an integral though subordinate part of the mind's whole working: 'with the subordination of the faculties to each other, according to their relative worth and dignity.'[42]

Of special interest to us are writers who, like Keats, contrast the poetic and scientific descriptions of the same natural object, but use the instance to demonstrate that the two outlooks are compatible and mutually invulnerable. In a passage which Keats probably remembered while writing *Lamia,* Hazlitt admitted that, as a matter of historical fact, 'it cannot be concealed' that the progress of knowledge and experimental philosophy 'has a tendency to circumscribe the limits of the imagination, and to clip the wings of poetry'; yet, he added, scientific and poetic observation are not exclusive alternatives. His example is the glow-worm, which the naturalist carries home to find it 'nothing but a little grey worm.' The poet visits it at evening when

it has built itself a palace of emerald light. This is also one part of nature, one appearance which the glow-worm presents, and that not the least interesting; so poetry is one part of the history of the human mind, though it is neither science nor philosophy.[43]

Leigh Hunt preferred the lily as his example:

Poetry begins where matter of fact or of science ceases to be merely such, and to exhibit a further truth; that is to say, the connexion it has with the world of emotion, and its power to produce imaginative pleasure. Inquiring of a gardener, for instance, what flower it is that we see yonder, he answers, 'a lily.' This is matter of fact. The botanist pronounces it to be of the order of 'Hexandria Monogynia.' This is matter of science. . .

> The plant and flower of *light,*

says Ben Jonson; and poetry then shows us the beauty of the flower in all its mystery and splendor.

That the ghost of Newton's *Opticks* continues to haunt this issue Hunt indicates by setting out to prove, through a most tenuous argument, that as 'light, undecomposed, is white; and as the lily is white . . . the two things, so far, are not merely similar, but identical.' [44] Hunt returned to the problem repeatedly in his essays; and his championship of Keats did not restrain him from taking strong issue, the year after his friend's death, with the rainbow passage in *Lamia.* He does not agree, Hunt says, 'that modern experiment has done a deadly thing to poetry,' for the man who thinks he is no poet 'as soon as he finds out the physical cause of the rainbow . . . need not alarm himself; he was none before.' [45]

To cite one other instance: Soon after his own conversion to Wordsworth and poetry, John Stuart Mill was confronted with the argument of John Roebuck, the Benthamite, that to cultivate feelings through imagination 'was only cultivating illusions.' 'In vain I urged on him,' Mill tells us, 'that the imaginative emotion which an idea, when vividly conceived, excites in us, is not an illusion, but a fact, as real as any of the other qualities of objects.'

To demonstrate the possibility of alternative perspectives, as each becomes relevant, Mill chose for his representative example the cloud.

The intensest feeling of the beauty of a cloud lighted by the setting sun, is no hindrance to my knowing that the cloud is vapour of water, subject to all the laws of vapours in a state of suspension; and I am just as likely to allow for, and act on, these physical laws whenever there is occasion to do so, as if I had been incapable of perceiving any distinction between beauty and ugliness.[46]

To validate the natural object seen by the poet, as against the object described by the natural scientist, became almost routine in Victorian criticism. 'The difference,' wrote Ruskin, 'between the mere botanist's knowledge of plants, and the great poet's or painter's knowledge of them' is that 'the one notes their distinctions for the sake of swelling his herbarium, the other, that he may render them vehicles of expression and emotion.'[47] In Matthew Arnold's version:

It is not Linnaeus or Cavendish or Cuvier who gives us the true sense of animals, or water, or plants, who seizes their secret for us, who makes us participate in their life; it is Shakespeare, with his

'daffodils
That come before the swallow dares, and take
The winds of March with beauty. . .'[48]

The belief, nevertheless, persists, even in our day, that the advances of science must shrink the province of poetry; and we still hear echoes of Keats's fallacy, that scientific description discredits the phenomena for which it is intended to account. As Keats had lamented the rainbow and the haunted air, so D. H. Lawrence has lamented:

'Knowledge' has killed the sun, making it a ball of gas, with spots; 'knowledge' has killed the moon. . . How are we to get back Apollo and Attis, Demeter, Persephone, and the halls of Dis?[49]

iii. Poetic Truth and Sincerity

It would have simplified the task of the historian if romantic theorists had ceded the word 'truth' to science, and adopted a different term to characterize poetry. (I. A. Richards has recently tried to do so, without being invidious, by suggesting a distinction between 'the *troth* of poetry' and 'the *truth* of science.') But of course, the power and prestige of 'truth' were too great to make the word dispensable, and nineteenth-century critics, like their neo-classic predecessors, continued to use 'truth' as a poetic norm, but with implicit semantic shifts which reflect the changes in their underlying theory. A frequent dialectic procedure was to allow truth to science, but to bespeak a different, and usually an even more weighty and important kind of truth, for poetry. It will be useful to block out the areas of significance in typical romantic predications of poetic truth—in those employments, at any rate, in which the context is at least roughly definitive.[50] It should be remarked that in practice, the following were neither fixed nor mutually exclusive senses of the word. In this most tangled of philosophical issues, a critic did not often proceed systematically from precise and stable definitions, but applied the term approximately and variably, in the significance most suitable to the question at hand.

(1) Poetry is true in that it corresponds to a Reality transcending the world of sense.

According to Blake, poetry is the vehicle of Vision, and 'Vision or Imagination is a Representation of what Eternally Exists, Really & Unchangeably,' outside 'the things of Vegetative & Generative Nature.'[51] For Shelley, one of the ways in which 'a poem is the very image of life expressed in its eternal truth' is that it accords with 'the unchangeable forms of human nature' and with the 'naked and sleeping beauty' of the 'forms' of the material world.[52] The poet, Carlyle proclaims, penetrates 'into the sacred mystery of the Universe,' revealing the Idea under appearance, the Infinite behind the finite, Eternity looking through time; and the poems of Shakespeare are 'truer than reality itself, since the essence of unmixed reality is bodied forth in them under more expressive symbols.'[53]

Statements in a similar vocabulary can occasionally be found in other critics, especially at moments of rhetorical climax, and have been greatly emphasized by later commentators. A recent writer has even built a book concerning English romantic poetry around the thesis that the major poets 'agreed on one vital point: that the creative imagination is closely connected with a peculiar insight into an unseen order behind visible things.'[54] It is clear that a salient and distinctive aspect of romantic theory was the recourse to the imagination (and to other powers and modifications of the mind) for the principles of the making and judging of poetry; that is, in fact, the thesis on which I have based this survey of romantic criticism. But it is, I think, ultimately misleading to put Blake and Shelley, instead of Wordsworth and Coleridge, at the intellectual center of English romanticism, and consequently to make the keystone of romantic aesthetics the doctrine that the poetic imagination is the organ of intuition beyond experience, and that poetry is a mode of discourse which reveals the eternal verities. One can, of course, adduce the statement in Wordsworth's *Prelude* that Imagination

> Is but another name for absolute power
> And clearest insight, amplitude of mind,
> And Reason in her most exalted mood.

Whatever may be its unspoken implications for poetry, however, such a passage is unique in Wordsworth, who was in this matter an honest heir to the centuries-old English tradition of empiricism. In his explicit prose comments, he says instead that 'imagination is a subjective term: it deals with objects not as they are, but as they appear to the mind of the poet'; [55] and his extended analysis of the poetic imagination, in the Preface of 1815, is in thorough accord with English sensational psychology. Coleridge, translating almost literally from Schelling, says that art imitates the *natura naturans,* the 'spirit of nature'; but in context, this turns out to be a way of saying that the 'idea,' or generative element in poetic composition, accords with that in external nature, in such a way as to insure a likeness between the evolving principle of a poem and what is vital and organic in nature. Coleridge does not make special cognitive claims for poetry. In his philosophy, it is specifically the reason, not the secondary imagination, which is 'the organ of the supersensuous,' with 'the power of acquainting itself with invisible realities or spiritual objects,' [56] with the result that religion and poetry remain distinct. The reason may co-operate with imagination, so that some religious statements are poetic, and the truth of 'invisible realities' sometimes finds expression in poetry; but this is an incidental question of subject matter, and not a matter of the essence of poetry. As for Keats, he was too occupied with the solid world of concrete objects to find congenial any aesthetic philosophy of a reality beyond sense. Keats's distinctions between 'the authenticity of imagination' and that which 'can be known for truth by consequitive reasoning,' [57] as well as the diverse asseverations about the equivalence of beauty and truth which have teased his commentators out of thought, do not justify an explanation in terms of 'an unseen order behind visible things.' If one had to venture an interpretation, one might list Keats's characteristic use of poetic 'truth' as fitting more readily the following classification, in which truth becomes primarily an attribution of value:

(2) Poetry is true in that poems exist, are very valuable, and are the product and cause of actual emotional and imaginative experiences.

What Keats wrote, in that extraordinary letter to Benjamin Bailey, was this:

I am certain of nothing but of the holiness of the Heart's affections and the truth
of Imagination— What the imagination seizes as Beauty must be truth—whether
it existed before or not—for I have the same Idea of all our Passions as of Love
they are all in their sublime, creative of essential Beauty. . . The Imagination
may be compared to Adam's dream—he awoke and found it truth.[58]

(The allusion is of course to Milton's Adam who dreamed of Eve and,
waking, found her to exist.) In an essay designed to prove 'The Realities of
Imagination' which Keats's friend, Leigh Hunt, wrote three years later, the
assertion becomes a virtual tautology—'This poem is true' is equivalent to
'This poem exists, and has effects':

'Whatever is, is.' Whatever touches us, whatever moves us, does touch and does
move us. We recognise the reality of it, as we do that of a hand in the dark. . .

The poets are called creators, because with their magical words they bring
forth to our eyesight the abundant images and beauties of creation. . . But
whether put there or discovered . . . there they are. . . If a passage in *King
Lear* brings the tears into our eyes, it is real as the touch of a sorrowful hand. If
the flow of a song of Anacreon's intoxicates us, it is as true to a pulse within us
as the wine he drank.[59]

(3) Poetry is true in that it corresponds to objects which contain, or have
been altered by, the feelings and imagination of the observer.

The eye of the scientist passively receives, while the eye of the poet receives
what it has itself supplemented or modified; scientific discourse reflects data,
but poetic discourse reflects data with emotional additions. As Wordsworth
put it, the ability faithfully to describe 'things as they are in themselves . . .
unmodified by any passion or feeling existing in the mind of the describer,'
though a power 'indispensable to a Poet, is one which he employs only in
submission to necessity, and never for a continuance of time. . .'[60] In this we
have the most common romantic differentiation between poetic and scientific
truth, grounded on the concept of the projective and modifying mind for
which the many alternative formulations have been inventoried in the third
chapter. To the passages cited there, I shall only add this one from Hazlitt.
Poetry, he says, 'is strictly the language of imagination.'

This language is not the less true to nature, because it is false in point of fact;
but so much the more true and natural, if it conveys the impression which the
object under the influence of passion makes on the mind.[61]

(4) Poetry is true in that it corresponds to concrete experience and integral objects, from which science abstracts qualities for purposes of classification and generalization.

This view is the converse of the preceding one. Instead of poetry originating in emotional additions to the facts dealt with by science, it is said to be the representation of plenary fact from which science, for its special purposes, pulls out a limited number of stable, and, therefore, manageable attributes. The world immediately given in experience is held to include not only primary and secondary qualities—size, shape, color, odor—but also the 'tertiary qualities' of beauty, emotion, and feeling-tones; and from this point of view, the supposed 'data' of science turn out to be high-order abstractions.

The background of this concept was the emphasis, in the latter eighteenth century, on the need for descriptive poetry to represent the particular and detailed, rather than the general or the abstract aspects of nature. Joseph Warton, who warned against the evidences in contemporary poetry of departing from *'true* and *lively,* and *minute,* representations of Nature, and of *dwelling in generalities,'* set up a distinction between poetry and history which nominally reversed Aristotle's assertion that poetic 'statements are of the nature of universals, whereas those of history are singulars.' According to Warton:

A minute and particular enumeration of circumstances judiciously selected, is what chiefly discriminates poetry from history, and renders the former, for that reason, a more close and faithful representation of nature than the latter.[62]

By the time Macaulay wrote his essay on Milton (1825), this distinction between poetry and history had been converted into the distinction between poetry and science. Language, Macaulay wrote, is best fitted for the poet in its rudest state, because nations 'first perceive, and then abstract. They advance from particular images to general terms.' This is

a change by which science gains and poetry loses. Generalization is necessary to the advancement of knowledge, but particularity is indispensable to the creatures of imagination.[63]

An able article 'On the Application of the Terms Poetry, Science, and Philosophy,' which appeared anonymously in *The Monthly Repository* for 1834, elaborates and systematizes this point of view. The author approvingly cites Wordsworth on the contradistinction between 'Poetry and matter-of-fact or Science,' but interprets the distinction in his own way. The 'essential attribute of all true Poetry' is the adherence 'to individual reality,' and the 'avoidance of the abstract and the general.' Its object is 'by the exhibition of objects, in their individual proprieties, as they act upon the senses and feelings, to excite emotion.' At the far extreme from poetry is science:

Science is any collection of general propositions, expressing important facts concerning extensive classes of phenomena; and the more abstract the form of expression, the more purely it represents the general fact, to the total exclusion of such individual peculiarities as are not comprised in it—the more perfect the scientific language becomes.[64]

Poetic statements thus represent the fuller, but correspondingly narrower, reality, and the statements of science a more meager reality, but a reality including a much greater number and variety of individual instances.

Poetry presents us with partial sketches, and transient glimpses of nature as it really exists; Science is the effort of reason to overcome the multiplicity of impressions, with which nature overwhelms it, by distributing them into classes, and by devising forms of expression, which comprehend in one view an infinite variety of objects and events.[65]

At the end of this development we may place a passage from J. S. Mill's review of Carlyle's *The French Revolution,* which Mill wrote in 1837, four years after he published his two articles on the nature of poetry. For terms such as 'particular,' Mill substitutes the old scholastic word, 'concrete'; and he describes the concrete object as including affective qualities as part of the given-in-experience. In poetry, and in poetic history,

not falsification of the reality is wanted, not the representation of it as being anything which it is not; only a deeper understanding of what it is; the power to conceive, and to represent, not the mere outside surface and costume of the thing, nor yet the mere logical definition, and *caput mortuum* of it—but an image of the thing itself in the concrete, with all that is lovable or hateable or admirable or pitiable or sad or solemn or pathetic, in it, and in the things which are implied in it.[66]

This difference between the concretely full and the abstractly partial, it is hardly necessary to add, has become the most popular distinction between poetry and science among those critics who hold that both modes of discourse yield knowledge. Poetry, John Crowe Ransom has said, is 'knowledge by images, reporting the fulness or particularity of nature,' while scientific truth 'is the abstracted or universal aspect of the picture'; and poetry 'is probably true in the commonest sense of true: verifiable, based on observation.'[67]

(5) Poetry is true in that it corresponds to the poet's state of mind: it is 'sincere.'

This usage was the natural corollary of an expressive poetics. It claims truth by the drastic expedient of reversing the criterion, so that poetic truth is to the poet what scientific truth is to the world without. By such a maneuver Wordsworth was able to achieve the paradox that poetry, though 'contradistinguished' from science, is itself a kind of science.

Words, a Poet's words more particularly, ought to be weighed in the balance of feeling. . . For the Reader cannot be too often reminded that Poetry is passion: it is the history or science of feelings. . .[68]

Later, Walter Pater transparently revealed the semantic tactic involved, in his restatement of Wordsworth's influential distinction. In science, the whole aim is 'the transcribing of fact,' but literary art 'is the representation of such fact as connected with soul, of a specific personality in its preferences, its volition and power.' For both modes of language, the sole standard is truth; but Pater's truth is Janus-faced, looking both out and in:

In the highest as in the lowliest literature, then, the one indispensable beauty is, after all, truth:—truth to bare fact in the latter, as to some personal sense of fact, diverted . . . from men's ordinary sense of it, in the former; truth there as accuracy, truth here as expression, that finest and most intimate form of truth, the *vraie vérité*.[69]

In this second sense, Pater's 'truth' approximates 'sincerity' which, significantly, began in the early nineteenth century its career as the primary criterion, if not the *sine qua non,* of excellence in poetry. The word, it would appear, had been popularized at the time of the Protestant Reformation to connote the genuine and unadulterated Christian doctrine, and secondarily, a lack of pretence or corruption in him who affirms a religious and moral sentiment.[70] One bridge by which this standard passed over from religious ethics to literary criticism was the discussion of pious poetry. In his essays 'Upon Epitaphs,' Wordsworth set as one of his aims 'to establish a criterion of sincerity, by which a writer may be judged.'

In this species of composition above every other, our sensations and judgments depend upon our opinion or feeling of the Author's state of mind. Literature is here so far identified with morals . . . that nothing can please us, however well executed in its kind, if we are persuaded that the primary virtues of sincerity, earnestness and a moral interest in the main object are wanting.[71]

John Keble, who viewed all poetry on the analogy of religion, proposed sincerity as the identifying mark of 'primary poetry,' no less than of moral character. 'For a simple and sincere mind declares itself by almost exactly the same manifestations, whether in poetry or in the common talk of daily life.' The first requirement is 'to thine own self be true'; this is one of the several touchstones 'of genuine and keenly felt emotion, as well as of transparently sincere poetry.' [72] In a passage from Carlyle, we can follow the movement of 'truth' as it turns on its heel to become equivalent to 'sincerity':

The excellence of Burns is . . . his *Sincerity*, his indisputable air of Truth. . . The passion that is traced before us has glowed in a living heart. . . To every poet, to every writer, we might say: Be true, if you would be believed. Let a man but speak forth with genuine earnestness the thought, the emotion, the actual condition of his own heart. . .[73]

For Carlyle, sincerity was the chief measure of his hero, whether in the avatar of prophet, priest, or poet. 'It is, after all, the first and last merit in a book'; and so judged, Dante's *Comedy*, for example, turns out to be 'at bottom, the sincerest of all Poems; sincerity, here too, we find to be the measure of worth. It came deep out of the author's heart of hearts.' [74]

In all these passages, sincerity retains its moral connotations, even in its use as aesthetic norm: good poetry is a test of character. But sincere could also be employed, with the moral overtones dampened, as the near equivalent of 'spontaneous' and 'natural,' in opposition to what is artful or contrived. So Leigh Hunt commends 'the passionate sincerity in general of the greatest early poets, such as Homer and Chaucer, who . . . were not perplexed by a heap of notions and opinions, or by doubts how emotion ought to be expressed.' In a comment on Keats, Hunt appeals jointly to spontaneity and sincerity in order to condemn neo-classic artifice. And though he retains the neo-classic standards of truth and fitness, these, too, are reversed to signify an aptness to the poet's unforced state of mind:

Let the student of poetry observe, that in all the luxury of the Eve of St. Agnes there is nothing of the conventional craft of artificial writers . . . no substitution of reading or of ingenious thoughts for feeling or spontaneity; no irrelevancy or unfitness of any sort. All flows out of sincerity and passion. The writer is as much in love with the heroine as his hero is; his description of the painted window, however gorgeous, has not an untrue or superfluous word. . .[75]

Sincerity, with persisting moral and characterological implications, became a favorite Victorian test of literary virtue. In *The Principles of Success in Literature*, George Henry Lewes posited 'The Principle of Sincerity,' comprising the 'qualities of courage, patience, honesty, and simplicity,' as one of the three laws of literature; and even for Matthew Arnold, the essential condition for 'supreme poetical success' was 'the high seriousness which comes from absolute sincerity.' [76] In reaction, such a deliberate craftsman as Henry

James (following the lead of proponents of *l'art pour l'art*) disengaged sincerity from its associations both with spontaneity and with morality and made it the indispensable attribute of a specifically aesthetic conscience and integrity. Eschewing 'the dull dispute over the "immoral" subject and the moral,' James proposed as 'the one measure of the worth of a given subject . . . is it valid, in a word, is it genuine, is it sincere, the result of some direct impression or perception of life?' Or as this criterion was later defined, in a purportedly anti-romantic sense, by T. E. Hulme:

If it is sincere in the accurate sense, when the whole of the analogy is necessary to get out the curve of the feeling or thing you want to express—there you seem to me to have the highest verse, even though the subject be trivial and the emotions of the infinite far away.[77]

iv. Poetry as neither True nor False

Most of the instances catalogued so far involve the assumption that there are two valid uses of the term 'truth,' one applicable to science and the other to poetry, each making reference to different elements or aspects of reality. Rigid empirical monists like Bentham, on the other hand, recognized only one kind of reality and one valid meaning of truth, and hence maintained that the single alternative to scientific truth is falsity. In a few writers, who wished to save both the premises of positivism and the validity of poetry, we can detect the emergence of an alternative theory. Poetry, they suggest, is neither true nor false, because, as the expression of feeling, it proffers no assertions about reality. and is therefore outside the jurisdiction of the criterion of truth. It will be recalled from the preceding chapter that some critics had earlier freed the supernatural poem from the obligation to conform to the empirical order of nature, on the philosophical premise that such a poem is its own created world, with its own beings and own laws. Now, on semantic and logical grounds, we find an attempt to disengage all poetic statements, even those purporting to describe existing objects of the empirical world, from any necessary correspondence to external fact.

John Stuart Mill found himself in a position without parallel to judge the soundness of Bentham's views on poetry. To test for posterity the efficacy of their principles, James Mill and Bentham brought up—or rather, fabricated—the boy to be what he himself called 'a mere reasoning machine.' As a result, John Mill tells us, he remained 'theoretically indifferent' to poetry, and read it only as a vehicle for truths in verse.[78] At the age of twenty-one came Mill's breakdown, from which the reading of Wordsworth's poetry helped him to recover. 'If John Mill were to get up to heaven,' observed Carlyle, 'he would hardly be content till he had made out how it all was.' [79] Having newly discovered the importance both of the feelings and of poetry, he at once set himself to re-cast the bases of his total philosophy to accommodate both these phenomena. For help in this reconstruction Mill applied himself to the writings of Goethe, Coleridge, and Wordsworth. The chief results of his speculations Mill incorporated in the two articles on poetry which he published in 1833. In them he undertook as a major task to refute the opinion of the doctrinaire Benthamite that poetry is trivial, and possibly pernicious, because it is not true.

He begins by opposing poetry to science in terms of a difference in objective. Science 'addresses itself to the belief,' poetry 'to the feelings.' But eloquence no less than poetry expresses and appeals to the emotions. To rehabilitate poetry, Mill is at pains to make a further distinction between these two modes of discourse, for in Bentham, as in earlier philosophers, the distrust of rhetoric as a method for marshaling the passions against the reason had flowed over into a distrust of poetry.[80] Mill's point is that the orator expresses feeling as a means to effect belief or action, whereas the poet expresses feeling as an end in itself. Thus, when the poet

turns round and addresses himself to another person; when the act of utterance is not itself the end, but a means to an end—viz. by the feelings he himself expresses, to work upon the feelings, or upon the belief, or the will of another . . . then it ceases to be poetry, and becomes eloquence.[81]

If the object of poetic discourse is not to assert propositions, or instigate belief, but expression for its own sake, what is its logical character? Although Mill had already begun work on his *System of Logic,* his dealings with this issue in his papers on poetry are indefinite and variable. But he indicates that poetry differs from science in being exempt from the criterion of truth; science asserts a proposition for assent or denial, but poetry merely presents an object for aesthetic contemplation. In Mill's own words, the former 'addresses itself to belief,' and 'acts by presenting a proposition to the understanding, the other by offering interesting objects of contemplation to the sensibilities.' Poetry may involve descriptions of objects, or include 'a truth which may fill a place in a scientific treatise,' but even so, 'the poetry is not in the object itself, nor in the scientific truth itself, but in the state of mind in which the one and the other may be contemplated.' He goes on to say (though not with the utmost perspicuity):

If a poet is to describe a lion, he will not set about describing him as a naturalist would, nor even as a traveller would, who was intent upon stating the truth, the whole truth, and nothing but the truth. He describes him by *imagery,* that is by suggesting the most striking likenesses and contrasts which might occur to a mind contemplating the lion, in the state of awe, wonder, or terror, which the spectacle naturally excites, or is, on the occasion, supposed to excite. Now this is describing the lion professedly, but the state of excitement of the spectator really. The lion may be described falsely or in exaggerated colours, and the poetry be all the better; but if the human emotion be not painted with the most scrupulous truth, the poetry is bad poetry, *i.e.* is not poetry at all, but a failure.[82]

At the root of the difficulty in Mill's account is his use of the same word, 'describe,' both for what language conveys of the qualities of the lion and what it conveys of the feelings of the speaker who contemplates the lion. Mill's reader properly wonders why, if the poet's underlying aim is to describe his own feelings, he should choose to complicate matters by bringing in a lion. 'The Philosophy of Poetry,' by Alexander Smith of Banff, which parallels Mill's approach, avoids the equivocation by distinguishing clearly between 'the description of the emotion, or the affirmation that it is felt,' and 'the expression of emotion,' or 'the language in which that emotion vents itself.' The difference, as Smith points out, is that between the statement, 'I feel pain,' and a groan.[83] Poetry characteristically expresses, rather than describes the poet's emotion; and though it describes—or makes reference to—external matters of fact, it is not its office to make assertions about them. Thus Smith is able to strike a sharper and more consistent discrimination than Mill between assertive and expressive language: prose asserts propositions of fact, while poetry alludes to facts as an indispensable means of specifying and conveying feelings. 'In prose, the main purpose of the writer or speaker is to inform, or exhibit truth. . . In poetry, on the other hand, the information furnished is merely subsidiary to the conveyance of the emotion.' For both the poet and reader of poetry, therefore, poetry is properly non-propositional, and its assertional truth or falsity is not a relevant consideration.

The poet—the reader of poetry—seeks not to know truth as distinct from falsehood or error—to reason or draw inferences—to generalize—to classify—to distinguish; he seeks for what may move his awe—admiration—pity—tenderness. . . Whether these scenes or these incidents are real or fictitious, he cares not. . . Behold . . . the philosophical enquirer, whose aim it is to *know*—to discover and communicate truth. . . Compare . . . the poet, whose aim it is to feel, and convey his feeling.[84]

We had earlier critical precedent for the removal of poetic sentences from the realm of assertion. 'Now, for the Poet,' Philip Sidney had replied to the Benthams of his day, 'he nothing affirmes, and therefore never lyeth. For, as I take it, to lye is to affirme that to be true which is false.' But as often in the history of criticism, a surface likeness veils a fundamental difference. Conceiving poetry as 'an arte of imitation' with the end 'to teach and delight,' Sidney had as his aim to validate narrative fiction, or 'feigning,' by demonstrating its moral intention and efficacy. According to his logic of poetic statements, therefore, the poet embodies a true 'generall notion' in an invented 'particular example,' and so, under the transparent guise of making declarative historical assertions, actually poses to the reader an implicit optative or imperative—the poet 'not labouring to tell you what is, or is not, but what should or should not be.' [85] To both John Mill and Alexander Smith, the essence of poetry is not narrative fiction (which on the contrary, as Mill says, is merely a non-poetic element frequently combined with poetry, though 'perfectly distinguishable'); [86] while any least evidence of an intention to work upon the will of the reader is enough to demonstrate that discourse is not poetry, but 'eloquence.' The essence and end of poetry is simply the poet's expression of feeling; hence poetry is independent, in its component sentences, from any judgment of truth to fact.

Mill, unlike Smith, also considered the matter from the point of view of the reader, and here the question becomes, not that of the intention of the poet, nor of the logical status of the poetic sentence, but of the role of belief or assent in the aesthetic experience. Mill wrote in his Diary:

Those who think themselves called upon, in the name of truth, to make war against illusions, do not perceive the distinction between an illusion and a delusion. A delusion is an erroneous opinion—it is believing a thing which is not. An illusion, on the contrary, is an affair solely of feeling, and may exist completely severed from delusion. It consists in extracting from a conception known not to be true, but which is better than the truth, the same benefit to the feelings which would be derived from it if it were a reality.[87]

To extract 'the same benefit to the feelings which would be derived from it if it were a reality'—here, in more than embryonic development, is I. A. Richards' influential distinction between 'scientific statement, where truth is ultimately a matter of verification,' and the 'emotive utterance' of the poet, which is composed of sentences which look like statements, but are actually 'pseudo-statements.' As Richards puts the matter, 'it is not the poet's business to make true statements,' for 'a pseudo-statement is "true" if it suits and serves some attitude.' 'Pseudo-statements to which we attach no belief and statements proper such as science provides cannot conflict.' [88]

In differentiating illusion from delusion, or the 'believing a thing which is not,' Mill probably had in mind Coleridge's description in the *Biographia Literaria* of 'that *illusion,* contra-distinguished from *delusion,* that *negative* faith, which simply permits the images presented to work by their own force, without either denial or affirmation of their real existence by the judgment.' [89] Coleridge's doctrine of the willing suspension of disbelief is cited by modern proponents of the view that truth or falsity is irrelevant to poetic statement; [90] and indeed, the logical and psychological concepts are natural correlates.

In the eighteenth century, discussions of belief in relation to poetry had centered on two problems—the state of mind of the audience at a theatrical performance,[91] and the psychological conditions that will make supernatural subject matter acceptable to a reader.[92] Coleridge followed these traditions by applying his analysis of the aesthetic attitude both to drama and to poems of the supernatural. The effect of stage presentations is 'a sort of temporary half-faith,' a 'negative belief,' voluntarily sustained; the state of mind is analogous to that in a dream, where 'we neither believe it, nor disbelieve' since 'any act of judgment, whether affirmation or denial, is impossible.' [93] In the *Biographia Literaria,* Coleridge applied the famous phrase, 'that willing suspension of disbelief for the moment, which constitutes poetic faith,' specifically to the reception of poetic characters which are 'supernatural, or at least romantic.' [94] But it is clear that Coleridge also enlarged his theory to account for the reader's attitude to realistic characters and events as well. In the quotation with which this section began, for example, the negative faith 'without either denial or affirmation' is adduced in a discussion of Wordsworth's 'adherence to *matter-of-fact* in characters and incidents,' and of the reader's attitude toward epics based on Scriptural history. Later in the *Biographia Literaria,* Coleridge uses the same concept to explain the effectiveness of characters such as Milton's Satan and Shakespeare's Iago and Edmund.[95]

In Coleridge's theory, then, theatrical representations, and the characters and events presented in narrative poetry, supernatural or realistic, when these have been properly managed by the author, are enjoyed without either affirming or denying their relation to fact. Recent discussions of the place of belief in poetry, however, have focussed rather on the state of mind in which we read seeming statements or generalizations—particularly, theological statements ('In Thy will is our peace'), or basic moral and philosophical generalizations ('Ripeness is all'). Did Coleridge also hold that poetic statements of such timeless religious and philosophical doctrines are properly read without either denial or affirmation?

There is evidence that he did, but within limits. Coleridge defined a poem as 'proposing for its *immediate* object pleasure, not truth,' and he chided Wordsworth for destroying the fundamental distinction, in some of his poems, 'not only between a poem and prose, but even between philosophy and works of fiction' by proposing truth for his immediate object, instead of pleasure.[96] Especially relevant is Coleridge's discussion of Wordsworth's Immortality Ode. Four decades after its composition Wordsworth himself protested against the conclusion that he meant in it to inculcate a belief in 'a prior state of existence.'

Archimedes said that he could move the world if he had a point whereon to rest his machine. Who has not felt the same aspirations as regards the world of his own mind? Having to wield some of its elements when I was impelled to write this Poem on the 'Immortality of the soul,' I took hold of the notion of pre-existence as having sufficient foundation in humanity for authorizing me to make for my purpose the best use of it I could as a Poet.[97]

There is a difference, to Wordsworth, between a forthright doctrinal assertion and a 'notion' taken by someone for his special purpose 'as a Poet'— one which is neither affirmed nor denied, apparently, but used as a poetic postulate on which to raise a structure incorporating elements taken from his inner experience. Some fifteen years earlier Coleridge had said very much the same thing, in the course of a critique of Wordsworth which that poet had taken very much to heart.

But the ode was intended for such readers only as had been accustomed . . . to feel a deep interest in modes of inmost being, to which they know that the attributes of time and space are inapplicable and alien, but which yet can not be conveyed save in symbols of time and space. For such readers the sense is sufficiently plain, and they will be as little disposed to charge Mr. Wordsworth with believing the Platonic pre-existence in the ordinary interpretation of the words, as I am to believe, that Plato himself ever meant or taught it.[98]

There are thus at least some apparent doctrinal elements in poetry which are read as assertions only by mistake, and which are properly entertained rather than assented to or denied. Yet, unlike some recent proponents, Coleridge set strict bounds to the application of this principle. Only a few pages earlier, he had circumstantially attacked those sentences in the Ode which address a six-year child as 'best Philosopher' and 'Seer blest,'

> On whom those truths do rest,
> Which we are toiling all our lives to find.

'In what sense,' Coleridge wants to know, 'is a child of that age a *philosopher*? In what sense does he *read* "the eternal deep"?' [99] Coleridge proposes that we suspend our disbelief of the postulate of metempsychosis, which is at least intelligible as a theory, though we need not credit it beyond the poem. But, it would seem, he will not grant the dispensation to poetic predications which, like these, do not have sufficient grounds for the mind to repose on even temporarily, for purposes of access to the poet's projected 'modes of inmost being.'

v. The Use of Romantic Poetry

The need to justify the existence of poets and the reading of poetry becomes acute in times of social strain. The English romantic era, which occurred hard upon the French Revolution, amid war and the rumors of war, and in the stress of social and political adjustments to the Industrial Revolution, was comparable to our own period between the two World Wars. Yet this was the very time when theorists of poetry, surrendering up traditional definitions of poetry as a mirror of truth, or as an art for achieving effects on an audience, concurred in referring poetry to the motives, emotion, and imagination of the individual poet. If poetry is the overflow of the poet's feeling, or is expression for its own sake—above all if poetry, in Mill's term, is 'soliloquy,' or as Shelley said, is the product of a poet singing 'to cheer [his] own solitude with sweet sounds'—it would seem that communication becomes inadvertent, and the audience merely eavesdroppers. The problem arises, of what use is such an activity, to anyone but the poet himself? When the Utilitarians attacked poetry for being an outmoded luxury trade, or a functionless vestige of a primitive mentality, they rudely posed a charge to which the romantic apologists, by the nature of their premises, were peculiarly vulnerable.

As a preliminary to considering their dealings with this problem, let us divide theories of poetic value into two broadly distinguishable classes:

(1) Poetry has intrinsic value, and as poetry, only intrinsic value. It is to be estimated by the literary critic solely as poetry, as an end in itself,

without reference to its possible effects on the thought, feeling, or conduct of its readers.

(2) Poetry has intrinsic value, but also extrinsic value, as a means to moral and social effects beyond itself. The two cannot (or at least, should not) be separated by the critic in estimating its poetic worth.

The first proposition is the common element in the diversified formulations of art for art's sake. Various tendencies in German criticism of the later eighteenth century converged toward this point of view. The analogy between a work of art and a natural organism opened the possibility that its end might be considered as simply the existence of the whole; as Goethe put it, 'a work of art must be treated like a work of nature,' in that 'the value of each must be developed out of itself and regarded in itself.' [100] The heterocosmic analogy, originally developed to free a poem from conformity to the laws of this world by envisioning it as its own world, with its own laws, suggested to some critics that it is also its own end. As early as 1788, Karl Philipp Moritz, writing 'On the Formative Imitation of the Beautiful,' claimed that a work of art is a microcosm, parallel in its structure to that of nature, and like that, 'a self-sufficient whole,' and beautiful only in so far as 'it has no need to be useful.' Utility is superfluous, accidental, and can neither increase nor diminish beauty; this 'needs no end, no purpose for its presence outside itself, but has its entire value, and the end of its existence, in itself.' For the energy of the artist

creates for itself its own world, in which nothing isolated has a place, but every thing is after its own fashion a self-sufficient whole.[101]

In Kant's *Critique of Judgment,* written two years later, the propensity is to separate the faculties of knowing, willing, and feeling, and therefore to isolate from each other the realms of truth, goodness, and beauty. And as Kant denied teleology to nature, so did he to its analogue, the work of natural genius. Beauty is purposiveness (*Zweckmässigkeit*) perceived in an object 'apart from the representation of an end'; and the observation of beauty is entirely 'contemplative,' 'disinterested,' indifferent to the reality of the object, and free from any 'representation of its utility.' [102] From Kant's writings, Schiller developed his own theory that art is the result of a 'play-impulse,' a free play of the faculties without ulterior motive; that an appearance is aesthetic only in so far as it 'expressly renounces all claim to reality'; and that this appearance must be enjoyed without desire and without 'asking after its purpose.' [103] In the course of the nineteenth century,

French writers, followed by the English, responded defiantly to the indifference or hostility of a utilitarian society by working these elements into the formula of *l'art pour l'art*. 'Humanity hates us,' wrote Flaubert, 'we shall not serve it and we shall hate it'; and he announced a retreat from this world, and consecration to 'la religion de la beauté.' [104] The varied slogans of this movement all announced that the value of a work of art is co-terminous with itself. The end of a poem is not to instruct, nor even to please. The end of a poem is simply to exist, or to be beautiful; and all art, as Wilde said, is quite useless.

The second proposition, which denies that the judgment of poetic value ought to be severed from the consideration of the effects on the reader, is one which had been held, with few exceptions, by critics from the ancient Greeks through the eighteenth century. In England, with much less qualification than in Germany, it continued to be affirmed by poets and critics right through the romantic period. 'If the English romanticist is a priest of art,' as Hoxie N. Fairchild has remarked, 'he remains a parish priest with a cure of souls.' [105] Keats, in his worship of beauty and his almost priestly consecration to his art, as well as in the character of many of his poems, came closest to the theory and practice of later proponents of art for the sake of art. He declared in his letters that the poet's approach to good and evil ends only 'in speculation'; he admonished Shelley that if we regard purpose as the God of poetry, then '*an artist* must serve Mammon'; and he derogated Wordsworth's compositions on the ground that 'we hate poetry that has a palpable design upon us.' [106] But his other comments make it clear that Keats objected to the manner in which Shelley and Wordsworth sought their moral and social effects, rather than to the inclusion of these effects in the judgment of poetic greatness. For Keats, the opposition between beauty and utility, like that between beauty and truth, seems to have been one more aspect of the division against himself which was resolved only by his premature death. He is the first great poet to exhibit that peculiarly modern malady—a conscious and persistent conflict between the requirements of social responsibility and of aesthetic detachment. In his earliest important poem, Keats had predicted that he must one day desert the realm of Flora and old Pan to 'find the agonies, the strife Of human hearts.' In his latest, he reiterated that none can usurp the height, 'But those to whom the miseries of the world Are misery.' His own poetry has been confessedly that of a visionary and a dreamer, without benefit 'to the great world,' but the greatest art cannot be judged solely by the standards of art:

> Sure not all
> Those melodies sung into the world's ear
> Are useless; sure a poet is a sage;
> A humanist, physician to all men.[107]

But if early nineteenth-century writers made the traditional claim that valid art has a use beyond beauty, it was with an important and characteristic difference. Earlier critics had defined poems primarily as a delightful way of changing the reader's mind; the Wordsworthian critic, primarily as a way of expressing his own. The product effects human betterment, but only by expressing, hence evoking, those states of feeling and imagination which are the essential conditions of human happiness, moral decision, and conduct. By placing the reader in his own affective state of mind, the poet, without inculcating doctrines, directly forms character.

The nature of the shift in perspective becomes clear if we set a comment of Dr. Johnson on Shakespeare beside a comment of Wordsworth on himself. According to Johnson, Shakespeare's primary defect is that he

> is so much more careful to please than to instruct, that he seems to write without any moral purpose. . . His precepts and axioms drop casually from him . . . he carries his persons indifferently through right and wrong, and at the close . . . leaves their examples to operate by chance.[108]

The author must set out purposefully to achieve a moral end, by the statement of doctrine and the presentation of moral instances; and the presumption is, as Pope had put it, that the audience will

> Live o'er each scene, and be what they behold.[109]

In his turn, Wordsworth conceived of the poet's social function no less gravely than had Spenser or Milton before him. He wrote to Sir George Beaumont, 'Every great Poet is a Teacher: I wish either to be considered as a Teacher, or as nothing.' [110] 'The poet,' he says, writes under the necessity 'of giving pleasure'; and in his defense of Robert Burns, Wordsworth attributed to poetry a double aim which, in a phrase that was already archaic, he denominated 'to please, and to instruct.' [111] And each of his own poems, he tells us in the Preface to the *Lyrical Ballads,* 'has a worthy *purpose.*' But this purpose, Wordsworth makes clear, in the act of composition itself, is neither deliberate nor doctrinal. 'For all good poetry is the spontaneous overflow of powerful feelings,' which by prior thought have become so habitually associated with important subjects that, by obeying blindly and mechanically the impulses of those habits, we shall describe objects, and utter sentiments, of such a nature, and in such connexion with each other, that the understanding of the Reader must necessarily be in some degree enlightened, and his affections strengthened and purified.[112]

In contrast to Johnson, Wordsworth maintains that, instead of telling and demonstrating what to do to become better, poetry, by sensitizing, purifying, and strengthening the feelings, directly *makes* us better. A great poet, he said, ought 'to rectify men's feeling . . . to render their feelings more sane, pure, and permanent.' And again: one man is superior to another in so far as he 'is capable of being excited without the application of gross and violent stimulants,' so that 'to endeavour to produce or enlarge this capability is one of the best services in which, at any period, a writer can be engaged.' In the statement that follows, Wordsworth indicated his explicit justification of poetry, the 'science of feelings,' in the contemporary world of international crises and social dislocation. Such a service, he said, was never more needed 'than at the present time,' when the brunt of 'great national events,' and 'the uniformity of . . . occupations' attendant upon 'the increasing accumulation of men in cities' tend to reduce the mind 'to a state of almost savage torpor.'[113] Nor, in this substitution of a predominantly emotional for a predominantly doctrinal culture, does the poet lose one whit of his Renaissance glory. Wordsworth's poet, 'carrying everywhere with him relationship and love, binds together by passion and knowledge the vast empire of human society, as it is spread over the whole earth, and over all time.' He utters feelings which by 'habitual and direct sympathy' connect 'us with our fellow beings,' so that, while the 'Man of science' converses with 'particular parts of nature,' the poet 'converses with general nature.' As a result, Wordsworth (in a way that anticipates, but reverses, Shelley's figure of the poet as a solitary nightingale) is able to claim that it is the scientist who cherishes truth 'in solitude,' and the poet who sings 'a song in which all human beings join with him.'[114]

The moral concept here implied—the turn from the rational and calculative ethics of Bentham and the early Godwin to other eighteenth-century theorists who had put sensibility and sympathy at the center of morality—comes out clearly, even crudely, in a disciple of Wordsworth, Thomas De Quincey. 'The literature of power' is opposed to 'the literature of knowledge.' 'What do you learn from "Paradise Lost"? Nothing at all.' Yet poetry, as a kind of emotional gymnastics, retains a non-cognitive moral efficacy:

Were it not that human sensibilities are ventilated and continually called out into exercise by . . . literature as it recombines these elements in the mimicries of poetry, romance, &c., it is certain that like any animal power or muscular energy falling into disuse, all such sensibilities would gradually droop and dwindle. It is in relation to these great *moral* capacities . . . that the literature of power . . . lives and has its field of action. . . And hence the pre-eminence over all authors that merely *teach* of the meanest that *moves,* or that teaches, if at all, indirectly *by* moving.[115]

To Plato, poetry had been bad because it aroused the emotions, and to Aristotle, poetry (or at least tragedy) had been good because it purged the emotions. To the Wordsworthian, poetry, because it strengthens and re-fines the emotions, is among the greatest of goods.

Shelley's 'Defence of Poetry' was by far the most elaborately reasoned and most impressive of all romantic statements of the moral value of poetry. In his *Four Ages of Poetry* Peacock may have used the Utilitarian argu-ments only as a satiric norm, but his arguments were taken very seriously by Shelley, who wanted intensely to unite the functions of poet and reformer. While still very young, Shelley had insisted that 'poetical beauty ought to be subordinate to the inculcated moral,' and that poetry ought to be 'a pleas-ing vehicle for useful and momentous instruction.'[116] The prefaces to his longer poems, however, show a mounting depreciation of teaching by moral proposition until, in the preface to *Prometheus Unbound,* he says flatly, 'Didactic poetry is my abhorrence.' He acknowledges, nonetheless, that he has not given up his 'passion for reforming the world.'[117]

A few years later, he set out in the 'Defence of Poetry' to show how poetry may achieve moral and social improvement without directly affecting 'a moral aim,' or attempting 'to teach certain doctrines.' In part, he explains this effect Platonically. Since the 'unchangeable forms' on which a poem is mod-eled incorporate not only the beautiful, but also the true and the good, poems that are beautiful automatically teach by moral contagion. Thus Homer's auditors admired, 'until from admiring, they imitated, and from imitation they identified themselves with the objects of their admiration.'[118] But after his wont, Shelley then transfers the discussion from Platonic forms to the concepts of psychology. He had defined poetry as 'the expression of the imagination,' and imagination, it eventuates, is the organ by which the individual identifies himself with other people. 'The great secret of morals is love; or a going out of our own nature, and an identification of ourselves with the beautiful which exists in thought, action, or person, not our own.'[119]

Shelley's theory is grounded, indeed, on the Eros-lore in Plato's *Symposium*

—'Love,' Shelley said in the same essay, 'found a worthy poet in Plato alone of all the ancients' [120]—but this is patently a Plato interpreted according to the current English psychology of the sympathetic imagination. The phenomenon of *Mitfühlung* had been a subject of intense speculation for a century, not only by sentimentalists, but by the acutest philosophical minds in England, including Hume, Hartley, Adam Smith, and Godwin. By the concept, these men had sought to bridge the gap between atomistic individualism (premised by the empirical philosophy) and the possibility of altruism —in eighteenth-century terms, the gap between 'self-love and social.' [121] And the upshot of Shelley's blend of Plato and English empiricism was, in effect, the antithesis to Diotima's recommendation in the *Symposium* that we disengage ourselves from the people and things of this world and, by a ladder of ascending abstractions, achieve the highest good in an other-worldly 'contemplation of beauty absolute.' [122] In complete contrast, Shelley conceives the highest good to lie in a progressive abolition of self-detachment and self-sufficiency, culminating in the identification of the one man with all men outside himself.

A man, to be greatly good, must imagine intensely and comprehensively; he must put himself in the place of another and of many others; the pains and pleasures of his species must become his own. The great instrument of moral good is the imagination; and poetry administers to the effect by acting upon the cause.

To Shelley, as to Wordsworth and De Quincey, the importance of poetry as a moral instrument lay in its exercising and strengthening the understructure of moral action, although to his view this is not so much a matter of feeling as of fellow-feeling. It is above all by conveying their power of universal sympathy and understanding that poets, though singing in solitude, become 'the hierophants of an unapprehended inspiration' and 'the unacknowledged legislators of the world.' [123]

Addressing himself now specifically to the Benthamites' claim that poetry lacks utility, Shelley admits the validity of the criterion, but broadens its significance. The utility of technological and scientific knowledge, which 'banishes the importunity of the wants of our animal nature' and disperses 'the grosser delusions of superstition,' is real but transitory. The higher utility, he admonishes Peacock, consists in a pleasure 'durable, universal and permanent'; in this sense, 'whatever strengthens and purifies the affections, enlarges the imagination, and adds spirit to sense, is useful'; and 'those who produce and preserve this pleasure are poets or poetical philosophers.' And Shelley, going over to the attack against the Utilitarians, lays the blame for the progressive ills of society on the great disproportion between the progress of science and that of the poetic and moral imagination in man. The following passage is the high point of Shelley's essay, and it remains a classic indictment of our technological, material, and acquisitive society.

The cultivation of those sciences which have enlarged the limits of the empire of man over the external world, has, for want of the poetical faculty, proportionally circumscribed those of the internal world; and man, having enslaved the elements, remains himself a slave. . . The cultivation of poetry is never more to be desired than at periods when, from an excess of the selfish and calculating principle, the accumulation of the materials of external life exceed the quantity of the power of assimilating them to the internal laws of human nature.[124]

It is fitting to close this subject with the deposition of a Utilitarian, who, in measured words, assigned to poetry a major part in restoring his capacity for happiness. In saying he found in Wordsworth's poems 'the very culture of the feelings' he needed at the time of his breakdown, John Stuart Mill joined a number of excellent readers—including Coleridge, Arnold, and Leslie Stephen [125]—who testify to Wordsworth's 'healing power'; and if it appears to many modern amateurs of poetry that this is to esteem his poems for what is extrinsic, and not truly poetry at all, it is still the praise Wordsworth deliberately sought, and would have valued most highly.

Bentham, Mill's early mentor, had taught that 'in regard to passion . . . repression, not excitation,' is the end to be sought; and James Mill, his son relates, 'regarded as an aberration of the moral standard of modern times . . . the great stress laid upon feeling.' [126] After his discovery of poetry in the late 1820's, John Mill did not abandon the Utilitarian theory of value, but, as Shelley had done, expanded it to include the area to which his vision had been raised. The new Utilitarianism, he wrote to Lytton Bulwer, 'holds feeling at least as valuable as thought, and Poetry not only on a par with, but the necessary condition of, any true and comprehensive Philosophy.' [127]

Like Wordsworth, to whom he turned for criticism as well as poetry, Mill assigned to the poet 'the cultivation of the feelings' and assistance 'in the formation of character.' His psychological grounds are that 'the capacity for strong feeling,' which is supposed to disturb judgment, 'is also the material out of which all *motives* are made,' so that 'energy of character is always the offspring of strong feeling.' [128] A poem is a soliloquy, but the very fact that the poet is oblivious of an audience, because it insures his expressing feelings 'exactly as he has felt them,' [129] serves all the better to warrant the integrity of the emotional effect. And though the momentum of Mill's reaction led him at first to make an untenable opposition between the role of intellection and feeling in poetry, he soon achieved a more balanced view. 'Every great poet . . . has been a great thinker,' he wrote in 1835; and only by fulfilling his emotional endowment by 'systematic culture of the intellect' can a poet achieve

the noblest end of poetry as an intellectual pursuit, that of acting upon the desires and characters of mankind through their emotions, to raise them towards the perfection of their nature.[130]

This is the view of a humanistic literary criticism, and Mill had excellent cause to protest Matthew Arnold's failure of discrimination in 'enumerating me among the enemies of culture.'[131] Indeed, after the farewell to partisanship best represented by his magnificent essays on Bentham and Coleridge, it may be said that Mill, as much as any Englishman, anticipated and concurred in the central tenets of Arnold's humanism—opposition to English insularity and complacency; recommendation of the best that has been thought and said in all ages; indictment of the brutalizing influence of an industrial and commercial society; and insistence on individual values against the growing pressures toward mass conformity.[132]

The parallel between these writers, so different in temper and intellectual training—and by that fact, so widely representative of the main lines of Victorian thinking—can be pursued even farther. In the Victorian age it was finally brought home to the generality of thoughtful men that if the methods and descriptions of natural science are taken to exhaust the possibilities of truth, the statements of traditional religion become no less fictions and illusions than those of traditional poetry. Subjected to 'scientific' criticism, the subjects of revelation were being reduced to the status of those figments of myth and superstition whose flight before the march of experiment had so rejoiced Bishop Sprat and other pious positivists in the seventeenth century. In Arnold's lifetime, the war between science and poetry was openly extending into a war between science and religion; and to save what he thought was essential in religion, Arnold extended to that area a strategy which had already been applied to poetry. We have noted the earlier tendency to yield truth of assertion to science, and to make poetry a realm of emotive discourse independent of factual truth or belief, from which, as Mill had put it, we extract from a conception known 'not to be true . . . the same benefit to the feelings which would be derived from it if it were a reality.' Arnold's innovation (in which, in our time, he has been followed by I. A. Richards) was to place on poetry, with this demonstrated power of achieving effects independently of assent, the tremendous responsibility of the functions once performed by the exploded dogmas of religion and religious philosophy. 'The future of poetry,' he said, and afterward quoted himself as having said, 'is immense.'

Our religion has materialised itself in the fact, in the supposed fact; it has attached its emotion to the fact, and now the fact is failing it. But for poetry the idea is everything. . . Poetry attaches its emotion to the idea; the idea *is* the fact.

And Arnold called on Wordsworth's statements about the relation of poetry to science and knowledge in order to confirm his own opinion that mankind will have to turn more and more to poetry 'to interpret life for us, to console us, to sustain us. Without poetry, our science will appear incomplete; and most of what now passes with us for religion and philosophy will be replaced by poetry.'[133]

In turn, John Mill tells us that when he was young, Bentham had furnished him 'a creed, a doctrine, a philosophy; in one among the best senses of the word, a religion.'[134] When he was older, however, he discovered that poetry 'is the better part of all art whatever, and of real life too'; and, his Benthamite friend and biographer, Alexander Bain, tells with some astonishment, 'he seemed to look upon Poetry as a Religion, or rather as Religion and Philosophy in One.'[135]

This had not been the attitude of the first generation of romantic critics, despite their lofty estimate of the nature of poetry and of its place among the major concerns of life. Arnold cited Wordsworth in his own support; but Wordsworth, though he made poetry, in relation to science, the Alpha and Omega—'the first and last of all knowledge'—did not in his criticism extend its claim to the province of religion. Coleridge very carefully kept science, poetry, and religion distinct by attributing each, primarily, to its appropriate faculty of understanding, imagination, and reason. It was only in the early Victorian period, when all discourse was explicitly or tacitly thrown into the two exhaustive modes of imaginative and rational, expressive and assertive, that religion fell together with poetry in opposition to science, and that religion, as a consequence, was converted into poetry, and poetry into a kind of religion.

Notes

1. Foreword to *Philosophies of Beauty,* ed. E. F. Carritt (Oxford, 1931), p. ix.
2. (5th ed.; London, 1934), pp. 6-7. Richards' later change of emphasis is indicated by his recent statement that ' "Semantics" which began by finding nonsense everywhere may well end up as a technique for widening understanding' (*Modern Language Notes,* LX, 1945, p. 350).
3. For a subtle and elaborate analysis of diverse critical theories, see Richard McKeon, 'Philosophic Bases of Art and Criticism,' *Critics and Criticism, Ancient and Modern,* ed. R. S. Crane (The University of Chicago Press, Chicago, 1952).
4. *Republic* (trans. Jowett) x. 596-7; *Laws* ii. 667-8, vii. 814-16.
5. See Richard McKeon, 'Literary Criticism and the Concept of Imitation in Antiquity,' *Critics and Criticism,* ed. Crane, pp. 147-9. The article exhibits those multiple shifts in Plato's use of the term 'imitation' which have trapped many later commentators as successfully as they once did the rash spirits who engaged Socrates in controversy.
6. *Republic* x. 597.
7. *Laws* vii. 817.
8. *Republic* x. 603-5; *Ion* 535-6; cf. *Apology* 22.
9. *Republic* x. 608.
10. *Poetics* (trans. Ingram Bywater) 1. 1447^a, 1448^a. On imitation in Aristotle's criticism see McKeon, 'The Concept of Imitation,' op. cit. pp. 160-68.
11. *Poetics* 6. 1449^b, 14. 1453^b.
12. Ibid. 8. 1451^a.
13. Ibid. 6. 1450^a-1450^b.
14. Ibid. 4. 1448^b, 17. 1455^a-1455^b.
15. *Republic* iii. 398, x. 606-8; *Laws* vii. 817.
16. *The Works of Richard Hurd* (London, 1811), II, 111-12.
17. Edward Young, *Conjectures on Original Composition,* ed. Edith Morley (Manchester, 1918), pp. 6, 18. See also William Duff, *Essay on Original Genius* (London, 1767), p. 192n. John Ogilvie reconciles creative genius and original invention with 'the great principle of *poetic imitation*' (*Philosophical and Critical Observations on the Nature, Characters, and Various Species of Composition,* London, 1774, I, 105-7). Joseph Warton, familiar proponent of a 'boundless imagination,' enthusiasm, and 'the romantic, the wonderful, and the wild,' still agrees with Richard Hurd that poetry is 'an art, whose essence is imitation,' and whose objects are 'material or animate, extraneous or internal' (*Essay on the Writings and Genius of Pope,* London, 1756, I, 89-90). Cf. Robert Wood, *Essay on the Original Genius and Writings of Homer* (1769), London, 1824, pp. 6-7, 178.
18. 'Originality,' *Gleanings* (London, 1785), I, 107, 109.
19. Charles Batteux, *Les Beaux Arts réduits à un même principe* (Paris, 1747), pp. i-viii.
20. Ibid. pp. 9-27.

21. Ibid. p. xiii. For the important place of imitation in earlier French neo-classic theories, see René Bray, *La Formation de la doctrine classique en France* (Lausanne, 1931), pp. 140ff.

22. Lessing, *Laokoon,* ed. W. G. Howard (New York, 1910), pp. 23-5, 42.

23. Ibid. pp. 99-102, 64.

24. *Three Treatises,* in *The Works of James Harris* (London, 1803), I, 58. Cf. Adam Smith, 'Of the Nature of that Imitation which Takes Place in What Are Called the Imitative Arts,' *Essays Philosophical and Literary* (London, n.d.), pp. 405ff.

25. Henry Home, Lord Kames, *Elements of Criticism* (Boston, 1796), II, 1 (chap. XVIII).

26. Thomas Twining, ed., *Aristotle's Treatise on Poetry* (London, 1789), pp. 4, 21-2, 60-61.

27. Sir Philip Sidney, 'An Apology for Poetry,' *Elizabethan Critical Essays,* ed. G. Gregory Smith (London, 1904), I, 158.

28. Ibid. I, 159.

29. Ibid. I, 159, 161-4, 171-80, 201.

30. See, e.g., his use of Aristotle's statement that poetry is more philosophical than history (I, 167-8), and that painful things can be made pleasant by imitations (p. 171); and his wrenching of Aristotle's central term, *praxis*—the actions which are imitated by poetry—to signify the moral action which a poem moves the spectator to practise (p. 171).

31. Cicero, *De oratore* II. xxviii.

32. 'The Concept of Imitation,' op. cit. p. 173.

33. Horace, *Ars Poetica,* trans. E. H. Blakeney, in *Literary Criticism, Plato to Dryden,* ed. Allan H. Gilbert (New York, 1940), p. 139.

34. *Essays on Poetry and Music* (3d ed.; London, 1779), p. 10.

35. 'Dryden,' *Lives of the English Poets,* ed. Birkbeck Hill (Oxford, 1905), I, 410.

36. 'Parallel of Poetry and Painting' (1695), *Essays,* ed. W. P. Ker (Oxford, 1926), II, 138. See Hoyt Trowbridge, 'The Place of Rules in Dryden's Criticism,' *Modern Philology,* XLIV (1946), 84ff.

37. *The Advancement and Reformation of Modern Poetry* (1701), in *The Critical Works of John Dennis,* ed. E. N. Hooker (Baltimore, 1939), I, 202-3. For Dennis' derivation of specific rules from the end of art, which is 'to delight and reform the mind,' see *The Grounds of Criticism in Poetry* (1704), ibid. pp. 336ff.

38. 'Dissertation on the Idea of Universal Poetry,' *Works,* II, 3-4, 25-6, 7. For a parallel argument see Alexander Gerard, *An Essay on Taste* (London, 1759), p. 40.

39. 'Idea of Universal Poetry,' *Works,* II, 3-4. On the rationale underlying the body of Hurd's criticism, see the article by Hoyt Trowbridge, 'Bishop Hurd: A Reinterpretation,' *PMLA,* LVIII (1943), 450ff.

40. E.g., Batteux 'deduces' from the idea that poetry is the imitation, not of unadorned reality, but of *la belle nature,* that its end can only be 'to please, to move, to touch, in a word, pleasure' (*Les Beaux Arts,* pp. 81, 151). Conversely, Hurd infers from the fact that the end of poetry is pleasure that the poet's duty is 'to illustrate and adorn' reality, and to delineate it 'in the most taking forms' ('Idea of Universal Poetry,' *Works,* II, 8). For purposes of a specialized investigation into the evidences for plagiarism among poets, Hurd himself, in another essay, shifts his ground, and like Batteux, sets out from a definition of poetry as an imitation, specifically, of 'the fairest forms of things' ('Discourse on Poetic Imitation,' *Works,* II, 111).

41. *Johnson on Shakespeare,* ed. Walter Raleigh (Oxford, 1908), pp. 10, 30-31.

42. Ibid. pp. 14, 39. Cf. pp. 11, 31, 33, 37, etc.

43. Ibid. p. 16.

44. Ibid. pp. 31-3, 41.

45. Ibid. pp. 9-12.

46. Ibid. pp. 15-17. See also Johnson's defense of Shakespeare for violating the decorum of character-types, by the appeal to 'nature' as against 'accident'; and for breaking the unities of time and place, by the appeal both to the actual experience of dramatic auditors, and to the principle that 'the greatest graces of a play, are to copy nature and instruct life' (ibid. pp. 14-15, 25-30). Cf. *Rambler* No. 156.

47. Ibid. pp. 20-21. The logic appears even more clearly in Johnson's early paper on 'works of fiction,' in *Rambler* No. 4, 1750 (*The Works of Samuel Johnson*, ed. Arthur Murphy, London, 1824, IV, 23): 'It is justly considered as the greatest excellency of art, to imitate nature; but it is necessary to distinguish those parts of nature which are most proper for imitation,' etc. For a detailed analysis of Johnson's critical methods, see W. R. Keast, 'The Theoretical Foundations of Johnson's Criticism,' *Critics and Criticism,* ed. R. S. Crane, pp. 389-407.

48. See the masterly précis of the complex movements within English neo-classic criticism by R. S. Crane, 'English Neoclassical Criticism,' *Critics and Criticism,* pp. 372-88.

49. *Letters of William and Dorothy Wordsworth: The Middle Years,* ed. E. de Selincourt (Oxford, 1937), II, 705; 18 Jan. 1816.

50. *Early Essays by John Stuart Mill,* ed. J. W. M. Gibbs (London, 1897), p. 208.

51. Ibid. pp. 228, 205-6, 213, 203-4.

52. Ibid. pp. 211-17.

53. Ibid. pp. 222-31.

54. Ibid. pp. 206-7.

55. Ibid. pp. 208-9. Cf. Hulme, 'If it is sincere in the accurate sense . . . the whole of the analogy is necessary to get out the exact curve of the feeling or thing you want to express . . .' ('Romanticism and Classicism,' *Speculations,* London, 1936, p. 138).

56. Review, written in 1835, of Tennyson's *Poems Chiefly Lyrical* (1830) and *Poems* (1833), in *Early Essays,* p. 242.

57. 'Hamlet,' *Selected Essays 1917-32* (London, 1932), p. 145.

58. *Early Essays,* pp. 208-9. Cf. John Keble, *Lectures on Poetry* (1832-41), trans. E. K. Francis (Oxford, 1912), I, 48-9: 'Cicero is always the orator' because 'he always has in mind the theatre, the benches, the audience'; whereas Plato is 'more poetical than Homer himself' because 'he writes to please himself, not to win over others.'

59. Preface to the *Lyrical Ballads, Wordsworth's Literary Criticism,* ed. N. C. Smith (London, 1905), pp. 30, 15-16.

60. *Letters,* ed. Maurice Buxton Forman (3d ed.; New York, 1948), p. 131 (to Reynolds, 9 Apr. 1818).

61. 'Defence of Poetry,' *Shelley's Literary and Philosophical Criticism,* ed. John Shawcross (London, 1909), p. 129.

62. 'Jean Paul Friedrich Richter' (1827), *Works,* ed. H. D. Traill (London, 1905), XXVI, 20.

63. See *Heroes, Hero-Worship, and the Heroic in History,* in *Works,* v, esp. pp. 80-85, 108-12. Cf. Jones Very's indignant denial of the inference that because the general ear takes delight in Shakespeare, 'his motive was to please. . . We degrade those whom the world has pronounced poets, when we assume any other cause

of their song than the divine and original action of the soul in humble obedience to the Holy Spirit upon whom they call' ['Shakespeare' (1838), *Poems and Essays,* Boston and New York, 1886, pp. 45-6].

64. 'Not every kind of pleasure should be required of a tragedy, but only its own proper pleasure. The tragic pleasure is that of pity and fear . . .' (*Poetics* 14. 1453ᵇ).

65. 'The Poetic Principle,' *Representative Selections,* ed. Margaret Alterton and Hardin Craig (New York, 1935), pp. 382-3.

66. See John Crowe Ransom, *The World's Body* (New York, 1938), esp. pp. 327ff., and 'Criticism as Pure Speculation,' *The Intent of the Critic,* ed. Donald Stauffer (Princeton, 1941).

67. 'Moore's *Life of Lord Byron,*' in *Critical and Historical Essays* (Everyman's Library; London, 1907), II, 622-8.

68. *Edinburgh Review,* VIII (1806), 459-60. On Jeffrey's use of an elaborate associationist aesthetics in order to justify the demand that an author or artist have as his aim 'to give as much [pleasure] and to as many persons as possible,' and that he 'fashion his productions according to the rules of taste which may be deduced' from an investigation of the most widespread public preferences, see his *Contributions to the Edinburgh Review* (London, 1844), I, 76-8, 128; III, 53-4. For contemporary justifications, on sociological and moral grounds, for instituting a petticoat government over the republic of letters, see, e.g., John Bowring's review of Tennyson's *Poems,* in *Westminster Review,* XIV (1831), 223; *Lockhart's Literary Criticism,* ed. M. C. Hildyard (Oxford, 1931), p. 66; Christopher North (John Wilson), *Works,* ed. Ferrier (Edinburgh and London, 1857), IX, 194-5, 228.

CHAPTER II

1. *Republic* x. 596.

2. Stephen C. Pepper, *World Hypotheses* (Berkeley and Los Angeles, 1942); see also Dorothy M. Emmet, *The Nature of Metaphysical Thinking* (London, 1945).

3. Coleridge, *Table Talk* (Oxford, 1917), p. 165; 27 Dec. 1831.

4. As quoted in K. E. Gilbert and H. Kuhn, *A History of Esthetics* (New York, 1939), p. 163.

5. *Leonardo Da Vinci's Notebooks,* ed. Edward McCurdy (London, 1906), p. 163; cf. pp. 165, 167, 169.

6. *Every Man out of His Humor,* III, vi, 201ff. For the wide currency of this definition, see *The Great Critics,* ed. J. H. Smith and E. W. Parks, p. 654; and *Elizabethan Critical Essays,* ed. G. G. Smith, I, 369-70.

7. Preface to Shakespeare (1759), *Johnson on Shakespeare,* p. 11. See also *Rambler* No. 4.

8. *The Works of Alexander Pope,* ed. Elwin and Courthope (London, 1871), II, 90.

9. J. J. Rousseau, 'De L'Imitation théatrale,' *Oeuvres complètes* (Paris, 1826), XI, 183ff.

10. 'A Discourse on Poetical Imitation,' *Works,* II, 111-12.

11. Irving Babbitt, *The New Laokoon* (Boston and New York, 1910), p. 3. For details see W. G. Howard, '*Ut Pictura Poesis,*' *PMLA,* XXIV (1909), 40-123; R. W. Lee, '*Ut Pictura Poesis:* The Humanistic Theory of Painting,' *Art Bulletin,* XXII (1940), 197-269.

12. *Idler* No. 34.

13. It may be relevant that in his *Rhetoric,* Aristotle classifies as a frigid metaphor,

because it is far-fetched and obscure, Alcidamus' saying that the *Odyssey* is 'a beautiful mirror of human life' (*Rhetoric* III. iii. 1406^{b}).

14. *Les Beaux Arts,* p. 27.

15. 'Of Simplicity and Refinement in Writing,' *Essays Moral, Political and Literary,* ed. T. H. Green and T. H. Grose (London, 1882), I, 240.

16. *Essays on Poetry and Music* (3d ed.; London, 1779), pp. 86-7; Johnson, *Rambler* No. 4, in *Works,* IV, 23.

17. 'Literary Criticism and the Concept of Imitation,' *Critics and Criticism,* ed. R. S. Crane, p. 162.

18. *Reflections on Aristotle's Treatise of Poesie,* trans. Rymer (London, 1694), p. 57.

19. 'Discourse on Poetical Imitation,' *Works,* II, 111.

20. *Naturalis historia,* XXXV. 36. On the vogue of the Zeuxis story in the Renaissance, see Panofsky, *Idea,* pp. 24ff.

21. 'On the Cultivation of Taste,' *The Works of Oliver Goldsmith,* ed. J. W. M. Gibbs (London, 1884), I, 337-8. Cf. e.g. Batteux, *Les Beaux Arts,* pp. 45ff.; and Beattie, *On Poetry and Music,* pp. 105-6.

22. Third Discourse, *The Literary Works,* ed. H. W. Beechy (London, 1855), I, 334. For a similar doctrine in Leon Battista Alberti's *De statua,* see Blunt's *Artistic Theory in Italy,* pp. 17-18.

23. *Rambler* No. 60 (1750), in *Works,* IV, 383. See A. O. Lovejoy, ' "Nature" as Aesthetic Norm,' *Essays in the History of Ideas* (Baltimore, 1948), pp. 70-71.

24. Preface to Shakespeare, *Johnson on Shakespeare,* p. 11. Cf. Reynolds, Third Discourse, *Literary Works,* I, 338; and Beattie, op. cit. p. 107.

25. Ibid. pp.11-12. Poetry, Johnson says (*Rambler* No. 36, in *Works,* IV, 237-8), 'has to do rather with the passions of men, which are uniform, than their customs, which are changeable. . .' In the version of James Beattie, the ideas of poetry are 'rather general than singular; rather collected from the examination of a species or class of things, than copied from an individual. And this, according to Aristotle, is in fact the case, at least for the most part' (*On Poetry and Music,* p. 56).

26. Johnson, *Rasselas,* in *Works,* III, 329.

27. See *Rambler* No. 36; and Reynolds, Eleventh Discourse, *Literary Works,* II, 22-3.

28. Joseph Warton, *Essay on the Writings and Genius of Pope* (3d ed.; London, 1772), I, 89. The passage is based on Hurd's exhaustive demonstration, in his 'Discourse on Imitation,' that the uniformity of perception and thought in all men makes it inevitable that the writings of poets will duplicate one another both in sentiments and descriptions. Johnson presented a similar thesis in *Rambler* No. 143, written in 1751, the same year as Hurd's 'Discourse.'

29. Eleventh Discourse, *Literary Works,* II, 22.

30. R. S. Crane, 'English Neoclassical Criticism,' *Critics and Criticism,* pp. 380-81. For a revealing application of this pattern of explanation to aspects of Dr. Johnson's criticism, see the note by W. R. Keast in *Philological Quarterly,* XXVII (1948), 130-32; and by the same author, 'Johnson's Criticism of the Metaphysical Poets,' *ELH,* XVII (1950), 63-7.

31. Preface to Shakespeare, *Johnson on Shakespeare,* p. 13. On pp. 37-9, Johnson elaborates on the 'vigilance of observation and accuracy of distinction' by which Shakespeare discriminates the mode of life and native dispositions of his characters. For Johnson's underlying philosophy of the uniformity within variety of human nature, see *Adventurer* No. 95, in *Works,* III, 213-19.

32. *Johnson on Shakespeare,* p. 39; 'Life of Thomson,' *Lives of the Poets* (ed. Hill), III, 299. 'Nothing in the art,' wrote Reynolds, the great proponent of Ideal

beauty, 'requires more . . . of that power of discrimination which may not improperly be called genius, than the steering between general ideas and individuality . . .' (*Literary Works,* II, 322).

33. *Rambler* No. 143, in *Works,* VI, 14; 'Life of Cowley,' *Lives of the Poets,* I, 20. Johnson objects to the novelty of the thoughts in the metaphysical poets merely because to exhibit only a half of an aesthetic virtue is to deviate into a fault: they 'are often new, but seldom natural.'

34. 'Life of Gray,' *Lives of the Poets,* III, 442. Thomson also 'is entitled to one praise of the highest kind: his mode of thinking, and of expressing his thoughts, is original' ('Life of Thomson,' *Lives of the Poets,* III, 298). On this issue see also Scott Elledge, 'The Background and Development in English Criticism of the Theories of Generality and Particularity,' *PMLA* (1947), 147-82.

35. *Essay on Pope* (London, 1782), II, 222-3, 230; cf. I, 40.

36. *Gleanings* (London, 1785), I, 29-30. In Germany, Novalis was to say: 'The more personal, local, temporal, peculiar a poem is, the nearer it is to the center of poetry' (*Romantische Welt: Die Fragmente,* ed. Otto Mann, Leipzig, 1939, p. 326).

37. Ibid. pp. 107, 109. See also Elizabeth L. Mann's compact summary of 'The Problem of Originality in English Literary Criticism, 1750-1800,' *Philological Quarterly,* XVIII (1939), 97-118.

38. *Enneads,* trans. Stephen MacKenna (London, 1926), v. viii. 1.

39. See Erwin Panofsky, *Idea* (Leipzig, 1924).

40. *Enneads* v. viii. 1.

41. *Ad M. Brutum Orator* ii. 8-10. Cf. Seneca, *Epistle* LXV.

42. Panofsky, op. cit. p. 56.

43. This scheme, developed in Ficino's important commentary on the *Symposium,* was applied to the theory of art by Giovanni Lomazzo, *Idea del tempio della pittura,* 1590. See Panofsky, op. cit. pp. 52ff. and pp. 122ff.; also Nesca Robb, *Neoplatonism of the Italian Renaissance,* Chap. III.

44. P. F. Reiff attributes to Plotinus a crucial formative influence on the early romantic theorists, directly upon Novalis and Schelling, and through them, upon the Schlegels. See 'Plotin und die deutsche Romantik,' *Euphorion,* XIX (1912), 591-612.

45. *Die Leiden des jungen Werthers,* entry of 10 May 1771.

46. See the survey by L. I. Bredvold, 'The Tendency toward Platonism in Neo-Classical Esthetics,' *ELH,* I (1934), 91-119.

47. *The Critical Works of John Dennis,* I, 418. Horace's doctrine, Hurd says, jibes with Aristotle's statement that poetry is more philosophical than history, and refutes Plato's argument 'that poetical imitation is at a great distance from truth.' 'For, by abstracting from existences all that peculiarly respects and discriminates the *individual,* the poet's conception, as it were neglecting the intermediate particular objects, catches, as far as may be, and reflects the divine archetypal idea, and so becomes itself the copy or image of truth' ('Notes on The Art of Poetry,' *The Works of Richard Hurd,* I, 255-7).

48. Ninth Discourse, *Literary Works,* II, 4. It was Coleridge's opinion that Reynolds rose above the standard theory and practice of his day because 'he had drunk deeply of Platonism' (*The Philosophical Lectures,* ed. Kathleen Coburn, New York, 1949, p. 194); see also Bredvold, 'The Tendency toward Platonism.' For a corrective to such views, see Hoyt Trowbridge, 'Platonism and Sir Joshua Reynolds,' *English Studies,* XXI (1939), 1-7; also, Elder Olson's Introduction to *Longi-*

nus on the Sublime and Sir Joshua Reynolds, Discourses on Art (Chicago, 1945), pp. xiii-xviii.

49. *Literary Works*, I, 330-33; cf. ibid. p. 351. For a similar reduction of the intellectual Idea to empirical psychology, see Beattie, op. cit. pp. 54-5; and Sir Richard Blackmore, *Essays upon Several Subjects* (1716) I, 19-21.

50. Tenth Discourse, *Literary Works*, II, 8.

CHAPTER III

1. A. W. Schlegel, *Vorlesungen über schöne Literatur und Kunst* (1801-4), Deutsche Litteraturdenkmale des 18. und 19. Jahrhunderts (Stuttgart, 1883), XVII, 91. In classical Latin, when *expremere* was used with reference to speech, the metaphor had already faded and taken the sense of 'signify' or 'stand for.' See J. C. La Drière, 'Expression,' *Dictionary of World Literature*, ed. J. T. Shipley (New York, 1943), pp. 225-7.

2. 'What Is Poetry?' (1833), *Early Essays*, p. 208.

3. 'The Philosophy of Poetry,' *Blackwood's*, XXXVIII (1835), p. 833. For the identity of the author, see p. 149.

4. Review of Lockhart's *Life of Scott* (1838), in *Occasional Papers and Reviews* (Oxford and London, 1877), pp. 6, 8.

5. *Coleridge's Miscellaneous Criticism*, ed. T. M. Raysor (Cambridge, Mass., 1936), p. 207.

6. Review of Coleridge's *Biographia Literaria*, in *Complete Works of William Hazlitt*, ed. P. P. Howe, XVI, 136.

7. *Shelley's Literary and Philosophical Criticism*, ed. John Shawcross, p. 121.

8. *Works of Lord Byron*, ed. E. H. Coleridge and R. E. Prothero (London and New York, 1898-1904); *Letters and Journals*, V, 318.

9. *Wordsworth, Shelley, Keats and Other Essays* (London, 1874), p. 202.

10. 'An Answer to the Question What is Poetry?' *Imagination and Fancy* (New York, 1848), p. 1.

11. 'What is Poetry?' *Early Essays*, pp. 208, 203, 223 (my italics).

12. 'Essay on the Drama' (1819), *The Prose Works* (Edinburgh and London, 1834-36), VI, 310.

13. *Don Juan*, IV, cvi.

14. Letter to Miss Milbanke, 10 Nov. 1813, *Works, Letters and Journals*, III, 405. Similar analogies were used by more sedate critics also. The Rev. W. J. Fox, reviewing the verse of Ebenezer Elliott, the 'Corn Law Rhymer,' spoke of 'humanity in poverty, pouring forth its own emotions,' and called Elliott's verse 'intense flashes of liquid lava from that central fire, which must have vent... .' As quoted by F. E. Mineka, *The Dissidence of Dissent* (Chapel Hill, 1944), pp. 301, 303.

15. *Childe Harold's Pilgrimage*, III, vi.

16. *Monthly Repository*, 2d series, VII (1833), p. 33; quoted by Mineka, op. cit. p. 307.

17. 'On Poetry in General,' *Complete Works*, V, 7.

18. *Romantische Welt: Die Fragmente*, ed. Otto Mann (Leipzig, 1939), p. 313.

19. *Sternbald*, in *Deutsche National-Litteratur*, CXLV, p. 300.

20. E.g., Hazlitt declares that in his *Excursion* Wordsworth 'paints the outgoings of his own heart, the shapings of his own fancy' (*Complete Works*, ed. P. P. Howe, London and Toronto, 1930-34, XIX, 10). And see Coleridge, *Miscellaneous Criticism*, p. 207.

21. *Phantasien über die Kunst* (1799), in *Deutsche National-Litteratur*, CXLV, p. 58.

22. *Prosaische Jugendschriften*, ed. J. Minor (Wien, 1882), II, 257-8.

23. 'On Poetry in General' (1818), *Complete Works*, V, 12. Cf. ibid. XVI, 136.

24. *Lectures on Poetry* (1832-41), trans. E. K. Francis (Oxford, 1912), I, 47-8.

25. For the history of the wind-harp and of allusions to it by poets, see Erika von Erhardt-Siebold, 'Some Inventions of the Pre-Romantic Period and their Influence upon Literature,' *Englische Studien*, LXVI (1931-2), 347-63. Robert Bloomfield, the farmer-poet, published an anthology of literature concerning the wind-harp in 1808; see *Nature's Music*, in *The Remains of Robert Bloomfield* (London, 1824), I, 93-143.

26. 'Defence of Poetry,' *Shelley's Literary and Philosophical Criticism*, ed. John Shaw-cross (Oxford, 1909), p. 121. In the opening passages of *The Prelude*, Words-worth had spoken in like terms of his attempt to poetize (1805 version, I, 101ff.): 'It was a splendid evening; and my soul Did once again make trial of the strength Restored to her afresh; nor did she want Eolian visitations; but the harp Was soon defrauded.'

27. 'Defence of Poetry,' ibid. p. 121.

28. *Complete Works*, V, 1.

29. Ibid. p. 3. Compare Goethe, in Eckermann's *Gespräche*, 29 Jan. 1826: 'Just so with the poet. So long as he only speaks out his few subjective feelings, he deserves not the name; but as soon as he knows how to appropriate to himself and express the world, he is a poet.'

30. As reprinted from Coleridge's *Literary Remains*, in *Biographia Literaria*, ed. Shaw-cross, II, 253-4, 258. Another and shorter version from one of Coleridge's note-books is published in *Coleridge's Miscellaneous Criticism*, pp. 205-13.

31. Preface to *Poems* (1815), in *Wordsworth's Literary Criticism*, p. 150. See also pp. 18, 165, 185.

32. *Letters of William and Dorothy Wordsworth: The Middle Years*, ed. E. de Selin-court (Oxford, 1937), II, 705; 18 Jan. 1816.

33. Notes to a partial translation of Lessing's *Laocoön*, in *Collected Writings*, ed. David Masson (Edinburgh, 1889-90), XI, 206.

34. 'What is Poetry?' *Early Essays*, p. 207. For an anticipation of such statements, see J. U. [James Usher], *Clio: or, a Discourse on Taste* (2d ed.; London, 1769), p. 140: 'You imagine [the man of sensibility] paints objects and actions, while he in reality paints passion, and affects us by the image of his own imagination.' See also J. Moir, *Gleanings*, I, 97-8.

35. *Early Essays*, p. 207. Keble: Poetry 'paints all things in the hues which the mind itself desires . . .' (*Lectures on Poetry*, I, 22). W. J. Fox: 'The changing moods of mind diversify a landscape with far more variety than cloud or sunshine in all their combinations; and those moods are in themselves subjects of descrip-tion . . .' (*Monthly Repository*, LXIII, 1833, p. 33).

36. 'On Poesy or Art,' *Biographia Literaria*, II, 254. See also Hazlitt: Poetry, 'the high-wrought enthusiasm of fancy and feeling,' in 'describing natural objects . . . impregnates sensible impressions with the forms of fancy . . .' ('On Poetry in General,' *Complete Works*, V, 4-5).

37. 'On Poetry in General,' *Complete Works*, V, 4. See also his analysis of Shakespeare's: 'Violets dim/ But sweeter than the lids of Juno's eyes/ Or Cytherea's breath,' as 'the intenseness of passion . . . moulding the impressions of natural objects according to the impulses of imagination . . .' (Preface to *Characters of Shake-speare's Plays*, ibid. IV, 176-7. Cf. Wordsworth, *Excursion*, I, 475ff.).

38. *Biographia*, II, 16. Cf. ibid. I, 59.

39. 'On Poetry in General,' *Complete Works*, V, 3.

40. Preface to *Lyrical Ballads* (added in 1802), in *Wordsworth's Literary Criticism*, p. 23.

41. 'Defence of Poetry,' *Shelley's Literary Criticism*, p. 155.

42. *Poetry and Prose of William Blake*, ed. Geoffrey Keynes (London and New York, 1939), p. 777. For an extreme view on the need for descriptive circumstantiality in a poem, couched still in the idiom of eighteenth-century criticism, see the review of Scott's *Lady of the Lake*, in *Quarterly Review*, III (1810), 512-13: Scott most strikingly exemplifies 'the analogy between poetry and painting. . . Whatever he represents has a character of individuality, and is drawn with an accuracy and minuteness of discrimination. . .' Much of this is the result of his genius, a natural 'intensity and keenness of observation' by which he is able 'to discover characteristic differences where the eye of dullness sees nothing but uniformity. . .' Cf. the passages from Moir's *Gleanings* in the preceding chapter.

43. 'The Ideal,' *Complete Works*, XX, 303-4. See also his essays 'Originality' and 'On Certain Inconsistencies in Sir Joshua Reynolds' Discourses.' On the related discussion of 'concreteness' in poetry, see Chap. XI, sect. iii.

44. *Wordsworth's Literary Criticism*, p. 25.

45. *Biographia*, II, 33n, 12; *The Friend*, in *The Complete Works of Samuel Taylor Coleridge*, ed. Shedd (New York, 1858), II, 416.

46. *Biographia*, II, 120.

47. E.g. *Thaeatetus* 191-5, 206; *Philebus* 38-40; *Timaeus* 71-2.

48. *De anima* II. ii. 424ª.

49. Locke, *Essay Concerning Human Understanding*, ed. A. C. Fraser (Oxford, 1894), I, 142-3 (II, i, 25): 'In this part the understanding is merely passive. . . These simple ideas, when offered to the mind, the understanding can no more refuse to have, nor alter when they are imprinted, nor blot them out and make new ones itself, than a mirror can refuse, alter, or obliterate the images or ideas which the objects set before it do therein produce.' The comparison of the mind, or at least the 'phantasy,' to a mirror had been common in the Renaissance; see, e.g., George Puttenham, *The Arte of English Poesie*, in *Elizabethan Critical Essays*, ed. G. G. Smith (Oxford, 1904), II, 20; and Bacon's discussion of this analogue in his passage on the Idols of the mind, *De Augmentis*, V, iv.

50. *Essay Concerning Human Understanding*, I, 121 (II, i, 2): 'Let us then suppose the mind to be, as we say, white paper, void of all characters, without any ideas.' See Locke's earlier draft, *An Essay Concerning the Understanding*, ed. Benjamin Rand (Cambridge, Mass., 1931), p. 61: The soul 'at first is perfectly *rasa tabula*, quite void. . .'

51. Ibid. pp. 211-12 (II, xi, 17).

52. Ibid. I, 48n, and 49. Cf. D. F. Bond, 'Neo-Classic Theory of the Imagination,' *ELH*, IV (1937), p. 248.

53. *Table Talk and Omniana of Samuel Taylor Coleridge* (Oxford, 1917), p. 188; 21 July 1832. Cf. ibid. p. 361 (1812): 'The mind makes the sense, far more than the senses make the mind.'

54. B. A. G. Fuller, *The Problem of Evil in Plotinus* (Cambridge, 1912), p. 70.

55. *Enneads*, trans. Stephen MacKenna (London, 1924), IV. vi. 1-3.

56. *The Cambridge Platonists*, ed. E. T. Campagnac (Oxford, 1901), pp. 283-4, 286-7, 292-3.

57. 'Of the Nature of a Spirit,' in V. de Sola Pinto, *Peter Sterry Platonist and Puritan* (Cambridge, 1934), pp. 161-2. Similar analogies are to be found in many writers in the Neoplatonic tradition. For example, see Boehme, in Newton P. Stallknecht, *Strange Seas of Thought* (Durham, N. C., 1945), p. 52. A. O. Lovejoy, in an early essay on 'Kant and the English Platonists,' cited many parallels between Kant's 'transcendental idealism' and the writings—more abstract and less riotously metaphorical than Culverwel's or Sterry's—of such English Platonists as Cudworth, More, Burthogge, and Arthur Collier (*Essays Philosophical and Psychological in Honor of William James,* New York, 1908, pp. 265-302). This essay, by the way, lends greater credibility than many students have granted to Coleridge's reiterated claim that through his early reading in Platonists and mystics, he had acquired the essentials of his idealism prior to his first knowledge of German philosophy.

58. *The Prelude* (1805), II, 378ff. See also ibid. XIII, 40ff., for the lovely passage in which Wordsworth finds in the naked moon shedding its glory over Snowdon, 'The perfect image of a mighty Mind.'

59. 'To a Gentleman,' ll. 12ff.

60. 'Tennyson's Poems' (May 1832), *Works of Professor Wilson,* ed. Ferrier (Edinburgh and London, 1856), VI, 109-10. We may add, as representative images out of the stream of post-Kantian German philosophy, these passages from Schleiermacher's *Monologen* (1800), ed. F. M. Schiele and Hermann Mulert (2d ed.; Leipzig, 1914), p. 9: 'Auch die äussere Welt . . . strahlt in tausend zarten und erhabenen Allegorien, wie ein magischer Spiegel, das Höchste und Innerste unsers Wesens auf uns zurük.' And pp. 15-16: 'Mir ist der Geist das erste und das einzige: denn was ich als Welt erkenne, ist sein schönstes Werk, sein selbstgeschaffener Spiegel.'

61. *The Prelude* (1850 ed.), VI, 743-5.

62. The theme is 'Of tides obedient to external force, And currents self-determined, as might seem, Or by some inner Power' ('To a Gentleman,' ll. 15ff.). Cf. the initial stanza of 'Mont Blanc,' in which Shelley likens the being-given and the given-forth to the interchange and indistinguishable union of water with water; see also ll. 34-40.

63. To Wordsworth's 'Aeolian visitations' of poetry (*Prelude,* 1805, I, 104), cf. his description of his perceptual commerce with the moods of nature (ibid. III, 136ff.): 'In a kindred sense Of passion [I] was obedient as a lute That waits upon the touches of the wind,' as a result of which 'I had a world about me; 'twas my own, I made it. . .'

64. On the history of the *camera obscura,* see Erika von Erhardt-Siebold, 'Some Inventions of the Pre-Romantic Period,' *Englische Studien,* LXVI (1931-2), pp. 347ff.

65. 'The Eolian Harp,' ll. 44ff. On Coleridge's intention to render Berkeley's subjective idealism in this passage, see his *Philosophical Lectures,* ed. Kathleen Coburn (New York, 1949), p. 371; also *Letters,* ed. E. H. Coleridge, I, 211.

66. 'Essay on Christianity' (1815), *Shelley's Literary and Philosophical Criticism,* pp. 90-91. Later, in his marginalia on Kant's *Critique of Pure Reason,* Coleridge was to declare, 'The mind does not resemble an Aeolian harp . . . but rather as far as objects are concerned a violin or other instrument of few strings yet vast compass, played on by a musician of Genius' (Henri Nideker, 'Notes Marginales de S. T. Coleridge,' *Revue de litterature comparée,* VII, 1927, 529). See also *Biographia,* I, 81.

67. *The Prelude* (1805), III, 142ff. The extremity of subjectivism, offered as a philosophical doctrine, is common enough among German followers of Fichte. Thus Tieck writes, in *William Lovell* (1795): 'Freilich kann alles, was ich ausser mir wahrzunehmen glaube, nur in mir selbst existieren.' 'Die Wesen sind, weil wir sie dachten.' 'Das Licht aus mir fällt in die finstre Nacht, Die Tugend ist nur, weil ich sie gedacht.' See Jenisch, *Entfaltung des Subjektivismus*, pp. 119-21.

68. 'Night VI' (1744), ll. 423ff.

69. *Essay Concerning Human Understanding*, I, 168-79 (II, viii, 7, 15, 23). See Addison's *Spectator* No. 413 (a kind of half-way house between the formulation of Locke and of Young); Akenside, *Pleasures of Imagination* (1744 ed.), II, 458-61, 489-514; and the quotations in Marjorie Nicolson, *Newton Demands the Muse* (Princeton, 1946), 144-64.

70. *The Prelude* (1805), II, 362ff.

71. Ibid. XI, 323-34.

72. *Treatise of Human Nature*, ed. L. A. Selby-Bigge (Oxford, 1896), p. 469 (III, i, i).

73. *An Enquiry Concerning the Principles of Morals*, in *Essays, Moral, Political, and Literary*, II, 263-5. Cf. David Hartley, *Observations on Man* (6th ed.; London, 1834), pp. 231-2 (III, iii, Prop. LXXXIX).

74. (1744 ed.), I, 481ff.; (1757 ed.), I, 563ff. William Duff, *Essay on Original Genius*, p. 67, describes 'the transforming power of Imagination, whose rays illuminate the objects we contemplate. . . The Imagination, enraptured with the contemplation of them, becomes enamoured of its own creation.' Archibald Alison, in a work written in 1790 to demonstrate that 'the qualities of matter are in themselves incapable of producing emotion,' but are perceived as beautiful or sublime through a process of association, thinks that his doctrine nevertheless coincides with 'a DOCTRINE that appears very early to have distinguished the PLATONIC school . . . that matter is not beautiful in itself, but derives its beauty from the expression of MIND' (*Essays on the Nature and Principles of Taste*, Boston, 1812, pp. 106, 417-18).

75. To Wordsworth, 30 May 1815, *Letters*, II, 648-9; to W. Sotheby, 10 Sept. 1802, ibid. I, 403-4.

76. *The Prelude* (1850 ed.), II, 232-60.

77. Ibid. ll. 382-418. Cf. ibid. (1805 ed.), VIII, 623-30; and see Stallknecht, *Strange Seas of Thought*, Chap. III. It is relevant to consider here the extraordinary weight that other romantic poets, as well as Coleridge and Wordsworth, placed on the experience of *Einfühlung*, or loss of distinction between self and external scene. E.g., Shelley, 'On Life,' *Literary and Philosophical Criticism*, p. 56: 'Those who are subject to the state called reverie, feel as if their nature were dissolved into the surrounding universe, or as if the surrounding universe were absorbed into their being. They are conscious of no distinction.' And Byron, *Childe Harold's Pilgrimage*, III, lxxii: 'I live not in myself, but I become Portion of that around me'; 'the soul can flee, And with the sky, the peak, and the heaving plain Of ocean, or the stars, mingle, and not in vain.' And ibid. IV, clxxviii: 'I steal From all I may be, or have been before, To mingle with the Universe.' Keats was exceptional, in that he felt an identification rather with individual things, such as sparrows and people, than with the total landscape; see the familiar passages in his *Letters*, ed. M. B. Forman (3d ed.; Oxford, 1948), pp. 69, 227-8, 241.

78. Included in the Preface to *The Excursion* (1814), ll. 47-71. The barely submerged analogy in this passage, by the way, presents an interesting parallel to cabalistic and other esoteric theóries of the sexual generation of the world.

79. Culverwel, e.g., joins the familiar concept of the first-order stars as angelic existences with the figure of the fountain of light: The Creator 'fill'd the *highest part* of the *World* with those *Stars* of the *first Magnitude,* I mean those *Orient* and *Angelic Beings,* that dwell so near the *fountain of Light,* and continually drink in the *Beams* of *Glory* . . .' (*The Cambridge Platonists,* ed. Campagnac, p. 283).

80. *Lay Sermons,* ed. Derwent Coleridge (3d ed.; London, 1852), pp. 75-7. Coleridge added in a note that this passage 'might properly form the conclusion of a disquisition on the spirit . . . without reference to any theological dogma. . .'

CHAPTER IV

1. Aristotle, *Rhetoric* i. i. 1356[a]; Cicero, *De oratore* ii. xxviii, xlv.

2. *Ars poetica,* ll. 99-103. Aristotle (*Poetics* xvii. 1455[a]) had already advised the practicing poet to act out the part and feel the emotions of his characters, in order to represent them more convincingly. Quintilian, who knew Horace's *Art of Poetry,* said that 'the chief requisite for moving the feelings of others, is . . . that we ourselves be moved' (*Institutes* iii. v. 2, vi. ii. 25-7). In the sixteenth century, Minturno explicitly added 'moving' to Horace's pleasure and instruction as the ends of poetry

3. 'Prologue at the Opening of the Theatre Royal, Drury Lane,' ll. 7-8; 'Life of Cowley,' *Lives of the Poets* (ed. Hill), i, 36-7.

4. *L'Art poétique,* iii, ll. 15-16, 25-6, 142. Cf. Dryden, 'Heroic Poetry and Poetic License,' *Essays,* ed. Ker, i, 185-6: '*Si vis me flere, dolendum est primum ipsi tibi;* the poet must put on the passion he endeavours to represent. . .'

5. 'Burns' (1828), *Works,* xxvi, 267-8.

6. *On the Sublime,* trans. Rhys Roberts, i. 3; viii. 1; xxxiii. 1-xxxvi. 4; viii. 4. For an analysis of the conceptual structure of the treatise, see Elder Olson, 'The Argument of Longinus' *On the Sublime,' Critics and Criticism,* ed. R. S. Crane, pp. 232-59.

7. Ibid. xxxii. 4; xxxix. 1-3.

8. Ibid. ix. 2.

9. For the new aesthetic tastes which developed in the eighteenth century under the aegis of 'the sublime,' see Samuel H. Monk, *The Sublime: A Study of Critical Theories in XVIII-Century England* (New York, 1935).

10. *The Critical Works of John Dennis,* i, 215.

11. Ibid. i, 336, 224.

12. *Advancement and Reformation,* in ibid. i, 215. It was probably by no accidental connection that Milton, immediately after referring to Longinus (apparently for the first time in England) went on to introduce the pithy phrase that poetry is 'more simple, sensuous, and passionate' than rhetoric. Dennis refers to Milton's Letter to Hartlib more than once during this period (see, e.g., *Critical Works,* i, 333, 335; ii, 389); if he is recalling this passage, he anticipates several romantic critics in converting Milton's passing differentiation between rhetoric and poetry as instruments of education into a statement of the essential character of a poem. See, e.g., *Coleridge's Shakespearean Criticism,* i, 164-6.

13. Ibid. i, 215-16.

14. *The Grounds of Criticism,* in ibid. i, 359.

15. Ibid. 1, 357, 376, 222, 340.

16. *Letters of William and Dorothy Wordsworth: The Middle Years,* 11, 617; cf. 11, 633. On 30 Aug. 1842, De Quincey wrote to Alexander Blackwood that 'I once collected (Dennis') ridiculous pamphlets to oblige Wordsworth, who (together with S. T. C.) had an absurd "craze" about him.' Wordsworth's request to De Quincey, however, could not have been made before the composition of the Preface of 1800. See E. N. Hooker's useful and copiously annotated edition of the *Critical Works of John Dennis,* 11, lxxiii, cxxv. By 1825, Wordsworth demonstrates that he had read Longinus carefully; see Markham L. Peacock, Jr., *The Critical Opinions of William Wordsworth* (Baltimore, 1950), pp. 157-8.

17. For a detailed discussion, see Vincent Freimarck, *The Bible in Eighteenth-Century English Criticism* (unpublished doctoral dissertation, Cornell University Library, 1950).

18. *Lectures on the Sacred Poetry of the Hebrews,* trans. G. Gregory (London, 1847), p. 156.

19. Ibid. p. 16.

20. Ibid. pp. 184-5, 188.

21. Ibid. pp. 50, 157; cf. p. 174.

22. *The Grounds of Criticism,* in *Critical Works,* 1, 364.

23. Lowth, *Lectures,* pp. 30, 50-4. See e.g., Hildebrand Jacob, *Of the Sister Arts* (London, 1734), p. 11; John Newbery, *The Art of Poetry on a New Plan* (London, 1762), 1, i-ii; and the essay in *British Magazine* (1762) attributed to Goldsmith, in *The Works of Oliver Goldsmith,* ed. J. W. M. Gibbs, 1, 341-3.

24. A number of passages from Greek and Roman theory concerning language origins are conveniently anthologized in Lovejoy and Boas, *Primitivism and Related Ideas in Antiquity* (Baltimore, 1935); see esp. pp. 207, 221, 245, 371-2, 219-22.

25. *De rerum natura,* trans. W. H. D. Rouse, V, 1041-90.

26. Strabo, *Geographica,* 1, ii. 6; Plutarch, 'De Pythiae oraculis,' *Moralia* 406 B-F. For a convenient summary of the doctrines and authorities on this subject current in the late seventeenth century, see Sir William Temple, 'Of Poetry,' *Critical Essays of the Seventeenth Century,* ed. Spingarn, 111, 79-89.

27. *Autobiography of Giambattista Vico,* trans. T. G. Bergin and M. H. Fisch (Ithaca, N. Y., 1944), p. 126; cf. Introduction, pp. 32, 36.

28. *The New Science,* trans. T. G. Bergin and M. H. Fisch (Ithaca, N. Y., 1948), pp. 63-8, 104-5.

29. Ibid. pp. 69, 116-18, 134-9.

30. Ibid. pp. 108, 118; cf. p. 142. This theory does not prevent Vico from maintaining also (p. 67) that 'the world in its infancy was composed of poetic nations, for poetry is nothing but imitation.'

31. Although M. H. Fisch thinks it 'scarcely credible' that Blackwell and his followers should not have been directly influenced by Vico, he also points out there has come to light no single British reference to Vico before Coleridge (*Autobiography of Vico,* Introduction, pp. 82-4).

32. *Enquiry into the Life and Writings of Homer* (2d ed.; London, 1736), pp. 38-44. Blackwell refers frequently to many of the classical writers who had been Vico's sources, including Lucretius and Longinus.

33. *Rambler* No. 36, in *Works,* IV, 233.

34. See e.g., Hugh Blair, *Critical Dissertation on the Poems of Ossian* (1763), in *The Poems of Ossian* (New York, n.d.), pp. 89-91; also, Blair's *Lectures on Rhetoric,* Lectures VI and XXXVIII. Cf. Adam Ferguson, *Essay on the History of Civil Soci-*

ety, 1767 (7th ed.; Boston, 1809), pp. 282-6. A compact treatment of these Scottish groups and their linguistic and aesthetic speculations will be found in Lois Whitney, 'English Primitivistic Theories of Epic Origins,' *Modern Philology,* xxi (1924), 337-78. Their more general sociological speculations are described by Gladys Bryson, *Man and Society: The Scottish Inquiry of the Eighteenth Century* (Princeton, 1945).

35. *A Dissertation on the Rise . . . and Corruptions of Poetry and Music* (London, 1763), pp. 25-8. On this topic, see René Wellek, *The Rise of English Literary History* (Chapel Hill, N. C., 1941), pp. 70-94.

36. Trans. Thomas Nugent (London, 1756), pp. 169-82, 227-30. See Paul Kuehner, *Theories on the Origin and Formation of Language in the Eighteenth Century in France,* Univ. Penn. Dissertations (Philadelphia, 1944).

37. *Oeuvres complètes* (Paris, 1826), xi, 221-4.

38. *Schriften,* ed. Roth and Wiener (Berlin, 1821-43), ii, 258-9; vii, 10.

39. *Treatise upon the Origin of Language* (London, 1827), pp. 45-6. Both Hamann and Herder knew Blackwell's *Homer* (see Lois Whitney, 'Thomas Blackwell, A Disciple of Shaftesbury,' *Philological Quarterly,* v, 1926, pp. 196-7). Herder also cites Condillac and Rousseau.

40. See e.g., A. W. Schlegel, *Briefe über Poesie, Silbenmass, und Sprache, Sämtliche Werke,* vii, 112-26, 136-53; and Eva Fiesel, *Die Sprachphilosophie der deutschen Romantik* (Tübingen, 1927), esp. pp. 47-84.

41. *Dissertation on Ossian,* pp. 91, 108.

42. *The Sacred Poetry of the Hebrews,* p. 36. For the eighteenth-century concept of primitive poetry, see Wellek, *The Rise of English Literary History,* pp. 61ff.

43. Joseph Warton, 'The Enthusiast' (1744), ll. 133-4. See also Thomas Warton, 'The Pleasures of Melancholy' (1745), ll. 150ff., and the opening section of Thomas Warton's *Observations on the Faerie Queene* (1754).

44. *An Essay on Original Genius* (London, 1767), pp. 270, 282-4.

45. *Dissertation on Ossian,* pp. 150, 175, 107-8.

46. *An Essay on the History of Civil Society,* 1767 (7th ed.; Boston, 1809), p. 285. The 'primitive' poetry uttered by the noble savages and noble peasants of the contemporary world was described in similar terms. The youthful Burns, 'bred,' as he put it, 'at a plough-tail,' even applied the stereotype (half ironically, perhaps) to his own early poetry. When I got heartily in love, 'then Rhyme and Song were, in a manner, the spontaneous language of my heart. The following composition was the first of my performances . . . when my heart glowed with honest warm simplicity; unacquainted, and uncorrupted with the ways of a wicked world' (*Robert Burns's Commonplace Book,* ed. J. C. Ewing and D. Cook, Glasgow, 1938, p. 3; April 1783). For similar opinions by contemporary reviewers of Burns, see *Early Critical Reviews of Robert Burns,* ed. J. D. Ross (Glasgow and Edinburgh, 1900).

47. *Dissertation on Ossian,* pp. 89, 179.

48. The usual attitude was to regret what poetry had lost by the development of art, refinement, and rules, without overlooking the fact that it had gained compensating advantages.

49. *Essay on Original Genius,* p. 192n.

50. In the attempt to subsume each species of poetry under the mimetic principle, Batteux claimed, in 1747, that even lyric poems, 'the songs of the Prophets, the psalms of David, the odes of Pindar and of Horace' are only to superficial inspection 'un cri du coeur, un élan, où la Nature fait tout, et l'art, rien.' Like

all poetry, lyric poetry is an imitation, but differs from the other forms in imitating sentiments rather than actions (*Les Beaux Arts*, Paris, 1773, pp. 316-25). Thomas Twining claimed, in 1789, that Batteux had here extended the limits of imitation beyond 'all reasonable analogy,' for when the lyric poet 'is merely expressing his own *sentiments*, in his own *person*, we consider him not as imitating . . .' (*Aristotle's Treatise on Poetry*, pp. 139-40).

51. Sidney, *Apology for Poetry*, in *Elizabethan Critical Essays*, ed. G. Gregory Smith, I, 201; Boileau, *L'Art poétique*, II, ll. 47, 57; Johnson, *Works*, IX, 39, 43-5, 152. See also Joseph Trapp, *Lectures on Poetry* (1711-15), trans. William Bowyer (London, 1742), p. 25. For the fortunes of the lyric in England, and a discussion of the relevance of the Longinian current to the theory and practice of the Pindaric Ode, see the excellent article by Norman Maclean, 'From Action to Image: Theories of the Lyric in the Eighteenth Century,' *Critics and Criticism*, ed. R. S. Crane, pp. 408-60.

52. *Reflections on Aristotle's Treatise of Poesie*, trans. Rymer (London, 1694), p. 4.

53. 'Of Poetry' (1690), *Critical Essays of the Seventeenth Century*, ed. Spingarn, III, 99. Cf. Hobbes, 'Answer to Davenant,' ibid. II, 57.

54. *The Grounds of Criticism in Poetry*, in *Critical Works*, I, 338. See also, e.g., Joseph Trapp, *Lectures on Poetry*, Lecture XII, and John Newbery, *The Art of Poetry*, I, 54. In his *Dictionary*, Dr. Johnson distinguished the 'greater' from the 'lesser' ode as possessing 'sublimity, rapture, and quickness of transition.'

55. See Lowth, *Lectures*, esp. Chaps. XXII, XXV-XXVIII. Also Sidney, *Apology for Poetry*, in *Elizabethan Critical Essays*, ed. Smith, I, 154-5; Cowley, Preface to *Pindarique Odes*, in *The Works of Mr. Abraham Cowley* (11th ed.; London, 1710), I, 184.

56. Trapp, *Lectures on Poetry*, p. 203; Young, *Poetical Works* (Boston, 1870), II, 159, 165. Cf. Hurd, *Horace's Art of Poetry* (1750), in *Works*, I, 104: 'Poetry, *pure Poetry*, is the proper language of *Passion*. . .' Anna Seward, letter to Dr. Downman, 15 Mar. 1792: '. . . what should be its essence, poetry, that is, the metaphors, allusions, and imagery, are the natural product of a glowing and raised imagination' (*Letters*, Edinburgh, 1811, III, 121). J. Moir, *Gleanings* (1785), I, 27: 'All true Poetry is the genuine effusion either of a glowing heart, or of an ardent fancy.' And see Paul Van Tieghem, 'La Notion de vraie poésie dans le préromantisme Européen,' *Le Préromantisme* (Paris, 1924), I, 19ff.

57. *Essay on the Writings and Genius of Pope*, I, iv-x; II, 477-8, 481.

58. *The Works of Sir William Jones* (London, 1807), VIII, 361-4.

59. Ibid. VIII, 371. Cf. the expressive theory of the poetic species held by John Keble and Alexander Smith, as described in Chap. VI, sects. iii and iv.

60. Ibid. pp. 372-6, 379. Of the various indices to the changing directions of criticism in the last decades of the century, Thomas Barnes's paper 'On the Nature and Essential Characters of Poetry' (1781) is of special interest. Like Jones, Barnes denies the validity of definitions of poetry as imitation, as fiction, or as 'the art of giving pleasure'; he appeals to the fact that 'the *original* language of mankind was poetical,' because all perception in the infancy of the world excited passion; and he proposes a pyramid of poetic value, in which 'the bursts of honest nature, the glow of animated feeling' are the properties of 'the *first order* of poetic excellence.' *Memoirs of the Literary and Philosophical Society of Manchester*, I (1785), pp. 55-6.

61. J. G. Sulzer, *Allgemeine Theorie der schönen Künste* (Neue vermehrte zweite Auflage; Leipzig, 1792), Preface to the first ed., I, xiii; and 'Erfindung,' II, 86. For a consideration of Sulzer's aesthetics, see Anna Tumarkin, *Der Ästhetiker*

Johann Georg Sulzer (Leipzig, 1933), and Robert Sommer, *Grundzüge einer Geschichte der deutschen Psychologie und Aesthetik* (Wurzburg, 1892).

62. 'Nachahmung,' ibid. III, 487.

63. 'Dichter,' ibid. I, 609.

64. 'Gedicht,' ibid. II, 322-3, 325. Sulzer adds that works which issue entirely out of simulated feeling and which achieve 'the tone and speech of natural poetry by rules,' will be 'abortions, which can be classified under none of the natural genres of speech' (ibid. pp. 323, 327).

65. Ibid. II, 325, 328-9. Cf. I, 619; II, 57.

66. 'Ode,' ibid. III, 538-9; and 'Lyrisch,' III, 299.

67. Review of *Die schönen Künste in ihrem Ursprung, aus den Frankfurter gelehrten Anzeigen* (1772), and *Goethe's Sämtliche Werke* (Jubiläums Ausgabe), XXXIII, 17-18. The book under review was an excerpt from Sulzer's *Allegemeine Theorie.*

68. *Ueber die neuere deutsche Litteratur,* 3d collection (1767), *Sämtliche Werke,* I, 394-5.

69. *Briefwechsel zwischen Schiller und Goethe,* II, 278-9 (27 Mar. 1801).

70. *Deutsche Litteraturdenkmale des. 18. und 19. Jahrhunderts,* XVII, 91-5.

71. Novalis, *Romantische Welt: Die Fragmente,* pp. 292, 313; cf. Schleiermacher, *Monologen,* p. 23. On this subject, see Erich Jaenisch, *Die Entfaltung des Subjektivismus von der Aufklärung zur Romantik* (Königsberg, 1929).

72. *De l'Allemagne* (Paris, 1852), pp. 140-42, 144.

73. *Politics* viii. 5. For Plato on the mimetic nature of music see *Laws* ii. 667-70.

74. *Critical Reflections on Poetry, Painting and Music,* trans. Thomas Nugent (London, 1748), I, 360-61. Du Bos says that instrumental music can also imitate non-human sounds such as the noise of tempests, winds, and waves (I, 363-4).

75. For a brief survey, see J. W. Draper, 'Poetry and Music in Eighteenth Century Aesthetics,' *Englische Studien,* LXVII (1932-3), 70-85; also H. M. Schueller, 'Literature and Music as Sister Arts: An Aspect of Aesthetic Theory in Eighteenth-Century Britain,' *Philological Quarterly,* XXVI (1947), 193-205.

76. *Essays on Poetry and Music,* p. 119.

77. (3d ed.; London, 1775), p. 3 (my italics). On the very limited sphere Avison allows to musical mimesis, see pp. 52, 60. For parallel uses of 'expression' in application to music, see Beattie, *Poetry and Music,* pp. 51-2; and Twining, *Aristotle's Treatise on Poetry,* pp. 21-2, 60-61.

78. 'Of the Nature of that Imitation . . . in What Are Called the Imitative Arts,' *Essays Philosophical and Literary* (London, n.d.), p. 431.

79. (London, 1763), pp. 74-6, 226-7. For French theories of music as expressive of feeling, see Rousseau, *Essai sur l'origine des langues,* and 'Lettre sur la musique française'; and L. G. Krakeur, 'Aspects of Diderot's Aesthetic Theory,' *Romanic Review,* XXX (1939), p. 257.

80. *Kritische Wälder,* Pt. IV, *Sämtliche Werke,* IV, 118, 162, 166. Cf. J. G. Sulzer, 'Ausdruck in der Musik,' *Allegemeine Theorie,* I, 271; II, 369; III, 421-2, 575.

81. *Phantasien über die Kunst* (1799), in *Deutsche National-Literatur,* CXLV, 71. See also Tieck, ibid. pp. 88-90, 94.

82. *Romantische Welt: Die Fragmente,* pp. 297-8.

83. *Vorlesungen über Philosophische Kunstlehre* (1798) (Leipzig, 1911), p. 136. Cf. Friedrich Schlegel, *Jugendschriften,* I, 62, 356; II, 257-8; and A. W. Schlegel, *Lectures on Dramatic Literature,* pp. 43-4. There are some later parallels to such opinion in England; see e.g., J. S. Mill, *Early Essays,* p. 210; and John Keble, *Lectures on Poetry,* I, 47-8.

84. Novalis, *Romantische Welt,* p. 300; cf. p. 313. See also Tieck, *Franz Sternbold's Wanderungen* (1798), in *Deutsche National-Literatur,* CXLV, 317. Goethe's statement (*Gespräche,* 23 Mar. 1829) that 'architecture is frozen music' is also to be found in Friedrich Schlegel, in Schelling's *Philosophie der Kunst,* and in de Staël's *Corinne,* IV, iii; see Irving Babbitt, *The New Laokoon* (Boston and New York, 1910), p. 62; and Büchmann, *Geflügelte Worte* (23d ed.; 1907), pp. 356-7.

85. *Essays on Poetry and Music,* p. 150.

86. See *The New Laokoon* (Boston and New York, 1910), esp. Chap. VI.

87. (London, 1823), Lecture XXXVIII, p. 511.

88. Ibid. pp. 512, 513-14, 518.

89. E. C. Knowlton reviews the evidence, in exploring the possible connection between Blair's treatment of the pastoral and Wordsworth's bucolic poems: 'Wordsworth and Hugh Blair,' *Philological Quarterly,* VI (1927), 277-81. Coleridge borrowed a volume of Blair's *Lectures* from Bristol Library in 1796; see Paul Kaufman, 'The Reading of Southey and Coleridge,' *Modern Philology,* XXI (1924), 317-20.

90. The identification is made in an obituary notice in *Monthly Magazine,* IV (1797), 400-02; see Lewis Patton, 'Coleridge and the "Enquirer Series," ' *Review of English Studies,* XVI (1940), 188-9. For Coleridge's connections with the magazine, which make it probable he had read Enfield's article, see Dorothy Coldicutt, 'Was Coleridge the Author of the Enquirer Series?' ibid. XV (1939), 45ff.

91. *Monthly Magazine,* II (1796), pp. 453-6. The similarity to Wordsworth's Preface was pointed out by Marjorie L. Barstow, *Wordsworth's Theory of Poetic Diction,* Yale Studies in English, LVII (1917), pp. 121-2.

92. *Coleridge's Shakespearean Criticism,* I, 226; Mill, *Early Essays,* p. 228.

93. *Oxford Lectures on Poetry* (London, 1926), p. 183.

94. Preface to *The Excursion* (1814), in *The Poetical Works,* ed. Thomas Hutchinson (London, 1928), p. 754. In *The Excursion,* planned to serve as the intermediate section of *The Recluse,* Wordsworth announces that 'the intervention of characters speaking is employed, and something of a dramatic form adopted'; but as de Selincourt says, even in this poem 'not only the hero but also the Solitary and the Vicar were thinly veiled portraits of their author . . .' (Introduction to *The Prelude,* text of 1805, ed. de Selincourt, Oxford, 1933, p. xi).

95. Preface to *The Excursion,* p. 754.

96. *Lectures on Poetry,* II, 92, 97.

CHAPTER V

1. *Wordsworth's Literary Criticism,* p. 21n.

2. 'The Philosophy of Poetry,' XXXVIII (1835), p. 828.

3. *Wordsworth's Literary Criticism,* p. 41.

4. *Miscellaneous Criticism,* p. 227. Cf. 'On Poesy or Art,' *Biographia Literaria,* II, 253.

5. E.g. 'Defence of Poetry,' *Shelley's Literary Criticism,* p. 121; De Quincey, 'Style,' *Collected Writings,* X, 171-3; Mill, 'What is Poetry?' *Early Essays,* pp. 203-4; Keble, *Lectures on Poetry,* I, 19-20, 58-9, 65; Jeffrey, Review of Goethe's *Wilhelm Meister,* in *Contributions to the Edinburgh Review,* I, 258.

6. *Wordsworth's Literary Criticism,* pp. 21-2.

7. See Chap. X.

8. *Wordsworth's Literary Criticism,* p. 23.

9. Ibid. p. 213.

10. *Biographia,* I, 30; II, 14-19.

11. *Shelley's Literary and Philosophical Criticism*, pp. 156-8; Mill's *Early Essays*, pp. 259-60; cf. ibid. 221-4, 229-30.

12. 'Alfred de Vigny,' *Dissertations and Discussions* (Boston, 1864), I, 348-9. On this question, see also: *Shelley's Literary Criticism*, pp. 154-8; Hazlitt, *Complete Works*, V, 129-30; VIII, 83; W. J. Fox, *Monthly Repository* (Jan. 1833), p. 31; A. Smith, 'The Philosophy of Poetry,' *Blackwood's*, XXXVIII (1835), p. 835.

13. *Wordsworth's Literary Criticism*, pp. 32, 27, 16. See Chap. XI, sect. v.

14. See esp. 'The Parallel of Deism and Classicism,' *Essays in the History of Ideas* (Baltimore, 1948), pp. 78ff.

15. Lecture XXXV, pp. 472-3; cf. Lecture II, pp. 19-20.

16. *Rasselas*, in *Works*, III, 327-8.

17. *A Critical Dissertation on the Poems of Ossian*, in *The Poems of Ossian* (New York, n.d.), pp. 89-90. For a consideration of what poetry has gained, as well as lost, in the progress of art and civilization, see his *Lectures*, Lecture XXXV, pp. 469-78.

18. For an amusing account of this fad and its rationale, see C. B. Tinker, *Nature's Simple Plan*, pp. 92ff.

19. *Wordsworth's Literary Criticism*, p. 62. To a passage in R. P. Knight's *Principles of Taste* which quotes Blair's speculations concerning primitive language, there is a marginal note in Wordsworth's hand expressing contempt for this 'dabbling with [man's] savage state, with his agricultural state, his Hunter state &c &c' (E. A. Shearer, 'Wordsworth and Coleridge Marginalia,' *Huntington Library Quarterly*, I, 1937-8, p. 73).

20. *Wordsworth's Literary Criticism*, pp. 6-7.

21. Ibid. pp. 14-15. Wordsworth originally wrote '*low* and rustic life,' and did not change this to '*humble* and rustic life' until the edition of 1832. Cf. ibid. p. 31: the most valuable object of writing is 'the great and universal passions of men, the most general and interesting of their occupations, and the entire world of nature. . .' See also the similar passage in *The Excursion*, I, ll. 341-7.

22. Preface to Shakespeare, *Johnson on Shakespeare*, pp. 19-20.

23. In a section of the Preface commenting on 'The Idiot Boy,' 'The Mad Mother,' 'We Are Seven,' and other poems; the passage was deleted in the edition of 1845. See *Poetical Works*, ed. de Selincourt, II, 388n.

24. *Wordsworth's Literary Criticism*, pp. 21-3, 29-30.

25. Ibid. p. 36. Rousseau had said that the heart, 'quand il est sincère, est toujours uniforme'; see Lovejoy, 'Parallel of Deism and Classicism,' p. 82.

26. *Wordsworth's Literary Criticism*, p. 30.

27. Ibid. p. 25; Johnson, 'Life of Gray,' *Lives of the Poets* (ed. Hill), III, 441. On this topic in Johnson, see W. R. Keast, 'Theoretical Foundations of Johnson's Criticism,' in *Critics and Criticism*, ed. R. S. Crane, pp. 402-3.

28. Chap. XXV, II, 383-4, 388-90.

29. *Wordsworth's Literary Criticism*, pp. 6-7.

30. Ibid. pp. 194, 200-01. See also Wordsworth's distinction between 'the *People*' and 'the *Public* (a very different Being),' in *The Letters: The Middle Years*, I, 169.

31. Ibid. pp. 11, 20-21; cf. pp. 13, 18.

32. Ibid. p. 29 (my italics).

33. Ibid. pp. 41, 14.

34. Ibid. p. 24.

35. *Wordsworth's Literary Criticism*, p. 113. He makes clear that his argument in this essay applies not only to epitaphs but to all poetic forms, since the 'primary sen-

sations of the human heart' are the vital springs of composition 'in this and in
every other kind' (p. 108).

36. Ibid. pp. 122, 128-9.

37. *Essay on Criticism*, ii, ll. 289ff.

38. See Chap. x, sect. v.

39. *Wordsworth's Literary Criticism*, pp. 18, 22-3; see also his note to 'The Thorn,'
Poetical Works, ed. de Selincourt, ii, 513.

40. Ibid. pp. 41, 43.

41. Ibid. pp. 15, 121, 18-19.

42. F. R. Leavis, 'Wordsworth,' *Revaluations* (London, 1949), p. 170.

43. Johnson, 'Life of Pope,' *Lives of the Poets* (ed. Hill), iii, 254; *Wordsworth's Literary Criticism*, p. 121 (my italics); cf. pp. 89-90, 93-4, 135. Johnson's 'Dissertation on the Epitaphs of Pope' appeared originally in the *Universal Visiter and Me-
morialist* (1756), was reprinted in the *Idler* (3d ed., 1767), and was then appended
to his 'Life of Pope.'

44. Novalis, *Romantische Welt: Die Fragmente*, ed. Otto Mann (Leipzig, 1939), p.
326.

45. Préface des Contemplations (1856), *Oeuvres complètes* (Paris, 1882), *Poésie*, v, 2.
Cf. Schiller: 'Totalität des Ausdrucks wird von jedem dichterischen Werk ge-
fordert, denn jedes muss Charakter haben, oder es ist nichts; aber der vollkom-
mene Dichter spricht das Ganze der Menschheit aus' (*Briefwechsel zwischen
Schiller und Goethe*, 4th ed., Stuttgart, 1881, ii, 279).

46. G. W. Allen and H. H. Clark, *Literary Criticism, Pope to Croce* (New York, 1941),
p. 221. For another extreme, but by no means unusual, view that Coleridge is a
good critic despite his philosophy, see R. W. MacKail, Introduction to *Coleridge's Literary Criticism* (Oxford, 1908), pp. viii-xviii.

47. *Coleridge's Shakespearean Criticism*, i, xlvii-xlviii, note.

48. *Biographia*, ii, 64.

49. Ibid. ii, 85.

50. Ibid. i, 14. Cf. his fragmentary essay with the revealing title, 'On the Principles of
Genial Criticism . . . Deduced from the Laws and Impulses which Guide the
True Artist in the Production of His Works,' ibid. ii, 219ff. On 17 Oct. 1815,
Coleridge wrote to Byron that the object of his *Biographia* was 'to reduce criti-
cism to a system, by the deduction of the Causes from Principles involved in our
faculties' (*Unpublished Letters*, ii, 143; cf. ibid. ii, 65-6).

51. *Letters*, i, 386-7; cf. 373-5.

52. *Biographia*, ii, 6-8; cf. p. 69.

53. *Wordsworth's Literary Criticism*, pp. 21, 31-6, 46.

54. *Biographia*, ii, 8-10.

55. *Shakespearean Criticism*, ii, 67 (my italics); cf. ibid. i, 163-6. These lectures were
given in 1811-12, and Coleridge did not then introduce the distinction between
'poem' and 'poetry' which became the pivotal point in the *Biographia*.

56. *Biographia*, ii, 9-11, 56 (my italics).

57. Ibid. ii, 12; *Shakespearean Criticism*, i, 166. R. S. Crane, one of the very few commentators who has taken Coleridge's distinction between poem and poetry to be
more than a show of perverse ingenuity, greatly clarifies the logic of this chapter
of the *Biographia*. See his 'Cleanth Brooks; or, the Bankruptcy of Critical Monism,' *Critics and Criticism*, ed. R. S. Crane, pp. 83-107.

58. See, e.g., I. A. Richards, *Principles of Literary Criticism*, pp. 239-53; Cleanth
Brooks, *Modern Poetry and the Tradition* (Chapel Hill, N. C., 1939), pp. 40-43,

and *The Well-Wrought Urn,* pp. 17, 230-31; Austin Warren, *Rage for Order* (Chicago, 1948), Preface.

59. *Biographia,* I, 196. Coleridge here follows the formulation of Schelling, but he was also familiar with the concept of the generative power of the conflict of opposites in such earlier thinkers as the Cabalists, Giordano Bruno, Boehme, and Swedenborg.

60. Ibid. I, 179-85.

61. Ibid. I, 183, 202. This passage is analyzed from a different point of view in Chap. x, sect. iii.

62. Ibid. II, 12. For some instances in which Coleridge applies this criterion to specific passages of poetry, see the early essay by Alice D. Snyder, *The Critical Principle of the Reconciliation of Opposites as Employed by Coleridge* (Ann Arbor, Mich., 1918).

63. Ibid. II, 28. Coleridge elsewhere maintains that all rhetorical figures must be justified by the genetic state of feeling; see e.g., ibid. II, 43; *Letters,* ed. E. H. Coleridge, I, 374; *Shakespearean Criticism,* II, 102-4, 122. But, he says, only in 'its lowest state' among savage tribes is art 'a mere expression of passion by sounds which the passion itself necessitates' ('On Poesy or Art,' *Biographia,* II, 253). On this aspect of the debate, see T. M. Raysor, 'Coleridge's Criticism of Wordsworth,' *PMLA,* LIV (1939), 496-510.

64. *Biographia,* II, 29-43.

65. Ibid. II, 45, 49.

66. Ibid. II, 49-50.

67. Ibid. II, 50. Cf. *Shakespearean Criticism,* I, 164, 166.

68. Ibid. II, 55-6. Cf. *Letters,* I, 374.

69. Ibid. II, 50-51. See also H. V. S. Ogden, 'The Rejection of the Antithesis of Nature and Art in Germany, 1780-1805,' *Journal of English and Germanic Philology,* XXXVIII (1939), 597-616.

70. *Biographia,* II, 63-5. See Chap. VIII, sect. v.

71. Ibid. I, 4.

CHAPTER VI

1. *The Works of Thomas Love Peacock,* ed. H. F. B. Brett-Smith and C. E. Jones (London, 1934), VIII, 5, 11, 24-5.

2. Ibid. VIII, 13, 17, 18-21. For a defense against attacks by contemporary reviewers of some of the very writers at whom he gibes in the 'Four Ages,' see Peacock's unfinished 'Essay on Fashionable Literature,' ibid. VIII, 263-91.

3. Letter of 15 Feb. 1821, *Shelley's Literary and Philosophical Criticism,* p. 213. Shelley's 'Defence' was planned as the first of three articles, but the last two remained unaccomplished.

4. See R. B. McElderry Jr., 'Common Elements in Wordsworth's "Preface" and Shelley's "Defence of Poetry," ' *Modern Language Quarterly,* V (1944), 175-81. Shelley may also have primed himself for the encounter with Peacock by rereading Sidney's *Apology for Poetry:* the parallels between the two essays are discussed by Lucas Verkoren, *A Study of Shelley's 'Defence of Poetry'* (Amsterdam, 1937). A less convincing case is made for Shelley's adaptation of Imlac's poetics, as expressed in Johnson's *Rasselas,* by K. N. Cameron, 'A New Source for Shelley's "A Defence of Poetry," ' *Studies in Philology,* XXXVIII (1941), 629-44. For a summary of the Platonic echoes in Shelley's 'Defence,' see James A. Notopoulos, *The Platonism of Shelley* (Durham, N. C., 1949), pp. 346-56.

5. See, e.g., Shelley's varied but fragmentary philosophical and ethical essays of 1815: 'On Life,' 'Speculations on Metaphysics,' and 'Speculations on Morals.' All are reproduced in *Shelley's Literary and Philosophical Criticism*.

6. *Shelley's Literary and Philosophical Criticism*, pp. 122-3, 152.

7. Ibid. pp. 155, 128; cf. pp. 131, 135.

8. Ibid. pp. 123-4.

9. Ibid. pp. 126-8. The language of poets is necessarily metaphorical, because these figures of speech disclose the unity behind the apparent diversity of phenomena ('unveil the permanent analogy of things by images which participate in the life of truth'); and it is necessarily 'harmonious and rhythmical,' because it is 'the echo of the eternal music.'

10. Ibid. pp. 124-5. On the difference between the 'restricted sense' and the 'universal sense' of the word 'poetry' see also p. 158. Cf. Peacock's mocking account of the sleights by which early poets acquire the reputation of being historians, theologians, moralists, and legislators, in 'The Four Ages,' *Works*, VIII, 6.

11. Plato, *Laws* vii. 817; Shelley, 'Defence of Poetry,' pp. 125-6.

12. 'Defence of Poetry,' pp. 124-5. Single poems, Shelley says later, may be regarded as 'episodes to that great poem, which all poets, like the co-operating thoughts of one great mind, have built up since the beginning of the world' (p. 139).

13. Ibid. pp. 134, 130. On this matter of the problem of the artist in his difficult poise between the 'sad reality' of 'that which has been,' and the direct depiction of 'beautiful idealisms of moral excellence,' see also Shelley's Dedication to *The Cenci*, and his Preface to *Prometheus Unbound*.

14. The unchangeable forms, said Shelley, exist 'in the mind of the Creator, which is itself the image of all other minds' (ibid. p. 128; see also p. 140). Cf. Chap. II, sect. iii.

15. Ibid. pp. 121-2, 125.

16. Ibid. pp. 155-6.

17. Ibid. pp. 124-5, 145.

18. Ibid. pp. 120, 129, 131, 153-5.

19. *The Poetry and Prose of William Blake*, pp. 626, 607, 637-9 (written 1809-10).

20. *Biographia Literaria*, ed. Shawcross, II, 255-9. Coleridge's basically psychological additions to Schelling's 'On the Relation of the Formative Arts to Nature,' by the way, are no less significant than his borrowings.

21. *Heroes and Hero-Worship*, in *Works*, V, 155-7.

22. *Blackwood's Magazine*, LXXIV (1853), pp. 738, 744, 748, 728.

23. Ibid. pp. 745, 748.

24. Ibid. p. 753. Cf. *Timaeus* 28-9.

25. *On the Sublime*, trans. W. Rhys Roberts, VIII. 4; I. 4; XII. 4-5. 'The design of the poetical image,' Longinus also says, 'is enthrallment, of the rhetorical—vivid description' (XV. 2).

26. *An Essay on the Genius and Writings of Pope*, I, iv-v; II, 477-8.

27. 'Life of Pope,' *Lives of the Poets* (ed. Hill), III, 251.

28. *The Works of Samuel Johnson* (London, 1825), VII, x, 'Prefatory Notice to the Lives of the Poets.'

29. 'Defence of Poetry,' *Shelley's Literary and Philosophical Criticism*, p. 153.

30. *Inquiring Spirit*, ed. Kathleen Coburn (London, 1951), p. 207; *Biographia*, II, 11-13, 84.

31. 'On Milton's Versification,' *Complete Works*, IV, 38. In West's 'Christ Rejected,' Hazlitt says, there is 'an absolute want of what is called *gusto* throughout,' as

against the paintings of Raphael, where 'every muscle and nerve has intense feeling' (*Complete Works*, XVIII, 33).

32. 'On Genius and Common Sense,' ibid. VIII, 31; 'On Criticism,' VIII, 217-18.

33. Gibbon's *Journal*, ed. D. M. Low (New York, 1929), pp. 155-6. Addison had lamented the lack of authors who, like Longinus, could 'enter into the very Spirit and Soul of fine Writing' (*Spectator*, No. 409); the phrase anticipates Hazlitt.

34. *Complete Works*, XX, 388; X, 32-3. Carlyle described Goethe's criticism of Hamlet as 'the poetry of criticism: for it is in some sort also a creative art; aiming, at least, to reproduce under a different shape the existing product of the poet' ('State of German Literature,' *Works*, I, 61).

35. *Letters of John Keats*, p. 368; Charles and Mary Cowden Clarke, *Recollections of Writers* (London, 1878), pp. 125-6. See also *Letters*, p. 65.

36. *Letters*, pp. 71, 108 (my italics); Longinus, *On the Sublime* VII. 2.

37. *Letters*, pp. 52-3. He adds, in an echo of a different tradition: 'Besides a long Poem is a test of Invention which I take to be the Polar Star of Poetry. . . This same invention seems indeed of late Years to have been forgotten as a Poetical excellence.'

38. 'Writings of Alfred de Vigny,' *Dissertations and Discussions*, I, 351-2.

39. *Edgar Allan Poe, Representative Selections*, ed. Margaret Alterton and Hardin Craig (New York, 1935), 'The Poetic Principle,' pp. 378-9, 389; 'The Philosophy of Composition,' pp. 367-8, 376.

40. *The Poetical Works of Matthew Arnold*, ed. C. B. Tinker and H. F. Lowry (Oxford, 1950), pp. xvii, xxi, xxiii, xxvi.

41. *On the Study of Celtic Literature and on Translating Homer* (New York, 1895), p. 264.

42. 'The Study of Poetry,' *Essays in Criticism*, 2d Series, pp. 17-20, 33-4. One element Arnold has in common with Longinus, as well as with Poe and many others in this tradition, is the emphasis on 'soul' as the province from which true poetry derives and to which it appeals. The poetry of Dryden and Pope, he says, in a passage that T. S. Eliot derided, 'is conceived and composed in their wits, genuine poetry is conceived in the soul.'

43. As quoted in W. F. Thrall and Addison Hibbard, *A Handbook to Literature* (New York, 1936), p. 325.

44. *The Name and Nature of Poetry* (Cambridge, 1933), pp. 12, 34-5, 46-7.

45. *Elizabethan Critical Essays*, ed. G. G. Smith (Oxford, 1904), II, 49. Puttenham explains this effect on the auditor by analogy with homeopathy in medicine, 'as the *Paracelsians*, who cure *similia similibus*, making one dolour to expell another . . .' (ibid. p. 50). Cf. Milton's homeopathic analysis of tragic purgation in his preface to *Samson Agonistes*.

46. Letter to Moore, 2 Aug. 1787, *The Letters of Robert Burns*, ed. J. De Lancey Ferguson (Oxford, 1931), I, 112.

47. 19 Mar. 1819, *The Letters of John Keats*, p. 318.

48. *Letters and Journals*, v, 215 (2 Jan. 1821); III, 405 (10 Nov. 1813).

49. *Poetics* 4. 1448^{b}.

50. *On the Sublime*, trans. W. Rhys Roberts, XXXV. 2-3.

51. *Advancement of Learning*, Bk. II, in *Critical Essays of the Seventeenth Century*, ed. Spingarn, I, 6; cf. *De augmentis scientiarum*, Bk. II, Chap. xiii.

52. 'On the Idea of Universal Poetry,' *Works*, II, 8-9. Addison, in *Spectator* No. 418, explains that it is the part of a poet to mend and perfect nature 'because the mind

of man requires something more perfect in matter than what it finds there.' See also Reynolds, Discourse XIII, *Works*, II, 78; and John Aikin, *Essay on Song-Writing*, 1772 (new ed.; London, 1810), pp. 5-6.

53. *Rasselas*, Chap. XLIII, *Works*, III, 419-21.

54. 'Life of Milton,' *Lives of the Poets* (ed. Hill), I, 170. The special and lowly exception is the prose romance; see *Idler* No. 24.

55. 'On Poetry in General,' *Complete Works*, V, 1, 4, 11.

56. Ibid. pp. 5, 17-18.

57. *Biographia* I, 172-3; II, 120.

58. *Complete Works*, XI, 8; XX, 47, 43. See also ibid. II, 113, and XII, 250-51; and Elizabeth Schneider, *The Aesthetics of William Hazlitt* (Philadelphia, 1933), p. 93.

59. Ibid. XII, 348-53.

60. Ibid. XII, 23. De Quincey, a greater expert in dreams, gives this even more startling capsule version of the theory of conflict, waking amnesia, and the compulsive repetition by each individual of the guilty, archetypal dream-myth of the human race: 'In dreams, perhaps under some secret conflict of the midnight sleeper, lighted up to the consciousness at the time, but darkened to the memory as soon as all is finished, each several child of our mysterious race completes for himself the treason of the aboriginal fall' ('The English Coach,' *Collected Writings*, XIII, 304; the passage came to my attention by its quotation in Harry Levin's *James Joyce*, Norfolk, Conn., 1941, p. 158). German theorists, Novalis and J. P. Richter most notably, had earlier brooded over the mysterious and guilty self opened up to us in our dreams; see Chap. VIII.

61. *Complete Works*, V, 3.

62. Ibid. IV, 151-2; XI, 308; cf. IV, 58.

63. *Confessions*, Book IX.

64. *The Autobiography of Goethe*, trans. John Oxenford (Bohn ed., 1903), I, 511.

65. See P. P. Howe, *The Life of William Hazlitt* (London, 1922), pp. 349-50.

66. 'On Poetry in General,' *Complete Works*, V, 7-8. Croce gives a terse summary of the more recent form of this doctrine (*The Essence of Aesthetic*, trans. Douglas Ainslie, London, 1921, p. 21): 'By elaborating his impressions, man *frees* himself from them. By objectifying them, he removes them from him and makes himself their superior.' For an expanded version, see Yrjö Hirn, *Origins of Art* (London, 1900), pp. 102ff.

67. *Collected Writings*, X, 48n. Cf. Essay Supplementary to the Preface (1815), *Wordsworth's Literary Criticism*, p. 198: 'Every great poet . . . has to call forth and to communicate *power*.'

68. 'The Poetry of Pope' (1848), ibid. XI, 54-5.

69. Ibid. X, 219-27. On romantic discussions of subjective and objective, see Chap. IX, sect. iii.

70. 'On Shakespeare and Milton,' *Complete Works*, V, 53.

71. Review of *Life of Scott* (1838), in *Occasional Papers and Reviews* (Oxford, 1877), p. 6.

72. *Lectures on Poetry*, trans. E. K. Francis, I, 19-20; 59-66.

73. Ibid. I, 42-7.

74. Ibid. I, 22, 53-4, 87-8. Relevant to the effect of the expressive point of view on the theory of genres is Wordsworth's attempt, in his 1815 Preface, to rationalize the curious classification of his poems in that volume, on the basis of 'the powers of mind predominant in the production of them.' See also Markham L. Peacock, Jr., *The Critical Opinions of William Wordsworth* (Baltimore, 1950), pp. 111-12.

75. Ibid. I, 88-9; see Quintilian, *Institutes* VI. ii.

76. Ibid. I, 92, 86, 90.

77. De Quincey, 'Charles Lamb,' *Collected Writings,* V, 231-2.

78. *Lectures on Poetry,* I, 21-2, 25-6.

79. Ibid. I, 22, 55-6. Cf. 'Review of Lockhart,' *Occasional Papers,* p. 24: 'The epic, there-fore, or any other form, may act, as was said, like a safety-valve to a full mind. . .'

80. Ibid. I, 73.

81. 'Review of Lockhart,' *Occasional Papers,* p. 11.

82. *Lectures on Poetry,* I, 20-22, 47.

83. Ibid. I, 13, 74.

84. J. T. Coleridge, *Memoir of the Reverend John Keble* (4th ed.; Oxford, 1874), pp. 302, 313. Keble himself, as a religious poet, was almost morbidly sensitive to the self-exposure involved in publication. See Walter Lock, *John Keble* (3d ed.; London, 1893), p. 57.

85. For a comment on the connection between Keble's theory of poetry and religion, see Cardinal Newman, 'John Keble' (1846), *Essays Critical and Historical,* II, 442-3.

86. *Lectures on Poetry,* I, 56 (cf. p. 66); *Occasional Papers,* pp. 24-5.

87. 20-22 Oct. 1831, *Letters of John Stuart Mill,* ed. H. S. R. Elliot (London, 1910), I, 11.

88. For a précis of the poetics of John Stuart Mill, see Chap. I, sect. iv.

89. The article, a long review of George Combe's *Moral Philosophy* (1840), is identi-fied as written by Alexander Smith, of Banff, in *Selections from the Corre-spondence of the Late Macvey Napier,* ed. by his son (Edinburgh, 1879), p. 371n.

90. 'The Philosophy of Poetry,' *Blackwood's Edinburgh Magazine,* XXXVIII (1835), 827.

91. Ibid. pp. 828, 833.

92. Ibid. pp. 835-7.

93. Ibid. p. 828.

94. *Leviathan,* ed. A. B. Waller (Cambridge, 1904), Pt. I, Chap. IV, p. 21.

95. *The Sublime and Beautiful,* Pt. V, sect. vii; *The Works of . . . Edmund Burke* (London, 1854), I, 178-80.

96. C. K. Ogden and I. A. Richards, *The Meaning of Meaning* (3d ed.; London, 1930), p. 149; I. A. Richards, *Principles of Literary Criticism* (5th ed.; London, 1934), pp. 267, 273.

97. *Philosophy and Logical Syntax* (London, 1935), pp. 26-31. For the most thorough exploration of the concept of emotive language as an approach to the problems of philosophy, see C. L. Stevenson, *Ethics and Language* (New Haven, 1944).

98. 'On Poetry in General,' *Complete Works,* V, 7.

99. 'The Philosophy of Poetry,' p. 828; see Stevenson, *Ethics and Language,* p. 213, for an analysis, as a 'persuasive definition,' of the assertion 'Pope is not a poet.'

100. For a recent instance of this objection to Richards' analysis—there are many earlier instances—see Max Black, *Language and Philosophy* (Ithaca, N. Y., 1949), pp. 206-9. In his 'Emotive Language Still,' *Yale Review* (XXXIX, 1949), pp. 108ff., Richards clarifies his intention by pointing out that almost all uses of language have multiple functions, and are 'descriptive and emotive together, at once refer-ential and influential.'

101. 'Philosophy of Poetry,' p. 829.

102. Ibid. p. 830.

103. Ibid. pp. 830-31. Smith also employs the interesting device of showing how poetry loses its essential quality when translated into a-rhythmic prose (p. 831), and

points out that terms like 'melodious,' 'harmonious,' and 'musical,' when transferred from music to versification, are only very distant metaphors (p. 832n.).

104. *Ibid.* pp. 832-5.

105. 'On Poetry in General,' *Complete Works*, v, 1-2. For this inconsistency in the use of 'poetry,' Gifford taxed him harshly in a review in the *Quarterly*, and Hazlitt reacted violently in a scathing 'Letter to William Gifford, Esq.' justifying his equivocality by appeal to current usage of the term. (*Complete Works*, IX, 44-6.)

106. *The Works of Professor Wilson*, ed. Ferrier (Edinburgh, 1856), VI, 109-11.

CHAPTER VII

1. C. D. Thorpe, in *The Aesthetic Theory of Thomas Hobbes* (Ann Arbor, Mich., 1940), gives an account of Hobbes's precedents and influence.

2. Preface to Rapin, *Critical Essays of the Seventeenth Century*, II, 165.

3. *Adventurer* No. 93.

4. *Biographia Literaria*, II, 120.

5. On the relations of Hobbes's theory of the mind to contemporary natural science, see E. A. Burtt, *The Metaphysical Foundations of Modern Physical Science* (London, 1925), pp. 118-27, 297; and on the geometrical background of the eighteenth-century topography of the mind, Walter J. Ong, 'Psyche and the Geometers; Aspects of Associationist Critical Theory," *Modern Philology*, XLIX (1951), 16-27.

6. *A Treatise of Human Nature*, ed. L. A. Selby-Bigge (Oxford, 1896), pp. xx-xxiii. Cf. Hume's *An Abstract of a Treatise of Human Nature*, published anonymously in 1740, ed. J. M. Keynes and P. Sraffa (Cambridge, 1938), p. 6; and his *Enquiry Concerning Human Understanding*, Sect. I, in Hume's *Essays*, II, 11-12. N. K. Smith summarizes Hume's relations to Newton, whom he venerated beyond all other men, in *The Philosophy of David Hume* (London, 1941), pp. 52-76.

7. *Observations on Man* (6th ed.; London, 1834), pp. 4-5.

8. *Elements of Criticism*, Introduction, I, 14, 21-4. Kames's friend and biographer, Alexander Fraser Tytler, expanded upon Kames's account of the scientific pretensions of his *Elements*, and claimed that Kames's method superseded that of all earlier critics, from Aristotle to the present (*Memoirs of the Life and Writings of the Honourable Henry Home of Kames*, 3 vols., Edinburgh, 1814, I, vii, 377-9, 388-9).

9. *An Essay on Genius* (London, 1774), pp. 1-4. For other claims that a valid criticism is based on inductively established laws of the mind, see, e.g.: Arthur Murphy, *Gray's Inn Journal*, No. 87; Edmund Burke, *On the Sublime and Beautiful*, 'On Taste' and Pt. I, sect. XIX; Joshua Reynolds, Discourse VIII, *Works*, I, 459; George Campbell, *Philosophy of Rhetoric*, 2 vols. (Edinburgh, 1808), I, vii-viii, I, 10.

10. *Essays on Poetry and Music*, pp. 5-6.

11. *Treatise*, p. 2; cf. pp. 8-9, 85-6.

12. *Essay on Genius*, p. 28.

13. *Biographia*, I, 74; cf. *Coleridge on Logic and Learning*, pp. 126-7.

14. *Elements of Criticism*, II, 403-4 (Appendix, No. 19). Locke (*Essay Concerning Human Understanding*, III, x, 3) had noted that abstract words like 'wisdom' or 'glory' may be used without determinate 'ideas'—i.e., images. Berkeley maintained that general and abstract words evoke passions without the intercession of ideas (*Principles of Human Knowledge*, in *Works*, ed. Fraser, Oxford, 1901,

1, 251-2); while Burke declared that we converse not only of abstract ideas, but even 'of particular real beings . . . without having any idea of them excited in the imagination' (*On the Sublime and Beautiful*, Pt. v, sect. v, in *Works*, 1, 175). The possibility, however, of an imageless process of thought did not, so far as I know, enter into eighteenth-century treatments of the productive poetic imagination, but was confined to discussions of the nature of the aesthetic response to a completed poem.

15. E.g., Lucretius, *De rerum natura* iv. 737ff.; Augustine, *De Trinitate* ii. 10. See M. W. Bundy, *The Theory of Imagination in Classical and Mediaeval Thought*, University of Illinois Studies in Language and Literature (1927), xii, pp. 102, 163.

16. 'Heroic Poetry and Heroic Licence,' *Essays*, 1, 186-7.

17. Hobbes, *Leviathan*, ed. A. B. Waller (Cambridge, 1904), p. 4; Hume, *Treatise*, pp. 9-10, and *Enquiry*, Sect. ii.

18. *Essay on Genius*, pp. 98-102.

19. *Elements of the Philosophy of the Human Mind* (London, 1792), pp. 475-9.

20. See J. W. Beach, *The Concept of Nature in Nineteenth-Century English Poetry*, pp. 54-78, for an account of the philosophical use of the term 'plastic.'

21. *Philosophical and Critical Observations on . . . Composition*, 2 vols. (London, 1774), 1, 101-2. Cf. William Duff, *Essay on Original Genius*, pp. 6-7: The imagination is the faculty which 'by its plastic power of inventing new associations of ideas, and of combining them with infinite variety, is enabled to present a creation of its own.' See also Owen Ruffhead, *Life of Pope* (London, 1769), p. 448; Burke, *On the Sublime and Beautiful*, in *Works*, 1, 58.

22. *Treatise*, pp. 10-11. See Aristotle on recalling a forgotten item, in *Parva Naturalia* 451^b 10-20. Hobbes extended the role of association from the act of remembering to all the 'consequence, or train of thoughts' composing 'mental discourse' (*Leviathan*, Pt. i, Chap. iii).

23. See, e.g., Gerard, *Essay on Genius*, pp. 108-25; and Kames, *Elements of Criticism*, Chap. i, pp. 25-6. For a study of the extent to which the concept of association permeated literary theory, see the series of articles by Martin Kallich in *ELH*, xii (1945), 290-315; *Studies in Philology*, xliii (1946), 644-67; *Modern Language Notes*, lxii (1947), 166-73.

24. *Treatise*, p. 366. Cf. Newton, *The Mathematical Principles of Natural Philosophy* (New York, 1846), p. 385: '. . . We conclude the least particles of all bodies to be also extended, and hard, and impenetrable, and moveable, and endowed with their proper *vires inertiae*.'

25. *Treatise*, pp. 10, 12-13.

26. Coleridge in *Biographia*, 1, 67, cited Sir James Mackintosh as having claimed that Hartley 'stood in the same relation to Hobbes as Newton to Kepler; the law of association being that to the mind, which gravitation is to matter.'

27. *The System of Nature*, 4 vols. (London, 1797), 1, 38-9; cf. pp. 200ff.

28. *Essay on Genius*, pp. 49-50; cf. p. 265.

29. *De natura deorum* ii. 37.

30. *Principia*, p. 504 (Bk. iii, 'General Scholium'); cf. *Opticks* (3d ed.; London, 1721), pp. 377-80, Query 31. See also Burtt, *Metaphysical Foundations of Modern Physical Science*, pp. 187-96, 280-99.

31. For the nature and currency of the theological argument, see N. K. Smith's Introduction to Hume's *Dialogues Concerning Natural Religion* (Oxford, 1935); and for some of its appearances in physico-theological poetry, Marjorie Nicolson, *Newton Demands the Muse* (Princeton, 1946), pp. 99-106.

32. 'To My Honor'd Friend Sir Robert Howard,' ll. 31-4.

33. *Essays,* ii, 19n. The passage was added in the edition of 1748, but canceled in the editions of 1777 and those that followed.

34. *Essay on Genius,* pp. 46-7. In the third chapter of the *Leviathan,* Hobbes had distinguished between a train of thought which, as in dreams and idle revery, is controlled only by contiguity in prior experience, and that which is directed by a 'passionate thought,' or 'design'; in the latter case we have 'the faculty of invention.' Thomas Reid, denying the adequacy of pure associationism to explain any regular or inventive thinking by inherent 'attractions and repulsions,' insisted that 'every work of art has its model framed in imagination,' by which the train of thought is 'guided and directed, much in the same manner as the horse we ride' (*Essays on the Intellectual Powers of the Human Mind,* London, 1827, pp. 219-20).

35. *Essay on Genius,* pp. 84-5. See also Reid, *Intellectual Powers,* p. 220; and Duff, *Essay on Original Genius,* pp. 8-9.

36. Burtt, *Metaphysical Foundations,* pp. 288-93.

37. See, e.g., Gerard, *Essay on Genius,* pp. 8-9. Something like the infinite regress I mention seems to characterize Hartley's one-page attempt to give a purely mechanical explanation of invention; see *Observations on Man,* pp. 272-3.

38. Ibid. pp. 60-64. To these passages, compare Akenside's description of aesthetic invention in *Pleasures of Imagination* (ed. of 1744), iii, 312-408, and notes.

39. *Essay on Genius,* p. 65.

40. *Biographia,* i, 73.

41. That is, Coleridge accepts as valid, not Hartley's determinism, but that combination of teleology and mechanism—of judgment operating on the offerings of the associative imagination—which characterized most eighteenth-century theories. See e.g., ibid. pp. 73, 76, 81, and 60: The law of association 'at the utmost . . . is to thought the same, as the law of gravitation is to locomotion. In every *voluntary* movement we first counteract gravitation, in order to avail ourselves of it' (my italics).

42. *Biographia,* i, 73, 193; *Anima Poetae* (Boston and New York, 1895), p. 199; *Miscellaneous Criticism,* p. 387.

43. *Biographia,* i, 163, and ii, 12, 123, 264n. It is an interesting possibility that Coleridge may have derived some of his terms for specifying the imagination from the associationists he opposed. Hume, e.g., had said that ideas are impenetrable, but that impressions and passions, 'like colours, may be blended . . . perfectly together' (*Treatise,* p. 366; cf. Gerard, *Essay on Taste,* London, 1759, p. 171). Hartley pointed out that simple ideas of sensation become associated in clusters and 'at last, coalesce into one complex idea,' in which the simple elements are no more identifiable than the several ingredients in a medicine, or the primary colors in white light (*Observations on Man,* pp. 47-8). Cf. Abraham Tucker, *The Light of Nature Pursued* (Cambridge, 1831), i, 135-8, 190; and Joseph Priestley, *Hartley's Theory of the Human Mind* (2d ed.; London, 1790), p. xxxviii. But it is evident that the concepts of blending and coalescence were forced on associationists by the very exigency of their rigid elementarism, which held that all complex ideas are images, composed of replicas of the parts into which objects of sense may be rationally analyzed. When such parts were not found by introspection, it was maintained that they had been 'fused' into a new unit-idea.

44. See e.g., *Biographia,* ii, 12-13, 19; *Shakespearean Criticism,* i, 209, ii, 341; *Letters,* i, 405; *Anima Poetae,* p. 199. Cf. his *Theory of Life,* ed. Seth B. Watson (Lon-

don, 1848), p. 22: 'Assimilation' is 'the phrase most in vogue at present' to stand
for nutrition 'for the purposes of reproduction and growth.' And p. 44: 'If life,
in general, be defined *vis ab intra, cujus proprium est coadunare plura in rem
unicam. . .*' See also his discussion of 'assimilation' as a metaphor in his *Letters*,
II, 710-11.

45. *Biographia*, I, 202, II, 65; *Miscellaneous Criticism*, pp. 387-8.

46. See conclusion of Chap. III; and I. A. Richards, *Coleridge on Imagination* (London, 1934), p. 52.

47. *Aids to Reflection* (London, 1913), pp. 268-9. Cf. Whitehead, *Science and the Modern World* (Cambridge, 1932), p. 70: 'The seventeenth century had finally produced a scheme of thought framed by mathematicians, for the use of mathematicians. . . The enormous success of the scientific abstractions . . . has foisted onto philosophy the task of accepting them as the most concrete rendering of fact.' And p. 80: 'A further stage of provisional realism is required, in which the scientific scheme is recast, and founded upon the ultimate concept of *organism*.'

48. *Letters*, II, 649. Cf. *The Philosophical Lectures of Samuel Taylor Coleridge*, ed. Kathleen Coburn (New York, 1949), especially Lectures XII-XIII.

49. To John Thelwall, 31 Dec. 1796, *Letters*, I, 211-12.

50. See Alice D. Snyder, *Coleridge on Logic and Learning* (New Haven, 1929), pp. 23-32; and *Biographia*, I, 103-4n., 138.

51. *Aids to Reflection*, pp. 40-41.

52. *Table Talk*, p. 163 (18 Dec. 1831).

53. *Philosophical Lectures*, p. 196.

54. Monologue on 'Life,' *Fraser's Magazine for Town and Country*, XII (Nov. 1835), 495.

55. *Shakespearean Criticism*, I, 233; *Miscellaneous Criticism*, p. 89.

56. Plato, *Phaedrus* 264; Aristotle, *Poetics* 7. See also Longinus, *On the Sublime*, XL.

57. *Statesman's Manual*, Appendix B, in *Lay Sermons*, p. 77.

58. *Coleridge's Treatise on Method*, ed. A. D. Snyder (London, 1934), p. 7; cf. pp. 37-8.

59. *Philosophical Lectures*, pp. 378-9.

60. 'On Poesy or Art,' *Biographia*, II, 258-9. Cf. *Statesman's Manual*, p. 25: 'But every principle is actualised by an idea, and every idea is living, productive, partaketh of infinity, and (as Bacon has sublimely observed) containeth an endless power of semination.'

61. *Statesman's Manual*, p. 77.

62. *Theory of Life*, p. 42; *Church and State*, in *Works*, VI, 140. Cf. *Coleridge on Logic and Learning*, p. 130, and his Monologue on 'Life,' p. 495.

63. *Shakespearean Criticism*, I, 223-4. In 'Poesy or Art,' *Biographia*, II, 262, Coleridge states the difference as one 'between form as proceeding, and shape as super-induced.'

64. *Aids to Reflection*, p. 267.

65. Ibid. p. 117n.

66. See Chap. VIII, sect. iii.

67. *Shakespearean Criticism*, II, 192.

68. *Statesman's Manual*, p. 76 (my italics); cf. *Biographia*, II, 257. A full account of Coleridge's governing analogues of mind would need to take in his statement, concerning the ethical and religious conduct of man, that 'the perfect frame of a man is the perfect frame of a state: and in the light of this idea we must read Plato's *Republic*' (*Statesman's Manual*, Appendix B, in *Lay Sermons*, p. 66. For a discussion of this Platonic element in Coleridge's view of mental order, see

I. A. Richards, Introduction to *The Portable Coleridge*, New York, 1950, pp. 44-54). A central problem in Coleridge's theory of the mind might be stated as the attempt to reconcile the sanctions of consciousness, authority, and will in the judicial, legislative, and executive elements of the archetype of the political state, with the attributes of unconscious and spontaneous self-evolution inherent in the alternative, and even more persistently employed, archetype of the growing plant.

69. *Theory of Life,* p. 44; cf. Kant, *Critique of Judgment,* ed. J. H. Bernard (London, 1914), pp. 277, 280.

70. MS note printed by A. D. Snyder, 'Coleridge's "Theory of Life," ' *Modern Language Notes,* XLVII (1932), p. 301; and *Theory of Life,* p. 63. As G. E. Moore has unsympathetically characterized this organismic thesis: 'Thus a "teleological" relation is supposed to be a relation which alters the things it relates, so that it is not they, but some two other things which are related' ('Teleology,' in *Dictionary of Philosophy and Psychology,* ed. J. M. Baldwin, II, 666).

71. *Church and State,* in *Works,* VI, 101. Cf. *Theory of Life,* p. 58.

72. *Shakespearean Criticism,* I, 223. See Gordon McKenzie, *Organic Unity in Coleridge,* Univ. of California Publications in English, VII (1939).

73. *Biographia,* II, 12. As part of the motto to Chap. XIII, 'On the Imagination,' Coleridge also quoted Milton's lines from *Paradise Lost,* v, 482ff.: 'Flowers and their fruit/Man's nourishment, by gradual scale sublim'd,/To *vital* spirits aspire: to *animal:*/To intellectual!'/

74. *The Art of Poetry,* I, 177-80.

75. *Anima Poetae,* pp. 142-3; see also pp. 124-5. In *Biographia,* I, 169-70, he holds that 'a true philosophy' must incorporate the fragments of truth from all existing systems—and he specifically includes the mechanical system—all ·'united in one perspective central point.' Cf. *Table Talk,* p. 157, and *Philosophical Lectures,* p. 313: 'Nature excludes nothing. . . The contrary method, exclusion instead of subordination' characterizes the history of human error.

76. *Table Talk,* p. 100; *The Friend,* in *Works,* II, 164; *Biographia,* I, 20; *Shakespearean Criticism,* I, 4-5. Coleridge holds, in accordance with the logic of organism, that genius and imagination must include, by transcending, the processes of talent and fancy, since 'the higher intellectual powers can only act through a corresponding energy of the lower' (*Table Talk,* p. 269).

77. *Miscellaneous Criticism,* p. 44n.; 88-9. See also *Shakespearean Criticism,* II, 170-71.·

78. *Miscellaneous Criticism,* p. 47.

79. Ibid. pp. 42-3.

80. Preface to James Mill's *Analysis of the Phenomena of the Human Mind,* ed. J. S. Mill (London, 1869), I, xii.

81. Ibid. I, 241-2.

82. 'The Two Kinds of Poetry' (1833), *Early Essays,* p. 232.

83. 'What Is Poetry?', ibid. pp. 208-9.

84. *Essay on Genius,* pp. 125-6, 147ff. Cf. Hume, *A Dissertation on the Passions,* in *Essays,* II, 144-5; Kames, *Elements of Criticism,* I, 27 (Chap. I).

85. 'The Two Kinds of Poetry,' *Early Essays,* pp. 223, 225. The extent to which, in Mill's theory, poetic invention was regarded as a special case of the general laws of association may be seen by comparing his exposition of those general laws in his *System of Logic* (VI, iv, 3), and his analysis of the special laws of poetic association in 'The Two Kinds of Poetry,' pp. 225, 230.

86. Ibid. p. 229. In the earlier stages of working his way out of Hartley's theory, Coleridge had himself emphasized the concept of emotional association: 'I hold that association depends in a much greater degree on the recurrence of resembling states of feeling than on trains of ideas. . . I almost think that ideas *never* recall ideas, as far as they are ideas. . .' But instead of regarding this observation as an addition to Hartley's doctrines, Coleridge thinks it subversive of the whole philosophy—'and if this be true, Hartley's system totters' (To Southey, 7 Aug. 1803, *Letters*, I, 427-8; cf. ibid. I, 347, and *The Friend*, in *Works*, II, 415).

87. 'On the Genius and Character of Hogarth,' *The Works of Charles and Mary Lamb*, ed. E. V. Lucas (London, 1903), I, 73-4.

88. *Anima Poetae*, p. 199. For Wordsworth's opinion of Lamb's comment see *Wordsworth's Literary Criticism*, p. 162. See also Shelley's brief distinction between the analytic reason and the synthetic imagination, in 'Defence of Poetry,' *Literary and Philosophical Criticism*, pp. 120-21.

89. 'On Poetry in General,' *Complete Works*, V, 4-5.

90. Ibid. p. 8.

91. 'Coleridge's Lay Sermon' (1816), ibid. XVI, 114.

92. Preface to Poems (1815), *Wordsworth's Literary Criticism*, p. 163.

93. Ibid. pp. 159-61; Coleridge, *Table Talk*, p. 309. See also Wordsworth's comment, cited in Christopher Wordsworth, *Memoirs of William Wordsworth*, II, 487: 'The imagination . . . is that chemical faculty by which elements of the most different nature and distant origin are blended together into one harmonious and homogeneous whole.'

94. *Biographia*, I, 64, II, 193.

95. *Wordsworth's Literary Criticism*, p. 165; and p. 156: Fancy insinuates herself 'into the heart of objects with creative activity.'

96. Ibid. pp. 151, 159.

97. Ibid. p. 163.

98. *Biographia*, I, 194.

99. *Science and the Modern World*, pp. 96, 117-18. Coleridge, however, was disappointed in *The Excursion* because it was neither explicitly enough anti-mechanical nor systematically enough organismic in its philosophy; see his letter to Wordsworth, 30 May 1815, *Letters*, II, 645-9.

100. *Imagination and Fancy* (New York, 1848), p. 2; cf. pp. 20-22.

101. See, e.g., the quotations in I. A. Richards, *Coleridge on Imagination*, pp. 31-43; also, F. X. Roellinger, 'E. S. Dallas on Imagination,' *Studies in Philology*, XXXVIII (1941), p. 656; F. L. Lucas, *The Decline and Fall of the Romantic Ideal* (New York, 1936), p. 176. The most recent example is Barbara Hardy, 'Distinction Without Difference; Coleridge's Fancy and Imagination,' *Essays in Criticism*, I (1951).

102. *Coleridge on Imagination*, pp. 18-19, 70, 78-85.

103. *Decline and Fall of the Romantic Ideal*, p. 164; cf. pp. 174-5.

104. *Table Talk*, p. 165; 27 Dec. 1831.

CHAPTER VIII

1. *Timaeus* 30.

2. See Burtt, *Metaphysical Foundations of Modern Physical Science*, p. 259. Newton is careful, however, to distinguish his 'Lord over all' from the concept of a 'soul of the world' (*Principia*, Bk. III, 'General Scholium,' p. 504).

3. *Characteristics*, ed. J. M. Robertson, II, 110-12.

4. *Aristotle*, trans. Richard Robinson (Oxford, 1934), p. 384.

5. *Dichtung und Wahrheit*, in *Sämtliche Werke*, XXIV, 52-4 (Pt. III, Bk. XI).

6. *Spectator* No. 160. See also *Spectator* No. 592.

7. *Poetics* 17. 1455ª. Horace attributed to Democritus the association (that Horace derided) between innate poetic ability and madness (*Ars Poetica* 295-7. See also Cicero, *Pro Archia* 18). William Ringler details the history of these ideas in 'Poeta Nascitur Non Fit,' *Journal of the History of Ideas*, II (1941), 497-504.

8. Cf., e.g., Thomas Lodge, *Elizabethan Critical Essays*, ed. G. G. Smith, I, 71-2. William Temple discusses the relation between inspiration and innate genius, and then goes on to contrast Homer and Virgil as different types of 'genius' in a way that anticipates Addison's theory ('Of Poetry,' *Critical Essays of the Seventeenth Century*, ed. Spingarn, III, 80-83).

9. Preface to *Works of Shakespeare*, in *The Works of Alexander Pope* (London, 1778), III, 270-72, 285.

10. Preface to the *Iliad*, in ibid. III, 244-5, 260.

11. *Ion* 533-4. On the early history of this concept see Alice Sperduti, 'The Divine Nature of Poetry in Antiquity,' *Transactions and Proceedings of the American Philological Association*, LXXXI (1950), 209-40.

12. For other examples see C. D. Baker, 'Certain Religious Elements in the English Doctrine of the Inspired Poet during the Renaissance,' *ELH*, VI (1939), 300-23; and Leah Jonas, *The Divine Science* (New York, 1940), 166-71. George Wither (quoted by Miss Jonas, p. 108), said that he did not know what he had to write, 'Until I read it over as you do . . . As if these writings had been none of mine.'

13. Answer to Davenant, *Critical Essays of the Seventeenth Century*, II, 59; cf. ibid. p. 25.

14. H. B. Charlton, *Castelvetro's Theory of Poetry* (Manchester, 1913), p. 22.

15. 'Life of Gray,' *Lives of the Poets* (ed. Hill), III, 433; 'Life of Milton,' ibid. I, 138.

16. Sixth Discourse, *Works*, I, 382. Henry Pemberton, after defining invention as the power of calling and assembling 'what images and conceptions may be subservient to the purpose, which shall be in view,' goes on to deny the 'fiction' of divine inspiration (*Observations on Poetry*, 1738, pp. 47-9).

17. *Reflections on Aristotle's Treatise*, trans. Rymer, p. 6.

18. *Essay on Genius* (1774), pp. 67-9. Longinus had early reduced myth to psychology when he held that genuine passion 'bursts out in a wild gust of mad enthusiasm and as it were fills the speaker's words with frenzy' (*On the Sublime* VIII. 4, p. 59). Building on Longinus, John Dennis accounted for poetical enthusiasm as passions 'whose cause is not comprehended by us,' because they 'proceed from Thoughts, that latently, and unobserv'd by us, carry Passion along with them' (*Advancement and Reformation of Poetry*, in *Critical Works*, I, 217).

19. *Shelley's Literary and Philosophical Criticism*, pp. 164, 213.

20. 'Defence of Poetry,' ibid. pp. 153-5.

21. Ibid. p. 157, and letter to Gisborne, 19 July 1821, *Complete Works of Percy Bysshe Shelley*, ed. Ingpen and Peck (London, 1926), X, 287.

22. In 'A Grace Beyond the Reach of Art,' *Journal of the History of Ideas*, V (1944), 131-50, S. H. Monk traces the concept of an indefinable aesthetic quality back through the Renaissance to Greek and Roman theories of rhetoric and painting. For the prevalence of the *je ne sais quoi* in French criticism, see E. B. O. Borgerhoff, *The Freedom of French Classicism* (Princeton, 1950), esp. Chap. V.

23. 'Of Beauty,' *Essays*, in *The Works of Lord Bacon* (New York, 1864), XII, 226.

24. *Entretiens d'Ariste et d'Eugène* (1671), ed. René Radouant (Paris, 1920), pp. 196, 199, 201, 209-12; and p. 202: This quality is like God himself, in that 'there is nothing in the world more known, nor more unknown.'

25. (London, 1694), p. 61.

26. See e.g., John Dennis, *Remarks on 'Prince Arthur,'* in *Critical Works,* I, 46.

27. II, i. 362; I, ii. 141-60. Cf. also Davenant, Preface to Gondibert (1650), *Critical Essays of the Seventeenth Century,* II, 20.

28. *Rambler* No. 92; cf. 'Life of Pope,' *Lives of the Poets* (ed. Hill), III, 259; and 'Life of Denham,' *Lives of the Poets,* I, 79.

29. Reprinted in *The Works of Alexander Pope,* ed. Elwin and Courthope (London, 1871), II, 90.

30. *Philological Inquiries* (1780-81), in *Works* (London, 1803), IV, 228-9, 234-5.

31. *Works,* I, 385-7.

32. 'Of Poetry,' *Critical Essays of the Seventeenth Century,* III, 83-4.

33. *Oeuvres* (Paris, 1790), I, 157.

34. 'On the Discrimination of Romanticisms,' *Essays in the History of Ideas,* p. 238.

35. See also *Spectator* No. 414. This parallel was deeply established in the eighteenth century; Johnson, e.g., called the composition of Shakespeare a forest, and that of a 'correct and regular writer' a garden (Preface to Shakespeare, *Johnson on Shakespeare,* p. 34).

36. *Critical Reflections on Poetry Painting and Music* (1719), trans. Thomas Nugent (London, 1748), II, 32. The recourse to plant life to illustrate the processes of genius did not pass without challenge. In his *Remarks on the Beauties of Poetry* (London, 1762), p. 36, Daniel Webb quotes Pope's description of Shakespeare as 'an instrument of nature,' and comments: 'These distinctions are too subtle for me. I shall never be brought to consider the beauties of a Poet in the same light that I do the colours in a Tulip.'

37. Ed. Edith J. Morley, pp. 15, 17, 13-14.

38. Ibid. pp. 6, 11, 21, 7.

39. *Spectator* No. 409. Both Rymer and Dryden had applied the epithet 'mechanical' to the unities and other rules (*Critical Essays of the Seventeenth Century,* II, 183; *Essays of John Dryden,* II, 158). Pope, in the *Guardian* No. 78, ironically compared such 'mechanical rules' to receipts for making puddings. For the discrimination between mechanical externals and the profounder requirements of great art, see also Welsted, in *Critical Essays of the Eighteenth Century,* pp. 364-5; Duff, *Essay on Original Genius,* p. 15; Reynolds, Sixth Discourse, *Works,* I, 386. The distinction survives in Hazlitt, *Table Talk,* in *Complete Works,* VIII, 82: 'To snatch this grace beyond the reach of art is . . . where fine art begins, and where mechanical skill ends'; this 'must be taught by nature and genius, not by rules or study.'

40. *Conjectures on Original Composition,* pp. 21-3.

41. Ibid. pp. 337, 327.

42. *Characteristics,* ed. J. M. Robertson (London, 1900), I, 136.

43. Ibid. I, 151-2, 172, 180, 214.

44. See p. 167. Lord Kames expressed an early, but passing, comparison between artistic unity and organic relations: 'Hence it is required in every such work, that, like an organic system, its parts be orderly arranged and mutually connected, bearing each of them a relation to the whole, some more intimate, some less, according to their destination . . .' (*Elements of Criticism,* I, 32).

45. E.g., see Locke's *Essay Concerning Human Understanding,* Bk. II, i, 9ff., for an attack against the thesis that there may be thought without consciousness.

46. Leibniz, *The Monadology,* in *The Monadology and Other Philosophical Writings,* trans. Robert Latta (Oxford, 1898), sects. 56, 61, 63. Leibniz also formulated a distinction between an organic body and 'a machine made by the skill of man,' which was often echoed in German aesthetics. The man-made machine 'is not a machine in each of its parts,' for it is composed of elements wrenched to their present use. 'But the machines of nature, namely, living bodies, are still machines in their smallest parts *ad infinitum.* It is this that constitutes the difference between nature and art' (ibid. sect. 64). On some related issues, see James Benziger, 'Organic Unity: Leibniz to Coleridge,' *PMLA* (LXVI, 1951), 24-48.

47. Introduction to *New Essays on the Human Understanding,* in *The Monadology,* ed. Latta, p. 370; cf. *Monadology,* sects. 19-21.

48. *Allgemeine Theorie der schönen Künste* (2d ed.; Leipzig, 1792), II, 88, 93-4. For Sulzer's reliance on Leibniz, see Robert Sommer, *Grundzüge einer Geschichte der deutschen Psychologie und Aesthetik* (Würzburg, 1892), pp. 195ff.

49. *Allgemeine Theorie,* I, 349, 352-3. Leibniz had already referred casually to the concept of the *je ne sais quoi* in connection with the *petites perceptions;* these, he said, form a 'something I know not what' (Introduction to *New Essays,* in *The Monadology,* ed. Latta, p. 372).

50. *Vom Erkennen und Emfinden der menschlichen Seele,* in *Sämtliche Werke,* VIII, 175-6. The passage resembles Coleridge's key description of the nature of a plant in Appendix B of *The Statesman's Manual.* There is a comparable passage in Giordano Bruno, Coleridge's favorite martyr, who of all earlier philosophers most approximated the elements of romantic nature-philosophy. See, e.g., Bruno's *Concerning the Cause, Principle, and One,* trans. Sidney Greenberg in *The Infinite in Giordano Bruno* (New York, 1950), p. 112.

51. *Von deutscher Art und Kunst* (1773), V, 217-18, 220-21; see also the earlier draft, pp. 238-9.

52. *Vom Erkennen und Empfinden,* VIII, 223, 226.

53. In Fichte's *The Nature of the Scholar* (1805), the Divine Idea whose possession is the mark of genius, turns out to be very like an internalized plant in its workings. It drives on 'through its own essential life,' impelling everyone even against his own wish 'as though he were a passive instrument,' never ceasing 'from spontaneous activity and self-development until it has attained . . . a living and efficient form.' But genius remains modest because this capacity 'works and rules with silent power, long before it comes to consciousness of its own nature' (Fichte, *Popular Works,* trans. William Smith, London, 1873, pp. 138, 163, 165).

54. 'Von deutscher Baukunst,' *Goethe's Sämtliche Werke,* XXXIII, 5, 9, 11. On the influence of Herder over this document, see Goethe's *Autobiography,* trans. John Oxenford (Bohn ed.; London, 1903), I, 441.

55. Letter of 20 Dec. 1786, in *Werke* (Weimar, 1896), IV Abtl., VIII, 100.

56. *Italienische Reise,* 6 Sept. 1787, *Sämtliche Werke,* XXVII, 107-8.

57. 'Über Wahrheit und Wahrscheinlichkeit der Kunstwerke,' *Sämtliche Werke,* XXXIII, 90; 'Einleitung in die Propyläen,' ibid. 108, 110. See also Eckermann's *Conversations,* 20 June 1831.

58. *Kampagne in Frankreich,* in *Sämtliche Werke,* XXVIII, 122; cf. *Einwirkung der neueren Philosophie* (1820), XXXIX, 31. See also the letter to Zelter of 29 Jan. 1830, *Briefwechsel zwischen Goethe und Zelter,* ed. F. W. Riemer (Berlin, 1834), V, 380.

59. *Critique of Aesthetic Judgement,* ed. J. C. Meredith (Oxford, 1911), pp. 168-9. Kant adds that in all art, after the initial material is furnished by nature, there must follow a mechanical process, subject to rules, in which the given material is artfully elaborated (pp. 170-71).

60. *Kant's Kritik of Judgement,* trans. J. H. Bernard (London, 1892), pp. 260-61, 272-80.

61. Ibid. p. 280.

62. 'Über Goethe's Meister,' *Jugendschriften,* ed. Minor, II, 170.

63. *System des transcendentalen Idealismus,* in *Sämtliche Werke* (Stuttgart und Augsburg, 1858), III, 349.

64. Ibid. p. 618.

65. Ibid. p. 617.

66. Ibid. pp. 616-17, 349, 626; see also pp. 612, 621-2. For Schelling's detailed analysis of the nature of a living organism, see his *Ideen zu einer Philosophie der Natur* (1797), in *Sämtliche Werke,* I, 690ff. Schelling, of course, attributes to the universe as a whole the qualities Kant had used to describe only the organic objects in nature.

67. 'Über naive und sentimentalische Dichtung,' *Werke,* ed. Arthur Kutscher (Berlin, Goldene Klassiker-Bibliothek, n.d.), VIII, 124, 167.

68. *Briefwechsel zwischen Schiller und Goethe* (4th ed.; Stuttgart, 1881), 27 March 1801, II, 278; 6 Apr. 1801, II, 280. See also Schiller's letter of 26 July 1800, ibid. II, 243. For Goethe's later theory of the daemonic spirit that activates a genius, see his *Conversations with Eckermann,* 8 Mar. 1831 and 20 June 1831.

69. *Vorschule der Aesthetik,* in *Jean Pauls Sämtliche Werke* (Weimar, 1935), Pt. I, vol. XI, 45-6, 49, 52. Richter also distinguishes sharply and at length between 'talent' and 'genius'—a distinction which Coleridge combined with the opposition between mechanical and organic and assimilated to his cardinal antithesis between fancy and imagination. For a history of the antithesis between talent and genius, see L. P. Smith, *Four Romantic Words,* pp. 108-12, and Julius Ernst, *Der Geniebegriff der Stürmer und Dränger und der Frühromantik* (Zurich, 1916), pp. 22, 63, 81-2. Cf. Schelling, *System des transcendentalen Idealismus,* in *Sämtliche Werke,* III, 624.

70. C. G. Jung, *Modern Man in Search of a Soul* (New York, 1934), pp. 180-81.

71. *Vorschule der Aesthetik,* XI, 50-51, 47n. For further discussion of the vast abysm of the unconscious, see Richter's unfinished work, *Selina,* in *Sämtliche Werke,* Pt. II, vol. IV, pp. 217ff. Richter was the most important source for De Quincey's extended discussions of the depth-psychology of the dreamer.

72. *Vorlesungen über schöne Litteratur und Kunst,* in *Deutsche Litteraturdenkmale des 18. und 19. Jahrhunderts* (Stuttgart, 1884), XVII, 101, 111; XVIII, 59.

73. Ibid. XVII, 102, 83.

74. *Vorlesungen über dramatische Kunst und Litteratur,* in *Sämtliche Werke* (Leipzig, 1846), VI, 157, 182. In his essay on *Romeo and Juliet* (1797), A. W. Schlegel had early demonstrated the conscious artistry of Shakespeare. For an example of the opposing tendency in deductions from the organicity of genius, we may note Novalis' objection that 'the Schlegels overlook, when they speak of the purposefulness and artistry of Shakespeare's works, that art belongs to nature, and is similar to self-contemplative, self-imitative, self-formative nature . . . Shakespeare was no calculator, no scholar. . . Nothing more senseless can be said [of his works] than that they are works of art in that confined, mechanical sense of the word' (*Romantische Welt: Die Fragmente,* pp. 355-6).

75. Ed. H. L. Mansel and John Veitch (Edinburgh and London, 1859-60), I, 338ff. John Stuart Mill, in his *An Examination of Sir William Hamilton's Philosophy* (6th ed.; London, 1889, pp. 341ff.), denied the validity of Hamilton's evidence for unconscious cerebration.

76. To Lady Louisa Stuart, 31 Jan. 1817, *Letters*, VI, 380-81.

77. Quoted from Woodhouse's manuscript by Amy Lowell, *John Keats* (Boston and New York, 1925), I, 501-2.

78. *The Plain Speaker*, in *Complete Works*, XII, 118-19.

79. *Lectures on the English Comic Writers* (1819), in *Complete Works*, VI, 109; 'Farington's Life of Sir Joshua Reynolds' (1820), ibid. XVI, 209-10.

80. To Thomas Butts, 25 Apr. 1803, *Poetry and Prose of William Blake*, pp. 866-7.

81. *Poetry and Prose*, p. 809; H. C. Robinson, *Diary, Reminiscences, and Correspondence*, ed. Thomas Sadler (Boston, 1898), II, 35.

82. 'State of German Literature,' *Works*, XXVI, 51-3. We may mention here the distinction by another Germanist, Thomas De Quincey, between an 'organic' and a 'mechanic' style, and his opposition of the style of Burke, which is governed by the 'very necessity of growth,' to that of Dr. Johnson, which exhibits neither 'process' nor 'evolution' ('Style,' *Collected Writings*, X, 163-4, 269ff.).

83. 'Characteristics' (1831), *Works*, XXVIII, 3, 5.

84. Ibid. pp. 3-5.

85. Ibid. pp. 5, 16. Cf. p. 40.

86. E.g., ibid. pp. 6-7, 10, 12.

87. *Heroes and Hero-Worship* (1835), in *Works*, V, 107-8.

88. 'Goethe,' *Works*, XXVI, 215.

89. 'Characteristics,' *Works*, XXVIII, 13; see also pp. 7, 41.

90. *Ueber das Studium der Griechischen Poesie*, in *Jugendschriften*, I, 145. Cf. *Gespräch über die Poesie* (1800), ibid. II, 339.

91. 'Characteristics,' *Works*, XXVIII, 38-9.

92. Preface to the *Works of Shakespeare*, *Works*, III, 273.

93. *Von deutscher Art und Kunst* (1773), in *Sämtliche Werke*, V, 217-18; the full development of Herder's ideas is to be found in his *Ideen zu einer Philosophie der Geschichte der Menschheit* (1784-91).

94. *Coleridge's Shakespearean Criticism*, I, 242-3. Cf. A. W. Schlegel, *Lectures on Dramatic Art and Literature*, p. 340. See also *Shakespearean Criticism*, I, 231, and *Miscellaneous Criticism*, pp. 159-60. For his organic theory of the English state, see Coleridge's *Church and State*, in *Works*, ed. Shedd, VI. Cf. *Lay Sermons*, p. 23, and *Table Talk*, pp. 163-4.

95. *Theory of Life*, p. 42; 'On the Principles of Genial Criticism,' *Biographia Literaria*, II, 232. The definition of beauty as the many-in-the-one is an old idea that readily lent itself to Coleridge's biological premises.

96. *Theory of Life*, pp. 44, 47-50.

97. 'On Poesy or Art,' *Biographia*, II, 255. Also *Table Talk* (27 Dec. 1831), p. 165; *Inquiring Spirit*, ed. Coburn, p. 158.

98. *Shakespearean Criticism*, I, 197-8; cf. *Miscellaneous Criticism*, p. 7.

99. *Shakespearean Criticism*, I, 224; II, 262-3; *Miscellaneous Criticism*, p. 190. On other theoretical bases for similar aesthetic preferences in this age, see A. O. Lovejoy, *The Great Chain of Being* (Cambridge, 1936), Chap. x.

100. 'Irony and "Ironic" Poetry,' *College English*, IX (1948), pp. 231-2, 237. See also his 'The Poem as Organism,' *English Institute Annual*, 1940, pp. 20-41.

101. See *The Well-Wrought Urn* (New York, 1947), p. 17.

102. 'On Poesy or Art,' *Biographia*, II, 257-8. For Coleridge's lifelong interest in the psychology of dreams, animal magnetism, and other mental phenomena whose causes lie in a realm, as he said, 'below consciousness,' see *Coleridge's Philosophical Lectures*, Introduction, pp. 44-7.

103. Robert Heron [John Pinkerton], *Letters of Literature* (London, 1785), pp. 207-8, 212.

104. See, e.g., the nineteenth book of *Dichtung und Wahrheit*, in which Goethe describes the *Sturm und Drang* conception of genius as 'declaring itself above all restraint.' Now, however, he sees that 'genius is that power of man which by its deeds and actions gives laws and rules.'

105. *Italienische Reise* (1787), *Sämtliche Werke*, XXVII, 108; *Diderot's Versuch über die Malerei* (1798-9), ibid. XXXIII, 212-13.

106. *Shakespearean Criticism*, II, 170; *Miscellaneous Criticism*, p. 43; *Biographia*, II, 65.

107. 'Coleridge,' *Appreciations* (New York, 1905), pp. 79-80.

108. *Biographia*, II, 19-20, 12; *Shakespearean Criticism*, II, 263 (my italics).

109. 'Coleridge as Aesthetician and Critic,' *Journal of the History of Ideas*, V (1944), p. 408.

110. *Coleridge on Logic and Learning*, p. 110; *Shakespearean Criticism*, I, 223-4. On this topic see also Charles Lamb, 'The Sanity of True Genius' (1826).

CHAPTER IX

1. 'The State of German Literature,' *Works*, I, 51.
2. *Monologen*, ed. F. M. Schiele, p. 22.
3. 'Vom Erkennen und Empfinden' (1778), *Sämtliche Werke*, VIII, 208.
4. *The Decline and Fall of the Romantic Ideal* (New York, 1936), p. 221.
5. *Axel's Castle* (Charles Scribner's Sons, New York, 1936), p. 176.
6. *The Geography of Strabo*, i. 2. 5; trans. H. L. Jones (Loeb Classical Library), I, 63. Cf. *Republic* iii. 400.
7. Dedicatory Epistle of *Volpone*, in *Critical Essays of the Seventeenth Century*, ed. Spingarn, I, 12.
8. Thus Cowley, defending himself as a writer of amatory verses, insisted that the mimetic mirror is turned strictly outward (Preface to *Poems*, 1656, in ibid. II, 85): 'It is not in this sense that *Poesie* is said to be a kind of *Painting;* it is not the *Picture* of the *Poet*, but of *things* and *persons* imagined by him. He may be in his own practice and disposition a *Philosopher*, nay a *Stoick*, and yet speak sometimes with the softness of an amorous Sappho.'
9. *Elizabethan Critical Essays*, ed. G. G. Smith, II, 142-3, 153-4. Puttenham adds the interesting suggestion that 'men doo chuse their subjects according to the mettal of their minds. . .' See also Ben Jonson, *Critical Essays of the Seventeenth Century*, I, 41: Language 'springs out of the most retired and inmost parts of us, and is the Image of the Parent of it, the mind. No glasse renders a mans forme or likenesse so true as his speech.' For ancient statements of the idea, see A. Otto, *Die Sprichwörter und sprichwörtlichen Redensarten der Römer* (Leipzig, 1890), p. 257.
10. *The Life of Dr. Johnson*, 13 April 1778. Cf. John Hughes, *Of Style* (1698), *Critical Essays of the Eighteenth Century*, ed. Durham, p. 83. For opposing views that there is only a single excellence in style, see Elizabeth L. Mann, 'The Problem of Originality in English Literary Criticism 1750-1800,' *Philological Quarterly*, XVIII (1939), pp. 113-14.

11. *Works of Richard Hurd,* II, 175-6, 184, 204, 213.

12. Quoted by Lovejoy, 'The Parallel of Deism and Classicism,' *Essays in the History of Ideas* (Baltimore, 1948), p. 92.

13. *Memoirs,* ed. Henry Morley (London, 1891), p. 35. Curiously, the famous statement, by the eighteenth-century naturalist, Buffon, 'le style est l'homme même,' which is often misquoted, and often misunderstood to epitomize the view that style reflects personality, says nothing, when read in context, about personality. Buffon's point is that the only guarantee of literary fame is not the content of knowledge and fact, which is common property, but the quality of style, which is the contribution of the individual author. See *Discours sur le style* (1753), Paris, 1875, p. 25.

14. *Works,* II, 204. For an expanded version of these doctrines, see J. G. Sulzer, *Allgemeine Theorie der schönen Künste,* the articles 'Manier,' and 'Schreibart; Styl.'

15. 1 (1760), p. 363, as quoted by Mann, 'The Problem of Originality,' p. 115. Similar scope was allowed for self-expression in painting; see e.g. Du Fresnoy, *De arte graphica,* trans. Dryden (2d ed.; London, 1716), p. 65; Roland Fréart, Sieur de Chambray, *An Idea of the Perfection of Painting,* trans. J. E[velyn] (London, 1668), p. 14.

16. *Critical Essays of the Seventeenth Century,* ed. Spingarn, II, 119, 128. Cowley himself had made the point that 'one may see, through the stile of *Ovid de Trist,* the humbled and dejected condition of *Spirit* with which he wrote it. . .' (Preface to *Poems,* in ibid. p. 81).

17. London (1697), p. xv.

18. *Essays of John Dryden,* II, 251, 253. Dryden similarly parallels Ovid with Chaucer (p. 254); see also Dryden's characterization of various Latin authors in his 'Preface to Sylvae,' 1685.

19. *Samuel Johnson* (New York, 1944), pp. 465-8. See also Johnson's 'Life of Swift,' *Lives of the Poets* (ed. Hill), III, 62-3. H. V. D. Dyson and John Butt had maintained earlier that Johnson's 'sense of the inseparability of a man and his works makes him the first of our Romantic critics' (*Augustans and Romantics,* London, 1940, p. 67).

20. E.g., more than fifteen years earlier James Beattie had gone much farther than Johnson in applying to Swift the concept that style is literary physiognomy: 'We often see an author's character in his works. . . All [Swift's] pictures of human life seem to show, that deformity and meanness were the favourite objects of his attention, and that his soul was a constant prey to indignation. . . Hence [an author's] work as well as face, if Nature is permitted to exert herself freely in it, will exhibit a picture of his mind' (*On Poetry and Music,* 1762, pp. 50-52).

21. Preface to Shakespeare, *Johnson on Shakespeare,* p. 10; and see W. R. Keast, 'The Theoretical Foundations of Johnson's Criticism,' pp. 404-5.

22. Preface to Shakespeare, pp. 30-31.

23. *The Works of James Thomson* (London, 1788), 1, ix. Cf. Beattie, *Poetry and Music,* pp. 50-51.

24. 'Life of Thomson,' *Lives of the Poets* (ed. Hill), III, 297-8.

25. *Transactions of the Royal Irish Academy,* v (1795), 40-41.

26. Ibid. pp. 48, 50.

27. Ibid. pp. 51-3, 56, 59, 87.

28. Ibid. pp. 83-4.

29. Quoted by A. C. Benson, *Walter Pater* (New York, 1906), pp. 48-9.

30. See Chap. II.

31. Herder's *Sämtliche Werke,* VIII, 207-8; cf. xii, 5-6. Schleiermacher's *Monologen* later exhibited a similar reasoning. He had long believed, he says, in the essential uniformity of human nature, until there dawned upon him his 'highest intuition' that 'each man is meant to represent humanity in his own way, combining its elements uniquely.' On this basis Schleiermacher concludes that 'language too should objectify the most interior thoughts. . . Each of us needs only make his language thoroughly his own and artistically all of a piece, so that [it] . . . exactly represent the structure of his spirit . . .' (*Soliloquies,* trans. H. L. Friess, Chicago, 1926, pp. 30-31, 66).

32. Friedrich Schlegel, *Prosaische Jugendschriften,* ed. J. Minor (Wien, 1882), I, 81; 140.

33. Kant had done much to popularize the latter-day use of these antonyms, which reverses the connotation they had had from the scholastic philosophers through Descartes. Descartes, for example, had defined the 'objective' as *'in nostra cogitatione,' 'in sola mente';* the 'subjective,' as *'in rebus ipsis,' 'extra nostram mentem.'* See the articles *Objektiv* and *Subjektiv,* in Rudolf Eisler, *Wörterbuch der philosophischen Begriffe* (4th ed.; Berlin, 1929-30).

34. *Prosaische Jugendschriften,* I, 81-2.

35. Ibid. I, 109; also I, 135. Schlegel thus uses 'manner' in the sense often given to 'style' in earlier criticism (Hurd, e.g., had defined 'style,' we remember, as an author's 'general turn or manner of writing'), and saves 'style' for a uniform norm of language, free from the intrusion of the individual differences of the author himself.

36. Ibid. I, 109; cf. I, 80-2.

37. *Fragment 116* in the Athenaeum of 1798, beginning 'Die romantische Poesie ist eine progressive Universalpoesie'—Schlegel's first formal definition of romantic poetry—again emphasizes the joint realism and self-revelation of this literary mode: 'Sie kann sich so in das Dargestellte verlieren, dass man glauben möchte, poetische Individuen jeder Art zu charakterisiren, sey ihr Eins und Alles; und doch gibt es noch keine Form, die so dazu gemacht wäre, den Geist des Autors vollständig auszudrucken' (*Prosaische Jugendschriften,* II, 220).

38. See Lovejoy's 'The Meaning of "Romantic" in Early German Romanticism,' and 'Schiller and the Genesis of German Romanticism,' in *Essays in the History of Ideas.*

39. *Über naive und sentimentalische Dichtung,* in *Schiller's Werke,* ed. Arthur Kutscher (Berlin, n.d.), VIII, 128, 135, 162; cf. 167-9.

40. Ibid. pp. 135, 138, 148.

41. Ibid. pp. 131-2.

42. *Prosaische Jugendschriften,* I, 107-9.

43. A. E. Lussky, *Tieck's Romantic Irony* (The University of North Carolina Press, Chapel Hill, N. C., 1932), pp. 67-70.

44. For a convenient summary, in another context, of the use of the Pauline passage by Tertullian, Augustine, Origen, and other early Christian theorists, see Ruth Wallerstein, *Studies in Seventeenth-Century Poetic* (Madison, Wis., 1950), pp. 27-48.

45. Lussky, *Tieck's Romantic Irony,* p. 69.

46. 'Nachricht von den poetischen Werken des Johannes Boccaccio,' *Jugendschriften,* II, 411-12; see also ibid. 151, 157, 348, 360, 370-71. It is an index to the medieval source of Schlegel's conception that in this same essay he comments, concerning Boccaccio's *Vita di Dante:* 'Remarkable also is the general view of poetry in this

document. He holds it to be the earthly covering and bodily vesture of invisible things and divine powers' (ibid. p. 407).

47. Hazlitt reviewed both these books, as well as Sismondi's *De la littérature du Midi de L'Europe;* see his *Complete Works,* vols. xvi and xix. Herbert Weisinger, in 'English Treatment of the Classical-Romantic Problem' (*MLQ,* vii, 1946, 477-88), gives a very incomplete survey of the currency in England of some of these terms; additions are made by René Wellek, 'The Concept of "Romanticism" in Literary History,' *Comparative Literature,* i (1949), 13-16.

48. *Modern Painters,* iii, iv, sect. i.

49. *Coleridge's Shakespearean Criticism,* i, 165-6. In *Biographia Literaria,* i, 109, Coleridge claims to have re-introduced into English the words 'objective' and 'subjective,' which were 'of such constant recurrence in the schools of yore.'

50. *Coleridge's Miscellaneous Criticism,* p. 148. Cf. *Table Talk,* p. 268, on 'the objective poetry of the ancients and the subjective mood of the moderns.' For some contemporary distinctions between 'subjective' and 'objective,' see: De Quincey, 'Style,' *Collected Writings,* x, 226; Jones Very, 'Epic Poetry' (1836), *Poems and Essays,* Boston and New York, 1886, p. 22; W. J. Fox's review of Tennyson, *Monthly Repository,* new series, vii (1833), p. 33; and the anonymous essay, 'On the Application of the Terms Poetry, Science, and Philosophy,' ibid. viii (1834), p. 326.

51. *Table Talk,* pp. 93-4. Cf. ibid. p. 213: In style, 'Shakespeare is universal, and, in fact, has no *manner.*'

52. Ibid. pp. 280-81. For contemporary gradings of poetic genres on a subjective-objective scale, see e.g., Macaulay, 'Milton' (1825), *Critical and Historical Essays,* i, 159; Jones Very, 'Epic Poetry' (1836), *Poems and Essays,* pp. 41ff.; J. Sterling, 'Simonides' (1838), *Essays and Tales,* i, 198-9.

53. Quoted by J. M. Baker, *Henry Crabb Robinson* (London, 1937), pp. 210-11. On the history of the *Monthly Repository,* see F. E. Mineka, *The Dissidence of Dissent* (Chapel Hill, N. C., 1944).

54. *Lectures on Poetry,* ii, 37.

55. 'Literature' (1858), *The Idea of a University* (London, 1907), p. 273.

56. *Table Talk,* p. 92 (12 May 1830). Cf. Henry Hallam, *Introduction to the Literature of Europe in the Fifteenth, Sixteenth, and Seventeenth Centuries* (1837-9), New York, 1880, ii, 270.

57. *Shakespearean Criticism,* ii, 117. Cf. Charles Lamb, 'On the Tragedies of Shakespeare' (1811), *Works,* ed. Lucas, i, 102-3.

58. *Table Talk,* p. 213 (17 Feb. 1833). Cf. *Shakespearean Criticism,* ii, 118n.: His plays are 'all Shakespeare;—and nothing Shakespeare.' For the qualities and powers of Shakespeare's mind which can nevertheless be discovered from his writings, see Coleridge's treatment of *Venus and Adonis,* in *Biographia,* ii, 13-14.

59. *Miscellaneous Criticism,* pp. 43-4.

60. *Biographia,* ii, 20. See also *Shakespearean Criticism,* i, 218; ii, 17, 96, 132-3.

61. *Table Talk,* p. 294 (15 Mar. 1834). Cf. *Biographia,* ii, 20. On the aesthetic history of the concept of sympathy, see W. J. Bate, 'The Sympathetic Imagination in Eighteenth-century English Criticism,' *ELH,* xii (1945), 144-64; and *From Classic to Romantic,* Chap. v.

62. 'On Genius and Common Sense' (1821), *Complete Works,* viii, 42.

63. 'On Shakespeare and Milton,' *Lectures on the English Poets* (1818), in *Complete Works,* v, 47-8, 50. See J. W. Bullitt, 'Hazlitt and the Romantic Conception of the Imagination,' *Philological Quarterly,* xxiv (1945), 354-61.

64. Marginal note, cited by Charles and Mary Cowden Clarke, *Recollections of Writers* (London, 1878), p. 156. Keats suggests, however, that Hamlet 'is perhaps more like Shakespeare himself in his common every day Life than any other of his Characters' (*Letters*, p. 347).

65. *Letters*, pp. 227-8 (27 Oct. 1818).

66. *Sämtliche Werke*, ed. Eduard Böcking (Leipzig, 1846), VII, 38n. On this subject, see Otto Schoen-René, *Shakespeare's Sonnets in Germany: 1787-1939*, unpublished doctoral thesis (Harvard University, 1941).

67. Trans. Black and Morrison (London, 1889), p. 352.

68. 'Scorn not the Sonnet.' Wordsworth had earlier said, in the essay added to his *Poems* of 1815: 'There is extant a small Volume of miscellaneous poems, in which Shakespeare expresses his own feelings in his own person' (*Wordsworth's Literary Criticism*, p. 179).

69. *Shakespeare's Autobiographical Poems* (London, 1838), pp. 3, 45-7, 181. For an account of the biographical reading of Shakespeare's sonnets, see Hyder E. Rollins' edition in the *New Variorum Shakespeare* (Philadelphia, 1944), II, Appendix IV.

70. 'Shakespeare,' *Poems and Essays*, pp. 39, 37, 40.

71. 'Hamlet,' ibid. pp. 53-5, 60.

72. 'Goethe' (1828), *Works*, XXVI, p. 245.

73. Ibid. pp. 244-6.

74. *On Heroes, Hero-Worship and the Heroic in History* (1841), in *Works*, V, 101, 104, 108-11. In his essay on Shakespeare in *Representative Men* (1850), modeled in part on Carlyle's *Heroes and Hero-Worship*, Emerson failed to discover even those limitations on self-revelation of which Carlyle had complained. 'What trait of his private mind has he hidden in his dramas? . . . So far from Shakspeare's being the least known, he is the one person, in all modern history, known to us.'

75. *Shakspere: A Critical Study of His Mind and His Art* (London, 1875).

76. *Table Talk*, pp. 92-3; 12 May 1830. Cf. *Shakespearean Criticism*, II, 96; and *Biographia*, II, 20.

77. Thomas Newton, in 1752, noted of Samson's great lament beginning with line 594, 'So much I feel my genial spirits droop': 'Here Milton in the person of Samson describes his own case. . . He could not have wrote so well but from his own feeling and experience' (*Paradise Regained . . . To which is added Samson Agonistes*, 2d ed., London, 1753). Cf. his comment on line 90, and *passim*. See also William Hayley, *The Life of John Milton* (London, 1835).

78. Dryden, 'Dedication of the Aeneas,' *Essays*, II, 165; Addison, *Spectator* No. 297 (9 Feb. 1712); Dennis, *The Grounds of Criticism in Poetry* (1704), *Critical Works*, I, 334; Chesterfield to his son, 7 Feb. 1749, *Letters*, ed. Bonamy Dobrée, 6 vols. (London, 1932), IV, 1306.

79. 'Life of Milton,' *Lives of the Poets* (ed. Hill), I, 157.

80. Burns to Mrs. Dunlop (30 Apr. 1787), *Letters*, I, 86; and to James Smith (11 June 1787), ibid. I, 95.

81. *The Marriage of Heaven and Hell*, in *Poetry and Prose*, p. 182.

82. *Shelley's Literary and Philosophical Criticism*, pp. 145-6. In the Preface to 'Prometheus Unbound' Shelley had called Satan 'the Hero of Paradise Lost,' but less 'poetical' in character than Prometheus because his virtues are tainted with ambition, envy, and revenge.

83. Review of Josiah Conder's *The Star in the East*, in *Quarterly Review*, XXXII (1825), pp. 228-9.

84. *Table Talk*, pp. 267-8.

85. The tenth in the Lectures of 1818, *Miscellaneous Criticism*, pp. 163-5. See also Coleridge's superb analysis of the moral psychology of Satan in Appendix B of *The Statesman's Manual*, in *Lay Sermons*, pp. 68-70. Macaulay, writing on Milton in 1825, fell in with Coleridge's interpretation; see his *Critical and Historical Essays*, I, 169-70.

86. 'On Genius and Common Sense,' *Complete Works*, VIII, 42.

87. *Lectures on the English Poets* (1818), ibid. V, 63, 65-7.

88. 'On the Writings of Thomas Carlyle' (1839), *Essays and Tales*, I, 340-41.

89. *Studies in Keats New and Old* (2d ed.; Oxford, 1939), p. 121.

90. 'John Milton,' *English Institute Essays*, 1946 (New York, 1947), pp. 11, 18. See also his *Paradise Lost in Our Time* (Ithaca, N. Y., 1945), Chap. III.

91. *Table Talk*, p. 93; 12 May 1830. On the currency at this time of the idea that the historical Homer was a nullity, see Georg Finsler, *Homer in der Neuzeit* (Leipzig and Berlin, 1912), pp. 202ff. Keble considers and rejects the possibility, *Lectures on Poetry*, I, 96-9.

92. *Lectures on Poetry*, I, 25-6, 259.

93. Ibid. II, 35-7. There is a curiously comparable passage in Keats's letters: 'A Man's life of any worth is a continual allegory—and very few eyes can see the Mystery of his life—a life like the scriptures, figurative. . . Shakespeare led a life of Allegory: his works are the comments on it—' (To George and Georgiana Keats, 14 Feb.-3 May 1819, *Letters*, p. 305).

94. Keble, *On the Mysticism Attributed to the Early Fathers of the Church*, No. 89 of *Tracts for the Times* (1841) (Oxford and London, 1868), pp. 6, 152; Wordsworth, 'The Simplon Pass,' ll. 18-20.

95. Ibid. pp. 169, 189, 152. See also the quotations from the Fathers, pp. 56-7, 155-6.

96. Ibid. pp. 147-8; cf. pp. 189-90. For an early connection of the rhetorical maxim that style reveals the man to the Logos-doctrine that God is partly revealed in His son, see Pierre de la Primaudaye, *L'Académie Françoise* (1577-94), quoted in John Hoskins, *Directions for Speech and Style*, ed. Hoyt Hudson (Princeton, 1935), pp. 54-6.

97. *Lectures on Poetry*, I, 93.

98. Ibid. I, 95, 100. Even the initial choice of the poetic genre is an index to character, for the poet 'fond of action' creates epic or drama, while the poet 'who loves restful things, the country, or quiet pursuits' will write georgics or eclogues (ibid. p. 92).

99. Review of Lockhart's *Life of Scott* (1838), in *Occasional Papers*, pp. 25-6.

100. *Lectures on Poetry*, I, 122, 147; cf. p. 107.

101. Ibid. II, 36, 97, 99. A somewhat earlier passage by Charles Lamb is strikingly similar in conception and phrasing: The skilful novelist implies and twines 'with his own identity the griefs and affections of another—making himself many, or reducing many unto himself. . . And how shall the intenser dramatist escape being faulty, who doubtless, under cover of passion uttered by another, oftentimes gives blameless vent to his most inward feelings, and expresses his own story modestly' (Preface to *The Last Essays of Elia*, 1833, in *Works*, II, 151).

102. Ibid. I, 122, 147, 167-8; II, 105. Cf. I, 159.

103. Ibid. I, 172. Cf. pp. 147-8. This stratagem had been suggested by Robert Burrowes (see page 235); and even earlier, by Robert Wood, for the restricted purpose of

discovering the milieu with which a poet was familiar: see e.g., his *Essay on the Original Genius and Writings of Homer* (1769), London, 1824, p. 23.

104. Caroline Spurgeon, *Shakespeare's Imagery* (New York, 1935), p. 4: 'The poet unwittingly lays bare his own innermost likes and dislikes . . . in and through the images, the verbal pictures he draws to illuminate something quite different in the speech and thought of his characters.'

105. *Lectures on Poetry,* i, 190.

106. Ibid. i, 190. Contemporaries of Keble also attempted, much more cursorily, to identify the clues to self-expression. C. A. Brown, writing in 1838 on Shakespeare's sonnets, suggested that even in his dramas, the poet may reveal himself by 'the selection or invention of his fables, or of the persons of his dramas, the bias of his mind in the management of them, his recurrence to certain opinions, or to his apparent likings or dislikings' (*Shakespeare's Autobiographical Poems,* p. 5). And Bulwer-Lytton pointed out that the sentiments an author's heroes utter 'are his at the moment; if you find them predominate in all his works, they predominate in his mind' [*The Student* (1835 and 1840), quoted by W. J. Birch, in *An Inquiry into the Philosophy and Religion of Shakespeare* (London, 1848), pp. i-ii]. From these, together with the passages quoted earlier from Robert Burrowes, we may extract two more canons of discovery. Both of these were employed, although not explicitly noted, by Keble as well:

6. The Canon of Recurrence. A persistent topic or allusion is the clue to a personal obsession of the author.

7. The Canon of the Gratuitous Interpolation. This was expressed as follows by Burrowes, p. 51: 'When a man quits the direct path, it is always to go by some way which he likes better.' Cf. Keble, ii, 105.

107. Donald A. Stauffer, *Shakespeare's World of Images* (New York, 1949), pp. 362-9; Henry A. Murray, 'Personality and Creative Imagination,' *English Institute Annual,* 1942 (New York, 1943), pp. 139-62. Murray's two main additions to the romantic canons derive respectively from Freud and Jung: (1) symbols which reflect 'a child's relationship to his parents, especially his mother,' and (2) themes paralleling ancient myth and folklore, best accounted for by 'inherited archetypal dispositions.'

108. Review of Lockhart's *Life of Scott,* in *Occasional Papers,* pp. 3, 25.

109. It is instructive to compare Keble's approach to Homer with that of the chief among his eighteenth-century predecessors. In his *Enquiry into the Life and Writings of Homer* (1735), Blackwell attempted to reconstruct the life and times of Homer by eking out ancient tradition with materials drawn from the epics themselves. But Blackwell, almost a complete literary determinist, emphasized race, moment, and milieu, and minimized—in fact, almost denied—the role of what he calls Homer's individual 'genius'; he is, therefore, a predecessor of Taine, rather than Keble. (See, e.g., the 2d ed., London, 1736, p. 345.) Robert Wood, writing in 1769, emphasized not the personality that Homer was, but the geographical, institutional, and religious facts that he knew (*An Essay on the Original Genius and Writings of Homer,* London, 1824, p. 15).

110. Flaubert, *Correspondence,* ed. Eugène Fasquelle (Paris, 1900), ii, 155; for similar passages, see ibid. ii, 379-80; iv, 164; v, 227-8; vii, 280. Cf. Stephen Dedalus' comparison of 'the mystery of esthetic' with 'that of material creation.' In the dramatic form, 'the artist, like the God of the creation, remains within or behind or beyond or above his handiwork, invisible . . .' (James Joyce, *A Portrait of the Artist as a Young Man,* Modern Library ed., p. 252).

111. *Shakespere* (Cambridge, Mass., 1926), pp. 11, 47, 51.
112. *The Personal Principle* (London, 1944), pp. 183-4.
113. W. R. Inge, *God and the Astronomers* (London, 1933), p. 16. Dorothy L. Sayers, in *The Mind of the Maker*, published in 1941, developed in great detail the theme that the concept of God the Creator is grounded in, and illuminated by, the creative experience of the artist. For example, the mind of a human author, in relation to its works, 'is both immanent in them and transcendent'; while it may also be said that in His creation, 'God wrote His own autobiography' (9th ed.; London, 1947), pp. 44, 70.

CHAPTER X

1. 'Épitre ix,' *Oeuvres complètes*, ed. A. Ch. Gidel (Paris, 1872), ii, 232. Voltaire remarked concerning this passage that Boileau himself 'was the first to observe the law which he gave. Almost all his works breathe this truth; that is to say, they are a faithful copy of nature' ('Du vrai dans les ouvrages,' cited ibid. note 2).
2. Epistle Dedicatory to *Liberty Asserted* (1704), in *Critical Works*, ii, 392.
3. Bishop Hurd so construed even a Neoplatonic version of poetic 'truth,' in his Notes on Horace's *Art of Poetry* (*Works*, i, 255, 257): '*Truth*, in poetry, means such an expression, as conforms to the general nature of things; *falshood*, that, which, however suitable to the particular instance in view, doth yet not correspond to such *general nature*. . .

    By abstracting from existences all that peculiarly respects and discriminates the *individual*, the poet's conception, as it were . . . catches, as far as may be, and reflects the divine archetypal idea, and so becomes itself the copy or image of truth.'
4. *The Philosophy of Rhetoric* (new ed.; New York, 1846), p. 55 (Chap. iv).
5. A. N. Whitehead, *Science and the Modern World* (Cambridge, 1932), pp. 68-9.
6. *Spectator* No. 413. On verse treatments of the distinction between primary and secondary qualities see Marjorie Nicolson, *Newton Demands the Muse* (Princeton, 1946), pp. 144-64.
7. (Cambridge, 1904), Pt. i, Chap. ii, p. 7. See also Hobbes's *Human Nature*, Chap. xi. John Sheffield, Earl of Mulgrave, with the tendency of his time to put the beginning of all enlightenment in the immediate past, wrote in his poem 'On Mr. Hobbs and his Writings': 'While in dark Ignorance we lay afraid/Of Fancies, Ghosts, and every empty Shade,/Great Hobbs appear'd, and by plain Reason's Light/Put such fantastick Forms to shameful Flight.'/
8. *The History of the Royal Society of London* (London, 1667), pp. 339-41.
9. 'Of Poetry' (1690), *Critical Essays of the Seventeenth Century*, ed. Spingarn, iii, 96.
10. See e.g., *Elizabethan Critical Essays*, ed. G. G. Smith, i, xxviii-ix, 341ff.
11. *John Dryden* (3d ed.; New York, 1946), p. 23. Davenant's Preface and Hobbes's *Answer* had been published separately from the poem at Paris the year before.
12. Preface to Gondibert, *Critical Essays of the Seventeenth Century*, ii, 3, 5. For similar developments in contemporary French epic theories see René Bray, *La Formation de la doctrine classique*, esp. pp. 235-8.
13. *Critical Essays of the Seventeenth Century*, ii, 61-2. Bishop Sprat, after his account of the flight of bogies before the bright face of the Royal Society, remarked that 'the *Wit* of the *Fables* and *Religions* of the *Ancient World* . . . have already serv'd the *Poets* long enough; and it is now high time to dismiss them' (*History of the Royal Society*, p. 414).

14. *Spectator* Nos. 315, 523..And see *The Letters of Sir Thomas Fitzosborne* (6th ed.; London, 1763), Letter LVII.

15. 'Essay on . . . Epick Poetry,' *Essays upon Several Subjects* (London, 1716), I, 33, 25.

16. 'Of Simplicity and Refinement in Writing,' *Essays,* ed. Green and Grose, I, 240.

17. *Elements of Criticism,* I, 86 (Chap. II, pt. i, sect. 7); II, 305 (Chap. XXII).

18. 'Life of Waller,' *Lives of the Poets,* I, 295; 'Life of Milton,' I, 178-9.

19. 'Life of Butler,' ibid. I, 213; 'Life of Milton,' I, 163-4; 'Life of Gray,' III, 439.

20. Pope, Preface to *The Iliad;* Bray, *La Formation de la doctrine classique,* p. 232. See also R. C. Williams, *The Merveilleux in the Epic* (Paris, 1925); and H. T. Swedenberg, Jr., *The Theory of the Epic in England,* 1650-1800 (Berkeley and Los Angeles, 1944).

21. *La Manière de bien penser dans les ouvrages d'esprit* (1687) (new ed.; Lyon, n.d.), pp. 13, 16.

22. *Essays on Poetry and Music,* p. 86.

23. *L'Art poétique,* III, 174-6, 189. He adds (237-8): 'La fable offre a l'esprit mille agrémens divers;/Là tous les noms heureux semblent nés pour les vers.'/

24. *Lectures on Rhetoric and Belles Lettres,* Lecture XLII, p. 583. See also Addison's *Spectator* No. 315.

25. In Bray, *La Formation de la doctrine classique,* p. 208. A passage from Condillac will illustrate how, in the pragmatic orientation, the criterion of 'truth' was often interpreted as truth to the propensities of the audience. The imagination may make use of the most absurd chimeras, 'whether they are false or not, if we are inclined to think them true. The chief point the imagination has in view is amusement; yet she is not at variance with truth. Her fictions are all just, when conformable to the analogy of our nature, to our knowledge, and to our prejudices' (*An Essay on the Origin of Human Knowledge,* trans. [Thomas] Nugent, London, 1756, p. 90).

26. *Aristotle's Treatise on Poetry* (London, 1789), Preface, pp. xv-xvi.

27. Ibid. p. xv. Cf. Aristotle, *Poetics* 25. 1460^b 32-9.

28. 'Of Heroic Plays' (1672), *Essays,* I, 153.

29. Ibid. p. 154.

30. *Spectator* No. 419. For similar arguments see Bray, op. cit. pp. 208ff.

31. *Essays on Poetry and Music,* p. 36.

32. *Analytical Inquiry into the Principles of Taste* (2d ed.; London, 1805), pp. 260-70.

33. *Aristotle's Treatise on Poetry,* notes, p. 487. Walter Scott later adopted this concept in discussing Mary Shelley's *Frankenstein:* 'We grant the extraordinary postulates . . . only on condition of his deducing the consequences with logical precision' (*The Prose Works,* Edinburgh and London, 1834-6, XVIII, 254).

34. *Letters on Chivalry and Romance,* ed. Edith J. Morley (London, 1911), pp. 143-4.

35. See Douglas Bush, *Mythology and the Renaissance Tradition in English Poetry* (Minneapolis, 1932), pp. 244-7.

36. Opponents of machinery in contemporary poems often made exception for burlesque, in which one aim, as Addison said, was that of 'ridiculing such kinds of machinery in modern writers' (*Spectator* No. 523). See: Johnson, 'Life of Pope,' *Lives of the Poets,* III, 232-4; Kames, *Elements,* I, 86-7; Fitzosborne's *Letters,* p. 303.

37. *Opere di Dante degli Alighieri . . . col Comento di Cristoforo Landini* (Vinegia, 1484), Preface, fol. a [vii]^v. For an earlier Neoplatonic concept of poetic invention, see Boccaccio, *Genealogia deorum gentilium* XIV. vii.

38. Shelley, 'Defence of Poetry,' *Shelley's Literary Criticism,* p. 156; cf. 'On Life,' ibid. p. 53, and letter to Peacock, 16 Aug. 1818, ibid. p. 164. In the third book of his *Discorsi del poema eroico* (1594), Tasso wrote that the operations of art 'appear to us to be almost divine, and to imitate the first Artificer. . .' 'The poet of excellence (who is called divine for no other reason than that, resembling in his works the supreme Artificer, he comes to participate in his divinity) is able to form a poem' which is like 'a little world.' (*Opere,* Pisa, 1823-5, xii, 65-6, 90. These passages are included in A. H. Gilbert, *Literary Criticism Plato to Dryden,* pp. 492, 500). See also Tasso's *Il mondo creato,* 'Giornata prima,' ibid. xxvii; the Argument (p. 1) says that 'l'arte umana, operando intorno alle cose create, imita l'arte divina.' For Leonardo on the painter's 'creation,' see Anthony Blunt, *Artistic Theory in Italy 1450-1600* (Oxford, 1940), p. 37.

39. *Poetices libri septem* (4th ed.; 1607), p. 6 (i. 1). For other comparisons between the making of a poem and the making of the world, see Giambattista Guarini, 'Il compendio della poesia tragicomica' (1599), *Il pastor fido,* ed. G. Brognoligo (Bari, 1914), p. 220; and Giordano Bruno, cited in Oskar Walzel, *Grenzen von Poesie und Unpoesie* (Frankfurt, 1937), p. 13.

40. *Elizabethan Critical Essays,* ed. G. G. Smith, i, 156-7.

41. *Art of English Poesy,* in *Elizabethan Critical Essays,* ed. G. G. Smith, ii, 4. Puttenham's treatise was published in 1589; Sidney's had been written about 1583, and had been circulated in manuscript before it was published posthumously, in two separate versions, in 1595. On the English use of 'create' with reference to literary activity, see L. P. Smith, 'Four Romantic Words,' *Words and Idioms,* pp. 90-95.

42. For Neoplatonic statements that the artist imitates God by creating 'a new world,' see, e.g., Federico Zuccari, *L'idea d'pittori, scuttori ed architetti* (1604), in Erwin Panofsky, *Idea,* pp. 48-50; and Peter Sterry, *Discourse of the Freedom of the Will* (1675), in F. J. Powicke, *The Cambridge Platonists,* pp. 185-6. For some applications to the poet of the term 'create,' and passing comparisons between poetic invention and God's creation, see: Donne, Sermon xxvi, from *Eighty Sermons* (1640), in *Complete Poetry and Selected Prose,* ed. John Hayward (London, 1932), p. 615; Temple, 'Of Poetry' (1690), *Critical Essays of the Seventeenth Century,* iii, 74-5; John Dennis, *Advancement and Reformation of Poetry,* in *Critical Works,* i, 202-3, 335; Pope, *An Essay on Criticism,* ii, 484-93. Relative to this subject, see A. S. P. Woodhouse's fine study, 'Collins and the Creative Imagination,' *Studies in English by Members of University College, Toronto* (Toronto, 1931), 59-130.

43. Cowley, in his Pindaric ode, 'The Muse,' described that goddess as voyaging even beyond the works of God—'Thou hast thousand *Worlds* too of thine *own.*/ Thou speak'st, great *Queen,* in the same *Stile* as *he*/And a *new World* leaps forth when *thou* say'st, *Let it be.*'/ He glossed his own passage thus: 'The meaning is, that Poetry treats not only of all things that are, or can be, but makes *Creatures* of her own, as *Centaurs, Satyrs, Fairies,* &c . . . and varies all these into innumerable *Systemes,* or *Worlds* of Invention' (*Works,* 11th ed., London, 1710, i, 220).

44. Preface to *Troilus and Cressida* (1679), in *Essays,* i, 219 (my italics).

45. *Spectator* No. 419; see also Nos. 421, 279. After Addison, references to supernatural poetry as a second creation became numerous. Edward Young pressed these, as he did other ideas from the *Spectator,* to an extremity: 'In the fairyland of fancy, genius may wander wild; there it has a creative power, and may

reign arbitrarily over its own empire of chimeras.' The human mind 'in the vast void beyond real existence . . . can call forth shadowy beings, and unknown worlds' (*Conjectures on Original Composition,* ed. Morley, pp. 18, 31). See also, e.g., Pope, Preface to the *Iliad,* in *Works* (London, 1778), III, 246; Johnson, *Lives of the Poets* (ed. Hill), I, 177-9, III, 337; J. Moir, *Gleanings* (1785), I, 31. For an objection against taking 'create' in any sense opposed to 'imitation,' see Batteux, *Les Beaux Arts,* pp. 31-3.

46. *Adventurer* Nos. 93, 97. William Duff spoke of 'creative Imagination' as 'the distinguishing characteristic of true Genius,' and cited invention of the supernatural as 'the highest efforts and the most pregnant proofs of truly Original Genius' (*Essay on Original Genius,* London, 1767, pp. 48, 143; cf. p. 89). In his *Essays on Song-Writing* (2d ed.; London, 1774, pp. 6-8), John Aikin said that the imagination cannot long be contented with 'the bounds of natural vision'—'it peoples the world with new beings, it embodies abstract ideas . . . it creates first, and then presides over its creation with absolute sway.'

47. *Spectator* Nos. 419, 279. Nicholas Rowe had already said in 1709 that 'the greatness of this Author's genius do's no where so much appear, as where he gives his imagination an entire loose, and raises his fancy to a flight above mankind and the limits of the visible world. Such are his attempts in *The Tempest, Midsummer Night's Dream, Macbeth,* and *Hamlet*' (*Some Account of the Life &c. of Mr. William Shakespear,* in *Eighteenth Century Essays on Shakespeare,* ed. D. N. Smith, Glasgow, 1903, pp. 13-14).

48. A few other instances of the extravagant praise of Shakespeare's supernatural imagination: Bishop Warburton wrote in 1747 that *The Tempest* and *Midsummer Night's Dream* are 'the noblest effort of that sublime and amazing imagination, peculiar to Shakespeare, which soars above the bounds of Nature, without forsaking Sense. . .' The passage was quoted by Mrs. Griffith, in *The Morality of Shakespeare's Drama* (Dublin, 1777), I, I, who added, 'He has, indeed, in both these exhibitions, created Beings out of all visible existence. . .' See also Mrs. Elizabeth Montagu's chapter on Shakespeare's 'Praeternatural Beings,' those elements from which 'Poetry derives its highest distinction,' in *An Essay on the Writings and Genius of Shakespear* (4th ed.; London, 1777), pp. 135ff. Even Dr. Johnson seems to echo the opinion that Shakespeare's special creative power is exhibited in the supernatural, in his 'Drury Lane Prologue'—'Each change of many-colored life he drew,/Exhausted worlds, and then imagined new'/—a tribute which was echoed by Garrick in his Shakespeare Ode: 'Not limited to human kind,/He fir'd his wonder-teeming mind,/Rais'd other worlds, and beings of his own!'/

49. Leibniz' cosmogony is conveniently described and glossed in Lovejoy's *The Great Chain of Being* (Cambridge, 1936), Chap. v; see also Bertrand Russell, *The Philosophy of Leibniz* (new ed.; London, 1937), esp. pp. 36-9, 66-9.

50. *Critische Dichtkunst,* sect. 6, in *Deutsche National Literatur,* ed. Joseph Kürschner, XLII, pp. 165, 175, 161.

51. *Von dem Wunderbaren* (Zürich, 1740), pp. 31-2; see also pp. 19-21. In his *Critische Betrachtungen über die poetischen Gemählde* (Zürich, 1741), Bodmer writes, pp. 13-14: 'All these numberless possible world-systems stand under the dominion of the imagination [Einbildungskraft].' And on p. 573: 'The mode of creation, in which the possible is executed by the power of the imagination, is particularly the province of the poet by virtue of his office, whence he is a creator, *poetes.*'

52. *Von dem Wunderbaren,* pp. 5-11.

53. Ibid. p. 165.

54. *Critische Dichtkunst,* pp. 160-62. Examples of the kind of contradiction which is impossible even for God's creation, Breitinger says (p. 160) are, that something should both be and not be, that a part should be as great as the whole, etc.

55. *Von dem Wunderbaren,* pp. 47, 49; cf. pp. 144, 151; and see his *Betrachtungen über die poetischen Gemählde,* pp. 594-5, where he attributes poetic truth and reasonableness to the order of a possible 'Welt-Systema.'

56. 'Über Wahrheit und Wahrscheinlichkeit der Kunstwerke' (1797), *Sämtliche Werke,* XXXIII, 87-91; 'Diderot's Versuch über die Malerei' (1798-9), ibid. p. 215. See also Eckermann's *Conversations of Goethe* (18 Apr. 1827), Everyman ed., p. 196.

57. *Letters on Chivalry and Romance,* pp. 131, 144, 153-4. Five years later, William Duff also opposed the 'other world' of supernatural poetry to the 'truth or strict probability' governing the realistic genres (*Essay on Original Genius,* pp. 142-3).

58. Ibid. pp. 137-9. On the basis of the traditional principle of the poetic decorum of parts, John Pinkerton turned the table on Hobbes entirely by skeptically denying that there is any 'truth of fact or historical truth, known to man,' and claiming as the one valid truth, 'that universal truth to be found in poetry and works of fiction,' consisting in 'the propriety and consistence' of the component parts. Thus Caliban is truer than any possible statement of fact, because his character *'is true to itself,* offends no idea of propriety, yet is not in nature' (*Letters of Literature,* London, 1785, pp. 216-18).

59. *Characteristics,* ed. J. M. Robertson (London, 1900), I, 222-3, 231.

60. Ibid. I, 135-6.

61. *Neue Jahrbücher für das klassische Altertum,* XXV (1910), 40-71; 133-65. Cf. Akenside, *The Pleasures of Imagination,* 1st ed., III, ll. 397-427: In the genesis of a poem in the mind of the poet, the images of memory fall into lucid order, as 'from Chaos old the jarring seeds/Of Nature, at the voice divine.' 'Then, with Promethéan art/Into its proper vehicle he breathes/The fair conception. . .'/ And thus 'mortal man aspires/To tempt creative praise.'

62. *Hamburgische Dramaturgie,* No. 34, in *Sämtliche Schriften,* ed. Karl Lachmann (Stuttgart, 1893), IX, 325; cf. No. 79, ibid. X, 120. For accounts of the poet's creation of another world which combine the statements of both Shaftesbury and Addison, see J. G. Sulzer, *Allgemeine Theorie,* articles: 'Einbildungskraft,' 'Erdichtung,' 'Gedicht,' 'Ideal.'

63. 'Zum Shakespeare's Tag' (1771), *Sämtliche Werke* (Jubiläums-Ausgabe), XXXVI, 6.

64. See Walzel, *Das Prometheussymbol,* pp. 133ff., and *Dichtung und Wahrheit,* Bk. XV, in which Goethe describes the origin of his 'Prometheus' ode. There came alive in him, he says, the fable of Prometheus, 'who, separated from the gods, peopled a world . . . I clearly felt that a creation of importance could be produced only when its author isolated himself.'

65. *Kritischen Wäldchen* (1769), in *Sämtliche Werke,* III, 103; also ibid. V, 238-9; XII, 7.

66. *Vorlesungen über schöne Literatur und Kunst* (1801-4), *Deutsche Litteraturdenkmale* (Stuttgart, 1884), XVII, 94-8. Also p. 261: Poetry signifies in general 'the artistic discovery, the marvelous act by which it enriches nature; as the name indicates, a true creation and production.'

67. Ibid. p. 102. He adds (p. 103), in a way that incorporates into this context Leibniz's notion of the soul as a monad which mirrors the universe: 'The fullness, the totality with which the universe is reflected in a human spirit . . . determines the degree of his artistic genius, and puts him in a position to form a world within the world.' For a distinction between Shakespeare's Promethean

creation of realistic characters, and his imaginative other-world of spirits and witches, see Schlegel's *Lectures on Dramatic Art and Literature,* p. 363; also, p. 378.

68. *Shelley's Literary and Philosophical Criticism,* pp. 125, 128, 156; cf. esp. pp. 137, 140, 143-4. See also the Platonic version of the artist's 'making' of 'a second creation,' in some respects superior to God's created nature, in Victor Cousin, *Lectures on the True, the Beautiful, and the Good* (1853), trans. O. W. Wight (New York, 1858), pp. 155-7.

69. *Heroes and Hero-Worship,* in *Works,* v, 80, 104; cf. 'Characteristics,' ibid. xxviii, p. 16.

70. To Thomas Poole, 23 Mar. 1801, *Letters,* I, 352; to Richard Sharp, 15 Jan. 1804, ibid. II, 450. 'Create' also was one of Wordsworth's favorite metaphors for the perceiving mind; see, e.g., *The Prelude* (1805), II, 271-3; III, 171-4; also above, Chap. III, sect. iii. For Wordsworth's frequent use of 'create' to apply to poetic production, see his Preface of 1815.

71. *Oxford Lectures on Poetry* (London, 1926), pp. 4-6, 23-4. David Masson used the concept that poetry is *'poesis,* or creation'—the imaginative production of 'a new or artificial concrete'—to set up a complete antithesis between poetry and science, and to establish the poet's freedom, in continuing 'the work of creation,' to condition 'the universe anew according to his whim and pleasure' (*The North British Review,* XIX, 1853, pp. 308-9; the article was republished in Masson's *Essays Biographical and Critical,* Cambridge, 1856).

72. (Chicago, 1948), pp. v-vi.

73. ' "Sailing to Byzantium": Prolegomena to a Poetics of the Lyric,' *The University of Kansas City Review* (Spring, 1942), VIII, No. 3, pp. 210-11, 216-17. For a warning against the advisability of utter freedom, in the fashion of miracle, either to the creative poet or God the Creator, see Dorothy Sayers, *The Mind of the Maker,* pp. 62-3.

74. *A Discourse of Ecclesiastical Politie* (London, 1671), pp. 74-6. See R. F. Jones, 'The Attack on Pulpit Eloquence in the Restoration,' *JEGP,* xxx (1931), 188-217; also 'Science and English Prose Style in the Third Quarter of the Seventeenth Century,' *PMLA,* XLV (1930), 977-1009.

75. *History of the Royal Society,* in *Critical Essays of the Seventeenth Century,* ed. Spingarn, II, 116-18.

76. *Leviathan* (Cambridge, 1904), pp. 14-15, 25, 42. Cf. Locke, *Essay Concerning Human Understanding,* III, x, sect. 34.

77. *Essays of John Dryden,* I, 185-9.

78. 'Of the Standard of Taste,' *Essays,* I, 269-70.

79. Addison, writing on 'True and False Wit' (*Spectator* No. 62), called Bouhours 'the most penetrating of all the French critics,' and Johnson held that he wrote true criticism in showing 'all beauty to depend on truth' (Boswell's *Life,* 16 Oct. 1769). See also A. F. B. Clark, *Boileau and the French Classical Critics in England* (Paris, 1925), pp. 262ff.

80. *The Art of Criticism,* trans. by a Person of Quality (London, 1705), pp. 5-12. For the justification of hyperboles as bringing 'the Mind to Truth by a Lye,' see p. 18. The ancient doctrine that all varieties of 'fiction' are the mystic veil of truth may be found conveniently summarized in Bk. XIV of Boccaccio's *Genealogia deorum gentilium.*

81. *Critical Essays of the Seventeenth Century,* III, 293. As a condition for admitting verse into his popular book of quotations, Edward Bysshe echoes Bouhours: 'As

no Thought can be justly said to be fine, unless it be true, I have all along had a great regard for Truth' (*The Art of English Poetry,* 1702, Preface). Trapp's discussion of this subject in his *Lectures on Poetry* (1711) is based largely on Bouhours, and similarly derives the criterion of truth from the principle that 'Thoughts are the Images of Things, as Words are of Thoughts . . .' (London, 1742, pp. 101ff.). As in the case of the poetic marvelous, 'truth' was used for internal appropriateness as well as correspondence to fact; see e.g. Bouhours, *Art of Criticism,* pp. 29-30.

82. *Essays on Poetry and Music,* p. 234.

83. *Spectator* Nos. 419, 421.

84. *Critical Essays of the Eighteenth Century,* ed. W. H. Durham (New Haven, 1915), pp. 89-92. Hughes cites Addison's theory (p. 95), and praises the allegorical visions in the *Spectator* papers themselves (p. 104).

85. *Adventurer* No. 57. Warton is writing in the assumed character of Longinus. Cf. Thomas Warton, *Observations on the Faerie Queene* (London, 1754), p. 13: *The Faerie Queene* is a poem 'where the faculties of creative imagination delight . . . because they are unassisted and unrestrained by those of deliberate judgment.' Spenser is at his best as allegorist 'where his imagination bodies forth unsubstantial things, turns them to shape . . . as in his delineations of fear, envy, fancy, despair, and the like.' On the relation of these ideas to the vogue of allegoric odes, see A. S. P. Woodhouse, 'Collins and the Creative Imagination.'

86. *An Essay on Original Genius,* pp. 177-9. Cf. John Aikin, *Essays on Song-Writing,* pp. 6-8. For other passages on the creativity of prosopopoeia, see E. R. Wasserman, 'The Inherent Values of Eighteenth-Century Personification,' *PMLA,* LXV (1950), 435-63.

87. 'Heroic Poetry and Heroic License,' *Essays,* I, 185-6.

88. 'Upon Epitaphs,' *Wordsworth's Literary Criticism,* pp. 126-9.

89. See Herder, *Ueber die neuere deutsche Litteratur,* in *Sämtliche Werke,* I, 396-7; and Schiller, *Ueber naive und sentimentalische Dichtung,* in *Werke,* VIII, 125-6. For an earlier use of the metaphor of body-and-soul as compatible with the matter-and-ornament concept of language, see, e.g., Ben Jonson, *Timber,* in *Critical Essays of the Seventeenth Century,* ed. Spingarn, I, 36-8.

90. 'Style,' *Collected Writings,* X, 229-30; and 'Language,' ibid. 259-62. Cf. Carlyle, *Sartor Resartus,* in *Works,* I, 57: 'Language is called the Garment of Thought: however, it should rather be, Language is the Flesh-Garment, the Body, of Thought.' See also the article, 'Real and Ideal Beauty,' *Blackwood's Magazine,* LXXIV (1835), p. 750; and G. H. Lewes, *Principles of Success in Literature* (1865), ed. T. S. Knowlson (Camelot Series, London, n.d.), pp. 118-19, 125.

91. Preface to the Lyrical Ballads, *Wordsworth's Literary Criticism,* pp. 17-18.

92. *Shakespearean Criticism,* II, 103; *Biographia Literaria,* II, 65-6. See also *Letters,* I, 373-4.

93. *Wordsworth's Literary Criticism,* pp. 19-20, 45-6, 185.

94. *The Excursion,* I, 475-81 (my italics).

95. *Shakespearean Criticism,* I, 212-13; *Biographia,* II, 16-18.

96. *The Piccolomini,* II, iv, 123-31. For Schiller's version, see his *Die Piccolomini,* III, iv, 1635ff. Coleridge worked from a transcript especially made by Schiller for the translation, and this may have differed from the published version of the play. See D. V. Bush, *Mythology and the Romantic Tradition* (Cambridge, Mass., 1937), p. 54n.

97. *The Excursion*, IV, 620-860. For Keats's more decorative version of the origin of myth, see 'I Stood Tiptoe,' ll. 163ff.; see also Byron, *Childe Harold's Pilgrimage*, Canto IV, stanzas CXV, CXXI.

98. Note to *Ode to Lycoris*, in *Poetical Works*, ed. de Selincourt and Darbishire, IV, 423. Even the austere occasion of a memorial in a Christian churchyard, Wordsworth said, may admit 'modes of fiction,' if they are those 'which the very strength of passion has created' ('Upon Epitaphs,' *Wordsworth's Literary Criticism*, p. 118). On various aspects of the romantic employment of myth, see Bush, *Mythology and the Romantic Tradition*, and Edward B. Hungerford, *Shores of Darkness* (New York, 1941).

99. *Essays and Marginalia*, ed. Derwent Coleridge (London, 1851), I, 18ff.

100. *Biographia*, I, 202.

101. To W. Sotheby, 10 Sept. 1802, *Letters*, I, 403-6; cf. the letter written to J. Wedgewood in 1799, *Unpublished Letters*, I, 117. For a perceptive correlation of Coleridge's theory with his own descriptive poetry, see W. K. Wimsatt, Jr., 'The Nature of Romantic Nature Imagery,' *The Age of Johnson* (New Haven, 1950), pp. 293-8.

102. *Miscellaneous Criticism*, pp. 148, 191; *The Statesman's Manual*, in *Lay Sermons*, p. 33. For Coleridge's echoes of A. W. Schlegel in some of his later discussions of myth, see *Miscellaneous Criticism*, p. 148n.

103. *Biographia*, II, 58-9.

104. *Statesman's Manual*, pp. 31-3.

105. *Wordsworth's Literary Criticism*, p. 162.

106. *Jerusalem*, I, 10. On the need of modern poetry for a 'mythology' as a central and unifying point, and the opinion that such a mythology is now developing from philosophical idealism and from the revelations of contemporary physics, see Friedrich Schlegel, *Gespräch über die Poesie* (1800), in *Jugendschriften*, II, 358-63.

107. *Biographia*, II, 124.

108. Ibid. II, 54-5.

109. On this topic see René Wellek, 'The Concept of "Romanticism" in Literary History,' Pt. II, *Comparative Literature*, I (1949), 147-72.

CHAPTER XI

1. *Lectures on Poetry*, II, 37.

2. Essay Supplementary to the Preface (1815), *Wordsworth's Literary Criticism*, pp. 169, 185.

3. Preface of 1800, ibid. p. 21n.

4. *Coleridge's Miscellaneous Criticism*, p. 277; cf. his discussions of the distinction between a poem and a work of science in *Biographia Literaria*, II, 9-10, and in *Coleridge's Shakespearean Criticism*, I, 163ff.

5. 'What Is Poetry?' *Early Essays*, p. 202. For other antitheses between poetry and science, see: Hazlitt, *Complete Works*, V, 9, 13; De Quincey, *Collected Writings*, X, 46-8, XI, 54-5; George Moir, 'Poetry,' *Encyclopaedia Britannica* (7th ed., 1842), XVIII, 140; Keble, *Occasional Papers*, p. 4; [Anon.], 'On the Application of the Terms Poetry, Science, and Philosophy,' *Monthly Repository* (N.S.), VIII (1834), 325-6; J. H. Newman, *The Idea of a University* (London, 1907), pp. 268, 273-5; [G. H. Lewes], 'Hegel's Aesthetics,' *British and Foreign Review*, XIII (1842), 9-10.

6. 'Cleanth Brooks; or, The Bankruptcy of Critical Monism,' *Critics and Criticism,* p. 105.

7. *The Advancement of Learning,* in *Critical Essays of the Seventeenth Century,* ed. Spingarn, I, 6; and *De augmentis scientiarum,* in *The Works of Francis Bacon,* ed. Spedding, Ellis, and Heath (New York, 1864), IX, 62.

8. *Essay Concerning Human Understanding,* III, x, 34 (cf. II, xi, 2); *Some Thoughts Concerning Education* (10th ed.; London, 1783), sect. 174, pp. 267-8.

9. As quoted by Douglas Bush, *Science and English Poetry* (New York, 1950), p. 40.

10. *Essay on Logic,* in *Works,* ed. John Bowring (Edinburgh, 1843), VIII, 272; *The Rationale of Reward* (1825), ibid. II, 253.

11. 'Bentham' (1838), *Early Essays,* pp. 379-80.

12. *The Rationale of Reward,* in *Works,* II, 253-4.

13. Ibid. II, 213.

14. *Autobiography of John Stuart Mill,* p. 78.

15. *Westminster Review,* I (1824), p. 19.

16. Ibid. IV (1825), p. 166.

17. Ibid. II (1824), 335-6. For Bentham's ridicule of an education devoted to 'dead languages,' see his *Works,* II, 258.

18. 'The Four Ages of Poetry,' *The Works of Thomas Love Peacock,* VIII, 11-12, 19, 21-2. The last paragraph, with its mock-heroic muster-roll of 'mathematicians . . . moralists, metaphysicians . . . political economists, who have built into the upper air of intelligence a pyramid,' is indubitably in the accent of Mr. MacQuedy.

19. *Benthamite Reviewing* (New York, 1934), p. 93.

20. *Complete Works,* ed. H. B. Forman (Glasgow, 1901), III, 232.

21. *The Autobiography and Memoirs of Benjamin Haydon,* ed. Aldous Huxley (London, 1926), I, 269.

22. *The History of the Royal Society,* pp. 414, 416.

23. (Warrington and London, 1777), pp. 25, 32-3.

24. 'Summer' (ed. of 1746), ll. 1711-13, 1730-54.

25. 'Spring' (ed. of 1746), ll. 208-15.

26. 'To the Memory of Sir Isaac Newton,' ll. 96-124. Cf. Akenside, *Pleasures of Imagination* (1744), I, ll. 103ff.; and see Marjorie H. Nicolson, *Newton Demands the Muse,* pp. 30-33.

27. *Opticks* (3d ed.; London, 1721), p. 27. For an exposition of the way a poet is able 'to inlist Imagination under the banner of Science,' through converting abstract into visual terms by means of such devices as personification and allegory, see Erasmus Darwin, *The Botanic Garden* (4th ed.; London, 1799), I, 'Advertisement,' and II, 63, 65.

28. *Letters on Chivalry and Romance,* Letter XI, pp. 154-5.

29. *The History of English Poetry* (ed. of 1824), III, 284-6. See also William Duff, *Critical Observations* (London, 1770), p. 303n.

30. *An Essay on the Writings and Genius of Shakespear* (4th ed.; London, 1777), pp. 149-50.

31. 'Thoughts on Ancient and Modern Poetry,' *The General Magazine and Impartial Review,* III (1789), 532-4.

32. 'Milton,' *Critical and Historical Essays,* I, 153-6.

33. Cf. Emily Dickinson's 'Arcturus is his other name,' as well as: 'I pull a flower from the woods,—/A monster with a glass/Computes the stamens in a breath/And has her in a class.'/

34. 16 Oct. 1842, in *Correspondence and Table-Talk*, with a Memoir by Frederick Wordsworth Haydon (London, 1876), II, 54-5.

35. *Prelude* (1850 ed.), III, 61-3. The passage was added after 1830.

36. 'The Tables Turned,' 'The Poet's Epitaph'; cf. *The Excursion*, IV, 961-2; also IV, 620ff., 1251ff. And see Douglas Bush, *Science and English Poetry* (New York, 1950), pp. 88-97.

37. *Wordsworth's Literary Criticism*, pp. 27-8. For Wordsworth's comment on the good and ill effects of the industrialization of England, see *The Excursion*, VIII, 87ff.; and for one of his own attempts at the poetry of the machine, the sonnet called 'Steamboats, Viaducts, and Railways.'

38. Note to 'This Lawn, a carpet all alive,' in *Poetical Works*, ed. de Selincourt, IV, 425.

39. *The Revolt of Islam*, ll. 2254-5; 'Defence of Poetry,' *Shelley's Literary and Philosophical Criticism*, pp. 151-2.

40. *Lectures on Poetry*, in *Prose Writings*, ed. Parke Godwin (New York, 1889), I, 27-31. Cf. George Moir, article 'Poetry,' *Encyclopaedia Britannica* (7th ed., 1830), XVIII, 145.

41. *Aids to Reflection*, pp. 268-9; *Lay Sermons*, pp. 63, 71-2; 80ff.

42. *Biographia*, II, 10-12.

43. 'On Poetry in General' (1818), *Complete Works*, V, 9.

44. 'What Is Poetry?' (1844), *Imagination and Fancy* (New York, 1848), p. 3.

45. Review of *Lamia*, in *The Indicator* (2 Aug. 1822); in Edmund Blunden, *Leigh Hunt's 'Examiner' Examined* (London, 1928), p. 147. In an essay written in 1824, Hunt again attacked the 'favorite remark with a pretty numerous set of writers' that knowledge of the nature of optical delusions has put poetry at a stand (*Men, Women, and Books*, London, 1876, pp. 3-4).

46. *Autobiography*, pp. 106-7.

47. Preface to *Moderr Painters*, 2d ed., 1844, *The Complete Works of John Ruskin*, ed. Cook and Wedderburn (London, 1903), III, 36.

48. 'Maurice De Guérin,' *Essays in Criticism* (London, 1891), p. 82.

49. *À Propos of Lady Chatterley's Lover* (London, 1931), pp. 86-7.

50. When Wordsworth, for example, citing Aristotle as evidence, said that the object of poetry 'is truth, not individual and local, but general and operative; not standing upon external testimony, but carried alive into the heart by passion; truth which is its own testimony,' we are justified in inferring little more than that poetic truth is in some sense general, and that its sanction is emotional effect rather than demonstrable correspondence to something external to itself. (*Wordsworth's Literary Criticism*, p. 25. Wordsworth may have had in mind a passage from Davenant as well as Aristotle; see the Preface to *Gondibert*, in *Critical Essays of the Seventeenth Century*, ed. Spingarn, II, 11.)

51. *The Poetry and Prose of William Blake*, pp. 637-8.

52. 'Defence of Poetry,' *Shelley's Literary and Philosophical Criticism*, pp. 128, 155.

53. *Heroes and Hero-Worship*, in *Works*, V, 80-81; 'State of German Literature,' ibid. XXVI, 51.

54. C. M. Bowra, *The Romantic Imagination* (Cambridge, Mass., 1949), p. 271; and see Chap. I.

55. *The Prelude* (1850 ed.), XIV, 189ff.; *Wordsworth's Literary Criticism*, p. 259.

56. 'On Poesy or Art,' *Biographia*, II, 257-9; *The Friend*, Essay V, in *The Complete Works*, II, 145. A poem, according to Coleridge, may incidentally involve truths, but 'is opposed to works of science, by proposing for its *immediate* object pleasure, not truth' (*Biographia*, II, 9).

57. Letter to Benjamin Bailey, 22 Nov. 1817, *The Letters of John Keats*, pp. 67-8.

58. Ibid.

59. Leigh Hunt, *Essays*, ed. Arthur Symons (Camelot Series, London, n.d.), pp. 67, 71-2.

60. Preface to *Poems* (1815), in *Wordsworth's Literary Criticism*, p. 150.

61. 'On Poetry in General,' *Complete Works*, v, 4.

62. *Essay on the Genius and Writings of Pope*, ii (London, 1782), p. 230; i (London, 1772), p. 47. See Chap. ii, sect. ii. Later, Erasmus Darwin said that the principal distinction between poetry and prose, next to meter, was 'that Poetry admits of but few words expressive of very abstracted ideas, whereas Prose abounds with them' (*The Botanic Garden*, 4th ed., London, 1799, ii, pp. 62-3).

63. Macaulay, *Critical and Historical Essays*, i, 153-4. For an anticipation of this idea in Giambattista Vico, see Chap. iv, sect. iii.

64. *The Monthly Repository*, New Series, viii (1834), pp. 324-7. In his *Dissidence of Dissent* (Chapel Hill, N. C., 1944), p. 419, on the basis of the British Museum's usually reliable manuscript key to the authorship of *Repository* articles, Francis E. Mineka attributed this article to J. S. Mill, and there are similarities between it and some of Mill's doctrines. But Professor Mineka now agrees, on several grounds, that it was probably the work of another author.

65. Ibid. pp. 326, 328.

66. *Early Essays*, p. 278; cf. p. 271, and p. 310: 'Mr. Carlyle brings the thing before us in the *concrete*. . .' For Mill's discrimination between the contraries, general-individual and concrete-abstract, see his *System of Logic*, i, ii, 3-4.

67. *The World's Body*, pp. 158, 156; cf., e.g., Donald Stauffer, *The Nature of Poetry* (New York, 1946), p. 125.

68. Note to 'The Thorn,' added in 1800; *Poetical Works*, ed. de Selincourt, ii, 513.

69. 'Style,' *Appreciations* (New York, 1905), pp. 3-5, 7, 31-2. Cf. p. 6: 'And further, all beauty is in the long run only *fineness* of truth, or what we call expression, the finer accommodation of speech to the vision within.'

70. See the *Oxford English Dictionary*, 'sincere' and 'sincerity'; also G. W. Allport and H. S. Odbert, *Trait-Names, a Psycholexical Study, Psychological Monographs*, XLVII (1936), p. 2.

71. *Wordsworth's Literary Criticism*, pp. 108, 115-16. See also pp. 112-13, 125. For an early but very limited use of the standard in literary criticism, see Boileau's Ninth Epistle, in which he discusses false flattery in poems: 'Rien n'est beau, je reviens, que par la vérité:/C'est par elle qu'on plaît, et qu'on peut longtemps plaire./ L'esprit lasse aisément, si le coeur n'est sincère.'/*Oeuvres complètes*, ii, 236; see also pp. 233-4.

72. *Lectures on Poetry*, i, 68-9, 73.

73. 'Burns,' *Works*, xxvi, 267-8.

74. *Heroes and Hero-Worship*, in *Works*, iv, 67, 91.

75. *Imagination and Fancy*, pp. 4, 233. Carlyle used sincerity as a sign of the spontaneous and organic growth of a work of art. Shakespeare's art 'is not Artifice. . . It grows from the deeps of Nature, through this noble sincere soul, who is a voice of Nature' (*Heroes and Hero-Worship*, in *Works*, iv, 108).

76. G. H. Lewes, *The Principles of Success in Literature*, pp. 87-8; Arnold, 'The Study of Poetry,' *Essays in Criticism*, Second Series (London, 1898), p. 48.

77. Henry James, *The Art of the Novel* (London, 1934), p. 45; T. E. Hulme, *Speculations*, p. 138.

78. *Autobiography of John Stuart Mill* (New York, 1924), pp. 76, 79.

79. Caroline Fox, *Memories of Old Friends*, ed. H. N. Pym (2 vols.; London, 1882), I, 309.

80. On the relation between Bentham's opinions about rhetoric and about poetry, see Mill's *Autobiography*, p. 78.

81. 'What Is Poetry?' *Early Essays*, pp. 202, 209.

82. Ibid. pp. 202, 206-7.

83. *Blackwood's Magazine*, XXXVIII (1835), p. 828. For the identity of the author, see Chap. VI, sect. iv.

84. Ibid. pp. 829, 835.

85. 'An Apology for Poetry,' *Elizabethan Critical Essays*, I, 158, 164, 184-5.

86. 'What Is Poetry?' *Early Essays*, p. 205; cf. Smith, 'The Philosophy of Poetry,' p. 836.

87. Entry for 11 Jan. 1854, in *Letters of John Stuart Mill*, II, 358.

88. *Science and Poetry* (London, 1926), pp. 56, 58-9, 61; see also the discussion of 'Poetry and Beliefs,' Richards' *Principles of Literary Criticism*, Chap. XXXV. Lyrical poems, Rudolf Carnap also said, express feeling, and 'are neither true nor false, because they assert nothing,' and lie completely 'outside the discussion of truth or falsehood' (*Philosophy and Logical Syntax*, London, 1935, p. 29).

89. *Biographia*, II, 107.

90. See, e.g., I. A. Richards, *Practical Criticism* (London, 1930), p. 277.

91. See: Preface to Shakespeare, *Johnson on Shakespeare*, pp. 25-8; Farquhar, *A Discourse upon Comedy*, in *Critical Essays of the Eighteenth Century*, ed. Durham, p. 281; DuBos, *Critical Reflections*, I, 349-50; A. W. Schlegel, *Lectures on Dramatic Art and Literature*, p. 246, and *Sämtliche Werke*, VI, 24. Walter Scott expanded upon Johnson's theory in his 'Essay on the Drama' (1819), *Prose Works*, VI, 308-12.

92. See: Kames, *Elements of Criticism*, II, i, 7 (I, pp. 77-9, 86); Hume, *A Treatise of Human Nature*, I, iii, 10 (p. 123); Hartley, *Observations on Man*, I, iv, 1 (p. 270); Hurd, *Letters on Chivalry and Romance*, Letter x; Twining, *Aristotle's Treatise on Poetry*, p. 487 (note 222).

93. *Coleridge's Shakespearean Criticism*, I, 199-203. See also his letter to Daniel Stuart, 13 May 1816, *Letters*, ed. E. H. Coleridge, II, 663-4.

94. *Biographia*, II, 6.

95. Ibid. II, 103, 186-9.

96. Ibid. II, 10-11, 104.

97. *Poetical Works*, ed. de Selincourt and Darbishire, IV, 464.

98. *Biographia*, II, 120-21.

99. Ibid. II, 111. I. A. Richards takes Coleridge to task for what he regards as his inconsistent literalism in this instance. We may, he says, 'take all the alleged attributes of Wordsworth's child as fictions, as part of the myth' exemplified in the notion of pre-existence (*Coleridge on Imagination*, London, 1934, pp. 136-7). Richards' judgment is corroborated by Cleanth Brooks in *The Well-Wrought Urn* (New York, 1947), pp. 129ff.

100. *Kampagne in Frankreich*, in *Sämtliche Werke*, XXVIII, 122.

101. *Ueber die bildende Nachahmung des Schönen*, in *Deutsche Litteraturdenkmale des 18. und 19. Jahrhunderts*, XXXI, 10-12, 16.

102. *Critique of Aesthetic Judgment*, ed. J. C. Meredith (Oxford, 1911), pp. 80, 48-9, 69.

103. *Ueber die ästhetische Erziehung des Menschen*, in *Werke*, VIII, 92-5.

104. *Correspondence*, III, 294; I, 225.

105. 'The Romantic Movement in England,' *Romanticism: A Symposium*, in *PMLA*, LV (1940), p. 26.

106. To Woodhouse, 27 Oct. 1818, *Letters*, p. 228; to Shelley, 16 Aug. 1820, p. 507; to Reynolds, 3 Feb. 1818, p. 96. Yet only three weeks before (ibid. p. 79), Keats had named Wordsworth's *Excursion* (which A. C. Bradley has justly called 'half poem and half lecture') as one of the 'three things to rejoice at in this Age.'

107. 'Sleep and Poetry' (1816), ll. 124-5; 'The Fall of Hyperion' (1819), Canto I, ll. 147-59; 166-7; 187-90. Cf. Keats's *Letters*, pp. 134-5.

108. Preface to Shakespeare, *Johnson on Shakespeare*, pp. 20-21. Cf. *Rambler* No. 4.

109. 'Prologue to Mr. Addison's Tragedy of Cato,' l. 4.

110. Jan. or Feb. 1808, in *The Letters of William and Dorothy Wordsworth: The Middle Years*, I, 170.

111. *Wordsworth's Literary Criticism*, pp. 25, 213; see also p. 217. So Coleridge: 'The poet *must* always aim at pleasure as his specific *means*; but . . . all ought to aim at something nobler as their end—viz.—to cultivate and predispose the heart of the reader . . .' (*Coleridge's Miscellaneous Criticism*, p. 321).

112. *Wordsworth's Literary Criticism*, pp. 15-16.

113. Letter to John Wilson, ibid. p. 7; Preface to *Lyrical Ballads*, ibid. pp. 16-17. Cf. p. 202.

114. Preface to *Lyrical Ballads*, ibid. pp. 27-8.

115. 'The Poetry of Pope,' *Collected Writings*, XI, 55-7.

116. To Elizabeth Hitchener, 5 June 1811, *The Complete Works*, ed. Ingpen and Peck, VIII, 100.

117. *Complete Poetical Works*, ed. Thomas Hutchinson, p. 207.

118. *Shelley's Literary and Philosophical Criticism*, pp. 132, 136, 129-30.

119. Ibid. pp. 121, 130-31.

120. Ibid. p. 144. Shelley had translated the 'Symposium' in 1818, three years before writing the 'Defence.'

121. For Godwin's analysis of sympathy as an ethical concept, see his *Enquiry Concerning Political Justice*, ed. F. E. L. Priestley (Toronto, 1946), I, 421-38; and for a discussion of Shelley's relations to Godwin's theory, ibid. Introduction, III, 108ff.

122. 'Symposium,' transl. Jowett, 211.

123. 'Defence of Poetry,' *Shelley's Literary and Philosophical Criticism*, p. 159; cf. p. 131.

124. Ibid. pp. 148-52. For William Hazlitt's reply to the Utilitarian depreciation of poetry, see *The Plain Speaker*, in *Complete Works*, pp. 161-2; 245-8.

125. J. S. Mill, *Autobiography*, p. 104; Coleridge, 'To William Wordsworth,' ll. 61ff.; Arnold, 'Memorial Verses'; Stephen, 'Wordsworth's Ethics,' *Hours in a Library* (London, 1907), II, 276, 299. See also John Morley, Introduction to *The Complete Poetical Works of William Wordsworth* (Globe ed.; London, 1926), pp. lxvi-lxvii.

126. Bentham, *Language*, in *Works*, VIII, 301; J. S. Mill, *Autobiography*, p. 34.

127. 23 Nov. 1836, *Letters of John Stuart Mill*, I, 104.

128. *Autobiography*, p. 106; *Early Essays*, p. 234.

129. *Early Essays*, p. 209.

130. 'Tennyson's Poems,' ibid. pp. 260-61.

131. To Alexander Bain, 4 Nov. 1867, *Letters*, II, 93.

132. See, e.g., Mill's essay on 'Civilization' (1836), and 'Inaugural Address Delivered at St. Andrews' (1867), as well as other essays collected in his *Dissertations and Discussions*.

133. 'The Study of Poetry,' *Essays in Criticism,* Second Series (London, 1898), pp. 1-3. (F. E. Mineka has pointed out to me that Arnold, in quoting part of this material from his own Introduction to the first volume of *The Hundred Greatest Men,* London, 1879, made interesting changes in the original text.) I. A. Richards' *Science and Poetry,* to which a part of this passage from Arnold serves as epigraph, is an expanded form of the theory that poetry enables us to retain the moral and emotional efficacy without the cognitive commitments of traditional religion. See his *Science and Poetry,* pp. 60-61.

134. *Autobiography,* p. 47.

135. J. S. Mill, *Early Essays,* p. 201; Alexander Bain, *John Stuart Mill* (London, 1882), p. 154.

Index

Books that have been cited frequently in the text are listed here at the end of the entry under the name of the author. The reference that follows the short title is to the note identifying the edition used.